Favorite Places
Of Worcester County

Worcester Telegram & Gazette
and Tatnuck Bookseller's

Favorite Places of Worcester County

A Guide To Shopping, Dining, Recreation,

Sightseeing, History, Facts & Fun

In Central Massachusetts

by Larry & Gloria Abramoff, Ann Lindblad,
and residents and fans of Worcester County

Published by Databooks
div Tatnuck Bookseller & Sons
335 Chandler Street
Worcester, MA 01602

FAVORITE PLACES OF WORCESTER COUNTY

For information address:
Favorite Places, C/O DATABOOKS, Publishing Division, 335 Chandler Street, Worcester, MA USA 01602-3402.

First Edition
Library of Congress Catalog Card Number: 94-093946
ISBN 0-9636277-7-5

Book design: Brady & Berg, Marianne Bergenholtz
Cover Design: Amorello Design, Janet Amorello
Cover Photo: Larry Stein, Technical Production, Art Director, June Greenman
Editing: Gloria Abramoff, Larry Abramoff
Printed in the U.S.A.

To order additional quantities of this book or the accompanying map, postcards and puzzles:
DATABOOKS
Mail Order Sales Desk
335 Chandler Street
Worcester, MA USA 01602-3402
FAX 508-756-9425
1-800-642-6657
1-508-756-7644
INTERNET: databooks@delphi.com
For more information see order form on last page.

The paper used in this publication meets the minimum requirements of the American National Standard for Information Sciences-Permanence of Paper for Printed Library Materials. ANSI Z39.48-1987.

Acknowledgements

Deep and sincere thanks go to Bruce Bennett, publisher of the Telegram & Gazette, for his early belief in *Favorite Places* and his unwavering support. Also, this book simply would not exist without the help and counsel of two very important people, Gloria Abramoff and Peter Lindblad.

We would also like to thank the following people for their assistance along the way: Tom Cole, marketing services director of the T&G; Bernadette Colburn, executive director of the Worcester County Convention & Visitors Bureau; Bud Paras, general manager WTAG/WSRS Radio; Skot Paré, program director of WTAG Radio; Steve Peck, program director WSRS Radio; Jack Foley, executive assistant to the president, Clark University; Beverly Osborn, formerly with the Worcester Historical Museum; Bill Grant of the Central Massachusetts Regional Planning Commission; Bill Densmore, former executive director of the Colleges of Worcester Consortium; and Annette Frongillo, Gail Wiles and Donna Cobb, all of Holden.

Special thanks go to the town clerks and historians from all 60 cities and towns for providing invaluable information, and to the hundreds of Worcester County "enthusiasts" who sent us their own *Favorite Places*.

- Larry Abramoff and Ann Lindblad

Introduction

Am I nuts or, why write this book?
(The book, what's in it, what's not, what's next.)

Twenty years ago, when I opened a bookstore in Tatnuck Square, the popular theory (even adopted by my future wife) was that I was probably nuts, a bookstore could not make it in sleepy old Tatnuck Square. And last year, when I announced I was going to write and publish a guide book to Worcester County, the popular theory was: he must be nuts; there's nothing to do in Worcester.

Well, for all those who considered me half-a-bubble out of plumb, a few sandwiches short of a picnic, or a few bricks shy of a load, here's the skinny: 20 years later the Tatnuck Bookseller is still going strong in a larger location. (See in Chapter 1, Worcester County's 101 Largest Employers); Gloria, who once said the major thing wrong with me was "Worcester," married me anyway and has been my wife for 17 years. More than 700 people entered our contest by sending in their "Favorite Places" in Worcester County and over 7,000 copies of this book were sold prior to publication. What this really means is, Worcester's a pretty nice place to live, and lots of people know it.

Yes, there really is a lot to do in Worcester -

A typical guidebook tells you about places to go and things to do. But this book is written for residents, as well as visitors and guests, and it also includes information about people and history as well. Now if anyone asks, "What's so special about Worcester County?" we can hand them this book, crammed with more than 1,400 listings of places to go, things to do, sights to see and chock full of information about the area's history and the people who live here now. Whether you're a native, or you're a visitor, Favorite Places of Worcester County is a fun and informative book you can use time and again.

Chapter 1-Discovering Worcester County is a sort of necessary evil. Those of us who live here may already know this stuff, but to visitors, it's news. It gives a brief overview of the County; major attractions, major employers, including a list of the top 101 employers in Worcester County, and industry highlights. In Chapter 12 - Town Profiles and Important Statistics, we've got the facts on each and every town in the County. You can compare tax rates, school expenditures, SAT scores, teacher salaries, house prices and crime rates. Find out where each town ranks in Chapter 13.

If you've ever wondered if anything important ever happened in Worcester County, we've got the answers. We found enough important stuff for a whole chapter: Chapter 2 - Famous People and Fabulous Firsts. Read about famous residents Johnny Appleseed, Grizzly Adams, Clara Barton and Cole Porter and Worcester area innovations such as the birth control pill, the modern rocket, anesthesia, wind chill, white chocolate and much more. This chapter is easy reading, full of trivia for your next date or dinner party, and will be expanded in the next edition. Due out late '96 or early '97 Favorite Places II will include notorious characters and haunted places. So don't forget to send in your suggestions.

Of course any good guidebook has information about getting around. Chapter 3 includes information about planes and trains, taxis, limos (even one that does historic tours). Chapter 4 has information sources such as, Tourist Info Centers, Chambers of Commerce, entertainment guides, and a special description and history of the Telegram & Gazette. Chapter 5 - Where to Stay, reminds us that you don't have to go very far for a romantic weekend or a family camping trip. We've included the usual hotels and motels, along with the offbeat: Bed & Breakfasts, campgrounds, and inns. So don't sit around this weekend; drive 10 or 20 miles and you can "take a vacation."

For fun look for bargain spots "beyond Spag's" in Chapter 6 - Shopping. We found factory outlets, flea markets, vintage fashions, and even a place that restores player pianos. Find out where you can get four star food at two star prices and where to visit all of Worcester's historic diners in Chapter 7 - Dining.

For the best places to ski, sled, swim, golf, fish, hike, pick blueberries or go hot air ballooning, see Chapter 8 - Recreation. We found that the best scenic views in Worcester County are free - find them in Chapter 9 - Sightseeing. Other cities may have only art and historical museums. We have those, too, but here you can also see antique toilets, old growth forests, Colonial clocks and Medieval battle armor. Find out where in Chapter 10 - Culture. Did you know there's a mountain range in Antarctica named after Clark University and five of its geography professors? Check it out in Chapter 11 - Colleges.

For history buffs, we've profiled all 61 Worcester County cities and towns including the "lost town" of Dana — do you know why it died? Where can you find Worcester County's only buffalo herd? Do you know where it "rained frogs" in 1953? Where the heck is Podunk? Which town has a windmill farm, and which one made most of the barbed wire for the western plains? Which town's farmers once attacked Worcester and which town had to "pick up and move?" Where did the Rolling Stones once record? Which town gave a piece of itself to the Statue of Liberty? And which spot in the county was seen from a ship in Boston Harbor in 1632?

Find the answers to these questions and more in Chapter 12 - The Towns of Worcester County. And don't forget to read the introduction to Chapter 12 by co-author Ann Lindblad who grew up in Tennessee. She gained a whole new perspective on the Civil War after learning of Worcester County's industrial power during that time.

We know you'll get your money's worth with this book. Compare: Fodors Guide to Cape Cod has about 250 pages and costs $13.00; Favorite Places is almost 400 pages and costs only $9.95! And please remember we can't be as comprehensive as the phone book. This book was meant to be just what the title says - a collection of favorite places.

Regarding our Favorite Places Contest, the grand prize is a trip to Worcester, England and the not-so-grand prize is a trip to Wooster, Ohio because they spelled it wrong! We're still receiving entries and notes today, and of the 700 entries the most impassioned votes went to Tower Hill Botanic Garden, Moore State Park, Spag's, Tatnuck Bookseller, Wachusett Reservoir and the Worcester Art Museum. We've quoted many of our enthusiastic "assistant authors" throughout the book.

Here's what to do if your favorite listing isn't here, if your favorite listing is wrong, if you have a "hot" new place, if you don't like our review, or if you do like our review, or if you find a mistake or know about a change... let us know! Drop a line to Favorite Places, C/O Tatnuck Bookseller Marketplace, 335 Chandler St., Worcester, MA 01602, or FAX (508) 756-9425. This is only the first edition of Favorite Places of Worcester County. With your help, the second edition will be even better. Thanks and have fun.

Larry Abramoff & Ann Lindblad

PS - Neither the author, editor, or publisher make any warranties about information contained in this book. Please remember, things change, call first and let us know your thoughts.

Table of Contents

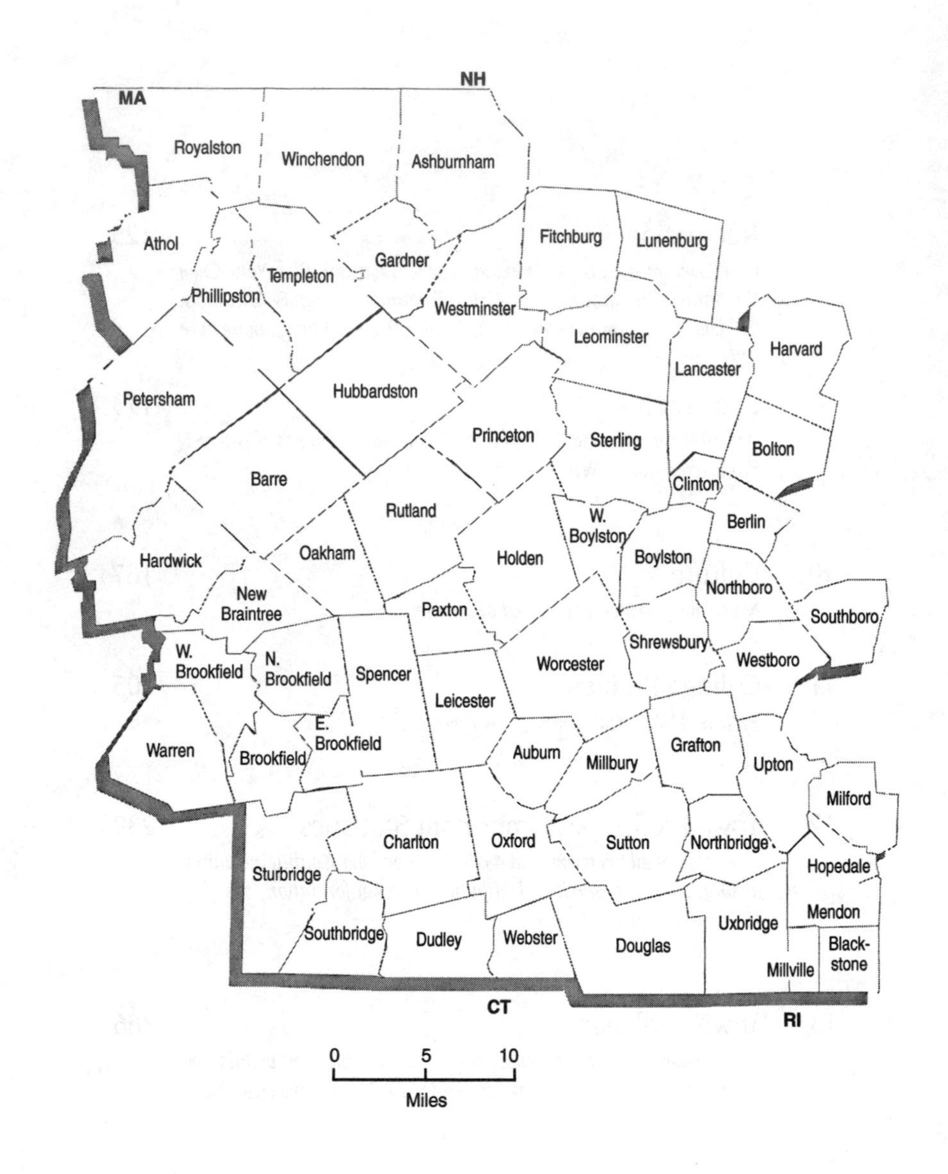

Location map of Worcester County

Chapter 1

Discovering Worcester County
or
Some Highlights, Major Attractions, Industry & General Chamber-of-Commerce-Type Information

Worcester, New England's second-largest city (pop. 169,759), is in the "heart" of Worcester County, the largest county in Massachusetts. Worcester County stretches from New Hampshire to the north, to Rhode Island and Connecticut to the south, with 4 cities and 56 towns (previously 57, see Dana) in between. The county's population of 709,705 represents 12% of the state's total, but its land area of some 1500 square miles comprises nearly 20% of the state.

Worcester County is home to 14 colleges, scores of unique museums and hundreds of sights to see. If you could pick up Worcester and plunk it down, say, in the Mid-west, it would no doubt be known as a cultural hub, attracting people from five states.

Indeed, Worcester does draw people from five states, but because the media "spotlight" tends to get stuck on Boston, just 40 miles to the east, many of Worcester County's attractions remain undiscovered (even by lots of "townies," myself included) — but also unspoiled and relatively uncrowded.

Diverse Cultures

In the last century, the area's booming mills and factories attracted immigrants from all over: Swedes, Finns, Poles, Russian Jews, Greeks, Irish, Lebanese, Lithuanians, Italians, French Canadians and Armenians. (My grandparents came from Azarbaijan, Latvia, Belarus, and Lithuania). Today, the descendants of these immigrants give Worcester a rich cultural diversity. The city continues to be enriched by more recent newcomers from India, Asia, South America, Africa and the Caribbean.

Worcester's central location is more important now than ever. Known as the "Heart of the Commonwealth," the area is nearly equidistant - an hour's drive or less - from Boston, Providence, Hartford, Springfield and Nashua, N.H., enabling many to take advantage of better home prices, and less congestion, even if they must work elsewhere. (Daily commuter rail service is finally available from Worcester to Boston. I can't wait for more frequent service, and my fervent hope is for regular train service to New York).

Into the Millennium

Heading into the 21st century, Worcester is in the right place at the right time. While the '80's building boom clogged and congested many cities, including some of Worcester, Worcester County remains accessible, affordable and it still has lots of open space left. The trick will be balancing economic development and environmental/quality of life needs. If Worcester can develop a philosophy and plan to encourage use and reuse, a powerful developmental force with little negative environmental impact may be achieved.

With over $1 billion in construction projects underway, including the Rte. 146 connector and Mass. Pike interchange, we'll finally have easy highway access to Boston. A planned renovation of historic Union Station as a transportation center, a new downtown convention center and a "Medical City" hospital complex all add to Worcester County's potential. But the area's future is best defined by these key facts:

9.2 million people live within a 75-mile radius of Worcester.

6 million people live within an hour's drive of Worcester.

The success of the Worcester Centrum off I-290 in Worcester's downtown is proof that these demographics count. The developers believed that "if you build it, they will come" and they were right. Opened in 1982 with Frank Sinatra headlining, the Centrum attracts international superstars like Janet Jackson, Bruce Springsteen and Billy Joel, who have launched world tours here because Worcester's easier accessibility draws bigger audiences. The $32 million convention center addition to the Centrum is set for completion in 1996.

More Major Attractions

Just across from the Centrum is the Worcester Common Fashion Outlets, the only enclosed (and carpeted) outlet mall in New England, which was revamped with Worcester's prime location in mind. With over 100 stores, anchored by Saks Clearinghouse, Filene's Basement and the Sports Authority, the mall attracts tour buses from as far away as New Jersey and New York. It's one of only two malls in the country with a professional theater company on site. Here the Foothills Theater, founded in 1969, performs some seven plays from October - March, offering evening performances and Thursday and Sunday matinees - a delightful complement to shopping excursions.

The Worcester Art Museum, the second-largest art museum in New England, is world-renowned for its permanent collection of over 30,000 works that span 50 centuries of art and culture. It is also recognized for its temporary exhibitions which have included "Haring, Warhol, Disney" and "Judith Leyster: A Dutch Master and Her World". The museum's holdings include works by Renoir, Monet, John Singer Sargent, and world art treasures such as St. John the Baptist by Renaissance painter Andrea del Sarto, and The Fur Jacket by James Abbott McNeill Whistler.

One of the most acoustically perfect performance halls in the country - Mechanics Hall - is on Worcester's Main St. Built in 1857 and restored in 1977, the hall has hosted Charles Dickens, Mark Twain, Caruso, Dvorak, Teddy Roosevelt, and Thoreau. Today, it is preferred by such world famous musicians as cellist Yo-Yo Ma, and violinist Midori, and is used for classical recordings by Sony and Telarc. The country's oldest music festival, the Worcester Music Festival, was launched in 1858, and has been an annual event for the past 135 years. Recently the first lady, Hillary Rodham Clinton, made it part of her whistlestop election year tour where she spoke in support of Democratic candidate Kevin O'Sullivan.

One of the country's largest independent bookstores is also in Worcester, Tatnuck Bookseller Marketplace, which has been featured on ABC's "Good Morning, America," and referred to by Boston's WBZ-TV newscaster, Jack Williams as a "world class bookstore". Housed in an historic brick factory building at 335 Chandler Street, with over 5 miles of books and a full-service 120-seat restaurant, the bookstore is also an official Massachusetts Tourist Information Center. Besides more than 500,000 books, Tatnuck also has a jeweler, clothier, candle shop and card store, and its book publishing and distribution division serves corporate customers in 48 states and 35 countries. World famous authors now regularly include Tatnuck on their book signing tours, including Pulitzer Prize winners David McCullough and Tracy Kidder. This book is the fourth in a series about Worcester recently published by the Tatnuck's Databooks division.

Spag's, one of the largest grossing stores in the world, is located in Shrewsbury, MA. With an eclectic selection of over 150,000 items, don't forget to bring your own bags because Spag's has no bags. This store is world renowned and estimates are that over 10,000 people visit each day. Now open Sundays and finally accepting credit cards, as you "tour" the store you are liable to run into Mr. Borghatti (Spag) himself. From clothing to food to fishing tackle, Spag's is definitely an event.

The one Worcester County attraction consistently mentioned in tourist guidebooks is Old Sturbridge Village, off the Massachusetts Turnpike(I-90) and I-84 in Sturbridge. A living history museum with 40 restored buildings and costumed interpreters, OSV recreates New England Village life in the 1830's. Visitors to OSV and the surrounding shops, restaurants and inns and motels number nearly half a million every year.

Some 300,000 skiers a year take advantage of the 18 trails at Wachusett Mountain Ski Area in nearby Princeton. With 100% snow-making, night skiing, and the state's only high speed quad lift, it attracts skiers from all over southern New England, N.Y. and N.J. In addition, Wachusett Mountain State Reservation attracts a half million visitors and hikers during the warmer months.

The Blackstone River Valley National Heritage Corridor is the birthplace of the Industrial Revolution, stretching from Millbury, MA to Pawtucket, R.I. The country's first water-powered mills were built in the 1700's along the Blackstone, taking advantage of the river's dramatic vertical drop from its headwaters in Worcester to the sea in Providence. Because of its many mills and the Blackstone Canal, built in 1820, the Blackstone was termed the "hardest working river in America."

Worcester County Job Opportunities

Many of the old mill buildings in the Blackstone Valley are being converted to new uses, making everything from recycled paint to plastic laminates. With a coming Mass. Pike interchange and connector to Worcester along Rte. 146, the valley is on the verge of another boom.

Elsewhere in the county, other industries are flourishing. To the southwest, the Tri-County area (Southbridge, Sturbridge, Charlton), home of American Optical, has at least five firms on the leading edge of fiber-optic research and development. To the north, the paper industry along Rte. 2 is finding new opportunities in recycling waste paper. The Leominster area is the fourth largest plastics manufacturing center in the country, with more than 100 manufacturers, a skilled labor pool, and a network of specialized suppliers.

To the east, the "borough" towns (Westborough, Southborough, Northborough) along Rte. 9, I-495, and I-290, have attracted hundreds of companies, including high tech (Chipcom Corp., Digital, Data General), telecommunications (Nynex), utilities (Mass. Electric, N.E. Electric), and many others, including pharmaceutical firms (Astra), manufacturers (Bose Corp.) and many distributors, suppliers and service companies.

Worcester's largest employer is University of Massachusetts Medical Center and Medical School, and clustered across the street is the second-largest concentration of biotechnology companies in New England — 18 biotech firms employing some 1,500 people in the 75-acre Mass. Biotech Research Park. The Park expects to grow to 4,000 employees. Some of the firms have relocated from Boston, preferring Worcester's lower overhead costs and less hectic commutes. The multi-national BASF conducts cancer research from a $100 million facility in the Park.

The area's second largest employer is the Fallon Healthcare System, an integrated medical delivery system comprised of a leading HMO (health maintenance organization), medical group practice and hospital. Worcester is considered a national model in medical managed care, and has the highest HMO enrollment in the country, at 54%. Health plan premiums in Worcester average some 30% less than those in Boston. Fallon's 22-acre "Medical City" complex directly across from the Worcester Centrum and the Worcester Common Fashion Outlets, is due for completion in 1998.

Traditional manufacturing has always been Worcester's mainstay, and the city is famous for its mechanics, metalworkers, and machine tool firms. The city has some 275 manufacturing firms; among the largest are abrasives manufacturer Norton Company, forger Wyman Gordon, steel rolling mill manufacturer Morgan Construction, boiler manufacturer Riley Consolidated and metals manufacturer Parker Affiliated.

Insurance firms Allmerica Financial and Paul Revere, both in Worcester, and Commerce Insurance Group in Webster employ more than 6,000 among them. The area's 14 colleges collectively employ more than 11,000 people, have an enrollment of more than 35,000 students, attract more than 1 million visitors annually, and have combined operating budgets of more than $775 million.
Job growth among small companies has been dramatic in recent years, with most new jobs coming from firms employing less than 500 people. Worcester has 4,000 small businesses, and Worcester County has 16,000 small businesses.1æ´Ω5~¢¢£§•¶Worcester County's 100 Largest Employers
from Worcester Area Chamber of Commerce, 1995

Worcester County's 101 Largest Employers

UMASS Medical Center
Employees: 6,300
55 Lake Ave. North
Worcester, MA 01605
(508) 856-0011
Aaron Lazare, M.D., Chancellor/Dean

Fallon Healthcare System
Employees: 5,000
Clinic: 630 Plantation St., Hospital: 25 Winthrop St.,
Clinic: Worcester, MA 01604
Hospital: Worcester, MA 01605
Clinic: (508) 852-0600; Hospital: (508) 798-1234
Clinic: Alan M. Stoll, VP/Admin.; Hospital: Denis J. Fitzgerald, M.D., President

Medical Center of Central Mass.
Employees: 3,700
119 Belmont St.
Worcester, MA 01605
(508) 793-6611
Peter H. Levine, M.D., President & CEO

Allmerica Financial
Employees: 3,450
440 Lincoln St.
Worcester, MA 01605
(508) 855-1000
John F. O'Brien, President & CEO

Worcester Public Schools
Employees: 3,000
20 Irving Street
Worcester, MA
01609
(508) 799-3020
James L. Garvey, Ed.D., Superintendent

City of Worcester
Employees: 2,500
City Hall, 455 Main St.
Worcester, MA 01608
(508) 799-1175
Thomas R. Hoover, City Manager

Norton Company
Employees: 2,500
One New Bond St.
Worcester, MA 01606
(508) 795-5000
Michel Besson, President & CEO

NYNEX
Employees: 2,400
15 Chestnut St.
Worcester, MA 01609
(508) 793-9966
Joseph H. Zukowski, Reg. Dir./Public Affairs

Digital Equipment Corp.
Employees: 2,260
Employees: 2,221
146 Main St.
Shrewsbury, MA 01545
(508) 493-9044
Robert B. Palmer, President (Corp. Offices, Maynard, MA).

Massachusetts Electric Co.
Employees: 1,803
25 Research Drive
Westborough, MA 01581
(508) 366-9011
John H. Dickson, President

Shaw's Supermarkets, Inc.
Employees: 1,695
15 Midstate Drive
Auburn, MA 01501
(508) 832-6780
Michael Goulart, District Manager

New England Electric System
Employees: 1,600
25 Research Drive
Westborough, MA 01581
(508) 366-9011
John W. Rowe, President

Paul Revere Insurance Group
Employees: 1,600
18 Chestnut St.
Worcester, MA 01608
(508) 799-4441
Charles E. Soule, President

Data General Corporation
Employees: 1,500
4400 Computer Drive
Westborough, MA 01580
(508) 366-8911
Ronald L. Skates, President

U.S. Postal Service
Employees: 1,302
4 East Central St.
Worcester, MA 01613-9998
(508) 795-3602
John P. Wellman, Postmaster

Wonder Market Companies
Employees: 1,200
P.O.B. 15055
Worcester, MA 01615
(508) 754-3255
Calvin C. Gould, President

Commerce Insurance Co.
Employees: 1,162
211 Main Street
Webster, MA 01570
(508) 752-1020
Arthur J. Remillard Jr., President

Holy Cross College
Employees: 945
One College Street
Worcester, MA 01610
(508) 793-2011
Rev. Girard C. Reedy, S.J., President

Wyman-Gordon Company
Employees: 942
244 Worcester Street/P.O. 8001
North Grafton, MA 01536
(508) 839-4441
David P. Gruber, CEO

Flexcon Company, Inc.
Employees: 930
Flexcon Industrial Park
Spencer, MA 01562-2642
(508) 885-3973
Neil McDonough, President & CEO

Neles-Jamesbury, Inc.
Employees: 850
640 Lincoln Street
Worcester, MA 01605
(508) 852-0200
Thomas Sturiale, President

T. J. Maxx/Newton Buying Co.
Employees: 840
135 Goddard Memorial Drive
Worcester, MA 01602
(508) 797-8600
Joseph DiRoberto, Assistant Vice President

Telegram & Gazette
Employees: 825
20 Franklin Street/P.O. Box 15012
Worcester, MA
01615-0012
(508) 793-9100
Bruce S. Bennett, President & Publisher

Allegro Microsystems, Inc.
Employees: 798
115 Northeast Cutoff/P.O.Box 15036
Worcester, MA 01615
(508) 853-5000
Allan S. Kimball, President

Commonwealth Gas Company
Employees: 774
157 Cordaville Road
Southborough, MA 01772
(508) 481-7900
Kenneth M. Margossian, President

Worcester Polytechnic Institute
Employees: 711
100 Institute Road
Worcester, MA 01609
(508) 831-5000
Dr. John Brown, Interim President

Chipcom Corporation
Employees: 675
118 Turnpike Road
Southborough, MA 01772
(508) 460-8900
Rob Held, President

Astra USA, Inc.
Employees: 650
50 Otis Street
Westborough, MA 01581
(508) 366-1100
Lars Bildman, President

Bose Corporation
Employees: 650
125 Fisher Street/P.O.Box 5028
Westborough, MA 01581
(508) 836-3200
Walter Hussey, Plant Manager

Shawmut Bank, N.A.
Employees: 600
446 Main Street
Worcester, MA 01608
(508) 793-4323
Michael J. Toomey, Senior Vice President

Morgan Construction Company
Employees: 549
15 Belmont Street
Worcester, MA 01605
(508) 755-6111
Philip R. Morgan, President

Clark University
Employees: 530
950 Main Street
Worcester, MA 01610
(508) 793-7711
Dr. Richard P. Traina, President

Millbrook Distributors, inc.
Employees: 530
Rt. 56/P.O. Box 35
Leicester, MA 01524
(508) 892-8171
Robert A. Sigel, President

Spag's Supply Inc.
Employees: 500
193 Boston Turnpike
Shrewsbury, MA 01545
(508) 752-8612
Anthony J. Borgatti, Jr., President

Quinsigamond Communty College
Employees: 470
670 West Boylston St.
Worcester, MA 01606
(508) 853-2300
Dr. Sandra L. Kurtinitis, President

Fairlawn Rehabilitation Hospital
Employees: 455
189 May Street
Worcester, MA 01602
(508) 791-6351
Ellen Ferrante, President & CEO

Banyan Systems, Inc.
Employees: 450
120 Flanders Rd.
Westborough, MA 01581
(508) 898-1000
Peter Hamilton, President

Assumption College
Employees: 437
500 Salisbury St.
Worcester, MA 01615-0005
(508) 752-5615
Joseph H. Hagan, President

Bay State/Sterling
Employees: 420
Union Street
Westborough, MA 01581
(508) 366-4431
Bernard Phaneuf, President

Bank Of Boston
Employees: 400
P.O.Box 15073
Worcester, MA 01615-0073
(508) 798-6400
Richard B. Collins, President

Riley Consolidated, Inc.
Employees: 400
P.O.Box 15040
Worcester, MA 01615
(508) 852-7100
Michael E. Bray, President

Visiting Nurse Association
Employees: 400
120 Thomas Street
Worcester, MA 01608
(508) 756-7176
Gloria S. Powaza, Executive Director

Sears Roebuck & Company
Employees: 390
Auburn Mall
Auburn, MA 01501
(508) 729-2200
William Richey, Manager

Worcester StateCollege
Employees: 375
486 Chandler Street
Worcester, MA 01602
(508) 793-8000
Dr. Kalyan K. Ghosh, President

Webster Spring Co.
Employees: 330
430 Main Street
Oxford, MA 01540
(508) 987-8706
Philip Good, Director/Manuf.

Worcester County's 101 Largest Employers (cont.)

BJ'S Wholesale Clubs/Auburn & Westborough
Employees: 305
290 Turnpike Rd.
Westborough, MA 01581
(508) 898-0009
Gail Vickstrom, Marketing Mgr.

David Clark Company
Employees: 300
P.O.Box 15054
Worcester, MA 01615-0054
(508) 756-6216
Robert Vincent, President

Reed-Rico
Employees; 300
18 Industrial Drive
Holden, MA 01520
(508) 829-4491
John Prosser, President

Madison Cable Corp.
Employees: 290
125 Goddard Memorial Drive
Worcester, MA 01603
(508) 752-7320
Harold Cotton, Chairman

Presmet Corporation
Employees: 270
112 Harding Street
Worcester, MA 01604
(508) 792-6400
Stephen H. Clinch, President

Proteon, Inc.
Employees: 270
9 Technology Drive
Westborough, MA 01581
(508) 898-2800
Michele Schoellkopt, Human Resources Mgr.

Imperial Distributors, Inc.
Employees: 265
33 Sword Street
Auburn, MA 01501
(508) 756-5156
Michael D. Sleeper, President

Thom Mcan Shoe Company
Employees: 260
67 Millbrook Street
Worcester, MA 01606
(508) 791-3811
Larry A. McVey, President

Adcare Hospital
Employees: 250
107 Lincoln St.
Worcester, MA 01605
(508) 799-9000
David W. Hillis, President

Goretti Supermarkets, Inc.
Employees: 250
One Providence Street
Millbury, MA 01527
(508) 865-4422
Mary Goretti, President

Quabaug Corporation
Employees: 250
18 School Street
North Brookfield, MA 01535
(508) 867-7731
Allan S. Dunkerley, President

The Devereux Foundation
Employees: 250
60 Miles Road
Rutland, MA 01543
(508) 886-4746
Stephen Yerdon, Director

YMCA Of Greater Worcester
Employees: 250
766 Main Street
Worcester, MA 01610
(508) 755-6101
Evan C. Page, President

Worcester Envelope Company
Employees: 241
22 Millbury St/P.O.Box 406
Auburn, MA 01501
(508) 832-5394
E. Dexter Pond, Jr., President

Liberty Mutual Insurance
Employees: 235
255 Park Ave.
Worcester, MA 01615
(508) 753-6000
William Payne, District Manager

Worcester-Berkshire Insurance Companies
Employees: 235
120 Front St., Suite 500
Worcester, MA 01608
(508) 754-6666
Keith Fry, President

Beaumont Nursing Home, Inc.
Employees: 230
85 Beaumont Drive
Northbridge, MA 01534
(508) 234-9771
Daniel J. Salmon, Administrator

Parker Affiliated Companies
Employees: 225
150 Grove St./P.O.Box 15052
Worcester, MA 01615-0052
(508) 791-7131
Jordan Levy, President

Westborough Marriott
Employees: 225
5400 Computer Drive
Westborough, MA 01581
(508) 366-5511
Mark O'Neil, General Manager

Edwards Food Superstore
Employees: 222
571 Boston Tunpike
Shrewsbury, MA 01545
(508) 842-1911
Michael W. Peters, Manager

St. Francis Home
Employees: 220
101 Plantation St.
Worcester, MA 01604
(508) 755-8605
Jacqueline Alix, Administrator

Worcester Marriott Inn
Employees: 220
10 Lincoln Square
Worcester, MA 01608
(508) 791-1600
Ed Walls, General Manager

Wright Line, Inc.
Employees: 218
160 Gold Star Boulevard
Worcester, MA 01606
(508) 852-4300
Philip Burkart, President

Big Y Supermarkets
Employees: 210
50 Southwest Cutoff
Worcester, MA 01604
(508) 752-2989
John Jendza, Store Manager

Worc. Area Transporation Co.
Employees: 203
207 Grove Street
Worcester, MA 01605
(508) 791-9782
Thomas Narrigan, General Manager

Bay State Gas Co.
Employees: 200
300 Friberg Pkwy.
Westborough, MA 01581
(508) 836-7000
David Reichman, Director/Public Affairs

Chase Paper Company, Inc.
Employees: 200
45 Oak Street
Westborough, MA 01581
(508) 366-4441
Phyllis Chase, President

Home Quarters
Employees: 200
571 Turnpike Rd.
Shrewsbury, MA 01545
(508) 842-1244
James Kuchta, General Manager

Polor Corporation
Employees: 200
40 Walcott Street
Worcester, MA 01603
(508) 753-4300
Ralph Crowley, Jr., President

Home Depot
Employees: 198
530 Turnpike Rd.
Shrewsbury, MA 01545
(508) 842-4100
Randy Nelson, Manager

R.H. White Construction
Employees: 195
41 Central Street`
Auburn, MA 01501
(508) 832-3295
David White, President

Tuthill Eng./Coppus Murray Group
Employees: 191
P.O. Box 8000
Millbury, MA 01527-8000
(508) 756-8391
William F. Jones, President

Central Mass. Health Care
Employees: 190
300 Mechanics Tower
Worcester, MA 01608
(508) 798-8667
John Powell, President & C.E.O.

Montrose/CDT
Employees: 190
28 Sword Street
Auburn, MA 01501
(508) 791-3161
George Graeber, Exec. V.P

National Envelope Corp.
Employees: 189
207 Greenwood Street
Worcester, MA 01607
(508) 798-8711
Timothy Chipman, General Manger

Elkay Products, Inc.
Employees: 186
P.O. Box 4247/800 Boston Tpke.
Shrewsbury, MA 01545
(508) 845-2116
Benson Kane, President

Polyclad, Laminates, Inc.
Employees: 180
86 Providence Street
Millbury, MA 01527
(508) 865-5211
Rodney L. Finne, Operations Manager

Cumberland Farms
Employees: 175
165 Flanders Road
Westborough, MA 01581
(508) 366-4445
Michael McGlain, Warehouse Manager

Northbridge Public Schools
Employees: 175
87 Linwood Ave.
Whitinsville, MA 01588
(508) 234-8156
Henry J. O'Donnell, Superintendent of Schools

Worc. Foundation/Exp./Biology
Employees: 175
222 Maple Ave.
Shrewsbury, MA 01545
(508) 842-8921
Dr. Thoru Pederson, President

Rob Roy Companies
Employees: 165
150 Pleasant Street
Worcester, MA 01609
(508) 754-8839
Robert D. Lapierre, President

Bioresearch Corp.
Employees: 160
100 Research Drive
Worcester, MA 01605
(508) 849-2500
Robert H. Foster, V.P./Adm. & Finance

Talbert Trading
Employees: 160
5 Quinsigamond Ave./P.O. Box 823
Worcester, MA 01613
(508) 755-1342
Robert I. Mantyla, Executive Vice President

Thermo Electron Web Systems
Employees: 160
35 Sword Street/P.O. Box 269
Auburn, MA 01501
(508) 791-8171
Edward J. Sindoni, President

American Optical Corp.
Employees: 155
14 Mechanic Street
Southbridge, MA 01550
(508) 765-9711
Neil Henderson, President

John J. Nissen Baking Company
Employees: 155
75 Quinsigamond Ave.
Worcester, MA 01610
(508) 791-5571
Gary Gonsalves, Plant Manager

AMI Companies
Employees: 150
46 West Boylston St.
P.O. Box 986
Worcester, MA 01613
(508) 852-5311
Eugene J. Ribakoff, President

Worcester County's 101 Largest Employers (cont.)

Cambridge Biotech Corp.
Employees: 150
365 Plantation St
Worcester, MA 01605
(508) 797-5777
Jeffrey Beaver, Acting President

Salisbury Nursing Home
Employees: 150
25 Oriol Drive
Worcester, MA 01605
(508) 852-3330
Lisa Kennedy, Administrator

Domino's Pizza of Worc., Inc.
Employees: 140
105 Hamilton St.
Worcester, MA 01604
(508) 795-7025
Donald Laing, President

Fleet Bank Of Massachusetts
Employees: 136
370 Main Street
Worcester, MA 01608
(508) 791-7811
John F. Merrill, Sr. Vice President

Automatic Rolls of New England
Employees: 125
131 Southbridge Street
Auburn, MA 01501
(508) 798-8858
Fred Sexton, General Manager

Holiday Inn Worcester
Employees: 120
500 Lincoln Street
Worcester, MA 01605
(508) 852-4000
Marcel Girard, General Manager

Stanley Tools-Worcester Plant
Employees: 120
149 Washington St.
Worcester, MA 01610
(508) 795-0909
Richard A. Edmond, Plant Manager

Tatnuck Bookseller
Employees: 100
335 Chandler Street
Worcester, MA 01602
(508) 756-7644
Lawrence Abramoff, President

Tropical Foods, Inc.
Employees: 100
50 Mill Street
Worcester, MA 01603
(508) 797-0363
Tom Lajoie, General Manager

Chapter 2

Famous People and Fabulous Firsts

This chapter highlights Worcester County's Famous People and Fabulous Firsts. For easy reference, the section is organized alphabetically by people and "firsts." Each listing includes some interesting facts, from the longest geographic name in the U.S., to Worcester County inventions that changed the world—anesthesia, the modern rocket, the birth control pill, and the sewing machine. Did you know that both the valentine and white chocolate got their start here? Or that pioneer legends Johnny Appleseed and Grizzly Adams were both born in Worcester County? Or that "Mary Had a Little Lamb" is a true story about a Sterling schoolgirl? We've tried to include it all, with highlights about baseball, strong women, and some odds 'n ends, but nobody's perfect so....

(*Did we miss anybody or anything?* Don't whine, *don't complain, just tell us. Send your comments, hot people or the latest local inventions to:* Favorite Places C/O Tatnuck Bookseller 335 Chandler Street Worc., MA 01602.)

About Baseball

Worcester County's baseball roots run deep. Athol's Candy Cummings invented the curve ball pitch in 1869; the catcher's mask was invented in Southborough; J. Lee Richmond of the "Worcesters" pitched baseball's first perfect game here in 1875; Worcester's Ernest Thayer wrote "Casey at the Bat" about a classmate in 1888. Baseball great Connie Mack was born in East Brookfield, and legendary Jesse Burkett called Worcester home for over 50 years.

Strong women

While the men were playing baseball, Worcester's women were fighting for equal rights. The first National Woman's Rights Convention was held in 1850 in Worcester, a natural choice since the area was home to Abby Kelley Foster and Lucy Stone. Both women were leaders in the equality movement, and were peers of Susan B. Anthony, who also spoke at the convention.

Other notable Worcester County women include Clara Barton of Oxford, founder of the American Red Cross; Lydia Pinkham, patent medicine entrepreneur, who first mixed her compound for "woman's troubles" using roots from a Lunenburg brook, and Frances Perkins of Worcester, FDR's Labor Secretary and the first female cabinet member.

Odds 'n Ends

This section details the wit and wisdom of the area's many authors, its Nobel and Pulitzer Prize winners, its Hollywood song and dance men, and the inimitable '60's radical leader Abbie Hoffman. And it includes some "fun facts" to file away. Not only was the 1960's icon, the yellow "smiley face" button, invented here, so was the ubiquitous "pink flamingo" lawn ornament. The world owes a debt to Worcester for both the rickshaw and the monkey wrench, and for shredded wheat and the steam calliope.

Famous People

James Capen Adams "Grizzly Adams" Charlton

Adams was the famed 19th century mountain man and P.T. Barnum performer known as "Grizzly Adams." He is buried in Charlton.

John Adams 2nd U.S. President Worcester

Adams (1735-1826) taught school in Worcester after graduating from Harvard College in 1755. His years as a Worcester schoolmaster are described in his diaries and autobiography.

George Bancroft Historian, founder of U.S. Naval Academy Worcester

Bancroft (1800-1891) wrote a popular six-volume history of the United States during the mid-1800's. He served as Secretary of the Navy under President James K. Polk and founded the U.S. Naval Academy at Annapolis.

Dave Bargeron Rock star Athol

Bargeron was the bass player for '60's rock group, "Blood, Sweat and Tears."

Clara Barton Founder of the Red Cross North Oxford

Known as the "Angel of the Battlefield" during the Civil War; Barton (1821-1912) founded the Red Cross. She was born in Oxford, and her home is now the Clara Barton Birthplace Museum, 68 Clara Barton Rd. (508) 987-5375.

Samuel N. Behrman Author, screenwriter Worcester

Behrman (1893-1973) wrote nostalgic and comic sketches about growing up in Worcester's Jewish community which were published in 1954 as *The Worcester Account.* The book was made into a Broadway play in 1958 starring Maureen Stapleton, Eli Wallach and Clifford David. His 1934 play, "Rain from Heaven," was the first American play to recognize what horrors the Nazi regime would wreak on the Jewish population.
"Used copies of The Worcester Account are still in great demand and sell anywhere from $10-$25.00 - a good read," Larry Abramoff, Worcester, MA.

Samuel Flagg Bemis Pulitzer Prize winner Worcester

Bemis (1891-1973) won his first Pulitzer Prize, in letters, in 1927, and won a second in history in 1950.

Robert Benchley Writer, actor Worcester

Benchley (1889-1945) was a famous New Yorker columnist and Algonquin Club wit who shared a cramped office with fellow writer Dorothy Parker. "One square foot less and it would have been adulterous," Benchley wrote. He was also an accomplished actor, star of some 4 dozen Hollywood short films. *The Oxford Dictionary of Modern Quotations* contains 16 famous Benchley witticisms, among them: "The surest way to make a monkey of a man is to quote him," and his famous telegram to a friend upon arriving for a Venice vacation, "STREETS FLOODED. PLEASE ADVISE."

Busby Berkeley Hollywood choreographer Athol

Berkeley's elaborate Kaleidoscopic production numbers are legendary. Born

William Berkeley Enos (1895-1976) in Los Angeles, he lived in Athol from 1914-1917 where he worked in the Lee shoe factory after his graduation from military high school. He and his actress mother, Gertrude Enos, performed *War Brides* in the Athol Opera House in 1917 before he shipped out to serve in France in WWI. After the war, he returned to Athol briefly, and then began his career in Hollywood, where he often worked with Ruby Keeler. His legendary films include *42nd Street* and *Footlight Parade*, both made in 1933.

Elizabeth Bishop Pulitzer-Prize winning poet Worcester

Bishop (1911-1979), a contemporary of fellow writer Mary McCarthy at Vassar, Bishop won the 1955 Pulitzer Prize for her *Poems: North and South, A Cold Spring.*

Mabel Caroline Bragg Children's author Milford

"Ms. Bragg wrote the Pony Engine, which...became the famous children's book, The Little Engine that Could *in the late '20's. Platt & Munk bought the rights... and published it in 1930 ...by Watty Piper (pseudonym for Platt & Munk),"* Pamela Fields, Milford, MA.

Luther Burbank Horticulturist Lancaster, Lunenburg

A famous horticulturist, Burbank (1849-1926) was born in Lancaster and planted the first of his famous potatoes in Lunenburg. He created hundreds of plant hybrids, including the Shasta daisy, and his Burbank potatoes are still grown today.

Jesse Burkett Baseball Hall of Famer Worcester

One of the great bunters in baseball history, Burkett (1870-1953) played for the N.Y. Giants, the Cleveland Indians, the St. Louis Browns and the Boston Americans. He was inducted into the Baseball Hall of Fame in 1946. Worcester's Jesse Burkett Little League honors Burkett, who had a .338 lifetime batting average, and lived in Worcester from 1890 until his death.

Ebenezer Butterick Founder of Butterick Patterns Sterling, Fitchburg

Butterick, a tailor from Sterling, with advice from his wife, Ellen, cut the first commercial paper patterns in Fitchburg on June 16, 1863. Early patterns were for Civil War uniforms. Later, demand for women's fashion patterns was so high that the firm moved to New York City. Within a decade, Butterick had offices in London, Paris and Berlin. Butterick Patterns are still sold today.

John Chapman "Johnny Appleseed" Leominster

Chapman (1774-1884), known as Johnny Appleseed, was a skilled nurseryman who planted apple trees in the frontier. He was born in Leominster and was regarded as a healer and almost a saint by settlers and natives alike.

Loretta Chase Romance novelist Worcester

Under the pen name Loretta Chase, Worcester's Loretta Chekani has written nine romance books and two novellas, all published by Avon books, a division of Hearst Publishing. Among her latest titles is *Lord of Scoundrels.*

"Look for Loretta's autographed picture in booth B-9 at Tatnuck Bookseller Marketplace," Gloria Abramoff, Worcester, MA.

Bob Cousy Basketball great Worcester

Former Boston Celtics star and broadcaster, Cousy (born 1928) led the 1947 Holy

Cross Basketball team to an NCAA Championship. With the Celtics, he was a master playmaker and regarded by many as the best passer in the game. He had a supporting role in the Hollywood movie, *Blue Chips*, and arranged for its world-wide opening in Worcester in 1994.

Harry Devine Olympic Bronze medalist Worcester

Devine won the 1928 bronze medal for boxing in the 126 lb. featherweight class at the Olympics in Amsterdam. Later, he fought as a welterweight. According to his wife, Mary, he saved all his fighting for her and hasn't won a round since they married in 1953. However, he did retire from professional boxing in the mid '30's .

Dorothea Lynde Dix Social reformer Worcester

Dix (1802-1887) opened a school for children in Worcester in 1816, when she was just 14. She was superintendent of Union Army nurses during the Civil War and later became known for advocating compassionate treatment of the mentally ill.

Harold D. Donohue Congressman who introduced resolution to impeach President Nixon Worcester

A 14-term congressman, Donohue (1901-1984) was a member of the House Judiciary Committee which conducted the Watergate hearings. He offered the resolution to impeach President Richard M. Nixon on July 24, 1974.

"The Durango Kid" Cowboy film star Athol

Charles Starrett (1903-1986) was born in Athol and won fame as "The Durango Kid" a western film star of the '40's and '50's. In all, he made 166 films, of which 136 were westerns. He started out as a Hollywood romantic lead before switching to the fast action Durango series. Local kids watching the Durango Kid on screen at Athol's Capitol Theatre circa 1943 got the thrill of their lives when, after the film ended, the real Durango Kid stepped on stage. They knew him forever after as a "good, home town guy."

Esther Forbes Author of *Johnny Tremain* Westborough, Worcester

Forbes (1891-1967) wrote *Johnny Tremain*, which won the 1943 Newbery Medal for most distinguished children's book. The movie version by Disney was released in 1957. Forbes also won the 1942 Pulitzer Prize for American history for *Paul Revere and the World He Lived In*. She was the first woman member of the American Antiquarian Society, which now houses her manuscripts.

Jedediah Foster Statesman West Brookfield

Foster (1726-1779) was one of three who drafted the Massachusetts Constitution. His work was completed by his son Dwight after his death. He was known to George Washington as "someone who could be relied upon" in Massachusetts.

Abby Kelley Foster Women's rights advocate Worcester

A member of the anti-slavery movement, Abby Kelley Foster (1811-1870) was a lecturer who influenced women's rights leaders Susan B. Anthony and Lucy Stone. She lived in Worcester as a child, and returned in 1847 with her husband, abolitionist Stephen S. Foster. Their Mower St. farm (today a private residence) was a stop on the Underground Railroad.

Nicholas Gage Author Worcester

Gage (born in Greece in 1939) wrote *Eleni*, the story of his mother's death in Greece during WWII, which was later made into an acclaimed film. Gage also wrote *A Place for Us*, which eloquently describes the immigrant experience in Worcester.

Rich Gedman Major League Baseball catcher Worcester

Gedman grew up in Worcester on Lafayette St. and graduated from St. Peter-Marian H.S. As a member of the Boston Red Sox he played in the 1986 World Series. He later joined the Houston Astros and the St. Louis Cardinals.

Jerome Geils Rock band leader Worcester

The "J.Geils" of J.Geils band fame is Worcester's Jerome Geils. The group was popular in the 1970's and '80's, and released a dozen albums over the course of 15 years. Guitarist Geils started out playing Worcester clubs. Among the band's hits were "I Want You to Want Me," released in 1981.

Georgia Gibbs Popular singer in 1940's-'50's Worcester

Nicknamed "Her Nibs" by Jimmy Durante, Georgia Gibbs was born Frieda Lipson and lived at the Jewish Foundling home on Coral St. She did USO tours with Bing Crosby and had a TV song show on NBC in 1957. Her 1940's hit "Kiss of Fire" was a million-seller.

Robert Goddard Father of modern rocketry Worcester

Goddard (1881-1945) invented the first liquid-fueled rocket. A graduate of South H.S. and a professor at Clark University, he launched the first liquid-propellant rocket in Auburn on March 16, 1926. He was the first to probe the potential of using rocket power to reach high altitudes. NASA's Goddard Space Flight Center is named in his memory. (See Auburn).

Emma Goldman Anarchist Worcester

Goldman (1869-1940) lived in Worcester in the 1890's where, in addition to her anarchist activities, she ran an ice cream parlor on Main St with her anarchist/lover Andrew Berkman. She participated in the Homestead Strike in 1892, was imprisoned for hindering conscription in 1917 and was deported to Russia in 1919.

Andrew Haswell Green "The Father of Greater New York" Worcester

Green (1820-1903) was from Worcester's wealthy "Green Hill Park" family, and as president of the Central Park committee, and later city comptroller, he was responsible for building New York City's Central Park, the New York Public Library, for the layout of N.Y.C. north of 125th St., and for smashing the notoriously corrupt Tweed ring.

Hank Greenberg Baseball Hall of Famer Blackstone Valley

Greenberg was one of several famous baseball players who got their start playing in the mill leagues of the Blackstone Valley (see Millville).

Lefty Grove Baseball Hall of Famer Blackstone Valley

Robert Moses "Lefty" Grove (1900-1975) got his start playing for the Blackstone Valley mill teams. Many consider him the greatest pitcher ever. He played for the Philadelphia Athletics and later the Boston Red Sox. He had a career total of 300 wins and 141 losses.

Danelle Harmon Romance novelist Sutton

Harmon has written several successful romance novels, among them *Pirate in My Arms* and *Captain of My Heart.*

Leo "Gabby" Hartnett Baseball Hall of Famer Millville

Hartnett played for the Blackstone Valley Mill League before the majors, as did many other famous baseball players.

Col. William Henshaw Coined the term, "Minute Men" Leicester

Henshaw suggested to the Continental Congress that a militia be "trained to march upon the minute," originating the term, "Minute Men."

Abbie Hoffman Sixties radical Worcester

Hoffman (1937-1989) founded the Yippie party and coined the phrase, "Never trust anyone over 30," when he was 32. He was born and raised at #5 Ruth St. in Worcester, and graduated from Worcester Academy. He stood trial as one of the "Chicago Seven" for leading the demonstration at the 1968 Democratic National Convention.

Elias Howe Sewing machine inventor Spencer

Howe (1819-1867) was the first to develop the lockstitch sewing machine, patented in 1846. (see Spencer).

Tyler Howe Inventor of the spring bed Spencer

Howe, related to Elias Howe, who invented the sewing machine, patented the first spring bed.

William Howe Inventor of the Howe truss bridge Spencer

A member of the famous Howe family of Spencer inventors, William Howe designed a strong wooden truss bridge which was named for him.

Dr. Elliot P. Joslin Diabetes specialist Oxford

Joslin was a leader in diabetes treatment and founded the Joslin Clinic in Boston.

Hannah Kalajian Co-founder of Near East Foods Worcester

Kalajian (1910-1994) and her husband, George, ran "George's Spa," which featured her rice pilaf and other Armenian specialties. They founded Near East Food Products, Inc. in 1962 to market packaged versions of her dishes. H.J. Heinz bought Near East in 1986. Kalajian later lived in Paxton and Northborough.

Arthur Kennedy Broadway and Hollywood actor Worcester

The late Kennedy, the son of a Worcester dentist, won a Tony in 1949 as Willie Loman's son, Biff, in Arthur Miller's *Death of a Salesman.* He went on to garner 5 Oscar nominations in his 55 year acting career, and starred in such films as *High Sierra, Peyton Place,* and *Lawrence of Arabia.*

Jacob Knight Folk painter West Brookfield

Knight (1938-1994) was an acclaimed folk artist whose paintings of N.E. town commons were published in Yankee Magazine. He also did paintings for the Smithsonian.

Stanley Kunitz   Pulitzer Prize-winning poet   Worcester

Kunitz, born in Worcester in 1905, won the 1959 Pulitzer Prize for *Selected Poems 1928-1958* written about his Worcester boyhood.

Denis Leary   Comedian   Worcester

Leary is a chain-smoking, irreverent stand-up comedian and movie actor. He recorded the popular "No Cure for Cancer" comedy album for A&M Records.

Connie Mack   Baseball player/manager   Brookfield, N. Brookfield

Cornelius Alexander McGillicuddy (1862-1956) was born in East Brookfield, and later lived in N. Brookfield. He holds the major league record for his 53 years as a baseball manager with Pittsburgh Pirates and Philadelphia Athletics. Mack's teams won 9 pennants and 5 World Series.

Milton Meltzer   Editor and historian

Meltzer (born 1915) a graduate of Classical High, wrote *Starting from Home,* a book about Worcester. He also wrote biographies on Langston Huges and Dorothea Lange.

Ebenezer Merriam   Famous printer   West Brookfield

Merriam started a family printing business in 1798, which branched into Springfield and printed Noah Webster's *First Dictionary of the English Language* in 1843. The company evolved into the current Merriam Webster publishing company.

Albert A. Michelson   The man who measured the speed of light Worcester - 1902

Michelson was chairman of Clark University's Physics Department. His prize-winning work concerned the measurement of light. He invented several interferometers, and his Michelson-Morely Experiment in 1887 marked the beginning of modern physics and opened the door to the relativity theories of Einstein who wrote, "I always think of Michelson as the artist in science."

Dr. Joseph E. Murray   Nobel Prize winner, performed the first human kidney transplant   Milford

Dr. Murray, born in 1919, graduated from Milford High School and later Holy Cross College.

"On Dec. 23, 1954, Dr. Murray transplanted a kidney...the landmark operation began the era of transplant surgery...Dr. Murray and several colleagues succeeded in solving the problem of organ rejection using the immunosuppressive drug Azathiaprine...The 1990 Nobel Prize in Medicine was awarded to Dr. Murray for his discoveries..." Pamela Fields, Milford, MA.

Eleanor Norcross   Impressionist painter and philanthropist   Fitchburg

The first woman to have a retrospective at the Louvre, Norcross (1854-1923) grew up in Fitchburg, graduated 2nd in her class from Fitchburg Academy at 16, went on to study painting in Paris, and regularly exhibited her work alongside Degas, Cassatt, Monet and others. She left funds to found the Fitchburg Art Museum, and she shipped home countless art objects, which are displayed at the museum, along with some of her paintings.

Jack O'Connell Mystery author Worcester

O'Connell's mysteries *Box Nine* and *Wireless* are both set in "Quinsigamond, " a mythical town he has based on Worcester. *Box Nine* won the 1990 Warner Books Mysterious Discovery Prize.
" O'Connell has appeared twice at the Tatnuck Bookseller Marketplace with his wife, Ruth, and daughter, Claire. Both books are great reads," Larry Abramoff, Worcester, MA.

Charles Olson Poet, critic Worcester

Olson (1910-1970) graduated from Classical High in 1928. His poetry influenced a generation of younger poets, including Allen Ginsberg. His work includes *The Maximus Poems* and *The Post Office.*
" My favorite place in Worcester County is 4 Norman Ave., 3rd floor - the building in which Charles Olson, one of the greatest 20th Century poets, was raised. The house is mentioned in many Olson poems," Jim Fay, Worcester, MA.

Orpheus 1960's Rock group Worcester

Orpheus, whose hits included "Can't Find the Time to Tell You," and "I've Never Seen Love Like This," had three members from Worcester - Bruce Arnold, John Eric Gulliksen and Jack McKenes.

Albina Osipowich Olympic Gold Medalist - 1928 Worcester

This 17-year old swimmer from Columbia St. won the gold medal for the 100-meter freestyle in Amsterdam.

Frances Perkins First Woman Cabinet member U.S. Secretary of Labor, 1933-1945 Worcester

Perkins (1880-1887) was appointed Secretary of Labor by FDR. She pioneered New Deal legislation that created the Social Security Act and laws governing child labor, the minimum wage, unemployment insurance, and the 40-hour work week. She gradu ated from Worcester's Classical High School in 1898.

Lydia Pinkham Patent medicine entrepreneur Lunenburg

Pinkham (1819-1883) began manufacturing her famous vegetable compound for "women's troubles" in Lunenburg in the 1870's with roots from Mulpus Brook. She later opened a factory in Lynn, MA.

Cole Porter Famous songwriter Worcester

Porter (1892-1964) graduated from Worcester Academy Class of 1909, saying later that his talent for songwriting first "came to light" in Worcester. He went on to write "Anything Goes," "I've Got You Under My Skin," "Begin the Beguine," and "Night and Day."

Alisan Porter Child actress Worcester

Born in 1981, Alisan starred with James Belushi in 1991 Hollywood film *Curly Sue.*

Olive Higgins Prouty Author of *Stella Dallas* Worcester

Author of the 1922 novel, *Stella Dallas,* Olive Prouty (1882-1974) was born in Worcester. *Stella Dallas* is the story of a poor mother rejected by her socialite daughter. The book was first made into a play, then a silent movie, and later into a sound movie starring Barbara Stanwyck. Bette Midler starred in the 1990 re-make.

Gen. Rufus Putnam The "Father of Ohio" Rutland, Sutton, Upton, N. Brookfield

Putnam (1738-1824) founded Marietta, Ohio's first permanent settlement. As Chief Engineer for the Continental Army, he built fortifications for George Washington in Brookline, Dorchester and Roxbury, as well as those at West Point. He was born in Sutton, grew up in Upton, apprenticed in N. Brookfield and moved to Rutland, where his house on Rte. 122-A is now a private home.

Luther Rice Founder of George Washington University Northborough

Rice, a Baptist missionary, was born in Northborough in 1783.

Mary Rowlandson First published female New England author Lancaster

Mary Rowlandson (1635-1678) wrote a "best seller" in 1682, *Narrative of the Captivity and Restoration,* the story of her capture by hostile natives and "redemption" four months later. (See Lancaster).

Deborah Sampson Revolutionary War soldier 1760-1827 enlisted in Worcester

Disguised as a man, Deborah Sampson joined the 4th Mass. regiment in Worcester on May 23, 1782, using her brother's name, Robert Shurtleff. She served honorably, was wounded twice, and won an $8 per month pension after the war from the U.S. Congress.

Mary Sawyer Sterling

Sawyer was the subject of "Mary Had a Little Lamb," written by John Roulstone in 1816 based on a true incident. (See Sterling)

Gen. Sidney Sherman First to yell, "Remember the Alamo!" Northborough

Sherman, who grew up in Northborough, is credited as the first to yell, "Remember the Alamo!" at the battle of San Jacinto.

Samuel Slater Father of the Industrial Revolution Webster

Slater (1768-1835) founded the town of Webster and built its first cotton mill in 1811. (see Webster).

John F. "Jack" Smith President and CEO of General Motors Worcester

Smith grew up in Worcester and graduated from Shrewsbury's St. John's High School in 1956. (Ironically, the previous GM Chairman and CEO, Robert Stempel, also had a Worcester connection, - he was a 1955 graduate of WPI).

Casey Stengel Baseball Hall of Famer Blackstone Valley

Stengel (1890-1975) played baseball for the Blackstone Valley Mill League before joining the majors. As manager of the New York Yankees from 1949-1960, he led the team to 10 pennants and 7 World Series titles. (See Millville).

Lucy Stone Women's rights leader West Brookfield, Warren

Stone (1818-1893) was a famous feminist speaker. Her marriage to Henry Blackwell in 1855 made news when she and her husband protested the suspension of women's rights in marriage. The term "Lucy Stoners" was applied to other feminists of the day. (See W. Brookfield, Warren).

Marshall "Major" Taylor World class cyclist Worcester

Called "The Worcester Whirlwind," Taylor (1878-1932) was the first black athlete to win an international competition. He moved to Worcester in 1895 from Indianapolis, and lived here 35 years.

Ernest Thayer Author of *Casey at the Bat* Worcester

First published in 1888, Thayer's famous poem was inspired by his schoolmate at Worcester's Classical High School, Henry Casey. The poem's last line is legendary, "But there is no joy in Mudville - mighty Casey has struck out."

Judge Webster Thayer Judge of the Sacco-Vanzetti trial Worcester

Italian immigrants and anarchists Nicola Sacco and Bartolomeo Vanzetti were charged with robbery of a paymaster in S. Braintree and were executed in 1927. Thayer (1857-1933) was criticized for his charge to the jury which resulted in conviction. In 1930 a bomb severely damaged his home and 17 others on Institute Road.

Isaiah Thomas Patriot, printer and member of the Sons of Liberty Worcester

Thomas (1749-1831) moved his printing presses to Worcester April 16, 1775, rode with Paul Revere, took part in the Battle of Lexington and Concord, and published an eye-witness account in his famous rebel newspaper, "The Massachusetts Spy." After the Revolution, Thomas printed America's first dictionary in Worcester in 1788. He founded the American Antiquarian Society, which houses his printing press.

Harry Tobias "Tin Pan Alley" Songwriter Worcester

Prolific songwriter who wrote more than 60 songs, Tobias (1895-1994) was raised in a Worcester triple decker at 79 Harrison St. He collaborated with brothers Henry and Charles to write, "Miss You," "Don't Sit Under the Apple Tree," "Rose O'Day," and "Lazy, Hazy, Crazy Days of Summer." "The Old Lamplighter" was written about a real Worcester lamplighter who tended the gas lamps on their street. His songs were recorded by Bing Crosby, Nat King Cole, Ella Fitzgerald and Bill Haley.

Eli Whitney Inventor of the cotton gin Westborough

Whitney, (1765-1825) was born in Westborough and is renowned for inventing the cotton gin, which removed seeds from raw cotton, making southern cotton profitable for the first time. But he was also the first to make muskets by machine. Before, they had been tediously hand-crafted. His breakthroughs of standard, interchangeable parts and the division of labor laid the foundation for today's mass production methods.

Alicia Witt Actress Worcester

Witt is a young pianist, actress and was a child prodigy. She has appeared in films with Madonna and Richard Dreyfuss, and in a TV series with Cybill Shepherd.

Fabulous Firsts

Anesthesia Dr. William Thomas Green Morton Charlton

A dentist, Morton was the first to use ether as an anesthetic in 1846. He later demonstrated its use at Mass. General Hospital in Boston in an amphitheater known today as the "Ether Dome."

Baseball Catcher's Mask St. Mark's School Southborough

First used in 1875 by St. Mark's School catcher, who modified a fencing mask to protect his broken nose. Later patented by a Harvard student, who was on the opposing team that day.

Birth Control Pill Developed by the Worcester Foundation for Experimental Biology Shrewsbury

Announced in 1957; approved by the FDA in June, 1960.
Developed by Drs. Gregory Pincus and Min-Chueh Chang.

Carpet Loom 1855 Clinton

Invented by Erastus Bigelow, whose carpet empire had the slogan, "A title on the door rates a Bigelow on the floor." (See Clinton)

Curve Ball Pitch W.A. "Candy" Cummings Athol

Cummings, later an Athol businessman, pitched the first curve ball in 1867 when playing for the Brooklyn Stars. A plaque at the Baseball Hall of Fame in Cooperstown credits Cummings with turning baseball into a science, transforming the sport. Cummings got the idea tossing clamshells on the beach in 1864, and spent several years perfecting his technique. After his retirement from major league baseball in 1877, he returned to Athol, where he ran a paint and wallpaper store and pitched for the amateur baseball team, the "Athols."

Elm Park Park and Elm Sts. Worcester

Elm Park, designed by Olmstead of Central Park and Boston's Emerald Necklace fame, is considered to be the nation's first public park

First American Nobel Prize Winner 1902 Albert A. Michelson Worcester

Michelson was chairman of Clark University 's Physics Department whose prize-winning work concerned the measurement of light. *(see Famous People)*

First Farmer's Almanac 1792 West Boylston

Robert B. Thomas, a West Boylston school teacher, published the first *Farmer's Almanac,* which farmers considered second in importance only to the Bible. The Almanac published weather predictions and other helpful hints.

First federally-licensed AIDS test Cambridge Biotech Corp. Worcester 1988

Cambridge Biotech, formerly Cambridge Bioscience Corp., received a federal license for its HIV-1 rapid diagnostic test on Dec. 13, 1988.

First Major League Baseball "Perfect Game" Pitched by J. Lee Richmond Worcester June 12, 1880

Richmond pitched for The Worcesters, a National League team from 1880-1882.

A perfect game is one in which no batter is allowed to reach base by any method. The Worcesters retired the Clevelands in 1-2-3 order nine successive times.

First National Woman's Rights Convention 1850 Worcester

Abby Kelley Foster spoke at both the first and second convention (also held in Worcester in 1851). Other notable attendees were Lucy Stone, Susan B. Anthony, Lucretia Mott and William Lloyd Garrison.

First Radio Station to play The Beatles WORC-Radio Worcester

Disc jockey Dick "The Derby" Smith introduced the Beatles to the country on Worcester radio station WORC. The Beatles were so thankful they gave Smith the gold record for their hit, "She Loves You," and inscribed it, "To America's first believer."

First Ted Williams home run in New England 1939 Worcester

Legendary Red Sox slugger Ted Williams hit his first home run in New England in 1939 during an exhibition game played against Holy Cross College at Fitton Field.

G Suit Developed by David Clark (1903 - 1989) Worcester

The famous "Anti-G" suit that prevents test pilots from blacking out when pulling out of high-speed dives was developed in Worcester by David Clark. Famous pilots to wear the suit include Chuck Yeager and Neil Armstrong. The company also manufactured all of NASA's Gemini spacesuits, including the suit worn by astronaut Ed White in the first U.S. spacewalk in June, 1965.

Hook Organ Mechanics Hall Worcester

The oldest unaltered instrument of its kind in the Western Hemisphere, believed to be the only four-keyboard organ built before 1900 left in existence. The 3,504 pipe organ was made by the E.& G.G. Hook company of Boston, and was dedicated in 1864. It was featured in the 1984 movie, "The Bostonians".

Liquid-fueled rocket Auburn

Invented by Robert Goddard, Clark University professor. (see Famous People).

Massachusetts' First Public Reading of the Declaration of Independence 1776 Worcester

Isaiah Thomas read the Declaration from the western porch of the meeting house, and his Massachusetts Spy was the first New England newspaper to print the Declaration.

Modern-day typewriter 1840 Worcester

Invented by Charles Thurber.

Monkey Wrench 1840 Worcester

Invented by Loring Coes. Coes Knife Co. was in business in Worcester on Coes Pond until the 1990's.

Pink Flamingo Lawn Ornaments 1950's Leominster

The ubiquitous plastic pink flamingos that decorate so many American lawns were first manufactured by Union Products in Leominster.

Postage Stamp Millbury

The country's first postage stamp was manufactured in Millbury, and the famous "Return to Sender" postal phrase was a Worcester invention.

Rickshaw 1846 Worcester

Albert Tolman built a "man-drawn lorry" in Worcester for a missionary heading to South America. From there, the rickshaw made its way to popularity in Asia.

Sewing Machine Spencer

Patented by Elias Howe in 1846 (see Spencer).

Sewing Machine Needle apparatus Silas Stuart Sterling

Stuart invented the device to make sewing machine needles.

Shay's Rebellion 1786 Worcester

First organized protest of the new government after the Revolution. Farmers led by Daniel Shays marched on the Worcester courthouse to protest high taxes. (See Hubbardston).

Shredded Wheat 1890 Worcester

Invented by Henry Perky in his Jackson St. factory. Worcester was once the "shredded wheat capital of the world."

Spring Bed Spencer

Developed by Tyler Howe, uncle of sewing machine inventor Elias Howe.

Steam Calliope Invented in 1855 by Joshua Stoddard (1814-1902) Worcester

Synonymous with the sound of the circus, the calliope has a keyboard connected by wires to valves that contain whistles. Stoddard's invention became a favorite during circus parades, political rallies, at carnivals and on riverboats.

Valentine 1847 Worcester

Esther Howland (1828-1904) was the first person to mass produce valentines in the U.S. She liked imported valentines, and began to make valentines with sentimental messages at home, later employing several women and using an assembly line method for her valentines decorated with doves, doilies and roses. By 1874 she was using the name, "The New England Valentine Company." Her business eventually grossed $100,000 per year, and she was later bought out by The George C. Whitney Co., also of Worcester.

Webster Lake Webster

Real name: Lake Chargoggagoggmanchauggagoggchaubunagungamaugg – The longest geographic name in the U.S., the longest lake name in the world.

White Chocolate Shrewsbury

Developed and first sold by Hebert's Candies in the early 1950's.

Windchill 1939

Windchill, which measures the combined effects of temperature and wind velocity on the loss of heat by human skin, was first defined by Clark University Ph.D. Paul A. Siple, (1909-1968) in 1939. On a 20 degree day with a 10 m.p.h. wind, the "windchill factor" is 3 degrees. Siple, an expert on cold weather, tested his theory in Antarctica, where he also named a previously uncharted 4,000' high mountain range the "Clark Mountains" in honor of his alma mater. *(He named five individual peaks after his favorite geography professors.)*

Worcester State Hospital 1833 - The country's first publicly financed insane asylum Worcester

Sigmund Freud visited Worcester State Hospital in 1909 during his first and only trip to America.

Yellow "Smiley Face" button 1963 Worcester

This "national icon" was designed by Worcester graphic artist Harvey Ball, for an in-house morale boosting promotion at The America Group Insurance Company in Worcester. The company wanted to promote a "smile attitude" among workers and with customers.The rest is history.

Sources: The Telegram & Gazette; The Worcester Historical Museum; various town historical societies; Grolier Academic American Encyclopedia; Forty Immortals of Worcester and Its County, Worcester National Bank, 1920; Heart of the Commonwealth, Margaret A. Erskine, Windsor Publications, 1981; Lunenberg, The Heritage of Turkey Hills, Nelde K. Drumm, Margaret P. Harley, Lunenberg Historical Society, 1977; More Once-Told Tales of Worcester County, Albert B. Southwick, Databooks, 1994; Northborough: A Town and Its People, 1638-1975, William H. Mulligan, Jr., Northborough American Revolution Bicentennial Commission, 1982; Once-Told Tales of Worcester County, Albert B. Southwick, Databooks, 1994;The City and the River, Vol. I, Doris Kirkpatrick, Fitchburg Historical Society, 1971; Worcester Area Writers 1680-1980, Michael True, Worcester Public Library, 1987, Worcester County residents.

Notes

Notes

Chapter 3

Getting Here - Travel Resources

Planes, trains and automobiles - also buses, limos, taxis and car rentals. This chapter has helpful travel listings organized first by category and town and then alphabetically by business name. For information on travel by water, on foot, on skis, or alternative air travel, (ballooning), see Recreation/Chapter 8. Any more hot tips on getting around - send comments and notes to Favorite Places C/O Tatnuck Bookseller 335 Chandler St. Worc., MA 01602. (Reminder, things change - call first.)

Airline Service

Continental Express

375 Airport Drive, Worcester Municipal Airport
Worcester
(800) 525-0280
Flights to Newark International Airport. Call for schedule information and reservations.

USAir Express
250 Commercial St., Suite 415
Worcester
(800) 428-4322
Flights to many areas. Call for schedule information and reservations.

Airports

Logan International Airport
Boston
(617) 561-1800
Boston's Logan International Airport is located about 40 miles outside of Worcester. To get there, take Route 122 South to the Mass Turnpike eastbound to Route 93 and on to the Callahan Tunnel; Logan is one-quarter mile further on the right. The Airport Handicapped Van provides free service between terminals from 4 am to 1 am daily. (617) 561-1769
Hot Tip
- if 93N is jammed try Atlantic Ave.

T. F. Green Airport
Warwick, R.I.
(401) 737-4000
Daily flights to various destinations. Call for directions and flight information, or contact a travel agent.

Bradley International Airport
Windsor Locks, Conn.
(203) 292-2000
Service to a variety of cities on many major airlines. Call for directions and flight information, or contact a travel agent.

Worcester Municipal Airport
375 Airport Drive Exit 10/Mass Pike
Exit 17/290 East
Exit 18/290 West
Worcester
(508) 754-2359
(508) 792-0610
Just four miles from downtown, Worcester Municipal Airport is 36 air miles from Boston and 136 air miles from New York City. Modern terminal building completed in 1994. Facilities include two runways, two jetways for passenger loading. Daily flights to Newark & Philadelphia. Served by Continental Airlines (800) 525-0280; USAir Express (800) 428-4322. Avis, Hertz, National.

Aviation (General)

Amity Flight School
375 Airport Drive
Worcester
(508) 791-0156
flight training (508) 756-7703
Flight Training; private, commercial, instrument, ATP, Multi-level engine instruction, FAA written exams, all instructor training; Complete aircraft maintenance; general aviation, corporate aircraft. Call for further information.

Bus Service

SCM Elderbus
Southbridge, Barre, & Sutton
124 Southbridge Road
Charlton
(508) 248-1050 all others, (508) 248-1051 Webster, Dudley, (508) 248-1054 Spencer, Brookfields
26 vehicles serving the following member towns: Barre, Brimfield, Brookfield, East Brookfield, North Brookfield, West Brookfield, Charlton, Douglas, Dudley, Holland, New Braintree, Oakham, Princeton, Rutland, Southbridge, Spencer, Sturbridge, Sutton, Wales, Warren, and Webster; also providing service to elderly, handicapped and clients of the state department of Public Health and Public Welfare.

MART - Montachusett Area Regional Transit
147 Water St.
Fitchburg
(508) 345-7711 or (800) 922-5636
Bus routes serving Fitchburg, Leominster, Lunenburg (to new Wal-Mart) and Gardner. Elderly/Disabled Dial-a-Ride Service available through Councils on Aging in Fitchburg 345-9598, Leominster 534-7511, Gardner 632-2839, Lancaster, 365-5388, Sterling 422-8111, Hubbardston, 928-5735, Ashburnham, 827-5000, Westminster 874-7402, Hardwick, (413) 477-8745, and Lunenburg 582-4166. For TDD Service for deaf or hearing impaired, call 1-800-789-0577.

Big Daddy Tours
3 Beverly St.
Oxford
(508) 987-8295
Tours throughout New England. Call for further information and reservations.

Fox Bus Lines
Silver Fox Drive P.O. Box 1042
Millbury, Worcester
(508) 865-6000
(800) 342-5998
Charter and tours available. Call for further information.

Greyhound Bus Lines
75 Madison St.
Worcester
(508) 754-3247 of (800) 223-0188
Daily service to various U.S. destinations. Call for schedule and fare information.

Peter Pan Bus Lines
75 Madison St.
Worcester
(508) 754-3247 (800) 231-2222
Service to destinations throughout the U.S, daily service to Boston. Call for schedules and information.

Worcester Regional Transit Authority (WRTA)
287 Grove St.
Worcester
(508) 791-WRTA
(508) 756-8321
Buses operate from 5:30 am until late evening on more than 28 routes, serving Worcester and 12 surrounding communities. Call for further information on routes, schedules and special services.

Car Pools

Mass Pike Car Pool
(617) 248-2833
Call for car pooling information along the Mass Pike. Parking areas located along or near the Mass Pike.
Millbury, Worcester, Auburn, Sturbridge, Charlton, Oxford, Upton, Grafton , Westborough, Hopkinton, Southborough.

Car Rentals

Avis
Worcester Municipal Airport, 375 Airport Drive
Worcester
(508) 754-7004 or (800) 831-2847
Luxury and compact cars available. Call for reservations.

Budget Rent-A-Car
33 Millbrook Street
(Corner Millbrook & Gold Star Blvd)
Worcester
(508) 852-0361
(800) 682-5231
Compact, Luxury cars, 7-15 passenger vans available. One way car and truck rentals nationwide. Service downtown and the airport. Call for reservations.

Enterprise Rent-A-Car
24 Portland St.
Worcester
(508) 792-4700 or 752-4100
Luxury to oompact cars, 8 passenger mini-vans. Call for reservations.

Hertz Rent-A-Car
375 Airport Drive
Worcester
(508) 753-7203 or (800) 654-3131
Luxury, compact cars and seven passenger vans. Call for reservations.

Children's Transportation

Safe Kids Shuttle
P.O. Box 7556
Worcester
(508) 791-6004
Childrens door-to-door transportation service to assist parents in Worcester County; service to and from school, dentist, soccer practice, etc. Call for details. Smoke-Free.

Robert L. McCarthy & Son, Inc.
Brookfield
(508) 885-2976
Destinations within Wachusett region, safe, reliable children's transportation 7 days a week, to day care, nursery school, after school activities, appointments. Fully insured, 2-way radio, licensed and certified drivers, clean late model vehicles.

Limousine Service

Aristocrat Limousine
32 Dodge Ave.
Worcester
(508) 854-3204
Limousine services for all occasions, concerts, sporting events, weddings, proms, Foxwood Packages, airport. Call for further information and reservations.

Baccarat Limousine Service
700 Plantation St.
Worcester
(508) 754-7226
(800) 654-5453
Limousines for all occasions, airport, weddings, proms, concerts, etc. Call for further information and reservations.

Capital Limousine Inc.
33 Chestnut St.
Winchendon
(508) 297-4400 or (800) 776-5466
All occasion limousine services, airport, weddings, proms, concerts, super stretch limousines available. Call for further information and reservations.

Comfort Limousine
69 Donovan Road
N. Brookfield
(508) 867-4000
Limousines for all occasions. Airport, weddings, proms, concerts and Foxwood 7-hour package. Call for further information and directions.

Corporate Limousine
1 Buckley Dr.
Auburn
(508) 852-5176
Specializing in airport transportation and historical tours around Worcester. Thorough knowledge of Worcester's most interesting historical and cultural sights to see and the fascinating stories behind each of them. Tours arranged according to interests: shopping, dining, museums, sightseeing, etc.

Dark Horse Limousine Service
30 Dustin St.
Worcester
(508) 756-0271
All occasion limousine service, airport, concerts, weddings, proms, nights out, etc. Call for reservations and further information.

Family Airport Shuttle
P.O. Box 7556
Worcester, MA 01605
(508) 791-6004
Airport transportation to Worcester & Boston airports; low rates, smoke-free, families, groups, individuals, college students, business travel; door-to-door service. Call for further information.

Flick's Limousine
513 Park Ave.
Worcester
(508) 752-3991 or 1-(800) 523-2466
All occasion limousine services, weddings, proms, 'baby's first ride home, nights out, etc. Call for further information and reservations.

Fuller Limousine Service
150 Shrewsbury St.
Boylston
(508) 869-3400
All occasion services, airport, weddings, proms, concerts, nights out, etc.

Knight's Airport Limousine Service
2000 Grafton Road
East Millbury
(508) 839-6252 or (800) 227-7005
Door-to-door to and from Logan & Worcester Airports. Call for further information and ask about super savers.

My Limousine Service
800 Main St.
Holden
(508) 829-5466
Airport, wedding, dinner packages, nights on the town, anniversaries, birthdays, bachelor & bachelorette parties; serving the Wachusett Area.

New England Livery
296 St. Nicholas Avenue
Worcester
(508) 853-7356
All occasion transportation services, airport, weddings, etc. Call for further information and reservations.

Premier Limousine Service
Union St.
Leominster
(508) 534-5489
Prompt, courteous, dependable service to and from Logan & Worcester airports.

Prestige Limousine
469 Central Turnpike
Sutton
865-0212
Red Sox – Boston Theatre – concerts - weddings – Great Woods – proms - corporate accounts.

Professional Limousine Services
81 Ballard St.
Worcester
(508) 754-1205
All occasion limousine service, airport, concerts, weddings, proms, nights out, etc. Call for further information and reservations.

Shrewsbury/West Boylston Livery Service
Quinsigamond Ave.
Shrewsbury
(508) 852-3800
Rolls Rental, Wedding Center
161 Turnpike Road, Route 9
Westborough
(508)366-9727
Special occasion services in Rolls Royce or Horse and Buggy. Call for further information and reservations.

Worcester Airport Limousine
310 Park Ave.
Worcester
(508) 756-4834 in Mass. (800) 660-0992, outside of Mass. (800) 343-3691
Transportation to and from Airports. Charters available. Call for further information and reservations.

Yaz Limousine
3 Beach Street
Milford
(508) 473-5952
All occasion limousine services, weddings, proms, airport, concerts, nights out, etc. Call for further information and reservations.

Taxis

Arrow Cab
1051 Southbridge St.
Worcester
(508) 756-5184, or 756-9000

Red Cab Taxi
50 Franklin St.
Worcester
(508) 792-9999

Yellow Cab
167 Grand St.
Worcester
(508) 754-3211

Trains

MBTA Commuter Rail
Rte 2A, east of junction with Rte 12
Fitchburg
(617) 722-3200
(800) 392-6100
SmarTraveler 374-1234-8-*
Fitchburg-Boston $4.75 one way
4 round trips daily M-F
Inbound (a.m.)
Fitch 5:45, 6:25, 6:55, 7:15
Arrive North Station
Boston 7:15, 8:00, 8:20, 8:49
Outbound (p.m.)
N. Stat. 4:50, 5:20, 5:30, 6:15
Arrive Fitchburg
6:25, 6:50, 7:00, 7:51

Amtrak
45 Shrewsbury St.
Worcester
(800) 872-7245 or 755-0356
Passenger rail service is provided to many destinations throughout the country. Call for schedule information.

MBTA Commuter Rail
45 Shrewsbury St. Amtrak Station
Worcester
(617) 722-3200 or (800) 392-6099 Hearing Impaired TDD (617) 722-5146
Worc-Boston $4.75 one way, free parking, 3 round trips daily M-F

Inbound (a.m.)

Worc	5:45	6:20	7:15
Fram.	6:15	6:50	7:45
S. Sta.	7:02	7:20	8:15

Outbound (p.m.)

S. Sta.	4:50	5:30	6:00
Fram.	5:25	6:19	6:30
Worc.	5:55	6:49	7:00

Half-fare, $2.35; 12-ride, 47.50; Monthly Pass, $136

Notes

Chapter 4

Support Services

If you're a "townie" like me, the following information may not seem the most vital, but there are a lot of people who are ready to help the traveler, visitor or resident. So here's a list: Chambers of Commerce, sources of information for entertainment, real estate, tourism and general visitor needs, along with an interesting history of one of this books main sponsors, the Worcester Telegram & Gazette. The following listings are sorted by category, by town. (Again, I hope we didn't miss anything but as I told you before; send us your notes, updates and comments and I'll try to include them in the next edition. Mail to: Favorite Places C/O Tatnuck Bookseller 335 Chandler Street Worc., MA 01602).

Chambers of Commerce

Clinton Chamber of Commerce
One Green St.
Clinton
(508) 368-7687
Serving Berlin, Bolton, Clinton, Lancaster, Sterling, Harvard.

Holden Chamber of Commerce
P.O. Box 377
Holden, MA 01520
(508) 829-9220; fax: same
Providing business support for Holden.

North Central Mass. Chamber of Commerce
110 Erdman Way
Leominster
(508) 840-4300
Serving Ashburnham, Ashby, Ayer, Fitchburg, Groton, Harvard, Lancaster, Leominster, Lunenburg, Pepperell, Princeton, Shirley, Sterling, Townsend, Westminster.

Greater Milford Chamber of Commerce
258 Main St. Suite 306, P.O. Box 621
Milford, MA 01757
(508) 473-6700; fax: 473-8467
Serving Milford, Hopedale, Mendon, Hopkinton, Upton, Medway, Millis, Holliston and Bellingham.

Tri-Community Chamber of Commerce
380 Main St.
Sturbridge
(508) 347-2761
Serving Sturbridge, Southbridge and Charlton.

Worcester Area Chamber of Commerce
33 Waldo St.
Worcester
(508) 753-2924
Business information and support services for towns in the Greater Worcester area. Chambers of Commerce for Northborough/Westborough, Auburn and the Blackstone Valley are also at this location.

Entertainment Information

Worcester Phoenix
314 Washington St.
Auburn
(508) 832-5317
A free weekly newspaper issued on Fridays, it also carries some of the same features as its parent publication, The Boston Phoenix. Includes news, features and entertainment listings.

Worcester Magazine
172 Shrewsbury St.
Worcester
(508) 755-8004
A free weekly newspaper issued on Wednesdays, Worcester Magazine has news, features, and a comprehensive listing of what to see and do in the area, including museums, restaurants, concerts and more.

Worcester Telegram & Gazette
"Datebook" and "Time Out" sections
20 Franklin St.
Worcester
(508) 793-9100
Comprehensive entertainment listings are included Sundays in the T&G's "Datebook" section, and also on Thursdays in the "Time Out" section.

General Information

Up to the Minute

Worcester Telegram & Gazette CityLine
20 Franklin St.
Worcester
(508) 792-9400
This popular service carries stock prices, soap opera updates, sports scores and school cancellations. It has received more than 10 million telephone calls from local residents since it began in 1989.

Realtor Information

Greater Worcester Board of Realtors
70 Elm St.
Worcester
(508) 752-2802; fax: 752-4960
For information on realtors in Worcester County.

Tourism Councils

Blackstone Valley Tourism Council
P.O. Box 7663
Cumberland, R.I. 02864
(401) 334-0837; 334-7773
Tourist information services.

Worcester County Convention and Visitors Bureau
33 Waldo St.
Worcester
(508) 753-2920
Convention, tour planning, housing bureau, transportation coordination, information packets, family tours, site inspections, spouse tours.

Tourist Information Centers

Massachusetts Turnpike Information Center
Mass Pike (I-90), eastbound after Exit 9
Charlton
(508) 248-4581
At the Charlton service area eastbound, a model of the John Ward House serves as the Tourist Information Center, restrooms.

Massachusetts Turnpike Information Center
Mass Pike (I-90), westbound before Exit 9
Charlton
(508) 248-3853
Tourist information center, restrooms, handicapped accessible.

Gardner Heritage State Park Visitor Center
26 Lake St.
Gardner
(508) 630-1497
Tourist information, handicapped access, restrooms.

Sturbridge Tourist Information Center
380 Main St., Rte. 20
Sturbridge
(508) 347-7594; 1-800 628-8379
Providing tourist information on Sturbridge, adjacent towns and Worcester, handicapped accessible, open 9 am -5 pm.

Tatnuck Bookseller Marketplace
335 Chandler St.
Worcester
(508) 756-7644
An official Mass. Tourist Information Center, also a bookstore, gift store, 125-seat restaurant. Complete section of books about Worcester and by Worcester-area authors; sportswear shop carries Worcester T-shirts, sweatshirts and novelty items, handicapped access, restrooms.

Worcester Lunch Car Diner Visitors Information Center
Highland St. & Main, next to "The Aud" - Worcester Memorial Auditorium, Worcester
Find out what's to see and do, and get a peek inside a vintage Worcester Lunch Car diner. (Open to the public, but not staffed).

Telegram & Gazette

by Kathleen Pierce

(*Editor's note: one of the most comprehensive information sources in Worcester County is the Worcester Telegram & Gazette. It is the state's third largest newspaper and its coverage area includes all of Worcester County and beyond. For information, call* (508) 793-9100.

When the building at 20 Front Street opened in 1910, its proud owner proclaimed it the "Temple of Truth."

To a local magazine, it was the "Newest Newspaper Plant in America."

Though the physical structure has changed much during the past 75 years, the work carried on inside is essentially the same.

The four-story building still houses the headquarters of the Telegram & Gazette. With a circulation of more than 112,000 papers daily and in excess of 140,000 on Sunday, the newspaper is by far the largest in Central Massachusetts and 96th in size in the country.

While the company's mission has changed little since it moved from its old offices on Main Street to the new Franklin Street building, it has expanded in size, products and technology. The paper now covers 64 Central Massachusetts cities and towns and has more than a dozen news offices around Worcester County and in Boston. Its 825 employees make it the 23rd largest employer in the county.

A state-of-the-art printing plant with two $8 million presses opened in 1991 in the Millbury Industrial Park off Route 20. Paper rolls weighing 2,700 pounds each and holding 10 miles of paper race through the clean, computerized machines at a speed of 2,400 feet per minute, or nearly 26.5 miles per hour.

The Scott presses installed at 20 Franklin St. in 1910 churned out 20,000 papers an hour. Each Goss Flexoliner press in Millbury today can run off 75,000 56-page papers in the same amount of time.

Besides its newspapers, the Telegram & Gazette also operates CityLine, a telephone information service. CityLine's more than 200 categories of information include stock prices, soap opera updates, sports scores and school cancellations. The popular service has received more than 10 million telephone calls from local residents since it began in July 1989. Callers plug into CityLine by dialing (508) 792-9400.

Since 1938, the Telegram & Gazette has published the city of Worcester's only daily newspaper. But much vigorous and vituperous competition preceded that achievement.

The roots of the Telegram & Gazette wind back to 1851 when The Morning Transcript first hit the streets. On January 1, 1866, that paper became the Worcester Evening Gazette after being bought by a Woonsocket, R.I., dentist and a Worcester financier and newspaperman.

In November 1884, Austin P. Cristy, a belligerent and revenge-seeking Worcester lawyer, borrowed $300 to start a weekly paper he named the Worcester Sunday Telegram. Two years later, Cristy founded the Worcester Daily Telegram.

By his own accounts, Cristy's goal was to use his papers to crush "the ring" that had thwarted his political ambitions. He pursued his aim relentlessly, spicing his paper with "lurid editorials and slanted news stories," wrote one historian. Christy's formula had politicians fuming, but it succeeded. He was soon the biggest player in the Worcester newspaper game.

At that point, there were four papers in Worcester: the Telegram, The Evening Gazette, the Worcester Spy and the Worcester Evening Post.

By 1899, the tepid afternoon Gazette was floundering. Circulation was down to 2,285 papers a day. Then out of New Haven, Conn., rode two rescuers, George F. Booth and John Day Jackson. The Connecticut newspapermen bought the Gazette for $35,000 and infused it with new vigor. Booth, who ran the day-to-day operation, revamped the sports department, started a women's feature, gave prizes for baby pictures and began to run cartoons and comic strips, according to a history of Worcester newspapers. In fact, The Evening Gazette became the first paper in the country to print daily colored comics. (The innovation, begun on July 5, 1922, ended a couple of years later because of costs.)

Booth also launched the Gazette Santa party for needy children. The event was a precursor to the present-day Telegram & Gazette Santa Fund, which today raises more than $160,000 annually and buys Christmas gifts for more 10,000 needy children.

Under Booth's able journalistic hand, the Gazette's circulation climbed to 15,000 within eight years, according to the histories.

The rival papers came under one ownership in 1920. A year earlier, T.T. Ellis, a former pressroom foreman at the Telegram, bought that paper from the weary Cristy. Ellis had made a fortune for himself with the invention of a new type of press blanket, a fiber mat used as a cushion between press cylinders. A year after buying the Telegram, Ellis snapped up the Gazette from Booth and his partner.

Booth clearly was not happy about the sale of his paper and vowed to be back in business within five years. True to his word, he and a new partner, Harry G. Stoddard, president of Wyman-Gordon Co., bought the papers in December 1925.

The Worcester Spy had expired in May 1904. And the Worcester Evening Post was bought by the Telegram in October 1938. Thus began the Telegram & Gazette's reign as the city's only daily newspapers.

The Booth and Stoddard families owned the papers until October 1986, when they were sold to The Chronicle Publishing Co. of San Francisco.

In April 1989, the morning Worcester Telegram and afternoon Evening Gazette merged into one a.m. paper called the Telegram & Gazette.

Notes and Comments

Chapter 5

Where to Stay

Is your mother-in-law coming to visit ... for three weeks? Is your sister Sally coming to stay, ... with her 6 kids? Is tonight the night you have to sleep on the couch? Did the painters just leave and your house smells so bad you've got a migrane? So, whether you're looking for a romantic escape weekend, just visiting or want to take the kids camping, here are some great "where to stay" options: from cozy bed & breakfasts to elegant hotels, this chapter lists a variety of places to stay in Worcester County, including inns, motels and campgrounds. Selections are listed by category first, and grouped by towns. For example, motels in Auburn are listed before those in Worcester. (But don't forget, call first and report back to us. How were the beds, water pressure, the food? Do they have non-smoking rooms? Send your notes and comments to: Favorite Places C/O Tatnuck Bookseller 335 Chandler Street Worc., MA 01602).

To help plan parties or business meetings, we have included meeting space available with many listings.

Bed and Breakfasts, Campgrounds, Hotels, Inns, Motels, Youth Hostels, Vacation Cottages, Corporate Apartments.

Bed & Breakfast Reservation Service

The Folkstone Bed & Breakfast Reservation Service
51 Sears Rd.
Southborough
(508) 480-0380 or 1-800-762-2751
Reservation service representing 26 B&B's, offering carefully selected lodging in homes and small inns, both in Worcester, and in the surrounding towns of Central Massachusetts, including elegant modern, Victorian, Colonial and remodeled farmhouse settings.

Bed & Breakfasts

John Adams Homestead
287 Russell Hill Rd
Ashburnham
(508) 827-5388
1770 Colonial with 3 rooms and continental breakfast . Beautiful roses in summer and working to bring the eastern bluebirds back to the area. Call for reservations and directions.

Captain Samuel Eddy House
609 Oxford St. South
Auburn
(508) 832-7282
Five nonsmoking overnight rooms in a historic 1765 Colonial. One large and 2 small rooms accommodate up to 20 people for a meeting. Full breakfast served. By reservation only. Call for directions.

Hartman's Herb Farm Bed & Breakfast
1026 Old Dana Rd.
Barre
(508) 355-2015
Country style farm house with 3 guest rooms and full breakfast served. Call for directions.

Jenkin's House Bed Breakfast and Restaurant
West St. On the Common
Barre
(508) 355-6444 or 1-800-378-7373
Victorian home with 5 guest rooms, 3 with private bath, period furnishings and full breakfast served. Restaurant is open to the public for lunch and dinner, Wed. through Sun. Call for reservations and directions.
"The atmosphere is terrific. It is so relaxing and the food and desserts are incredible," Judy Kelley & Ed Wadleigh, Barre, MA.
"This is a beautifully restored home with unique furnishings, many rooms have fireplaces and lovely views of the Barre Common," Susan Morrall, Barre, MA

Stevens Farm Bed & Breakfast
749 Old Coldbrook Rd.
Barre
(508) 355-2227
Family farm for over 200 years, 5 rooms, outdoor pool, X-country skiing, hiking, banquet hall for small parties/conferences can accommodate up to 30 people, Continental breakfast served. Call for reservations and directions.

Ford's View Bed & Breakfast
179 Linden St.
Berlin
(508) 838-2909
200 year old farm house has 2 rooms, continental breakfast, outdoor pool, fishing pond and hiking trails. Call for reservations and directions.

The Fieldstone Victorian
40 Edgewater Dr.
Blackstone
(508) 883-4647
Victorian home, 2 rooms, overlooking the reservoir. Full breakfast served. Call for reservations and directions.

Colonial Bed & Breakfast Resort
625 Betty Spring Rd.
Gardner
(508) 630-2500
109 rooms, 5 meeting rooms, conference and ballroom facilities available for 30 to 300 people. Full-service restaurant and lounge. Suites, room service, indoor pool and parking available. Handicapped accessible. Call for directions.
"Its packages are very affordable. Fun, relaxing, very comfortable," Madaline Ruggiere-Danzilio, Shrewsbury, MA.

Hawke Bed & Breakfast
162 Pearl St.
Gardner
(508) 632-5909
Built around the late 1700's the three guest rooms are simply decorated with braided rugs and flowered spreads. Breakfast is a no-nonsense affair of expertly cooked eggs or pancakes. Call for reservations and directions.

Captain Slocomb House
6 South St., off the Common
Grafton
(508) 839-3095
Victorian home, 3 guest rooms, each with private bath, full breakfasts.

Heritage House
28 North St.
Grafton
(508) 839-5063
1795 Federal Colonial with 3 guest rooms furnished with European feather beds and antiques. Wonderful full breakfast served. Call for reservations and directions.

Carter Washburn House
34 Seven Bridge Rd.
Lancaster
(508) 365-2188
Federal house built in 1812, furnished with antiques and original art work. 4 rooms available, call for reservations and directions.

College Town Bed & Breakfast
12 Old Common Rd.
Lancaster
(508) 368-7000, or (508) 365-5016
5 rooms in a contemporary style home, deluxe continental breakfast served. Can accommodate up to 10 people for business meetings. Call for reservation and directions.

Deershorn Manor Bed & Breakfast
357 Sterling Rd.
Lancaster
(508) 365-9022
Historic Victorian estate, ideal for weddings and conferences. Antique furnishings, library, deluxe continental breakfast served. Call for reservations and directions.

Pine Hill Farm Bed & Breakfast
Pond St.
Paxton
(508) 791-1762
Historic 1750 house, furnished with antiques, 3 rooms, full hearty breakfast served. Call for reservation and directions.
"I love the smell of pine woods, the sight of crystal clear water in the nearby Pine Hill Reservoir, and the comfort of country furnishings and a home-made hearty breakfast," Barbara Sayre, Fayetteville, New York.
"It boasts old mill sites, lovely woodlands, many birds, including loons, delicious breakfasts and great hospitality," Sally Fay, Paxton, MA

Fernside Inn
162 Mountain Rd.
Princeton
(508) 464-2741
Restored historic vacation lodge dating to the mid-1800's, opening Fall '95; a tradition of rest and relaxation. 8 rooms with private baths, 4 with fireplaces. Close to Mt. Wachusett; beautiful view of Boston.

Apple Tree Bed & Breakfast
51 Sears Rd.
Southborough
(508) 460-6960
Farm house with antique furnishings, 3 guest bedrooms, 2 with private bath. Hearty continental breakfast served. Call for reservations and directions.

Spencer Country Inn
500 Main St., Rte. 9
Spencer
(508) 885-9036
10 rooms, in circa 1740 house, Continental breakfast served; 5 dining rooms seating 140; Banquet hall holds 250 for weddings, functions. Hogshead Pub has live entertainment on weekends. Call for reservations and directions.

Zukus Farm Bed & Breakfast
89 Smithville Rd.
Spencer
(508) 885-5320
Country post and beam is a working farm with one 3- room suite. Full breakfast served. Call for reservation and directions.
"Private, romantic, great secret escape from reality," Kathy Culver, Barre, MA.
"Fantastic food, fireplace, 'farm quiet' and massage," Judy Willey, North Brookfield, MA.

Sterling Orchards Bed & Breakfast
Kendall Hill Rd.
Sterling
(508) 422-6595
Restored 1740 Colonial with working orchard; 2 private guest rooms with private bath. Can accommodate meetings of up to 20 people.

Bethany Bed & Breakfast
5 McGregory Rd.
Sturbridge
(508) 347-5993
4 guest rooms with Laura Ashley linens throughout. Full breakfast served, outdoor dining in summer, lovely sitting room and private dining area. Special corporate rates, business meetings and Victorian Tea Parties available. Call for reservations and directions.

Colonel Ebenezer Crafts Inn
Fiske Hill Rd.
Sturbridge
(508) 347-3313
On the highest point in Sturbridge, this 18th Century Colonial has 8 rooms and is furnished with antiques and period reproductions. Deluxe Continental breakfast served. Call for reservations and directions.

Putnam House
211 Putnam Hill Rd.
Sutton
(508) 865-9094
18th Century hill-top farmhouse, with 1.5 rooms, fireplace in the bedroom, private adjoining bath. No smoking or animals. Children welcome, can provide crib, full breakfast. Close to the Mass Pike, I-395 and Rte.146.

Charles Capron House
2 Capron St.
Uxbridge
(508) 278-2214
Victorian B&B listed on the National Register of Historic Places, full breakfast, call for reservations and directions.

Rose Cottage Bed & Breakfast
24 Worcester St., Rte. 12
West Boylston
(508) 835-4034
1850 Gothic Victorian, 5 rooms with long stay accommodations available, full breakfast served. Conference room can accommodate up to 12 people. Decorated for the seasons and has won top honors for their Christmas decorating.

Worcester
For Bed and Breakfasts in and around Worcester, call Folkstone Bed and Breakfast Reservation Service 508-480-0380 or 1-800-762-2751

Campgrounds

Coldbrook Resort
Old Coldbrook Rd.
Barre
(508) 355-4648
106 sites, 55 full hookups, a/c allowed, tenting available, RV rentals, camping cabins, handicap restroom facilities, laundry, country grocery store, ice, tables, fire rings and grills. 2 swimming pools, wading pools, pond fishing, golf, hiking trails and more. Open April 15 through Oct 15. From jct Rte.122 & Fruitland St. go 1/4 mile East on Fruitland St. then 1 mile south on Coldbrook Road.

Crystal Springs
Rte. 117
Bolton
(508) 779-2711
219 sites, some full hookups available, tenting, group sites for RV's, laundry, grocery store and public phone. Swim pool, pond swimming, mini-golf, playground, 2 tennis courts, basketball, shuffleboard courts, sports field, horseshoes, volleyball, planned group activities. Open April 1 to Oct 15. From jct I-495 exit 27, go 1 3/4 mile west on Rte. 117.

Applewood Campgrounds
44 King Road
Charlton
(508) 248-7017
77 sites, full hookups, tenting available, group sites, grocery store, swimming pool, wading pool, basketball, playground, sports field, horseshoes, volleyball. Call for directions.

The Woodlot Campground
72 Stafford St.
Charlton
(508) 248-5141
91 sites, hookups, pull-thrus, tenting available, grocery store, laundry, coin games, swimming pool, wading pool, basketball, playground, planned group activities, movies, badminton, horseshoes, volleyball. Open May 1 through Oct 15. Call for directions.

Winding Brook Campground
Rte. 96
Douglas
(508) 476-7549
A campground with leveled sites among the pines. 145 sites, full hookups, tenting available, grocery store, rec room, swim pool, pond swimming, pond fishing, playground, planned group activities, sports field, horseshoes, hiking trails and volleyball. Open May 15 through Oct 1. Call for directions.

Lake Manchaug Campground
76 Oak St.
East Douglas
508) 476-2471 in season; off-season 476-2328
200 sites on 80 acres; crystal-clear lake; half mile of lake frontage; all sites have 5-way hook-ups available; swimming, boating, row boats allowed. Open May 1-Sept. 15.

Lake Dean Campgrounds
North Brookfield Rd.
Oakham
(508) 882-3125
Seasonal camping area on Lake Dean, fishing, swimming, boating, full hook-up sites, no tenting. Playground area and basketball. Call for further directions and reservations

Pine Acres Family Campground
203 Becham Rd.
Oakham
(508) 882-9509
350 campsites on Lake Dean; open year-round; full hook-ups, pull-through sites, full store, restaurant, adult lounge, and recreation building, children's playground, volleyball, tennis courts, horse-shoe pits, three beaches, lake front sites, rental R-V's, full-time activities director in summer.

Lamb City Campground
85 Royalston Rd.
Phillipston
(508) 249-2049 or out of Mass. 1-800-292-5262
150 sites, full hookups, pull-thrus, tenting available, RV rentals and supplies, laundry, convenience store, camping cabins, coin games, pools, wading pool, pond swimming, boating, electric motors only, ramp dock, canoe boat rentals, pond fishing, basketball, playground, shuffleboard, planned group activities (weekends only), sports field, horseshoes, hiking trails, volleyball. Open all year.

Pout & Trout Campgrounds
94 River Rd. (off Rte. 68)
Rutland
(508) 886-6677
156 sites, full hookups available, tenting available, group sites and limited grocery store. Coin games, swim pool, boating, no motors, pedal and row boat rentals, river/pond fishing, basketball, playground, planned group activities, field, horseshoes, volleyball. Call for directions. *"Peace and quiet, always something going on,"* Colleen Rochefort, Rochdale, MA

Yogi Bear Jellystone Park
30 River Rd.
Sturbridge
(508) 347-2336/(508) 347-9570
Open all year, 409 sites, full hookups, pull-thrus, cable TV, tenting available, camping cabins, handicap restroom facilities, grocery store, recreation hall, pools, lake swimming, whirlpool, water slide, boating, no motors, canoeing, row and pedal boat rentals, lake fishing, mini-golf, basketball, playground, shuffleboard, planned group activities, movies, badminton, horseshoes, hiking trails, volleyball, cross country skiing, snowmobile trails. Call for directions.

Kings Campgrounds
24 Holt Rd.
(Lake Manchaug)
Sutton
(508) 476-2534
On Lake Manchaug, 120 full hookups, tenting when space is available. Lake swimming, fishing, paddle boat rentals, grocery store, playground, volleyball, basketball, sports field, planned activities especially for children, handicapped accessible. Call for directions.

Indian Ranch Campgrounds
Rte. 16
Webster
(508) 943-3871
110 sites, full hookups, lake swimming, fishing, grocery store within walking distance. Banquet facilities, corporate outings, novelty store, golf nearby, handicapped accessible. Open on Sundays to the public; paddle and excursion boats, outdoor cocktail lounge, Country Western entertainment. Call for directions.

KOA-Sturbridge Webster Family Kampground
Rte. 16
Webster
(508) 943-1895
102 sites, hookups, pull-thrus, tenting available, limited grocery store, swimming pool, laundry, playground, shuffleboard courts, horseshoes, hiking trails and volleyball. Open April 15 through Oct 15. From Jct. I-395, exit 2, go 2 1/2 miles east on Rte. 16.

High View Campground
58 John Gilbert Rd.
West Brookfield
(508) 867-7800
163 sites, 110 full hookups, tenting available, convenience store, pool, pond fishing, playground, rec hall, adult lounge, vast hiking trails, 10 golf courses nearby. Opening April 15 through Oct 15. Call for directions.

The Old Sawmill Campground
Longhill Rd.
West Brookfield
(508) 867-2427
120 sites, full hookups, tenting available, limited grocery store, rec room, coin games, swim pool, wading pool, basketball, playground, planned group activities (weekends only) horseshoes, hiking trails. Open May 1 through Columbus Day. Call for directions.

Sutton Falls Camping Area
Manchaug Rd.
West Sutton
(508) 865-3898 or 1-800-439-3898
A lakeside campground with rolling terrain and semi-wooded sites. 100 sites, full hookups, tenting available, limited grocery store, equipped pavilion, lake swimming boating, electric motors only, canoeing, row boat rentals, lake fishing, playground, planned group activities (weekends only), horseshoes and hiking trails. Open mid April through Columbus Day. Call for directions.

The Old Holbrook Place
114 Manchaug Rd.
West Sutton
(508) 865-5050
A lakeside campground in a pine grove

with open and shaded sites. 66 sites, full hookups, limited grocery store, lake swimming, boating, canoeing, ramp, row boat rentals, lake fishing, hiking trails, day picnicking. Recreation open to public. Open Memorial Day through Labor Day. Call for directions.

Lake Dennison State Recreation Area
Rte. 202
Winchendon
(508) 939-8962
Beautiful place to camp and swim in a nice clear lake. Good campsites at reasonable rates. 151 sites, no hookups, tenting available, swimming, boating, no motors, canoeing, ramp fishing, planned group activities, hiking trails. Recreation open to the public. Open Memorial Day through Columbus Day. Call for directions.

Otter River State Forest
Rte. 202
Winchendon
(508) 939-8962
97 sites, no hookups, tenting available, pavilion, lake swimming, stream fishing, planned group activities, sports field, hiking trails. Recreation open to the public. Open Memorial Day through Columbus day. Go 7 miles south on US 202.

Hotels

Best Western Royal Plaza Hotel & Conference Center
Jct. Rtes. 2 & 31, (exit 28) 150 Royal Plaza Drive
Fitchburg
(508) 342-7100
325 rooms, restaurant, lounge, indoor pool, sauna, Jacuzzi, sun deck, exercise room, jogging trails. 59,000 s.f. of exhibit space that accommodates 340 exhibit booths or a meeting of 3,000 people. Hotel has 12 function rooms.

Sheraton Leominster Inn & Conference Center
Erdman Way, off Rte. 2
Leominster
(508) 534-9000
Modern hotel and conference center; 187 rooms, 12 meeting rooms, amphitheater, restaurant seats 100 and 120 in lounge, entertainment on weekends, recreation facility, indoor pool, 9,728 s.f. exhibit space available, free parking, handicapped accessible. Call for directions.

Milford Courtyard by Marriott
10 Fortune Blvd.
Milford
(508) 634-9500 or 1-800- 321-2211
152 rooms, breakfast, dining area, lounge, indoor pool, hot tub, 2 conference rooms can accommodate up to 32 people, exercise room, handicapped accessible.

Sheraton Milford Inn
11 Beaver St.
Milford
(508) 478-7010
Modern hotel, 173 rooms, restaurant, lounge, entertainment, indoor pool, 12 meeting rooms, 5800 s.f. exhibit space available, handicapped accessible. Off Rte. 495 and Rte. 109.

Tage Inn
24 Beaver St.
Milford
(508) 478-8243
93 rooms, restaurant within walking distance, 1 meeting room can accommodate up to 12 people, handicapped accessible.

Chocksett Inn Hotel & Conference Center
59 Laurelwood Rd.
Sterling
(508) 422-3355 or 1-800- 439-7829
25 suites with full kitchen. Meeting and function rooms for up to 125 people.

Lounge, continental breakfast, handicapped accessible. Golf nearby.

Apple Inns Motor Lodge
478 Main St.
Sturbridge
(508) 347-5141
65 rooms, conference room can accommodate up to 40 people, restaurant within walking distance, handicapped accessible. Call for directions.

Sturbridge Host Hotel
366 Main St., opposite Old Sturbridge Village
Sturbridge
(508) 347-7393
Open year round on the shores of Cedar Lake; 241 rooms, canopy bedroms with fireplace, restaurant, lounge, entertainment, 15 meeting rooms, 12,100 s.f. exhibit space, tennis, racquetball, health and fitness center, indoor pool, whirpool, miniature golf. Beach for swimming & boating. Cross country skiing. Special group of VIP rooms, with private lounge. Antique, country and Christmas shops nearby. Handicapped accessible. Call for directions.

Residence Inn by Marriott of Boston
25 Connector Rd.
Westborough
(508) 366-7700 or 1-800- 331-3131
109 rooms, 1 & 2 bedroom suites with fully equipped kitchens, 1 meeting room can accommodate up to 15 people, outdoor pool, exercise room, Continental buffet breakfast served, handicapped accessible.

Westborough Marriott
5400 Computer Drive, Rtes. 9 and 495
Westborough
(508) 366-5511
223 guest rooms and suites, Chipperfield's Restaurant, and the Scoreboard Bar & Grill; indoor pool, whirlpool, saunas, fitness center; Grand ballroom accommodates 800, 12 additional meeting rooms, 8500 s.f. exhibit space, recreational facilities, handicapped accessible.

Beechwood Inn
363 Plantation St. off Rte. 9
Worcester
(508) 754-5789 or 1-800-344-2589
Adjacent to UMass. Medical Center and the Biotech Park, the Beechwood is renowned for fine cuisine and impeccable service. 58 rooms, restaurant, lounge, entertainment, handicap access, 5 meeting rooms and 2,400 s.f. exhibit space.

Clarion Suites Hotel
70 Southbridge St.
Worcester
(508) 753-3512
100 rooms, 65 restaurant and 65 lounge seating. Exercise room, outdoor pool, 2 meeting rooms and 1,400 s.f. exhibit space. Handicap access.

Holiday Inn
500 Lincoln St.
Worcester
(508) 852-4000 or 1-800- 465-4329
Beautifully renovated facility located in Central Massachusetts. 142 guest rooms, restaurant, lounge, entertainment on weekends, exercise room, saunas, indoor pool, handicap access, 15 meeting rooms and 19,638 s.f. of exhibit space. Call for directions.

Marriot Hotel
10 Lincoln Sq.
Worcester
(508) 791-1600
250 rooms, downtown Worcester near Centrum. Restaurant, Murphy's Chop House, lounge, exercise room, sauna, indoor/outdoor pool, grand ballroom seats up to 500, 8 small meeting rooms. Handicapped accessible and parking.

Inns

Grafton Inn
25 Central Square
Grafton
(508) 839-5931
7 rooms, 96 restaurant seating, banquet room accommodates up to 150 people, handicapped accessible. Call for directions.

Winterwood at Petersham
19 North Main Street
Petersham
(508) 724-8885
Built as a private summer home in 1842, on the National Register of Historic Places; 6 rooms with private baths, decorated with antiques, designer wallpapers, fabrics. Across from wildlife preserve; views of Mt. Wachusett. Meeting space available. Continental breakfast served. Call for directions.
"It's a lovely Greek Revival inn with congenial hosts," Allen Young, Royalston, MA.
"A bed & breakfast, Winterwood, has Colonial furnishings that are delightful. Meals are also served here by reservation only, or the entire home may be reserved for weddings, etc. Former President Bush was here for his niece's wedding and reception," Susan Morrall, Barre, Ma.

The Harrington Farm Country Inn
178 Westminster Rd.
Princeton
(508) 464-5600
Restored 20 room farmhouse, 6 guest rooms, main dining room accommodates up to 35 people. Can seat a total of 70 in three rooms. Available for business meetings or parties. Call for directions.

Sterling Inn
240 Worcester Rd., Rte. 12
Sterling
(508) 422-6592
6 rooms, 4 meeting rooms can accommodate up to 100 people. Restaurant and lounge. Call for directions.

Old Sturbridge Village Lodges and Oliver Wight House
Rte. 20; adjacent to Old Sturbridge Village, 1/2 mile from I-84 and Mass. Pike
Sturbridge
(508) 347-3327
Oliver Wight House, circa 1789, offers 10 rooms decorated in the Federal style. Dennison Cottage houses two luxury suites; and the 47 Village units are ideal for families, private entrances, curb side parking, outdoor pool, handicapped accessible.

Publick House Historic Inn & Country Motor Lodge
On the Common
Sturbridge
(508) 347-3313 or 1-800-PUBLICK
Choose from the charm of the Publick House Historic Inn, built in 1771, spacious rooms of the Country Lodge; or a suite in the Chamberlain House or Colonel Ebenezer Crafts Bed and Breakfast Inn (built in 1786, furnished with antiques). Swim, play tennis or jog on their sixty acres. Dine graciously in the Publick House Restaurant or enjoy a lighter fare at Crabapples. 3 restaurants, 12 meeting rooms, banquet facilities up to 250 people, handicapped accessible. Call for directions.

Quality Inn Colonial
Rte. 20
Sturbridge
(508) 347-3306 or 1-800- 228-5151
64 rooms, restaurant and lounge within walking distance, outdoor pool, handicapped accessible. Call for directions.

Sturbridge Country Inn
530 Main St.
Sturbridge
(508) 347-5503

9 rooms, restaurant within walking distance, limited handicap access. Call for directions.

Westborough Inn
62 Milk St., Rte. 135
Westborough
(508) 836-1900
25 rooms, kitchen and laundry room available. Restaurant within walking distance, meeting room accommodates up to 10 people, handicap access. Call for availability and directions.
"Cozy rooms with fireplaces and hay rides with a stop for hot chocolate around a crackling fire," Serena E. Leiser, Worcester, MA.

The Victorian
583 Linwood Ave.
Whitinsville (Northbridge)
(508) 234-2500
Former mansion of a wealthy mill owner overlooks 5-acre woodland estate. Home to one of New England's great restaurants. Dark walnut and mahogany woodwork and wallpaper and drapes of the period. 8 spacious rooms with private baths.
"Restored Victorian mansion built in 1871 by a wealthy mill owner. A fine restaurant, too," A.L. Rutland, MA.

Motels

Budgetel Inn
444 Southbridge St.
Auburn
(508) 832-7000
102 rooms, 1 meeting room can accommodate up to 10 people, free in-room Continental breakfast and coffee, handicapped accessible. Call for directions.

Days Inn-Auburn
426 Southbridge St.
Auburn
(508) 832-8300 or 1-800- 325-2525
70 rooms, 15 meeting rooms, restaurants nearby, handicapped accessible. Call for directions.

Ramada Inn
624 Southbridge St.
Auburn
(508) 832-3221 or 1-800- 228-2828
A long tradition of hospitality. 159 rooms, restaurant, lounge, entertainment on weekends, indoor pool, hot tub, handicap access, 10 meeting rooms, 5,000 s.f. of exhibit space. Call for directions.

Clinton Motor Inn
146 Main St.
Clinton
(508) 368-8133
21 rooms, restaurants nearby. Call for directions.

Thunderbird Motor Inn
299 Lunenburg St.
Fitchburg
(508) 342-6001
60 rooms, restaurant nearby, outdoor pool. Call for directions.

Super 8 Motel
22 Pearson Blvd.
Gardner
(508) 630-2888
48 rooms, conference room accommodates up to 15 people. Dining and shopping nearby. Handicapped accessible. Call for directions.

Leominster Motor Inn
665 Central St., Rte. 12
Leominster
(508) 537-1741
40 guest rooms, affordable prices, weekly rental, efficiency rooms available.

Motel 6
Commercial Rd.
Leominster
(508) 537-8161 or (508) 891-6161
115 rooms, restaurants nearby, outdoor pool, handicap access. Call for directions.

Super 8 Motel
Main St.
Leominster
(508) 537-2800 or 1-800-800-8000
101 rooms, restaurant nearby, 1 conference room can accommodate up to 15 people, handicap access. Call for directions.

The Inn on the Hill
1 Lindell Ave.
Leominster
(508) 537-1661
98 rooms, restaurant, lounge, outdoor pool, 3 meeting rooms can accommodate up to 125 people. Call for directions.

Super 8 Motel
880 Lynch Blvd., (exit 25 off I-290)
Marlborough (near Northborough line)
(508) 460-1000
Affordable prices, 64 luxurious rooms, in-room movies, major credit cards accepted, conference room accommodating 25, handicap accessible, free Continental breakfast.

Friendship Inn
Junction of Rtes. 9 and 20
Northborough
(508) 842-8941 or 1-800-424-4777
Economy daily and weekly rates, free Continental breakfast, 80 rooms, efficiencies; J.J. O'Rourkes Restaurant, meeting and banquet rooms. Handicapped accessible. Call for directions.

Days Inn-Shrewsbury
889 Boston Turnpike (Rte. 9)
Shrewsbury
(508) 842-8500 or 1-800- 548-0058
101 rooms; 250 restaurant seating; 198 lounge seating, entertainment. Pass to fitness center available. Handicap access, meeting rooms available.

Red Roof Inn
367 Boston Turnpike Rd.
Southborough
(508) 481-3904 or 1-800- 843-7663
108 rooms, restaurants nearby, morning coffee, daily newspaper, handicap access. Quiet location at the junction of Rte. 9 and I-495. Twelve miles east of Worcester.

Best Western American Motor Lodge
Rte. 20
Sturbridge
(508) 347-9121
55 rooms, 2 meeting rooms can accommodate up to 50 people, lounge, restaurant, indoor pool. Call for directions.

Carriage House Inn
358 Main St.
Sturbridge
(508) 347-9000
79 rooms, restaurant/lounge within walking distance, free complimentary breakfast, outdoor pool, handicap accommodation. Meeting space available for up to 40 people. Call for directions.

Econolodge
682 Main St.
Sturbridge
(508) 347-2324 or 1-800- 424-4777
48 rooms, restaurants nearby, passes to fitness center available. Seasonal outdoor pool. Handicapped accessible. Call for directions.

Old Sturbridge Motor Lodge
Main St., Rte. 20
Sturbridge
(508) 347-3327
59 rooms, restaurants nearby, outdoor pool, handicap access. Call for directions.

Sturbridge Coach Motor Lodge
408 Main St. opposite Old Sturbridge Village
Sturbridge
(508) 347-7327
54 rooms, outdoor pool. Dining and shopping nearby. Call for directions.

Sturbridge Motor Inn
Service Rd., I-84-exit 2
Sturbridge
(508)347-3391
32 rooms, restaurant nearby, outdoor pool, handicap access.

Pleasant View Motor Lodge
Rte. 146
Sutton
(508) 865-5222
55 rooms, restaurant, lounge, meeting room for up to 100 people, handicapped accessible. Call for directions.

Quaker Motor Lodge
Off Rte. 146 , (take Rte. 146A, Chockalog Rd. exit).
Uxbridge
(508) 278-2445
23 rooms, restaurants nearby, 1 meeting room can accommodate up to 35 people, outdoor pool. Call for further directions.

Friendship Inn North
90 Sterling St.
West Boylston
(508) 835-6247 or 1-800-453-4511
40 rooms, restaurant nearby, outdoor pool. Call for directions.

Howard Johnson's Motor Lodge
181 West Boylston St.
West Boylston
(508) 835-4456
48 rooms, restaurant nearby, call for directions.

Comfort Inn
Rte. 9
Westborough
(508) 366-0202
98 rooms, 4 meeting rooms accommodate 10 to 65 people. Restaurant, lounge, coffee shop, handicapped accessible. Call for directions.

Town Crier Motel
Rte. 2A
Westminster
(508) 874-5951
31 rooms, restaurant nearby, handicap access. Call for directions.

Days Inn/Days Lodge
50 Oriol Drive, off Lincoln St.
Worcester
(508) 852-2800 or 1-800- 932-3297
118 rooms, lighted tennis courts, outdoor pool, handicap access, includes Continental breakfast. Directions I-290, Exits 20 & 21.

Econolodge
531 Lincoln St.
Worcester
(508) 852-5800
48 rooms, handicapped accessible, dining and shopping nearby, passes for fitness center available. Behind Lincoln Plaza. Call for directions.

Hampton Inn
110 Summer St.
Worcester
(508) 757-0400
97 rooms, 2 meeting rooms, hospitality suites for up to 50 people. Handicapped accessible. Complimentary breakfasts and passes for fitness center. Call for directions.

Youth Hostels, Vacation Cottages, Corporate Apartments

Dudley Home Hostel
Marsh Rd.
Dudley
(508) 943-6520
Youth hostel, 7 beds. Open April through November.

Church's Vacation Cottages
73 Wallis St.
East Douglas
(508) 476-7752
On the pristine Whitin Reservoir, summer rentals May 15-Oct. 15.

Princeton Place - Corporate Apts.
285 Plantation St.
Worcester
(508) 754-6777
Corporate furnished suites. Full amenity package within a serene and private setting. Located near UMass Medical Center and major highways. Restaurants, shopping and entertainment nearby. Outdoor pool, tennis, club house, security entry building.
"In addition to providing excellent traditional apartments, they provide fully furnished corporate apartments on a month to month basis," Rob Flaherty, Salem, MA

Notes

More Notes

Chapter 6

Shopping

I have at least two occupations, retail merchant and author. I have been a retail merchant for twenty years and an author for about fifteen minutes. One of the guiding principals in writing this chapter has come out of my retail experience. Shopping should be fun because if it's not fun, then It's work and who wants more work? In fact, at work, the more fun I have, the more successful I am. Because when it's not fun it's work and I'd rather be golfing.

So, the stores in this chapter are, to say the least, an eclectic mix, guaranteed to make your shopping fun. We list malls, but if you're looking for a guide to chain stores in Worcester County, you won't find them here. The only chains listed are those that started here, like Worcester-based Maurice the Pants Man and Thom McAn Shoes. Included here are places offering unusual, one-of-a kind, or handmade items and places that still offer old-fashioned service. Stores are listed by category first, (see below) and grouped by towns. For example, gift stores in Athol are listed before those in Worcester. And remember, things change, call first.

And a final note: Shopping is like the old west. You are the scout, help show us the way. When you find a good, or not so good, watering hole (store) tell us. Give us your reviews, notes and comments and the next edition of *Favorite Places* will be even better...and you can join us as authors. Send your reviews, notes, comments and hot tips to: Favorite Places C/O Tatnuck Bookseller 335 Chandler Street Worc., MA 01602.

Antiques & Art; Bicycles; Bookstores; China; Clothing (including Children's, Consignment, Men's, Women's, Vintage); Collectibles; Country Stores; Discount Stores; Factory Outlets; Flea Markets; Food (including Dairy Stores, Ethnic Markets, Farmstands, Fish Markets, Gourmet, Home Brewing; Organic); Furnishings (including Baby, Curtains, Lighting, Restoration, Rugs, and Used); Gardening; Gifts, Crafts, Flowers; Golf Stores; Jewelers; Malls; Music; Shoes; Sporting Goods; Stationery; Toys; and Miscellaneous.

Antiques & Art

Haley's Antiques
488 South Main St., P.O. Box 248, Athol
(508) 249-9400
Collectibles, appraisals, local art gallery, and publishing.
"It's a large home and barn filled with goodies for novice and serious lookers," Nita Bates, Athol, MA.

Skinner Auction Gallery
Rte. 117 (Main St.), Bolton
(508) 779-6241
New England's largest auction gallery, and the 5th largest in the nation. Synonymous with fine antiques, with a name nearly as famous as Sotheby's.

Prindle Ridge Antiques
212 Main St., Rte. 20, Charlton
(508) 248-6893
Country antiques, field wagons, wheelbarrow reproductions, call for hours.

Pewter Owl Antiques
3 East Broadway, Rte. 2A, Gardner
(508) 632-2157;632-0608
Glass, china, books on antique subjects, and all general antiques.

Apollo Piano
77 Potter Hill Rd., Grafton
(508) 839-9547
Comprehensive piano rebuilding, refinishing, specializing in antique player pianos, grands and uprights.

Grafton Antique Exchange
Grafton Common, Grafton
(508) 839-2314
Victorian setting, the George W. Fisher House. Consignment, furnishings, china, glassware, books, Wed.-Sat. 11am-5:30pm, Sun. 1-5:30pm.

Jack Haringas Antiques
40 N. Main St. (Rte. 140), Grafton
(508) 865-9322; (508) 832-7334
General merchandise, 8:30am-5pm.

Little Richard's Auction Gallery
16 Ferry St., Grafton, off Rte. 122-A
(508) 799-5165 or 839-3136
Antique and estate auctions every other Sat.

Puddin Stone
Rte. 68, Breezy Hill Corners
Hubbardston
(508) 928-1371
Antiques and gift items, some jewelry; Mon.-Sat. 10am-5pm; Sun. 10am-4pm, Tues. by chance.

Nipmuc Trading Post
Rte. 16, Mendon
(508) 634-8300
Antiques & collectibles, multi-dealer shop and consignment, oak, mahogany antique furniture, toys, military memorabilia, hunting and fishing items, Tues.-Sun. 10am-5pm; Wed. 10am-8pm.

Gina's Antiques
24 Main St., Millbury
(508) 865-2299
Fine furniture, oak, mahogany, walnut, glass, china, collectibles.

Country Corner Antiques
48 Donovan Rd., North Brookfield
(508) 867-5378
Extra-special antiques, great browsing, Mon.-Fri. 9am-3pm; Sat.-Sun. by chance.

Deacons Bench
18 North Main St., Rte. 140
Oakdale (W. Boylston)
(508) 835-3858
Three floors of antiques, something for everyone, Tues.-Sat. 10:30am-4:30pm, Sun. 12-5pm.

Whiting Farm
Rte. 2A, Phillipston
(Exit 19 off Rte. 2, Phillipston)
(508) 249-7637
Crafts, antiques, collectibles, dried flowers, candles, pottery. April-Dec.

Prudence Shop
Ridge Rd. (Rte. 68 to Wachusett St. to Ridge Rd.), Rutland
(508) 886-4483
Antiques; woodenware, primitives, furniture.

Art Pottery Antiques
333 Redemption Rock Trail, Rte. 140, Sterling
(508) 422-6882
Furniture, glassware, tools, and other general antiques, open Sat. & Sun. 10am-5pm.

Antique Center of Sturbridge
426 Main St., Route 20 across from Basketville, Sturbridge
(508) 347-5150
Many dealers under one roof.

Fairgrounds Antique Center
362 Main St. (Rte. 20) above Piccadilly Pub, Sturbridge
(508) 347-3926
Multi-dealer shop with over 120 booths & showcases, Mon.-Sat. 10am-5pm., Sun. 12-5pm.

New England Graphics
Sturbridge Marketplace, Sturbridge
(508) 347-9655
Framed pictures & prints; limited editions, Wild Wings, Wysocki, Rockwell, Wyeth, Amish, Victorian, Classics & more, daily 10am-6pm.

Rob & Ruth Lyon Sturbridge Antique Shops,
Rte. 20, Sturbridge
(508) 867-7316 or 347-2744
Fine antique iron for hearth and home, cooking utensils, and door hardware.

Showcase Antique Center
Rte. 20 (OSV entrance), Sturbridge
(508) 347-7190
160 showcases displaying quality small items plus paintings and small furniture, Mon.-Fri. 10am-5pm, Sun. 12-5pm, closed Tues.

Sturbridge Antique Shops
Route 20 - 1/2 mile E of Mass Pike and I-84, Sturbridge
(508) 347-2744
75 dealers under one roof, Mon.-Fri. 9am-5pm, Sat. & Sun. 10am-5pm.

Wright Tavern Antiques
129 Boynton St. (on the Common next to library), Templeton
(508) 939-8879
Country furniture, kerosene lamps, mini/full size, tinware, woodenware, kitchen collectibles, etc. Open year round by chance or appt.

Upton Country Store and Antique Center
62 Main St., Upton
(508) 529-3163
Furniture, glass, jewelry, penny candy, jellies, consignments, country antiques, M-F 10am-5pm, Weekends 12-5pm.

Uxbridge House Antiques
117 Douglas St., Rte. 16, Uxbridge
(508) 278-2635
Cobalt and Depression glass, antiques, collectibles, advertising memorabilia.

Waucantuck Bargain Shop
325 Mendon St. Rte. 16, Uxbridge
(508) 278-5022
Used furniture and appliances, antiques, collectibles.

Nancys Antiques
271 W. Boylston St., Rte. 12, West Boylston
(508) 835-6889
Many dealers under one roof, Tues.-Sat. 11am-5pm, Sun. 12-5pm.

Obadiah Pine Antiques
160 West Boylston St., Rte. 12, West Boylston
(508) 835-4656
Variety of antiques, call for hours.

Robert & Co. Antiques,
271 West Boylston St., Rte. 12, West Boylston
(508) 835-6550
Many dealers under one roof, closed Mon.

Yankee Heritage Antiques
44 Sterling St., Jct. Rtes. 12 & 110, West Boylston
(508) 835-2010 .
Antiques, collectibles, primitives, furniture, glass, anything old, specializing in oak, M-F 10am-5:30pm, Sun. 9am-5:30pm, closed Sat.

Rays Wayside Furniture, Antiques & Collectibles
Rtes. 12 and 140, West Boylston
(508) 835-4690
Many dealers under one roof, open 10am-5pm daily.

West Boylston Antiques
277 W. Boylston St., West Boylston
(508) 835-8853
Many dealers under one roof, Tues.-Sat. 11am-5pm, Sun. 12-5pm.
"Wonderful gift source for weddings, showers, etc. I've located beautiful items for myself, friends and family," Gregory O'Connor, Worcester, MA.

Two Seater
Rte. 9 on the Common, West Brookfield
(508) 867-5787
Antiques and collectibles, 9:30am - dusk everyday and on Tues by chance.

David Rose Antiques
Rte. 140, West Upton
(508) 529-3838
18th and 19th century furniture and decorative accessories.

Attic Treasures
32 South St., Rte. 135, Westborough
1- 800-367-2870; (508) 366-2888
Full-service antiques, specializing in Nippon China, Limoge, antique toys, trucks, cars, pedal cars, always buying metal toys, Tues.-Thurs. 10:30am-5pm; Fri. 10:30am - 9pm; Sat. 10:30am-5pm; Sun. 1-6 pm; Mon. by chance.

Regan Antiques
302 Worcester Rd. (Rte. 140), Westminster
(508) 874-5793
General line of antiques, open by chance.

Factory Flea
100 Grove St., Worcester
(508) 754-6003
Gifts, cards, candles, art supplies, antiques, used furniture, one-of-a-kind gifts.
"They always have a great variety of items to buy as gifts or as fun things for yourself at very affordable prices," Andrea N. Driscoll, Worcester, MA.

Vaillancourt Folk Art and Friends
145 Armsby Rd., Rte. 146, Sutton
(508) 865-0434
Featured in Yankee Magazine. America's largest and best known producer of Christmas collectibles. Located in 1820 farmhouse, the 40 painters of Vallaincourt produce 800 different Christmas and Easter collectibles, sold in over 2500 stores in 6 countries. Vallaincourt originals are known for their high quality. Studio tours available, retail store.

Bicycles

Bicycle Barn
123 Boston Turnpike Rte. 9, Westborough
(508) 366-1770
Bicycles, parts, accessories, service.

Bicycle Alley
1073-A Main Street, Worcester
(508) 752-2230
Home of the Worcester Road Club,

TREK Mountain Road, MultiTrack, Touring and Tandem models, M-F 10am-8pm, Sat. 9am-6pm, (Sun. 12-5 pm in season)

Eastern Cycle Supply Co., Inc.
1103 Main St., Worcester
(508) 752-5301
Complete stock of bicycles and supplies.

Fritz's Bicycle Shop,
328 W. Boylston St., Rte. 12, Worcester
(508) 853-1799
Specializing in repair, mechanics trained at Barnett's Bicycle Institute and United Bicycle Institute.

O'Neils Bicycle & Ski Shop
1094 Main St., Worcester
(508) 798-0084
Full line of bicycles and supplies. Call 1-800-638-6344 for free national catalog; Also on-line shopping: Call on Internet address: oneils@bikenet.com. Open 'til 8pm M-F; Sat. 'til 5pm.

Bookstores

Chapters Book Shop
108 Pleasant St., East Brookfield
(508) 867-7187
Beautiful lakeside setting, special orders, cards and papers, new and collectible books, Tues.-Thurs. 10 am-5:30pm; Fri. 10am-6pm; Sat. 10 am-4 pm.

Just Plain Words
507 Electric Ave., Parkhill Plaza, Fitchburg
(508) 345-5590
Hours: Weekdays 10am-6:30 pm; Weekends - call ahead.

Book Corner #1
354 Timpany Blvd.,
Timpany Plaza, Gardner
(508) 632-7733
Hours Mon.-Sat. 9:30 am - 9 pm; Sun. 12:30-6:00 pm.

Book Corner #2
1 Searstown Mall, Leominster
(508) 537-0942
Hours: Mon.-Sat. 9:30am-9:30 pm; Sun. 11 am-6 pm.

Little Professor Book Center
98 Boston Turnpike, White City East, Shrewsbury
(508) 752-1512
Hours: Mon.-Sat. 9am -9pm; Sun. 12 noon- 5pm.

Book Corner #4
184 Main St., Sturbridge
(508) 347-9334
Hours: Mon.-Sat. 9:30am-9pm; Sun. 10am - 6pm.

Cricket Book Shop
76 Hall Road, Sturbridge
(508) 347-3574
Used, rare, out-of-print (also at booth #25 every day at Sturbridge Antique Shops) by chance or appointment.

Old Sturbridge Village New England Bookstore
1 Old Sturbridge Village Rd., Sturbridge
(508) 347-3362
Located in Old Sturbridge Village gift shop, historical books. Apr.1-Nov. 5, daily 9am-5pm.

Haunted Book Shop
Centerwood Terrace, Rte. 12, W. Boylston
(508) 835-4738
Used and rare books; specializing in art & history, collectible card games, including Magic, The Gathering & Expansions; will buy select books, call for hours.

Book Bear
86 West Main St. Rte. 9, West Brookfield
(508) 867-8705
Daily 10am-6pm; wide variety of subjects, used books.

Open Book
18 Lyman St., Westborough
(508) 366-8448
Hours: Mon.-Sat. 9am.-9pm; Sun. 9am-5 pm.

Afro Books
927A Main St., Worcester
(508) 799-9799
Books about African-Caribbean and African-American cultures, fiction, nonfiction, children's books; 10am-6pm Tues.-Sat.

Another Story
1145 Main St., Worcester
(508) 752-3566
Used and rare books, lots of scholarly books and recent best sellers; 30,000 titles, all different; Mon., Tues., Sat. 10am-6pm; Wed., Thurs., Fri. 10am-8pm; Sun. noon-6pm.

Book Owl
59 Ward St., Worcester
(508) 831-1113
Thurs., Fri., Sat., 10 am-5pm.

Clark University Bookstore
918 Main St., Worcester
(508) 792-5330
Trade books, special orders, school supplies, gifts, greeting cards, clothing.

Fabulous Fiction Book Store
984 Main St., Worcester
(508) 754-8826
Science fiction, fantasy, comic books, fantasy war games, 100,000 back issue comics. Mon., Fri., Sat: 10am - 7pm; Tues., Wed., Thurs.10am - 6pm; Sun: Noon-6:30pm.

Quinsigamond College Bookstore
670 W. Boylston St., Worcester
(508) 853-2300
Hours: Mon.-Thurs. 8am - 4pm; Fri. 8am - 3pm.

Tatnuck Bookseller
335 Chandler St., Worcester
(508) 756-7644 ; fax: (508) 756-9425
One of the largest independent bookstores in the world, over 5 miles of books, full-service restaurant; serves customers in all 50 states and over 35 foreign countries. Expert booksellers, special orders their specialty. Mon.-Thurs. 8am-10pm, Fri. 8am-Midnight, Sat. 9am-Midnight, Sun. 9am-6pm.

"It's a cornucopia of art, literature, food, and friendship. They also sell books," Richard Tauber, Marlboro, MA.
"It's funky, interesting, stimulating..." Joan McGinn, Worcester, MA.
"It is a cool place - I can be me - get centered, read books, talk to God and drink coffee!" Marina Jardo
"The atmosphere is happy, welcoming. It's the hot gathering place with something wonderful to buy and something wonderful to eat," Anne McNulty, Newton, MA.
"A place with essence and warmth, where I feel comfortable alone (sipping hazelnut coffee and reading) or for a business lunch," Joyce DiBacco, East Brookfield, MA.
"My three favorite things are under one roof, good books, great food and bargains," Bernice Chandonnet, Rutland, MA.
"A special world inside Worcester," Debra Burbine.

The Ben Franklin Bookstore
21 Salem St. (across from Worcester Public Library), Worcester
(508) 753-8685
Rare, out-of-print books; selected CDs and prints; some new books.

"The best selection of used/antiquarian books in Worcester. Superb selection of foreign language literature!" Michelle M. Donabedian, Holden, MA.
"My favorite place is really two places in the city of Worcester itself: The Tatnuck Bookseller and the Ben Franklin Bookstore. The offerings and ambiance of these two book stores complement each other very well," Frank Simpson, Springfield, MA.

Univ. of Mass. Medical Center Bookstore
55 Lake Ave., N., Worcester
(508) 856-3213
Hours: Mon.- Fri. 8:30 am- 5pm.

China

Allen's
26 Main St., Leominster
(508) 534-3111
China, crystal, stoneware, bridal registry, Mon.-Sat. 9:30am-5:30pm, Thurs. till 8:30pm, open Sun. from Labor Day-Xmas.

Clothing

T.J. Maxx
Auburn Plaza, Auburn
(508) 832-5361
Clothing, gifts for men, women, and children, housewares.
"I can always find a bargain," Catherine St. Cyr, N. Brookfield, MA.

Maurice the Pants Man
Locations in:
Fitchburg (508) 345-0290; Milford 478-5889; Sturbridge 347-7859; Worcester 754-0781.
Casual clothing for the entire family: Levis, Champion, Timberland, & OshKosh, open daily.

Millbury Trading Post
40 Main St. (across from Brooks Drug) Millbury
(508) 865-8531
Sweatshirts, pants, youth, regular & big sizes; flannel jackets, call for hours.

Calverts
Old Shrewsbury Village, Rtes. 9 & 20 Shrewsbury
1-(800) 371-4200; (508) 842-4200
Discount clothing for the entire family, Carter's brand kids clothes, and much more, Mon.-Sat. 9am-9pm, Sun. 12-6pm.

Alan Bilzerian
143 Highland St., Worcester
(508) 757-3000
Cutting edge fashion with a national reputation.

Anya
70 James St., Worcester
(508) 791-8589
Eclectic clothing, accessories & gifts, call for hours.

El / Elle
108 June St., Worcester
(508) 831-0850
A new concept boutique for men and women, Mon.-Wed. 10:30 am-6pm; Thurs., Fri. 10:30am-7pm; Sat. 10:30 am-5pm.

Modern Classics
Cottage Place, 1200 West Boylston St. (Exit 4 off 190, next to Steves Pizza) Worcester
(508) 854-3030
Mens and womens fashions—unique selection, Mon.-Sat. 10am-5:30pm, Wed. & Fri. till 7pm, Sun. 12-5pm.

Clothing - Children's

Raschels, Inc.
Westmeadow Plaza, Rtes. 9 & 135, Westborough
(508) 366-0221
Over 550 brands at discount prices; child-friendly atmosphere, call for hours.
"Worth the trip," A.L. Rutland, MA.

New Arrivals
117 June St., Worcester
(508) 792-1575
Quality kids fashions, everyday and special occasions, Hartstrings, Plum Pudding, Flapdoodles, Sweet Potatoes, more. Mon.-Fri.- 10am.- 5:30pm; Wed. till 6:30pm; Sat. 10am - 4pm.

Clothing - Consignment

Courtney and Company
1215 Main Street, Holden
(508) 829-7400
Household goods, clothing, kids, antiques & assorted goodies.
"Lots of used clothing, antiques and craft store is chock full of goodies," Cheryl Hannon, Leicester, MA.

Hand Me Downs
79 Reservoir St., South Plaza, Holden
(508) 829-0439
Barely worn casual and dress children's clothing. Tues.-Sat. 10am - 5pm

Up Scale ConsignMINTs
TwinCity Mall, Leominster
(508) 534-3322
Used clothing and accessories for men, women, and children, Mon.-Sat. 10am-6pm, Thurs. & Fri. till 8pm, Sun 12-5pm.

New-2-You Clothing Boutique
165 Church St., Northbridge
(508) 234-9484
Formerly stylish clothes, old toys, used furniture, etc. womens and childrens (2T & up), Tues.-Thurs. 11am-6pm, Fri. & Sat. 11am-4pm.

Loose Threads, Etc.
8 Maple Ave., Rutland
(508) 886-2464. Quality used clothing.

M.T. Pockets
46 Main St., Sterling
(508) 422-8360
Top quality used and vintage clothing; One-of-a-kind treasures not found anyplace else, Tues.-Sat. 10am-4pm; Thurs. 10am-7pm.
"Small, but stylish, very reasonable, always different items," Kathleen Morell, Leominster, MA.

Kids Go Round
145 N. Main St., Webster
(508) 943-9922
Children's consignment infants-size 14, large selection.
"A large, always changing selection of nice used kids' clothes," Valerie Sampson, Oxford, MA.

Clothespins
West Boylston St., Rte. 12 in the Meadowbrook Plaza, West Boylston
(508) 853-5666
Children's consignment shop; boys and girls sizes 0-14, open daily 10am-5pm; Thurs. 10am-6pm, closed Sun.

Dollar's Worth
4 Quinsigamond Ave., Worcester
(508) 793-9810
A little bit of everything for the whole family, M-F 10am-4pm, Wed. till 7pm, Sat. 8am-3pm.
"Clothes are sold by the pound, both new and used merchandise, recycled, affordable to every class and age," Nancy Held, Sutton, MA

Easy Pieces
4 Quinsigamond Avenue, Worcester
(508) 791-7533
Mens womens, and childrens clothes, M-F 10am-5pm, Sat. 10am-4pm.

Forget-Me-Not
360 West Boylston St., Worcester
(508) 853-3038
Women's consignment.
"Variety, quality, low prices, helpful staff," Sandy Busnak, Worcester, MA

Rishay's
214 Shrewsbury St., Worcester
(508) 756-1344
Semi-formal, holiday dresses, after 5 wear, interview outfits, 10% off with college i.d.; Wed. 10:30am-6 pm; Thurs.-Fri. 10:30am-9pm; Sat.10:30 - 6pm; Sun. Noon-6 pm.

Sally's Boutique
(Salvation Army Thrift Shop)
72 Cambridge St., Worcester
(508) 797-4407
Great stuff from clothes to couches, proceeds help a good cause.
"I'm a college student and I don't have a lot of money to buy clothes, but I love these old, funky clothes," Kate Clark, Clark Univ., Worcester, MA.
"I find great clothes and what I buy goes to helping someone," Louise M. Buma, Northbridge, MA.
"You can buy neat things for $1," Janice V. Lebonte, Wocester, MA.

Clothing - Leather-goods

Best Bib & Tucker
538 Main St., Sturbridge
(508) 347-2229
Artifacts and skulls of the Southwest; leather and Australian outback clothing and accessories, open 10am-5:30pm, Sun. 11am-5pm, closed Tues.

Moccasins
Sturbridge Marketplace, Sturbridge
(508) 347-2353
Hand made sandals, belts, handbags, custom work, Sperry Topsiders, leather, snakeskins, gloves and other leather goods, M-F 10am-6pm, Sat. & Sun. 10am-5pm.

Clothing - Mens

Trippi's for Men
268 Boston Turnpike, Rte. 9, Shrewsbury
(508) 755-4721
Big-tall-short-small & regular; free alterations, Trippi's Uniform Company downstairs, call for hours.
"In 1979-80 I had a bookstore next to Trippi's in White City Shopping Plaza. The sidewalk sales were carnivals. The Trippi's have fun, selling Nehru jackets and old ties, making jokes, while expertly clothing and tailoring you." Larry Abramoff, Worcester, MA.

Armando's
254 Grafton St., Worcester
(508) 757-1530
Quality men's fashions at modest prices; expert tailoring, Mon.,Tues.,Sat. 10am-6pm Wed-Fri.10am-9pm.

Authentic Crew
335 Chandler St. (In the Tatnuck Bookseller Marketplace) Worcester
(508) 799-0222
Worcester wear, sweats and T's for the whole family.

Lujon Men's Clothing Inc.
35 Pleasant St., Worcester
(508) 752-3289
Fine men's clothing, Mon.-Sat. 9am-5:30pm, Wed. till 8 pm.

Mozart Custom Shirts
11 Pleasant St., Worcester
(508) 831-7321
Custom shirts, suitings, also ready-made clothing, everything from suits, trousers, sport coats and shoes. Mon.-Sat. 9 am-6pm; closed Sun.

Viapiano's Clothier
386 Chandler St., Worcester
(508) 757-0926
Handmade men's suits, specializing in English and Italian fabrics. 8:30am-6 pm daily.

Clothing - Mens and Boys

Shack's Clothes
403 Main St., Worcester, (also at the Auburn Mall)
(508) 753-8188; 832-6358
Tailored men's and boy's clothing; updated sportswear, Mon.-Sat. 9am-5pm, Wed. till 8:45pm.

Clothing - Vintage

Vintage Clothing
44 Main St., Gardner
(508) 630-3710
1800s - 1960 period clothing, wedding gowns, furs, military, textile, linens, jewelry, and accessories. Photography in vintage clothing, 7 days 10am-6pm except Sun. 12-4pm.

Linda White
100 Main St., Upton
(508) 529-4439
Rare, excellent quality antique clothing, some museum-quality, by appointment only.

Pastiche Vintage Goods
85 Harding St., Worcester
(508) 756-1229
Antiques, vintage clothing for men and women, and accessories, Call for hours.

Ragtime Ann-tiques
70 James St., Worcester
(508) 752-6638
Specializing in vintage clothing for men & women; accessories, jewelry, Halloween costumes.
"Theater clothes galore - fashions from the '30's and '40's with all accessories from funk to frivolous." N.N., Worcester, MA.
"Whenever I go to a special affair, whether Halloween, Mystery Party, I go here. Clothes from the '20's to the '90's, decorated elegantly," Linda McMahon, Chandler St., Worcester, MA.

Shaky Jakes Vagabond Vendors
123 Highland St., Worcester
(508) 754-2123
Men's, women's, and children's vintage clothing, Tues. 1-6pm, Wed.-Fri. 11am-6pm, Sat. 10am-6pm. Open since the 1960's!

Clothing - Women's

Talbot's
1063 Main St., Holden
(508) 829-9993
Top-quality women's fashions, Weekdays, 10am - 6 pm; Thurs. till 8pm, Sun. 12noon - 5pm.

Allen's
26 Main St., Leominster
(508) 534-3111
Women's, children's apparel, china, crystal, stoneware and bridal registry. Orthopedic and comfort shoes; post-mastectomy products, Mon.-Sat. 9:30am-5:30pm, Thurs. till 8:30pm., open Sun. from Labor Day-Christmas.
"The salespeople are fantastic; a Main St. institution since 1910," A.L., Rutland, MA.

Elizabeths Fashions 247 W. Main St., Northborough
(508) 393-2024
Quality women's apparel

Ike's Den
284 Boston Turnpike (Rte. 9 Eastbound), Shrewsbury
(508) 752-4014
Unique designer fashions, petite to large sizes, great for special occasions; hours: Mon.- Fri. 10am. - 6pm.; Wed. till 9pm, Sat. till 5pm.

Back Street
194 Elm St., Southbridge
(508) 764-2799
A boutique with thrift shop prices, new merchandise daily, open Wed.-Sat.

Lee Ann's
374 Main St., Southbridge
(508) 764-8380
Ladies casual fashions, Mon.-Sat. 10am-4pm,closed Sun.

Paradise Found
Sturbridge Marketplace, Rte. 20, Sturbridge
(508) 347-7384
Fine larger women's clothing, super selection of sizes 16W to 56, open daily 10am-6pm.

Definitely Wendy
Westboro Shopping Center, Rte. 9 & Lyman St., Westborough
(508) 366-7696
Award-winning specialty store, the definition of style in women's fashions, Mon.,Tues.,Wed.,Fri.10am-6pm, Thurs. 10am-7pm, Sat. 10am-5pm.

Elegant Expressions
12 Lake Ave., Worcester
(508) 799-7309
Specialty boutique, fine women's fashions also mother-of-the-bride and bridal fashions.

Slovin
121 Higgins St. off Brooks St. near the Summit, Worcester
(508) 853-4289
Worcester's true factory outlet; first quality fabric & tailoring; Missy, regular & petite sizes, open Mon.-Fri. 9am-5pm.

Top It Off
133 Highland St., Worcester
(508) 753-9651
Worcester's largest selection of hand-crafted specialty women's fashions; visit the backroom consignment shop, Mon-Sat. 10am-6pm.

Collectibles

Douglas Collectibles
Rte. 16, Douglas
(508) 476-3049; 1-800 476-3049
Sports cards and stamps; large stock of Magic cards. Mon.-Fri. 11am-7pm; Sat. 9 am-5 pm; Sun. 12 noon-5 pm.

Skip and Sue's Collectibles
697 Main St., Holden
(508) 829-4393
Sports cards, Magic cards, coins, yard sale items, Mon.-Sat. 10am.- 7:30pm; Sun. 11am. - 5pm.

Dan's Cards and Comics
276 West Main St., Northborough
(508) 393-1395
Comic books or sports, TV and movie cards, daily 12-6pm, Thurs. & Fri. till 7pm.

Jack's Trains
Christmas Tree Lane
(call for directions), Rutland
(508) 886-4394
Model trains, HO and N scale, Mon.-Fri. 6- 9pm.

JC's Dugout
129 Marcy St., Southbridge
(508) 764-7455
Sportscards & memorabilia; hockey, racing, baseball, basketball, football, nonsports cards, buy-sell-trade, M-F 10am-8pm, Sat.& Sun. 12-8pm.

A Child's Dream
Sturbridge Marketplace, Rte. 20, Sturbridge
(508) 347-7282
Comic books (new & old), trading cards, Star Trek & Star Wars, Magic and Jyhad playing cards, daily 10am-6pm.

Hog Heaven Hobbies
3 Arnold Rd (right turn at Sr. Center), Sturbridge
(508) 347-9350
Radio control model aircraft, cars, boats, trains, plastic models, Legos, Klutz, kites, Olde Time crafts & collectibles, call for hours.

Stan's Toy Chest
8 West Main St., Westborough
(508) 366-5091
Comic books or sports, TV and movie cards, Tues.-Fri. noon-7pm, Sat. 10am-4pm.

Dragon's Lair East
1147 Main St., Webster Sq., Worcester
(508) 752-6862
Marvel comics, role playing military & fantasy games, sports & non-sports cards, video games bought & sold, M-F 10am-7pm, Sat. 11am-6pm, Sun. Noon-5pm.
"They have great variety of video games and comics and a place to sit and talk. Great prices, too!" Sean McGinn-Murtha, age 11, Worcester, MA.

Grand Slam Sports Cards
382 W. Boylston St., Worcester
(508) 853-8829
Nearly 2 million cards in stock, buy & sell, baseball, football, basketball, hockey, sets, star cards, starting line-ups, complete supplies, M-F 10:30am-6:30pm, Sat. 10am-6pm, Sun. 12-5pm.

That's Entertainment
244 Park Ave., Worcester
(508) 755-4207
Comic books, collectible & new; wide selection of trading cards, sports & non-sports; collectible toys, Star Trek, Star Wars, etc., 7 days 10am-6pm.
"They have the best selection of comic books, baseball cards, Star Trek stuff and other collectible toys," Marilyn Howley, Bolton, MA..

Country Stores

Hartman's Herb Farm
1026 Old Dana Rd., off Rtes. 122 and 32, Barre
(508) 355-2015
300 different varieties of herbs, perennials, and annuals; display gardens; and a variety of craft classes, 500 lb. pig and other animals; great place for family fun Bed & Breakfast. Call or write for current catalog, 7 days 10am-5pm.
"There's something for everyone. Craft store, cards, books, gardens, greenhouses, animals (pigs, goats, sheep, rabbits, chickens, cats and sometimes kittens, dogs that are very friendly with kids, munchies for tasting, lots of room to run for kids while you browse. The Hartmans are so knowledgeable they are able to answer all questions. They also have catalog sales," Catherine Prentiss, Barre, MA.

Marshall Farm
340 Marshall Road, Fitchburg
(508) 343-6255;
Apple-related gifts and apple foods, open 8:30am to 5pm daily in season.

Grafton Country Store
On the Common, Grafton
(508) 839-4898
A gathering place for shoppers and browsers, Tues.-Sun. 10am - 5pm.

Country Store Petersham
Common, Petersham
(508) 724-3245
Homemade breads, soups, sandwiches, convenience store/deli, small gift shop.

Discount Stores

Christmas Tree Shops
Rtes. 9 and 20, Olde Shrewsbury Village, 1000 Boston Turnpike Shrewsbury
(508) 842-5945
Something for everyone at great prices—not just Christmas items, Mon.-Sat. 9am-9pm, Sun. 9am-6pm.
"*They have creative items at very reasonable prices!*" Deborah Webb, Shrewsbury, MA.

Spag's Supply
Rte. 9, Westbound, Shrewsbury
(508) 799-2570
Spag's has everything - 150,000 items; great for bargain hunters,(10,000 customers daily from all over N.E.) everything from auto supplies to beauty aids, toys to fishing tackle.
"*It's funky and wonderful,*" Valerie Sampson, Oxford, MA.
"*Always a bargain, it has everything!*" Katheryn Freeman, Westborough, MA.
"*It's unique, traditional, fun, it's Spag's,*" Claude Wooden, Shrewsbury, MA.
"*It's never boring, always something new and different, like a treasure hunt.*" *Sheila Bissonnette, Paxton, MA.*
"*I have never, ever gone there without running into one or two friends I know!*" Paul Krasnov, Holden, MA.
"*Where shopping and parking are perfected to an art form. Both men and women love shopping there. Spag's also supports the community and local charities,*" Louise Erskine, Worcester, MA

Building 19 1/10
949 Grafton Street, Worcester
(508) 791-0190
Salvage and surplus, M-F 9:30am-9:30pm, Sat. 9am-9:30pm, Sun. 11am-5pm.
"*Best inexpensive gift wrapping department, best cheap toys,*" U.K., Worcester, MA.
"*Not only great buys, but also entertainment and amazement at the many items for sale,*" Kathleen M. Toomey, Worcester, MA.

Duffy's Discount
1511 Main St., Worcester
(508) 757-6940
Mon.-Sat. 9am-5pm, Thurs. till 7pm, Sun. 10am-5pm.
"*There are great prices on health and beauty aides, food, toys and miscellaneous,*" Joanne Williamson, Leicester, MA.

Factory Outlets

Giovannio Factory Outlet
308 Providence Rd., Rte. 122, Grafton
(508) 839-9011
Hats made on premises, ladies' straw and felt designer styles at discount prices, Mon.-Sat. 10am-4:30pm.

Factory Outlet at Russell Harrington Cutlery
44 River St (off Hamilton St.), Southbridge
(508) 765-0201
Americas oldest cutlery maker; world famous brands cutlery, sporting knives, hand tools; seconds available; all at discount prices; Open Thurs. 5-9pm, Sat. 8am-12 Noon.

Flea Markets

Auburn Antique & Flea Market, Inc.
773 Southbridge St. (Rte. 12), Auburn
(508)832-2763
Everything from antiques to new merchandise; something for everyone, great indoor flea market, indoor/outdoor, Sun. 9am-4pm.

Douglas Flea Market, Antiques, Collectibles, & Furniture
N.E. Main St., E. Douglas
(508) 278-6027
Thirty dealers year-round. Snack bar serves all homemade food, clean restrooms, on historic 50-acre Bosma Farm, free parking, free admission, all antiques, collectibles inside; in summer, outside new merchandise, Sat. 10am-2pm, Sun. 8am-4pm.

Grafton Flea Market
33 Upton St. Rte. 140 (Grafton-Upton line), Grafton
(508) 839-2217
Every Sun. 7am-5 pm, antiques, china, jewelry, stamps, baseball cards, coins, knick knacks, open mid-March till end of Dec.

Rietta Flea Market
Gardner Rd., Rte. 68, Hubbardston
(508) 632-0559
"I can always find a bargain and get exercise," Jane McCauley, Hubbardston, MA.
"Nice ride into the country, excellent selection of antiques, collectibles, new items, furniture, free kittens, collection of trains, free entrance," Mona Golen, West Boylston, MA.

Whalom Park
Rte. 13, Lunenburg
(508) 342-3707
Sat. and Sun. after Thanksgiving-Jan. not open holidays, call ahead.

Edgemere Drive-In Theatre
Rte. 20, Shrewsbury
(508)798-4200
Seasonal, adult admission 50 cents; children free.

Westboro Antique & Flea Market
Rtes. 9 & 135E, Westborough
(508) 836-3880
Indoors/outdoors; 200 dealers New merchandise section, open Sun. 7am-4pm.

Worcester Flea Market
72 Pullman St. (I-190 2N-3S to W. Mtn. St. at bottom of hill).
Worcester
(508) 852-6622
Weekend bargains; fun for all ages, year round Sat. & Sun. 9am-4:30pm.

Food - Dairy Stores

Westfield Farm
Worcester Rd., Rte. 68, Hubbardston
(508) 928-5110
Gourmet goat cheese distributed to area restaurants and supermarkets, also Gouda and smoked cheddar, locally made.

Lundgren & Jonaitis
237 Main Street, Shrewsbury
842-2881 or 1-800-799-MILK
Wholesome, fresh, convenient; free home delivery or stop by the store, open 7 days Mon.-Sat. 8am-6pm, Sun. 8am-1pm.

Smith Country Cheese
20 Otter River Road, Winchendon
(508) 939-5738
Farmstead cheeses—Gouda, cheddar, baby Swiss; handcrafted gifts, Mon.-Sat. 10am-5pm; Sun. 1-6pm; Winter Thurs.-Sat. 10am-5pm, Sun. 1-6pm.

Cheese Shop
131 Gold Star Blvd., Worcester
(508) 852-6593; 1-800-400-6593
Cheeses from 15 different countries, Gouda, Fontina, Gruyere, Jarlsberg, local goat cheeses, French Brie, Danish blue, and more, gourmet mustards, pastas, crackers, oils, vinegars.

Food - Ethnic Markets

D'Errico's Market 145 East Central St., Worcester (see dining)
(508) 754-8630
All kinds of fresh meats and cheeses, beef, pork, lamb, veal, poultry. Imported products from Italy and France.

Ed Hyder's Mediterranean Marketplace
408 Pleasant St., Worcester
(508) 755-0258
Located in an old fire station with Old World charm, foods from 40-50 countries, exotic items, nine types of olives, five types of feta cheese, hummus, baba ghanoush, fresh filo dough, basil, green almonds, and more, open M-F 9am-6pm; Sat. 9am-5pm.

George's Fruit Store
347 Chandler St., Worcester
(508) 755-8793
Fresh produce and gourmet specialties, imported pasta, candies, nuts, dried fruits, fruit baskets.

Tom's International Delicatessen
118 Water St., Worcester (see dining)
(508) 755-7295
Cold cuts, cheeses, Hungarian, Russian, Polish and German specialties.

Tropical Foods Webster Sq. Plaza, Worcester
(508) 797-0363
Traditional grocery store offerings and Caribbean ingredients, chayote, sugar cane, malanga, recao, plantains, cilantro, fresh and dried chiles, deli, bakery, fresh and dried seafood and meat depts.

Twin's Oriental Market
118 Cambridge St., Worcester
(508) 798-2547
Oriental produce, lemongrass, ginger, black beans, Chinese cabbage, noodles, sushi, mushrooms, lotus root, ginseng, sauces, cooking utensils.

Worcester India Grocery
256 Shrewsbury St., Worcester
(508) 754-3407
Chinese okra, fresh chilies, coconuts, cilantro, curry pastes, chutneys, pickles, Indian sweets, syrups, Indian cookbooks.

Food - Farmstands

Bolton Spring Farm
149 Main St (495 to Rte. 117, Exit 27, 2 miles East, Bolton
(508) 779-2898
Apples, pears, peaches, vegetables, pumpkins.

Blue Plate Farm Stand
661 Main St (Rte. 122A), Holden
(508) 829-4083
Bedding plants, Mother's Day, hardy mums, Fall plants, native fruits & vegetables, pumpkins, open in season.

Chris Farm Stand
Worcester Rd. 1/2 mile N of Rte's 68/62 on 68, Hubbardston
(508) 928-4732
Organic produce, NOFA Certified, summer specialty—sweet corn, May-Oct., first 3 weeks in Dec.

Flat Hill Orchards
321 Elmwood Rd., Lunenburg
(508) 582-6756
Apples, peaches, pears, plums, and nectarines; mums, wreaths,and Indian corn, open 8/1-12/25.

Berberians' Farm Stand
68 Otis St., Northborough
(508) 393-8079
75 varieties of homegrown vegetables, herbs, full line fresh fruits, breads, frozen meat pies, fruit pies, honey, syrup, dressings and more, mid-May through end of Oct., call for hours.

Davidian Brothers Farm Stand
500 Church St., Northborough
(508) 393-3444
"Fruits and vegetables - excellent produce, locally grown, better flavor than produce shipped in from out of state," Jo-Ann Sullivan, Northborough, MA.

Derrick Farms
301 Sanders Rd., Oakham
(508) 882-5591
Blueberries!

Alta Vista Farm Store
80 Hillside Road, Rutland
(508) 886-4365
Worcester County's only buffalo herd! Featured on WCVB-TV's "Chronicle," Naturally raised American Bison, fresh low cholesterol buffalo roasts, burgers, steaks etc. Gift shop, buffalo-related gift items, farm store. Buffalo graze in scenic pastures. Call for hours and directions. Come see the live herd of buffalo roam.
"It's fun for all ages, the buffalo are unique, the view breath taking and the gifts wonderful," Betty & Katherine Muir, Rutland, MA.

Capasso Farms
118 Framingham Rd., Southborough
(508) 485-1680
Strawberry picking in June, bedding plants, fresh vegetables grown on premises in season, other produce available all year long, cheese, crackers, jellies, local wines, bakery items and fresh cut flowers, fresh cut Christmas trees.

Henshaw Farm & Gardens (The Kitchen Garden)
268 Baldwinville Rd (Exit 21 off Rte. 2, head N) Templeton
(508) 939-8558
Strawberries, pumpkins, herbs, vegetables, fresh & dried flowers, homemade breads and pies, seasonal.

Pease Orchard
Brooks Village, 11 Phillipston Rd., Templeton
(508) 939-5324
Apples, peaches, pumpkins, vegetables.

Dick Kelly's Farm Stand
10 Gable St., Upton
(508) 529-6258
Corn, vegetables, peaches, strawberries, raspberries, blueberries.

Food - Fish Markets

Captain Ron's
385 Cambridge St., Worcester
(508) 795-7703
Fresh seafood and Italian dishes, prime rib, steak, chicken, for eat in or take out. Mon.-Tues. 11 am - 9 pm; Wed.-Thurs. Sun., 11am. - 10pm; Fri., Sat. 11am - 11pm Full bar.

Coral Seafood Restaurant
112 Green St., Kelley Square, Worcester
(508) 755-8331
Fresh seafood, good prices, swordfish, salmon and more, homemade soups (see dining).

Sole Proprietor Fish Market
118 Highland St., Worcester
(508) 798-3477
Fresh fish daily, M-F 10am-8pm; Sun. 12-6pm (see dining).

Tatnuck Seafood
1102A Pleasant St., Worcester
(508) 755-3025
Fresh Atlantic seafoods, fish delivered twice daily, many homemade items like chowders, stuffed clams, lobsters cooked to order. Tues.-Fri. 8am-6pm; Sat., 8am-2pm.

Food - Gourmet

Baskets of Thoughts
63 Auburn St., Drury Square, Auburn
(508) 832-0772
Gourmet gift baskets and gourmet goodies for all occasions. UPS shipping available, call for hours.

Gourmet Cookie Bouquet
P.O. Box 546, Milford
(508) 478-8711
Gourmet cookie bouquets by mail order, great alternative to flowers from $13.95. Phone orders only. Mon.-Sat. 9am - 6pm.

Armeno Coffee Roasters, Ltd.
75 Otis St. - 3/4 mile north of Rte. 9 past Fountainhead Apts.
Northborough
(508) 393-2821 or 1-800-ARMENO-1
A micro-coffee roaster, retail store in an old grist mill on Smith's Pond in Northborough. Free coffee cupping workshops (similar to wine tastings) and roaster demonstrations by appointment. Arabica coffees from 25 countries in 1/2- and 1-lb packages; grinding/brewing equip. & accessories, M-F 9am-5pm, call for weekend hours.

Hebert Candy Mansion
Rte. 20, 575 Hartford Pike, Shrewsbury
(508) 845-8051
Gourmet confections, novelty items, chocolates, candy made on the premises. Mon.-Sat. 9am-8pm, Sun. 10am-8pm.
"The famous Hebert's Candy Mansion - even though the structure itself is not made of candy, I always stop here on my journeys to see the sights, smell the smells and pick up a box of white chocolate mansionettes. Hebert's invented white chocolate and I think they still do it best," Elizabeth Lennon Keilty, Stoneham, MA.
"A turn of the century Tudor mansion that hosts a candy factory...quite picturesque and it always has a great aroma. Every holiday the Mansion is a host to special events, like Santa Claus or the Easter Bunny. I have been coming to Hebert Candies since I was a little boy." Paul B. McMahon, Newton, MA.

Food - Home Brewing

Stella Brew
Rte. 20 (inside A & J Pool), Charlton
(508) 248-6823
Homebrew supplies, beer, wine, soda, herb mixes, quality selection at low prices; catalog available, call for hours.

Keg & Vine
697 Main St., Holden
(508) 829-6717
Home brew supplies, Hours. Tues.-Fri. 10am. - 7pm, Sat. 9am - 5pm.

The Vineyard
123 Glen Ave, Upton
1-800-626-2371
Grains, hops, yeast, extract, vintner's supplies and more, worth the trip, call for hours.

Food- Organic

Living Earth
232 Chandler St., corner of Park Ave., Worcester
(508) 753-1896
Environmentally safe, all natural food products; gourmet, ethnic foods, bakery items, coffees, cheeses, low cholesterol buffalo meat; vitamins; wheat-free, salt-free, allergy-free foods and nutritional substitutes; organic wines; cosmetics; gift baskets; bulk purchases; and much more, Mon.-Fri. 9 am-9 pm; Sat. 9am-6pm; Sun. 11am-5pm, (see dining, Healthy.).

Furnishings

Angel House Designs
Rte. 148 (7 miles N of OSV), Brookfield
(508) 867-2517
Fine sofas & wing chairs, cupboards, beds, fabrics, antiques reupholstery too, daily, 10am-5pm; closed Tues.

Charlton Furniture Co., Inc.
Rte. 31, Dresser Hill Road, Charlton
(508) 248-5566 .
Fine Shaker furniture, Nichols & Stone, Declaration Americana, American Antiquity, M-F 10am-8pm, Sat. 10am-5pm, Sun. 12-5pm, closed Wed.

Chair Shoppe
101 Depot Road, E. Templeton
(508) 939-8524
Master craftsman in 20 different methods of seat weaving; antique specialist, complete restoration, wicker repair, call for hours.

Factory Coop
45 Logan St Exit 23 off Rte. 2, Gardner
(508) 632-1447
Outlet savings everyday; first quality furniture & accessories, Mon.-Fri. 9am-5pm; Sat. 9am-6pm; Sun. 12-5pm.

Gardner Furniture Outlets
25 Kraft St. Exit 22 off Rte. 2, Gardner
(508) 632-9661
Outlet savings everyday, first quality furniture & accessories, Mon.-Wed. & Sat. 8am-5pm; Thurs. & Fri. 8am-8pm; Sun. 12-5pm.

R. Smith Furniture Co.
289 S. Main St. Exit 23 off Rte. 2, Gardner
(508) 632-3461
First quality furniture at outlet savings, accessories, Mon.-Sat. 8am-5pm; Fri. 8am-9pmM; Sun. 1-5pm.

Rome Furniture
210 Main St; warehouse and showroom, Sherman St., Gardner
(508) 632-0687; 632-1320
Large display of glider rockers, country, traditional, Shaker, and some contemporary; bedding.

Farmer's Workshop
154 Goddard Rd., Hardwick
(413) 477-8819
Custom made country furniture—cabinets, desks, jewelry boxes, and made-to-order, Mon.-Sat. 8 am- 1 pm or by appt.

Sargent's Country Barn
18 Sargents, Leicester
(508) 892-4077
Country furniture, accessories, also unfinished pieces.

Linwood Mills Furniture, Inc.
665 Linwood Avenue, Northbridge
(508) 234-8003
Brand name furniture, accessories and mattresses.

Ralph Curcio Co., Inc.
372 East Broadway, Rte. 2-A,
South Gardner
(508) 632-1120
Traditional N.E. ladderback chairs, hand-woven fiber rush seats made on site.

Bay Path Furniture & Gift Shoppe
N. Spencer Rd. (Rte. 31), Spencer
(508) 885-9041
Traditional and country furniture; Pfaltzgraff, Byers Choice Carolers, Walt Disney Classics, Hummels, June McKenna, and more, Sun. 12-5pm; Tues.-Fri. 10am-8pm, Sat. 10am-5pm.

Spencer Furniture
Rte. 9, Spencer
(508) 885-3678 ; (800) 233-0123
Yield House, Lazy Boy, Bassett, Broyhill, Hitchcock, Lane, Temple Stuart; also bedding, accessories, appliances, carpets; Yield House Gift Shop on premises. Free shipping anywhere in U.S. on Yield House purchases over $50. "*Warm and friendly atmosphere, great gift selections at great prices and helpful sales people!*" Joanne Simonovitch, Spencer, MA.

Shaker Shop
454 Main St. 1/2 mile W of OSV,
Sturbridge
(508) 347-7564
Shaker, contemporary furnishings custom-made including dovetail cherry desks, Shaker sofa tables, pencil-post and rope beds. Stencil cutting and chair weaving classes, kits, woodworker's accessories, Shaker milk paint, open 7 days; winter 11am-5pm; summer 10am-6pm.

Sturbridge Furniture Warehouse
Sturbridge Marketplace, Rte. 20, Sturbridge
(508) 347-7069
Largest clock gallery in N.E.; grandfather clocks, wall clocks, mantel clocks; curio cabinets; discount prices, 10am-6pm 7 days.

Templeton Colonial Furniture Factory Store
Jct. Rte. 2 and Baldwinville Rd.,
Exit #20 off of Rte. 2 Templeton
(508) 939-5504; 1-800-729-5504
Shaker to traditional furniture at low discount prices, Mon., Wed., Sat. 9am-4:30; Thurs & Fri. 9am-8:30pm; Sun. 1-5pm.

Ray's Furniture Warehouse
1 High St., just off Rte. 12, Winchendon
(508) 297-3454
Furniture made in the Winchendon area by affiliated factories, Colonial to contemporary, kitchen to dining, chairs, any need, any room. Tues.-Sat. 9am - 5pm; Sun. noon-5 pm.

Ron & Peg's Reflections
178 School St. (Rte. 12), Winchendon
(508) 297-2411
Furniture-new and factory seconds-accessories, Boyds, Hancock, baskets and more, Wed.-Sun. 10am-5pm.

Winchendon Furniture Co., Inc.
13 Railroad St. Exit 24 off Rte. 2,
10 miles to center of Winchendon
(508) 297-0131
Outlet savings everyday, first quality furniture and accessories, Tues., Wed., Sat. 9am-5:30pm; Thurs & Fri. 9am-8pm; Sun. 1-5pm, closed Mon.

Dovetail Wood Works
114 W. Boylston St., Worcester
(508) 853-3151
Hand crafted hardwood furniture featuring time-proven joinery, and beautiful hand-rubbed finishes, the antiques of tomorrow, call for hours.

Empire Furniture Showrooms
40 Jackson St., Worcester
(508) 753-5483
Wholesale showrooms open to the public, prestigious brand names, interior design staff, furniture, bedding, carpeting, lighting, window treatments.

Futon Company
129 Highland St., Worcester
(508) 831-7170
Worcester's only futon store; the most unique gifts in town; lamps, picture frames, clocks etc., Mon.-Sat. 10am-6pm, Thurs. till 8pm, Sun. 12-5pm.

O'Coin's
239 Mill St., Worcester
(508) 791-3411
Furniture, window treatments and bed and bath; video, audio and high fidelity; major appliances, locally owned, operated and staffed by people that care, free parking; Mon.- Fri. 10am - 9pm; Sat. 9am-6 pm; Sun. 12noon-5pm, closed Sun. in the summer.
"Have fun. Ask for Jimmy O. Tell him Larry sent you," Larry Abramoff, Worcester, MA.

Rotman's
725 Southbridge St., Exit #11 off I-290, Worcester
(508) 755-5276
Enormous selection of furniture, carpets, bedding, lamps, and accessories for all decorating needs, M-F 9:30am-9:30pm, Sat. 10am-9pm, Sun. 12-6pm.

Furnishings - Baby

Norm's Discount House
55 Airport Rd., Fitchburg
(508) 345-1137
Carriages, playpens, dresses, cribs, also teen furniture.

Webster Baby
168 Main, Webster
(508) 943-4161
Complete line of baby furniture and accessories, crib bedding.

Baby Specialties
100 Grove St., Worcester
(508) 791-2599
Discount prices on baby furniture, also teen and juvenile furniture.

Rock-A-Bye Baby
1141 Main St., Worcester
(508) 753-3350
Juvenile furniture and accessories, infant clothing 0-24 months.

Furnishings - Curtains

Country Curtains
The Lincoln House , Rte. 20 , Sturbridge
(508) 347-2158
At the entrance to Old Sturbridge Village; hundreds of window treatments, home decorating ideas, mail order catalog service.

Furnishings - Lighting

Lampshades, Etc.
33 Main St. Rtes. 12 and 62, Sterling
(508) 422-7787
Custom-designed shades, lamps, repairs, supplies, classes.

Hammerworks
6 Fremont St., Worcester
(508) 755-3434
Hand crafted Colonial reproduction lighting fixtures, post lanterns, wall lanterns, chandeliers, wall sconces. Everything made on the premises.

June Street Lampshades
118 June St., Worcester
(508) 754-9119
Specializing in antique and unique lighting; lamp, shade, & clock repairs; lamp & shade sales. Custom orders on hard-to-find items, M-F 10am-5pm, Sat. 10am-4pm.

Furnishings - Restoration

Reliable Finishing Co. & Antiques
177 West St, Rte.. 68N
(Exit 22 off Rte. 2), Gardner
(508) 632-6657 or 1-800-675-6657
Furniture refinishing and sales, Mon.-Fri. 8:30am-5pm; Sat. 9am-3pm.

Furniture Rehab
139 Central St., Leominster
(508) 534-6549
Furniture restoration and repair.
"Tell Danny Larry sent you," Larry Abramoff, Worcester, MA.

Hanson's Refinishing Co.
10 Lyons Rd., Princeton
(508) 464-5800
Furniture refinishing, Mon.-Fri. 8am-5pm; Sat. 8am-3pm.

Custom Craftsmanship
S. Gardner
(508) 630-1644; By appointment only
Restoration of antique furniture; some items for sale.

Furnishings - Rugs

New England Braided Rug Manufacturing Co.
Rte. 148, Brookfield
(508) 867-5460
Custom wool braided rugs, made to order, call for hours.

North Oxford Mills
Clara Barton Road (off Rt 12) North Oxford
(508) 987-8521
Factory outlet, wool custom braided rugs, broadloom carpet, residential and commercial.
Mon - Sat 9 -5; Weds until 9pm.

The Carpet Lover
Rte. 16 at Rte. 146 interchange
, Uxbridge
(508) 278-5657
Floor covering for all your needs; Large selection of carpet remnants, spacious warehouse, Mon.,Wed.,Fri. 9am-6pm, Tues.-Thurs. 9am-8pm, Sat. 9am-3pm.

Furnishings - Used

Commonwealth Stationers
90 Grove St., Worcester
(508) 755-3177 or (800) 649-3177
Specializing in office furniture, new and used. A complete facility for all office furniture needs, M-F 7:30am-5:30pm; Sat. 9am-2pm.
"I bought a $2,000 Chippendale desk-beautiful - for $400. Great deals, great bargains, beautiful office furniture. Ask for Tony, tell him Larry sent you," Larry Abramoff, Worcester, MA.

Encore Pre-Owned Goods
417 Park Ave., Worcester
(508) 754-4666
Good quality furniture on consignment.

Rainbow Furniture
112 Grove St., Worcester
(508) 752-9143
Good bargains on furniture liquidated from hotels and motels.

Gardening

Perennial Peddler 156 Perry St., East Douglas
(508) 476-3647
Perennial display gardens, specializing in Astilbes and Daylilies.

Mendon Greenhouse Rte. 16, Mendon
(508) 478-3425
Flowers and gifts, plants, lawn care supplies. Mon.-Sat., 8:30am- 5:30pm.

Pleasant View Nursery
242 Pleasant St., Paxton
(508) 752-5967
All gardening needs, annuals, perennials, seeds, evergreens, trees, shrubs, good advice. Open 7 days a week.

Rutland Nurseries
Emerald Rd., off Rte. 56, Rutland
(508) 886-2982; 1-800-540-5678
Design and landscaping, lawn maintenance, and more, garden center, open 8am-5pm, closed Sun.

Shrewsbury Nurseries
957 Boston Turnpike (Rte. 9), Shrewsbury
(508) 842-2831
Complete line of nursery plants and related products, landscaping.

Curtiss Garden Concepts
Rte. 9, Southborough
(508) 460-1440
Nursery stock, annuals, perennials, house plants, mulch, soils, lawn ornaments, gardening tools.

Gulbankian's Florist Shop & Garden Center
40 Mt. Vickery Rd., Southborough
(508) 485-8979
Growers of quality plants and flowers, 9am - 6pm.

Bemis Nursery
29 N. Brookfield Rd. off Rte. 31, Spencer
(508) 885-4247
Mass. certified horticulturists, guaranteed plants, free delivery.
"Lots of fun, a beautiful place to wander and enjoy the plants," Gloria Abramoff, Worcester, MA.

Jack Straw Garden Designs
South Street (Rte. 135, 9/10 mile South of Westborough rotary) Westborough
(508) 366-4713
Nursery specializing in perennials and unusual annuals, workshops, consultants in garden design, installation, and maintenance; April-Oct.
"You can wander among rows and fields of brilliant blooms, poppies, bluebells, daisies and lilies that are native grown. It's the garden that grows in my dreams and keeps me digging," Kris Allen, Westborough, MA.

Gifts, Crafts, Flowers

Hobbit Doorway Books & Gifts
362 Main St., Athol
(508) 249-5988
Unique jewelry, Gargoyles, Guatemala bags, replicas and reproductions of distant times and places, bath & body products, books, and more, call for hours.

Appletree Fabrics
59 Auburn St., Drury Square, Auburn
(508) 832-5562
Full line of quilting supplies and fabrics, Mon.-Wed. 10am-8pm, Thurs.-Sat. 10am-5pm, Sun. 12-3pm.

Country Supply
1 Maple Street, Off Route 202, Baldwinville
(508) 939-5767;-800-540-5767;
Mon.-Wed. 9-5, Thurs.& Fri. 9am-7pm; Sat. 10am-4pm.

Country Gourmet Corner
Route 122 and Valley Rd., Barre
(508) 355-6999
Green Mountain Coffee; pottery; linens; gift baskets; gourmet foods; and cooking gadgets, call for hours.

Knitwitts
111M Allen Rd., Brookfield
(508) 867-9449
Retail yarn shop, specializing in designer yarns,"serious yarns for the serious knitter."

Charlton Mills, Inc.
Rte. 20, Charlton
(508) 248-7976
Box factory outlet, wrapping paper, shopping bags, crafts, laces, silk flowers, wedding supplies; weekly craft classes. Will package and ship items anywhere in the country. Basket supplies and classes, open daily 9am-6pm; Sun.12-5pm.

Country Barn Gift Shop
Rte. 16 across from Cong. Church, Douglas
(508) 476-7669
An array of handcrafted gifts-antique teddy bears, Yankee candles, lamps & shades & more; Wed.-Sun. 10am-5:30pm.

Calico Crib
252 Howe St., East Brookfield
(508) 867-7389
Quilt and fabric shop, quilting classes, supplies; hand-made quilts for sale, custom work. 9 am-5 pm weekdays; Sat. 11am-5 pm; Sun. 1-4 pm.

Apple Tree Barn
9 West St., East Douglas
(508) 476-2291 Call for hours
Cafe and Victorian gift shop all on one floor.
"Lots of charm, Victorian and country gifts, great staff, great food," Linda Rousseau, East Douglas, MA.

New England Living
45 Logan St., Gardner
(508) 630-1415
Features home and garden accessories handcrafted by local artisans; contemporary, floral sprays, pottery, foundry items, stained glass and more, Tues.-Sat. 10am-5pm; Sun. 12-5pm or by appt.

Grafton Greenhouses & Flower Shop
43 South St., Grafton
(508) 839-5596 Mon.-Sat. 9-5
Flowers, plants, also the Country Room gift shop.

Heather Shop
1061 Main St. Rte. 122A, Holden
(508) 829-4005
Quality gifts and collectibles for showers, weddings, and special occasions; yarn shop; free wrapping, Mon.-Sat. 10am-6pm, Thurs. 10am-7pm, Sun. - call for hours.

Unreal Silk Plants & Trees
1505 Lancaster Ave., Lunenburg
(508) 534-4591
Silk plants, trees, hanging plants, and floor plants for home and commercial use, call for hours.

Jan-Dec Vintage Boutique and Yarn Shop
16 Hastings St., Rte. 16 (above Lowell's), Mendon
(508) 634-3937
Antique and vintage clothing, jewelry, accessories, yarns, sweaters and more.

Mendon Country Gift Barn
Rte. 16, Mendon
(508) 473-1820
Quality country furnishings, decorative accessories, Christmas shop, open daily.

Crafters Choice
Rte. 146, Millbury/Sutton line
(508) 865-5591
Ceramics, needlework, crafts supplies and classes, dollhouses, trains and accessories, M-F 10am-8pm, Sat. 10am-6pm

Blue Cupboard
24 Bates St. (just off Rte. 67)
North Brookfield
(508) 867-9869
Finely hand-crafted gifts and collectibles, hand-painted earthenware pottery created on premises, in an early 1800's farmhouse, open Wed.-Sat. 11am-5pm; Sun. 1-5pm.

Country Candle & Crafts
42 Whitney St., Northborough
(508) 393-6480
Crafts, candles, silk flowers, stationery, penny candy, wedding accessories, open daily 9am-9pm, Sun. 12-6pm.

Craftworks
3 Pierce St. (Northborough Ctr.), Northborough
(508) 393-9435
Unique cooperative of 25 talented artisans; quality hand-made gifts and treats for all occasions, open 7 days 10am-6pm.

GraffiTee
3 Sutton Ave., Oxford
(508) 987-7950
Custom screen prints & graphic design shirts, hats, all printables, business cards, airbrushing. Gift-canning, an unusual way to wrap your gift, Tues.-Fri. 12-6pm, Sat. 10am-3pm.

Paxton Village Florist
679 Pleasant St., Paxton
(508) 754-5597
Variety of flowers, plants, all floral needs.

Doll House
43 West St., Petersham
(508) 724-3454
Doll houses, miniatures, and old dolls, Wed. 10am-5pm, or by chance or appt.

Petersham Crafts Center
Main St., Petersham
(508) 724-3415
Seasonal, April through Dec.; craft classes for adults and children, everything from doll clothes, caning, Lithuanian eggs and more. Variety of crafts by local artisans for sale.

Gathering Shed
Ridge Rd., Rutland
(508) 886-4531
Dried flowers & arrangements.

Skaff Floral Creations, Inc.
621 Main St., Shrewsbury
(508) 842-0304
Creative, unique, one of a kind designs; wedding specialists; exotic material from all over the world. Mon.-Tues., Wed., Sat., 9am.-5pm; Thurs.-Fri., 9am-6pm.
"Skaff's is a must-see, the owner Michael Skaff restored a Shrewsbury historical site, creating a place of elegance. If you like to take a trip back in time, this is the place to visit. Michael was one of the florists chosen to create the floral displays for the 1993 Presidential inauguration," Mary Ann Shannon, Worcester, MA.
"Fresh varieties of exotic flowers from around the world," Zinta Moskalew, Worcester, MA.

Oakwood Farm Christmas Barn
Rte. 31, Spencer
(508) 885-3558
Housed in 175-year-old barn; ornaments, wreaths, garlands, music boxes, nutcrackers, etc., call for hours, seasonal.
"*There's somtehing for every occasion and holidays,"* Jane M. Mosher, Rutland, MA.
"A world of its own, lovely, unique," Susan Johnston, North Brookfield, MA

Little Lamb Keepsakes
237 Worcester Rd. (Rte. 12), Sterling
(508) 422-8700
Herbs, gifts,and cards, call for hours.
"Nice country gift shop in Sterling. Smells great," Cindy Wilder, Worcester, MA.

Basketville
410 Main St. (Rte. 20), Sturbridge
(508) 347-3493
Shaker baskets; unique collection of handwoven designs, low prices, open 7 days.

Briar Patch
541 Main St. (Rte. 20) Sturbridge
(508) 347-3091
Where decorating is an art. Victorian, traditional and country accessories, pictures, lamps, flowers, vines, berries, custom floral designs in dried or silk. Largest collection of Beatrix Potter in N.E, open 7 days at 9 am, call for summer hours.

Colonial Crafts
479 Main St (Rte. 20), Sturbridge
(508) 347-3061
Stencilling, rubber stamps, quilting, folk doll patterns, homespun, rug hooking, painting classes, open daily 10am-6pm.

Coppersmith Factory Store
1 Snell St. (behind Yankee Candle)
Sturbridge
(508) 347-7038
Candles, candleholders, and tinware, open Fri.-Mon. 10am-5pm.

Country Friends
425 Main St., Rte. 20, Sturbridge
(508) 347-9003
Handcrafted gifts by local artisans—quilting, folk dolls, basketry, stained glass, calligraphy, and much more, open Fri.-Mon. 11am-5pm.

Crabtree & Evelyn
Rte. 20, Main St at entrance to OSV,
Sturbridge
(508) 347-2910
Fine toiletries and gourmet food items, custom gift baskets available; Mon.-Sat. 10am-5pm, Sun. 12-5pm.

East X Southwest
Sturbridge Marketplace, Rte. 20,
Sturbridge
(508) 347-3140
Products of New England & New Mexico, Native American & Mexican arts, Navajo and Zuni Jewelry, Western book shelf, Zapotec weavings, western art tiles, open daily 10-6pm.

Green Apple, Inc.
On the Common on Rte. 131,
Sturbridge
(508) 347-7921
New England antiques-all periods-American folk art; country furnishings, hand-made clothing. High quality items crafted by local artisans, open daily 10 am, evenings in season.

Handmaiden
Sturbridge Marketplace, 2nd Floor
Sturbridge
(508) 347-7757
For the discriminating shopper; distinctive handcrafted country gifts; Cats Meow, June McKenna Daddys Long Legs, Boyds Bears collectibles, Open 7 days, 10am-6pm.

League of American Crafters
Sturbridge Marketplace 559 Main St.,
Sturbridge
(508) 347-2323
New England's largest permanent indoor craft show 10,000 sq. ft., 150 crafters; purchase direct from fine artisans, Open 7 days 10am-6pm.

Made in Massachusetts
Route 15 (Exit 2/84)
next to Hebert's Candy, Sturbridge
(508) 347-5672
Gifts, crafts, and food items from more than 150 vendors all "Made in Massachusetts"- syrup, herbs, vinegars, relishes, cheese, baskets, mittens, vests, tapestries, and more, call for hours.

Peter Shawn & Company
423 Main St (next to Basketville), Sturbridge
(508) 347-8130
Pilgrim cranberry glass, Annalee dolls, Dedham pottery, Linden clocks, Baldwin brass & more.

Sadie Green's Curiosity Shop
On Rte. 131, (opposite the Common next to Publick House); (also 423 Main St. Rte. 20 next to Basketville), Sturbridge
(508) 347-1449; 347-7057
Lamps, antique reproductions, furniture, Americana, textiles, art glass & gifts. Designer, sterling & marcasite jewelry, Sun.-Wed. 10am-6pm; Thurs. 10am-8pm; Fri. & Sat. 10am-10pm.

Sturbridge Isle Craft Shoppe
Sturbridge Isle, Old Rte. 15, Sturbridge
(508) 347-7200
Handcrafted merchandise ranging from childrens items to adults.

Sturbridge Pottery
99 New Boston Rd., Sturbridge
(508) 347-9763
Spacious gallery, working clay studio, handcrafted pottery, daily 9am-5pm.

Sturbridge Yarn-Mill Outlet
450 Main St. (Rte. 20), Sturbridge
(508) 347-8258
Largest selection of yarn in N.E. latch hook, cross stitch, needlepoint kits & supplies & more, Mon.-Sat. 9am-6pm, Sun. 12-6pm.

Susan's Secret Garden
531 Main St., Sturbridge
(508) 347-9303
Victorian gifts, hand-embroidered linens, collectible teapots, fine writing paper, wedding gifts, baby gifts, call for hours.

The Quilt and Cabbage
538 Main St. (Rte. 20), Sturbridge
(508) 347-3023
Quality fabrics, quilts & supplies, gift items, Mon. & Wed.-Sat. 9:30am-4:30pm, Sun. 11am-4pm, closed Tues.

Traditions International, Ltd.
538 Main St., Sturbridge
(508) 347-7606
Ethnic folk art, jewelry & giftware from every region of the world, Swedish Dala, European crystal, African ceremonial dolls, gold filigree Russian tea glasses, Judaic gifts, & much, much more, daily 10am-6pm, closed Tues.

Wright's Factory Outlet
Rte. 20 Exit 9 off Mass Pike, Sturbridge
(508) 347-2839
Low prices, huge selection; trim, ribbon, craft supplies, craft books, bridal accessories, wreaths; also knitting, quilting and crochet supplies, Mon.-Sat. 9am-7:30pm; Sun. & Holidays, 10am-5pm.

Yankee Candle Co.
434 Main St., Rte. 20, Sturbridge
(508) 347-5500
Handcrafted candles in many fragrances, make your own colorful candle souvenirs, seconds available. Open daily 9:30am-5:30pm.

Yankee Crafter's Shoppe
Rte. 20, 446 Main St., Sturbridge
(508) 347-1348
Dolls, jewelry, ceramics, dried flowers, baskets, small furniture-all handcrafted by local artists, call for hours.

Country Mischief
Templeton Common (exit 21 off Rte. 2, to East Templeton), Templeton
(508) 939-5460
Montage of a bygone era-gifts housed in historic 220-year-old house built with bricks used for ballast in ships coming from England in the 1770's. Country,

Victorian, Colonial and Primitive folk art and crafts. Christmas room with Santa Clauses and Father Time figures, Mon.-Sat. 9am-5pm; Sun. 11am-5pm.
"Gail, her family and staff have transformed the historic Stone House into a veritable museum of crafts. Every inch of the 17 rooms is a feast for aesthetic sensibilities. The "decor" changes with the seasons and whether you buy or browse through the thousands of offerings, the welcome is always warm and the coffe (free!) hot," Charlene Zimkiewicz, Barre, MA

Sandra's Workshop
116 Partidgeville Rd., Templeton
(508) 939-2703
Handpainted items in folk-art style, dolls, custom, personalized items, by chance or appt.

New England Rocking Horse
81 West St., Uxbridge
(508) 278-2836
Handcraft woodworkers, 17 artists hand paint all products, which include kitchen and bath accessories, bread boxes, centerpieces, children's chairs, occasional tables, corner cupboards and bookcases. For a catalog, send $2 to N.E. Rocking Horse, 81 West St., Uxbridge, MA 01569. Catalog fee refunded with first order.

Raspberry Patch
2 S. Main St., Uxbridge
(508) 278-7476
Jewelry, watches, T-shirts, gifts.

Yarns...and Sweaters
1 Mendon St., corner Rte. 16 and S. Main St., Uxbridge
(508) 278-7733
An eclectic collection of yarns, sweaters and accessories, call for hours.

Basket Case Distinctive Gifts
Wachusett Plaza, Rte. 12; Exit #4 off I-190, W. Boylston
(508) 835-2250; 1-800-273-2205
Distinctive cards; fine china; elegant crystal; Victorian handcrafts; Crabtree & Evelyn, Waterford Crystal, Godiva, gift baskets, and more.

Parkers Gifts & Collectibles
9 Maple St., Rte. 140, W. Boylston
(508) 835-4173
Lizzie High, Cats Meow Villages & more; Country & Victorian giftware; Christmas ornaments, Snowbabies, Annalee; packaged cocoa, coffee, tea, penny candy, truffles; free gift wrapping, Mon.-Sat. 10am-6pm, Sun. 12-5:30pm.

Mission Bay Candle Co.
750 Main St., Rte. 67, Warren
(413) 436-5695
Over 130 fragrances; aroma therapy candles, earth treasures jewelry, open Fri. & Sat. 10am-5pm.

Red Clover Gift Shoppe
At Salem Cross Inn, Rte. 9,
West Brookfield
(508) 867-2939
Unique collection of antiques and handicrafts from local townspeople, closed Mon.

Social Etc...
Rte. 9 on the Common, West Brookfield
(508) 867-8731
Full service distinctive florists, unique gifts, fresh, silk and dried flowers, 7 days 8:30am-6 pm.

The Post and Boot
Rte. 9 on the Common, West Brookfield
(508) 867-5934
Home accents, mailboxes, bird feeders and houses, house numbers and plaques and antiques. 10 am-5 pm., Tues. by chance.

Flight of Fancy Dollhouse Shoppe
45 East Main Street, (Rte. 30), Westborough
(508) 366-0775
Dollhouses and supplies; miniatures; custom work; largest dollhouse shop in Central Mass., Tues.-Sat. 10am-5pm, Sun. 1-5pm.

Mugford Farm Stand & Flower Shop
8 Warburton Lane, Westborough
(508) 836-5554; 1-800-645-6495
Specializing in wild flowers and garden flowers.

Stained Glass by Ann Marie
Westminster
(508) 874-1211
Suncatchers, ornaments, Christmas wreaths, many styles and designs to choose from. By appointment only.

Bhadon Gift Shop
1075 Pleasant St., Worcester
(508) 798-0432 or (800) 294-4483 .
Unusual gifts, attractively displayed, jewelry, clothes, American handcrafts, Crabtree & Evelyn, free gift wrapping, open daily, call for hours.

Higgins Armory Museum Gift Shop
100 Barber Ave., Worcester
(508) 853-6015
Gifts, books, Tues.-Sat. 10am-4pm, Sun. 12-4pm.

Tatnuck Candle
335 Chandler St., Worcester
(508) 756-7644
Within Tatnuck Bookseller Marketplace. Candles, oil lamps, glassware, gifts.

Vuoman's Originals
339 W. Boylston St.
(next to Steves Pizza), Worcester
(508) 854-0660
A wide variety of gifts including Scandinavian, crystal, dried flowers, children's wear, something for every occasion, Tues.-Fri. 10am-6pm, Sat. & Sun. 10am-5pm.

Worcester Art & Frame
34 Mechanic St., Worcester
(508) 753-8604
Custom picture framing, dry mounting, needlepoint, prints, graphics, volume discount wholesale/retail, M-F 10am-5pm, Sat. 10am-3:30pm.

Worcester Art Museum Gift Shop
55 Salisbury St (290-W Exit 18/290E Exit 17 follow signs, Worcester
(508) 799-4406
Truly original gifts, hundreds of unique items—jewelry, prints, stationery, sculpture & more. Moderately priced; museum admission not required, Tues.-Fri. 11am-4pm, Sat. 10am-5pm, Sun. 1-5pm.

Golf Stores

Pin Hi Golf Crafters
244 W. Boylston St.
(Dunkin Donuts Plaza), West Boylston
(508) 835-3456
Pro quality custom golf clubs; brand look and play alikes, for men, women, lefties, seniors, youths, beginners, call for hours.

Fore Season Golf Center
258 Park Ave., Worcester
(508) 752-6116
Pro Shop—full line of golf apparel, teaching area, putting green, indoor hitting nets.
"They made me the best set of clubs I've ever hit. Good practice facility, good lessons," Kevin McCann, Worcester, MA.
"Indoor practice, video lessons, discount prices," Joel Buduski, Worcester, MA.
"You can get good compression all year long," Jim Boudreau, Worcester, MA.

Jewelers

Jefferson Square Jewelers
1655 Main St., Holden
(508) 829-9670
Family-owned, new and antique watches, watch repair, good selection of quality jewelry, established 1980.

Ludvigson Jewelers
19 Main St., Millbury
(508) 865-6686
Watches, collectibles, Mayflower glass, Seiko clocks, Andrea giftware; jewelry repair, engraving, appraisals, and more, M-F 10am-6pm, Thurs. till 8, Sat. 10am-4pm.

Silver Chief
57 Central St., Southbridge
(508) 765-0615
New & estate gold & silver jewelry, coins, diamonds, flatware, candle sticks, etc., M-F 10-4, call for Sat. hours.

Cormier Jewelers
136 Main St., Spencer
(508) 885-3385
Full service jewelry store-goldsmith & watchmaker on premises; 14kt. white gold collection, Tues.,Wed.,Fri. 9am-5pm1-5pm, Thurs. 9am-7:30pm, Sat. 9am-4pm.

Neal Rosenbloom Goldsmith
261 Park Ave., Worcester
(508) 755-4244
Specializing in custom goldsmithing, gem sales, and designer, hand-made jewelry, call for hours.

Tatnuck Jeweler
335 Chandler St., Worcester
(508) 756-7644
Located in the Tatnuck Bookseller Marketplace, specializing in watch and clock sales and repair and fine jewelry. Also estate watches.

The Source of Distinction
123 West St., Worcester
(508) 757-6836
Bridal and formal jewelry, unique gifts, American Indian jewelry, holistic crystals, aroma therapy, housed in Gothic Victorian, Mon.-Sat. 10am-6pm.

Malls

Auburn Mall
385 Southbridge St Exit 9 off I-290, Exit 10 Mass. Pike, Auburn
(508) 832-6000 or 832-3488
Anchored by Caldor and Sears, 70 specialty shops and cart vendors; plenty of free parking.

Searstown Mall
Commercial Rd. Junction Rtes. 2 and I-190, Leominster
(508) 537-7500
Enclosed mall with 75 stores,anchored by Sears, Bradlees, Toys R Us, and J.C. Penney, plenty of free parking.

Greendale Mall
7 Neponset St Exit 19 I-290 West to I-190, Exit 1, Worcester
(508) 856-9400
Anchored by Lechmere and Marshalls; free enclosed parking; 56 unique and distinctive stores and restaurants; The Gap, Eastern Mountain Sports, Kay-Bee Toys.

Worcester Common Fashion Outlets
100 Front St. Exit # 16 off I-290 Worcester
(508) 798-2581
The nations first enclosed cosmopolitan outlet mall; 1 million sq. ft. of carpeted shopping space with a 4,500-car garage; Filene's Basement, Saks Clearinghouse, DKNY, Bed, Bath & Beyond, The Sports Authority, Kay Bee, Bass, London Fog, and more. Food court overlooking Worcester Common,

Mon.-Sat. 10am-9pm, Sun.11am-6pm. *"It's a rainbow! It's alive, vibrant, posh. Downtown Worcester is back,"* Claude Wooden, Shrewsbury, MA.
"It is a boom to Worcester. Newly opened it is Awesome..it's brought life back to Worcester, no need to ride to Kittery," Margaret Leonard, Worcester, MA.

Music

Record Town
Auburn Mall , Auburn
(also Greendale Mall, Worcester)
(508) 832-7126; 856-9666.
First rate service, and always a sale going on, CD's, tapes, singles, over 1,000 videos. Greendale Mall location also has TicketMaster for concerts and events. Bring cash for concert tix; charge cards not accepted.

Strawberries Records and Tapes
Locations in:
Auburn (508) 832-5761; Leominster 537-6240; Shrewsbury 757-3443; Westborough 366-0017; and Worcester 831-3535.
Latest selection, the place to go for same-day releases, wide selection of CD's, tapes.

M.H. Guitar & Fiddle Shop
300 Main St. (Rte.. 9) E. Brookfield
(508) 867-6793
Sound systems, lessons in fiddle, mandolin, guitar, bass, piano, voice & banjo; instruments and accessories for sale. Gibson, Deering Banjo & more, M-F 10am-7pm, Sat. 10am-6pm.

Gordon/LaSalle Music Stores
133 Merriam Ave, Twin City Mall
Leominster
(508) 537-1200
Over 250 product lines, used equipment bought and sold, rent to buy, school band instruments.

The Gig Stop
316 N. Main St., Rte. 122,
North Uxbridge
(508) 278-7211
New and used musical instruments sales and service, call for hours.

Newbury Comics
551 Boston Turnpike, (Rte. 9W)
Shrewsbury
(508) 845-3391 Call for hours
CDs, tapes, T-shirts, and comics.
"Music, music, and more music. The people who work there are very helpful. Anybody can go there and find something they like," Loren Haberski, age 13, Northborough, MA.

Gordon/LaSalle Music Stores
333 Southbridge St., Southbridge
(508) 765-9352
Over 250 product lines, used equipment bought and sold, rent to buy, school band instruments.

Spencer Music Shop & Studio
23 Pleasant St (Rte. 31N), Spencer
(508) 885-9684
Crate amplifiers, retail, repairs, full teaching studio, lay-a-ways, call for schedule.

Al-Bums
149 Highland St., Worcester
(508) 798-3657
New and used music; a favorite of the college crowd. Mon.-Wed. 11am-7pm, Thurs.- Sat. 11am-9pm, Sun. 12-6pm.

Gordon/LaSalle Music Stores
484 Main St. (Denholm Bldg.)
Worcester
(508) 753-8724
Over 250 product lines, used equipment bought and sold, rent to buy, school band instruments; free parking in rear.

Kurlan Music Center
17 E. Mountain St. -
The Summit, Worcester
(508) 853-6417
New musical instruments, lessons, accessories, rentals for school lessons sheet music and books.

Mars Records
146 Highland St., Worcester
(508) 798-7884
Specialize in college rock and oldies, Mon.-Sat. 11am-6pm, Sun. 12-5pm.

Music Quest 1
46 Grafton St., Worcester
(508) 754-9597
Used music and CD's at low prices, comic books, posters, memorabilia.

Reaction Records
13 Mechanics St., Worcester
(508) 799-4240
All types of recordings.

Union Music
142 Southbridge Street (Next to Coney Island Hot Dogs), Worcester
(508) 753-3702
Voted Worceter's Best Music Store 1994. Guitars, amps, keyboards,drums, effects, band instruments, lessons, rentals and some philosophy.

Shoes

Thom McAn
Locations in:
Auburn Mall, Auburn (508) 832-2783; Timpany Blvd.; Gardner 632-9770; Searstown Mall, Leominster 534-9764; White City, Rte. 9, Shrewsbury 752-9464; Greendale Mall 852-3294, Worcester; Lincoln St.; Worcester 853-9832; Webster Sq., Worcester 752-9395. Men's and women's casual and dress shoes; children's shoes in sizes 3 and up. Thom McAn is headquartered at 67 Millbrook Street, Worcester, MA 01606, (508) 791-3811 and employs 260.

Hyde Factory Outlet
15 Mechanic St., East Brookfield
(508) 867-7406
Name brand shoes at discount prices for the whole family. Boots, sneakers, soccer shoes, roller skates, and much more, Mon.,Tues.,Wed.,Fri., 10am-5:30pm, Thurs. 10am-8pm, Sat. 10am-5pm.

Allen's
26 Main St., Leominster
(508) 534-3111
Orthopedic and comfort shoes; shoes for the diabetic foot covered by Medicare; Xtra Depth shoes by P. W. Minor, Josef Seibel, New Balance; Mon.-Sat. 9:30am-5:30pm, Thurs. till 8:30pm, open Sun. from Labor Day-Xmas.

ProFeet
Quinsigamond Plaza, Rte. 9, Shrewsbury
(508) 756-5866
Top quality athletic footwear & apparel; Nike, Reebok, Avia, Danskin, Nike Gortex, Tinley tights & more, call for hours.

Westies
Westboro Shopping Center, Westborough
(508) 366-7494
Women's shoes featuring 9 West, Mon.-Sat. 10am-8pm, Sun. 12-5pm.

B.T. Footwear
35 E. Main St., Westborough
(508) 366-3615
Florsheim, Sebago, Munro, Lake of Woods, Sorel, Defroster, Keds, BT, Herman, Skyr, Carolina, Maine Trotter and more for men, women, and children, M-F 10am-6pm, Sat. 10am-5pm, Sun. 12-5pm.

Charlie's Surplus
116 Water St., Worcester
(508) 752-7121
Boots, sneakers at great prices.

Churchill's
16 Austin St., Worcester
(508) 753-0932
Top quality men's shoes, Cole-Haan, Dr. Martens, Timberland, New Balance, Florsheim, Rockport.

KangaRoo Crossing
180 Main St., Worcester
(508) 791-9206
Branded athletic footwear and clothing; outdoor/casual shoes; shoes for all individual sports. Team and club sales, Sun. 12-4pm, M-F 9am-8pm, Sat. 9am-5:30pm.
"Great soccer shoes, always fun to shop," Thomas A. Deune, Worcester, MA.
"Knowledgeable, friendly, strong inventory," Charlie Bibaud, Worcester, MA.
"No matter what type of shoe I'm looking for, they have it," Kevin Asplund, Worcester, MA.

Mortt's Shoes
120 Stafford St., Worcester
(508) 752-9931
Family department shoe store, men's, women's, kids', dress shoes, boots, brand name shoes at lower prices, Nike, Keds, Reebok.

RoMo Boutique for Feet
131-A Highland St., Worcester
(508) 754-3398
Original Dr. Martens shoes and boots, clothing and accessories, Mon.-Sat. 10am-6pm; Thurs. 12-8pm.

Sneakerama
Main St., Webster Square, Worcester
(508) 799-7278
Brand name athletic footwear for the whole family.
"Say 'Hi' to Lou and Mrs. G.," Larry Abramoff.

Shoes - Children's

Mr. Ed's Kids Bootery
Heritage Mall, Auburn
(508) 832-4238
Specializing in narrow to extra wide widths, 32 years experience, locally owned.

Curran's
1207 Main St., Holden
(508) 829-2080
Discount prices, old-fashioned service, name brands for less, soccer, basketball, ballet, tap and more.
"Great prices, people come from miles around," A.L., Rutland, MA.

Sporting Goods

Play It Again Sports
Auburn Plaza, 711 Southbridge St
. (next to T.J. Maxx), Auburn
(508) 832-7985
Buy, sell, trade and consign used and new sporting goods. Hockey, golf, exercise equipment & weights, skis, baseball, softball, skates, tennis, camping, boxing, football, soccer.

White Ski & Sport, Inc.
60 Main St., Boylston
(508) 869-2351
Ski and snowboard equipment, expert advice, seasonal, call for hours.

John's Sport Shop
38 Main St., Gardner
(508) 632-0620 or (800) 439-0620
All kinds of sporting goods; BSA and GSA authorized dealer, M-F 9am-5:30pm; Thurs. 9am-7pm; Sat. 9am-4pm.

Spencer Billiards North Brookfield Rd., Spencer
(508) 885-5236
Custom-built pool tables, manufactured on the premises.

Nevada Bob's
1 Oak St. at Rte. 9, Westborough
(508) 870-0520
Discount golf and tennis equipment. 9:30 am - 8 pm weekdays; 9:30 am - 6 pm Sat.; Sun., noon to 5 pm.

City Sporting Goods
154 Blithewood Ave (off Grafton St.), Worcester
(508) 755-3957
Trophies, monogramming, silk screening; equipment and uniforms for all sports, M-F 8am-5pm, Sat. 8am-12pm.

Eastern Mountain Sports
Greendale Mall, Worcester
(508) 856-9606
Top-quality hiking and camping equipment, clothing, sleeping bags, back packs, ski wear and more.

IceCats Corner Team Shop
303 Main St., Worcester
798-5400; 1-800-830-CATS
Complete selection of authentic IceCats (Worcester's AHL hockey team) merchandise, clothing for infants-adults, souvenirs, and more, M-F 10am-6pm; Sat. 10am-4pm.

Mac-Ben Tatnuck
649 Chandler St., Worcester
(508) 797-9101
Large selection Nike clothing; free parking.

New England Backpackers, Inc.
6 East Mountain St., Worcester
(508) 853-9407
Specialists in lightweight camping gear, canoes, kayaks, climbing equip. X.C. skis, backpacks; official Boy Scouts of America distributor.

Strand's Ski Shop
1 West Boylston Dr., Worcester
(508) 852-4333
Full range of ski equipment, over 60 years of experience; all types of ski clothing; open year round, in- season weekdays 10am - 8pm; Sat. 10am-4:30pm; Sun. Noon - 4:30pm.

Stationery

Bradford Stephen
623 Chandler St. at Tatnuck Square, Worcester
(508) 752-8642
Fine paper goods, stationery, including Crane engraved wedding invitations, computerized calligraphy machine, call for hours.

Paper Emporium
113 Highland St., Worcester
(508) 756-1722
Great cards & gifts; holiday cards & invitations, calendars, gifts, wrappings, stationery, Tues.-Fri. 10am-6pm, Sat. 10am-5pm.

Paperworld Party Center
30 Prescott St. at Lincoln Sq., Worcester
(508) 751-8500
Supplies for weddings, showers, birthdays, anniversaries, holiday parties, cake and candy making supplies, balloons, helium tank sales and rentals, invitations, napkins and much more.

Toys

Bears Unlimited
139 Worcester St., North Grafton
(508) 839-4308
Teddy bear store, "collectible and huggable plush," Steiff, North American, Russ brands. Open by chance or by appointment.

Gentle Elephant Toys & Books
276 West Main St. (Rte. 20), Northborough
(508) 393-9999
Educational toys and books-Ravensburger, Brio, Ginny, Corolle, etc., programs & playgroups for children and

parents. Call for more information and catalog, M-F 9:30am-6pm, Sat. 9:30am-5pm.

Classic Toy Shop
580 Main St., Shrewsbury,
(also 198 Park Ave. Worcester)
(508) 845-9303; (508) 755-3629
Just as the name implies-classic toys like Brio, Playmobil, Ravensburger, Madame Alexander and Ginny dolls, top-notch educational learning toys and games, unique items. Mon.-Sat., 9:30am-5:30pm, Sun. 12 noon-5 p.m.(in Worcester).

Whitco Toy
140 Main St. Spencer (508) 885-9343
Hard-to-find toys; Mattel; Playskool; Little Tykes; bicycles, Mon.-Sat.,10am-9pm, Sun. 12-7pm.

The Whiz
Westboro Shopping Center,
Rte. 9 & Lyman St., Westborough
(508) 366-2030; 1-800-649-Soft
Software, hardware, gifts, hobbies, games, toys, crafts, everything from rubber chickens to computers, Mon.-Sat. 9am-9pm, Sun. 12-5pm.
"Wonderful, creative toys for kids of any age. Here the unusual is usual," A.L. Rutland, MA.

Brown Toy House Creative Playthings
79 William St. (near Elm Park),
Worcester (508) 798-3607
Playmobil and Brio, lots of creative playthings, puzzles, games. Mon.-Fri. 10 am-4 pm.

John's Toys
70 James St., Worcester (508) 797-0023
Star Wars, Star Trek & collectible toys; TV movie and celebrity related toys and gifts. M-F 9:00 am-7:00 pm; Sat. 10am - 5pm, mail order catalogue available.

Miscellaneous

Higgins Energy Alternatives
Jct. Rtes. 122 & 32, Barre
1-(800) 424-6343
Fireplace/stove showroom, gifts for the hearth, fireplace, or stove owner; tool sets, hearth rugs, bellows, steamers, log carriers, log baskets, lawn & garden, Mon.-Sat. 8:30-5pm; Thurs. till 8:30pm.

Fuller Flag Company
1025 Main St., Holden
(508) 829-6016
Wonderful hand-made flags, banners, flags from all states, countries. Tues.-Fri. 9am - 5pm, Sat. 9am - 3pm.

Halloween Outlet
246 Park Avenue (across from Park Ave Towers), Worcester 1-800-HALWEEN
The largest exclusive Halloween store on the East Coast. Over 4,000 masks; 10,000 costumes for kids & adults; sales, rentals, haunted houses.

MacKoul's Cars
220 Worcester St., N. Grafton
(508) 839-2324
Specializing in Volvo & Saab repairs, foreign, used car sales, body shop.
"Selection, service, price," Michael Plante, Worcester, MA.

The Owl Shop
416 Main St., Worcester
(508) 753-0423
Pipe, cigar and cigarette tobaccos. Music boxes, fine pens and cutlery, darts, cribbage and chess boards, Swiss Army knives and watches, model cars, candy and fine wines, Mon.-Sat. 9am-6pm.
"It's one of the oldest businesses (circa 1915) that takes care of its customers like the way business used to. It's a classic," David W. Fulgham, Worcester, MA.

Chapter 7

Dining

I know there are lots more places to dine out there. And I can't blame you for not telling us. After all, who wants to wait in line while out-of-towners discover your special spot? The next thing you know they'll be raising the prices because of the "tourist" market. All I can say is, " Don't be selfish, think globally, share your favorite spot with us and read on so you can share our favorite spots."

If you're tired of meat and potatoes, you can get fried cassava roots, oxtail and curried goat without leaving the county, along with Osso buco, Churrasco a Rodizio, basmati rice and Kang ped Yaang. Worcester is a place where sushi, kibbe, calamari and baba ghanoujh are commonplace. In the mood for Brazilian? Vietnamese? Caribbean? No problem. One restaurant here even specializes in Armenian, Israeli, Russian and Greek food all under one roof. And if you find the right local spot, you may even get free wisecracks; no extra charge!

In this chapter, we've put diners first because Worcester has so many unique and historic "lunch cars." And for special occasions, we've listed Extra-Fine Dining next. The remaining categories are in alphabetical order, and are grouped by town. For example, "Family" restaurants in Auburn are listed before "Family" restaurants in Worcester. And remember, things change, call first, send us your review. Whether it's the latest new pub, hot dog spot or an update on one of our listings send your comments, suggestions, notes and reviews to: Favorite Places C/O Tatnuck Bookseller 335 Chandler Street Worc., MA 01602, or FAX 508-756-9425.

Diners; Extra-Fine Dining; American Traditional / Country Dining; Bagels; Bakeries; Bistros; Cinema Pubs; Clubs;Coffee Houses, Cafes, Tea Rooms; Country Clubs; Deli's; Ethnic: (Armenian, Israeli, Russian, Austrian, Hungarian, German, Brazilian, Caribbean, Chinese, Greek, Indian, Italian, Japanese, Mexican, Middle Eastern, Southwestern, Thai, Vietnamese); Family; Healthy; Historic; Hot Dog Stands; Ice Cream; Pubs & Taverns; Seafood; Steak Houses.

Special thanks to the Telegram & Gazette, Worcester Magazine, and the Worcester Phoenix, whose restaurant reviews were an invaluable resource.

Nothing Could Be Finer Than to Eat in Worcester's Diners

Worcester is a "living diner museum" according to the Roadside, a newspaper devoted solely to preserving that most unique of American institutions - the Diner. Indeed, Worcester has so many living, breathing diners that Roadside editor Randy Garbin moved his whole funky publication here. As he notes in the Spring, 1994 issue, which is devoted to Worcester's diners, "...the diner is king here...the issue isn't finding a diner, it's deciding on which one."

Why is Worcester lucky enough to have so many diners still operating? Because the famed Worcester Lunch Car Company manufactured them here at 2 Quinsigamond Ave. until 1961, numbered them, and shipped some 850 of them all over the country. Other Worcester-made diners around New England include The Four Sisters in Lowell, The Blue Bonnet in Northampton and The Hop in Lynn. Henry's Diner in Allston is Worcester #841, and Ann's Diner in Salisbury is Worcester #824.

The Roadside defines a diner as a "prefabricated structure with counter service, hauled out to its site." But anyone who has visited a true Worcester diner knows it can be like stepping back into the 1940's, with polished quartered oak booths and paneling, trademark curved ceilings, brass foot rests, real tile and real marble counters. The food varies from diner to diner, but in most you'll find home-cooked food at a bargain, with an ambiance hard to match anywhere else.

Today, Worcester's Diners serve an eclectic mix of old-timers, college students, factory workers, office workers, families - anyone who wants good food, cheap, served with a neighborhood feel. For more on diner history, write the *Roadside*, 11 Homer St., Worcester, MA 01602-2114. The publication's goal is "to get America out of the franchises, the malls, the interstates, bland suburbia, and back into the real things...diners, drive-ins, trains, porches, and anything locally owned."

Diners

Woody's Main St. Diner
311 Main St., Athol
(508) 249-8529
Mon.-Fri. 5am-2pm; Sat. 5am-11am, closed on Sunday.
"The food is great, low-cost, and smoking is not allowed," Allen Young, Royalston, MA.

Moran Square Diner
6 Myrtle Ave., Fitchburg
(508) 343-9549
Authentic diner, Worcester Dining Cart # 765; classic diner food including New England boiled dinner; also healthy choices like fat-free cream cheese and egg substitutes (one co-owner is a nutritionist). Mon.-Fri. 5am-2pm; Sun. 6am-noon breakfast only, closed on Sat.

Skip's Blue Moon Diner
102 Main St. (Exit 22 off Rte. 2, follow Rte. 68 North), Gardner
(508) 632-4333
Vintage 1948 Worcester Lunch Car diner, home-style cooking; Mon.-Fri. 6am-2pm; Sat. 6am-1pm; Sun. 7am-1pm; Dinners Thurs.-Sat., 5pm-8pm, prime rib a bargain. On the National Register of Historic Places.

Big Ts Little Kitchen
48 Central St., Leominster
(508) 537-3433
Home-made pasta; open Tues.-Sat. 5am-2pm; Thurs.-Sat. 10pm-2pm; Sun. 5am-noon, closed Monday. An historic Worcester Lunch Car.

Chet's Diner
Rte. 20, Northborough
(508) 393-9403
A Worcester Lunch Car diner, installed at its present location July 2, 1931, open Mon.-Fri. 5am-2pm; Sat. 5am-11am; Sun. 8am-2pm. Daily specials, breakfast all day.

Carl's Oxford Diner
291 Main St., Oxford
(508) 987-8770
Burgers, pancakes, home fries, a stand-out diner, Mon.-Fri. 6am-1:30pm; Sat. 6am-noon; Sun. 7:30am - noon.
"The food is excellent! It speaks of days gone by, the owner is charming, and entertaining and the price is right," Barbara T. Brimer, Worcester, MA.
"Great meals! Good food," Pat and Richard Casagranda, Oxford, MA
"Carl's Diner was one of the hot topics on several call in radio shows I had for this book on WTAG/WSRS radio." Larry Abramoff, Worcester.

Windsock Diner
Southbridge Airport, Federal Hill Rd., Southbridge
(508) 765-0226
Thurs.-Fri. 11am-9pm; Sat. 7am-4pm; Sun. 7am-1pm.
"Good, stick-to-your-ribs food; close to Old Sturbridge Village," Lynda Nesbitt, Spencer, MA.

Art's Diner
541 West Boylston St., Worcester
(508) 853-9705
Pasta, sandwiches, soups, just lunch, 11am -3pm daily.

Blue Belle Diner
47 Prescott St., Worcester
(508) 755-8191
Family-owned since 1979, open Mon.-Fri. 6am - 2pm; a favorite of students from nearby Worcester Voc-Tech H.S.; good prices.

Boulevard Diner
155 Shrewsbury St., Worcester
(508) 791-4535
Italian specialties; an historic Worcester Lunch Car, beautiful exterior. Open Mon.-Sat. 7:30am-3am; Sun. 6am-1:30pm.
"The best Italian food at all hours of the night," Michelle Donabedian,

Holden, MA.

"At 2am on January 11, 1984, in a raging snowstorm, three hours after my birthday present was born, I had a hearty breakfast here with the city plow drivers on break," Larry Abramoff, Worcester, MA.

Broadway
100 Water St., Worcester
(508) 753-3233
Prices: Inexpensive. Homemade ice cream. A Worcester institution, great Sunday am breakfast, open other days for lunch and dinner, Mon.-Thurs. 5am-8pm; Fri.-Sat. 5am-9pm; Sun. 5am-3pm.
"From the time I was 9, my father took me here to breakfast every Saturday. He even had a charge account," Larry Abramoff, Worcester, MA.
"Satisfying Sunday morning breakfast that brings in the crowds, offering everything from eggs Benedict to blintzes," Telegram & Gazette.

Charlie's Diner
344 Plantation St., 200 yards off Rte. 9 across from UMASS and Biotech Park, Worcester
(508) 752-9318
Elegantly maintained classic Worcester diner, 2nd generation family-owned; clean, hearty portions, a tradition. Mon.-Fri. 6am-2:30pm; Sat. 7:30 am-11:30am, closed Sunday.
"Great authentic diner atmosphere. Stick-to-your ribs diner food, great pancakes and coffee. Off the beaten path but accessible," Dana O'Connor, Worcester, MA.

Corner Lunch
Lamartine St. and Quinsigamond Ave., Worcester
(508) 755-5576
Only 1950's diner in Worcester still in original condition. Open 7 days; hours until 9pm Mon.-Fri. - Cool neon sign, great flame-grilled burgers, steak 'n eggs, home fries.

Emerald Isle
49-53 Millbury St., Worcester
(508) 798-9747
Not far from George's Green Island diner, a 1946 O'Mahony diner, which has been completely remodeled. Look for its leprechaun hat on the roof from I-290. Open Mon.-Thurs. 6:45am-9pm; Fri.-Sat. 6:45am-10pm, only bar open on Sunday.

George's Green Island
162 Millbury St., Worcester
(508) 753-4189
A mainstay in a working class neighborhood, basic diner experience, a Worcester Lunch Car diner.
Open daily 10:30pm-11:30am.

Gold Star Restaurant
68 West Boylston St., Worcester
(508) 852-7900
Not in a classic diner car, but good quick, inexpensive breakfast or lunch fare. Open Mon.-Sat. 6am-3pm; Sun. 7am-3pm.
"Try the homemade corned beef hash. Service casual but efficient," Telegram & Gazette.

Kenmore Diner
250 Franklin St., Worcester
(508) 753-9541
A 1940 O'Mahony diner updated save for the black marble counter. Night owl hours - 11pm - 11:30am, low prices.
"Late hours for nighthawks, great hash browns, super prices for great dineresque foods...steak 'n eggs, etc. retro-atmosphere with old fashioned diner coffee mugs and interesting patrons to observe," Michelle Donabedian, Holden, MA.

Miss Worcester
300 Southbridge St., Worcester
(508) 752-1310
Affectionately called the "Miss Woo" by regulars; a 1948 Worcester Lunch Car, located just across from where it was made; family-owned. Open Mon.-Fri. 6am-2pm; Fri. 11pm-4am; Sat. 8am-noon, 11pm-4am, closed on Sunday.

Parkway Diner
148 Shrewsbury St., Worcester
(508) 753-9968
A Worcester Lunch Car, covered by a facade on the outside; untouched on the inside; 20 stools, no booths; Italian specialties; fresh Italian bread; food a local legend. Open Mon.-Sat. 5am-10pm; Sun. 7am-1pm.
"John Evangelista cooks me a great meal, tells me my boyfriend is a lucky man and reminds me of my father. It's like home away from home," Anita Kostecki, Worcester, MA.

Ralph's Chadwick Square Diner
95 Prescott St., off Grove St., Worcester
(508) 753-9543
Burgers and chili famous in diner, live entertainment famous in attached club portion. Open Wed.-Sat. 6pm-2am - a local legend (see also "Clubs").
"It's my favorite because of the atmosphere," Rick Conorole, Auburn, MA.
"Best live music club, 1994," Worcester Magazine.

Wendy's Clark Brunch
934 Main St., Worcester
(508) 756-1550
A Clark Univ. favorite. Open Mon.-Sat. 6am-3pm, closed Sunday.

Extra-Fine Dining

Victorian House
16 Maple Ave., Ashburnham
(508) 827-5646
Pork Dijonnaise, filet of sole with crabmeat, lobster tails, pasta primavera, elegant desserts, entrees $11-$31. Open Wed.-Sat. 5pm-9:30pm.
"This country gem offers top-flight food at prices that can be quite reasonable if you choose carefully. And don't deny yourself dessert; the Creme Royale is a heavenly combination of mascarpone cheese, raspberry puree and fresh raspberries," Worcester Magazine.

Athol Steak House
14 Grove St., Athol
(508) 249-2624
American and continental cuisine, intimate setting in a turn-of-the-century mansion. Lunch served Mon., Wed., Thurs., Fri. 11:30am-2pm, dinner 5pm-9pm; Fri.-Sat. till 10pm; Sun. brunch 10:30am-2pm, dinner 12:30pm-8pm.

Axe Mill Tavern
306 Main St., Rte. 16, East Douglas
(508) 476-1276
Prices: Moderate. Expect the unexpected - alligator Pomodora, Montego Bay chicken, seafood Jonathan, venison Vancouver and more, creative wine list. Closed Sun.-Mon.; Tues.-Thurs.3:30-11pm; Fri.-Sat. 11am-11pm.
"Great food, wide variety of items on the menu and excellent service," Jackie Gaskin, Douglas, MA.
"Definitely worth a special visit. The out-of-the-ordinary menu is very refreshing," Telegram & Gazette.

Abigail's
625 Betty Spring Rd., Gardner
(508) 630-2322
Formal dining; seats 300; Steaks, Boston Clam Chowder very special;

6 function rooms; part of Colonial Bed & Breakfast. Open Mon.-Thurs. 6:30am-9:30pm; Fri.-Sat. till 10:30pm; Sun. 6:30am-9:30pm. (See where to stay.)

Castle Restaurant
1230 Main St., Leicester
(508) 892-9090
Lobster, venison, shrimp and more in medieval castle atmosphere; women's menu lists no prices. Open Tues.-Sat. 11:30am-9pm; Sun. 2pm-9pm, closed Mon.
"It's one of a kind," James A. Pijus, Lavallee, Tennessee.
"Because of the romance and ambiance," Betty and Don LeBlanc, W. Millbury, MA.
"The Castle's Patio - cool breezes, great music, relaxing atmosphere and great food," Joanne Williamson, Leicester, MA.
"It's so damn romantic," T. Bradley Jarvis, Paxton, MA.

Harrington Farms
178 Westminster Rd., Princeton
(508) 464-5600
Gourmet menu changes seasonally. Main dining room accommodates up to 35 people. Can seat a total of 70 in three rooms. Available for business meetings or parties. Call for directions and reservations. Open Wed.-Sun. 5pm-9:30pm.
"Dinner at Harrington Farms embodies the charm that we love about Princeton and New England at its best," Christine Nichols, Princeton, MA.
"Quiet elegance on the mountain... what impresses is the palpable peacefulness. The background noises of our lives, the jangling telephones, the rat-a-tat of video games, the clamor of traffic, are replaced by the plaintive hoot of an owl, the whistle of the wind in the treetops," Worcester Magazine.

Le Bearn Restaurant Francais
12 Cedar St., Sturbridge
(508) 347-5800
Fine French cuisine, roast duckling, coq au vin, bouef bourguignon. Wonderful for an intimate dinner or special occasion. Entrees $17-$24. Open daily 5pm-closing.
"Traditional French cuisine in a charming setting. Nestled on a side street, away from the tourist bustle, Le Bearn plays the role of a country cottage, lovingly decorated by Madame Marty," Worcester Phoenix.

Whistling Swan
502 Main St., Rte. 20, Sturbridge
(508) 347-2321
Housed in an elegant Greek Revival mansion, fine service, creative menu, mustard-herb rack of lamb, roast duckling with Madeira sauce and more. Wonderful for special occasions. More casual Ugly Duckling Loft is upstairs. Open Tues.-Sat. 11:30am-9pm; Sun. noon-9pm, closed Monday.
"The food is terrific!" Barbara Hane, Dudley, MA.
"The crab cakes with watercress mayonaisse are among the best we've sampled, the rack of lamb flavored with breadcrumbs, garlic and herbs moist, savory and delicious. I can't get the white chocolate moussse with raspberry puree out of my mind," Worcester Magazine.

Victorian
583 Linwood Avenue, Whitinsville (Northbridge)
(508) 234-2500
All entrees $24. Restored mansion, special place for special occasions. Superb service, outstanding food, Wed.-Sat. 5:30pm-9:30pm; Sun. brunch 11:30am-2:30pm, dinner 4pm-8pm, closed Mon.-Tues.
"Find any excuse for a special occasion to visit the Victorian, an authentically restored mansion where service bor-

ders on polite pampering and the food has few peers," Worcester Phoenix.

Arturo's Ristorante
411 Chandler Street, Worcester
(508) 755-5640
Northern Italian menu, elegant atmosphere. Pizzeria open Sun.-Sat. 11:30am-11:30pm; dining room open Mon.-Sat. 5pm-10pm.
"Of two restaurants I ate in while in Worcester County, this one was fun. Great ambiance phenomenal desserts." Nadine Liebling, Long Beach, New York.
"Great food, great atmosphere," Darlene Post, Princeton, MA.
"The atmosphere is inviting, the food is consistently delicious, the prices are reasonable,and Arturo and his staff do everything they can to make your visit enjoyable," Debbie Goldsmith, Worcester, MA.

Beechwood Inn & Restaurant
363 Plantation St., off Rte. 9 near Biotech Park and UMASS Worcester
(508) 754-5789
Elegant setting, extensive wine list, Mix of American cuisine and out of the ordinary offerings. Open Mon.-Fri. 6:30am-10:30am breakfast, 11:30am-2:30pm lunch, 6pm-10pm dinner; Sat. 7:30am-10:30am breakfast, 11:30am-2:30pm lunch, 6pm-10pm dinner; Sun. 10am-2pm brunch, 3pm-9pm dinner.
"Fine dining for any occasion and upscale accommodations for guests at reasonable prices," Rob Webb, Shrewsbury, MA.
"Near perfection is right here in Worcester," Worcester Magazine.

Maxwell-Silverman's Tool
house, 25 Union St., Worcester
(508) 755-1200
In a restored 100-year old factory building, steak, seafood, Club Maxine's for parties, meetings and Sunday brunch, dancing Fri. and Sat. night. Full bar. Open Mon.-Thurs. 11am-9:30pm; Fri.-Sat. 11am-11pm; Sun. brunch 11am-2:30pm, dinner 4pm-9pm.
"This factory-turned restaurant is back near the top of the area's favorite eateries. The combination of comfortable surroundings and the work of three new chefs is hard to beat," Telegram & Gazette.

Stendahls
8 Austin St., Worcester
(508) 752-0600
Superb gourmet French dining, elegantly prepared, fine attention to details, 7 wild lettuces in the salad; duckling and fresh fruit zabaglione are legendary, over 50 wines offered. Regularly gets top marks from area food reviewers. Wonderful for special occasions. Entrees $17-$25. Open Tues.-Sat. 5pm-10pm.
"Stendahls: the word is 'sublime,' a bit of Europe in downtown Worcester. Stendahls is the crown jewel in Worcester's downtown. And you may not be a crown prince, but you can dine like one," Worcester Magazine.

Struck Cafe
415 Chandler Street, Worcester
757-1670
Exquisite food; entrees $14-$21. Homebaked carrot pineapple bread is legendary; creative cuisine; unusual combinations, including charming mix and match china place-settings. Reservations recommended. Open Tues.-Fri. 11:30am-2pm; Tues.-Thurs. 5pm-9pm; Fri.-Sat. 6pm-10pm.
"Elegant yet comfortable, with a new affordable menu featuring lighter, fresher entrees and the most creative cooking in town," Worcester Magazine.

Thyme's Square on Hudson
455 Pleasant St., Worcester
(508) 791-6102
Extra-fine dining without the extra-high cost. Creatively prepared dishes; grilled blue marlin, cajun dishes , European Bistro atmosphere, homemade desserts, smoke-free dining; Tues.-Fri. lunch 11:30am-2:30pm; dinner 5-9pm Tues.-Sat.
"Thymes Square impresses immediately with its handsome facade, and imaginatively prepared food entirely lives up to that first impression," Worcester Magazine.

Tiano's
108 Grove St.,
Northworks Marketplace, Worcester
(508) 752-8901
Classic and modern Italian dishes; Baked Shrimp Tiano a favorite; impeccable service, wonderful ambience. Open Mon.-Fri. 11:30am-2:30pm, 4:30pm-10pm, Fri.-Sat. 4:30pm-11pm; Sun. 4pm-9pm.
"Tiano's does it up right: service, ambience and food on a recent visit were virtually flawless," Worcester Magazine.

American Traditional / Country Dining

Col. Isaac Barre Restaurant
Off the Common, Barre
(508) 355-4629
Rustic charm, cozy elegance, moderate prices, sauteed chicken Marsala; baked haddock and more, 20 mins. from Worcester. Entrees $11-$16. Open Mon.-Sun. 11:30am-2pm; Tues.-Sun. 5pm-9pm.
"They have a wonderful Sunday brunch which gives us a chance to relax, listen to beautiful piano music and enjoy delicious food at very reasonable prices. The atmosphere is terrific and the ride there from Worcester is breathtaking," Marion H. McShera, Worcester, MA.

Top of the Town
500 Main St., Clinton
(508) 365-6500
Seafood, beef, pasta, moderate prices $8-$13. Open Mon.-Sat. 11:30am-3pm lunch, Mon.-Thurs. 5pm-9pm dinner; Fri.-Sat. dinner 5pm-10pm; Sun. 9am-1pm brunch, 1pm-9pm dinner.
"The financially challenged -which is most of us these days - will find Top of the Town's prices right in line. Prime rib au jus is the priciest splurge at $12.95. baked stuffed breast of chicken is $7.95," Worcester Magazine.

Grafton Inn
25 Central Square, Grafton
(508) 839-5931
Blackboard specials, home-style American dishes, full bar. Open Mon.-Thurs. 11am-9pm; Fri.-Sat. 11am-11pm; Sun. noon-9pm.

Sheraton Inn
99 Erdman Way, Leominster
(508) 534-9000
Varied menu in beautiful hotel, moderate prices. Open Mon.-Sun. breakfast 6:30am-11am, lunch/dinner 11:30am-10pm in Masquerades Pub, dinner 5pm-10pm.
"An attractive room in a beautiful hotel, offering some of the finest dining in the area. A great value," Telegram & Gazette.

Corner Stone's
616 Central St., Leominster
(508) 537-1991
Inexpensive prices, steak, veal dishes, prime rib, cocktail lounge. Open Mon.-Sat. 11:30am-10pm; Sun. 11:30am-9pm.
"Imaginative offerings with fresh ingredients. The house salad can be a meal, but save room for the veal Marsala or prime rib," Telegram & Gazette.

The Grille
35 Solomon Pond Road,
Northborough
(508) 393-2681
Basic American menu, steaks, chops, seafood, specials, $8-$15, bar. Open Mon.-Wed. 11:30am-2:30pm lunch, 4pm-9pm dinner; Thurs.-Sat. 4pm-11pm dinner; Sun. noon-9pm.

Fox Run Restaurant
Exit 19 off Rte. 2, Phillipston
(508) 249-8267
Seasonal; Easter to Thanksgiving, private Christmas parties. Fine country dining, call for hours, seats 150, up to 75 in a function room; known for plank steak, rack of lamb, and Chateau Briand for two.
"Suzanne Hooley, owner-chef of Fox Run, long known for her apple pies and apple crisp...credits Red Apple Farm less than two miles down the road with supplying all her apples..." Worcester Phoenix.

Ladd's Restaurant
Barre-Paxton Rd., Rte. 122, Rutland
(508) 886-4771
Informal full service restaurant. Open Wed.-Thurs. 4pm-8:30pm; Fri.-Sat. 4pm-9:30pm; Sun. noon-6pm; closed Mon.-Tues.
"Large portions of well-prepared staples," Telegram & Gazette.

Andrea Restaurant
241 Turnpike Rd., Rte. 9,
Southborough
(508) 481-0727
Fresh seafood, Italian, steaks, kid's menu, famous for the veal Parmesan, family-owned and operated for 29 years, $6.95 and up, early bird dinners from 4:30-6pm, entrees $8-13. Open Tues.-Sat. 11:30am-2pm lunch, 4:30pm-8:30 dinner; Fri. dinner till 9:45pm, Sat. noon-3:30pm lunch, 3:30pm-9:45 dinner; closed Sun.-Mon.
"Best lunch on Rte. 9," according to several residents of Southborough, MA.

Spencer Country Inn
500 Main St., Spencer
(508) 885-9036
Beautiful country setting, circa 1740 house, 5 dining rooms seating 140; banquet hall holds 250 for weddings, functions. Hogshead Pub has live entertainment on weekends. Open Tues.-Sat. 11:30am-3pm lunch, 5pm-9pm dinner; sun. 10am-1pm brunch, 1pm-8pm dinner.
"Fine country dining in a lovely setting without cliched hooey. The kitchen displays a keen sense of preparation for creative tastes," Telegram & Gazette.

Sterling Inn
240 Worcester Rd., Rte. 12, Sterling
(508) 422-6592
Quaint and rustic atmosphere, tender meats, broiled seafood, and duck l'orange, entrees, premier wine by the glass and Sterling cider. $11-$17. Open Tues.-Sat. 11:30am-3pm lunch, 5pm-9pm dinner; Sun. 10am-1pm brunch, 1pm-8pm dinner, closed Mon.
"Quiet, elegant dining," Mary Ann Macleod, Sterling.
"Classic American cuisine served in a charming country setting by a friendly staff," Telegram & Gazette.

Steamer's Grille
Sturbridge Host Hotel & Conference Ctr.,
366 Main St.,
Sturbridge
(508) 347-7393
Seafood, beef in casual setting, full bar.

Ugly Duckling Loft
502 Main St., Sturbridge
(508) 347-2321
Upstairs from the more formal Whistling Swan (see Extra-Fine Dining), this is less expensive and more casual,

but still has great food. Menu choices include Italian, Caribbean, French, Swedish and English offerings. Open Tues.-Sat. 11:30am-11pm; Sun. noon-9pm, closed Monday.
"In the hands of masterful chef-owner Carl Lofgren, even a meatloaf becomes something special: meatloaf Wellington," Telegram & Gazette.

White Pillars
33 West Main St., Rte. 9,
West Brookfield
(508) 867-5986
Creative menu, American offerings with a gourmet flair. Top quality dining at moderate prices. Open Sun.-Mon. 11:30am-8pm; Tues.-Thurs. 11:30am-9pm; Fri.-Sat. 11:30am-9:30pm.
"A menu that dares to be different ... American standards with a haute cuisine twist. Almost a four-star restaurant at two-star prices," Telegram & Gazette.

Too Shea's
Rtes. 2 and 140, Westminster
(508) 874-0833
Friendly atmosphere, big portions, seafood sampler is a specialty, reasonable prices, entrees $5-$16. Open Mon.-Thurs. 11:30am-8:30pm; Fri.-Sat. 11:30am-9pm; Sun. 7:30am-8:30pm.
"The signature dish, a seafood sampler, is simply amazing. When you want a good meal at a reasonable price, this North County spot is hard to beat," Worcester Magazine.

Brass Pineapple
302 Spring St., Winchendon
(508) 297-0312
American favorites, casual atmosphere, specialties Long Island Duck and pork tenderloin Dijonnaise, homemade desserts, moderate prices. Open Thurs.-Sat. 11:30am-2pm lunch; Wed.-Sat. 4:30pm-9pm dinner; Sun. 7:30am-noon breakfast only, closed Mon.-Tues.
"This casual, homey North County restaurant offers basic American standards prepared with flair and a surprisingly ambitious selection of specials," Telegram & Gazette.

Old Traveler's Restaurant
102 Front St., Winchendon
(508) 297-0740
"From scratch" cooking, family style casual dining, full service breakfast, homemade soups and chowders, large dessert selection, full bar, lunches $4-$7; dinners $6-$11, function room available. Open Mon.-Thurs. 6am-3pm; Fri.-Sat. 6am-8pm; Sun. 7am-1pm breakfast only, closed Tues.

Bagels

Bagel Inn,
Main St., Holden
(508) 829-3550
Open Mon.-Sat. 5:30am-4pm, Sun. 5:30am-2pm.
"Wonderful, tasteful, greatest bagels around," Darlene Post, Princeton, MA.

Arthur's Bagels & Friends
June Street, Worcester
(508) 757-3835
Considered one of area's best bagel shops, open daily 5:30am-2pm.
"Every time I go I leave feeling good, smiling and with the distinctive odor of Arthur's lingering with me all day," Rachel Scanlon, Worcester, MA.

Arthur's Manhattan Bagel Factory
43 West Boylston St., Worcester
(508) 856-9311
Arthur's branches out: Bagels, sandwiches, salads, soups, pizza bagels, muffins, pastries. Open Mon.-Fri. 6am-5pm; Sat. 6am-3pm; Sun. 6am-1pm.

Bagel Time
194B Park Ave., Worcester
(508) 798-0440
Lots of fun flavors, and traditonal basic bagels. Open Mon.-Fri. 6am-6pm; Sat.-Sun. 6am-3pm.
"A bakery shop that puts its competitors to shame with its big, dense, chewy bagels," Worcester Phoenix.

Bakeries

As You Like It
362-370 Main St,12 Mill St. (Restaurant) Fitchburg
(508) 345-6407
Variety of baked goods, frozen dinners, and mead (Honey Wine) as well as Native American art, Colonial china, new age gifts, and more in the gift shop. Bakery open Tues.-Sat. 8am-5pm; restaurant Tues.-Fri. 11am-4pm; Sat. 8am-2pm, closed Sun.-Mon.

Baldwin Hill Bakery
Baldwin Hill Road Phillipston
(508) 249-4691
Commercial baker of all natural bread. Open Sun.-Thurs. 8am-8pm.

Darby's Bakery
76 Central St., West Boylston
(508) 835-6789
Open Tues.-Fri. 7:30am-6pm; Sat. 8am-5pm; Sun. 8:30am-1pm, closed Monday.
"Everything tastes homemade and is homemade. The breads are the best in the Worcester area and what variety. Great pastries, too," Gretchen Ellison, Shrewsbury, MA.
"High quality baked goods, family business, friendly, inviting atmosphere, personal touch definitely apparent," Martha Page, West Boylston, MA.
"Tell Darby that Gloria sent you," Larry Abramoff, Worcester, MA.

Bahnan Bakery
369 Pleasant St. Worcester
(508) 791-8566
Syrian and Lebanese bread. Other Middle Eastern, Armenian and Greek foods.

Crown Bakery
133 Gold Star Blvd., Worcester
(508) 852-0746
Legendary Swedish bakery delights. Consistently ranked one of area's top bakeries. Open Mon. 8am-5pm; Tues., Wed. Thurs., Sat. 6am-6pm; Fri. 6am-7pm, closed Sunday.

Lederman's Bakery
108 Water St., Worcester
(508) 753-9487
Open Sat.-Thurs. 3am-7pm; Fri. 3am-6pm.
"You can buy delicious baked goods and have a cheese and egg on a bulkie served at the coffee bar," Anthony Dzindolet, Leicester, MA.
"Tell Alan that Larry sent you," Larry Abramoff, Worcester, MA.

Scano's
352 Shrewsbury St., Worcester
(508) 757-5481
Bakery, breakfast and lunch, no lunches on weekends, no bar, cash only. Open Mon.-Fri. 6am-2pm; Sat. 6am-1pm; Sun. 6am-1pm.

Sweet Treats
932A Main Street, Worcester
(508) 755-4562
Ice cream, coffee, desserts, a Clark Univ. favorite. Open Mon.-Fri. 6am-2pm; Sat.-Sun. 6am-1pm.
"Donna makes the most wonderful chocolate raspberry cake. All the pastries, ice creams and coffees are like Paris," Susan Starr, Worcester, MA.

T.J. Cinnamon's Bakery
221 Park Ave.- in Big D Market, Worcester
(508) 753-0724
Cinnamon buns, hazelnut coffee, fresh baked goods, baked stuffed croissants, more. Open Mon.-Fri. 6am-8pm; Sat.-Sun. 6am-6pm.
"They have the greatest fat-free muffin..." Theresa Monteith, East Brookfield, MA.

Widoff's Bakery
129 Water St. Worcester
(508) 752-7200
Traditional Jewish Bakery.

Bistros

P.T. Beanie's
385 Main St., Worcester
(508) 752-9688
Busy bar and creative dining, including lamb, duckling and blue-cheese potato pancakes. Dinner and jazz entertainment served only on Thurs., Fri. and Sat. nights, lunch throughout the week, full bar. Closed Sun.-Mon.
"Excellent food, reasonable prices, nice, relaxed atmosphere, jazz music," Carol Jette, Shrewsbury, MA.
"Food so wonderful it makes me want to burst into song" Gabriele Goszcz, Auburn, MA.

Pasta Pantry
806 Pleasant St., Worcester
(508) 756-4560
European style bistro atmosphere, bring your own wine; garlic bread pizza, crab ravioli, fettucine, capellini and more, entrees $4-$9. Open Mon.-Sat. 11:30am-9pm, closed Sunday.
"You'll have to look far to find a wider, or fresher variety of pasta - capelli, fettucine, linquine - in more 'flavors' such as tomato and basil, cracked black pepper, red hot chili pepper, lemon-and-lime, and garlic-and-herb," Worcester Phoenix.

Tatnuck Bookseller Restaurant
335 Chandler St., Worcester
(508) 756-7644
A mix of well-prepared dishes, from soups and sandwiches to elegant daily specials. A great spot for coffee, a hearty lunch, or elegant dinner. Some of the best food in Worcester. BYOB. Mon.-Thurs. 8am-10pm; Fri. 8am-Midnight; Sat. 9am-Midnight; Sun. 9am-6pm.
"I can read and eat at the same time. What I like to do best," Debra Williams.
"There's a whimsy, a warmth, and a touch of funkiness that makes this place - set in a 27,000 square foot historic factory building among 500,000 books - special. The choices are creatively eclectic, absolutely fresh, and reasonably priced," Worcester Phoenix.
"Sunday morning brunch! It's great in winter or on rainy days. You can spend the entire day just looking at all the nice things and special books," Sonja Hulspas, Worcester, MA.

Cinema Pubs

Last Strand Cinema and Drafthouse
58 High St., Clinton
(508) 365-5500
Pizza, nachos, beer, 320 seats, tickets around $4, reasonable food prices, matinees on Sat., Sun.
"The idea is to provide a kind of one-stop-shopping date or family experience. You don't have to go out before and/or after the movie because you can eat and drink right in the theater," Telegram & Gazette.

Elm Draughthouse Cinema
35 Elm St., Millbury
(508) 865-2850
Serving beer, wine and pizza, admission, $3.00.

Clubs

Quarter Keg
Rte. 20, Charlton
(508) 248-3191
Entertainment, also volleyball in summer. Open daily 11:30am-Midnight.

Oxford Tavern
314 Main St., Oxford
(508) 987-5397
Rock 'n roll, 21 and over, no cover. Open Tues.-Sat. noon-2am; Sun.-Mon. noon-1am.

Foggy's
1041A Lyman St., Westborough
(508) 366-5435
Live entertainment. Open Tues.-Sat. 11:30am-10pm; Sun.-Mon. 11:30am to 9pm.

21 Club/Pub
Higgins Univ. Center, Clark Univ., Worcester
(508) 793-7711
Live performers, dancing, bar for patrons over 21.

Aku-Aku
11 Central St., Worcester
(508) 792-1124
Dick Doherty's Comedy Hut. Shows at 8pm & 10:30pm.

Algiers
21-23 Foster St., Worcester
(508) 754-7742
Casablanca-style decor, targeted to 21-25 year olds. Open Thurs.-Sat.,
"A flashy, college-oriented Top 40 dance club," Telegram & Gazette.

Eleni's Midnite Cafe
831 Franklin St., Worcester
(508) 754-0996
Acoustic folk, jazz and blues Thurs., Fri., Sat. 9pm-midnight; poetry Sun. 8pm-midnight. Full restaurant, BYOB, no credit cards.

Espresso Bar
70 James St., Worcester
(508) 770-1455
Under-21 dance club, alcohol-free, specialty coffees and desserts from late afternoon through evening. Open Wed.-Sat., live bands, open mike Thurs.

Gilrein's
802 Main St., Worcester
(508) 791-BLUE
Legendary blues club, live entertainment. Wed.-Thurs. 8pm-2am; Fri.-Sat. 5pm-2am; Sun. 8pm-2am.
"It connects me with my soul and the souls of others. It expands my joy of life. It's real," Elizabeth Adams-Oliva, Princeton, MA.

Izzi's
70 James St., Worcester
(508) 799-7665
Dance club in the back of London Billiards, over-head laser lights, dance tunes. Open daily 4:30pm-12:30am.

Penitentiary
70 James St., Worcester
(508)767-1444
Country dance club, country dance lessons on Tues., Wed., ballroom dance lessons Mon.; live country entertainment Fri. and Sat., Spanish music on Sun., a 2,500 sq. foot maple dance floor, dinner menu, snacks. Opens daily at 3pm.
"It has become one of the city's hottest nightspots...a full, cleverly written menu for dinner and munchies," Telegram & Gazette.

Plantation Club
151 Plantation St., Worcester
(508) 752-4666
Live entertainment most evenings. Open Mon.-Tues. at 4pm; Wed.-Thurs. at 2pm; Fri.-Sun. at 11:30am.

Ralph's Chadwick Square Diner
95 Prescott St., Worcester
(508) 753-9543
Live music club adjacent to diner (see diners). Open Wed.-Sat. 7pm-2am.

Sh-Booms /Polly Esta's
213 Main St., Worcester
(508) 752-4214
Dance club, Polly Esta's is a separate room within Sh-Booms, a college favorite, music from the '50's, '60's and '70's. Open Wed.-Sat. 7pm-2am.
"Best dance club, best singles club, the emporium of all things recorded circa 1959," Worcester Magazine.

Coffee Houses, Cafes, Tea Rooms

Jenkins House Tea Room
On the Common, Barre
(508) 355-6444 or 1-800-378-7373
Open Wed.-Sun. noon-8pm.
"Food is great, surroundings extremely pleasant, most welcome atmosphere," Rita M. Robinson, Barre, MA
"The food is always fresh, light and healthy" There is an open, airy dining room, plus tables on side porches and in a beautiful manicured garden," Susan Morrall, Barre, MA

Apple Tree Barn
9 West Street, East Douglas
(508) 476-2291
Open Tues.-Wed. 7am-5:30pm; Thurs.-Sat. 7am-8pm; Sun. 7am-6pm, closed on Monday.
"Great food, great setting, lots of charm, Victorian and country gifts, pleasant staff," Linda Rousseau, E. Douglas, MA.
"The food is great, the menu quite varied, the gift shop is quaint and lends a country atmosphere to your dining," Mary Ann Keinan, Worcester, MA.

Beanery
79 Worcester Rd., Grafton
(508) 791-7747
Lunch, great cappuccino, dinners on Saturday nights. Open Mon.-Fri. 6:30am-4pm; Sat. 7am-11pm; Sun. 8am-12:30pm.

Special Teas
1 Grafton Common, Grafton
(508) 839-7447
Tea room on the green; in former town hall circa 1862; unusual breakfasts, lunches, crepes, imported teas, soups, low-fat menu choices; 11am. - 4pm Tues.-Fri.; 11am.-5pm Sat.-Sun.
"It is the closest thing to an English tea room in this area. They serve cream teas!" Linda McCulloch, Shrewsbury, MA.

Tea Room at Fruitlands Museum
102 Prospect Hill, Harvard
(508) 456-9028
Open year round. Hours Tues.-Sun. Mon. holidays 10am-4pm, May through October.
"The view is spectacular of Nashoba Valley, four museums ... and excellent tearoom," Elizabeth Vesenka, Littleton, MA

Coral Seas Coffee House
110 Water Tower Plaza, Leominster
(508) 534-1446
Gourmet coffee and teas, breakfast and lunch menu, live entertainment every Fri. night. Open Mon.-Sat. 6am-9pm; Sun. 8am-6pm.

Coffee on the Common
681 Pleasant St., Paxton
(508) 754-1381
Blackboard specials, homemade breads, full breakfasts, lunch, soups, sandwiches, chicken and seafood dinners, bakery items, 7 days 5am - 8pm.
"The hash doesn't come out of a can. The blueberry pancakes aren't taken out of a freezer. And the pie crust isn't shaken out of a box," Worcester Magazine.

Coffee on the Common
Gregory Hill Princeton Center, Princeton
(508) 464-5211
Homemade soups, bread, gourmet flavored coffees. 8am-3pm weekends, 7am - 3pm weekdays, full breakfasts, bagels, muffins; sandwiches, soups for lunch.
"Old fashioned atmosphere and old-fashioned prices. There's no more pleasant place for breakfast or lunch, coffee and conversation," Susanne Rubenstein, Princeton, MA.

Coffee Garden
Corner of Middle Rd. & Rte. 9, Southborough
(508) 229-2019
Cozy interior, tasty pastries and 10 flavors of coffee, even butterscotch. Mon.-Sat. 6:30am-5pm; Sun. 8am - 1pm.

Sterling Orchards Appleseed Tearoom
Kendall Hill Rd., Sterling
(508) 422-6595
Private dinner parties, luncheons, or breakfasts, 6 or more people. Open to public Mother's Day-Father's Day, by appointment only.

Sturbridge Coffee House
504 Main St. Rte. 20, Sturbridge
(508) 347-7125
Gourmet coffee, espresso, cappuccino, latte and French pastry. Open Mon.-Thurs. 6am-6pm; Fri. 6am-9pm; Sat. 8am-10pm; Sun. 8am-6pm.

Bean Counter
113 Highland St., Worcester
(508) 754-3125
Gourmet coffee; A Clark Univ. favorite. Sun.-Wed. 7am - 10pm; Thurs.-Sat. 7 am - 11pm.
"It's where we hang out and do nothing," Nelly Ramos, Worcester, MA.

Chestnuts Cafe
10 Chestnut St. (at Chestnut Place office building), Worcester
(508) 757-7984
Soups, sandwiches, pizza, daily specials from chicken stir-fry to Fettuccinne Alfredo, prices $2.89-$4.25, open 7:30am - 2:30pm. daily, closed weekends.

Coco Bean Cafe
264 Park Ave., Worcester
(508) 757-3754
Live music Wed.-Sun., a college favorite, open Wed.-Sat. 8pm-closing, acoustic open mike Wed. and Fri.

Coffee Kingdom
2 Richmond Ave., Worcester
(508) 755-8936
Fresh ground coffee, bistro, candies, cookies. Mon-Fri 7am - 11pm.; Sat. Sun- 11am - 11pm. A college favorite.
"It is a place where you can go to, be social, have fun and drink the best coffee," Catey Driscoll, Holden, MA.
"If a food or beverage can be made from a coffee bean, it's available here..." Worcester Phoenix.
"I love to go there on Sunday and have capuccino, read and eat a scone," Tian Morrier, N. Oxford, MA.
"It's a veritable "coffee shop" complete with great espresso-based drinks and regular "Joe" plus the atmosphere allows for never-ending philosophical conversation, chess or reading - depending on the cafe-goer," Michelle M. Donabedian, Holden, MA.

Lucky's Cafe
102 Grove St., Worcester
(508) 756-5014
Great home cooked meals, Mon.-Fri. 7:30am-3:30pm; Sat. 8am-2pm, closed Sunday.

Plantation Cafe
26 Mechanic St., Worcester
(508) 798-5460
Breakfast pastries and fresh roasted coffee; quiches, crepes and pasta of the day for lunch. Fri.-Sat. evenings, gourmet entrees moderate prices, lunch $4-$6; dinner $6-$13. Open Mon.-Wed. 7:30am-4pm; Thurs.-Sat. 7:30am-9pm, closed Sunday.
"...the Plantation Cafe feels like the Florida Keys: bright, cheery, festive, and a tad funky. On Friday and Saturday evenings, try more gourmet fare, such as shrimp with apples and snap peas served with wild and long grain rice," Worcester Phoenix.

Tatnuck Bookseller Restaurant
335 Chandler Street, Worcester
(508) 756-7644
In the midst of one of the largest bookstores in the universe; bottomless coffee, special teas, homemade desserts, books on the tables, house rootbeer, BYOB, great food, classical music. In a converted historic factory building you'll be part of the action as the book business, serving customers all over the world, continues to function. Daytimes you can often find the owner, author Larry Abramoff, behind door number two, ready and willing to give a fascinating tour.

Worcester Art Museum Cafe
55 Salisbury St., Worcester
(508) 799-4406
11:30am-2pm, Tues.-Sat.
"Nestled in a gallery setting, this cafe offers such light cuisine as soups, salads and a daily entree. Try dessert and espresso or cappuccino before browsing in the museum," Telegram & Gazette.

Deli's

Dagwood's Deli
490 Main St.,Fitchburg
(508) 345-2141
Open Mon.-Fri. 7am-3pm; Sat. 8am-3pm, closed Sunday.
"They have the best food around!" Katrina Cote, Fitchburg, MA.

Rutland Deli & Sandwich Shop
Rutland Plaza, 87 Main St., Rutland
(508) 886-6069
Fast, fresh hot pizza, great crust, choice toppings. Open Mon. 6am-3pm; Tues.-Fri. 6am-7pm; Sat. 6am-3pm, closed Sunday.

Albrizio's
389 Main St. , Worcester
(508) 799-0099
Prices: Inexpensive prices, sandwiches, soups, salads, pasta. Open Mon.-Fri. 7am-5:30pm; Sat. 8am-2pm, closed Sunday.

Elsa's Bushel and Peck
358 Main St., 643 Chandler St. and
17 East Mountain St., Worcester
(508) 752-9001
Offers 125 different sandwiches, regularly voted one of area's best deli's, cash only. Main St. open Mon.-Fri. 7am-5pm; Sat.-Sun. 9am-3pm. Chandler & Mountain Sts. open Mon.-Sat. 8am-7pm, closed Sunday.
"...a menu of more than 100 sandwiches. Named combo sandwiches (e.g. the $4.25 Connie-C: grilled turkey with cheddar, sauteed onions, mushrooms, and barbeque sauce on a bulkie) they dominate and get huge points for creativity and flavor," Worcester Phoenix.

Homsey's Middle-Eastern Deli
1241 Millbury St., Worcester
(508) 798-3113
Inexpensive lunch or dinner, grinders, ice cream, pastries. Open Mon.-Fri. 7am-8pm; Sat. 7am-2pm, closed Sunday.
"George makes great lentil soup," Joan Webster, Worcester, MA.
"Mouth-watering specialties such as baba ghanouj, hummus, stuffed grape leaves and kibbe make for an inexpensive lunch or dinner," Telegram & Gazette.

Maury's
1125 Main St., Worcester
(508) 754-4446
Open Mon.-Sat. 9am-4pm, closed Sunday.

Picnic on Park
318 Park Ave., Worcester
(508) 797-3663
Deli, bakery, coffee bar and ice cream parlor; soups, sandwiches, muffins, cheesecake and other homemade delights; picnic boxes prepared on 48 hrs. notice. Open Mon.-Tues. 6:30am-6pm; Wed.-Fri. 6:30am-7pm; Sat.-Sun. 7:30am-5pm.
"This upscale deli also could be considered a bakery, coffee bar and ice cream parlor. Pleasant place for an indoor picnic," Telegram & Gazette.

Regatta Deli
28 Lake Ave., Worcester (also Colonial Dr., Westborough)
(508) 756-6916
Standard and unusual sandwich selections, Mon.-Sat. 7am-6pm, closed Sunday.
"Awesome meats, delicious," Alyssa M. Brocho, Worcester, MA.
"...famous for its Italian club (the Regatta, $2.75) but has an extensive menu that shouldn't be overlooked," Worcester Phoenix.

Tom's International Delicatessen
118 Water St., Worcester
(508) 755-7295
Known for great cold cuts, homemade cream cheeses, cash only. Open Tues.-Sun. 8am-6pm, closed Monday.
"Where in Worcester can you buy delicious cold cuts, cheeses, Hungarian, Russian, Polish and German specialties. Also at Tom's you can buy Chicopee's famous blue seal fresh and smoked kielbasa," Rita Ann Dzindolet, Leicester, MA.

Weintraub's
126 Water St., Worcester
(508) 756-7870
Great deli dishes, Romanian pastrami, catering, takeout, cash only. Open Mon. 9am-4pm; Tues.-Sun. 9am-8pm.
"Because of nostalgia - the best delicatessen." Bertha Jonas, Worcester, MA.

Ethnic - Armenian

Ararat Family Restaurant
367 Burncoat St., Worcester
(508) 856-0100
Shish kebab, hummus, baba ghanoujh and Chicken Kievski, Armenian, Greek, Israeli and Russian dishes, inexpensive, no entree more than $7.95, BYOB. Open Tues.-Wed. 11am-9pm; Thurs.-Sun. 11am-10pm, closed Monday.
"Ararat is unique and should be tried. The food is good and the service friendly," Worcester Business Journal.

Aris's Armenian Bakery
432 Pleasant St., Worcester
(508) 754-7424
Bakery open Mon.-Sat. 9am-9pm, restaurant 11:30am-8pm, closed Sunday.
"Armenian cuisine, small, home-cooked (like Nana's) with good prices

and great selection of specialty dishes," Michelle Donabedian, Holden, MA.

Armenia
68 Stafford St., Worcester
(508) 756-4660
Fine Armenian and Middle Eastern cuisine, baba ganoujh, hummus, stuffed grape leaves, Armenian pizza, etc. BYOB, Mon-Sat 10am-9pm; Sun noon-9pm; take-out, catering available.
"The Kazanchian family will treate you to their homeland's finest. Make sure to order the foule, fava beans cooked and seasoned with garlic, cumin, lemon and fiery pockets of red pepper, all in an olive oil base," Worcester Phoenix.

Shiraz Armenian Cuisine
259 Park Ave., Worcester
(508) 767-1639
Middle Eastern and Armenian recipes, hours Mon.-Tues. 11am-8pm; Wed.-Thurs. 11am-9pm; Fri.-Sat. 11am-10pm, closed on Sunday.

Ethnic - Austrian, Hungarian, German

Old Vienna Restaurant and Kaffeehaus
22 South St., Westborough
(508) 898-2230
Top name folk, jazz entertainment; restaurant has Wienerschnitzel, Sauerbraten, extensive wine, legendary beer offerings.
"Fabulous music/entertainment, great food, too!" Elaine Quigley, Westborough, MA.
"Interesting, well-prepared food with a German motif. Good wine and beer offerings," Telegram & Gazette.

Ethnic - Brazilian

Ipanema
106 Southville Rd., Southborough
(508) 460-6144
Churrasco a rodizio, indoor barbeque and other foreign specialties, fried cassava roots and dried beef, boiled, spiced and deep fried, entrees $5-$16., Wed.-Fri. 5-10pm., Sat.-Sun. noon - 10 pm.
"If you've never tried Brazilian food and can't make it to Boston's better churrascarias, it's worth the trip to Ipanema," Worcester Phoenix.

Ethnic - Caribbean

Caribbean Cuisine
5 East Mountain St. "The Summit"
Worcester
(508) 856-9199
Authentic Caribbean cuisine; oxtail with rice & peas; curry chicken and Jamaican Jerk Pork; Mon.-Fri. 11:30am-9 pm, Sat. 9am-9 pm, closed on Sunday.
"Recent renovations have given the inside of the restaurant the look of an outdoor veranda overlooking the soft blue Caribbean. Come listen to the reggae music and enjoy that laid back Island atmosphere..." Worcester Magazine.

Ethnic - Chinese

Golden Lion
547 Southbridge St., Auburn
(508) 832-3209
Traditional Chinese and American choices, full bar, takeout. Hours Mon.-Sat. 11:30am-1am; Sun. & holidays noon-1am.

Yong Shing Restaurant
338 Southbridge St., Auburn
(508) 832-0622
Traditional Chinese cuisine. Hours Mon.-Thurs. 11:30am-10pm; Fri.-Sat. 11:30am-1am; Sun. noon-10pm.
"Yong Shing Restaurant has the best Chinese food around," Ron Prouty, Auburn, MA.

Jade Lee Kitchen
96 Franklin Rd., Fitchburg
(508) 343-8249
Szechuan specialties, takeout, cash only. Open Mon.-Thurs. 11am-10pm; Fri.-Sat. 11am-11pm; Sun. noon-10pm.

Singapore Restaurant
South St., Twin City Mall, Fitchburg
(508) 345-0132
Szechuan, Mandarin, fresly made food, crab rangoon a specialty. Open daily noon-midnight.

Chum Lees
50 Boston Turnpike Rte. 9, White City Shopping Plaza, Shrewsbury
(508) 798-2220
Traditional Chinese dishes, excellent food, egg drop soup, scallion pancakes, and house specials Sizzling Seafood Fantasia, Kung Po Three Delights, Five Flavored Shrimp. $8-15. Mon.-Thurs. 11:30am-10pm; Fri-Sat; 11:30am-11 pm.;Sun. noon-10pm., full bar.
"Everything was excellent. Chicken fingers, spareribs, beef teriyaki, chicken wings and fried shrimp were all piping hot and delicious; we especially liked the shrimp and the crab Rangoons," Worcester Magazine.

Lih Garden Restaurant
97 Boston Turnpike, Shrewsbury
(508) 793-2950
Oriental dishes in a casual setting, orange-flavored beef a lunch time favorite, takeout. Open daily 11:30am-10pm.

Chef Sau Gourmet Chinese
Restaurant 148 Main St., Spencer
(508) 885-3995; 885-3996
Original cooking, moderate prices. Specialties include: Chef Sau's Crispy Spiced Beef Filet; Imperial Hunan Chicken, Scallops in Chef Sau's Sauce. Open Tues.-Thurs. 11:45am-9:30pm; Fri. 11:45am-10:30pm; Sat. 4pm-11:30pm; Sun. 4pm-9:30pm, closed Monday.
"The ingredients are fresh, the flavors clear and distinct, the sauces unique, the quality high, the service pleasant and the prices reasonable. And Chef Sau's Secret Sauce enlivens anything it touches," Telegram & Gazette.

Mayling's Chinese Restaurant
131 East Main St., Webster
(508) 943-6963
Szechuan, Cantonese, casual setting with Szechuan and Cantonese offerings, beer, wine. Open Mon-Thurs. 11am-9pm; Fri.-Sun. 11am-10pm.

Nancy Chang Restaurant
Rtes. 12 & 110, West Boylston
(508) 835-3663
Szechuan, Mandarin, Oriental grille and pasta, Peking duck and pasta; chicken & cashew ; shrimp with peanut sauce, piano music 4 nights a week; full bar, wide-screen TV in lounge. Open Sun.-Thurs. 11:30am-9:30pm; Fri.-Sat. noon-10:30pm.

Cheng-Du
Rte. 9, 157 Turnpike Rd., Westborough
(508) 366-7489
Szechuan food served with style and grace, separate lounge, function room. Open Sun.-Thurs. 11:30am-10pm; Fri.-Sat. 11:30am-midnight.
"Cheng-Du has been described as the Asian wing at the museum jazzed up with flash and dazzle, and that is just what it is," Worcester Magazine.

Mandarin Westborough
57 East Main St., Westborough
(508) 366-2288
Excellent food, flavorful, attractively served, full bar; Entrees $6-$22. Open Mon.-Thurs. 11:30am-10pm; Fri.-Sat. 11:30am-11pm; Sun. noon-10pm.
"Intriguing decor and a remarkably diverse menu make this a Chinese-American restaurant worth a visit," Telegram & Gazette.

Chopsticks
1083 Main St. (Webster Sq.), Worcester (also Leominster)
(508) 755-1075
Imaginative fine Chinese cooking, good service, great reputation, entrees $4-$14. Open Sun.-Thurs. 11:30am-10pm; Fri.-Sat. 11:30am-11pm.
"Fine Chinese cooking presented with imagination and care, every dish a delight. For a special treat, try the dim sum siu mi appetizer and pine nuts chicken," Worcester Phoenix.

Peking Wok
7 West Boylston Street, Worcester
853-3088
$5-$22. Specialties such as Hunan crispy whole fish, sizzling calamari, and fried ice cream. Reasonable prices. Open daily 11:30am-10pm.
"This isn't just another Chinese restaurant. The service is superb, the setting peaceful, and the prices quite reasonable. Fast for a few days, and then try the all-you-can-eat-buffet," Worcester Phoenix.

Ping's Garden
60 Madison St., Worcester
(508) 791-9577, 791-9578
Szechuan, Mandarin, Hunan, consistently voted one of the area's best restaurants. A college favorite, all-you-can eat Sunday buffet 4:30-9 pm; $8-$15 per person. Open daily 11:30am-Midnight.
"Lunch buffet is a popular draw. For a better value, try an 'Authentic Chinese Lunch'... an impressive amount of food with choices of pork vegetable, beef and chicken dishes," Telegram & Gazette.

Quan Yin
56 Hamilton St., Worcester
(508) 831-1322
All meatless menu, mock meats look and taste like the real thing. Store front seating 10 people, call ahead or take-out. $4-$8 entrees. Open Mon.-Thurs. 10am-9pm; Fri.-Sat. 10am-10pm, closed Sun.
"There's not a meat dish on the menu, but the flavors are so rich, the vegetables so fresh and abundant, and the spices so pungent, that you'll forget you're eating vegetarian," Worcester Phoenix.

Ethnic - Greek

Athens Restaurant
785 N. Main St., Leominster
(508) 840-3343
Pizza, pasta, seafood, sandwiches, moussaka, pastitso. Open Sun.-Thurs. 11am-10pm; Fri.-Sat. 11am-12pm.

Ethnic - Indian

Dehli Palace
200 Lunenburg St., Fitchburg
(508) 342-3873
All-you-can-eat lunch buffet, hearty and mildly spicy menu offerings, chicken masala, basmati rice, and more. Entrees $7-$11; luncheon specials $5-$6.50. Open Mon.-Thurs. noon-9:30pm; Fri.-Sat. noon-10pm; Sun. 5pm-9:30pm.

House of India
439 Park Ave., Worcester
(508) 752-1330
Inexpensive prices, Eastern spices, sitar music in the background; kebabs, lamb chops and more, entrees $8-$11. Open daily 11:30am-10:30pm.
"Try the berra kebab, six small lamb chops served on a bed of onions and covered with fresh green peppers and tomato served on a sizzling platter like a fajita," Telegram & Gazette.

Sweetheart
270 Shrewsbury St., Worcester
(508) 752-3700
Classic Indian cuisine, pungent curry, fish masala a favorite, great reputation. Open Mon.-Sat. 11am-3pm, 5pm-10:30pm; Sun. 5pm-10pm.
"Cooked-to-order versions of creative Indian cuisine," Telegram & Gazette.

Ethnic - Italian

Eddie's,
46 South St., Athol
(508) 249-3236
Fine Italian dining, open Wed.- Fri. 11:30am - 4pm lunch, 4pm-8pm dinner, Fri.-Sat. till 9pm; Sun. noon-8pm, closed Mon.-Tues.

Silvester's Restaurant
544 Wattaquaddock Hill Road, Bolton
(508) 365-5757
Wonderful veal dishes; large menu, great bread, over 103 entrees, Tues., Wed., Thurs., Sun.: 11:30am- 9pm; Fri. 11:30am-10 pm; Sat. 4-10 pm. Closed Mon.
"Good food, reasonable prices, excellent wait staff," Fred Viles, Harvard, MA.
"Caring management. Superb service. Irresistible bread," Telegram & Gazette.

Il Forno
27 Airport Rd., Fitchburg
(508) 345-2511
Italian restaurant with loyal following, brick-oven pizza, veal Francese, BYOB. Open Tues.-Thurs. 11am-10pm; Fri. 11am-11pm; Sat. 4pm-11pm; Sun. 4pm-9pm, closed Monday.
"This little Italian spot is attracting quite a following and shows true signs of greatness...veal Francese was just an explosion of garlic/lemon taste in the mouth. A short wait is likely on weekends, but it's worth it," Worcester Magazine.

Jefferson House Grille
1 Princeton Rd., (visible from Rte. 122-A), Holden
(508) 829-9090
Moderate prices, Northern Italian and American dishes, pasta, huge portions, full bar, $7-$10 entrees. Open Tues.-Sun. 11:30am-10pm, closed Monday.
"Superb renderings of Northern Italian and American classics at great prices," Telegram & Gazette.

Vinny's
700 Main St., Rte. 122-A, Holden
(508) 829-3141
Good food, great prices; haddock, chicken teriyaki, baked lasagna, baked manicotti and more, full bar. Open Sun.-Thur 11:30am-9pm; Fri.-Sat. 11:30am-10pm.
"This longtime family restaurant offers good, solid food at reasonable prices. Friendly, efficient service," Telegram & Gazette.

Vittorio Italian Cucina
861 Main St., Leicester
(508) 892-8923
Classic Italian specialties, family atmosphere, great homemade bread, professional service, moderate prices. Open Thurs. & Fri. 4pm-10pm.
"Creative approaches to classic Italian dishes...outstanding bread made on

the premises," Telegram & Gazette.

Il Camino
Rte. 12, Leominster
(508) 537-5083
Family-style casual Italian dining, Sun.-Mon. 11:30-9pm; Tues.-Sat. 11:30am-9:45pm.
"The 'exclusive dinners' range from $10.50 to $15; they're six-course meals with everything included, from soup to dessert," Worcester Magazine.

Monty's Garden
35 Central St., Leominster
(508) 537-6302
Homemade pasta, inexpensive; all-you-can-eat lunch buffet Mon., Wed., and Thurs.; pasta, pizza, and salads, plus many more regular menu items, full bar. not handicapped accessible. Open Wed.-Mon. 11:30am-10pm, closed Tuesday.
"Despite its popularity prices are still reasonable. Pasta is either imported or comes from the adjoining Pasta Company and the tomato sauce is satisfyingly heavy," Worcester Magazine.

Peppercorns
231 E. Main St., Rte. 16, Milford
(508) 634-8933
Interesting, creative menu; lobster corn chowder a specialty. Sandwiches have out-of-the ordinary combinations, pasta, pizzas, shrimp scampi. Entrees $6-$12; lunches $5-$7.
"This neatly decorated restaurant, owned by the same folks who run Bushel 'N Peck in Worcester, serves up a variety of tasty soups, sandwiches and burgers for lunch," Telegram & Gazette.

Vellante's
Rte. 109, Milford
(508) 473-9001
Country style Northern Italian dishes, casual atmosphere, moderate prices, full bar. Open Tues.-Fri. 11:30am-2:30pm lunch, Mon.-Sat. 4:30pm-9:30pm dinner; Sun. 4:30pm-8:30pm dinner.
"Try the osso buco, veal shank cut crosswise in a thick slice and braised, served in a mushroom sauce with creamy polenta," Telegram & Gazette.

A.J.'s Pub and Restaurant
411 West Main St., Northborough
(508) 393-5245
Italian favorites and American standards. Fried calamari a hit, burgers, deli sandwiches. Entrees to $11. Open Mon.-Thurs. 11:30am-10pm; Fri.-Sat. 11:30am-11pm; Sun. 4pm-9pm.
"Afficionados of Italian will remember A.J. Tomaiolo's on Route 9. The same loving touch with calamari and cacciatore is evident at A.J.'s Pub," Worcester Magazine.

Primo Pasta
5 Fairlawn Ave., Oxford
(508) 987-0273
Fresh ingredients, antipasto, filet of sole, ziti, linguine, swordfish, chicken and sausage cacciatore, fresh bread, inexpensive prices, a true find, no credit cards. Open Tues.-Sat. noon-2:30pm lunch, Mon.-Thurs. 4pm-9pm dinner; Fri.-Sat. till 10pm; Sun. 4pm-8pm all you can eat buffet.
"...In the same ordinary brick building as the local video store. But don't be fooled by appearances, Primo Pasta has fabulous food," Telegram & Gazette.

Michele's
Rte. 31 Post Office Place, Princeton
(508) 464-5669
Italian dishes and daily specials, entrees ranging from $6-$13, charge cards accepted. Open Wed.-Sun. 5pm-9pm.
"The atmosphere is wonderful, the food is absolutely delicious, the desserts are to die for, especially the Tiramisu," Cindy LaRivere, Worcester, MA.

"It's my favorite because of its great Italian food and small-town hospitality. And you never go home hungry!" Richard M. Knight, Princeton, MA.

East Side Mario's
Rte. 9 Westbound
(on Lake Quinsigamond), Shrewsbury
(508) 755-0900
Very popular with families, extensive kids menu; decor reminiscent of Manhattan's Little Italy in the 1940's, moderate prices, entrees $7-$11. Open 11am-1am daily.
"The linguine chicken tettrazine is a treasure hunt in which pieces of chicken breast gently sauteed with mushrooms, garlic and fresh chopped tomatoes keep turning up in a mound of linguine and just enough Alfredo sauce to hold it all together," Worcester Magazine.

White's Corner Restaurant
154 Turnpike Rd., Southborough
(508) 485-9833
Seafood, steaks, pasta, entrees $11-$21. Open Mon.-Sat. 11:30am-10pm; Fri.-Sat. till 11pm; Sun. noon-9pm.

Rom's Restaurant
Rte. 131, Sturbridge
(508) 347-3349
American/Italian cuisine; plentiful portions, affordable prices. Originally a roadside sandwich stand, now it seats up to 700, Wed. night smorgasbord 5pm-9 pm; Thurs. lunch buffet 11:30 am-2 pm
"It's my favorite because of the food and atmosphere," Frank Cameron, Leicester, MA.

Joseph's at Indian Meadows
275 Turnpike Rd., Rte. 9,
Westborough
(508) 366-6526
Italian-American cuisine, dinner and dancing every Sat.-Sun. Buffet brunch 11am - 3pm. Overlooking Indian Meadows Golf Course. Lunch Tues.-Fri. 11:30am.-3:00pm; dinner Tues.-Sat. 5-10pm.

Scioletti's
18 Lyman St., Westborough
(508) 366-9044
Homemade breads, soups, pasta and entrees like veal Marsala, sirloin, and grilled chicken breast. Open Mon.-Sat. 11am-10pm; Fri.-Sat. till 11pm; Sun. noon-9pm.
"This trattoria boasts an upscale, classy dining room that's a pleasant surprise in a mall restaurant. The food is very good and prices are low enough to accommodate the whole family," Worcester Magazine.

Ziti's Italian Trattoria
Rte. 9, Speedway Shopping Center,
Westborough
(508) 898-2282
Italian favorites, BYOB. Open Mom.-Sat. 10am-10pm; Sun. noon-10pm.
"Ziti's at first glance may seem just another fast-food place, but follow your nose to the open kitchen where some impressive Italian cooking is in progress. Chicken marsala was first-rate," Worcester Magazine.

Angela's
257 Park Ave., Worcester
(508) 756-7995
Inexpensive home-style Italian dishes, complimentary fried dough, chicken cacciatore and more, cash only, not handicapped accessible, entrees $7-$8. Open Sun.-Thurs. 4pm-10:30pm; Fri.-Sat. 4pm-11:30pm, closed Monday.
"Just one of Worcester's answers to the North End, Angela's holds its own admirably amidst the city's wealth of good Italian spots," Worcester Magazine.

Brick Oven Bakery
80 Franklin St., Worcester
(508) 757-1611
Breakfast, lunch, dinner, daily pasta specials, pizza by the slice, cookies, breads, eat in or take-out. Open Mon.-Fri. 7am-5pm; Sat. 7am-11pm, closed Sunday.

Caffe Espresso
19 Wall St., Worcester
(508) 753-9986
Generous servings of Italian dishes, excellent desserts. No credit cards, inexpensive prices, BYOB, open daily 6am-11pm.
"Huge portions of Italian favorites mixed with imaginative specials make this cozy neighborhood spot a real find," Telegram & Gazette.

Caffe Giacomo
214 Shrewsbury St., Worcester
(508) 831-9696
Open Mon.-Wed. noon-Midnight; Thurs.-Sat. noon-2am; Sun. 5pm-Midnight.
"An escape from reality! No phones, no TV, beautiful atmosphere. Relaxing! Romantic!" Brenda MacDonald, Worcester, MA.

D'Errico's Restaurant
145 Central St., Worcester
(508) 754-3743
Ample portions, thick bread, next to D'Errico's Market, grill choices include salmon, steak, BYOB.
Open Mon.-Thurs. 8am-8pm; Fri.-Sat. 8am-9pm, closed Sunday.
"It is nostalgic, serves great ethnic Italian food, has ambience, marvelous low prices, great staff and customers," Barbara Brandt Happy, Worcester, MA.

Dino's
13 Lord St. (off Plantation St.), Worcester
(508) 753-9978
Tasty Italian and American dishes at moderate prices; friendly family style, $4-$15. Open Mon. 4pm-10pm; Tues.-Thurs. 11:30am-10pm; Fri. 11:30am-11pm; Sat. 4pm-11pm; Sun. 1pm-9pm.
"Check out the chicken Pietro, chicken sauteed with mushrooms, fresh tomato and artichoke hearts in a gorgonzola cream sauce - a dish so scrumptious it could easily have commanded a price tag of $20 or more in a New York restaurant," Telegram & Gazette.

East Park Grill
172 Shrewsbury St., Worcester
no phone
Value and tasty food; arrive early to avoid a line; large servings, fresh ingredients and pasta, informal setting, cash only.
"It offers a great selection of excellent pasta dishes at very reasonable prices. I also like the very easy-going relaxed atmosphere it offers," Victoria Brainard, Worcester, MA.
"The value- and taste-conscious citizenry turns out nightly in droves to enjoy tasty entrees all under $10," Worcester Phoenix.

Italian Kitchen
169 Shrewsbury St., Worcester
(508) 752-9404
Family-style Italian specialties, full bar, cash only, Sun.-Thurs. 11am-9pm; Fri.-Sat. 11am-10pm.
"...home-made pasta that's served perfectly al dente under a tasty blanket of sauce - $4.50 buys you an overflowing plate," Worcester Phoenix.

Leo's Ristorante
11 Brackett Court, Worcester
(508) 753-9490
Lots of Italian favorites, veal dishes, good bread, homemade pasta; moderate prices. Mon-Fri lunch 11:30am- 2pm; dinner 5-10:30pm seven days a week.
"The Veal d'Angelo is a sure-fire winner and the warm bread with dip is a nice touch," Telegram & Gazette.

Milano
592 Main St., Worcester
(508) 753-2994
Superb pizzas, both deep dish and thin cruct; other Italian specialtles, entrees $4-$12. Open Sun. 1pm-9pm; Mon.-Wed. 11am-9pm; Thurs.-Sat. 11am-11pm.
"The pizzas are imaginative and superb...Two examples: the Venetian, with marinated steak, five cheeses, spinach, and onions: and the Tuscany, with eggplant, peppers, mushrooms, onions, plum tomatoes, and five cheeses," Worcester Phoenix.

Pizzeria at Arturo's
411 Chandler St., Worcester
(508) 755-5640
Casual dining in one room, elegant dining in another, full bar, open daily 11:30am-11:30pm.
"It has my favorite food," Emily Ruth Egan (age 7), Worcester, MA.
"It's the best of both worlds, one is the romantic, quiet side of the restaurant, and the other side is a great family place to go with great pizza," Linda Brideau, Hudson, MA.

Porto Bello
156 Shrewsbury St., Worcester
(508) 753-9865
Under same management as former Libby's II, homemade soups, lasagna, shrimp scampi, broccoli manicotti Mon.-Thurs. 11am-9pm; Fri. 11am-10pm, Sat. 5-10pm. Closed Sun., holidays.
"Exceptional food quality, preparation, presentation and service," K. Thomas, Sutton, MA.

Shorah's Ristorante
27 Foster St. across from Worcester Common Fashion Outlets, Worcester
(508) 797-0007
Great downtown location, gourmet pizza and veal specialties, calzones. Open Mon. 11am-3pm; Tues.-Thurs. 11am-9pm; Fri.-Sat. 11am-10pm; Sun. 4pm-9pm.
"Conveniently located in the heart of the city and the food is top-notch. Like pesto? You'll love scallops and shrimp pesto - marvelous," Worcester Magazine.

Wonder Bar
121 Shrewsbury St., Worcester
(508) 752-9909
Pizza, Italian dishes in family setting, full bar, cash only, great date spot. Open Tues.-Thurs. 11am-11pm; Fri.-Sat. 11am-Midnight, closed Sunday & Monday.
"The Wonder Bar is my favorite casual place to eat in Worcester County because of the great homemade Italian food and because it reminds me of the neighborhood restaurants my grandparents and parents talk about when they were growing up when you walk in and people know you by name," Elizabeth M. Cox, Auburn, MA
"Best cheap date place around. Good pizza and Chianti. Nicest wait staff and proprietors," Dana O'Connor, Worcester, MA.
"Check out the juke box," Larry Abramoff, Worcester, MA.

Black Orchid
92 Shrewsbury St., Worcester
(also 185 W. Boylston St., West Boylston)
(508) 752-2488; 835-2224
Casual Italian dining, pizza, chicken Marsala, pasta, steak. Open daily 11:30am-1:30am.
"They serve wonderful food and they have quick service, I love it," Cara Ann Biscalia, Worcester, MA.

Ethnic - Japanese

Sakura Tokyo
640 Park Ave., Worcester
(508) 792-1068
Features of a traditional Japanese restaurant, sushi bar, table grills offer

meals prepared as you watch, complete with juggling knife performances by expert chefs. $10-22. Open Mon.-Thurs. 11:30am-10:30pm; Fri.-Sat. 11:30am-11:30pm; Sun. 11:30am-10pm.
"Watch as skillful, entertaining chefs work at your table using immaculately fresh ingredients," Telegram & Gazette.

Ethnic - Mexican

Acapulco Mexican Restaurant
107 Highland St., Worcester
(508) 791-1746
Good, basic Mexican fare, inexpensive prices, good late night spot, prices from $3.95, no bar. Open Mon.-Wed. 4pm-3am; Thurs. 11am-3am, Fri.-Sat. 11am-4am. Sun. 1pm-3am.

Taco Amigo
976 Main Street, Worcester
(508) 793-8226
A college favorite, fajitas, other Mexican fare, BYOB, takeout, cash only, inexpensive. Open Mon.-Fri. 11:30am-2:30pm, 5pm-9:30pm; Sat. 5pm-9:30pm, closed Sunday.
"Atmosphere is quaint, service always with a smile and sincerity, food portions are excellent, prices are very good," Tammy Ann Benoit, Worcester, MA.

Ethnic - Middle Eastern

Aris' Cafe
432 Pleasant St., Worcester
(508) 754-7424
Genuine Middle Eastern cuisine, lovingly prepared, savory baba ghanouj, tabbula, chicken kebab, spinach pie, homemade desserts, entrees $4-$8, cash only, Mon. - Sat. 11am-7:30pm, (till 9pm in summer), closed Sun., patio dining available in warm weather.
"This is Middle Eastern cuisine at its best, presented with pride, care, and love," Worcester Phoenix.

Beirut Restaurant
102 Belmont St. Rte. 9, Worcester
(508) 753-1299
Deli-style setting, American dishes and Middle Eastern dishes. The shawarma is a tasty specialty, entrees $3-$7. Open Mon.-Wed. 10am-8pm; Thurs.-Fri. 10am-9pm; Sat. 4pm-9pm, closed Sunday.

El Basha
424 Belmont St.Rte. 9, Worcester
(508) 797-0884
Homemade Middle Eastern & Lebanese cuisine; lamb shish kebab. Open Mon.-Sat. 11:30am-10pm, closed Sunday.
"Fantastic grape leaves," Darlene Post, Princeton, MA.
"Middle Eastern fare is done very well... the food is authentic and top-notch," Worcester Magazine.

El Morocco
100 Wall St., Worcester
(508) 756-7117
Legendary food and jazz. Traditional Middle Eastern fare, kibbee, stuffed grape leaves, kebobs. Famous visitors to the "El" include Frank Sinatra, Nat "King" Cole, Stan Kenton, Harry James and Rodney Dangerfield, who made the infamous remark gazing from the patio over industrial Worcester, "It's a nice view, if only there was a view." Open daily 11:30am-10pm, Sun. 9am brunch.
"The patio at the El Morocco - in warmer weather, there are few city sights as impressive as the Worcester vista from this urban garden setting - plus live jazz and great food," Susan L. Smith, Worcester, MA.
"It's the most lovable restaurant in the USA," Amen Esper Jr., Worcester, MA.

Ethnic - Southwestern

Cafe Santa Fe
Rte. 12 , West Boylston
(508) 835-6733
Real Texas BBQ, steaks, New Mexican dishes, fajitas, live country entertainment on weekends. Open Mon.-Sat. 11am-10pm; Sun. noon-10pm.
"Solid Southwestern favorites in a place that looks right and feels right. You won't go wrong here with the Chicken Fajitas or the Cowboy Steak," Telegram & Gazette.

Willy's Genuine Texas Pit Bar-B-Q
344 Turnpike Road, Rte. 9,
Westborough
(508) 366-1881
Barbecue ribs cooked over hardwood coals, also Cajun food, fajitas, enchiladas. Entrees $6-$17. Open Mon.-Thurs. 11:30am-10pm, Fri.-Sat. 11:30am-midnight; Sun. noon-10pm.
"Some of the best barbecue you'll find in these here parts, pardner, surrounded by Texas kitsch. Cajun specialties and imaginative appetizers round out the menu- and the belly," Worcester Phoenix.

Cactus Pete's Steak House & Saloon
400 Park Ave., Worcester
(508) 752-3038
Pub fare with a Southwestern tang, Mon.-Thurs. 11:30am-10pm; Fri.-Sat. 11:30am-11pm; Sun. 4pm-11pm.
"They serve very good food," Jessica Adams, (age 10), Worcester, MA.
"The chili has taken first place two years in a row at the Boston Chili Fest, and the restaurant has won Best Barbecue the past two years in Worcester Magazine's reader's poll," Worcester Magazine.

Ethnic - Thai

Bangkok City Restaurant
66 John Fitch Highway, Fitchburg
(508) 342-3100
Thai food served in a casual setting, beer and wine. Open Sun.-Thurs. 11:30am-9pm; Fri.-Sat. 11:30am-10pm.

Thai Pochana
21 South Street, Westborough
(508) 836-3236
Dishes featuring all the flavors of ethnic - Thai cuisine: cilantro, lemon grass, ginger, onions and more. Fresh ingredients, large portions, reasonable prices. The house special duck won't disappoint, entrees $6-$13. Open Mon.-Fri. 11:30am-3pm; Sat.-Sun. 5pm-10pm.
"Thai Pochana offers large portions, attractive presentations, and reasonable prices, all in a quietly elegant setting. Best bets: the nam sod with minced chicken, sliced ginger, roasted peanuts, red onions, scallions, lemon juice, cilantro and some zesty chili paste; and the house special duck, worth the trip alone," Worcester Phoenix.

Thai Cha-Da
264 Park Ave., Worcester
(508) 752-2211
Diners can create their own dishes,by choosing chicken, beef, duck, tofu, or shrimp combined with different curries vegetables and spices, entrees $6-$14. Open Mon.-Fri. 11am-10pm; Sat. noon-10:30pm; Sun. 4pm-10pm.
"Consistently excellent. A wide selection of meat, fish and vegetable dishes served efficiently in comfortable, gracefully decorated surroundings," Telegram & Gazette.

Thai Orchid
144 Commercial St., Worcester
(508) 792-9701
Inexpensive to moderate prices, lunch

buffet, Mon.-Fri. 11:30am-3pm lunch, 5pm-10pm dinner; Sat. noon-10pm; Sun. 4pm-10pm.
"They have the best Thai food," Ana Prince, Hudson, MA.
"All-you-can-eat lunch buffet offers a pleasurable taste of Thai treasures for $6.95 a person," Telegram & Gazette.

Ethnic - Vietnamese

Da-Lat Restaurant
425 Park Ave., Worcester
(508) 753-6036
Vietnamese cuisine, a college favorite. Nearly 120 items, soup and noodle dishes a specialty, seasoned with lemon grass, basil, chili, peanut sauce, curry , etc., entrees $5-$8, BYOB, cash only, open weekdays 11am-10pm; Sat.-Sun. 10am-11pm.

Four Sea Restaurant
27 Millbury St., Worcester
(508) 756-8049
Formerly Quan Binh Dan. Authentic Oriental dishes, hot and sour soup, garlic shrimp, and creative dishes like braised cow stomach. Fresh fruit drinks, entrees $4-$11, open daily 11am-10pm.
"A hidden gem featuring Oriental cuisine so authentic they don't even translate part of the menu," Worcester Phoenix.

Minh Garden Restaurant
521 Main St., Worcester
(508) 799-0803
Unusual Vietnamese dishes, exotic flavors, creative salads, lots of noodle and soup varieties, also traditional Chinese offerings. Entrees $4-$9, open daily 11am-10pm.
"This frill-less storefront restaurant distinguishes itself with its unusual Vietnamese dishes that offer subtleties of flavor and fragrance often lacking in Chinese food," Worcester Phoenix.

Family Dining

Gauthier's Family Restaurant
442 Southbridge St., Auburn
(508) 832-2021
Open Mon.-Fri. 5:30am-2pm; Sat. 5:30am-noon; Sun. 7am-11:30am.
"Gauthier's Family Restaurant is a favorite breakfast and lunch spot and meeting place for Auburn politicians," Beth Prouty, Auburn.

Calico & Creme
Williamsville Rd., Hubbardston
(508) 928-5150
50 flavors of home-made ice cream; home-made yogurt and pies. Pizza, sandwiches, light dinners. Smoke-free dining; farm animals to pet as well; April - Oct., Mon.-Sat. 8am-9pm; Sun. noon-9pm.

Mountain Barn
174 Worcester Road (Route 31), Princeton
(508) 464-2044
Rustic decor and view of Mount Wachusett. Good food, reasonably priced. One-price children's menu.
Open Thurs.-Sat. dinner at 4:30pm, Sun. at noon; Sat. lunch at 11am; Sun. breakfast 8am-11am.
"Great atmosphere and excellent service...the kitchen does an admirable job preparing familiar mainstays with style," Telegram & Gazette.

Uncle Tannous'
Rte. 12, Webster
(508) 949-6189
Family-style offering burgers to fettuccine Alfredo to fried scallops. Open Tues.-Thurs. 11:30am-8pm; Fri.-Sat. 11:30am-9pm; Sun. 8am-8pm, closed Monday.
"Our reviewers were more than pleased

with the veal Parmesan with spaghetti and the stir-fried chicken and vegetables," Worcester Magazine.

Parent's Village Square Restaurant,
Rte. 202, Winchendon
(508) 297-3034
Roast pork, beef stir fry, swordfish, baked scallops, lobster roll, specials change daily. Entrees $4-$9, small portions available and priced accordingly. Open Mon.-Wed. 6am-2pm; Thurs.-Sun. 6am-8pm.

Windon Motel & Restaurant
Spring St., Winchendon
(508) 297-0677
Family-style casual dining, seafood, prime rib, lobster, hamburgers. Entrees $7-$13. Open Tues.-Sat. 4pm-9pm; Sun. 11:30am-8pm, closed Monday.

Boynton
117 Highland St., Worcester
(508) 756-8458
Basic family food and prices; meatloaf dinner, burgers and broiled scrod, cash only. Open Mon.-Sat. 11am-10pm.
"Family fare at family prices," Worcester Phoenix.

Coes Cafe
242 Mill St. next to Coe's Pond, Worcester
(508) 754-9622
Weekly specials like chicken Kiev, trout, lemon veal, roasted pork loin. Mon.-Sat.11 am-1 am; Sun. noon-midnight.
"One of those finds that hides itself nicely behind a straight forward family fare facade but delivers on a varied and challenging menu. Where you might expect mozzarella sticks, you find shiitake ravioli, Japanese dumplings and baked brie," Worcester Phoenix.

Sisters Breakfast and Lunch
171 Stafford St., Worcester
(508) 755-2604
Good food, great service, Mon.-Fri. 6am-2pm; Sat. 6am-1pm; Sun. 7am-1pm.

Tatnuck Bookseller Marketplace
(What again?) Well, it is our book.!
335 Chandler St., Worcester
(508) 756-7644
Pasta, pizza, daily specials, soups, gourmet entrees at a reasonable price. Great coffee, homemade desserts, elegant dinners. They get an early breakfast crowd, mid-morning coffee klatch. From time to time authors write their books here and business gets conducted. Lunches are popular and the specials change daily. Early dining favors families and later becomes more elegant and romantic. Homemade potato chips, cole slaw and house root beer a special treat. The kids' menu is a sure-fire hit, and even offers spaghettios. Read'm and eat. Non-smoking, BYOB. Open Mon.-Thurs. 8am-10pm; Fri. 8am-midnight; Sat. 9am-midnight; Sun. 9am-6pm.
"This is a great family place because the kids can jump up and browse the bookstore while parents can actually complete a sentence!" A.L., Rutland, MA.

Theo's Restaurant
151 Highland St., Worcester
(508) 791-9300
Sandwiches, pizza, open daily 7am-midnight.
"Delicious food, but most important by far BEST FRENCH FRIES on earth! (fresh, not frozen). Try the gravy on them!" Thomas Fisk, Worcester, MA.

Webster House
One Webster St. (Webster Sq.), Worcester
(508) 757-7208
Basic New England fare, chicken pot pie, Yankee pot roast, atmosphere like a homey parlor, good value. Entrees

$2-$11. Open daily 7am-11pm.
"Food is good, and reasonable," Ed Murphy, Worcester, MA
"Generous portions ...extensive vegetable offerings," Telegram & Gazette.

Healthy Dining

Living Earth Garden Cafe
232 Chandler St., corner of Park Ave., Worcester
(508) 753-1896
Fresh, local, all-natural, free-range, organically grown, hormone-free, pesticide-free, fat-free, low sodium, vegetarian, low cholesterol dishes, including Roaming Thunder buffalo meat, delicious buffalo chili. Gourmet and ethnic foods, fresh bakery items. Mon.-Fri. 9am. - 9pm; Sat. 9am - 6pm; Sun. 11am.- 5pm.
"Shop for natural foods at Living Earth, and have a delicious vegetarian dinner in the cafe," Lorraine Mason, Worcester, MA.
"Healthy, natural and organic foods," Marianne Brannan, Shrewsbury, MA.

Historic Dining

White Cliffs
Rte. 20, Northborough
(508) 393-3695
1886 Historic mansion, once the "summer cottage" of Daniel Wesson; traditional cuisine. Open Thurs.-Sat. 5pm-9pm; Sun. 1pm-5pm.

Winterwood at Petersham
19 North Main Street, Petersham
(508) 724-8885
Elegant restaurant in an historic inn, by reservation only.
"It's a lovely Greek revival Inn with congenial hosts," Allen Young, Royalston, MA.

Publick House
Route 131 (on the Common), Sturbridge
(508) 347-3313 or 1-800-PUBLICK
A 200-year-old Colonial tavern and pub. Romantic and relaxed setting; gourmet, and traditional offerings, $15-$24, Mon.-Sat. 7am-10:30am breakfast, noon-4pm lunch, 4pm-8:30 dinner; Sun. breakfast buffet 8am-10:30am, dinner noon-8pm.
"The food is great and atmosphere wonderful," Annette McCaullum, East Douglas, MA.
"Traditional American cuisine with a gourmet twist in an historical setting. Efficient management plus fine food make for a memorable experience," Telegram & Gazette.

Cocke 'N Kettle
240 South Main St., Uxbridge
(508) 278-5517
American traditional food with extras like popovers and corn fritters. Open Tues.-Fri. 4pm-9pm, early bird specials 4pm-5:45pm; Sat. 5pm-10:30pm; Sun. 1pm-8:30pm.
"Superb in every way," Floyd Cranska, Millbury, MA.
"Good food, pleasant atmosphere, historic setting, enjoyable family business," Alexandra Cesaroni, Uxbridge, MA.
"The ambience is steeped in history and some tantalizing mystery as well - how did the Hessian sword get into the wall? Arrive after dark to appreciate the full impact of the mansion, ablaze with lights," Worcester Magazine.

Pub Max and Maxfield's Restaurant
Rtes. 122 & 16 at the Old Uxbridge Inn, Uxbridge
(508) 278-0005
Renovated "painted lady" Victorian on the National Register of Historic Places, pub fare downstairs, more formal restaurant upstairs, 7 days a week, 11am - midnight.

"Nostalgia buffs will be warmed to know that some of the glorious old Eden Restaurant of Franklin St., Worcester, was incorporated into the decor for a sense of continuity and splendor," Worcester Magazine.

Salem Cross Inn
Rte. 9, Ware Rd., West Brookfield
(508) 867-2345
Great food in a wonderful Colonial setting, inn built in 1705, on the National Register of Historic Places. Filled with antiques - the real thing, with an antique roasting jack used for special "Hearthside" feasts; working "beehive" oven. Entrees $11-20. Open Tues.-Sun. at 11:30am-9pm, Sat. till 10pm, Sun. till 8pm.
"Traditional American food with a Continental touch served in an extraordinary Colonial-era setting," Telegram & Gazette.

Bergson's 1790 House
Rte. 9, Westborough
(508) 366-1707
Romantic antique Colonial setting. Homemade breads, fine, traditional food, open Tues.-Fri. 11:30am-2:30pm lunch, 5pm-10pm dinner; Sat. 5pm-10pm; Sun. noon-9pm.
"Dining here is as if you stepped into an elegant private home in the 1830's where the host is a hospitable, vastly talented cook."

Old Mill Rte.
2-A, Westminster
(508) 874-5941
Quaint and cozy old mill setting, traditional New England offerings. Great place to take guests from outside New England. Open Mon.-Thurs. 11:30am-9:30pm; Fri.-Sat. 11:30am-10pm; Sun. 9am-8:30pm.
"Unadulterated early New England charm" Richard Hildreth, Westminster, MA
"It hasn't changed much in 30-40 years, great place for duck," Walter W. Horan, Marblehead, MA.

Hot Dog Stands

Hot Dog Annie's
250 Paxton St. Rte. 56, Leicester
(508) 892-9059
Hot dogs with a very special sauce. Open daily 9am-9pm.
"Food is great and price is low," Tom Revane, Worcester, MA.
"Famous barbecue sauce is out of this world!" Laura Berthiaume, Worcester, MA.
"I like the food and it's a nice ride out there," Steve Martineau, Worcester, MA.
"Great food, the best dogs," Donna Pomeroy, Leicester, MA.
"The barbecue dogs are best in New England, so voted by Yankee Magazine," Joanne Williamson, Worcester MA.

Four Corners
Pleasantdale Rd. at Rte. 122, Rutland
(508) 886-6666
Open spring fall only; free volleyball on 2 sand courts, picnic tables. Hot dogs, burgers, ice cream.
"On hot nights, the whole town comes here," A.L. Rutland, MA.

Bob's Hot Dogs Rest
stop near Wachusett Reservoir at Rtes. 12 and 140, West Boylston
no phone
Blue and white lunch truck a tradition here for 20 years. Bob's trademark quote: "Have a salubrious day!"

Coney Island Lunch
Southbridge St., Worcester
(508) 753-4362
A Worcester legend. Open daily 9:30am-8pm, Fri.-Sat. till 10pm, closed Tuesday.
"Every time I go there it brings memories," Kathy Howard, Barre, MA.
"The sign is great. Tell Andy to smile

and tell 'em Larry sent ya!" Larry Abramoff, Worcester, MA.

Hot Dog Express
281 Park Avenue (Corner of Park Avenue and Pleasant Street), Worcester
(508) 755-333
Excellent tube steaks and sausages. Chips, sodas, fresh rolls, and a wisecrack if you need one.

Ice Cream

Dresser Hill Dairy Bar
Dresser Hill Rd., Charlton
(508) 248-7870
Open Apr.-Oct. 11am-10pm daily.
"The Snicker's bar ice cream cones are HUGE and inexpensive and the view is extraordinary," Jane Reynolds, Charlton, MA
"Great ice cream, best onion rings, beautiful view at sunset," Linda Strickland, Charton Depot, MA..

Pine Croft Dairy
555 Prospect St., West Boylston
(508) 853-0717
Open Mon.-Thurs. 8am-8pm; Fri.-Sat. 7am-9pm; Sun. 7am-8pm.
"Best ice cream in Worcester County," Michelle Donabedian, Holden, MA.
"Very good ice cream," Ed Murphy, Worcester, MA.

Pubs & Taverns

Piccadilly Pub
602 Southbridge St. Rte. 12, Auburn
(508) 832-4762
One of the area's most popular spots, burgers, fish, lobster, steaks. Open Mon.-Sat. noon-1am; Sun. 11am-11pm.
"Piccadilly Pub is a favorite eating place," Betty Jane Weagle, Auburn, MA.
"You can't beat the burger here - there are all kinds of add-ons available; fish 'n chips is the most-ordered item. And with good reason," Worcester Magazine.

Station House Pub
200 Main St., Blackstone
(508) 883-1619
Housed in former fire station building, open daily 11am-2am.

Union House Pub
18 Bridge St, .Monument Square, Blackstone
(508) 883-5353
Overlooks Saranac Dam, pub, entertainment. Open Tues.-Sun. 11:30am-1am, closed Monday.

Old Timer
155 Church St., Clinton
(508) 365-5980
Irish flavor; casual dining, piano bar and buffet, full bar. Open daily 11:30-2:30 lunch, 5pm-9pm dinner, closed Tues. evening only.
"Inside, you'll find the McNally's dining room looking as it must have on opening day in 1932...Singing Chef McNally will carve your delicious - and endless - roast beef to order...Some day, places with this much character will be extinct. Long live the McNally's!" Telegram & Gazette.

Sully's
74-76 Parker St., Gardner
(508) 632-7457
Pub fare, reasonable prices, relaxed atmosphere, function room available, comedy on Sat. night. Burgers, sandwiches, entrees include poached salmon with dill Hollandaise, steak au poivre, veal Marsala, blackened catfish, fajitas, quesadillas and more. Open daily at 11:30 am.
"A nice little spot to grab a bite. An extensive and varied menu for a pub. Sully's offers 12 drafts, among them Mill City Amber Ale, Rhino Chaser,

Guinness, Newcastle Brown Ale and Harpoon Winter Warmer," Worcester Magazine.

DiNardo's New York Style Eatery
14 Monument Sq., Leominster
(508) 840-0133
Italian, seafood, prime rib, casual, family style. Open daily 11am-2am.

E.J. Marrone's
700 Central St., Leominster
(508) 537-6029
Pub fare and extra's, Mon.-Sat. 11:30am-11pm, Sun. till 10pm.
"E.J.'s is a homey, down-to-earth place that reliably serves up all the pub fare you'd expect - burgers, nachos, prime rib - and some surprises too, such as veal Florentine and lobster Newburg pie," Worcester Magazine.

Teddy's
Providence Rd., Linwood (Northbridge)
(508) 234-9256
Open Mon.-Thurs. 11:30am-9pm; Fri. 11:30am-10pm; Sat. 5pm-10pm, closed Sunday.
"It's the best pub in Worcester County," Gerry Shugrue, Whitinsville, MA.

One Flight Down
89 Main St., Milford
(508) 473-7669
Steaks, sandwiches, full bar, entrees $5-$12. Open Mon.-Sat. 11:30am-1am; Sun. 4pm-9pm.
"One of Milford's fine restaurants in the historic Thom Block. This restaurant features many fine entrees," Lyn Lovell, Milford, MA.

Fireside Restaurant & Pub
Rte. 146, Millbury
(508) 865-5595
Reasonable prices, excellent food, informal setting, traditional steaks, chicken and seafood. Open Sun.-Wed. 11:30am-9pm; Thurs.-Sat. 11:30am-10pm.
"The menu offers some very good choices, including a wide-ranging appetizer sampler and the traditional steaks, poultry and seafood entrees, all carefully prepared," Telegram & Gazette.

Olde Post Office Pub
Ray Street and Rte. 140, North Grafton
(508) 839-6106
Fresh food, large servings, cheery setting. Low prices, good family style service. Seafood, chicken, beef, pasta, sandwiches, and burgers, full bar. $4-13. Open Mon.-Fri. 11:30am-9pm; Sat.-Sun. 8am-midnight.
"This pub is done to the rafters with post office memorabilia, which creates a unique, fun atmosphere. The prime rib was superb, a seafood platter fresh-tasting and piping hot...leave room for the homemade desserts," Worcester Magazine.

Periwinkles & Giorgio's Italian Pub
892 Southbridge St., Auburn
(508) 832-9705
Family fare and Italian cuisine. Outdoor seating in warm weather, inexpensive prices. Open Mon.-Sat. 11:30am-1am; Sun. noon-midnight.
"This is a great spot if some in your group feel like Italian food and others want steak or seafood...Service was fast and efficient, despite the fact that the place was mobbed," Worcester Magazine.

J.J. O'Rourke's
Rtes. 9 and 20, Northborough
(508) 842-8420
Pub, billiard parlor, family style dining, interactive trivia in the lounge on the NTN network, Sat. night karaoke. Open daily 11:30am-midnight.
"Hearty burgers, fresh seafood, a variety of Mexican specialties..." Worcester Magazine.

Whistle Stop
85 A Main St., Oxford
(508) 987-3087
Open Tues.-Thurs. 11:30am-3pm; Fri.-Sat. 11:30am-9pm, bar open Sun. only, closed Monday.
"It's great for a couple beers after work, good food and keno," Roger Bates, Oxford, MA.

Forefathers Pub
Rte. 122 on the Common, Paxton
(508) 756-9662
Dinner specials $8.95; traditional menu offerings, steak, chicken pie, prime rib, seafood. Open Wed.-Sat. 11:30am-9pm; Sun. noon-9pm, closed Mon.-Tues.

Lantern Room II
2 Grafton St., Shrewsbury
(508) 842-7220
Hearty sandwiches, fish, veal, chicken and steak, entrees $6-$12. Open Mon.-Thurs. 11:30am-10pm; Fri.-Sat. 11:30am-11pm; Sun. 11:30am-9pm.
"It's known as 'the Cheers of Shrewsbury,' and I thought I heard someone yell 'Norm!' when I walked in," Worcester Phoenix.

Xavier's
31 Pleasant St., Spencer
(508) 885-7705
Seafood, steak, pub fare, fish 'n chips, casual, full bar. Cash only, open Mon.-Fri. 5:30am-2pm; Sat.-Sun. 6am-1pm.

Charlie Brown's Steak House
Haynes St., Rte. 131, Sturbridge
(508) 347-5559
Traditional pub fare in a Victorian setting, open Mon.-Sat. 11:30am-5pm lunch, 5pm-9pm dinner; Sun. 10am-2pm brunch, 2pm-9pm dinner.

Old Sturbridge Village Tavern
One Old Sturbridge Village Rd., off Rte. 20, Sturbridge
(508) 347-3362
Open to patrons of Old Sturbridge Village.
"The village takes you to simple times away from today's stress and the tavern is cozy with a fire and the food is satisfying to your stomach and frame of mind," Irene LaFlamme Shrewsbury, MA.

Oxhead Tavern 3
66 Main St., off Rte. 20, Sturbridge
(508) 347-9994
Roadside tavern atmosphere and fare. Open Mon.-Thurs. 11am-10pm; Fri.-Sat. 11am-11pm; Sun. noon-11pm.

Beaman Tavern
171 West Boylston St. Rte. 12, West Boylston
(508) 835-3707
Creative selections in addition to pub fare. Jalapeno bites, crab cakes, jambalaya, seafood Alfredo, queso crisp. Entrees $4-$13, deck for outdoor dining. Open Tues.-Thurs. 11;30am-10pm; Fri.-Sat. 11:30am-11pm; Sun.-Mon. 11:30am-9pm.
"You'll find one of the nicer Worcester-area venues for alfresco dining...the deck is delightful. Try the boneless buffalo chicken appetizer," Worcester Magazine.

Ye Olde Tavern
Main St., West Brookfield
(508) 867-9709
Was the historic David Hitchcock Tavern, where Washington, John Adams and LaFayette stopped to dine. Open daily noon-1am.

Tom Foolery's
95 Turnpike Road (Route 9), Westborough
(508) 366-5959
Menu selections from all over - Chicago, Europe, New Orleans and New England. Good choices are the seafood gumbo, and chicken piccata, wide selection of foreign beers, entrees $5-$15. Open Mon.-Sat. 11:30am-midnight; Sun. 11am-midnight.

"Food - excellent; service - excellent - clean men's room," Paul F. Quinn, Worcester, MA.
"The solid, simple food is well-prepared," Telegram & Gazette.

Barber's Crossing
Rte. 12, 325 West Boylston St., Worcester
(508) 852-3435
Open Mon.-Sat. 11am-1:30am; Sun. 11am-12:30am.
"Food is always good especially the lobsters," Rita Wasielewski, Webster, MA.

Eddy's Pub
317 West Boylston St., Worcester
(508) 853-2269
Inexpensive; good, simple food, huge menu, turkey pot pie, meat loaf, full bar, cash only. Open daily lunch and dinner specials 11am-1:30am.
"There are no highfalutin airs at Eddy's but if you're in the mood for a terrific pizza or any of a wide selection of sandwiches or even a steak, this pub will fill the bill - and all at prices kind to the wallet," Worcester Magazine.

Firehouse Cafe
One Exchange Place, across from Worcester Common Fashion Outlets, Worcester
(508) 753-7899
Lunch, dinner, bar, mix and mingle, burgers to dinners, live entertainment. Open Mon.-Thurs. 11:30am-9pm; Fri.-Sat. 11:30am-10pm; Sun. noon-6pm.
"Before its restaurant incarnation it was actually a fire station. The menu is basically pub-style; baked sea scallops and Oriental shrimp stir-fry were both top-notch. Deli sandwiches and burgers are a big draw, too," Worcester Magazine.

Leitrim's Pub
265 Park Ave., Worcester
(508) 798-2447
A college favorite, open Mon.-Fri. 4pm-2am; Sat.-Sun. noon-2am.
"Atmosphere, cheap beer, friendly people," John Best, Worcester, MA.
"Best college bar, 1994," Worcester Magazine.

Main Street Brewing Co., Ltd.
244 Main St., Worcester
(508) 753-6700
June '95 opening; housed in renovated former Coghlin's Furniture building. Open daily 11am-2am.

Ninety-Nine Restaurant
900 West Boylston St., Worcester
(508) 852-2999
A sports pub, but also intimate seating and a pleasant setting. Good service, food quality. Entrees $5-$14. Open daily 11:30am-11:30pm.

Northworks Eatery and Drinkery
106 Grove Street, Worcester
(508) 755-9657
In the historic Washburn & Moen Manufacturing building, basic, good food, seafood, beef, chicken, tasty and at reasonable prices, entrees $4-$12. Open Mon.-Sat. 11:30am-10pm; Sun. 4pm-9pm.
"It's my favorite because: atmosphere and good food," Geri Elmer, Holden, MA.
"Price is right, food more than all right. Waitresses bright, atmosphere just right," Athina Simonian, Worcester, MA.

O'Connor's Restaurant & Bar
1160 West Boylston Street, Worcester
(508) 853-0789
A restaurant with the feel of an Irish pub. The signature dish is the Famous & Enormous Beef, also corned beef shillelagh and Bailey's Irish Cream Pie, entrees $4-$14. Open Mon.-Sat. 11:30am-10pm, closed Sun.
"Atmosphere!" Gill Greenman, Honolulu, Hawaii
"It serves creative food, the best variety of beer and it's a great place to socialize," Deborah Barrett, Worcester, MA.

Piccadilly Pub Restaurant
480 Shrewsbury Street
(Rte. 9), Worcester
(508) 755-1808
Casual dining; reasonable prices, decent food, especially appetizers and desserts, entrees $4-$10. Open 11am-midnight.

Hotel Vernon
kelley Square, Worcester
An old fashioned bar. Worth the trip to see the Mayflower Room. Built like the inside of an old ship. Great hand painted walls. Al Capp and Al Banx used to hang out here. First building in Worcester constructed with all union labor. For an excellent guided tour, ask for Red.

Tweed's
231 Grove St., Worcester
(508) 755-8047
Worcester's first pub-style restaurant, opened 1979, steak sandwiches, Guinness, pub fare. Open Mon.-Sat. 11:15am-1am; Sun. noon-Midnight.
"Roomy booths, quick service. Try the prime rib and the sauteed chicken Mariano," Telegram & Gazette.

Seafood

SS Lobster
691 River St. (Rte. 12), Fitchburg
(508) 342-6135
Fresh seafood, lobsters a specialty, cholesterol-free frying; dining room, take-out. Retail seafood market. Cash only. Open daily 11am- 8pm, Fri. and Sat. till 9pm.

Point Breeze Restaurant
Point Breeze Road, Webster
(508) 943-0159
On a peninsula jutting into Webster Lake. One of the top dining views in the Worcester area, coho salmon, blue fish, squid, oysters, mussels, swordfish, clams, scrod, scallops, rainbow trout, $8-$20. Open daily 11am-11pm.
"Veal Oscar and roast pork show gourmet touches at excellent prices," Telegram & Gazette.

Harry's Restaurant
149 Turnpike Rd., Rte. 9,
Westborough
(508) 366-8302
Fried clams, seafood, sandwiches, dinner platters, quick, friendly service. Open Mon.-Fri. at 7am, Sat.-Sun. 11am, close 1am Sun.-Thurs., Fri.-Sat. till 2am.

Harbor Restaurant
463 Maple St., Winchendon
(508) 297-2133
Shrimp boats, lobster rolls, Gulf shrimp, haddock, fried lobster chunks $6-$14. Open Tues.-Thurs. 4pm-8pm; Fri.-Sat. 11:30am-9pm; Sun. 11:30am-8pm, closed Monday.

Little Anthony's Seafood Emporium
678 Spring St., Winchendon
(508) 297-2669
All kinds of seafood, chicken, pork, fettuccine, daily specials entrees $6-$13. Open daily 11am-9pm, closed Tuesday.

Coral Seafood Restaurant
112 Green St., Kelley Square,
Worcester
(508) 755-8331
Fresh seafood, good prices, swordfish, salmon and more, homemade soups. Open Mon.-Thurs. 11am-10pm; Fri.-Sat. 11am-11pm; Sun. noon-9pm.
"It has friendly atmosphere, home cooked food at reasonable prices and with interesting flavors," Bobbie Chase, Worcester, MA.
"Consistently well prepared, top-quality fish. Deliciously decadent desserts made on premises," Telegram & Gazette.

Sole Proprietor Seafood and Spirits
118 Highland St., Worcester
(508) 798-FISH ; 798-3474
Ever-popular, fresh seafood, always good. Open Mon.-Thurs. 11:30am-10pm; Fri. 11am-11pm; Sat. noon-11pm; Sun. 4pm-9pm.
"Purists can ponder the 33 varieties of alphabetical fishes - from amberjack to wahoo - broiled, baked, fried, steamed, sauteed, mesquite grilled, or even blackened Cajun style," Worcester Phoenix.

Steak Houses

Chuck's Steak House
10 Prospect St., Rte. 20, Auburn
(508) 832-2553
Extensive menu, moderate prices. Fresh-baked bread, fully-stocked salad bar. Open Mon.-Thurs. 5pm-10pm; Fri. 5pm-10:30pm; Sat. 5pm-11pm; Sun. 2pm-9pm.
"Plenty of good choices from an extensive menu. And, for salad bar aficionados, there are munchies galore," Telegram & Gazette.

New England Steak and Seafood
16 Uxbridge Rd., Mendon
(508) 473-5079
Family-style, casual, full bar, live country entertainment, open Mon. 4pm-10pm; Wed.-Fri. 11am-11pm; Sat. 4pm-11pm; Sun. 5pm-11pm, closed Tuesday.

Steakloft
369 West Main St., Northborough
(508) 393-8134
Steak a specialty of the house, other dishes, too, full bar. Open Mon.-Fri. 11:30am-10pm; Sat.-Sun. 4pm-11pm.
"My prime rib and lazy lobster entree was terrific. I would definitely go back for this dish. Try the Steakloft; it's a reliable spot for good beef and seafood," Worcester Magazine.

Murphy's Chop House
Worcester Marriott, 10 Lincoln Sq., Worcester
(508) 791-1600
Prime rib buffet Fri.-Sat.; more than a steak house; much better than the usual hotel restaurant, wide range from clam chowder to escargots; clams casino, wontons of duck and a "Woosta" steak specialty. Entrees $14-$21. Open daily 7am-10:30am breakfast, 11am-2pm lunch, 5pm-10pm dinner.
"Murphy's offers a refined dining experience in a pleasantly appointed dining room," Worcester Magazine.

Notes

Chapter 8

Recreation

Don't be bored - find out:

Where can you see July 4th fireworks from Boston, Worcester and Framingham — at the same time? Where can you watch hawks migrate? Where can you play boccie or the ancient Scottish sport of curling? Which public golf course was designed by the famed Donald Ross? Which one is the site of a rocket launch? Where can you take a hot air balloon ride? Where you can enjoy horseback riding even if you can't walk? Which sledding area has a lift to the top? Where is the only technical rock climbing area in Worcester County? Where can you take the kids to pick apples? berries? or to watch maple sugaring? What's the "fishing hot-line" phone number?

All of these answers and more are in this chapter. People in Worcester County take their recreation very seriously, and the size of this chapter is proof. Listings are grouped by category and town. For example, golf courses in Athol are listed before those in Worcester. Please note that campgrounds are listed in Chapter 5 - Where to Stay. One distinction — Wildlife Management Areas are open spaces that are often stocked with game for hunting; Wildlife Sanctuaries are open spaces where wildlife is protected. Remember, things change, call first. (P.S. - for the answers to the previous paragraph's questions, turn to the last page of this chapter).

And - don't forget we need your reviews and comments. Help us update our book, fill in the blanks, give us your help: Send notes and comments to: Favorite Places C\O Tatnuck Bookseller 335 Chandler Street, Worc., MA 01602 or FAX (508)756-9425.

Amusement Parks & Centers; Animal Farms; Balloon Rides & Flying; Biking; Billiards; Boating, Sailing, Canoeing, Rowing; Bowling; Christmas Tree Farms; Fairs; Fishing & Wildlife Information; Forests, Conservation Land & Open Space; Golf Courses; Golf Driving Ranges; Hiking/Nature Walks; Hockey; Horseback Riding; Ice Skating; Maple Sugaring; Orchards/Pick Your Own; Parks, Playgrounds & Recreational Areas; Ponds, Lakes, Rivers & Reservoirs; Recreation Centers; Roller Skating; Skiing and Sledding; Sports Clubs; Swimming Pools; Tennis, Waterfalls; Wildlife Management Areas; Wildlife Sanctuaries.

Amusement Parks & Centers

Spooky World 100 River Rd., Berlin
(508) 838-0200
"America's Haunted Theme Park," 24-acre Halloween extravaganza, attracts 200,000 people during Halloween season; celebrities like Elvira, Tiny Tim and Linda Blair have performed here. Houses American Horror Museum, with props from Hollywood horror films. Handicapped accessible. Call for hours and directions.

Whalom Park Rte. 13, (Ex 32 off Rte. 2), Lunenburg
(508) 342-3707
102 years in operation. Beach, water slide, picnic area, rides, miniature golf, miniature train and boat rides. Seasonal, opens April 1st weekends only. June 23rd daily until Labor day. Open till Columbus Day, weekends only. Call for hours and directions. For history of the park, see Chapter 12, Lunenburg.
"My dad had his company picnic here when I was young - great fun," L. Abramoff, Worcester.

Millbury Amusement & Sports Center Rte. 20, Millbury
(508) 799-9033
Miniature golf, a par 3 golf course, driving range, batting cages and arcade. Also has bumper boats, tank tag, and two go-cart tracks.. Call for hours and directions.
"It's my favorite because of the arcade, batting cages, go carts," Shaun Wise, age 11, Worcester, MA.
"I like to ride the cars. This is my favorite place to go!" Jose Santiago, age 10, Worcester, MA.

Animal Farms

Southwick Zoo Millville St. off Rte. 16 (from 146 take Uxbridge exit, to Rte. 16 East to Mendon) Mendon
(508) 883-9182
New England's largest zoo, with more than 100 different species. Fascinating collection of over 600 rare birds, unusual animals. Pony and elephant rides, children's petting zoo, animal circus with Arabian horses and elephant ballerina; 30-acre deer forest. Educational programs, picnic grove, snack bars, gift shop. 10am-5pm daily. For more info., see Mendon.

Heifer Project International Wachusett St., Rutland
(508) 886-2221
285-acre farm with panoramic views of Boston's Prudential and Hancock Towers. HPI raises and ships farm animals to Third World Countries to end world hunger. School tours, special events, birthday parties, hayrides, sleigh rides, picnicking, Gift shop. Volunteers and visitors welcome, call ahead.
"Meet Kate the sweet border collie, and other bred animals and unusual species, lambs in the spring (May), goats, yaks, rabbits, chickens, ducks, cows," Helen Carter Worcester, MA.
"It's a wonderful farm with interesting animals located at the exact center of Massachusetts with a beautiful view of the surrounding area. They also send the animals to help alleviate world hunger," Irene T. Amsden, Rutland, MA.
"It's not far from Worcester, but the area is rural and is a peaceful place to be, with the

animals. They provide a great service and people can volunteer," Marla Welsford, Worcester, MA.

Farmland Petting Zoo Redstone Hill Rd. (off Rte. 62), Sterling
(508) 422-MOOO (6666)
Over 100 farm animals to pet and feed, wagon, pony rides, birthday and group parties, picnic tables under large tented area, snack bar. Open May 15-Oct. 31. Call for hours and directions.

Homecroft Farm 101 Leland Hill Rd., Sutton
(508) 865-4387
Petting farm, miniature horses, goats, sheep, cows, chickens, ducks, rabbits, lots of baby animals, visitors can bottle feed calves daily at 10 am, kids can help plant a community garden, from which produce is donated to shelters and soup kitchens. Open 7 days a week during warm months, 9am-5pm, call for winter hours. Adults $4, kids under 12, $3; directions from Worcester, Rte. 146 South, left on Central Turnpike, Leland Hill Rd. is 3rd left, follow yellow dots on telephone poles.

Green Hill Park Skyline Drive, Worcester
(508) 779-1290
Playground, picnic area, barnyard zoo.

Balloon Rides & Flying

Sterling Airport Club 121 Greenland St., Sterling
(508) 422-8860
Flying lessons are available; location of the MIT Soaring Association. Restaurant open weekends in winter, ice cream stand and restaurant open daily spring through fall. Call for further information and directions.

Worcester County Hot Air Ballooning 57 Shore Road, North Brookfield
(508) 867-2008
Hot-air balloon rides, great for anniversaries, weddings, sightseeing, advertising, birthdays, gift certificates available, $150 per person; $275 for two, prices subject to change, includes champagne, cheese, crackers and breakfast.

Amity Flight School Worcester Airport, Worcester
(508) 756-7703
Flying lessons, scenic flights.

Bella Via Balloon Co. 9 Bates Ave., Worcester
(508) 853-6101
Since 1978 balloon rides, instructions, sales and champagne flights. Call for further information and directions.

Skywords Unlimited Aerial Adventures 255 Beverly St., Worcester
(508) 852-3980
Specializing in hot air balloon adventures. Leave from Auburn and go where the wind takes you. Average 1 hour flights. Call for reservations and directions.

Biking

Tufts Health Plan / Fitchburg Longsjo Classic   Fitchburg
(508) 343-4281, phone or fax for information.
Second oldest bike race in the country, attracts over 650 riders, including national and international professionals, past and present Olympians. 4-day stage race, July 1-4 annually.
"Contact Dr. Ray Wolejko who organizes this event each year. Attracts big names in biking," U.K., Fitchburg, MA.

Blackstone Valley Alternatives Valley Tour   54 Douglas Rd., Whitinsville
(508) 234-6232
Bike event (fund raiser) held in October, goes through all 11 towns of the Blackstone Valley. Call for further information.

Seven Hills Wheelmen   Greendale Station, P.O. Box 24, Worcester
(508) 831-0301
Group offers two to three rides a week most of the year for all ages and abilities. Road and off road biking. Also, hiking, cross-country and snowmobiling and snowshoeing. Call or write for further information.

Billiards

Boston Billiard Club   454 Grove St., Worcester
(508) 852-2121
Pool hall with 30 tables, pool leagues, pub style restaurant, bar. Boat house deck, music, open in summer. Call for hours and directions.

Jillian's Billiard Club   315 Grove St., Worcester
(508) 793-0900
Combination pool hall and pub style restaurant. Ping pong tables, electronic dart boards, video games, two full service bars. Call for hours and directions.

London Billiards   70 James St., Worcester
(508) 799-7665
Pool hall, full bar and pub style restaurant. "Izzi's" night club. Call for hours and directions.

Rack-N-Rhythm   100 Grove St., Worcester
(508) 831-7665
Combination pool hall and dance club. Pub style restaurant. Call for hours and directions.

Boating, Sailing, Canoeing, Rowing

Note: for more boating spots, refer to the Ponds, Lakes, Rivers and Reservoirs section.

Nashua River Watershed Association (NRWA)   592 Main St., Groton
(508) 448-0299
The NRWA is responsible for restoring the Nashua River to its orginal unpolluted beauty. A guide to the 60-mile river and Stillwater River, Nissitissit River and Squannacook River

is available for canoeists.
"The river is cleaned for canoeing and its miles of greenway have wonderful hiking, picnicking and horseback riding areas for peaceful and interesting get-aways," Lee (Bill) Farnsworth, Lancaster, MA.

Blackstone River Canoeing
From Plummer's landing, Northbridge to Rice City Pond, Uxbridge, Northbridge to Uxbridge
(508) 278-9400 (401) 334-0837
Hawk and great blue heron sightings possible. A nice canoe trip. For canoe guide for other trips, call the Blackstone River Valley National Heritage Corridor.

Donahue Rowing Center   237 North Quinsigamond Ave., Shrewsbury
(508) 845-9121
State-of-the-art rowing facility constructed by the Town of Shrewsbury. Lake Quinsigamond, home of the Eastern Sprints, is considered one of the best bodies of water in the U.S. for the sport of rowing. The Donahue Rowing Center is home to the rowing programs of Holy Cross, WPI, St. John's, Shrewsbury High and the Quinsigamond Rowing Association. Boat Ramp. For introductory programs, contact the Shrewsbury Parks and Recreation Dept.

Blackstone River - Canoe Rentals -Finn & Feather Sports   Rte. 140, Upton
(508) 529-3901
Canoe Rentals for trips on the Blackstone River. Fish and tackle shop. Call for hours and directions.

Regatta Point Community Sailing   55 Lake Ave. North, Lake Quinsigamond, Worcester
(508) 757-2140
Sailing, instructions, social functions throughout the season. Open Apr. through Oct. Call for hours and directions.
"To sit and view the lake is beautiful," Russell S. Matison, Worcester, MA.
"It's like a sanctuary in the city," Berina Grover, Worcester, MA.

Shore Park   Shore Dr., Worcester
(508) 779-1326
Wind surfing, recreational sailing, sailing instruction and social activities are offered through the Worcester Parks and Recreation Department. Family, individual and junior programs are offered. Call for hours and directions.

Bowling

Auburn Ten-Pin Bowl   101 Southbridge St., Auburn
(508) 791-5700
Youth and adult leagues. Call for hours and directions.

Thunderbird Bowl   38 Southbridge St., Auburn
(508) 755-4304
Youth, adult and senior leagues; programs for hearing and visually impaired. Call for hours and directions.

Palace Bowling Alleys   78 Daniels St., Fitchburg
(508) 345-0731
Candlepin alleys, adult leagues only, snack bar.

Putnam Street Bowling Alleys   14 Putnam St., Fitchburg
(508) 343-9664
Candlepin alleys, adult and youth leagues available. Call for hours and directions.

Gardner Ten Pin   560 West Broadway, Rte. 2A, Gardner
(508) 632-0010
Ten pin alleys, lounge, snack bar, adult and youth leagues. Call for hours and directions.

Fairlanes Town & Country Bowl   405 Boston Turnpike, Rt. 9, Shrewsbury
(508) 754-7050
10 pin alleys, adult/youth leagues, snack bar and lounge.

Bayberry Bowling Center   326 Main St., Spencer
(508) 885-4876
Candlepin bowling alleys. Youth and adult leagues. Call for hours and directions.

Sparetime Recreation   117 Church St., Whitinsville (Northbridge)
(508) 234-2077
Twelve new bowling lanes and 8 billiard tables, plus 8 renovated lanes downstairs. A big, clean family fun spot in the Blackstone Valley. Call for hours and directions.

Colonial Bowling Center   248 Mill St., Worcester
(508) 754-7645
Candlepin alleys, adult leagues. Call for hours and directions.

Christmas Tree Farms

Hillcrest Farm   153 Millbury St., Auburn
(508) 832-2995
Cut your own tree. Open 9am to 8pm daily. "Farmer's Daughter" shops.

Chandler's White Christmas Tree Farm   189 Crosby Road, Berlin
(508) 838-2660
Cut your own tree. Open 9am to dusk daily.

Carlson Christmas Tree Farm   69 N. Sullivan Rd., Charlton
(508) 248-7450
Cut your own tree. Open 9am to dark, daily.

D & M Tree Farm 82 Dresser Hill Road, Rte. 31, Charlton
(508) 248-6780
Cut your own tree. Open 9am to dark daily.

Bingham Tree Farm Kendall Rd., Fitchburg
(508) 345-9971
Cut your own tree. Open 8am to 5pm daily.

Pell Farm Soap Hill Rd., Grafton
(508) 533-4559
Cut your own tree. Open 10am to 4pm daily.

Dresser Tree Farm 550 Manning St., Holden
(508) 829-4894
Cut your own tree. Open 9am to dusk weekends.

Southwick Tree Farm 132 Marshall St., Leicester
(508) 791-5258
Cut your own Christmas tree. Open 10am to 4pm daily.
"The old farmhouse (circa 1800) and barns overlook a small pond with rows and rows of Christmas trees in various stages of growth. Happy faces of all ages choosing & cutting their tree add to the excitement of a wonderful season!" Sonia Southwick, Leicester, MA.

Pierce's Tree Farm Rte. 13, Lunenburg
(508) 8-582-4723
Cut your own tree. Open 8am to dark daily.

Choose & Cut Tree Farm Old Common Rd., New Braintree
(508) 867-2423

Walker's Greenery 568 Main St., Rte. 12, Oxford
(508) 987-8936
Cut your own tree. Open 10am to dark daily starting November 1st.

The Whiting Farm Rte. 2A, Phillipston, Exit 19 off Rte. 2, Phillipston
(508) 249-7637
Christmas trees, herbal wreaths, dried flowers, pottery, antiques & collectibles. Open April- Dec., call for hours and directions.

Deer Run Tree Farm Calamint Hill Rd., Princeton
(508) 464-2932
Cut your own tree. Hay rides, scenic vistas, tree bailing and cider. Open weekends 9am to 4pm.

Greenmantle Tree Farm Gates Rd., Princeton
(508) 464-2071 or (508) 464-5080
Cut your own tree. Open 10am to dusk daily.

Lone Maple Farm 106 Rhodes Rd., Princeton
(508) 464-2476
Cut your own tree. Proceeds benefit the Boys & Girls Clubs of Worcester. Open 8:30am to dark daily. Call for directions.

Bo-Bar Plantation 255 Pleasantdale Rd., Rutland
(508) 886-6227
Cut your own tree. Open 8:30am. to 4:30pm, call for directions.

Love's Tree Farm Glenwood Road, off Rte. 122-A, Rutland
(508) 886-4931
Acres of cut-your-own trees, seasonal.

Oliver's Christmas Tree Plantation Rte. 56, Rutland
(508) 886-4844
Cut your own tree. Open weekends 9am to dark, starting after Thanksgiving.

Wolf Hill Farm 30 Jericho Hill Rd., Southborough
(508) 485-5087
Cut your own tree. Open 10am to dusk Thurs.-Sunday.

Carlson Tree Farm 126 Arnold Rd., Sturbridge
(508) 248-7450
Cut your own tree. Open 11am. to dusk weekends.

Star Of The East 15 DeWitt Rd., Sutton
(508) 865-3292
Tree farm, gift shop and group hay rides. Open 9am to dark Mon.-Sat. noon to dark, Sunday.

Fairs

Hardwick Fair Rte. 32A, On the Common, Hardwick
The oldest in New England. It is not commercial and has good wholesome family fun and lots of agricultural exhibits. Held in August.

Spencer Fair Grounds Smithville Rd.,off Rte. 31, Spencer
Country fair held Labor Day weekend.
"Rides, entertainment, livestock judging and demolition derby," G.A., Worcester, MA.

Fishing & Wildlife Information

Statewide Fishing Information
1-800-ASK-FISH
Fishing information through the use of your 'touch tone' phone! Lists of stocked waters for trout, bass and pike, boat ramp access areas near your location, answers to commonly asked questions and much more.

Mass. Div. of Fisheries & Wildlife Off Rte. 9, north on Rte. 135, Westborough, MA 01581
(508) 792-7270
Field headquarters building with an excellent reference library. Resources for fish and wildlife topics, including "Central Mass. Pond Maps" booklet containing 50 maps of Worcester County ponds. Educational programs for adults and children are offered. Call for hours and directions.

Forests, Conservation Lands, Open Space

Mt. Watatic, Ashburnham State Forest Rte. 119, Ashburnham
A moderate 2.3 mile day hike to the 1832' summit of Mt. Watatic is a good family outing. Hiking time is 2.5 hours. From the junction of Rtes. 101 and 119, travel west for 1.4 miles on Rte. 119 and park in the off-road area on the right. Follow the sign for the Wapack Trail and Mt. Watatic. Look for second sign called the Blueberry Ledges Trail. After a mile, this trail ends and the Wapack Trail enters from the left, follow to the top, where there are views of Boston, Vermont the Adirondacks and Mt. Greylock.

Bearsden Watershed Off South Royalston Rd., Athol
Hiking, horseback riding, cross-country skiing, walking and snowmobiles. No dirt bikes or 4-wheel drive vehicles allowed.

Lawton State Forest Townsend Rd., Athol
(508) 249-4551
Wooded area for hiking. Call town office for directions.

Gilbert-Stockwell Conservation Land Barns St., across Gilbert Way, Auburn
(508) 832-7701
Wooded area for walking. Call Town Clerk's office for directions.

Granger Ledges Oxford St., South, Auburn
(508) 832-7701
Hiking area, rock ledges. Call Town Clerk's office for further directions.

Brewer Brook Area Rte. 62, to Pleasant St., off Pleasant St., Berlin
(508) 838-2931
Walking, cross-country skiing, snowshoeing. No sign to indicate location off Pleasant St. Call Town Clerk's office for further directions.

Gates Pond Reservoir Off Rte. 62 , Taylor St., Berlin
(508) 838-2931
Walking, cross-country skiing, snowshoeing. Call Town Clerk's office for further directions.

Philbin Conservation Area Off Rte. 117, Bolton
Hiking trails.

Bement Center   Jones Rd., Charlton
(508) 248-7811
Biking, boating, camping, fishing, swimming, hiking, tennis.

Gardner Heritage State Park   Lake St., Gardner
(508) 630-1497
Visitors Center. Historical site, leashed pets allowed, restrooms, handicapped accessible restrooms available. Park area located on Rte. 101, Dunn Pond State Park.
"My father took me fishing there as a boy, and now I take my children and grandchildren. What memories!" Roger L. Gerard, Gardner, MA
"It offers unique appropriate activities all year for all ages," Ann Gerard, Gardner, MA.

Mt. Wachusett Community College Land   444 Green St., Gardner
(508) 632-6600
Biking, cross-country skiing, hiking or walking the nature trails, all weather track for jogging and tennis. Call for further directions.

Perley Brook Headwaters   Wheeler St., Gardner
Walking trails, picnicking. Call Town Clerk's office for further directions.

Fletcher Reservation   Rte. 140 toward Upton, Old Upton Rd. On Silver Lake, Grafton
Town beach, fishing and canoeing.

Gummere Woods   Wheeler Rd., & Worcester St., Grafton
40 acres on the western side of Quinsigamond and Lake Ripple. Hiking, walking, bird watching area and a good location to find wild mushrooms.

Marsters Property   Wheeler Rd. & Worcester Rd., adjacent to Gummere Woods Area, Grafton
A very nice hiking, picnicking and bird watching area.

Merriam Road Conservation Area   Merriam Rd., Grafton
50 acres, nice walking trails, cross-country skiing and bird watching area.

Parker Macomber Land Area   Keith Rd. & Sailsbury St., Grafton
An interpretive trail is currently under development here. A nice place for archeologists to study the old Indian village area.

Clapp Scorgie Tufts Smith   Still River Rd., Harvard
80 acres, cross-country skiing, fishing, horseback riding, hiking, ice skating, nature walks, snowmobiling. (Resource: Harvard Trails, published by Harvard Conservation Trust, on sale at Harvard Pharmacy).

Holy Hill Conservation Area   South Shaker Rd., Harvard
(508) 456-3607
A sanctuary named for a Shaker holy hill where religious services were held outside. The worship area sometime called the 'dancing ground', is 1/2 mile up a trail. Shaker barn foundations, a Shaker cemetery and stone bridge are found here. A trail guide is available at Town Hall on the town common.

Town Forests, Conservation Lands, Open Space   off Harris St., Holden
Hiking and walking trails, snowshoeing and cross-country skiing.

Trout Brook Reservation   Rte. 31 North, to Manning St., Holden
A very nice walking and hiking area. Several well marked hiking trails with a brook that runs along some trails. You can also see a small waterfall. Cross-country skiing, snow-shoeing and ice skating on a small pond. Parking area.
"*You can walk there in summer and ski in winter,*" Judy Savage, Rutland, MA.

Hubbardston Forest   New Westminster Rd., off Rte. 68, Hubbardston
Large area for walking, hiking, picnicking, cross-country skiing and snowshoeing.

Cook Conservation Area   Rte. 70 north on Lunenburg Rd., Lancaster
240 acres cross-country skiing, hiking or walking. Trail along the river shows an old mill foundation, a very pretty river.

New England Forest Foundation   Accessible on George Hill on West George Hill Rd., Lancaster
91 acres cross-country skiing, hiking and walking area.

Town Forest   Brockerlman Rd., Lancaster
286 acres, cross-country skiing, hiking, horseback riding, hunting, beautiful mountain laurel area to view (blooms in June).

Lane-Comerford Area Conservation Land   Johnny Appleseed Lane, off I-190, Leominster
220 acres, boating, cross-country skiing, fresh water fishing, hiking, hunting, nature walks, picnicking. Access through Oxbow Wildlife Refuge, Lancaster.

Clarks Hill Reservation   Lancaster Ave., Lunenburg
17 acres, with a steep climb to the top of the hill top you'll find an open field with views. Picnic under the hickory tree at the top. Walking/hiking area.

Henry E. Cowdrey Nature Center   Rte. 2A, Massachusetts Ave., Lunenburg
(508) 582-4130
Family hiking area on 300 acres, streams, swamp, forest and beaver dam. Many forms of wildflowers, shrubs and ferns can be seen along the nature trails. Picnic area. Maps are located at the Town office.

Jenks Woods   Burrage St., Lunenburg
74 acres of wooded and swampy terrain for walking/hiking. A small pond here makes for good skating in winter and the small hill on the eastern shore provides a good overlook of the area. Maps can be obtained at the Town Clerk's office.

Lunenburg Town Forests   Gilchrest St., Lunenburg
121 acres to walk along the bubbling brook and forest area with glacial features.

Town Forest   Off Rte. 2A, Lunenburg
Hiking and walking trails.

Brierly Pond West Main St. (near convergence of West Main and Sutton Rd.), Millbury
22 acre area has marked nature trails for walking/hiking through hills, streams, woods, waterfront area on Brierly Pond.

Davidson Sanctuary West Main St., Millbury
Located between Carleton Rd. and Stone Rd. This area has 1.25 miles of marked trails, has woodlands, streams, hills and springs for your viewing and bird watching pleasure.

Stowe-Day Sanctuary Auburn Rd. (near Old Commons end), Millbury
This 130 acrea area has marked nature trails of hills, woodlands, springs, wetlands streams and Ramshorn Brook.

Edmond Hill Woods Off Rice Ave., Northborough
Thick woods area, hiking.

Mt. Pisgah Smith Rd., Northborough
Hiking trails, horseback riding, snowshoeing, parking.

Shiny Rocks Off School St., Northbridge
40 acres, walking trails to cliff that overlooks valley.

Oakham Forest Spencer Rd., Rte. 148, Oakham
Hiking trails, cross-country skiing, snowshoeing.

Conservation Commission Land #1 Asnebumskit Rd., off Rte. 122, Paxton
Built as a passive recreational area. Hiking, bird watching, wildlife & nature studies. Cross-country skiing, snowshoeing.

Conservation Commission Land #2 Smith Property, opposite Town pool, near Paxton Center School, Paxton
Passive recreational area. Hiking, bird watching, wildlife & nature studies. Cross-country skiing, snowshoeing.

Moore State Park Mill St. (Rte. 2 west, Rte. 31 south, cross over Rte. 122, continue and follow signs), Paxton
(508) 792-3969
432 acres, canoeing, fishing, historical site, non-motorized boating, fishing, hunting, hiking trails, flowering bushes, waterfall, four season open space for the public, cross-country skiing, showshoeing. Call for hours and directions. For more background, see Paxton.
"*It is one of the smallest state parks; it has a beautiful waterfall and a peaceful, secluded hiking trail around a pristine, wooded pond,*" Mike McDonald, Southbridge, MA.
"*Fabulously beautiful grist mill and pond, a setting of unspoiled nature,*" Lorraine Kokocinski, Paxton, MA.
"*Beautiful waterfalls, flowering plants, fall foliage, one room schoolhouse, historic significance, quiet beauty, a little known gem,*" Marianne Bourgault, Rutland, MA.
"*Its beauty and serenity provide a welcome respite...especially in the late spring when the many rhododendrons are in bloom!*" Susan Jacques, Millbury, MA.

Federated Women's Club State Forest   Rte. 122, Petersham
(508) 939-8962
Six wilderness campsites, 1,035 acres. Hiking, camping, fishing, hunting, leashed pets allowed, cross-country skiing, scenic viewing area. Call for hours and directions.

Harvard Forest   Rte. 32, Harvard Pond, Petersham
(508) 724-3302
Hiking, nature walks and the Fisher Museum of Forestry are located here. Hiking trails begin on New Salem Rd. Call for hours and directions.

Roaring Brook   East St., Petersham
A very nice walking area.

Swift River Reservation   Nichewaug Rd., Rte. 32 & Rte. 122, Petersham
An area for walking, hiking and bird watching. Trails lead through old pasture and woodland area to a viewing area of the Swift River.

Elliott Laurel Reserve   Rte. 101, near Bakers Lane, Phillipston
Nature trails for walking, hiking and bird watching are located here.

Wachusett Mountain State Reservation   Mountain Rd., Princeton
(508) 464-2987
Auto road leads to the top of Mt. Wachusett. Mountain biking allowed only on road. Hiking trails, cross-country skiing, historical site, restrooms handicapped accessible, leashed pets allowed, scenic viewing area, walking, parking. Access road to mountain open May through October.
For historical background, see Chapter 12, Princeton.
"Our favorite hike is in the Mt. Wachusett Reservation along the south edge. We've led a yearly trek to a little known clearing there, just north of Blueberry Hill where, on July 4th evenings we enjoy seeing the fireworks of Boston, Framingham and Worcester simultaneously. An incredible display!" George Mahowald, Rutland, MA.
"One place stands above the rest, literally and figuratively - Wachusett Mountain. At all times and in all seasons, it is a delight to eye and soul. It's the only place I have ever seen a scarlet tanager," Peter B. Baker, Worcester, MA.
"Mountain biking on the carriage roads (West, North, Echo Lake, Administration, and Balance Rock Roads) makes 'mountain' biking more like it was intended to be — biking in the mountains," Ellen Gugel, Westborough, MA.
"It's my favorite because it's a four-season place - cool in summer, picnicking, blueberry picking, foliage, hawk migration, and skiing," Marie Heenan, Rutland, MA.

Jacobs Hill Reservation   Rte. 68, head northwest from center, Royalston
A short hike through the hemlock-beech woods on Jacobs Hill leads to a ridge-top overlook, with the clear waters of Long Pond and the east branch of the Tully River some 300 feet below.

Lawrence Brook Access   Rte. 68, Mill Yard Rd., Royalston
Brook runs through town, hiking, fishing, horseback riding, nature trails, bird watching.

Royalston State Forest   Rte. 32, Royalston
Walking trails.

Rufus Putnam Park   Rte. 122-A, Rutland
17 acres, fishing, ice skating, nature walks, picnics, benches installed by Eagle Scout Jared Faucher.

Westville Reservoir & Dam   South St., Southbridge
A nice area for walking. Two mile walk along the Quinebaug river.
"Lovely in any season. Peaceful. Parallels Old Grand Trunk railroad site, tranquil, brings relaxation," Ralph C. Monrow, Southbridge, MA.

Buck Hill Conservation Land   McCormick Rd., off Rte. 31 adjacent to 4-H Camp Marshall, Spencer
(508) 885-2595
Walking trails through forest and around the pond.
"A self-teaching series of trails...great place to visit with family, friends, lover or alone," William Goss, Shrewsbury, MA.
"Many interesting trails through woods, fields and around the pond. Nice to visit winter or summer," Tom Bair, Upton, MA.

Rocky Brook Conservation Area   Osgood Rd., Sterling
Cross-country skiing, hiking, nature walks and picnicking.

Streeter Point Recreation Area   Rte. 20, Sturbridge
(508) 347-9257
Picnicking, hunting, fishing, leashed pets allowed. Call for hours and directions.

Tantaisquis Historical Reservation   Leadmine Rd., Sturbridge
Walking Trails

Purgatory Chasm State Reservation Purgatory Rd., Off Rte. 146 South to Purgatory Rd.,follow signs, Sutton
(508) 234-3733
Breath-taking 70' gorge with caves, hidden chambers, cross-country skiing, hiking, picnicking, hunting, leashed pets allowed, picnicking, restrooms, scenic viewing area. A geological wonder, this fissure is between two ledges that are 40 to 70 feet deep and a half-mile long. Call for hours and directions.
"Unique chasm, cool in summer, not too crowded, play area, fun for children, free, natural setting," Mrs. Nancy Heck, Sutton, MA.
"Best place in the state to get caught on top of a large rock formation with no apparent way down!" Kerry Walker, age 10, Auburn, MA.

Upton State Forest   Westborough Rd., Upton
(508) 278-6486
Cross-country skiing, hiking, horseback riding, hunting, leashed pets allowed, snowmobiling and walking trails. For further information call Blackstone Heritage State Park. Mass. Pike west to Rte. 495 south (Hopkinton exit). At Pratt Pond take right onto Westborough Rd.

Capron Park   Rte.16, at the waterfall, Uxbridge
Includes 4-mile self-guided walk along the Blackstone Canal, starts near Cross St. by the Stanley Woolen Mill, (park in Tri-River Family Health Center lot); or for the hike to King Philip's Rock, go over the bridge to the Dept. of Environmental Management building on the left. Boat tours (seasonal) leave from Oak St. & East Hartford Ave.

Lucy Stone Park   Old West Brookfield Rd., Warren
Walking, hiking, fishing, shore fishing in Quaboag River.

Conservation Land   Bowman St., Westborough
Hiking and walking around the reservoir. Very peaceful.

Sudbury Valley Trustees   Off Friberg Parkway Rte. 9, Westborough
Walk-Up reservation for hiking, nature walks, bird watching, cross-country skiing and snowshoeing.
"Families can wander in pine woods with Lady Slippers, marveling at the tranquility,"
Kris Allen, Westborough.

New England Wild Flower Reserve   West St., Winchendon
Nature walking trails. Not maintained, but a nice area for quiet walks.

Golf Courses

Ellinwood Country Club   1928 Pleasant St., Athol
(508) 249-7460
A challenging 18-hole course, yards: 5,737, practice putting and pitching areas, pull & power carts, food served, pro shop. Call ahead for tee times and directions.

Pakachoag Golf Club   20 Upland St., Auburn
(508) 755-3291
Town owned, 9th fairway site of Robert Goddard's first rocket launch, 9-hole course, 3,237 yards, pull carts, putting green, snack bar. Great for sledding and cross-country skiing. Call for tee times and directions.

Berlin Country Club   25 Carr Rd., Berlin
(508) 838-2733
9-hole course, yards 2,300, pull/ power carts, pro shop, snack bar, bar/lounge, clubhouse. Tee times are not required, but call for further directions.

Twin Springs Golf Course   Wilder Rd., Bolton
(508) 779-5020
9-hole course with varied terrain and small greens. Come see the new clubhouse, just built in '95. Yards 2,612, carts available, practice putting/pitching area, lessons, pro shop, club rental, snack bar. Call ahead for tee times and directions.

Heritage Country Club   Sampson Rd., Charlton
(508) 248-5111
18-hole public course, yards: 5,505, driving range, practice putting and pitching areas, pull & power carts, pro shop, lessons and food available. Call for tee times and directions.

Nichols College   46 Dudley Hill Rd., Dudley
(508) 943-4534
A relatively level 9-hole course, yards: 3,241, practice putting and pitching areas, pull & power carts, snack bar/lounge, pro shop. Tee time reservations are not required, but call for further directions.

Bay Path Golf Course   North Brookfield Rd., East Brookfield
(508) 867-8161
9-hole course, yards: 3,015, pull & power carts, lessons, pitching practice area, driving range, pro shop, food served. Tee times are not required, call for further directions.

Gardner Municipal Golf Course   Eaton Rd., Gardner
(508) 632-9703
18-hole course with the first nine wide open and the back nine tree lined and tight. Yards: 6,200, putting area, pull & power carts, restaurant, bar/lounge, pro shop. Call for tee times and directions.

Dunroamin Country Club   Rte. 32, Hardwick(Gilbertville)
(413) 477-8880
9-hole course, 3,028 yards, pull & power carts, practice putting/pitching areas, driving range, lessons, clubhouse, snack bar, bar/lounge. Course is closed to the public on Sundays. Call for tee times and directions.

Shaker Hills Golf Club   Shaker Rd., Harvard
(508) 772-2227
18-hole course opened in 1991, has the feel of a 'private' course. Yards: 6,850, driving range, putting area, pull & power carts, clubhouse, snack bar, bar/lounge, lessons and pro shop. Call for tee times and directions.

Holden Hills Country Club   1800 Main St., Rte. 122A, Holden
(508) 829-3129
A challenging 18-hole course among the hills and streams. Yards: 5,826, pull & power carts, practice putting & pitching area, club rentals, pro shop, snack bar, restaurant, bar/lounge. Call for tee times and directions.

Hillcrest Country Club   325 Pleasant St., Leicester
(508) 892-8616
12 hole course, (the first 6 are re-played), 6,350 yards, practice putting and pitching areas, lessons, club rental, snack bar, clubhouse, bar/lounge. Call for tee times and directions.

Strawberry Hills Country Club   1430 Main St., Leicester
(508) 892-1390
18-hole course, the fairways are tree lined and narrow, yards: 5,740, practice putting and pitching areas, pull & power carts, snack bar, pro shop. Call for tee times and directions.

Grand View Golf Course   Wachusett St., Leominster
(508) 537-0614
18-hole very scenic golf course, water comes into play on several holes. Yards: 6,744, putting area, pull & power carts, snack bar, pro shop and club house. Call for tee times and directions.

Monoosnock Country Club   Monoosnock Ave., Leominster
(508) 537-1872
9-hole course with narrow fairways and brooks. This course is closed to the public on Fri., Sat. and Sun. Yards: 6,107 (3,050 per nine, second nine uses different tee markers), driving range, practice putting & pitching area, pull & power carts, pro shop, lessons, club rentals, restaurant, bar-lounge. Call for tee times and directions.

Maplewood Golf Course   994 Northfield Rd., Lunenburg
(508) 582-6694
A nice scenic 9-hole course. Yards: 2,685, driving range, putting area, pull & power carts, lessons, club rentals, snack bar and pro shop. Call for tee times and directions.

Clearview Country Club   66 Park Hill Ave., Millbury
(508) 753-9201
9-hole hilly course, yards: 3,000, pull & power carts, lessons, snack bar, restaurant, bar-lounge and pro shop. Tee times are not required but call for further directions.

Juniper Hill Golf Club   202 Brigham St., Northborough
(508) 393-2444
Two beautiful 18-hole courses, with some holes overlooking Lake Chauncey. Lakeside course-yards: 6,140, Riverside course-yards: 6,306, pull & power carts, putting area, pro shop, teaching center, club rentals, clubhouse, bar-lounge and snack bar. Call for tee times and directions.

Quail Hollow Golf & Country Club   1822 Old Turnpike Rd., Oakham
(508) 882-5516
9-hole course just opened in '92. Yards: 3,045, driving range, practice putting and pitching areas, pull & power carts, club rentals, lessons, clubhouse, full restaurant, bar/lounge, pro shop. Call for tee times and directions.
"I can watch the sun setting behind the western hills while enjoying tasty, reasonably priced meals, which are served on a glass enclosed porch," Anne Marie Buron, Oakham, MA.

Pine Ridge Country Club   28 Pleasant St., Oxford
(508) 892-9188
18-hole hilly course, yards: 6,100, putting area, pull & power carts, lessons, club rentals, pro shop, clubhouse, restaurant, bar-lounge. Call for tee times and directions.

Petersham Country Club   North Main St., Rte. 32, Petersham
(508) 724-3388
Beautiful scenery at this 18-hole course, yards: 6,115, practice putting and pitching areas, pull & power carts, lessons, club rentals, pro shop, club house, snack bar, bar-lounge. Call for tee times and directions.

Bedrock Golf Club   87 Barre-Paxton Rd., Rutland
(508) 886-0202
9-hole newly constructed course, yards: 3,486, putting green, pull & power carts, pro shop, snack bar. Call for tee times and directions.

St. Mark's Golf Course   Cordaville Rd., Rte. 85, Southborough
(508) 485-6145
9-hole hilly course, yards: 3,200, putting area, snack bar. Tee times not required, but call for further directions.

Stonybrook Golf Course   Valley Rd., Southborough
(508) 485-3151
9-hole course, yards: 1,170, pull carts, snack bar, practice green, lessons, club rentals. Tee times not required, but call for further directions.

Pleasant Valley Country Club and the New England Classic   Armsby Rd., off Rte. 146, Sutton
(508) 865-5244
Site of Pleasant Valley Classic professional golf tournament, which the public can attend. Otherwise, this 18-hole private course is open to members and guests only.
"It brings the excitement and professionalism of golf to New England every year. Supporting local charities and involving all local volunteerism, it truly is an annual New England tradition," Stephen J. Mingolla, Sutton, MA.

Blissful Meadows Golf Course   801 Chockalog Rd., Uxbridge
(508) 278-6113
9-hole public course, yards: 3,011, driving range, putting green, pull & power carts, pro shop, snack bar, lounge, handicap service. Call for tee times and directions.

Edgewood Golf Course   757 West Hartford Ave., Uxbridge
(508) 278-6027
This 9-hole very challenging course has pull & power carts, practice putting/pitching area, lessons, club rentals, restaurant & lounge, club house, league play. Call for tee times and directions.

Wachusett Country Club   187 Prospect St., West Boylston
(508) 835-4453 or (508) 835-2264
A Donald Ross course, with rolling terrain, this 18-hole course has superbly manicured greens. Yards: 6,600, driving range, putting green, pull & power carts, pro shop, food available at the "Slice It Right" Restaurant, bar-lounge. Call for tee times and directions.

Westborough Country Club   121 West Main St., Westborough
(508) 366-9947
Small greens and hilly, this 9-hole course has yards: 3,045, putting area, pull & power carts, pro shop, restaurant, bar-lounge. Call for tee times and directions.

Indian Meadows Golf   275 Turnpike Rd., Westborough
(508) 836-5460
9-hole course where water comes into play on several holes. Yards: 6,018, pull & power carts, pro shop. Call for tee times and directions.

Westminster Country Club   51 Ellis Rd., Westminster
(508) 874-5938
A nice and challenging 18-hole course. The front nine is flat, with the back nine hilly. Yards: 6,473, practice putting/pitching area, pull & power carts, clubhouse, lessons, club rentals, pro-shop. Restaurant overlooks 18th hole. Call for tee times and directions.

Winchendon Country Club 160 Ash St., Winchendon
(508) 297-9897
This 18-hole course has narrow fairways and small greens. Yards: 5,317, putting area, power carts, pro shop, lessons, club rentals, restaurant, bar-lounge. Cross-country skiing in winter. Call for tee times and directions.

Green Hill Municipal Golf Course Green Hill Ave., Worcester
(508) 852-0913
18-hole municipal golf course, very challenging. Yards: 6,487, putting area, pull & power carts, pro shop, snack bar, club rental. Call ahead for tee times and directions.
"It's my favorite because of its beauty! The scenic views around the course, especially the 3rd and 9th fairways, are unparalleled, especially in May and October," Leo Coleman

Golf Driving Ranges

Auburn Golf Ranges 541 Southbridge St., Auburn
(508) 832-0559
Driving range on grass and mat areas, very nice flowers decorate the area. Call for hours and directions.

South Meadow Golf Range 317 South St., Berlin
(508) 838-2333
Many grass and mat teeing areas, 18-hole miniature golf course, lessons available. Call for hours and directions.

Lancaster Golf Center 438 Old Union Turnpike, Exit 34 off Rte. 2, Lancaster
(508) 537-8922
70 grass & mat stations for driving range, putting green and sand bunker area, pro shop and PGA professional. Also, hardball and softball batting cages. Call for hours and directions.

Mendon Driving Range Rte. 16, Mendon
(508) 478-6295
Golf driving range, clubs available and teeing areas.

Golf Dome Walnut St., Off Rte. 9, Shrewsbury
(508) 845-1001
Indoor driving range, 23 tee areas, golfers can also hit shots from 25 to 40 yards away to a pair of chipping greens. A PGA pro is on duty at all times. 9am to 9pm, seven days a week. Call for directions.

Spencer Driving Range 500 Main St., Spencer
(508) 885-2694
Driving range with mat teeing areas, pro shop and lessons. Call for hours and directions.

Rotary Driving Range Rte. 9, Westborough
(508) 366-5327
Golf driving range, mat teeing areas, and grass areas as well. Lessons given, call for hours and directions.

Hiking/Nature Walks

Good hiking areas exist all over Worcester County - check these other sections: Forests, Conservation Lands & Open Space; Ponds, Lakes, Rivers & Reservoirs, Waterfalls; Wildlife Management Areas; and Wildlife Sanctuaries.

Mid-State Trail From N.H. to R.I. through Worcester County, Ashburnham to Douglas
(508) 874-5629 for information; also (508) 797-9744
You can walk about 95 miles, the length of Worcester County on the Mid-State trail, from Mt. Watatic in Ashburnham to Douglas State Forest. The trail passes by Redemption Rock on Rte. 140 in Princeton, and goes over the Mt. Wachusett State Reservation. It passes Sampson's Pebble, the giant rock at Treasure Valley Boy Scout Reservation. Mid-State Trail Guides ($5.95) can be ordered by calling 1-800-64-BOOKS, and are available at N.E. Backpacker, 6 East Mountain. St., Worcester (508) 853-9407, and at EMS, Greendale Mall (508) 856-9606, Worcester.

Forty Caves off Lancaster Rd., Berlin
(508) 838-2931
Ravine, exposed cliffs, some 50' in height, caves where native tribes sought shelter on trips north. Call Town Clerk's office for further directions.

Worcester County Horticultural Society Tower Hill Botanic Garden, 11 French Dr., Boylston
(508) 869-6111
Flower shows, lectures walking trails, workshops and concerts. Educational programs year round. Garden gift shop, unique garden gifts. Hours Tues.-Sun. 10 am-5pm April through Dec., 10am - 5pm. Tues.-Fri. Jan., Feb. & Mar., call for directions.
"Tower Hill is a fascinating newly evolving botanic garden. Not only sophisticated gardens but also walking paths in fields and woods, an educational center for plant displays, classes, and lecturer, sound gatherings and much more," Sandra Kocher, Spencer, MA.
"The formal gardens inspire tranquillity, yet the wooded trails provide a more rugged kind of escape," Jean M. Langley Boylston, MA.
"It must be 'Prelude to Heaven!" Fabulous in all seasons, hiking, picnicking, and just to look around," Kathleen Grimley, Boylston, MA.

Southern New England Trunk Line Trail Rte. 96, South St., Douglas
Dirt walking and hiking trails go from Douglas to Franklin. Horseback riding, snowmobilling and mountain bikes can be used as well. 50 miles long and open to the public.

Fisher Museum of Forestry Rte. 32, Petersham
(508) 724-3285
Dioramas of New England's changing countryside, hiking trails, call for hours and directions.

Heritage Nature Walk off West St., behind West St. School, Southbridge
Along the Quinebaug River from Southbridge to Sturbridge. Hundreds of daffodils planted by students from West St. School and the Southbridge Garden Club.
"It's new, it's nature, and it's wonderful for all the family," Evelyn A. Petrell, Southbridge, MA.
"Two mile walk... along Quinebaug River, lovely in any season, peaceful, tranquil, brings relaxation. It parallels the old Grand Trunk Railroad site, " Ralph C. Munroe, Southbridge, MA.

King Philip's Rock Hike from Visitors Center, East Hartford Ave., Uxbridge, Northbridge/Uxbridge
(401) 762-0250
30 minute scenic walk along the footpath from Blackstone River Heritage State Park Office to 408' high King Philip's Rock.
"The view from atop the rock offers the most beautiful view out of anywhere in the county, and the hike is easy!" Paul Meleski, Appalachian Mt. Club, Worcester MA.
"Overlooks the Blackstone Valley Heritage Corridor," Albert Dubois, Uxbridge, MA.

River Road Off Thomas St., West Boylston
Nice walking area, runs parallel to the Quinapoxet River.
"A wonderful walk along Quinapoxet River," Tom Dewitt, West Boylston, MA.

Hockey

Worcester IceCats Worcester Centrum, Worcester
(508) 798-5400
A member of the American Hockey League, the IceCats are playing to sometimes sell-out crowds at the Worcester Centrum. Opponents often include the Providence Bruins and the Springfield Falcons. Great family recreation. Prices $7.50-$12.50.

(Note: for information about hockey rinks, see Ice Skating section).

Horseback Riding

Grafton Stables & School 137 Upton Rd., Grafton
(508) 839-6367
Lessons, boarding, pony rides for parties available. Call for further information and directions.

Ridge Valley Stables Rte. 140, Grafton
(508) 839-3038
Lessons, training, boarding, transporting. Pony rides for all occasions. Call for appointment and further information.

Special Equestrians, Inc. at White Oak Farm 411 North St., Jefferson (Holden)
(508) 829-0611
Therapeutic riding for handicapped adults and children, dressage and huntseat, boarding and lessons available. Largest dust-free indoor arena in area. Call for hours and directions.

Stony Acres Stable 90 Schoolhouse Rd., Philipston
(508) 249-2582
Trail rides, lessons, sales and boarding. Call for hours and directions.

Holiday Acres Equestrian Center 333 Main St., Rte. 122-A, Rutland
(508) 886-6896
Riding lessons, boarding, summer camps, training.

Ice Skating

Daniel S. Horgan Rink Memorial Skating Rink Oxford St. North, Auburn
(508) 832-5932
Learn to skate, skating leagues for all ages. Public skating Mon.-Fri. 10am-12pm, Wed. 3pm- 5pm, Sat. & Sun. 2pm-4pm, skate rentals. Call for directions.

George R. Wallace, Jr. Civic Center Complex 1000 John Fitch Highway, Fitchburg
(508) 345-7593
Two public ice-skating rinks. Home of the Fitchburg State College's championship hockey program. Public skating Sun. 1:30-3:00pm. The complex also has a 100 seat planetarium, two function rooms and 4,200 seat concert arena. Call for further information and directions.

Veteran's Memorial Skating Rink 45 Veterans Dr., Gardner
(508) 632-7329
Public skating, open hockey, street hockey (summer), skate rentals and lessons. Call ahead for public skating times and directions.

The "REZ" High St., Southbridge
An old reservoir that the fire fighters made into an outdoor skating rink.

Central Massachusetts Skating School Bridal Lane, Westborough
(508) 366-9373
Private lessons, group lessons and hockey leagues. Call for further information and directions.

Worcester Skating Rink 284 Lake Ave., Worcester
(508) 755-0582
Public skating rink, hockey leagues and skate rentals. Call for hours and directions.
"It is a place where I can skate, play hockey and I can relax because I'm with my friends," Ryan Salmon, age 13, Worcester, MA.

Maple Sugaring

Legassey's Sugar House 1277 North Orange Rd., off Rte. 2A, Athol
(508) 249-6687
Maple sugar house, small group tours given for school, etc. Syrup on sale year round. Call ahead for hours and directions.

Coolidge Farm 168 Berlin Rd., Bolton
(508) 779-6633
Maple sugar house, syrup sales, call ahead for operating times, tours and directions.

Ewen's Sleepy Hollow Sugar House and Cider Mill 66 Elmwood Rd., off Rte. 2A, Lunenburg
(508) 582-6655

Maple syrup made locally, open Sat.-Sun. 12-4pm, late winter-early spring. Farmstand, syrup and cider. No admission fee, call for hours and directions.

K.E. Farm   317 Leadmine Rd., Sturbridge
(508) 347-9323
Maple sugar house, starts boiling in Feb. Group tours welcome, call ahead for hours and directions.

Sunny Knoll Farm   Off Rte. 12, Westminster
(508) 874-0627
Maple sugar house and dairy farm, call ahead for hours and directions.

Orchards/Pick Your Own

Indian Head Farm   232 Pleasant St., Berlin
(508) 838-2942
Farm has been in operation since 1782. Pick your own blueberries, strawberries and fresh vegetables. Farm stand also open. Call for hours and directions.

Wojcik Farm   65 Milk St., Blackstone
(508) 883-9220
Pick your own apples and farm stand.

Bolton Orchards   Wilder Rd., Rt. 110 and 117, Bolton
(508) 779-2898
Bulk harvest apples, peaches, plums, pears and a variety of vegetables, open year round.

Nashoba Winery Orchard   100 Wattaquadoc Hill Rd., Bolton
(508) 779-5521
Pick your own apples, press your own cider, wine tasting and sales daily. Wine tours from 11am-5pm.

Nicewicz Farm   116 Sawyer Road, Bolton
(508) 779-6423

Charlton Orchards   Old Worcester Rd., Charlton
(508) 248-7820
Pick your own blueberries, apples, peaches and pears. Call for hours and directions.

Fay Mountain Orchards   Stafford St., Charlton
(508) 248-7237
Pick your own apples 15 varieties, cider, cider mill demonstrations and wagon rides. Baked goods and preserves.
"The Gilmore family is great; the cider is the best around; their Macs are crisp and tart!" Valerie Sampson, Oxford, MA.
"It is a delight of hills, ponds and orchards where one can pick favorite apples or watch a cider press squeeze out the golden juice, or buy a hot apple pie," William Hultgren, Charlton, MA.

Douglas Orchard 36 Locust St., Douglas
(508) 476-2198
Pick your own blueberries, raspberries and apples in season.

Apple Barn at Marshall Farms 340 Marshall Rd., Fitchburg
(508) 343-6255
Pick your own Macs, Cortland, Delicious, pumpkins; farmstand, gift shop, fresh baked goods and a country store. Picnic area. Call for hours and directions.
"*Apple picking, homemade desserts, crafts,*" Ruth Penka, Fitchburg Historical Society.

Carlson Orchards Oak Hill Rd., Harvard
(508) 456-8263
Pick your own apples: Macintosh, Cortland, Red Delicious, Macoun. Cider Mill, year round farmstand.

Doe Orchards 324 Ayer Rd., Harvard
(508) 772-4139
Pick your own apples, farmstand; Macs, Cortlands, Delicious, Macoun, Empire. Cut your own tree. Open 10am to 4pm Friday through Sunday. Call for picking hours and directions.

Hammerhead Farm 56 Westcott Rd., Harvard
(508) 456-6858
Pick your own apples. Call for hours and directions.

Hazel U-Pick 13 Westcott Rd., Harvard
(508) 456-9092
Pick your own apples. Macs, Cortlands. Children welcomed.

Phil's Apples 24 Prospect Hill Road, Harvard
(508) 456-3361
Pick your own apples; Macs, Red Delicious. Pumpkins, honey, flowers, pies are also available. Cider pressed in the orchard. Call for hours and directions.

Pick a Peck Apples 46 Westcott Rd., Harvard
(508) 456-8521
Pick your own apples; Macs, Cortlands and pick your own pumpkins.

Wade Orchard 62 Westcott Rd., Harvard
(508) 456-3926
Pick your own apples.

Westward Orchard Massachusetts Ave., Rte 111, 1/2mi. west of Rte. 495, Harvard
(508) 456-8363
Pick your own apples, peaches, pears, pumpkins, blueberries, perennials, corn, and cut your own Christmas tree. Call for hours and directions.

Hubbardston Orchards High St. and Rt. 62, Hubbardston
(508) 928-5431
Pick your own apples. Children welcome. Apple pies, doughnuts and dumplings.

Nampara Farms 3 Bemis Road, Hubbardston
(508) 928-4487
Apples, gourds, Indian corn, squash, jellies, pies, pick your own pumpkins.

Deershorn Farm Stand 205 Chase Hill Rd., Rte. 62, Lancaster
(508) 368-7603
Pick your own Macs, Cortland, Delicious, Romes, and choose from 26 varieties at the stand. Farmstand open year round, gifts, fruit baskets, vegetables.

Appleseeds Applesales 143 Joslin St., Leominster
(508) 534-7960
Pick your own apples, strawberries, pumpkins, and farmstand. Macs, Cortlands, Red and Golden Delicious, more varieties available. Call for hours and directions.

Kimball Farm 321 Elmwood Rd., Lunenburg
(508) 582-6756
Farmstand with a variety of apples. Mums, wreaths, Indian corn are also available.

Lanni Orchards 294 Chase Rd., Rte. 13, Lunenburg
(508) 582-6246
Pick your own apples, cider mill, homemade pies, herbal vinegars. Daily, 9am.-6 pm.

Hawk Hill Orchards West Main St. & Carleton Rd., Millbury
(508) 865-4905
Pick your own apples, peaches, plums and country store with jams, jellies, pies, cider.
"Hawk Hill has good apples," Michael T. Macnultz

Stowe Farm Orchards and Stables 15 Stowe Rd., Millbury
(508) 865-4818
Pick your own apples, beautiful setting on what is the oldest farm in Millbury. Unique petting zoo, country store, apple pies, jellies and candies, Sept.- end of Dec.
"Nearby, quaint, affordable fun with variety of offerings for children and families," Sandra Ellis, Worcester, MA.
"It has a beautiful meadow and horses," Megan Tamalavitch, Worcester, MA.

Brookfield Orchards 12 Lincoln Road, off Rtes. 67 and 31, North Brookfield
(508) 867-6858
Open year round. Apple picking in Sept.-Oct., cross-country skiing in winter. Trails marked for novice, intermediate, expert, picnic areas available. Country Store, apple dumplings, pies, fresh cider, cheddar cheese, gift baskets.
"It was so much fun picking apples and the kids would stuff themselves with their favorite kind of apple. The only time we would allow our children candied apples was at the orchard. It always remained a favorite treat. The gift shop is also very unusual with its many natural displays and lots to see and fun for browsing, and penny candy too! Apple dumplings to die for!" Doris Richard, Worcester, MA.

Tougas Family Farm   246 Ball St., Northborough
(508) 393-6406
Pick your own fruits in season. Numerous apple varieties, kitchen with fresh pie, ice cream, coffee and wonderful homemade strawberry donuts. Kid's Hay Mow play area, barnyard animals and wagon rides.
"Picking berries is very soothing. You're outside and the conversation in the other rows is always fascinating. Plus the freezer has berries for months after a visit," Jean M. Langley, Boylston, MA.
"Tougas Family Farm is a fun filled relaxing way to spend an afternoon enjoying the splendor of the trees, the plump pumpkins and the juicy apples," Lynn Marie Carroll.

Red Apple Farm   Highland Ave., Phillipston
(508) 249-6763
Pick your own apples. Dozens of apple varieties and hay rides during foliage season.

Clearview Farm   4 Kendal Hill Rd., Sterling
(508) 422-6442
Pick your own apples, peaches, raspberries & pumpkins. Stand is open 10am-6pm at the start of peach picking season. Honey and cider sales as well. Hay rides and seasonal produce available.

Old Oak Apple Farm   182 Justice Hill Cutoff, Sterling
(508) 422-8303
Pick your own apples. Fresh vegetables, gourds and pumpkins. Open Sat.-Sun. and holidays 10am-5pm. Call for further directions.

Breakneck Farm   21 South Rd., Sturbridge
(508) 347-5620
Farm stand and "Made in Massachusetts" specialty foods. Pick your own pumpkins in fall. Open Jan. & Feb., Wed-Sun, 10am-6pm, starting in March, open daily 9am-7pm. Call for further direcitons.

Keown Orchards Farm Stand   9 McClellan Rd., Sutton
(508) 865-6706
Open mid-July through Christmas, 7 days a week. Pick-your-own apples from Labor Day, Pumpkin Patch open weekends in Oct.; Christmas trees, and special festivals, Peach Party, etc. School groups welcome, wagon rides.
"The Keown family has owned this farm for 70 years, although it was operated for 200 years before they acquired it...the specialty remains more than 60 varieties of apples — many antique or Massachusetts cultivars and over a dozen kinds of peaches and nectarines."

Breezelands Orchards 1791 Southbridge Rd., Warren
(413) 436-7100
100-acre farm, 10,000 trees, harvesting 30,000 bushels of apples annually. Pick-your-own apples; 20 varieties from all over the world. Gift baskets shipped; fresh pressed cider, peaches, pears, corn, honey. Kids can ride the hobby horse, pet the bunnies and choose pumpkins for Jack-O'lanterns. Call for hours and directions.

Ragged Hill Orchard John Gilbert Rd., West Brookfield
(508) 867-2187
Pick your own apples. Children welcome. Apples, cider, jam sales as well.

Arnold's Orchards 15 Spring Rd. (Rte. 135 to Upton Rd. to Spring Rd.), Westborough
(508) 366-2845
Second orchard on high hill above Mass. Pike bridge. Hiking trails, pick your own apples (several varieties) and pumpkins. Group picking and children welcome. Farm animals petting area, apple and cider sales.

Harvey's Farm & Garden Center 120 South St., Westborough
(508) 366-1545
Pick your own apples, organically grown. Pick your own berries in season. Barnyard critters, hay rides, gift barn birthday parties arranged. Open Apr. 1-Jan. 1, 9am-6pm daily.

Nourse Farm Strawberry Fields 80 Nourse St. (Rte. 30), Westborough
(508) 366-2644
Pick luscious strawberries in the sun, also raspberries, blueberries; farm store with corn, vegetables; hayrides, pick-your-own pumpkins, also farm-raised turkeys.

Parks, Playgrounds & Recreational Areas

Auburn Recreation Center Oxford St., Auburn
(508) 832-7701
Outdoor recreational area, great for sledding, soccer, basketball, baseball fields, Rocket Land playground is located here as well. Call Town Clerk's office for directions.
"It's a fun place to go with your friends so you can act like a kid again," Kate Casavant, Oxford, MA.
"It's so much fun - you can roller blade or bike ride and there is a playground," Navah Meller (age 8), Worcester, MA.

Goddard Park Near Auburn Public Library at 369 Southbridge St., Auburn
(508) 832-7701
Two-acre park, benches, shade trees, waterway with dam, falls. Model of Robert Goddard's first rocket, and a Polaris A2 rocket.

South Commons Off Rte. 62, South St., located off South St., Berlin
(508) 838-2931
Tennis, basketball, soccer and baseball fields. Call Town Clerk's office for further directions.

Derby Land Off Berlin Rd. at Emerson School, Bolton
(508) 779-2771
Soccer fields and playground. Call Town Clerk for further directions.

Morningdale Manor Orient St., off Rte. 70, Boylston
Playground and baseball field.

Central Parks Church St., Clinton
Walking, bike riding, benches in the center of town. Nice area for children to bike.

Clinton High School Church St., Clinton
Baseball, football fields.

Clinton Middle School Rte. 110, Clinton
Playground, soccer fields, jogging, softball fields.

Fuller Field High St., Clinton
Sports fields, football, baseball, softball, field hockey.

Vale St. Playground Vale St., Clinton
Softball and little league fields.

Nichols College Center Rd., Dudley
(508) 943-1560
Outdoor tennis and volleyball. Check with the school for utilization of gym, basketball courts and football field. Call for further directions.

The Fun Zone Community Playground Rte. 197, West Main St., behind Dudley Elementary School, Dudley
Newly constructed playground for children.

Coggshall Park 244 Mt. Elm Rd. off Electric Ave., Fitchburg
(508) 345-9550
Lake Mirror, hiking trails, picnicking, swans, fountain, playground, lake, skating in winter, (warm up at the Stonehouse). Park renovated in 1994. Contact the Town Clerk's office for further directions.
"In the winter you can go ice skating; spring, you can look at the pretty flowers ...summer, you can watch a band concert, buy a hot dog, popcorn, soda from the vendor man, have a family picnic, feed the ducks; fall you can collect pinecones, view the foliage...they even have a playground for kids. It's a nice place for memories of good times and learning about nature," Laura Anderson, Fitchburg, MA.
"Provides a peaceful setting away from the noise and bustle of the city," Jean C. McCarthy, Fitchburg, MA.

Coolidge Park John Fitch Highway, Fitchburg
Ball fields, football field, soccer, jogging track. Call Town Clerk's office for further directions.

Dawson Recreation Area Salisbury St., Holden
Outdoor swimming pool, baseball field, basketball, tennis courts and playground area.

Mountview School 270 Shrewsbury St., Holden
Soccer, baseball, softball fields, tennis and basketball courts, permit needed.

Ralcigh B. Bubar Building 1128 Main St., Holden
Building has gymnasium and can be rented, contact the DPW (829-0249), grounds have a soccer and baseball fields and playground area, gazebo for concerts.

Mellen St. Playground Mellen St., Hopedale
Playground area for children, softball and basketball area.

Kid's Kingdom Playground Rte. 2A, Mass Ave., Lunenburg
Children's playground, newly constructed. Near T.C. Passios Elementary School.

Marshall Park Rte. 2A, Mass Ave., Lunenburg
Sports field, soccer, baseball and jogging track.

Fino Field Off Sumner St. which is off Main St., Milford
Two baseball fields and a football field, outdoor pool. Swimming lessons through the Recreational Department.
"Milford's first large athletic field, built after WWII to honor Milford boys in the war. Named after Rudoph Fino, the first boy from Milford to be killed...lighted baseball and football field...swimming pool," Lyn Lovell, Milford, MA.

Town Park Congress St., Milford
Tennis, basketball, baseball, playground, summer concerts.

East Millbury Park Wheelock Ave., Millbury
Baseball fields, basketball courts and a tot lot play area for children.

Elmwood St. Field Elmwood St. (Elmwood Street School), Millbury
Basketball courts, soccer field and swing set.

Greenwood St. Playground Greenwood St., near Rte. 20, Millbury
Baseball, softball fields, basketball and tennis courts, swings and slides.

James Direnzo Playground Millbury Ave. (near Dorothy Landing), Millbury
Basketball court and tot lot play area for children.

Millbury Memorial Jr.-Sr. High School Field Martin St., Millbury
Football and baseball fields, open field track, tennis courts.

Thomas E. Morey Memorial Park Washington St. Park, Millbury
Wooly World Playground is located here, as well as, lighted little league field, soccer field, basketball court, restrooms and concession stand.

West Millbury Playground West Main St. (Northeast of Oxford Rd.), Millbury
Softball, soccer fields, basketball court and swing set.

Windle Field **Canal St. (at Canal St., Elm St. and Providence Rd.), Millbury**
Lighted football/soccer field, baseball, tennis courts and a tot lot play area for children.

Assabet Park **Rte. 135, South St., Northborough**
Playground, basketball, wading pool, picnic table, parking.

Ellsworth/McAffe Park **Rte. 135, South St., Northborough**
Playground, soccer fields, volleyball, pavilion, picnic, concerts at the gazebo in summer, life exercise stations area, sledding, parking.

Vail Field Playground **Crescent St., Northbridge**
Playground, soccer and baseball fields.

Wright Memorial Park **Ware Corner Rd., Oakham**
Baseball, soccer fields, playground area.

Greenbriar Recreation Area **Rte. 12, Oxford**
Tennis, baseball, cross- country skiing, walking trails. A very nice area.

Treasureland Joslin Field **off Church St., Oxford**
Public playground planned and built by community group.

Anna Maria College **Sunset Lane, Paxton**
(508) 849-3341.
Gym, basketball, 2 soccer fields, baseball/softball open for public use. Call for reservations.

Dean Park **Main St., Shrewsbury**
It's got all the necessary 4 season park things and close to good food for a picnic pickup. Baseball, softball fields, tennis, walking and cross-country skiing.
"It is there that stillness and beauty abound, it's invisible walls are impervious to violence and only love dwells there," Judith K. Aplowe Gilbert, Worcester, MA.

Shrewsbury Parks and Recreation
Shrewsbury
(508) 845-9121
For information on areas, permits for tennis, contact the Recreation Dept.

Globe Village Recreation Area **West St., Southbridge**
Heritage nature trail starts here. Baseball, softball, soccer and field hockey fields, tennis and Tot Lot play area.

Henry Street Field **Henry St., Southbridge**
Basketball, softball, baseball fields, tennis and playground.

McMahon Park **Dresser St., Southbridge**
Basketball and tennis courts, track, football and baseball fields.

Morris Street Field **Morris St., Southbridge**
Little league fields, basketball and tennis, playground.

Sterling Memorial Area   Cross St., Sterling
Gazebo for band concerts, weddings, etc., also location for the Christmas tree lighting ceremony.

West Sterling Park   Princeton Rd., Rte. 62, Sterling
Tennis courts and ball fields.

Taft Memorial Park   Hecla St., Uxbridge
Baseball field, basketball, tennis, jogging track and playground area.

Town Park   Marywood St., Uxbridge
Playground for children.

Cutter Park   West Main St., Warren
Playground area and youth size baseball fields.

Gendron Park   Dean St., Warren
Baseball field, walking area.

Quaboag Regional High School   Old West Brookfield Rd., Warren
Athletic fields, tennis.

West Boylston Pride Park   Crescent St. (adjacent to Major Edwards Elementary School),West Boylston
Playground area, tennis, baseball, town pool, wading pool, jogging track, football, soccer, nature trail.
"*Best playground,*" Kyle McDonald, Boylston, MA.

Fales Elementary School   Eli Whitney St., Westborough
Playground area for children.

Haskell Street Playground   Haskell St., Westborough
Basketball, tennis, soccer and baseball fields, playground area and walking.

Hastings Elementary School   East Main St., Westborough
"Pipe Dreams" style playground for children.

Tot Lot   Ruggles St., Westborough
'Pocket size' playground area just right for toddlers.

Boynton Park/ Cascades Park   Off Mower St. (out of Tatnuck Sq. near Worcester/Paxton line), Worcester
Softball, playground, picnic area. Park at Boynton Park, follow posted signs to trails leading to Cascades Park, a beautiful waterfall, watch for "No Trespassing" signs protecting Worcester's watershed.
"*Easy to get to. Quiet, scenic, good inexpensive family hiking, picnicking area,*" Brenda McCann, Worcester, MA.

Christoforo Columbo Park Shrewsbury St., Worcester
Entrance marked by historic lion statues from former Union Station. Also known as East Park. Football, little league, softball, boccie court, baseball, basketball, tennis and playground.
"It's where I grew up and they've made a lot of improvements; new lights, walking paths and concerts," Mary A. D'Argenis, Worcester, MA.

Elm Park Park Ave. and Elm St. Street, Worcester
Designed by Olmstead, it is the nation's first public park, ducks, geese, arched bridges, children's playground, ice skating in winter. Picturesque, picnic grove, basketball and monuments too.
"It has it all, history in spades, natural beauty, outdoor concerts, ice skating, and people from every corner of the earth playing with their children, and their children playing together. It is truly the heart of the heart of the commonwealth," Libby Westie.
"Ice skating under the lights at Elm Park- romance!" Margaret M. and William Moynihan, Dennis, MA.
"It's beautiful in the summer with all it's flowers and shrubbery. A place to think and relax and it's the oldest park in the US," Terry Doyle, Holden, MA.
"Feeding the ducks, typically New England," Helen A. Sachs, Worcester, MA.

Green Hill Park Skyline Dr., Worcester
(508) 779-1290
Playground, picnic area, barnyard zoo and public golf course. This park is the location of many annual special events in Worcester. Little league and volleyball area also. For information on public tennis courts, telephone the Worcester Recreation Department.
"It's the jewel of commonwealth. Beauty all times of the year," Patricia A. Murphy-Knights, Worcester, MA.
"It is the best place to go sledding during the long, snowy weekends and especially on snow days off from school. You will meet wonderful families from all over Worcester County. Everyone is having so much fun! It brings out the kid in me when I spend a day at Green Hill Park with my children. Also, they have the Barnyard Zoo, which is a fun place to visit," Stephanie Ann Bourgeois, Manchaug, MA.

Hadwen Park Heard St., Worcester
Football, baseball, basketball, tennis, shuffleboard, playground and sledding.
"It's got everything I like. Baseball field, basketball court, beautiful quiet woods, a river to fish in, a great place for a cookout, a marsh with water fowl. It's Worcester's best kept secret," Jaime Grimes, Worcester, MA.

Institute Park Salisbury St., Worcester
Football, three tennis courts, band stand for summer concerts.

Lake Park Lake Ave. (on Lake Quinsigamond), Worcester
Football field, softball, baseball, basketball, playground.
"Circular track - entire perimeter a great mile walk or run. You get a good mile walk on one complete rotation and most of it is in view of the lake. In early morning the sunlight can be seen dancing off the water and the college rowing teams sing their merry cadences as they do their practice runs... a delightful, soul-filling way to exercise," Jean C. Lorusso, Worcester, MA.

Quinsigamond Community College 670 West Boylston St., Worcester
(508) 854-4317
Soccer, jogging, walking, the best hill around for sledding and with membership you can utilize the gym, basketball and indoor pool. Call for further information and directions.

Ponds, Lakes, Rivers & Reservoirs

Tully Lake St. Recreation Area Rte. 32, Athol / Orange
(508) 249-4551
Lake fishing, boat ramp, small motorized boats allowed, picnicking, grills, no swimming. For directions call the town clerk of Athol.

Auburn Town Beach Gleason Park off Central St., Auburn
(508) 832-7813
Swimming, swim programs available through the Auburn Parks Dept, boat ramp off Eddy Pond.

Eddy Pond Off Rte. 52, Cedar St., Auburn
A paved boat launching ramp and parking area can be found off of Rte. 52, on Short Rd. Best fishing is in early spring.

Quabbin Reservoir Visitors Center Off Rte. 9, Belchertown (near Ware)
(413) 323-7221
Although the Visitors Center isn't in Worcester County, much of the Quabbin is, and this is a good place to learn about rules of visiting this "accidental wilderness." The Quabbin is a man-made reservoir, and has hiking trails, bird and eagle watching, and fishing (no swimming, hunting or pets). Advance notice is required for student and other groups. The observation tower offers a great view of the whole reservoir. Call for information on hunting, fishing and special programs. Open 8:30 am-4:30 pm 7 days a week.

Breezy Picnic Grounds and Waterslides 538 Northwest Main St., Whitins Reservoir, off Rte.16 and West St., Douglas
(508) 476-2664
Two 300' waterslides, picnics, swimming in the Whitins Reservoir, video games, snack bar, restrooms and changing facilities. Family and company outings welcomed. Call for hours and further directions.
"*It's fun for all ages! It's a lovely clean swimming lake, grass picnic grounds and two waterslides,*" Geri Fuhrmann, Holden, MA.

Douglas State Forest Wallum Lake Rd. (Mass Pike to exit 10, Rte. 395 south, Rte. 16 east for 5 miles, follow signs), Douglas
(508) 476-7872
4,595 acres, swimming in Wallum Lake, showers, picnic areas, fishing, boating, boat ramp, hiking, horseback riding, hunting, x-country skiing, canoeing, horseback riding, leashed pets allowed, interpretive programs, snowmobiling, walking. Cedar Swamp boardwalk trail. Call for hours and direction.
"*It is the best pristine area in Mass.-recreation for picnics, horse trails, bike trails scenery,*" U.K. Douglas, MA.

Dunn Pond State Park   Rte. 101, Gardner
(508) 632-7897
115 acres, boating, boat ramp, canoeing, cross-country skiing, fishing, hiking, leashed pets allowed, interpretive programs (seasonal), picnicking, swimming, walking, restrooms, handicapped accessible, call for further directions.

Silver Lake   Rte. 140, Grafton
Lake swimming, beach area, picnicking, concession stand.

Hardwick Pond   Hardwick Pond Rd., Hardwick
Fishing, boating, boat ramp.

Bare Hill Pond   Off Pond Rd., Harvard
Boating, fishing, swimming, ice skating, nature walks, 320 acres.

Asnacomet Pond   Just off Rtes. 68 & 62, Hubbardston
Also known as "Comet Pond." Swimming for town residents in summer. One of the most popular trout ponds in Central Massachusetts. A paved ramp for boat access is located just off Rte. 62, there is also good shoreline access here.

Brigham Pond   Off Rte. 68, Wachusett Road & Depot Rd., Hubbardston
Warm water pond is the headwater for the West Branch of the Ware River. Car-top or small trailer boats can be launched off a gravel ramp located off of Wachusett Rd. Shore access is available in the area between the dam and ramp area.

Moosehorn Pond   Old Princeton Rd., off Rte. 68, Hubbardston
Access to this 62 acre pond is provided by a gated public ramp off Hubbardston Rd. for car-top boats and canoes. Shore access is available in the area of the ramp and off the railroad track on the east side of the pond.

Fort Pond   Lunenburg Rd., north of Rte. 2, Lancaster
Boat access for fishing is available at a gravel ramp off of Fort Pond Rd. Shoreline access is limited to the area immediately adjacent to the ramp. Fort Pond is a managed trout pond.

Louisa Lake   Dilla St., Milford
Row boats, fishing, no motorized boats allowed.

Lake Lashaway   North on Rte. 9, North Brookfield
293-acre warm water pond. Boat access is available through a paved ramp at the north end of the pond off of Harrington St. Shore access is limited to the area adjacent to the ramp and along Rte. 9.

Little Chauncey Pond   Lyman St., Northborough
Located just north of Big Chauncey Pond, this small 45-acre pond offers an opportunity to fish in a relatively unspoiled, tranquil setting. Boat access off Lyman St. is a dirt ramp suitable for small boats and canoes.

Buffumville Reservoir   Putnam Rd., Oxford / Charlton
Putnam Rd. bisects the reservoir into a 265-acre north basin and a 186-acre south basin. Boats can be launched at the north end of the south basin off Putnam Rd. Public swimming area is found on the east shore of the north basin. Shore fishing is accessible along the entire reservoir.

Paradise Pond   Off Rte. 31, (2 miles northeast of Princeton center), Princeton
A dirt boat launch is available for canoes and car-top boats. Limited parking.
"Meditation is possible here, spirits live there and every season has its own beauty," Mary Garvin, Northborough, MA.

Tully Reservoir Area   Rte. 32, Royalston
Fishing, ice skating, cross-country skiing, parking, boat ramp.

Long Pond   Rte. 122, Rutland
Fishing, boating. Boat ramp available.
"Great place to go fishing, relax. Scenery is beautiful, peaceful," Linda L. Fielding, Worcester, MA.
"What an awesome spot to be at on a Sunday morning with a cup of coffee and newspaper in hand, while husband and kids fish nearby," Donna Cobb, Holden, MA.
"Every year I take my boys fishing here - we bring our inflatable boat and motor to a great spot where we swing off a rope high over the water and take the plunge." L. Abramoff, Worcester, MA.

Rutland State Park   Rte. 122-A, Rutland
(508) 886-6333
1,420 acres surrounding Whitehall Pond, boating, canoeing, cross-country skiing, fishing, swimming, hiking, hunting, picnicking, snowmobiling, restrooms, scenic viewing area, walking, leashed pets allowed. Lifeguard not on duty after Labor Day, but Park remains open. Car-top boats and canoes can be launched off Whitehall Road. Call for hours and directions.
"We held our first annual Tatnuck Bookseller company outing here, - 150 people came and I think we left two or three behind," Larry Abramoff, Worcester, MA.

Ware River Access   Rte. 122, Rutland / Barre
88 acres, boating, shore fishing, nature walks; canoeing from Rte. 122 bridge crossing between Rutland and Barre, boat ramp.

Howe State Park   Howe Rd., Spencer
(508) 885-2320
Swimming, shore fishing, picnic area with grills, horseback riding, walking trails.
"Spencer's finest, quietest and most relaxing spot... it relieves stress and calms the nerves...I feel like a whole new person...marked trails for nature walks where you can find beaver, porcupine, deer, birds, and more...you can camp there also...the lake is always stocked, and there are many open spaces for the unskilled fisherman." Jason Marhefka, Spencer, MA.
"I am reluctant to share this treasured spot. What a place of peace and tremendous beauty, especially in the spring and summer. I particularly enjoy the 1/2mile walk into the sanctuary. The no-auto distance helps me feel more detached and removed from the

hustle of my work day. The sound of the running water through the old mill; the fragrance of the flowers and the flowering shrubs; the tranquillity of the pond — a true resting place," Joe Verla, North Uxbridge, MA.

Spencer State Forest Howe Pond Rd. (Rte. 9 west to Rte. 31 south to Howe Pond Road), Spencer
(508) 886-6333
965 acres, canoeing, cross-country skiing, fishing, hiking, historical site, horseback riding, hunting, picnicking, restrooms, scenic viewing area, snowmobiling, swimming, walking.

Sholan Park Swett Hill Rd., Sterling
East Lake Waushacum, off Swett Hill Rd., swimming (for Sterling residents only), boating, ice skating.

West Waushacum Pond Worcester Rd. to Gates Rd., Sterling
142-acre cold water pond is located on the Wachusett Reservoir watershed. A popular stocked trout pond in Worcester County. No boat ramp, but car-top boats and canoes can be lifted over the guard rail along Gates Road.

Big Alum Pond off Clark Rd., Sturbridge
195 acre lake. Its shoreline is 80% developed with year-round homes and summer cottages. Shore fishing is somewhat limited.

Wells State Park Walker Pond Rd., off Rte. 49, Sturbridge
(508) 347-9257
59 camp sites, 1,470 acres, boating, canoeing, boat ramp, camping, cross-country skiing, fishing, hiking, historical site, horseback riding, hunting, interpretive programs (seasonal), leashed pets allowed, restrooms, scenic viewing area, showers, snowmobiling, swimming, walking trails, trailer/RV.

Manchaug Pond Manchaug Rd., Sutton
Fishing, boat ramp located on Manchaug Rd.

Otter River State Forest & Lake Dennison Recreation Area, Templeton /Baldwinville
(508) 939-8962
1,220 acres, 100 campsites, cross-country skiing, fishing, hiking, hunting, interpretive program (seasonal), picnicking, restrooms, snowmobiling, swimming and walking trails. Call for directions.

Wildwood Lake Off Rte. 140 & Williams St., Upton
Bass are the game fish here. Car-top boats and canoes may be launched at a town park off Williams St. Shore access at this park is available and along Rte. 140.

Blackstone River and Canal Heritage State Park East Hartford Ave , Uxbridge
(401) 762-0250 (508) 278-6486
1,005 acres, canoeing, cross-country skiing, hiking, historical site, leashed pets allowed, picnicking, scenic viewing area and walking trails. The Blackstone Valley is "history with a view," Includes mills, villages, canal remnants, greenways, etc. Contact the Visitors

Center for historic sightseeing tours by car, foot, riverboat or canoe. Once called the "hardest working river in the world," the Blackstone begins in Worcester and flows through two dozen Massachusetts and Rhode Island towns. In 46 miles it drops 438 feet, which made the river an excellent source of water power. (Directions: Mass Pike to exit 11, Rte. 122 south to N. Uxbridge, set of lights, left onto East Hartford Ave., follow signs.)
"The 1100 acres in Northbridge and Uxbridge... the pastoral beauty of the views from look-out rock, the canal lock at Goat Hill, the serenity of a canal walk at Riverbend Farm," Spaulding R. Aldrich, Whitinsville, MA.

Pout Pond Off West Hartford Ave., Uxbridge
Swimming, picnicking and shore fishing.

Comins Pond Comins Pond Rd., Warren
For a cooling swim, fishing or a leisurely walk around its boundaries.

Memorial Beach Thompson Rd., Webster
Swimming, picnic area.

Webster Lake Lakeside Ave. (I-290, to Rte. 52, Exit 1), Webster
Boating, limited shore fishing, swimming. The Indian name is Lake Chargoggagomanchauggagoggchubunagungamaugg (longest geographic name in the U.S.) translation: *"I fish on my side of the lake, you fish on your side, and no one fishes in the middle."* Boat launching area on Memorial Beach Drive.

Wachusett Reservoir Access off Rtes. 12, 140, 110 & 70, West Boylston / Boylston / Clinton/ Sterling
(508) 792-7270; (508) 365-3272; (508) 368-0474
This reservoir is bordered by 37 miles of shoreline. A wonderful place for walking, hiking, cross-country-skiing and snowshoeing. Absolutely no boats may be put on the reservoir and no ice fishing is allowed. Shore fishing is allowed in zoned areas, stocked with trout in the spring. For further informational and directions contact the Mass. Div. of Fisheries & Wildlife.
"The water, the walking trails, the wildlife, the dam, and all the town around it," Kris Hillenburg, Clinton, MA.
"Always beautiful all seasons! A little country atmosphere, always tranquil," C.C. Doe, West Boylston, MA.
"It's my favorite because of its unique walking trails," Cynthia Cannon, Sterling, MA.

Lake Wickaboag Off Rte. 9, West Brookfield
More than 300 acres, close to the center village, surrounded by seasonal and year round homes. Swimming, boating, fishing.
"Probably West Brookfield's most important asset," Pat Turner, West Brookfield, MA.

Lake Chauncy Lyman St., off Rte. 9, Westborough
Beach swimming, parking and volleyball area. One of the most consistently fished warmwater ponds in central Massachusetts. 185 acres, access for boats off Lyman St. gravel ramp. Shore access is along the southern and eastern shores. Largemouth bass are abundant.

Sandra Pond Upton Rd., Westborough
Skate and fish on this trout-stocked pond. Fishing derby open to the public is held here each fishing season.

Suasco Project Mill Rd., on Mill Pond, Westborough
Car-top boats can be launched for fishing. Ice skating in winter.

Leominster State Forest Princeton Rd., Westminster
(508) 874-2303
4,126 acres, boating, canoeing, boat ramp, cross-country skiing, fishing, swimming, hiking, horseback riding, hunting, historical site, leashed pets allowed, restrooms, walking trails, picnicking, snowmobiling, scenic viewing area.
Crow Hill outcrop has scenic views; and is the only technical rock climbing spot in Worcester County. Paradise Pond great for canoeing, quiet spots along eastern shore; blueberry picking on the islands. Rte. 2 west to Rte. 31 south, look for signs.

Wyman Beach Narrows Rd., Westminster
Beach area for swimming.

Coes Pond 200 Mill St., Worcester
Swimming, lifeguard on duty, restrooms. Car-top boats can be launched at Columbus Park across the lake from the town beach. Shore access is available at Columbus Park, town beach and along Mill St. and at the dam. Rainbow trout are stocked here.

Indian Lake Rte. 122A, Worcester
204-acre warm water pond, swimming, fishing, parking area. A paved boat launching ramp is provided by the city off of Salisbury St. (Rte. 122A).
"*It has everything close to home,*" Marion Bundza, Worcester, MA.

Quinsigamond State Park 10 North Lake Ave., Worcester
(508) 755-6880
51 acres, picnicking, fishing on Lake Quinsigamond, swimming, restrooms, handicapped accessible restrooms, showers, leashed pets allowed.

Recreation Centers

YMCA 55 Wallace Ave., Fitchburg
(508) 343-4847
Swimming pool, racquet ball courts, gym, Nautilus area, free weight room, cardiovascular room, fitness classes, teen center, summer day camp. Mon.-Fri- 5:30 am-9:30 pm; Sat. 7am -7pm; Sun. 8am-5 pm.

Becker College Leicester and Worcester campuses
(508) 791-9241
Athletic facilities available to the public by request.

John Smith Sports Center Sumner St., near Rte. 495, Milford
(508) 634-8080 or (508) 634-8234
42,000 square foot multipurpose facility with soccer as its main highlight; founded by for-

mer premier place kicker for the N.E. Patriots - John Smith, who runs successful soccer clinics. Two indoor soccer arenas are available for leagues, tournaments. Basketball, volleyball, street hockey, facilities, as well as baseball and softball pitching machines, a golf driving range, a miniature golf course, tennis court, lacrosse and field hockey facilities.

Mid-Town Fitness and Racquetball Club 16 Pine St., Milford
(508) 478-3030
Racquetball courts, exercise room, free weights, Nautilus and aerobics. Contact the club for daily guest and membership information.
"Built in 1881 as a music hall, many famous people performed here...later it was a movie theater, now it is a fine racquetball club and has a complete fitness program," Lyn Lovell, Milford, MA.

Northbridge Senior Center Highland St., Northbridge (Whitinsville)
"When you can no longer play baseball, basketball or football, this place is Utopia! It is a place where 32 men shoot league pool each Wednesday and enjoy the competition and friendships!" Maurice J. Murray, Whitinsville, MA.

Whitin Community Center 60 Main St., Northbridge / Whitinsville
(508) 234-8184
Health club, fitness center, racquetball, indoor pool, gym, child care, three lighted tennis courts, exercise room, 11-acre park. Daily guest passes and memberships available. Call for hours, directions and further information.

Paxton Sports Center, Inc. 603 Pleasant St., Paxton
(508) 755-8223
Fitness center with daily guest passes and full memberships available. Indoor heated pool, life cycles, treadmills, stair master, four tennis courts, aerobics, nursery and adult and junior programs. Call for further information and directions.

Petersham Curling Club North Main St., Petersham
(508) 724-3210
Worcester County's only curling club. Indoor curling rink, adult leagues, fall-spring, instruction for juniors available. Curling is a unique 400-year old game, brought to Canada by the Scots Highlanders. The object of the game is to slide a stone over an ice course 138' x 14' 2"; the stone closest to the "button" wins the point; players sweep the ice with brooms to help the stones glide better.

Tri-Community YMCA 43 Everett St., Southbridge
(508) 765-5466
Daily guest passes and memberships are available. Full size gymnasium, indoor pool, strength training area, cardiovascular fitness center, pre-school and youth programs, racquet ball courts, aerobics. Camp Foskitt is used by members and guests in the summer as well. Call for membership information, hours and directions.

Griffin Road Athletic Facility Griffin Rd. at Chocksett Elementary School, Sterling
New playground built in fall 1994, ball fields, track, football and soccer fields.

Friendly House 36 Wall St., Worcester
(508) 755-4362
Friendly House serves children ages 5-15, Tot Lot program, teen programs, basketball leagues, from age 9, and lots more.
"I can just chill with my friends or play basketball," Colonel Boothe, age 13, Worcester, MA.

Jewish Community Center (JCC) 633 Salisbury St., Worcester
(509)756-7109
Recreational facility for the entire family, pre-school and toddler child care center. After-school child care program with transportation from selected neighborhood schools. Indoor and outdoor pools, squash, recquet ball and outdoor tennis, Nautilus fitness center, extensive aerobics program, summer day camp, sports specialty camp, ptograms for older adults. Call for membership information.

YMCA - Central Branch 766 Main St., Worcester
(508) 755-6101
Daily guest passes and memberships available. Indoor pool, racquetball, squash, handball, tennis, basketball courts. Rock climbing gym and Nautilus program center with the latest in exercise equipment. Call for hours and directions.
"At the YMCA is a climbing wall. I love rock climbing," Naomi Meller, age 11, Worcester, MA.

YMCA - Greendale Family Branch 75 and 100 Shore Dr., Worcester
(508) 852-6694
Guest passes and full memberships are available. There are programs, activities for the entire family. Child care, nursery school, swimming pools and lessons, kids gym, tennis, basketball, floor hockey, aerobics, summer camps, and much more. Wonderful programs for 'active' older adults, call for further information, hours and directions.

YWCA of Central Massachusetts 1 Salem Square, Worcester
(508) 791-3181
Guest and memberships are available. There are several 'drop-in' programs and activities, as well as fitness and wellness classes, swimming lessons for all ages, aerobics and more. Call for further information, hours and directions.

Roller Skating

Roll-On-America Rte. 2, Exit 34, Lancaster
(508) 534-8303
Public skating, private parties, indoor mini-golf, laser tag facility and much more for the whole family. Call for hours and directions.

Cheap Skate Rte. 12, Oxford
(508) 987-3561
Roller skating, lessons, rentals, birthday and private parties. Call for hours and directions.

Skylite Roller Skating Center 648 Park Ave., Worcester
(508) 757-8640
Roller skating, lessons, birthday and private parties. Call for hours and directions.

Skiing and Sledding

(Note: For some great places to sled, see the Parks, Playgrounds & Recreational Areas section, most notably Auburn Recreation Center, Green Hill Park and Quinsigamond Community College in Worcester. For more cross-country skiing spots, check these sections: Golf Courses; Forests, Conservation Land & Open Space; Ponds, Lakes Rivers & Reservoirs; Sports Clubs and Wildlife Management Areas.

Pine Ridge   Valley Rd., Barre
(508) 355-6446
Great downhill learn-to-ski and family area, 270' vertical drop, one T-bar, snowmaking, ski school, 2 trails. Call for hours and directions.

Mid State Snow Tubing   Rt. 169 (just off Rt. 20), Charlton
(508) 248-4641
Snow tubes and lift to the top provided. Snowmaking for great sledding conditions. Weekdays 4-9pm, weekends 10am-11pm, vacation and snow days same as above, call for directions.

Country Meadow Farm Sleigh Rides   11 Glover St., Millbury
(508) 865-2675
Horse-drawn sleigh and hay rides by appointment only, birthday parties, country gift shop, Christmas room open year round, call for hours and directions.

Brookfield Orchards   12 Lincoln Rd., off Rtes. 67 and 31, North Brookfield
(508) 867-6858
Cross-country skiing on 12 kilometers of groomed trails, snowfall permitting, through March. Adults pay admission. Call for directions.
"*Brookfield Orchards in winter — cross-country skiing around the orchard and going in for coffee & doughnut,*" Dr. V. Persons, West Brookfield, MA.

Wachusett Mountain   Mountain Rd., Princeton
1-800-SKI-1234 for snow conditions; (508) 464-2300
Downhill skiing with new high speed detachable quad chair lift plus 1 triple chair, 1 double chair, 1 pony lift, 1 Poma Lift. 100% snowmaking on all trails, Ski Magazine recently rated Wachusett among the best in New England for snowmaking and grooming. Rentals, lessons for all ages, special beginner packages and kids' programs. NASTAR racing, special group rates and corporate outings. The lodge is of post and beam architecture, has four food and beverage locations, a coppertop fireplace in the very center and a ski shop.
"*The ski area in winter is a sheer delight - the best available within a hundred or more miles and only a half hour from downtown Worcester. Seen from the surrounding countryside, Wachusett's profile is an exclamation point in an otherwise featureless view. It is truly a special place, used and cherished by many thousands of people,*" Peter B. Baker, Worcester, MA.
"*It offers great skiing, gorgeous views, and excellent hiking trails,*" Melissa Durfee, Grafton, MA.
"*It has one of the nicest base lodges in the country, plus they just installed a high speed quad chair lift, the only one in Massachusetts,*" W. Lyedecher, Westminster, MA

Wachusett Mountain State Reservation   Mountain Rd., Princeton
(508) 464-2987
"My first choice in cross-country skiing. Why? It's not 'just another' boring flat golf course. It's significant work to ski up it, but the glide down on the closed, unplowed auto road and carriage roads are definitely worth it," Ellen Gugel, Westborough, MA.

Ski Ward   1000 Main St., Rte. 20, Shrewsbury
(508) 842-6346
Downhill skiing with chair lift, T-bars, 2 pony lifts, 2 rope tows, 200' vertical drop, 8 trails, snowmaking, ski school, great learn-to-ski and family area. Call for hours and directions.

Sports Clubs

Auburn Sportsman Club   50a Elm St., Auburn
(508) 832-6492
Private club, but surrounding area is available to the public for hiking, cross-country skiing, snowshoeing and walking. Pond, archery and firing area is for members only. Contact the club for membership information and directions.

North Worcester Fox & Coon Club   399 Masson Rd., Holden
(508) 829-5199
Family-oriented sportsman's club. Public welcome to use the 110 acres for cross-country skiing, snowshoeing, walking. Call for further membership information and directions.

Leominster Sportsman's Association   Elm St., Leominster
(508) 534-9755
209 acres-open to the public, biking, boating, cross-country skiing, fishing, hiking, horseback riding, hunting, ice skating, nature walks, picnicking, snowmobiling, target archery. To join, contact the club or a member.

Bay Path Archers Inc.   243 Guelphwood Rd., Southbridge
(508) 765-9505
Memberships for family, single and juniors (ages 16-17) are available. Special group instructions for Boy & Girl Scouts as well. Call for hours, directions and further information.

Swimming Pools

Note: all pools listed are open from June to late August. Call ahead for specific information, hours and directions.

Philip J. Weihn Memorial Pool   Rte. 110, Clinton
(508) 365-4684
Outdoor state swimming pool, with swimming programs available.

Gustave Johnson Memorial Pool   35 Wanoosnock Ave., Fitchburg
(508) 342-6510-pool
Outdoor state swimming pool, with swimming programs available.

Greenwood Memorial Pool 69 Park St., Gardner
(508) 632-0678
Indoor swimming pool, youth lessons, free senior swim.

Leominster State Pool Viscoloid Ave., Leominster
(508) 537-8268-pool
Outdoor state swimming pool, with swimming programs available.

Sen. P. Eugene Casey Memorial Pool Rte. 140, Milford
(508) 473-5998
Outdoor state swimming pool, with swimming programs available.

Andrew J. Petro Memorial Pool Gilbrater Field, Randolph St., Southbridge
(508) 764-7352
Outdoor state swimming pool, with swimming programs available.

Bennett Field Pool 1260 Main St., Worcester
(508) 792-5515-pool
Outdoor state swimming pool, with swimming programs available.

Dennis F. Shine, Jr. Memorial Pool 184 Providence St., Worcester
(508) 792-0727-pool
Outdoor state swimming pool, with swimming programs available.

Tennis

For tennis court information, refer to these sections: Parks, Playgrounds & Recreational Areas; and Recreation Centers.

Waterfalls

For more information about these waterfalls, see Chapter 12, Royalston.

Doane's Falls Athol Rd., Royalston
200' waterfall, views of cascading Lawrence Brook and Tully Mountain. Mountain biking, cross-country skiing, snowshoeing, hiking and horseback riding.

Royalston Falls Falls Rd. (off Rte. 2 near Athol line), Royalston
Trail is one half mile long leads to falls which drop 70' over a granite ledge The trail is suitable for mountain biking, rock outcrops are perfect for picnicking and contemplation; a very beautiful area.
"A wonderful place in the spring following the snow melt and any time after major rainstorms. The water rushes over a series of falls and on into a tight squeeze where nature shows its tremendous power," William Goss, Shrewsbury, MA.

Spirit Falls Jacob Hill, Rte. 68, Royalston
Located one mile west of Royalston Common. Foot access by forest roadway north from Doane's Hill Rd., just west of bridge over Tully River east branch at base of Doane's Hill. Walking trails, cross-country skiing.

Wildlife Management Areas

Many Wildlife Management Areas listed here are stocked with wildlife for hunting. For further information and directions, call the Mass. Division of Fisheries & Wildlife at the number listed.

High Ridge Wildlife Management Area Rte. 140, parking off Smith and Chapel Sts., Ashburnham / Gardner
(508) 792-7270
2,018 acres, walking, hiking trails, snowshoeing, it is also a pheasant stocked area for hunting.

Millers River Wildlife Management Area Off Rte. 68, Athol / Royalston / Phillipston
(508) 792-7270
2,351 acres for walking, cross-country skiing, snowshoeing.

Barre Falls Wildlife Management Area Off Rte. 56, Coldbrook Rd., Rutland Rd., Barre / Hubbardston / Rutland / Oakham
(508) 792-7270
10,557 acres within four towns, canoe access for the Ware River and Barre Dam. Walking, picnicking, cross-country skiing, snowshoeing and is a pheasant stocked area for hunting.
"...A fun place year round. The beautiful grassy bowl behind the dam is perfect for sunning, trails, including a portion of the Mid-State, invite the nature-lover...well-kept picnic area and covered pavilion that can be reserved for larger groups, several parking areas and rest rooms...There is a stretch of the Ware River where you may put in your canoe. In winter those trails which extend into MDC land beckon the cross-country skier," Albert L. Clark, Barre, MA.

Delaney Wildlife Management Area Access area off Harvard Rd. in Stow, Bolton / Lancaster / Harvard
(508) 792-7270
923 acres crossing three towns. Cross-country skiing, walking and a pheasant stocked area for hunting.

Quaboag Wildlife Area & River System Longhill Rd., Rte. 148, Brookfield / West Brookfield
(508) 792-7270
1,007 acres for nature walks, cross-country skiing, snowshoeing, horseback riding, this is also a pheasant stocked area for hunting. A boat ramp is located at the north end of Quaboag Pond off Shore Rd.
"It is a great place to canoe, fish, bird watch, and it has historical significance," Roger Jones, Holden, MA.
"Excellent for canoeists," William Goss, Shrewsbury, MA.

Richardson Wildlife Management Area   Off Rte. 9, Brookfield /West Brookfield
(508) 792-7270
350 acres, walking, hiking and is a pheasant stocked area for hunting.

Bennet Meadows Wildlife Management Area   Gould Rd., Charlton
(508) 792-7270
281 acres, hiking, walking, cross-country skiing, snowshoeing, stocked pheasant area for hunting.

Hubbardston Wildlife Management Area   Off Rte. 68, Westminster Rd., Hubbardston
(508) 792-7270
600 acres for walking, hiking, cross-country skiing, pheasant stocked area for hunting.

Moose Hill Wildlife Management Area   Paxton Rd., off Rte. 9, Leicester / Paxton / Spencer
(508) 792-7270
552 acres in three towns, cross-country skiing, walking, snowshoeing and is a pheasant stocked area for hunting.

Winimusset Wildlife Management Area   Off Rte. 67, Hardwick Rd. & Thompson Rd., New Braintree
515 acres, hiking, walking, cross-country skiing, snowshoeing and is a pheasant stocked area for hunting.

West Hill, E. Kent Swift Wildlife Management Area   Northbridge / Upton / Mendon / Uxbridge
(508) 792-7270
1,717 acres, for walking, cross-country skiing, snowshoeing and pheasant stocked areas for hunting. Off Rte. 16, (West River St. to Upton Rd. to Pudding St.)

Phillipston Wildlife Management Area   Off Rte. 101, Phillipston / Barre / Petersham
(508) 792-7270
2, 855 acres for walking, cross-country skiing, snowshoeing and is a pheasant stocked area for hunting.

Popple Camp Wildlife Management Area   Popple Camp Rd., near Rte. 101, Phillipston / Petersham
(508) 792-7270
1,232 acres for walking, cross-country skiing, snowshoeing and is a pheasant stocked area for hunting.

Birch Hill Wildlife Management Area   Off Rte. 202, Royalston / Templeton/ Winchendon
(508) 792-7270
3,210 acres, located in three towns, snowshoeing, cross-country skiing, walking, is a pheasant stocked area for hunting.
"Large, undeveloped, almost wilderness area, with very few tourists, except during bird season," Robert Hubbard, Otter River, MA.

Four Chimneys Wildlife Management Area   Off Rte. 31, Borkum Rd., Spencer
(508) 792-7270
200 acres for walking, cross-country skiing, snowshoeing and is a pheasant stocked area for hunting.

Leadmine Wildlife Management Area   Leadmine Rd., Sturbridge
(508) 792-7270
Walking, hiking, cross-country skiing, is a pheasant stocked area for hunting.

Breakneck Brook Wildlife Management Area   Breakneck Rd., Sturbridge / Southbridge
(508) 792-7270
707 acres, walking, hiking, cross-country skiing and snowshoeing.

Westborough Wildlife Management Area   Rte. 135, Westborough / Northborough
(508) 792-7270
428 acres, walking, cross-country skiing, snowshoeing, pheasant stocked area for hunting.

Wildlife Sanctuaries

Note: Wildlife Sanctuaries are open spaces where wildlife is protected. Call ahead for hours and directions.

Cook's Canyon Wildlife Sanctuary   South St., Barre
(508) 355-4638
Two sanctuaries adjoin each other, Cook's Canyon (47 acres) and Williams Woods (12 acres). Trails lead you through forest, meadows to a shallow pond. Programs are offered by the Worcester County Property Office.

Flat Rock Wildlife Sanctuary   Ashburnham Hill Rd., Fitchburg
(508) 355-4638
340 acres includes a unique 'bald' at the highest point, mature beech/forests and sphagnum wetland. Nature trails throughout the sanctuary for wonderful bird watching.

Brigham Wildlife Preserve   North Brigham Hill Rd., Grafton
Nature trails, open fields for cross-country skiing. There is also a canoe launching area off Wheeler Rd.

Oxbow Nature Wildlife Management Area Off Rte. 110 Still River Depot Rd., Harvard
1600 acres, nature walks, beaver houses, is an important habitat area for the threatened species Blanding's turtle, a wonderful area to watch birds, especially the Woodcock mating dance, and you may find some blue spotted salamanders. Also cross-country skiing, snowshoeing.

Lincoln Woods Wildlife Sanctuary Union St., off Rte. 12, Leominster
(508) 464-2712
68-acre sanctuary has six ponds, owned by the Massachusetts Audubon Society. Programs are available through its program office operated by Lincoln Woods.

Brooks Wildlife Management Area East St., Petersham
Nice, quiet hiking trails for bird watching and cross-country skiing. Old growth forest.
"There are no man-made distractions here, just well-marked trails through forest and along the marge of the burbling Swift River. As you tread the pine needle carpeted path, you feel as though you're stepping back in time an find yourself mouthing Longfellow's 'This is the forest primeval, the murmuring pines and hemlocks,'...be on the watch for a sign that points out where the Indians frequently stopped and ground their parched corn in a rock by the side of the trail..." Julie Clark, Barre, MA.

Wachusett Meadow Wildlife Sanctuary 113 Gooodnow Rd., off Rte. 62, Princeton
(508) 464-2712
Trails wind over hills, through forests and fields and through a maple swamp, home to the Crocker Maple, one of the largest sugar maples in the United States. Educational programs year round. Trail maps are available.
"My favorite place is the huge tree at the base of Wachusett Meadow — if you go visit, you'll know why!" Alan Kanner, formerly of Worcester; Susan Sanders, Worcester, MA.
"It has a great frog pond, neat trails, and most of all, the Glacial Boulder to climb on!" Sean McGinn-Murtha, age 11, Worcester, MA.
"A wonderful place to catch your breath and walk where only woodland sounds are heard. Special spots - Crocker Maple (estimated 300 years old), a tiny stream bordered by ferns and a little tree-bordered pond. Over 1000 acres of woods, swamps, rocky uplands and scenic views from Brown Hill," Jo-Ann Sullivan, Northborough, MA.

Millers River Wildlife Management Area Birch Hill Rd. to River Rd., Royalston
Nature trails, bird watching.

Rock House Reservation & Quaboag Wildlife Management Area Rte. 9, West Brookfield
Bird watching, walking trails.
"It is a quiet, peaceful place; one combining beauty of water, flowers, birds and animals, amid 12,000 year old large cave-like rock shelter. A unique spot to enjoy," Gertrude L. Hill, West Brookfield, MA.
"It's my favorite because of its awesome natural beauty and connections to the past," Peggy Miller, West Brookfield, MA.

Broad Meadow Brook Wildlife Sanctuary 414 Massasoit Rd., Worcester
(508) 753-6087
Maintained by the Audubon Society, wildlife preserve, in an urban setting. Six trails winding through 287 acres of marsh, meadow and woodland. Educational programs for both children and adults. Open year-round during daylight hours, closed Mondays.
"The largest inner city sanctuary in the universe, over 270 acres only 10 minutes from City Hall," Larry Abramoff," Worcester, MA.
"The oasis in the center of Worcester i.e. a haven of peace and tranquillity and free during the week for all Worcesterites," Betsy Shapiro, Worcester, MA.

Answers to questions in the Chapter 8 introduction: July 4th fireworks from Boston, Framingham and Worcester can be seen by hiking Mt. Wachusett, as can the annual hawk migration, see Forests, Conservation Land & Open Space: Wachusett Mountain State Reservation, Princeton. For boccie, see Christoforo Columbo Park, Worcester, in the Parks, Playgrounds & Recreational Areas section. For curling, see Recreation Centers: Petersham Curling Club. For a Donald Ross course, see Golf Courses: Wachusett Country Club, Worcester. For the site of the first liquid fueled rocket launch, see Golf Courses: Pakachoag Golf Course, Auburn. Check for hot air ballooning under the Balloon Rides & Flying section. In the Horseback Riding section, Special Equestrians in Jefferson helps handicapped riders. Under Skiing and Sledding, Mid State Snow Tubing in Charlton has a lift to the top. For the only technical rock climbing spot in Worcester County, see Ponds, Lakes, Rivers & Reservoirs: Leominster State Forest, Crow Rock outcrop. For apple and berry picking, see the Orchards/Pick Your Own section, and to see how sap turns into sugar, turn to Maple Sugaring. For the fishing "hot-line," call 1-800-ASK-FISH.

Chapter 9

Sightseeing

As a child my dad would take the back seat out of the car, a blue '53 Plymouth, and pile the kids in back, light up a cigar, and take us for a drive to see the sights and get some ice cream. Seat belts had not yet been invented, and mandated, so Dad avoided jail. We opened all the windows wide to avoid second hand smoke because even at a young age we knew smoking was bad (and smelly). We kids had some great times.

You might know about the views from atop Boylston's Tower Hill Botanic Garden, but have you seen the view from Charlton's Dresser Hill Road? You might know about Worcester's historic Salisbury Mansion, but do you know where the "Whispering Wall" is?

Interesting places that are both easy to see and worth seeing are listed here. A good rule of thumb - if it's a scenic view that you must hike to, it's in Chapter 8 - Recreation. If you can drive to it, it's listed here. For example, the view from the top of Mt. Watatic is in Recreation, because it's a hike; but the spectacular view from Airport Hill in Worcester is listed here, because you can drive there.

Some places like Moore State Park, Tower Hill Botanic Garden, Wachusett Mountain and Wachusett Reservoir are listed in both sections because they offer easily accessible sightseeing and more adventurous hikes. Sightseeing destinations that are more educational in nature, such as museums, are listed in Chapter 10 - Culture.

Listings are grouped by category and town. For example, historic graveyards in Charlton are listed before those in Worcester. We know you'll find places you didn't know about listed here, and if we haven't listed your favorite place for sightseeing, let us hear from you. Send your notes, hot tips and comments to: Favorite Places C/O Tatnuck Bookseller 335 Chandler Street, Worcester, MA 01602 or FAX (508) 756-9425.

Historic Graveyards; Points of Interest (Architectural, Historic, Natural, Religious); Scenic Views: (also Foliage, Gardens; Sightseeing Tours; Winery Tours).

Historic Graveyards

Bay Path Cemetery Dresser Hill Rd.,off Rte. 31, Charlton
"Grizzly Adams of Rocky Mountain fame is buried here. His gravestone features Adams' portrait with his bear, Big Ben," William Hultgren, Charlton.

Old Settler's Burial Grounds Behind Main St. and Bolton Rd., Lancaster
Approval from the DPW or police before entering is required. Revolutionary soldiers are buried here as well as the first marker of John Houghton buried in 1684. There are 270 stones dating between 1684 and 1878. Information on who is buried here listed by the Historical Commission. (508) 368-4355.
"Oldest burial ground in Worcester County," Lancaster Historical Commission.

Rawson Brook Cemetery Main St., Leicester
Very old cemetery.

Spider Gates Off Marshall St., Leicester
"The place is surrounded by natural beauty and folklore tales of death, murder and suspense; it is also a very old cemetery dating back to the 1800's," Lucy Hoisington, Worcester, MA.

Rutland (The Old Burial Ground) Main St.,Rte. 122A (next to churches, primary school),
Rutland
Many 18th century headstones.
"Look closely and you'll find headstones of two 18th century women with the unfortunate first names of "Submit" and "Mindswell," A.L., Rutland, MA.

Beaman Cemetery Rte. 12, West Boylston
A section of the Mount Vernon cemetery, located behind the common in West Boylston.
"It has the oldest stones I've found anywhere!" Evelyn B. Cox, Lubec, Maine.

New Boston Cemetery off Rte. 202, Templeton Line, Winchendon
Gravestones dating back to the 1700's.

The Old Centre Cemetery Hall Rd., Winchendon
Of note is the grave of Eden London, a black Revolutionary War veteran who served in his master's place (see Chapter 12, Winchendon).
"It connects us to the Revolutionary War and helps to educate on Black history, the Continental Army, and the slaves' role in that Army!" Sherrill Murphy, Winchendon, MA.
"Dating back to the 1700's, it is a wealth of historical information about the town. Many gravestones have little stories to tell, like the man who invented sweetened milk for ocean voyages," Jennifer Whitaker, Winchendon, MA.

Hope Cemetery 119 Webster St., Worcester
Chartered in 1853, 18th century graves from the Old Worcester Common cemetery were moved here in the 1960's. Graves of Robert Goddard and women's rights leader Abby Kelly Foster are here.
"It is a beautiful park setting to reflect on life, history, nature and whatever else may be on your mind," Cookie Nelson, Worcester, MA.
"Children's section, historic people dating back over 200 years," John Savastano.

Rural Cemetery   Grove St., Worcester
Dedicated in 1838, burial site of Worcester's most prominent early leaders, Isaiah Thomas, Gov. Levi Lincoln, the Salisburys, the Washburns, the Bancrofts and many more. Wonderfully elaborate monuments.

Worcester Common   Franklin St., Worcester
"Worcester Common is a piece of Worcester's history that has not become lost in the shuffle of the new. The Timothy Bigelow graveyard reminds us of the Revolutionary War, and the giant monument, and the reflecting pool allow your eyes to dance along with the past of Worcester," Hillary Yaffe, age 13, Worcester MA.
"Our Worcester History lies under that ground," Russell G. Hakenson Jr., Worcester, MA.

Points of Interest - Architectural

Barre Common   Barre Center, Rte. 122, Barre
Monuments are found here of the Civil War, World War I & II, Soldier Boy and Vietnam Memorial. On the National Register of Historic places.
"By golly, there's no place like home! There's great dining, a beautiful historic Common, lots of interesting roads off the Common, a wildlife sanctuary, farmer's market, band concerts, historical society building and much more," Mary Ellen Radziewicz, Barre, MA.

Historic Rider Tavern   Stafford St., Charlton
This was a regular stopping place along old stagecoach routes.
"An unchanged coaching inn of the Federal period in a picturesque setting, showing how our ancestors traveled, lodged, drank and were entertained," William Hultgren, Charlton, MA.

Northside Village   Stafford St., Northside Rd., and Cemetery Rd., Charlton
An old one-room schoolhouse is here, near the historic Rider Tavern.
"Northside is a New England gem, whose facets reflect a by-gone era with a contemporary face. Old one-room schoolhouse, an old tavern near an orchard where cider is pressed and crafts people continue their skilled works," William Hultgren, Charlton, MA.

Bigelow Estates   Church and Chestnut Sts., Clinton
From the Bigelow Carpet Mills family, now used by the Holy Rosary church as a rectory.

Sawyer/Philbin House   156 Main St., Clinton
Circa 1763, one of the oldest standing house in Clinton, built by Moses Sawyer.

Hardwick Center   Rte. 32, Hardwick
Beautiful fountain and monuments are located here.
"It's the home of the oldest country fair in the U.S., the epicenter of the latest earthquake, and has beautiful scenery and foliage," Tracey Hahns, Hardwick, MA.
"A perfect balance of 'park land' with historic architecture and country charm - white steepled church, Carnegie Library, fountain and general store," Pamela Beall, Brimfield, MA.

Bulfinch Church First Church of Christ   Town Common, Lancaster
(508) 365-2427
Built in 1816 by famed architect Charles Bulfinch, its bell was cast by Paul Revere. For complete guide to Lancaster's more than 80 historic buildings, (over 300 years of American history in wood and stone) see Lancaster Historical Commission, (508) 368-4355.
"It's the oldest congregation in Worcester County (1653), a beautiful building designed in 1816 by Charles Bulfinch, who also did the State House, Boston. It's a National Historic Landmark and a magic spot," Thomas Wintle, Lancaster, MA.

Downtown Milford's Pink Granite Buildings   Town Hall, 52 Main St., Milford
Milford has a number of historic buildings built from the world famous pink granite quarried locally. In addition to the town hall (1854), they include the police station (1912), the Middle School West and Stacy complex, the Milford Armory on Pearl St., the Thom Block, 89 Main St., and Memorial Hall on School St.
"This great building (Town Hall) is on the National Register, built in 1854 in Italianate architecture, very beautiful," Lyn Lovell, Milford, MA.

First Congregational Church   Main St., Milford
"Built in 1820, a typical lovely New England church," Lyn Lovell, Milford, MA.

Gillon Block   Main St., Milford
"Fancy brickwork and a fine onion tower, built in 1888, on the National Register," Lyn Lovell, Milford, MA.

Irish Round Tower St. Mary's Cemetery   Cedar St., Milford
A replica of one in Ireland, where monks would hide with their precious manuscripts from invading Danes and Norsemen.
"The only one in America, built of Milford granite by Fr. Patrick Cuddihy to keep silent vigil. It is a replica of one in Glenalough, Ireland," Anne L. Lamontagne, Milford, MA.

Little Brick Schoolhouse   Purchase St., Milford
Built in 1832, Milford's oldest school - in operation until 1938.

St. Mary's Church   Winter St., Milford
(508) 473-2000
"The church is an elegant edifice of Milford pink granite in the English Gothic style, built in 1870. It is magnificent," Anne L. Lamontagne, Milford, MA.

Chestnut Street Meeting House and Historic Cemetery   Chestnut St., Millville
An 18th century meeting house built in 1769 and preserved in its original condition.
"This church has been in three different towns (Mendon, Blackstone, Millville) without moving an inch," Margaret Carroll, Millville.

Petersham on the Common   Rte. 32, Main St. and Common St., Petersham
A beautiful common with Town Hall, bandstand, library and Civil War monuments.
"Petersham has some of New England's most beautiful homes and a fantastic old time country store. You can eat there, pick up a few groceries, and even find some unique

gifts," Susan Morrall, Barre, MA.

Royalston Common Rte. 68, Royalston Center, Royalston
Beautifully preserved New England common.
"It is an architectural treasure, beautifully preserved," Allen Young, Royalston, MA.

Sterling Historical Society House Corner of Pine and Maple, Sterling
(508) 422-6139
Call for information on historic buildings and graveyards.

Knowlton Buildings Upton Historical Society Upton
(508) 529-6600
Walking tour outlined in a pamphlet researched by Thomas Gorman of Troop 132 for his Eagle Scout project, available at the Town Clerk's office, cost $1.00. Historic background is given of many area buildings.
"The buildings remind us of our heritage. The Knowlton Hat Factory was world known and sustained the economy of Upton for almost 100 years," Barbara Burke, Upton, MA.

Cornet John Farnum House Mendon St., Rte. 16, Uxbridge
Built between 1710-15; this house was the site of early town meetings. Now home to the Uxbridge Historical Society, it is open the 3rd Sunday of each month from 1-4pm.

Quaker Meeting House (circa)1770 Rte. 146A, Quaker Highway, 3 miles south of town center, Uxbridge
This meeting house exists virtually in its original form. Huge fireplaces heat either side of the main room, while heavy wooden curtains divide the room when lowered for separate worship service. Open Sundays July & August, 2-4pm, Thanksgiving Day for services.

Old Stone Church Rte. 12 & Rte. 140, West Boylston
Built in 1892 with granite from local quarries. This church is located on the Wachusett Reservoir, right on the water's edge, the only remaining building from the original West Boylston.
"A great place to spend a warm summer afternoon or cool fall day or bright spring day. Even beautiful in the winter" Cindy Wilder Worcester, MA.
"Peace & quiet, the most beautiful place to be at sunset," Kelly Gracey, Worcester, MA.
"Close to city yet serene and tranquil enough to feel far away. Great place to lie on a blanket with a good book," Tom Morrissette, Worcester, MA.
"It's so peaceful, has fresh air, no cars or buildings, no noise, no pollution, just nature all over. A great place to pray," John Finn, Worcester, MA.
"Where my wife and I spent our first date. I grew up on Cape Cod and it reminds me of home," Walter Selens, Worcester, MA.

Bancroft Tower Bancroft Hill off Beechmont St., Worcester
A Worcester landmark, this 56' tower is on one of the highest points in the city and resembles a miniature feudal castle. It was built by Stephen Salisbury III in 1900 in memory of Worcester historian George Bancroft.
"I take visiting friends and relatives there all the time. It feels like a piece of English countryside. The view of the city and its surrounding towns is fabulous," Joyce Tamao, Worcester MA.
"The view is amazing," Timothy O'Donnell, Shrewsbury, MA.

"The tower where you can see all of Worcester. I can think and look over the beautiful city," Kim O'Connell, Worcester, MA

Clock Tower Building at Worcester State Hospital Off Rte. 9 and Plantation Street, Worcester
High on a hill, this has been a local landmark for more than a century. Designed in 1877 by Weston & Raud, this Victorian Gothic style structure is built of gneiss rubble trimmed with rock faced granite and red brick. The clock itself is made of cast iron cresting trimmed with pointed arches and polished trefoil columns.

First Unitarian Church 90 Main Street, Worcester
Sidney M. Stone, architect (1851); reconstructed after the 1938 hurricane.

Higgins Armory Museum 100 Barber Ave., Worcester
Now a museum, this structure was the first glass curtain wall building, built as the offices of Worcester's Pressed Steel Co. and to house the personal metalwork collection of company president John Woodman Higgins. Great example of modern architecture's roots, designed by architect Joseph Leland in 1931. (See Chapter 10, Culture- Museums).

Mechanics Hall Main St., Worcester
Designed by architect Elbridge Boyden, in 1855, this Federalist hall has a handsome facade and beautiful, acoustically perfect interior space. (See Culture - Auditoriums).

New Aud, Worcester Memorial Auditorium Lincoln Square, Worcester
(508) 798-8888
Lucius Briggs, Frederic C. Hirons architect (1932). A memorial to all war veterans, hosts various entertainment events. The imposing classical revival building is set on a base of "Deer Island Granite." The upper portion of the structure is faced with Indiana limestone.

Preservation Worcester 20 Washington Sq., Worcester, MA 01604
754-8760
Worcester's many historic buildings have lots of stories to tell, and the best authority on the subject is Preservation Worcester, a group dedicated to preserving Worcester's architectural heritage. To learn more about "the way things were," and to help protect historic buildings from the wrecking ball, contact PW. The group sponsors many informative lectures, seminars and tours annually.

Salisbury Mansion 40 Highland Street, Worcester
(508) 753-8278
Provincial classical mansion built by Stephen Salisbury in 1772, architect, Abraham Savage. Presently restored to how it appeared in the 1830's, the home includes some of the original furnishings. Tours and exhibitions offered by the Worcester Historical Museum and the mansion is available for small group meetings and receptions. Stephen Salisbury II helped found WPI. Stephen III started the Worcester Art Museum.

Union Station Washington Square, Worcester
Watson & Huckel, architects; built between 1909-1911, the station accommodated 162 trains daily in its prime; thousands of troops passed through during WWII. Now vacant, renovation as an inter-modal transportation center is planned. A citizens' group dedicated to saving the station and ensuring its complete restoration is the Union Station

Alliance (508) 795-3456, P.O. Box 218, Worcester, MA 01613-9904.
"It could be what Union Station is in Washington, D.C.!" Claude Wooden, Shrewsbury, MA.
"Despite its ruin, it's still majestic and has a soul," Susan Berthiaume, Worcester, MA.
"Majestic beauty - I've always wished I could live there like a mansion with a circular rotary driveway," Kathy Martinelli, West Boylston, MA.

Vernon Hill Three-Deckers   127-137 Providence Street, Worcester
These triple deckers, circa 1925, are among the city's best. Three-deckers were favored by immigrant families because of their spaciousness; front and back porches, (fresh-air clothes dryers) front parlors and suitability for extended families.

Worcester's Diners   Worcester
Worcester Lunch Car Company was located at 2 Quinsigamond Ave., right across from where the Miss Worcester diner is today. Many Worcester Dining cars are still in operation. (See Chapter 7, Dining for a complete listing).

Worcester City Hall   Main Street, Worcester
Peabody & Stearns, architects (1898); Four story symmetrical rectangular block construction of gray Milford granite. Marble stairway and distinguished council chambers.

Worcester Market   631 Main Street, Worcester
Oreste Ziroli, architect (1914); Believed to be the largest grocery supply store when owned by Providence Public Market Co. Currently the state welfare office. Famous for its steer head ornamentation.

Worcester Polytechnic Institute Alumni Gym Gargoyles   100 Institute Rd., Worcester
Built in 1916, WPI's Alumni Gym features 36 unique gargoyles around the top of the building. Each gargoyle is playing a different sport!

Points of Interest - Historic

Blackstone Canal   Oak Street, behind River Bend Farm, Blackstone
"A place of quiet beauty," Richard T. and Joanne Moore, Uxbridge, MA

Triad Bridge   Visible from Rte. 122 at Blackstone/Millville line, Blackstone
Three different railroad bridges intersect here; one still in use by Providence & Worcester RR.
"If you're lucky, you'll see a train pass," Thomas Bik, Blackstone, MA.

Hassanamisco Indian Reservation   80 Brigham Hill Rd., off Rte. 122, Grafton
(508) 393-2080
State's smallest and oldest Indian Reservation, owned by Nipmuc Council of Hassanamisco band, never owned by settlers. Open to the public in summer for tribal functions, annual Native American Fair held in July. (see Chapter 12, Grafton).

Harvard Historic District Shaker Road, Harvard
(508) 456-3607
Shaker houses built by Harvard's Shaker community. Plain, attractive clapboard houses painted in pastel colors, complemented by stone stairs, barns, and trees.

Rowlandson Garrison Site and Rowlandson Rock Main St., Lancaster
Large pine tree stands where the Garrison was located, which was burned to the ground in 1676 (see Chapter 12, Lancaster).
"Scene of the principal massacre in the Indian attack of 1676. Rowlandson Rock, where captives spent their first night after capture is near the water tank on George Hill.

Johnny Appleseed Birthplace Marker off Mechanic St., near Rte. 2, Leominster
Stone marker at site of Johnny Appleseed's birthplace. He was born John Chapman to Nathaniel and Elizabeth Symond Chapman in 1774 (see Chapter 12, Leominster).

Redemption Rock Rte. 140 "Redemption Rock Trail", Princeton
Look for a state highway historic marker along Rte. 140 heading toward Wachusett Mountain Ski Area. Redemption Rock is on the left side of the highway, and is the spot where a ransom was paid to warriors to release Mary Rowlandson and her son in 1675 (see Lancaster). This spot is also on the route of the Mid-State Trail (see Chapter 8, Recreation).

Sterling Town Common Main St., Rte. 12, Sterling
Statue of Mary's little lamb is located here.
"I often see children and adults admiring and touching the bronze statue ...of a lamb which commemorates the poem, 'Mary had a little lamb...'" - Ruth Hopfman, Sterling, MA.

Winchendon Toy Town Horse Junction of Rtes. 12 and 202, Winchendon
Originally built in 1914 by the Morton E. Converse Co. Toy Manufacturer. The one standing now is a reproduction.
"Depicts the historical nature of the Toy Town image. Great picture opportunity," Burton E. Gould, Jr. Winchendon, MA.
"Giant rocking horse, symbol of 'Toy Town' since 1914. Also great furniture shopping," Lois Regan, Winchendon, MA.

"Whispering Wall" WWI Memorial Lincoln Sq., across from the Worcester Memorial Auditorium, Worcester
Sit at one end of the Memorial's elliptical bench, and you can plainly hear what's baraly whispered at the other end.

Points of Interest - Natural

Rockingstone Park (Cradle Rock) Rockingstone Rd., Barre
Large glacial boulder deposited on rock ledge. Used to rock in the 1800's, required large team to stabilize, 2 miles N.W. of Barre Common, Rte. 122 left on Old Dana Rd., right on Rockingstone.

Rollstone Boulder Fitchburg Common, Fitchburg
Giant glacial granite rock, once perched atop Rollstone Hill. Moved to safer location on the common by dynamiting it, removing the pieces, and reassembling it on the Common.

Tantiusques Reservation Site Leadmine Rd., Sturbridge
Site of first mine in New England, and possibly the country. Lead, or graphite was mined here beginning in 1641. (see Sturbridge).

Points of Interest - Religious

Cross 33 Harty Rd. (from Barre Common, take School St., to Harty Rd.), Barre
A cross 200 feet long, 25' wide, with words of the Ten Commandments painted in 3' high letters easily seen from the air. Built by John P. Harty, in answer to a "voice."
"It is surrounded by wooded land in the quiet country, and I pray where only a few special people come out.," Raymond M. Cyr, Hubbardston, MA.

St. Joseph's Abbey 167 North Spencer Rd., Rte. 31, Spencer
(508) 885-3901; 885-3010
Trappist monastery, offering community Mass Mon.-Fri. at 6:25 am, and on Sat. and Sun. at 7am. The Abbey is is located high on a hill with wonderful views. The monks are the makers of Trappist Preserves, 11 flavors sold in grocery stores and the Abbey gift shop. Shop hours are Mon.Sat. 9am-4:30pm and Sunday 1-4:30pm. Call for further information.
"You experience exquisite beauty and unrivaled tranquillity at this Trappist Monastery where you hear monks' heavenly chanting. A great stress-buster for believers and atheists alike," Joan McGinn, Worcester, MA.
"Both the marvelous design of the Abbey interior/exterior and the way it is placed on a hilltop is magnificent ...peaceful in all seasons, rabbits that are wild graze unafraid by the entrance drive," Sue M. Leonard Hyannis, MA.
"It's so open, quiet and beautiful, especially after a heavy snow storm on a sunny day! You can see so far in all directions, without street lights and traffic, loud boom boxes intruding on your thoughts! You can take pictures capturing all you can see," Henry Kasabilla, Spencer, MA.
"Attend the 3a.m. sunrise service on Easter Sunday. The chapel is blacked out; no lights or candles, when from the depth of the Abbey songs and chanting are heard as lights from candles are slowly brought by the Trappist monks," Helen Carter, Worcester,MA.

St. Anne's Shrine 16 Church St., off Rte. 20, Fiskdale (Sturbridge)
(508) 347-7338; gift shop
Votive shrine and Chapel to St. Anne; outdoor mass pavilion; way of the Cross; gift shop; 2 ton crucifix; icon exhibit with more than 80 Russian icons collected by Assumptionist priests serving in Russia from 1906-1941. Lighted path for evening walks, picnic grove. Open year round, church open 7 am-9 pm. Gift Shop hours 10am-4pm weekdays, 10am-6pm weekends. Call for further information.
"It's relaxing and peaceful and beautiful," Ann Burinsky, Millbury, MA.

Cathedral Church of St. Paul   38 Chatham St., Worcester
Completed in 1874, architects E. Boyden & Son, Victorian Gothic church constructed of gray granite.
"It is very pretty and fantastic, Catholic, beautiful and sensational place to be," Lindsay Martinelli, age 10, Worcester, MA.
"It's my favorite because of inner peace and contentment there," Bernice M. McNeil, Worcester, MA.

Scenic Views

Route 122 from Paxton to Petersham
"The road has lots of diversity in scenery including beautiful open space, distinctive New England town appeal and lots of sky," Carol Bedrosian, Grafton, MA.

Quabbin Park Observation Tower   Rte. 9, Belchertown, Ware
(413) 323-7221
Although the Quabbin Park Visitor's Center isn't in Worcester County, much of the Quabbin Reservoir is. After the dams were completed, it took seven years for the lake to fill, and today it is 18 miles long, 150 deep in some places, covering 39 square miles and is filled with 412 billion gallons of water. On a clear day, nearly the whole reservoir can be seen from the glassed-in observation floor of the 85-foot stone tower on top of Quabbin Hill. What used to be the Worcester County town of Dana lies to the northeast (see Chapter 12, Dana).

Blackstone Gorge   County St., off Rte. 122 South, Blackstone
Only unspoiled banks left along the Blackstone, 90' rock precipices tower over the river.
"Walking through the hemlocks along the forested banks here transports you to a different point in time," Thomas Bik, Blackstone, MA.

Wilder Rd   Off Rte. 117, Bolton
On the hill facing west you can see Mount Wachusett.
"Wonderful place to watch the sun set," Karen A. LeCompte, Lancaster, MA.

Dresser Hill Scenic Outlook   Off Rte. 31, Dresser Hill Rd, Charlton
Located just off Rte. 31, very nice scenic area to drive.
"When looking from Dresser Hill Road down onto the Town of Southbridge at sunset - fabulous! It's peaceful, lovely and looks very New England with all the individual points of interest in the valley and on the horizon. One looks over Charlton, Southbridge and Sturbridge from this historic spot," Helen I. Lenti, Southbridge, MA.
"When fall season arrives and that warm autumn breeze splashes on your face, another world is created," Linda Grigas, Oxford, MA.
"The view over cattle-filled fields and orderly rows of corn stretches to the horizon where three states are seen," William Hultgren,Charlton, MA.

Wachusett Dam   Rte. 70 just entering Clinton from the south, Clinton
An impressive dam on the Nashua River at Clinton - the north dike is nearly two miles across and 114 feet high (See Chapter 12, Clinton).
"Wachusett Dam is a place of beauty, 'a joy forever,' at all seasons of the year," Jennie E. Mayberry, Clinton, MA.

"The water fountain- located at the base of the Wachusett Dam - beauty and serenity," Sandy Hudson, Lunenburg, MA.
"Standing on Clinton's water dam-a serene and beautiful view," Hazel I. Fox, Clinton, MA.
"It's my favorite place because of its beauty and usefulness," Patricia Bell, Clinton, MA.

Prouty Road Off Rt. 32, Hardwick
Historical homes and beautiful foliage drive.
"A fantastic ride in Hardwick. Scenes from this road have been on the cover of Yankee Magazine," Susan Morrall, Barre, MA.

Prospect Hill Rd. Off Rte 110, Stillriver Rd., Harvard
Nice viewing area.
"The views are spectacular," Karen A. LeCompte, Lancaster, MA.

Moore State Park Rte 31, Paxton
(58) 792-3969 or (508) 368-0126
Self-guided tours through this 400-acre park take you on a journey around a sawmill and gristmill, old tavern, 1-room schoolhouse, blacksmith shop, and mill owner's house. Noted for its beautiful spring display of azaleas and rhododendrons as well as one of the oldest standing sawmills in New England still on its original site. (see also Chapter 8, Recreation - Forests)
"In spring azaleas bloom. In summer all is green. In autumn trees burn with color — a park for all seasons," Katherine Stannard, Paxton, MA.

Princeton Intersection of Rte. 31 and Rte. 62, Princeton
On a clear day you can see Boston, looking in the direction of the Prince of Peace Church.
"I love this town's beauty - the Audubon Sanctuary, the beautiful Victorian homes and Wachusett Mountain," Kathy Winaco, Holden, MA.

Wachusett Mountain Mountain Road, Princeton
(508) 464-2300 chair lift; (508) 464-2987 State Reservation.
You don't have to be able to hike to catch the view from the summit. In the warmer months, the auto road to the summit is open from the State Reservation headquarters, or you can take the Skyride chairlifts from the ski lodge at the base. Call ahead for chair-lift information.

Cooper's Hilltop Farm 515 Henshaw Street, Rochdale (Leicester)
(508) 892-3720
Farm located on the hilltop which makes this a nice scenic viewing area, especially during foliage season. Fresh milk produced is sold in its convenient store located at the farm.
"The milk tastes great, the people are friendly, the scenery is bucolic, and the sunsets spectacular," Patricia M. Faron," Rochdale, MA.

Waters Farm Waters Rd., off Central Turnpike Rd., Sutton
(508) 865-4886
Historic 1757 family farm, panoramic views, Waters Farm Day annual autumn event. Call for hours.
"The scenic beauty, especially at fall foliage time," Michael A. Chizv, Sutton, MA.
"It's an extremely beautiful place in God's creation that allows you to "let the rest of the

world go by," Sandra Haagsma, Worcester, MA.
"It's historical and very beautiful," Mary B. King, Sutton, MA.

Wachusett Reservoir Rte. 140, West Boylston
"The lovely setting made for a great picnic and the beginning of a new love, a beautiful place to speak beautiful thoughts", Linda Privitera, Worcester, MA.
"It has such a beautiful, peaceful sunset," Art Dufault, Worcester, MA.
"It's a beautiful place to relax and collect my thoughts," Rebecca Kelly, Palmer, MA.

Airport Drive Goddard Memorial Dr. (near Worcester Municipal Airport), Worcester
Heading up Airport Dr. from Mill St., straight past right hand turn to Worcester Airport, the road becomes Goddard Memorial Dr. Look for sign on left saying "Future Home of Goddard Memorial Park." Walk just a short distance from the road for a spectacular view of the city.
"It's my favorite view particularly during autumn you can see much of the city and surrounding countryside. It's nice to sometimes stop and take a nature appreciation break," Mark Rubin, Worcester MA.

Holy Cross College 1 College Street, Worcester
On the hill near Holy Cross College.
"It provides a spectacular view of the city," Randall S. Blanchard, Carlisle, MA.
"The top of the main hill - great view of the city and surrounding area- it's very peaceful and noise free," James R. Carey, Cambridge, MA.

Worcester Municipal Airport Airport Drive, Worcester
(508) 754-2359
"Airport Hill" has great views all around. On a clear day you can see the Prudential and Hancock Towers in Boston.
"Standing in an open field while an airplane comes straight at you and then passes twenty feet overhead makes you feel like Cary Grant in North By Northwest," Paul Gallagher, Worcester, MA.
"Airport Hill in the fall is the best place to go to see the fall foliage," Courtnay Davenport, Worcester, MA.

Scenic Views - Foliage

T & G City Line Worcester
(508) 792-9400 Enter 3255 (FALL)
To enjoy New England color at its best, get foliage updates every fall on City Line, free 24-hour, up-to-the-minute leaf-color updates.

Tufts Univ. Veterinary School Rte. 6 (former Grafton State Hospital), Grafton
"The colors are just great," Carmella M. Keyes, Worcester, MA.

Becker College Rte. 56 North to Paxton Street, Leicester
"The views from Becker College are awesome during the foliage season, and it's free," Robbin Miller, Worcester, MA.

Westborough Road   From Rte. 20 to Westborough Rd., Worcester
"My worries seemed to hide in the colors," Jillian Balser, age 13, Worcester, MA.

Scenic Views - Gardens

Tower Hill Botanic Garden   11 French Drive, Boylston
(508) 869-6111; 869-0314
Worcester County Horticultural Society 132 acres with lawn and secret gardens, cottage, vegetable, and wildlife gardens; walking trails with panoramic views. Garden trips and tours available; gardening library; apple orchard.
"Its location on a hill over-looking Wachusett Reservoir and its natural beauty, breathtaking," Susan Reed, Boylston, MA.
"It has the best view of the reservoir - Wachusett Mt. in spring, summer, fall, winter. They have the best all around programs and a neat gift shop with a proposed restaurant in 1995, best gardens in summer, spring and fall" Doris M. Blondin, E. Douglas, MA.
" The uppermost bench on Tower Hill overlooking the reservoir (walk there from the visitor center). It restores my sanity and perspective on a beautiful spring or fall afternoon. Especially nice with a good book," Cassandra Camp, Westborough, MA.
"It provides an escape from stress of everyday life..." Elnora King, South Lancaster, MA.
"It's so peaceful, like heaven on earth," Carolyn Roux, Sterling, MA.

Sightseeing Tours

Corporate Limousine   1 Buckley Dr., Auburn
(508) 852-5176
Specializing in airport transportation and historical tours around Worcester. Thorough knowledge of Worcester's most interesting historical and cultural sights to see and the fascinating stories behind each of them. Tours arranged according to interests: shopping, dining, museums, sightseeing, etc.

Blackstone River Valley National Heritage Corridor Commission Visitors Center   East Hartford Ave. Uxbridge
(508) 278-9400
Blackstone Valley is "history with a view," Includes mills, villages, canal remnants, greenways, etc. Contact the Visitor's Center for historic sightseeing tours by car, foot, riverboat or canoe.

Blackstone Valley Explorer Riverboat
Departs from several locations along the Blackstone area.
Blackstone Valley Tourism Council
(401) 334-0837
River tours on a 49 passenger riverboat, the only river tour in the valley since 1848. Historical interpretation and environmental guided tours, some tours are scheduled to depart from Blackstone, Northbridge and Uxbridge. Operating spring through fall. Group rates, boat leaves rain or shine, 7 days a week. Call for schedule and reservations.
"River rides are entertaining and informative way to experience natural and historical resources," Val Stegemoen Millville, MA.

Southbridge Airport Clemence Hill Rd., Southbridge
(508) 765-0226
Lessons, scenic flights. Call for further information and directions.
"Airplane rides, sightseeing by air," Lynda Nesbitt, Spencer, MA.

Amity Flight School Worcester Airport, Worcester
(508) 756-7703
Scenic flights are available. Call for further information and reservations.
"15 minute flight over Worcester," Andrew Salek, Worcester, MA.

Winery Tours

Nashoba Valley Winery 100 Wattaquadoc Hill Rd. Bolton
(508) 779-5521 (800) 286-5521
Daily, year round wine tastings, wine and gift sales, scenic picnics, orchard walking tour, festivals, and pick-your-own fruits in their season. Rt. 117W 1 mi to Bolton Center, left at blinking light, 1/4 mile. Winery tours Fri.-Sun. 11am-5pm, $1.

Mellea Winery 108 Southbridge Rd., off Rte. 131, Dudley
(508) 943-5166
Three acres of vineyards, wine-tastings, gift shop, hand-operating bottling, corking and capping machines. French-American varieties, two red, four white grapes. Open weekends Jan. through April; Wed. through Sun., May through Dec. Call ahead for hours and further directions.

Chapter 10

Culture

In Worcester County, you'll find the full range of the cultural arts, from the most traditional, a classical concert at Mechanics Hall - to the funkiest - touring toilets at the country's only Sanitary Plumbing Museum. Millions have visited Old Sturbridge Village and the renowned Worcester Art Museum. But did you know that Higgins Armory Museum has the largest display of arms and armor in the western hemisphere? Go there and you'll see armor made for a dog, and even a Medieval chastity belt.

Among Worcester County's museums, you'll find the homes of Clara Barton (Oxford) and Louisa May Alcott (Harvard), historic country stores (Douglas), clock-making shops (Grafton), and even a museum about the history of plastics (Leominster) where the admission price is two plastic milk jugs which will be pulverized before your eyes, melted and recycled into a key chain.

As with earlier chapters, the listings here are grouped first by category and town, and then alphabetically by name. For example, the Athol Historical Society Museum is listed before the Worcester Historical Museum. And remember, things change, call first. (Don't forget: We want to hear from you. Additions, deletions, notes and comments for the next edition. Send information to: Favorite Places C/O Tatnuck Bookseller Marketplace 335 Chandler Street, Worcester, MA 01602 or FAX (508) 756-9425).

Art Galleries; Arts Festivals; Continuing Education; Libraries; Movies; Museums; Music; Theater Groups.

Art Galleries

Graceworks Gallery 716 Main St., Bolton
(508) 779-5272
Hours: Wed.-Sun. noon-6pm, closed Mon.-Tues.

Brookfield Gallery of Fine Arts 39 Upper River Street, Brookfield
(508) 867-9233
Hours: Mon.-Sat. 9am - 5pm, free admission.

Hammond Gallery Fitchburg State College, 160 Pearl Street, Fitchburg
(508) 345-2151
Hours: Mon.-Fri. 8am-6pm, Sat. 2pm-5pm, Sun. 2pm-6pm, free admission.

East Wing Gallery Mount Wachusett Community College, LaFontaine Fine Arts Center
444 Green St., Gardner
(508) 632-6600
Hours: 8am-9pm, Mon.-Thurs. 8am-5pm.

Surroundings Gallery 377 Main St., Gardner
(508) 630-2340
Visual arts created by local artists, Mon.-Sat. 10am-6pm.

Gallery Corucopia Appleworks 325 Ayer Road, Harvard
(508) 772-6701
Crafts, gifts, sculpture, decoys, pottery, all work of local artists.
Hours: noon-5pm. Wed.-Sun., or by appointment.

JaNan Gallery 138 South Main St., Milford
(508) 473-1504 or toll free in MA 1-800-660-1504
Custom framing shop and art gallery featuring local artists, posters, limited edition prints, Native American pottery. Hours: Mon.-Wed. 10am-6pm, Thurs.-Fri. 10am-8pm, Sat. 10am-5pm, Sun. 1pm-4pm.

Craftworks 3 Pierce St., Northborough
(508) 393-9435
Theorem paintings and marbleized fabric. Watercolors and flags ongoing. Handmade gifts by more than 30 local artists, 10am-6pm daily.

San Francisco Gallery 10 South West Cutoff, Northborough
(508) 393-2266
Featuring contemporary and traditional works, Mon. 1pm-6pm, Tues.-Sat. 10am-6pm.

Bartlett Art Gallery Atlantic Union College, Main Street, South Lancaster
(508) 368-2153
Hours: Sun.-Thurs. 1pm-5pm.

Arts Center at Southborough 21 Highland Street, Southborough
(508) 481-9351
Collection of prints from Worcester Art Museum Print Studio Workshop. Hours: Mon. 10am-1pm, Thurs. 11am-1pm, Sun. 2-4pm through Oct., donations welcome.

Arts Center Gallery 111 Main St., Southbridge
(508) 764-3341
Local and regional artists located in a Victorian mansion. Exhibits, workshops and classes. The Gateway Players, a community theater group are also featured here. Private functions can be held here. Hours by appointment.

Gifted Hands 186 Main Street, Spencer
(508) 885-0271
Crafts and art by local artists. Hours: Tues.-Fri. 10am-6pm, Sat. 10am-4pm, Sun. noon-5pm.

Sterling Artist's Cooperative Sterling Center, 15 Waushacum St., Sterling
(508) 422-3200
Historic Faneuil Cider Mill, one of the largest gallery spaces in New England, working artisans, exhibitions, demonstrations, classes, and special events also home of Sterling Glass Works, glass blowing studio, demonstrations. Open daily 10am-6pm, closed Tues.

Traditions International LTD 538 Main Street, Sturbridge
(508) 347-7606
Hours: Mon.10am-6pm.

Vaillancourt Folk Art & Friends 145 Armsby Road, Sutton
(508) 865-0434
Hours: Mon.-Sat. 9am-5pm, Sun. 11am-5pm.
(See Chapter 6, Shopping: Antiques & Art for more information.)

Gold Swan 45 Sterling Street, West Boylston
(508) 835-9044
Works of four artists, Tues.-Thurs. 10am- 7pm, Wed.-Sat. 10am-5pm.

Studio 31 Gallery 31 Elm Street, West Boylston
(508) 835-4921
Landscapes, seascapes, florals, portraits, Mon.-Fri. 10:30am-4pm or by appointment.

African Heritage Gallery 930 Main St., Worcester
(508) 752-1199
Displays of jewelry, wood carvings, masks, beads and more. Hours: Mon.-Sat. 10am-7pm, free admission.

ART Works Gallery 261 Park Avenue, Worcester
(509) 755-7808
Original limited edition prints, watercolors, oils by artists, gallery posters and custom framing, Tues., Wed., Fri. 10am-6pm; Thurs. 10am-8pm, Sat. 10am-5pm.

Artistic Presentations   629 Cambridge Street, Worcester
(508) 757-1429
Hours: Thurs.-Fri. 10am-5:30pm, Sat. 10am-5pm.

Arts Worcester   349 Main St., Worcester
(508) 755-5142
Weekdays, 11am-2pm, Sat. 1pm-4pm or by appointment, free admission.

Atlantis Art Gallery   198 Park Ave, Worcester
(508) 752-9023
Displays of etchings, lithographs, serigraphs, paintings and photographs by local artists, Mon.-Fri. 10am-5:30 pm, Sat.10am-4pm through Dec. 30, free admission.

Charlotte Wharton Studio   594 Chandler Street, Worcester
(508) 754-4013
Collection of portraits and landscapes, classes available to the public. Hours: 9am-5pm Mon.-Sat. or by appointment..

Collector's Gallery   142 Highland Street, Worcester
Blown glass, etchings, lithographs, serigraphs, and paintings. Hours: Mon.-Fri. 9am-5:30pm, Sat. 9am-5pm.

Fletcher/Priest Gallery   5 Pratt Street, Worcester
(508) 791-5929
Nationally recognized artists, Wed., Thurs., and Fri. Noon- 6pm, Sat. 10am- 3pm and by appointment.

Gallery of Visual Arts   108 Grove Street, Worcester
(508) 755-1880
Featuring local artists, Tues.-Fri. 10:30am-9:30pm.

Grove Street Gallery   70 Winter Street, Worcester
(508) 755-7931

Iris and B. Gerald Cantor Art Gallery   O'Kane Hall, Holy Cross College, Worcester
(508) 793-3356
Permanent collection displayed, works by Rodin and pieces by 20th century German sculptors. Mon.-Fri. 11am- 4pm, Sat.-Sun. 2pm-5pm. Free admission.

Kaleidoscope Gallery   Worcester Public Library, Salem Square, Worcester
(508) 799-1655
Works of local artists, paintings, sculptures, prints and photographs, informational exhibits.

Prints & the Potter Gallery   142 Highland Street, Worcester
(508) 752-2170
Hand-crafted jewelry, ceramics, wood, glassware, limited edition prints and posters, custom framing, Mon-Fri. 9am- 5:30pm, Sat. 9am- 5pm.
"This is where you can find the wonderful hand painted and glazed "Worcester Ware'

pottery created by Elisabeth Donker," A.L., Rutland, MA.

Quinsigamond Gallery Quinsigamond Community College, 670 West Boylston St., Worcester
(508) 853-2300
Hours: Mon.-Fri. 4-7pm, or by appointment.

Rader Art Gallery Worcester Academy, 81 Providence St., Worcester
(508) 754-5302
Hours: Mon.-Fri. 2pm-4pm, or by appointment.

Rose Madder Gallery 102 Grove Street, Worcester
(508) 755-1064
Oil paintings, watercolors, antique prints. Hours: Mon.-Fri. 10am-6pm, Sat. 10am-5pm, Sun. noon-5pm.

University Gallery Clark University Goddard Library, Worcester
(508) 793-7572
Small, student run, offering exhibitions of contemporary artists, focusing on work of New England artists. In April the final exhibit features work by graduating art students. Hours: Wed.-Sun. noon- 5pm.

University of Massachusetts Medical Center Gallery Medical School Lobby, 55 Lake Avenue, North, Worcester
(508) 856-2000
Featuring local and national artists. Monthly exhibits. Noontime performing art series offered, daily 9am-9pm, free admission.

Upstairs Gallery 565 Main Street, Rte. 9 Cherry Valley, Leicester
(508) 892-1620
Hours: Tues.-Sat. 11am- 5:30pm.

Wawrzonek Gallery 70 Webster Street, Worcester
(508) 798-6612
Hours: Mon.-Fri. 11am-5pm and by appointment.

Worcester Center for Crafts 25 Sagamore Rd., Worcester
(508) 753-8183 or 753-6140
Founded in 1856 as the Worcester Female Employment Society, the Center now provides a facility of almost 30,000 sq. ft. dedicated to contemporary craft education for children and adults in 10 fully-equipped studios, a library, two Craft Galleries with over 2,205 sq. ft. of exhibition space and a gallery gift store, which features the work of over 400 artisans in all media. Bridal Registry and special gifts registry. Free parking and admission.Contemporary crafts, gift shop, pottery, jewelry, furniture, blown glass, leather goods. Open Tues.-Sat. 10am-5pm.
Classes offered for ages 5-17 concentrating on woodworking, enameling, photography, multi-media, pottery. Summer camp for children available. A two year school for woodworking etc. offered. Two craft fairs per year.

Arts Festivals

First Night
Worcester
(508) 799-4909
The place to be on New Year's Eve in Worcester, a city-wide event. Late afternoon until midnight; music, puppet shows, ballet and opera for entire family in dozens of downtown locations. Fireworks ring in the new year. First Night is truly unique family entertainment.

Auditoriums

George R. Wallace Civic Center 1000 John Fitch Highway, Fitchburg
(508) 345-7593
Concerts, family entertainment, bingo nights, public ice skating rinks.

Memorial Hall Cultural Center Main St., Milford
(508) 478-7044

Centrum 50 Foster Street, Worcester
(508) 798-8888
Worcester's civic center opened in 1982 with Frank Sinatra headlining, and today attracts international superstars like Janet Jackson, Bruce Springsteen, U2, and Billy Joel, who have performed here because Worcester's easier accessibility draws bigger audiences. A $32 million convention center addition to the Centrum is set for completion in 1996. Home to the Worcester IceCats AHL hockey team, the Centrum also books trade shows, ice shows, sporting events and family entertainment (see Chap. 1)
"Now you walk to the Fashion Outlet and The Marriot after or before a show," Claude Wooden, Shrewsbury, MA.

Mechanics Hall 321 Main St., Worcester
(508) 752-5608; ticket office: 752-0888
Among the great concert halls of the world; Mechanics Hall was built in 1857 and has excellent acoustics and a rare Hook pipe organ. Dickens, Twain, Caruso and Teddy Roosevelt are just a few of the famous people who have appeared here. It is the site of the annual Worcester Music Festival and International Artists Series concerts, and the popular (and free) lunch-time Brown Bag Concerts (see this chapter, Music). It is a National Historic Landmark, and free tours are available by appointment. (see Mechanics Hall, Chapter 1 and Hook Organ, Chapter 2).
"Wherever you sit, you'll have the best seat in the house," Cristin Alberts, Worcester, MA.
"...painstaking restoration and stunning colors,... how proud I feel when guests such as Sen. Robert Dole and First Lady Hillary Clinton say it is one of the best halls in America," Mike McDonald, Southbridge, MA.
"A work of architectural beauty with superior acoustics," Paul Schwam, Holden, MA.
"Heavenly," Rena Miller, Worcester, MA.
"The place has true class. A place to feel elegant," Jean Langley.

Worcester Memorial Auditorium, the "New Aud" Lincoln Square, Worcester
(508) 798-8888
Built in 1932; the Aud offers a variety of entertainment, including plays and concerts.
"Historical events, Sonny & Cher, Rolling Stones, Holy Cross basketball, boyhood memories," Robert M. Cloutier, Thompston, CT.

Continuing Education

Night Life
Adult Education courses at various sites around Worcester
For information, call (508) 799-3091.
Night Life is one of the largest and most popular enrichment programs in the country, offering hundreds of classes including sports, Spanish, crafts and computers.

Libraries

Richard Sugden Library 8 Pleasant Street, Spencer
(508) 885-7513
Town's history and artifacts pertaining to the town's history as a manufacturing center for shoes and wire. Antique collection of sewing machines, Mon.-Thurs. 10am-8pm, Fri. 10am-5pm, and Sat. 10am-1pm.

American Antiquarian Society 185 Salisbury St., Worcester
(508) 755-5221
The country's first national historical society. This independent research library was founded in 1812 by Isaiah Thomas, and has the largest single collection of printed source materials relating to U.S. history and culture from 1640-1876 and the world's most extensive early American newspaper collection, Mon.-Fri. 9am- 5pm, free public tours Wed. at 2 p.m.

Clark University Goddard Library Clark University, 950 Main St., Worcester
(508) 793-7461
Open to the public, Mon.-Thurs. 8am-Midnight; Fri. 8am-10pm, Sat. 10am-10pm; Sun. noon-Midnight. Exhibit of Robert Goddard's (father of modern rocketry) equipment, family photos, rocket frame, and the library houses all of Goddard's papers (see Chapter 2).

Dinand Library Holy Cross College, Worcester
(508) 793-2642
Hours: Sun.-Thurs. 8:30am -1am, Fri.-Sat. 8:30am-1pm, open to the public.

George C. Gordon Library Worcester Polytechnic Institute, 100 Institute Road, Worcester
(508) 831-5410
Hours: Mon.-Fri. 8am-11pm, Sat. 8am-9pm, Sun.noon-11pm, open to the public.

Guy H. Burnham Map and Aerial Photography Library Clark University, Worcester
(508) 793-7322
One of several repositories in Massachusetts for all maps of the U.S. Geological Survey, Defense Mapping Agency, open to the public, 190,000 maps, source for genealogical research, railroad routes and battle maps.

Hurlburt Reading Room Worcester Historical Museum 30 Elm St., Worcester
(508) 753-8278
"A wonderful place for research and reading - high ceilings, wood paneling, and large windows letting in a lot of light," A.L., Rutland, MA.

Worcester Public Library Salem Square , Worcester
(508) 799-1655
"Incomparable collection; finally (again) great hours, and because I worked there 12 years (1972-84) and love it still," Harry Roger Williams, III.
"It's democratic, it's free, it's got everything one needs," Veronica Griffin, Worcester, MA
"The people who work there are helpful and pleasant. The selection of books is outstanding. The variety of subjects is extensive. The programs offered cover a large range of interests. The parking is convenient. I love to go there," Maureen W. Hanigan, Sturbridge, MA.

Movies

Last Strand Cinema and Drafthouse 58 High St., Clinton
(508) 365-5500
Pizza, nachos, tickets around $4, reasonable food prices, matinees on Sat., Sun.

Elm Draughthouse Cinema 35 Elm Street, Millbury
(508) 865-2850
Serving pizza, beer, wine, and movies for a reasonable price. Presenting second run features
"Great place to see a movie at reasonable prices," Nancy T. Watts, Millbury, MA.

Cinema 320 Clark University, Worcester
(508) 793-7477
Excellent schedule of foreign and art films.

Museums

Athol Historical Society Athol
President Howard Wilson (508) 249-4217
Curator M. Dexter Gleason (508) 249-6598
The museum is filled with artifacts from Athol's past, from a Bible printed in England in 1599, to a permit written in Vietnamese to bring a Russian-made rifle back to the U.S.A. Open Sun. 2-4pm in July and Aug. or by special appointment.

Henry Woods Museum Barre Public Library   On the Common   Barre
(508) 355-2533
Large collection of Indian artifacts, enough preserved animals to stock a taxidermy's store and many other interesting items. Hours by appointment.

Boylston Historical Society   Old Town Hall, Boylston
(508) 869-2720
Open Tues. and Thurs. 9am-noon.

Holder Memorial Museum   210 Church St., Clinton
(508) 368-0084
Original patent models for the Bigelow looms, samples of each type of tree flooded by Wachusett Reservoir and more. Open Sat. 9am-noon, free admission.

E.N. Jenckes General Store & Museum   Main St., East Douglas
(508) 476-2433
Many artifacts remain from this country store, established in 1833. Restored by the Douglas Historical Society, the Jenckes Store is a typical country store of a hundred years ago which sold everything from ladders to lace, furniture to feather plumes. The store's original counters are stocked with goods sold during its heyday — galoshes and boots, brushes, bed linens, straw hats, shaving soap and razors. The dry goods section has original (but empty) tins of codfish, cocoa, cereals, mustard, molasses and more. Visitors, groups welcome by appointment (see Chapter 12, Douglas).
"This wonderfully preserved 19th century Greek revival commercial building is open to the public. It is a well preserved 19th century general store! Wow!" John Petraglia, East Douglas, MA.

Fitchburg Art Museum   185 Elm St., Fitchburg
(508) 345-4207
A variety of works focusing on contemporary New England artists. Permanent collection of works by American and European artists; two exhibits on the history of art; year-round art classes and seminars. Four galleries offering works of contemporary New England artists. Paintings exhibiting the Tombs and Temples of Ancient Egypt also featured. Tours available. Hours: Tues.-Sat. 11am-4pm, admission $3. Seniors $2. Students and children free.
"Its art collection is outstanding!" Judith A. Foster, Leominster, MA.
"They own a small but diverse collection of art in a comfortable museum setting and they do great work with the community's school system," Susan DiBattista, Westminster, MA.

Fitchburg Historical Society & Museum   50 Grove St., Fitchburg
(508) 345-1157
Artifacts of the city's past, including clothing, inventions, Victorian furniture and Civil war memorabilia and uniforms. Public programs and publications, such as "Fitchburg's Golden Age", covering the area's rich industrial history. Mon.-Tues. 9am-4pm, Wed.-Thurs. 10am-4pm, free admission.

Gardner Museum   28 Pearl St., Gardner
(508) 632-3277
Entrance-way in shape of chair, exhibits of local furniture makers, artisans, large doll house collection. Tues.-Sun. 1pm-4pm, free admission.

Willard House and Clock Museum, Inc. 11 Willard St., Grafton
(508) 839-3500
Oldest house in Grafton, circa 1718, birthplace and original clock-shop of Willard clock-makers, Simon, Ephraim, Benjamin and Aaron; 70 Willard clocks and family heirlooms. Country furniture of the 18th & 19th centuries. Tues.-Sat. 10am-4pm, Sun.1pm-5pm, admission $3; children ages 6-12 $1, groups by appointment.

Fruitlands Museum 102 Prospect Hill Rd., Harvard
(508) 456-3924
Four collections of American art and history, 200 acres offering picnicking and hiking. Mid-May through Oct. Shaker House, Native American Museum, Picture Gallery, Fruitlands (Alcott house). Off-season "Tea Room" open. American Indian museum. Tues.-Sun. plus Mon. holidays free, programs with admission. 10am-5pm; $6; Seniors $5; college students $3.50 with ID; ages 4-17 $2.50; under 3 free.
"It's my favorite place in Worcester County because of 1) the spectacular view of Nashoba Valley, 2) four museums honoring American Indians, American Painters, the American Shakers and the self-taught man, Bronson Alcott, American...and an excellent Tea Room!" - Elizabeth Vesenka, Littleton, MA.

Leominster Historical Society 17 School Street, Leominster
(508) 537-5424
Civil War exhibit along with largest hair comb collection in the country. Leominster was once known at "Comb City of the World." Included in the collection are a carved tortoise shell with scrolled, floral designs, dragonflies and studded rhinestones or pearls. Exhibits relating the story of Johnny Appleseed. Mon.-Fri. 8am-2pm, Sat. 8am-noon or by appointment, free admission.

National Plastics Center and Museum 210 Lancaster St., Leominster
(508) 537-9529
History of plastics, children's hands-on Discovery Corner with plastic building toys, Plastic Lab! and Kid Lab! by reservation. Pin ball machine teaches recycling message. School programs offered, live demonstrations. Admission $2 or two plastic milk bottles. Children and Seniors $1 or one plastic milk bottle. Hours: Wed.-Sat. 11am- 4pm, call to book visits and programs.
"Awesome! The 'micromolder' crunches milk jugs and makes key chains out of them," Andy Lindblad, Rutland, MA.

Mendon Historical Museum 3 Main St. at Founder's Park (corner of Rte. 16 and Main), Mendon
(508) 473-7672
Native American artifacts, early household utensils and furnishings. Open May - Sept. at scheduled hours or call for appointment, curator: Alice Pickering Palladini.

Cooke's Rolls Royce Museum 106 South Main St., North Brookfield
(508) 867-2892
Large collection of Rolls Royce cut-away engines and working engines; also a working garage. Open 8am-5pm, call for appointment.
"No one knows about this place, but it has the world's largest collection of Rolls Royce engines, all maintained by Frank Cooke, an 82-year-old genius who repairs and restores Rolls as well," Andy O'Donnell, Worcester, MA.

North Brookfield Historical Museum Haston Public Library, 3rd Floor, Main St., North Brookfield
(508) 867-0208
Displays regarding early industries in town, Quabaug Rubber Co., Quaboag Water Co., local Indian artifacts, historical pictures; open summers.

Northborough Historical Society Museum Rt. 20 (Main St.), Northborough
(508) 393-2011
Open May, Jun., Sept., Oct. Sun. 2pm-4pm, by appointment during summer months. Research material also available by appointment.
"Interesting, informative changing exhibits relating to the Town's growth from a small outpost in the early 1700's through the Industrial Revolution on into the 20th century. Enthusiastic and knowledgeable curator and guides. Town was home to Gov. "Honest" John Davis and Luther Rice (Baptist missionary)," JoAnn Sullivan, Northborough, MA.

Clara Barton Birthplace Museum 68 Clara Barton Rd, off Rte. 12, Oxford
(508) 987-2056
Home of the founder of the American Red Cross; includes Barton family furnishings, Civil War memorabilia and Red Cross mementos. Built between 1818 and 1820. Open April-Oct. Tues.-Sun. 11am-5pm, tours by appointment.

Fisher Museum of Forestry Harvard Forest Rte. 32, Petersham
(508) 724-3302
Dioramas and other exhibits describing history, ecology, and local forest management are on permanent display. Trails available for hiking in the 900-acre forest, Mon.-Fri. 9am-5pm, Sat.-Sun. noon-4pm, closed on holidays, free admission.

General Artemus Ward 786 Main St., Shrewsbury
(508) 842-8900
Ward was commander of the Continental Army before George Washington. Built in 1727, the homestead is owned by Harvard Univ. and furnished as it was 150 years ago. Free admission, open April-Nov., call for hours.
"It is a beautiful step back in time to the 1700's," Patricia Hine, Worcester, MA.

Old Sturbridge Village One Old Sturbridge Village Rd. off Rte. 20, Sturbridge
(508) 347-3362
Non-profit, world-renowned, educational outdoor living history museum on 200 acres with more than 40 restored buildings. Costumed interpreters depict life as it was in the 1830's. Open year-round, call for hours and schedule of special events. Buildings include a church, meeting house, tavern, bank, homes, a working farm and a mill. Demonstrations of cider production, fireplace cooking, making of scones, bread making, and wall cabinet making. School groups accepted beginning in Jan. by reservation only. Sign-language interpretation offered. Tues.-Sun. 9am-5pm.
"It depicts New England's finest hour of the past in it's truest form," Helen E. Erickson, Worcester, MA.
"I can go back to another time of life, a less complicated life, a quieter way of life," Phyllis Carter, Worcester, MA.

"It gives me an opportunity to put my life in perspective," Heather Krasnov, Holden, MA.
"The picnic spot at Old Sturbridge Village, on the hillside between the covered bridge and the sawmill— it is secluded, but has views of the OSV buildings, duck ponds and ox-cart trails. When you are there, you feel far removed from the 20th century," A. Kenary, Worcester, MA.

American Sanitary Plumbing Museum B. J. Manoog's Plumbing
39 Piedmont St., Worcester
(508) 754-9453
The country's only such museum, opened in 1988. Copper lined and clawfoot bathtubs, lavatories, kitchen sinks and sitz baths, assortment of plumbers' tools and blowtorches, "electric sink" circa 1928 was the first attempt at a dishwasher. Plumbing materials, tools, catalogs and books available, open Tues. and Thurs. 10am-2pm, free admission, closed July and Aug.
"It's the best way to learn history", Nancy Ford, Worcester, MA.

Higgins Armory Museum 100 Barber Ave. (exit #1 off I-190 to Rte. 12, to Barber Ave.), Worcester
(508) 853-6015
Housed in one of the country's first multi-storied all steel and glass buildings, on the National Register of Historic Places, the museum has the largest display of arms and armor in the Western Hemisphere. Founded by John Woodman Higgins, the museum opened in 1931. Here you'll find mail, armor made for a dog, suits of armor used for jousting on horseback, Maximillian-style armor with web-shaped feet (which legend says were made to accommodate Maximillian's 6 toes), and even an actual chastity belt; Tues.-Sat. 10am-4pm; Sun. noon-4pm. Admission $4.75; Seniors: $4; children: $3.75. Special programs offered throughout the year, gift shop. A popular site for Cub Scout "Over-Knight" sleep-overs.
"After touring museum, kids can go to the Quest Gallery, try on Medieval clothes, and make crayon rubbings of actual funerary brass artwork. A one-of-a-kind experience," A.L., Rutland, MA.

Mass. National Guard Military Museum 44 Salisbury St., Worcester
(508) 797-0334
Built in 1889, the oldest armory in the state houses military memorabilia dating back to 1636, including full-dress uniforms from the 1880's, a Civil War uniform from 1862, and weapons recovered from the Boxer Rebellion in China. Includes items from the American Museum at Ft. Devens, which is closing. Open Tues.-Fri. 9am-3pm, or by appointment, free admission.

New England Science Center 222 Harrington Way, Worcester
(508) 791-9211
Museum and wildlife center with 3 floors of interactive exhibits, including planetarium and outside observatory. Indoor & outdoor animal exhibits on 40 acres, with 26 different animal species, including Worcester's famous Polar bears, otters, mountains lions, eagles, owls and more. Narrrow gauge "Explorer Express" train ride, snack bar, gift shop. and on-going special events, like "Jazz at Sunset" summer concert series. Mon.-Sat. 10am-5pm; Sun. Noon-5pm, call for directions.
"Both my kids and my husband and I love the animal focus and our kids are preschoolers," Ann R. Greenawalt, Shrewsbury, MA.

Worcester Art Museum 55 Salisbury Street, Worcester
(508) 799-4406
The second-largest art museum in New England, it is world-renowned for its permanent collection of over 30,000 works that span 50 centuries of art and culture. The museum's holdings include works by Renoir, Monet, John Singer Sargent, and world art treasures such as "St. John the Baptist" by Renaissance painter Andrea del Sarto, and "The Fur Jacket" by James Abbott McNeill Whistler. Tues.-Fri. 11am-4pm, Sat. 10am-5pm, Sun.1pm-5pm, Seniors: $5, ages 13-18 and full-time college students with ID: $3. ages 12 and under free. Art classes offered for all ages. Free to all every Saturday 10am-noon.
"It is one of the very best museums in the whole U.S.A. There are changing exhibits, permanent collections and an excellent teaching art education program and museum shop," Carole Francis, Paxton, MA.
"I'm proud of the quality and prestige here," Linda Knowlton, Holden, MA.
"A superb museum - small enough to see in a day with a charming cafe for gourmet eating," Michelle M. Donabedian, Holden, MA.
"You can learn about life from 2000 years B.C. to the present in two hours," Paula Travers, Worcester, MA.
"The collection is the heart of the museum, but the effort that goes into conservation, framing, display and acquisition is its pulse," Frances Jacobson, Westborough, MA.

Worcester Historical Museum 30 Elm St., Worcester
(508) 753-8278
A wonderful chronicle of Worcester's past, offering permanent and changing exhibits, collections of things made in Worcester, old photos, chronicles of the immigrant experience, library services, special events. Tues.-Sat. 10am-4pm, Sun. 1pm-4pm. Worcester Historical Museum also operates Salisbury Mansion, 40 Highland St. (see Chapter 9, Sightseeing).

Music

Holden's 250th Bandstand Memorial Community Park 1128 Holden St., Holden
"Built to commemorate Holden's 250th anniversary, 11 free family concerts are presented each Sunday during the summer. The park also provides a place for solace, rest and reflection for all," Susan McNamara, Holden, MA.

Thayer Symphony Orchestra Atlantic Union CollegeMain St., Lancaster
(508) 368-0041
Six concerts per season, one summer concert, 55-60 professional musicians from all over MA, RI and CT, founded over 20 years ago, performances in Machlin Auditorium on the campus of Atlantic Union College, Lancaster, MA.
"Wonderful concerts with top musicians performing in a delightful setting," Lancaster Historical Commission, Lancaster, MA.

Worcester Area Folk Society 45 Elmwood St., Millbury
(508) 752-2019 or 757-2155
Sponsors folk performances from traditional folk to bluegrass and blues and ethnic music also. Performances are held at John Henry's Hammer Coffeehouse at the First Unitarian Church, 90 Main St., Worcester

Assabet Valley Mastersingers Box 911, Northborough
(508) 562-9838
Season runs September through May with three concerts. Presenting a December Messiah Sing.

The Sweet Adelines, Int'l. Post Rd. Chapter Trinity Episcopal Church 440 Main St., Shrewsbury
(508) 852-4493
Local organization of worldwide women singers. Four-part harmony and barbershop-style.

Worcester Music Festival Mechanics Hall, Worcester
(508) 754-3231
The country's oldest continuous music festival, started in 1859 and sponsored by the Worcester County Music Association. Concerts include symphony and chamber orchestras, ethnic dance ensembles. Concerts held in the fall, winter and spring. Performances by individual artists also offered.

Brown Bag Concerts Mechanics Hall, Main St., Worcester
(508) 752-5608; (508) 752-0700 for schedule info
Free, bring your own lunch concerts sponsored by WICN Public Radio, Call (508) 752-0700 for schedule information.
"This concert series gives my daughter and I a chance to spend an afternoon together appreciating something we enjoy very much together - music. What a beautiful place and to be lucky enough to have this in our own backyard. From jazz to blues to mariachi, this series is free. Of course you may give a donation if you choose -we do," Stephanie A. Bourgeois, Manchaug, MA.

Cathedral Music in Worcester Saint Paul's Cathedral corner of Chatham and High Streets, Worcester
(508) 798-0417 (Mon-Fri) or (508) 799-4193 (Sat. and Sun.) for concert schedule
Performing Arts Series Sept.-June. features choral, organ and instrumental concerts.

Central Massachusetts Symphony Orchestra Tuckerman Hall, 10 Tuckerman Street, Worcester
(508) 754-1234
Regional community orchestra performs outdoor summer concerts at Institute Park, indoor concerts at Tuckerman Hall and Mechanics Hall. Tickets available through the Symphony Office P.O. Box 70, West Side Station or at M.T. Plante Ticket Agency 321 Main Street, Worcester.

Chorus of the Retired Men of Greendale c/o 16 Calumet Avenue, Worcester
(508) 853-9182
Chorus of over 50 seniors trained for performances for residents, senior groups and various community organizations. Performing at over 70 sites from Sept. through June.

International Artists Series Box 16356, 6 Chatham Street, Worcester
(508) 75-MUSIC or 756-8742 for tickets and information.
Annual series of more than a dozen concerts featuring internationally renowned performers such as the Vienna Choir Boys, Ladysmith Black Mambazo, and the Kremlin

Chamber Orchestra each year in Mechanics Hall, 321 Main St., Worcester. Subscriptions, single tickets or group sales available.

Master Singers of Worcester, Inc. **P.O.Box 761, Worcester**
(508) 874-5830 for ticket information and membership.
45-voice choral group presenting concerts including a Christmas concert in Dec. Major choral presentation each spring.

Opera Worcester, Inc. **10 Winthrop Street, Worcester**
(508) 752-8201
Live opera in Worcester. Bus trips available for performances in Boston and Metropolitan in New York.

Salisbury Singers, Inc. **500 Park Ave., Worcester**
(508) 366-4164
60 singers, ensemble-in-residence at the Worcester Art Museum. Tickets available at M.T. Plante Ticket Agency and Ben Franklin Bookstore.

Trinity Choir **Trinity Lutheran Church, 73 Lancaster, Worcester**
(508) 753-2989
Performances of sacred music from sixteenth century to present day.

Worcester Chorus **Worcester County Music Association Memorial Auditorium, 1 Highland Street, Worcester**
(508) 754-3231
120 member local singing group performing with major orchestras and the Worcester Orchestra. Yearly Musical Festival. Appearances abroad as well as Mechanics Hall.

Worcester Orchestra **1 Highland St., Worcester**
(508) 754-3231
Performances with the Worcester Chorus regularly. Annual salute to young artists. Summer pops concerts.

Theater Groups

Stratton Players **60 Wallace Ave., Fitchburg**
(508) 345-6066
Live theater presented by the Stratton Players.

Theater at the Mount **Mount Wachusett Community College, 44 Green St., Gardner**
(508) 632-6600 Children's programs call (508) 632-2403
Performing theater group, also summer drama camp co-ed for grades 3-8

Masque Theatre Company, Inc. **Milford's Memorial Hall Cultural Center P.O. Box 106, Milford**
(508) 478-7044 Box office

Calliope Productions 40 Church Street, Northborough
(508) 842-6437
Non profit theater presentations. Six plays per season March -December. Fri.- Sun. evenings.

New England Theatre Company Anna Maria College, Paxton
(508) 849-3300

Toy Cupboard Puppet Theater and Museum 57 East George Hill Rd., South Lancaster
(508) 365-9519
Features paper dolls, toys, books, doll houses, puppets and marionettes. Performance every Sun. at 2pm. Museum closed Jan-mid-Feb. Museum open Sun. 2:30-5pm or by appointment.
"Puppet theater for children seating 100 persons. Where one or two performances are given weekly in the summer or by appointment. An extremely entertaining place to visit," Joan Richards, Lancaster, MA.

Clark University Center for Contemporary Performance and Theater Program 950 Main St. Clark Univ. Dept. of Visual and Performing Arts., Worcester
(508) 793-7113
Directors, composers, playwrights, choreographers, film/video makers and critics directing productions. Students and guests make up crew.

Little Theatre Worcester Memorial Auditorium, Worcester
(508) 755-1257
Performances Nov.-Jan. presented by the Kenon K. Rockefeller Traveling Playhouse, usually sold out far in advance, tickets can be reserved early.

Masque WPI 100 Institute Rd., Worcester
(508) 831-5946
Partially funded by Worcester Polytechnic Institute, features a three-part performance each November and February. Also featured is the M.W. Repertory theatre Company a student-run group performing two to three shows per year on campus.

Peter Pan Players 846 Millbury St., Worcester
(508) 791-8288
Performances by children staged in seven in-house productions.

Worcester Children's Theater Center for The Performing Arts 6 Chatham Street, Worcester
(508) 752-7537
Professional group presenting live theatre to children. Workshops available. Plays presented for schools, libraries and parks. Summer camps available.
"I take acting lesson there and I'm learning to sing and dance there too," Megan Frost (age 8).

Worcester County Light Opera Company, Inc. 21 Grand View Avenue, Worcester
(508) 753-4383
Worcester's oldest active theatre group, since 1937. One major Broadway musical presented each year and a variety of other productions. Children's summer theater workshop.

Worcester Foothills Theatre Company 100 Front Street (In Worcester Common Fashion Outlet Mall complex). Worcester
(508) 754-3314 (Business Office)
(508) 754-4018 (Box Office) Voice/TDD
Professional theater company offering over 200 live performances from Oct.- May, musicals, drama, comedy. Past performances include Anastasia, The Lion in Winter, Pump Boys and Dinettes, and The All Night Strut. Internships available. Listening devices for the hearing impaired. One performance per season is sign language interpreted.
"It provides the quality of professional theater without the inconvenience of the trip to Boston", Scott Bianchi, Worcester, MA
"It is an essential cultural center for the whole county, offering excellent live theater," George Doyle, Holden, MA.
"Two hours of great entertainment," Tina Kotseas, Worcester, MA.
"I get season tickets for great nights out all year," Sybil LaBaire, Shrewsbury, MA.
"It's next to the Worcester Common Fashion Outlets- for shopping and a show," A.L., Rutland, MA.

Worcester Forum Theater Ensemble 6 Chatham Sq., Worcester
(508) 799-9166
A professional theater company, Forum operates a spring-summer schedule of two indoor productions at Forum Theater, 6 Chatham St. and two outdoor Shakespearian productions at Green Hill Park. Group rates, student rush tickets and discounted season subscriptions available.
"Great theater that tackles tough issues," Erin Sellers, Worcester, MA.
"A performance includes the ABC's, art, beauty, comfort, delight, enlightenment, fun, glamour, happiness, insight, joy, knowledge, love, music, neatness, order, peace, quality, rest, style, tension, unity, vision, wisdom, X-tras, youth and zest", Jane A. Richardson, Douglas, MA.
"Gorgeous scenery, reminds us of Vermont, and wonderful, accessible productions," Dick Seder, Southborough, MA

Notes

Chapter 11

Colleges

"Every great American city has at least one college. Worcester has ten."

This famous billboard on I-290 in downtown Worcester seen by millions of motorists is funded by the Worcester Consortium for Higher Education. It emphasizes what many tend to forget: Worcester is a college town.

Maybe they don't eat goldfish or streak anymore, but the college kids do count, and there are lots of them.

The Consortium may have 10 members, but there are actually 14 colleges in Worcester County which collectively employ more than 11,000 people, have an enrollment of more than 35,000 students, attract more than 1 million visitors annually, and have combined operating budgets of more than $775 million.

The following profiles were prepared and submitted by each college.

Worcester County's Colleges

Anna Maria College, Paxton, MA
Assumption College, Worcester, MA
Atlantic Union College, South Lancaster, MA
Becker College, Leicester and Worcester, MA
Clark University, Worcester, MA
College of the Holy Cross, Worcester, MA
Fitchburg State College, Fitchburg, MA
Mount Wachusett Community College, Gardner MA
Nichols College, Dudley, MA
Quinsigamond Community College, Worcester, MA
Tufts University School of Veterinary Medicine, North Grafton, MA
University of Massachusetts Medical Center, Worcester, MA
Worcester Polytechnic Institute, Worcester, MA
Worcester State College, Worcester, MA

Anna Maria College

Paxton, MA

Anna Maria College was founded in 1946 by the Sisters of St. Anne. The college is dedicated to providing a balanced integration of liberal arts education and career preparation skills. This is accomplished within the context of today's complex and demanding job market through the Universal Curriculum of Anna Maria College. The curriculum is designed to help AMC students become well-rounded enough to balance the demands and pressures of their careers and personal lives so they can become responsible, productive members of our society .

The college offers over 30 undergraduate and eight graduate degree programs on its 180 acre campus. In 1994, its undergraduate student population was 775, with 1,100 students enrolled in its graduate programs in Paxton and at eight other sites located in Massachusetts. Class size averages betweeen 15 and 20 students, with a faculty/student ratio of 1:16.

Extracurricular, social and athletic opportunities are plentiful, and are an important component in a student's experience. Among the clubs and organizations are the International Club, Campus Ministry, Drama Club, History Club, Music Therapy Club, Science Club, College Chorus, Student Government Association and honor societies.

The college competes in nine varsity athletic programs at the Division III level as a member of the National Collegiate Athletic Association, the Eastern Collegiate Athletic Conference and the Commonwealth Coast Conference. These include soccer, basketball, baseball and golf for men and volleyball, soccer, field hockey, basketball and softball for women.

What AMC Offers the Community and Students:

The original Karas art collection consisting of oil paintings, sculpture, wood cuts and pastels housed in the library (open year round).
The New England Theater in Residence at Anna Maria College, which performs threee musical/dramas per academic year. (various times).
Drama Club plays (various times).
Senior art exhibit (November).
Various music faculty/student recitals
Annual craft fair sponsored by the Alumni Association (November).
Mass of the Holy Spirit (September).
Tuxedo Classic Jazz Band Concert (September).
Variety Show (April).
Spring/Christmas choral concerts.
Black History Month activities (February).
Athletic sporting events (various times - baseball, basketball, soccer, softball, field hockey, volleyball).
Christmas tree lighting party (December).
Spiritwoods Pub DJ parties (various

times). Must be 21 or over and be escorted by an of-age AMC student.
College book store (various times).
Mass and other religious events (various times).
Spiritual Enhancement/Cultural Appreciation/Professional Development/Wellness Days events (various times).
Late afternoon and evening academic courses.

Where to Find Things:

Campus map at college entrance; campus center
College monthly calendar of events available from the Campus Center or Public Affairs Department in Socquet House.
Call the Public Affairs Department: (508) 849-3337.

Important Information:

Anna Maria College
One Sunset Lane
Paxton, MA 01612

Main Switchboard:
(508) 849-3300
Athletic Department:
(508) 849-3446
Book Store:
(508) 849-3461
Library:
(508) 849-3405
Public Affairs:
(508) 849-3337
Registrar:
(508) 849-3400
Zecco Performing Arts Center
(508) 849-3410

Assumption College

Worcester, MA

History

Assumption College was founded in 1904, in the Greendale section of Worcester, by the religious congregation of the Augustinians of Assumption. As a combination seminary and preparatory school for men, the College's original goal was to provide clergy for the French-speaking population of New England. At its inception, classes were taught in French and the faculty:student ratio was 1:1; four faculty and four students. As the student body grew, the College quickly expanded its curriculum to include pre-law and pre-medicine programs. In 1917, Assumption received a charter to grant Bachelor of Arts degrees from the Commonwealth of Massachusetts.

Assumption remained a bilingual institution until the late 1940s. The next decade was a period of steady growth for the College. Then, in June of 1953, a tornado destroyed much of the College's physical plant, killing one priest and two nuns. For the next three years, Assumption operated out of make-shift classrooms generously provided by community organizations until the current campus was ready.

In 1956, when the College moved to its present site, student enrollment was 165. Optimistic trustees and faculty predicted an eventual student body of 500. That goal however, was soon exceeded. By 1969, the undergraduate student population was 929. Faced with changing times and inspired by Vatican II, Assumption became one of the nation's first Catholic colleges to invite laymen and laywomen to serve on its board of trustees. At the same time, the school decided to admit women.

Since 1978, under the guidance of President Joseph H. Hagan, solid financial leadership has enabled the College to operate in the black. It has placed remaining operating funds into an endowment for the financial needs of students and faculty development, and continued physical plant expansion.

General Description

Today Assumption College is a four-year, private, coeducational, Catholic liberal arts college. It educates students in the traditions of Christianity and liberal arts, and promotes Christian living; it expands professional possibilities and deepens spiritual resolve.

The primary focus of Assumption's faculty members is teaching. Ninety percent of them have doctorate degrees in their fields. The ratio of students to faculty is l5: I, and the average class size is 24. Total undergraduate enrollment is 1,750 and the ratio of men/women students is approximately 40% to 60%.

There are 24 undergraduate majors offered at Assumption. Some special programs offered include: Medical Technology/ Pre-Med, Pre-Dental, Pre-Bio Tech, Pre-Theology, Natural Science Research, Pre-Law, and Secondary and Elementary Certification. Cross-registration and special combined degree programs, such as the 3/2 Engineering Program or the Gerontology Studies Program, are encouraged within the consortium of colleges in the Worcester area. Other combined programs with outside professional schools include Podiatric Medicine, Optometry, and Banking. A unique academic opportunity, the Community Studies Program, teaches geography, history, and sociology research skills in the hands-on study of Worcester's ethnic neighborhoods. In addition, students, in most disciplines, may design an independent study course. They may also take advantage of internships, for credit, in local businesses and organizations.

Through courses in philosophy, literature, history, and theology, Assumption provides students with the basic tools for lifelong learning, such as how to think, how to write, how to understand people and live with them. The unique 2-year Foundations Program helps students reflect on the heritage of the Western world. Each year, a select number of highly qualified sophomores participate in the University of Dallas' Semester in Rome Program, which reinforces this program. Students take advantage of other study abroad opportunities. Assumption will soon have its own program, Assomption-France, in Cannes, France, which will emphasize opportunities for integration into the French culture as well as internships.

College organizations and the Diocese of Worcester provide opportunities for the students to learn and use leadership skills. In addition, students are known for their contributions and service to the Worcester area civic, cultural, educational and business community. They also volunteer, internationally and nationally, for the Mexico Mission, and the New York City, Appalachia, and Philadelphia projects.

Affordable, Assumption is highly regarded for its astute administration and its fiscal responsibility. The College continually upgrades its academic programs and facilities to provide an excellent learning and physical environment for its students.

Sports

The College is a member of the National Collegiate Athletic Association (NCAA), the Eastern College Athletic Conference (ECAC), the New England Collegiate Football Conference, and the Northeast-10 Conference. Assumption competes in men's and women's basketball, soccer, tennis, cross country, baseball, softball, women's field hockey and volleyball, and men's football, lacrosse, and golf in the NE-10.

The College conducts its varsity basketball games in the Andrew Laska Gymnasium. On the lower lever are offices of the athletic staff, showers and lockers. Outdoor athletic facilities include tennis courts and the H.L. Rocheleau Field (baseball, soccer, football, lacrosse) and the Norman Marois field (softball and field hockey).

The College has constructed a new recreation complex, the Plourde Recreation Center. The first floor of the complex features four racquetball courts, an aerobics room, a standard size pool, 6 lanes by 25 yards, and a field house, which boasts three full-size, multi-purpose courts. On the second floor of the field house is a suspended, three lane track, with views of the nearby playing fields. Also located on the second floor is the weight training room, and a lounge. All intramural activities are held in the Plourde Center. Over 500 students and 50 faculty, administration and staff use the facility on a daily basis.

Most of Assumption sporting events are free and open to the public. There is a nominal admissions fee for basketball and hockey games. Tickets can be purchased at the door before the games.

Assumption College Facts:

500 Salisbury St.
Worcester, MA 01609
(508) 767-7000
Enrollment: 1,750

Alumni: Massachusetts: 7,670; New England: 9,670; Other: 2,000
Number of Transfer students: 150
Percent of 1st year students graduating within 5 years: 76%
Percent of 1st year students who return for sophomore year: 84%
Percent of students on campus: 87%
Percent of faculty/staff residing in:
Worcester: 41%
Worcester County: 77%
Other: 23%

Accreditation:
New England Association of Schools and Colleges
State of Massachusetts Department of Education
Council of Rehabilitation Education
Massachusetts Association for Colleges for Teacher Education
National League for Nursing

President: Joseph H. Hagan (508) 767-7000
Dean of Students: Mr. J. Richard Christiansen (508) 767-7325
Associate Dean of Students: Ms. Maureen Killay (508) 752-6515
Admissions Director: Mr. Thomas Dunn (508) 767-7285
VP for Student Life: Father John Frank (508) 752-6515
Director of Public Relations: Ms. Nancy McBride (508) 752-5615

Facilities on campus:

Emmanuel d'Alzon Library:
180,000 volumes
Chapel of the Holy Spirit
Computer Center, Founder's Hall
Plourde Recreation Center

Atlantic Union College

South Lancaster, MA

Innovative Programs in an Historic Setting

Founded in 1882, Atlantic Union College offers a strong liberal arts program founded on Christian values. A truly multi-cultural campus, AUC draws students from around the world and is one of the most culturally diverse liberal arts colleges in the country. Extracurricular activities as well as academic programs emphasize the value of living with cultural variety. Atlantic Union College is associated with the Seventh-day Adventist church, whose nineteenth century beginnings still are felt in some of the early architecture on campus:

Founder's Hall, a three-story clapboard building, orginally the administration building for what was once South Lancaster Academy and then Lancaster Junior College, has been renovated and returned to much of its original form. The building contains a collection of Adventist memorabilia and is open to the public by appointment.

The G. Eric Jones library also holds an extensive collection of early Seventh-day Adventist documents as well as considerable materials relating to the history of the college and regional Adventist church. The library also houses the Ottilie F. Stafford Modern Poetry Collection. The curators of the collection sponsor lectures, tours and use the library for special research.

The Thayer Conservatory of Music is housed in one of the homes of the Thayer family and one of the best examples of late nineteenth century domestic architecture in the area. Thayer Hall's central staircase is the largest one of its kind - and one of the most beautiful - in the state of Massachusetts. Musical practice as well as chamber and orchestral concerts take place in the larger drawing rooms, as do occasional wedding receptions and other special events. Tours and interviews can be arranged by calling the Thayer Conservatory.

Built in 1883 by Eugene Van Renssalaer Thayer, "The White House" now is home to the study of literature and writing at AUC. The main fireplaced parlor provides a lovely Victorian setting for discussion groups and various humanities-oriented activities and receptions.

The Mabel R. Bartlett Art Gallery, also built in the latter part of the nineteenth century, houses one of the region's loveliest small art galleries. Home to the art faculty, the gallery also houses a small permanent collection and presently provides space for materials owned by the Weidner Center for the Cultivation of the Altruistic Spirit.

The Weidner Center is one of two special college programs especially designed with the community in mind. Named for John H. Weidner, rescuer of over a thousand members of the European Jewish community, Allied personnel and other threatened peoples from the Nazi regime during WWII, the center hosts exhibits and offers lectures on the nature and necessity of Christian ethics and humanitarian behavior and gives tours to off-campus groups. The center is an integral part of AUC's curriculum, which emphasizes the mandate to afford others dignity and selfless aid and support.

The W.G. Nelson Field House is home to "Kinesis, a Lifestyle", a program of total fitness and wellness. Seventh-day Adventists believe in the need to be healthy and fit in order to be a clear-thinking and ethical human being. Classes in nutrition, muscular movement, and the ethics of sportsmanship complement an athletic and fitness program that is also an integral part of the college curriculum.

The Chan Shun Dining Commons, scheduled for completion in the summer of 1995, will provide meeting and conference rooms for students, faculty, staff and the community and will serve healthful and attractive vegetarian meals. The 18,350 square-foot dining facility will be one of the largest in the region.

Atlantic Union College is committed to educating people toward fulfilling their highest potential - academically, healthfully and ethically and provides a curriculum that requires the exercise of the mind and body and the active exercise of principle-driven ethics in today's multi-cultural and multi-faceted world. This triple approach to education also energizes AUC's Adult Degree Program and Electronic Distance Learning, two other innovative programs that make high-quality education available to a growing number of non-traditional students who are unable to participate in regular classes.

The college does not discriminate on the basis of gender, race, culture, nationality, or age in any of its admission or educational policies. The community is welcome to visit the campus at any time. Please call the office of public relations at (508) 368-2248 for an appointment for further information.

Important Information

Main Street
South Lancaster, MA 01561-1000
(508) 368-2000

Students: 500 Day/traditional;
500 non-traditional
Faculty: 50
President: James J. Londis

Dean of Student Services:
Ciro Sepulveda
Academic Dean: Carol Allen
Director of Admissions: Osa Canto
Director of Financial Aid:
David Rawson
Director of Adult Degree Program:
Ian Bothwell

Becker College

Leicester and Worcester, MA

Located in the heart of Massachusetts, Becker is a unique New England college and one of the oldest two-year colleges in America. The institution comprises two separate campuses located six miles apart, each with its own dormitories, library, dining hall and academic facilities.

The Leicester campus began as an academy in 1784 — the 19th oldest campus in the country. The Worcester campus was founded in 1887 by E.C.A. Becker. Both schools have sustained a long-standing tradition of quality education. In 1974 Becker and Leicester began working together to expand academic offerings and provide broader social and recreational opportunities for their students. As a result of their close cooperation, the two were formally consolidated in 1977 as the Worcester campus and Leicester campus of Becker College.

Today the college offers 27 associate degree and three bachelor degree programs and its student body has grown to a full-time enrollment of 1,000. Men and women from across the United States and many foreign countries have selected Becker to provide the necessary education and professional training to achieve their goals. Becker is a small, coeducational college offering career-focused programs designed for both the two-year student and for the student seeking to transfer to a four-year college or university.

Despite all its diversity, Becker proudly retains its "small college" reputation for personal attention and individual student concern.

The Becker Student

With 1,000 full-time students and an additional 2,800 students enrolled in Continuing Education, Becker's student population is wonderfully diverse, and includes individuals from 15 states and 20 foreign countries. Fully one-third are enrolled in academic concentrations that have been added to the curriculum in the past seven years!

Well over half of Becker's students come from Massachusetts. And while the majority of the full-time student body matriculates immediately after high school graduation, there are growing numbers of older, non-traditional students in the mix.

Students young and old choose Becker for a variety of compelling reasons, not the least of which is Becker's reputation for high quality and challenging academic programs. Many are attracted by the specific, career-oriented education they will receive and by the promise of meaningful and fulfilling employment upon graduation.

Others want the total educational experience and enrichment that is unique to a residential college experience. Still more are attracted by tuition/room and board costs that are the lowest of any private college or university in Massachusetts.

Did You Know:

John Hancock and Samuel Adams signed the incorporation papers of Leicester Academy.

Eli Whitney, inventor of the cotton gin, and William P. Morton, father of modern anesthesia, attended Leicester Academy.

Leicester Academy once owned a township in Maine.

Robert Goddard, father of modern rocketry, studied penmanship at Becker.

Becker offered the first course in typewriting available in Worcester; when Myron Converse graduated in 1894, Worcester Five Cents Savings Bank bought its first typewriter because of his skill. Eventually he became president of the bank.

Harry G. Stoddard, president and chairman of the board of Wyman-Gordon Company, graduated from Becker in 1893.

In the early days of Becker the executive secretarial program was a popular course of study for male students; it included "Pitmanic Pothooks," a method of taking short-hand.

Louisa May Alcott frequently visited her Uncle Reverend Samuel May, an active abolitionist, at his home in Leicester. The house is now a Becker residence hall and is said to be haunted.

Becker offered the first journalism major in the east and the first Retail Merchandising program in Massachusetts.

Becker is the single largest holder of historic properties in Central Massachusetts with 25 buildings listed on the National Register of Historic Places.

William Marcy and Richard Olney, both graduates of Leicester Academy, went on to become Secretary of State.

The first perfect game in professional baseball was pitched by J. Lee Richmond on a site near Becker's present-day Worcester Campus ("Worcesters" -1; Cleveland - 0).

Ralph Crowley, chairman of the board of Polar Corporation, graduated from Leicester Junior College.

Important Information

Address:
61 Sever Street
Box 15071
Worcester, MA 01615-0071

3 Paxton Street
Leicester, MA 01524-1197

Telephone: (508) 791-9241

Student Population: 1,150 (full time equivalent, headcount: 1,745)
Faculty Size: 120

President: Arnold C. Weller, Jr. ext. 205
Dean of Students: Carlton A. Perry, ext. 260, 460
Dean of Admissions: Brian P. Davis, ext. 240, 440
Student Services Director:
Worcester: Jodi Donohue-Aja, ext. 261
Leicester: Timothy Chiasson, ext. 462

Academic Buildings: 52
Dormitories: 26
Campus Acreage: 100

Clark University

Worcester, MA

Clark University, founded in 1887, is the oldest graduate institution in New England and the second-oldest in the nation. Clark was founded by

Jonas Gilman Clark, a Worcester-area merchant, and G. Stanley Hall, a prominent psychologist who was Clark's first president.

Clark has played a prominent role in the development of psychology and geography as distinguished academic disciplines in the United States. In addition to maintaining an impressive record of research, Clark faculty have extended their influence through professional organizations and publications. For example, both the American Psychological Association and the journal "Economic Geography" were founded at Clark.

In 1909, Clark brought Sigmund Freud to America to lecture on psychoanalysis - the only U.S. institution to have done so. Clark's faculty has included Robert H. Goddard, the "father of the space age," and Albert A. Michelson, the first American to win a Nobel Prize in science. Other researchers here first measured the wind-chill factor, conducted research that led to the creation of the birth control pill and made the first breakthroughs in understanding how brain tissue regenerates itself.

Clark is the smallest research university in the country - the smallest member of the Association of American Universities, which includes the nation's leading research universities. As such, Clark combines the academic opportunities of a large research university with the atmosphere of a small college.

Students who come to Clark are seeking close interaction with professors who are nationally known researchers. Clark students have an opportunity rarely found at other colleges and universities to engage in research and other creative scholarship. Clark's strong graduate programs give undergraduates an opportunity to incorporate advanced studies into their undergraduate program.

Clark is also attractive to students interested in making a difference, socially and intellectually, on their campus and in their communities. Clark students have a well-earned reputation for social awareness and activism. Clark's internationally oriented faculty, curriculum and student body help students achieve a global understanding that will be critical to professional success.

Clark's unique five-year BA/MA, BA/MBA and BA/MHA programs offer students the chance to earn a master's degree in five years for the same cost as a bachelor's degree. Clark offers the fifth year of the accelerated programs for free to students who maintain a 3.25 grade point average.

A new Environmental School has been established at Clark to address the crucial issue of reconciling economic and technological development with long-term environmental sustainability. The new school, which will enroll its first students in the fall of 1995, is an "alternative" liberal arts program of study that can be combined with a number of existing Clark majors. The Environmental School will provide students an understanding of our physical environment, the way we use and alter the earth, and the meaning we give to aspects of the environment.

The new school will be based on Clark University's 75-year history of specializing in the study of humankind and their environment. Clark has made its mark in environmental education through such research centers as the George Perkins Marsh Institute, the first university research center dedicated to the human causes of environmental change, and such international conferences as "The Earth as Transformed by Human Action" in 1987. Nearly a quarter of Clark University's faculty are involved in research and study on the environment.

Clark is located on 50 acres, with more than 56 campus buildings, including the Robert Hutchings Goddard Library housing more than 500,000 volumes. Clark provides housing for approximately 1,500 students in eight residence halls and eight houses.

Degree Choices:

Bachelor of Arts, Bachelor of Science, Master of Arts, Master of Business Administration, Master of Health Administration, Master of Public Administration, Master of Science in Professional Communication, Master of Arts in Liberal Arts, and the Ph.D.

Sports:

Clark has 17 NCAA, Division III teams including baseball, basketball, crew, cross country, field hockey, lacrosse, soccer, swimming and diving, tennis and volleyball.

Important Information

Address:
Clark University
950 Main St.
Worcester, MA 01610-1477

Phone Numbers:

Information: (508) 793-7711
University President:
Richard Traina:(508) 793-7320
Dean of Students, Catherine Maddox-Wiley: (508) 793-7423
Director of Admissions:
Kristin Tichenor: (508) 793-7431
Higgins University Center:(508) 793-7549

Student Population:
Approximately 3,000 undergraduate and graduate students. Students hail from some 42 states and territories and 82 countries.

Faculty Size:
175 full-time instructional faculty, 98 percent with doctoral degrees.
11-1 student/faculty ratio (more than 70 percent of classes have 20 or fewer students).

Majors:
Clark offers 28 undergraduate majors and the option to self-design a major. Clark also offers 23 minors and 12 interdisciplinary concentrations.

Did You Know:

When Clark opened its doors in 1889, it was the first all-graduate institution in America.

The first Ph.D. in psychology to be granted in the United States was awarded to G. Stanley Hall, Clark's first president, who earned the degree from Harvard in 1878.

In 1914, Robert H. Goddard, in his first year as a member of the Clark faculty, secured his first rocket patents. These patents embodied the principles that, 45 years later, sent a man to the moon.

In 1911, Clark neurology professor Clifton F. Hodge worked with the Telegram & Gazette's widely publicized effort to make Worcester "the first fly-free city in America." Schoolchildren were offered prizes for killing and delivering the common pests. More than 16 million flies died in the process.

America's first Ph.D. in anthropology was awarded at Clark in 1892 to Alexander F. Chamberlain, who worked under the direction of Clark anthropologist Franz Boas, considered the "father of American anthropology."

In 1982, Clark opened the nation's first U.S. Department of Energy-supported demonstration model for efficient energy cogeneration. The idea for the project had been suggested some years earlier by three Clark students as part of their independent coursework for classes on energy policy and alternative energy sources. The cogeneration plant continues to serve Clark.

In 1967, Alice Higgins became chair of the Clark University's Board of Trustees, the first woman in the country to head the governing board of any private university.

The Marsh Institute at Clark is the first university research center dedicated to studying the human dimensions of global environmental change.

Clark geographer Paul Siple, a renowned polar explorer, invented the "wind-chill" factor. On one of his trips, he carried the flag of Clark's Graduate School of Geography, charting an Antarctic mountain range and naming it for Clark and the individual peaks for his professors.

Lewis Terman, a graduate student at Clark, was responsible for developing the concept and design of the first widely used American I.Q. tests.

The first study of maze learning by white rats was done at Clark in 1900 by Willard Small, a candidate for a Ph.D., who took as a model King Henry's VIII Hampton Court maze.

Since its founding in 1921 as the second independent doctoral program in geography in the United States, Clark's Graduate School of Geography has awarded more Ph.D. degrees in geography than any other American university.

Clark University philosopher Christina Hoff Sommers' *Who Stole Feminism? How Women Have Betrayed Women*, Simon & Schuster (1994), kicked off a new round of national debate on feminist issues.

Clark's undergraduate college recently ranked 18th in the nation among 925 undergraduate colleges in producing graduates who go on to earn Ph.D.s. Clark was first in geography and related disciplines, third in psychology, 10th in the sciences and 11th in political science and international relations.

IDRISI, a geographic information system (GIS) software developed by Professor Ron Eastman in the School of Geography at Clark, is the best-selling software of its kind in the world. Officially endorsed by the United Nations, more than 11,000 registered users in more than 100 countries use IDRISI for research, resource management, local planning and education.

Clark's Jacob Hiatt Center for Urban Education, an innovative educational partnership with the Worcester public schoools, is a national model for university/public school collaboration.

Clark was one of the first universities to call for a divestiture of South African holdings decades ago because of South Africa's apartheid policies, and one of the first to move toward reinvesting endowment funds following Nelson Mandela's call to lift economic sanctions.

College of the Holy Cross

Worcester, MA

The College of the Holy Cross has been ranked among the top 25 national liberal arts colleges for the last several years in U.S. News and World Report's annual college survey. Founded by the Society of Jesus in 1843 and the oldest Catholic college in New England, Holy Cross began with one wooden building, a half-finished brick structure, and 52 acres of land in Worcester on Pakachoag Hill, also known as Mount St. James. Today Holy Cross is a large educational complex with nearly 30 major buildings, including libraries, a modern science center, classrooms, music and art centers, extensive facilities for information technology, residence halls, chapel, football stadium, hockey rink and campus activity center, spread over 174 sloping acres.

A community of 2,600 students, evenly divided between men and women, Holy Cross offers a curriculum leading to the Bachelor of Arts degree with majors in 17 fields. In addition, its Center for Interdisciplinary and Special Studies offers non-traditional programs such as concentrations, multi-disciplinary majors, and academic internships in Worcester and Washington, D.C. The college also offers a special First-Year Program for about 165 students.

Indicative of its academic leadership has been such recognition as grants of more than $1.27 million in the past four years to support its modern language program and Multimedia Resource Center, which are expected to put Holy Cross in the forefront of changes in the way colleges and universities across America teach modern foreign languages. In recent years Holy Cross also has received: a National Endowment for the Humanities challenge grant of $600,000, creating a $3 million fund to endow three professorships in the humanities; a $300,000 grant from the W.M. Keck Foundation for the renovation of its chemistry laboratories; and challenge grants from the Kresge Foundation totaling $900,000 for new scientific instrumentation and for extensive renovation of music and concert facilities. Holy Cross also has established a Luce Professorship in Religion, Economic Development and Social Justice supported by a total of $690,000 in grants from the Henry Luce Foundation.

The college actively supports the enhancement of public education in Worcester with several programs. Among them are the Youth Exploring Science program, which brings minority 6th, 7th and 8th graders to campus during vacations for intensive science education, a five-year program of year-long learning sabbaticals at Holy Cross for 11 secondary science teachers; summer workshops for two dozen Worcester science teachers at least through 1997, and a collaborative effort between Worcester teachers and Holy Cross faculty to develop new science curricula for Worcester schools, to be tested in the schools in the 1996-97 school year.

Important Information

Address:
1 College St.
Worcester MA 01610-2395
508-793-2011

Enrollment: 2,600
Full-time faculty: 213; Part-time faculty: 51
President : Rev. Gerard Reedy, S.J, . (508) 793-2525
Dean of Students: Rev. Earle L Markey, S.J., (508) 793-2414
Admissions Director:
Ann Bowe McDermott, (508) 793-2443
Student Activities Director:
Peter W. Simonds , (508) 793-3487
Facilities on the 174-acre campus:

- 7 academic buildings
- 9 residence halls
- Dinand Library
- O'Callahan Science Library
- Music Library
- Hogan Campus Center
- Millard Art Center
- Brooks Center for Music
- Hart Recreation Center
- St. Joseph Memorial Chapel
- Kimball Dining Hall

Did You Know:

Unlike some "colleges" that actually are universities with graduate programs and enrollments of more than 10,000 or 15,000, Holy Cross is strictly undergraduate with only 2,600 students.
The college is ranked in the top 4 % of 877 private four-year colleges in the number of its students who earned doctorates.
The college's grounds department won nine national grounds maintenance awards since 1977, including the Grand Award for the Best Maintained Campus in the U.S. from the Professional Grounds Management Society in 1977 and 1983.
United States Supreme Court Justice Clarence Thomas is a 1971 Holy Cross graduate.
Originally an all-male school, Holy Cross admitted women for the first time in 1972 and within four years there was an equal number of men and women.
In 1990 Joseph B. Murray, M.D., a 1940 graduate, was awarded the Nobel Prize in Medicine for performing the first human kidney transplant.

A recent Fortune Magazine survey examined which American colleges and universities produce the most CEOs of Fortune 500 and Service 500 companies. Holy Cross ranked in the top 25 overall and placed in the top 10 when the size of each graduating class was taken into account.

Boston lawyer and 1949 graduate Barry Reed is the author of the best-selling novel, the *Verdict*, which became a major motion picture starring Paul Newman.

The Holy Cross libraries acquired their 500,000th volume during the 1994-95 academic year.

More than 75 percent of Holy Cross students graduated in the top 20 percent of their high school classes.

About 500 students annually participate in some form of community service activity, ranging from volunteering at Abby's House, a women's shelter, and at the Mustard Seed, a soup kitchen, to tutoring in after-school programs, to visiting nursing homes and participating in the "grandkids" program.

The first valedictorian, in 1849, was an African-American man, James A. Healy, who became the Catholic Church's first African American bishop. His brothers also attended Holy Cross and one, Patrick, became a Jesuit priest and served as president of Georgetown University.

FITCHBURG STATE COLLEGE

Fitchburg, MA

Fitchburg State - "the uncommon public college" - has come to be recognized as one of the finest colleges of its kind in New England. A top-flight faculty outstanding academic programs, attractive grounds and a family-like atmospher‹ combine to create an extraordinary all-around educational experience.

The college - now celebrating its centennial - offers 60 programs of stud within 23 majors, and boasts an innovative new Liberal Arts and Sciences program that emphasizes such crucial skills as writing, critical thinking, listening, speaking and quantifying. Regardless of their major, all students study the history of our great civilizations and explore the world of ideas that have forged our many cultures.

While the focus of the college's outstanding faculty is on teaching and advising, scholarly writing and research are very much a part of their academic lives. Many have published books, and in the last few years two were named Fulbright Scholars. The faculty-student ratio is 1:15. Nearly all students participate in the college's extensive internship program, which offers real world experience and a head start on the job search.

Fitchburg State was among the first to have a fiber optic network and now operates 14 computer laboratories, some general, some focused specifically on such fields as graphics, business, nursing, technical writing and geography.

The college has long been a leader in the education of future teachers, and operates a laboratory school where undergraduates earn teacher certification, take classes, conduct observation and work with schoolchildren and teachers. In recent decades, Fitchburg State has earned a reputation for excellence in other fields. Nursing majors study in one of the oldest and most respected programs in Massachusetts. Communications/Media students have access to a fully stocked television studio, unparalleled darkroom facilities and an equipment laboratory that allows them to make the world their lab.

The list goes on: one of the finest medical technology labs in New England; laboratory and greenhouse facilities to perform cell and tissue cultures and advanced biochemical analyses; field locations to study forest, bog, marsh, lake and coastal habitats; zoological and botanical specimen collections; robotics and computerized manufacturing equipment for industrial technology majors; modern typesetting and Mac labs for graphic arts; extensive exercise science equipment and metabolic measurement instruments; and the Montachusett Economic Center, where students can work with nonprofit agencies and businesses.

Students at Fitchburg State take an active role in the governance, judicial and planning processes. There are clubs, groups, teams and organizations for just about every interest. Since education involves much more than classroom learning, there are films, lectures, concerts, seminars, tournaments, exhibits and coffeehouses. The Visiting Artists and Lecturers Series brings to campus some of the country's most thought-provoking speakers.

A college's success may be difficult to measure, but all indications are that we're achieving the results that matter. Despite a difficult economy, just four percent of our recent graduates were unable to find work. Seventy-three percent had jobs related to their college studies, and 95 percent felt they got a good education at the college.

Important Information

College address: 160 Pearl St., Fitchburg, MA 01420-2697
Telephone: (508) 345-2151; Fax: (508) 665-3693

President: Vincent J Mara, Ph.D., 508-665-3112
Vice President for Student Affairs: Charles Ratto, 508-665-3130
Director of Admissions: Marke Vickers, 508-665-3144

Character
Four-year, public, coeducational college of liberal arts and professional programs. Undergraduate, graduate, and continuing education programs available on full- and part-time basis.

Location
Fitchburg, Massachusetts, a city of 39,000 located in the North Central part of the state, close to the New Hampshire border, about 50 miles from Boston.

Main campus: 32 buildings (some nearly a century old, most post-60's) on 35 acres.
McKay Teacher Education Center: 12 acres.
Athletic Fields: 35 acres.
Calendar:
Two semesters: Early September to mid-December, and late January to early May. (Two summer sessions and a winter session are also offered by Graduate and Continuing Education).

History:
Established in 1894 as the State Normal School in Fitchburg, offering a two-year teacher training program for women. In 1910, Edgerly School on campus became one of the first junior high schools in the United States. The following year, a practical arts teacher training course for men, the first of its kind in the country, was instituted. Beginning in the early 1930s, four-year degrees were offered in practical arts and all levels of education. Graduate courses were added in 1935.

In 1960, the college became the State College at Fitchburg, and began to award degrees in disciplines other than education. In 1965, the name was officially changed to Fitchburg State College. Today the college offers 32 undergraduate degree programs in 20 academic fields.

Majors:
Undergraduate majors: biology, business administration, chemistry, communications/media, computer science, early childhood education, economics, elementary education, English, general studies, geography, history, human services, industrial technology, mathematics, medical technology, middle school education, nursing, psychology, sociology, special education, technology education/industrial technology.

Graduate majors: English, education, communications/media, computer science, MBA, counseling.

Enrollment Day Division Undergraduates: 3,075 - 55% female, 45% male;
Resident: 1,200
Fields of study: Professional: 50%, Education: 16%, Arts and Sciences: 24%, Undeclared: 10%.
Evening Division Students : (excluding graduate): 1,216
Graduate Students: 861
Degrees awarded (1994):
Baccalaureate: 831; Master's: 245
Faculty:
Full-time faculty: 246
Part-time faculty: 150 (day and evening)
Percent with doctorate or highest degree in field: 61%
Student-faculty ratio: 15:1

Library:
Library services include instruction classes, interlibrary loans, free CD-ROM computer-based literature searching, a fee based on-line service, 75 hours of reference, 98 hours of operation, and an automated circulation system. The library contains 175,854 volumes, including a children's literature collection of 7,000 volumes, an 11,900 item reference collection and the McKay Campus School Library. It also houses the papers of author Robert Cormier. There are 387,513 microfilm/fiche items, including the Educational Resources Information Center (ERIC) with its 327,000 items. It currently receives 1,381 periodical subscriptions.

Accreditation: New England Association of Schools and Colleges, National League for Nursing, Council for Standards in Human Service Education, Council of Graduate Schools.

Financial aid:
Federal state and philanthropic programs provide students with more than $6 million in grants, loans, work-study awards and scholarships. 58% of undergraduates receive financial aid from federal loans and grant programs, and 36% receive scholarship assistance from private donations.

Revenues:
Net state appropriations: $9,660,378.
Total revenue: $28,096,134.
Endowment:
$3.5 million, managed by the Fitchburg State College Foundation
Economic impact:
$126 million
Total employees: 525
Annual payroll: $15.5 million
Cultural events:
The college annually sponsors a Visiting Artists and Lecturers Series and a Performing Arts Series. The Stageright theatre group, the band, chorus and jazz groups, and the dance dub offer performances throughout the year. The Campus Center Art Gallery hosts a series of exhibits annually.

Alumni Association: The Alumni Association offers a number of programs and services to the college's graduates. It serves the campus community with scholarships, equipment grants and library materials. Its official publication is the quarterly magazine Contact. Total living alumni: 20,904 Percent living in Massachusetts: 79.

Athletics : College teams compete in NCAA Division III. Men's varsity sports: baseball, basketball, cross country, football, ice hockey, indoor track, soccer, track and field. Women's varsity sports: basketball, cross country, field hockey, indoor track, softball, soccer, track and field, volleyball. Many intramural activities are also offered.

Did You Know:

Fitchburg State just celebrated its 100th birthday.

It was the first college in the country to offer a practical arts teacher training course.

It is the only four-year college in North Central Massachusetts, and the only public college in central Massachusetts to offer the MBA degree.

The college has a private foundation with an endowment of $3.5 million.

Six thousand students study at the college, both full- and part-time, graduate and undergraduate, in some 30 academic fields.

The college's archives house the papers of novelist Robert Cormier.

The college is the second largest employer in the area with 525 employees.

The college has a $100 million economic impact on the surrounding towns, and attracts 25,000 annual visitors to the area.

Fitchburg State features a multicultural environment including 85 international students from 18 countries.

Mount Wachusett Community College

Main Campus: Gardner, Massachusetts
Secondary Sites: Leominster, Clinton, Fort Devens, Athol

Mount Wachusettt Community College students come from all walks of life, with varying academic credentials, to pursue many different goals. The College, founded in 1963, serves the 29 cities and towns in Northern Worcester County. Located on 269 scenic acres in Gardner, MA, the campus includes a main academic building with fully equipped classrooms, laboratories, studios, library and theater. In addition, a state-of-the-art recreational complex consists of a gymnasium, athletic field, running track, handball and racquetball courts, pool, weight room and fitness center. The College's facilities are also accessible to persons with disabilities. In addition to the Gardner campus, MWCC holds classes at its Leominster, Fort Devens, Athol and Clinton campuses.

The Associate Degree and Certificate programs at Mount Wachusett offer multiple options to help students achieve their goals. The degree programs meet transfer requirements at most public and private four-year colleges and universities across the nation. The career and technical curricula are designed to provide students with distinctive advantages to enter a wide variety of occupations in a rapidly changing and highly competitive global economy. The College is fully accredited by the New England Association of Schools and Colleges.

The General Education core, required in all degree programs, is an essential component to student education. These courses assist the students to speak, write, think and analyze. As a result of MWCC's academic and co-curricular experiences, students can gain greater self-awareness and self-confidence and acquire effective leadership skills. Student success is MWCC's primary concern.

A number of support systems are in place to serve students at MWCC. Academic, career, transfer and personal counseling; assessment; professional and peer tutoring; instruction in basic skills; English-as-a-second-language; and services to students with learning disabilities are offered.

The library at Mount Wachusett contains 60,000 volumes, with additions made daily. Subscription to nearly 300 magazine titles and substantial media and publication collections represent a small portion of the services provided by the MWCC Library.

The services of the Financial Aid Office are used by three-quarters of the day students at the institution. An active student government supports 20 student organizations and clubs, and funds numerous events during the year. There is also a child care center on campus.

Class size at MWCC is kept small in order to maximize faculty-student interaction, and the College places a strong emphasis on the academic advising process. The concern and competency of the faculty, in addition to a college-wide dedication to relevance and currency in instructional programs, materials and equipment are largely responsible for retention rates and student satisfaction ratings that are well above the national average.

Did You Know:

100% of the Nursing Class of '94 passed the National Registered Nursing Exams.

Over 20,000 patrons per year enjoy Theater at the Mount theatrical presentations.

Each semester, MWCC offers more than 500 courses and programs.

Students in MWCC's Broadcasting and Telecommunications Department air their programming live on CATV in three communities.

A new Physical Therapy Assistant Degree Program began in the Spring '95 semester.

35% of MWCC graduates transfer to four-year colleges.

13 sports and drama camps are offered each summer for children ages 8-15.

There are 20 student clubs and organizations.

MWCC has been nationally recognized for its services to students with disabilities.

The "Mount Advantage" Financial Aid Program guarantees full tuition and institutional fees to eligible students.

MWCC has 46 transfer agreements with baccalaureate institutions.

Joint Admission agreements exist with the University of Massachusetts at Amherst, Fitchburg State College and Worcester State College.

A dual enrollment program allows high school juniors and seniors to take college courses.

MWCC offers January intersession and two Summer session semesters.

MWCC's computer courses are taught by Novell Inc. Certified Netware instructors.

Important Information

Address:
Mount Wachusett Community College
444 Green Street
Gardner, MA 01440-1000
Telephone: (508) 632-6600; (508) 222-MWCC; (508) 632-6155
Fax: (508) 632-6155

Student Population: 1,800 Day; 3,000 Division of Continuing Education
Faculty Size: 76 full-time; 150 adjunct
President: Daniel M. Asquino, ext. 101
Dean of Students Services: Mary E. Solomita, ext. 104
Director of Admissions: Maria A. McCarthy, ext. 134
Director of Financial Aid: Dr. Richard Pastor, ext. 117
Dean of Continuing Education and Community Services: Dr. Richard Fox, ext. 123

Campus Locations: Gardner, Leominster, Fort Devens, Athol and Clinton
Gardner Campus Acreage: 269

Nichols College

Dudley, MA

Nichols College has a long tradition of educating young adults for careers in business. Founded in 1931 by Col. James Conrad as a junior college for men, Nichols has evolved to a four-year co-educational institution with a separate evening division offering undergraduate and graduate programs at four campus locations.

Students choose Nichols College for its strength in business education. The faculty provides a blend of academic and professional experience which gives students a unique perspective on business and public service. A small 22:1 student/faculty ratio offers the personal attention lacking at larger institutions.

One way Nichols stands out from almost every other college in the country is through the College's commitment to computer technology. The PC-Plan requires every incoming freshman to own and use a laptop computer, a vital piece of equipment used to complemnt a wide range of subject matter. Students become familiar with the latest software programs and offer valuable skills to future employers.

The Institute For American Values is also a unique part of the Nichols experience. As the public policy arm of the College, the Institute brings noted speakers to campus to discuss a wide range of timely topics - from subjects debated in Congress to international crises, to historical lectures. Institute events are free and open to the public.

With 11 varsity sports for men and women, athletics plays an important role in the Nichols education. Close to 40 percent of students play on some varsity team, and a strong intramural program offers an additional athletic outlet. A new outdoor recreation complex offers six lighted tennis courts, two basketball courts and a volleyball pit.

Nichols offers a bachelor of science in business administration with specialties in General Business, Marketing Management, Management Information Services, Accounting, Finance, Real Estate Finance, Economics, and Entrepreneurship. Also offered are a bachelor of science in public administration and bachelor of arts degrees in American Studies, History, Psychology, Industrial Psychology and Social Services.

The evening program offers the same quality business education for working professionals at four campus locations - Dudley, Leominster, Auburn and Southborough. Students either work toward a certificate, associates or bachelors degree in business or liberal arts in the undergraduate programs or a master of business administration in the graduate program. Classes are offered at night during the week and on Saturday mornings.

Important Information

Address:
Nichols College
Box 5000 Center Road
Dudley, MA 01571
(508) 943-1560

Student population: 750 full-time day undergraduate, 75 percent residents; 725 part-time evening undergraduate; 500 part-time evening graduate.

College President: Lowell C. Smith
Dean of Students: Roger Carney
Admissions Director: Tracey Dysart
Student Activities Director: Roxanne Castaldy

Buildings: 44 including 14 residence halls. The largest residence hall is Shamie Hall, completed in 1991, which houses 246 students. Shamie Hall rooms have private bathroom, individually controlled heat and air conditioning, cable and computer hookups. Other residence halls can accommodate 92 to 15 students. Several are renovated private homes located right on campus.

Davis Hall was completed in 1991 and offers an updated and fully-networked academic environment. The building houses 10 classrooms, two lecture halls, a seminar room, six faculty offices and a lounge.

Nichols is located on 210 acres of land in the center of Dudley. Adjacent to the campus is a nine-hole golf course operated by the College and available for student use.

Did You Know:

Environmental Science Professor Mauri Pelto directs the largest glacial research program in North America. Every summer, Dr. Pelto travels to the glaciers of the North Cascades of Washington state to study 50 of the 700 glaciers in the area and record changes in size, health and movement over time.

Famous Graduates:

Fred Friendly '36, retired president of CBS News, and producer of "See it Now" television series in collaboration with Edward R. Murrow.

Richard Hebert '69, vice president, and Frederick Hebert '70, treasurer of Hebert Candies, founded by their father 77 years ago.

Quinsigamond Community College

Worcester, MA

It's a place where "age" doesn't matter. I discovered a whole new life there after kitchen and kids," Idamay Arsenault, Worcester, MA.

For 30 years, Quinsigamond has been committed to responding to individual and community needs by providing a broad range of programs to students of all ages and backgrounds. Established in 1963 as the sixth community college in Massachusetts, it is located on the former campus of Assumption College in north Worcester and consists of 7 buildings on 50 acres. Quinsigamond's student body has grown from under 300 to over 7,000 full-time and part-time students. The college's transfer programs provide the broad foundation necessary for further study at four-year colleges and universities. Career programs prepare men and women for immediate entry into a variety of fields.

Those who wish to continue their education through evening, afternoon or weekend study can do so at Quinsigamond's Center for Lifelong Learning. At the center, students can earn an Associate's Degree, or enroll in selected courses for personal or professional enrichment. The college's extensive Community Services Program, which is administered by the center, sponsors a variety of workshops and seminars of interest to the community. The Center for Education and Training develops custom in-service courses and programs for business and industry.

Students attend Quinsigamond because it offers them an opportunity to achieve both personal as well as educational goals, in a supportive environment. The College offers over 40 study options, ranging from Liberal Arts to such career fields as Engineering, Technology, Health Care, Business and Office Management. In addition, Quinsigamond offers custom training and education to area business and industry and is a participant in local economic development activities, notably in Biotechnology.

Quinsigamond's strengths according to its 15,000 alumni, are a) its diversity of programming which prepares students for immediate entry into the workplace or for immediate transfer to four-year colleges and universities; b) the personal attention of both faculty and staff to the personal as well as educational needs of students; c) the support services available to non-traditional students which ease the transition back to a formal educational setting; d) its affordability for first-generation college students; e) its accessibility to commuting students in Central Massachusetts; and f) a very good reputation among employers and four-year colleges and universities for high-quality graduates.

Quinsigamond offers over 40 study options in the fields of Liberal Arts, Applied Arts, Business, Engineering and Technology, Health, Human Services. Individual programs of study include: Administrative Office Management; Automotive Technology; Basic Engineering; Biotechnology; Business Administration (career and transfer options); Computer Information Systems; Computer Maintenance Technology; Criminal Justice; Dental Hygiene; Early Childhood Education; Electronics; Emergency Medical Training; Environmental Health/Safety; ESL; Fire Science, Graphic Arts; Health; Hotel/Restaurant Management, Human Services; Liberal Arts; Mental Health; Nurse Education; Occupational Therapy, Paramedic Technician; Radiologic Technician; Respiratory Therapy; TQM; Visual Arts.

Quinsigamond is fully accredited by the New England Association of Schools and Colleges (NEASC), the regional accrediting body. Individual programs of study are also accredited by their own professional associations, especially in the field of Health.

Important Information

Address: 670 West Boylston Street, Worcester, MA 01606
Phone: (508)853-2300
Fax: (508)852-6943

Student Population: Approximately 7,000 full-time and part-time students annually, 63% female; 37% male; Minority enrollment: approximately 15%
Faculty Size: 96 full-time; 273 part-time* (*unduplicated headcounts)

Important Numbers:

President: Dr. Sandra L. Kurtinitis (508) 854-4203
Acting Dean/Students: Ann R. Carroll (508) 854-4375

Admissions Director: Ronald C. Smith (508) 854-4218
Student Activities Director: Patrick T. Tran (508) 854-4294

Tufts University School of Veterinary Medicine —— North Grafton, MA

Tufts University, founded in 1852, is a small but complex university, which enrolls about 7,900 students in eight undergraduate, graduate and professional schools on three campuses (each in a different county!) in Medford/Somerville, Boston and North Grafton, Massachusetts. John DiBiaggio was named the university's 11th president in 1992.

Tufts established the School of Veterinary Medicine in 1978. It is the only veterinary school in New England and one of just 27 veterinary schools in the United States. Tufts' veterinary school is fully accredited by the American Veterinary Medical Association. Dr. Franklin M. Loew has been dean of the veterinary school since 1982.

First-year veterinary students study at Tufts' Boston health sciences campus, the site of Tufts' School of Medicine, School of Dental Medicine and Sackler School of Graduate Biomedical Sciences, as well as the U.S. Department of Agriculture's Jean Mayer Human Nutrition Research Center on Aging.

Second-, third- and fourth-year students are based at the veterinary school's 634-acre campus in North Grafton, MA, about 7 miles east of Worcester, where the facilities include: Tufts New England Veterinary Medical Center with the Hospital for Large Animals; the Henry and Lois Foster Hospital for Small Animals; the Franklin M. Loew Veterinary Medical Education Center; the Wildlife Clinic; the Center for Animals and Public Policy; and the Tufts Veterinary Diagnostic Laboratory. The school also maintains the Tufts Ambulatory Farm Service in Woodstock, Conn., and a research laboratory at the Marine Biological Laboratory in Woods Hole, MA.

Tufts' veterinary school attracts highly qualified candidates from throughout the United States as well as from other countries. The school enrolls about 300 students in its four-year professional program that leads to a doctor of veterinary medicine (D.V.M.) degree. With 673 applications to the Class of 1999, the application rate has increased 14 percent over the previous year, providing almost nine prospective students for each available space. Women account for about 70 percent of the enrollment. In addition, the school annually serves over 1,100 part-time students through its continuing education programs for veterinarians, veterinary technicians, animal owners and breeders, and the biotechnology industry.

From its beginning, Tufts has differentiated itself from other veterinary schools and colleges by developing five "signature programs," which have depth and relevance to society and the future practice of veterinary medicine. These are: Ethics and Values in Veterinary Medicine, Wildlife Medicine, Equine Sports Medicine, International Veterinary Medicine and Biotechnology.

Tufts has nine combined or joint degree programs: D.V.M./Ph.D. with the University of Massachusetts Medical Center; B.S./D.V.M. and D.V.M./M.S. with Worcester Polytechnic Institute; D.V.M./M.A. with Tufts' Fletcher School of Law and Diplomacy; B.S./D.V.M. with the University of Massachusetts at Amherst; B.S./D.V.M. with the University of Vermont; D.V.M./M.S. with the veterinary school's Center for Animals and Public Policy; D.V.M./M.P.H. with Tufts' School of Medicine; and D.V.M./Ph.D. with Tufts' Sackler School of Graduate Biomedical Sciences.

The primary goal of the veterinary school is to prepare talented enthusiastic students to successfully meet the present and future demands for their professional services, including research, private practice, teaching or public service. Competence is expected of students in the traditional aspects of the profession, such as food, fibre, companion and sporting animal medicine and surgery, preventive medicine and public health. The school also emphasizes newer dimensions, such as ethics, wildlife medicine and human-animal relationships, where contributions of veterinary medical knowledge are of increasing value to all of society.

With the graduation of its 12th class in 1994, Tufts' veterinary alumni now number 710. Graduates pursue careers in small- and large-animal medicine, zoo and wildlife medicine, international development and biomedical research. With nearly two-thirds of its graduates residing in New England, the school has had a dramatic impact on animal health, veterinary education and biomedical research in the region.

A program in biomedical research complements and enhances the school's educational objectives. Tufts currently ranks fifth among U.S. veterinary schools in the amount of research funding it receives from the National Institutes of Health. Studies are conducted in established fields of animal health as well as in fields where human and animal medicine interact. For example, Tufts has an academic and research emphasis on biotechnology, a rapidly expanding industry in the region. Plans are underway for Tufts Biotechnology Corp., a wholly owned subsidiary of Tufts University, to develop a biotechnology research park on the Grafton campus.

Important Information

Tufts University School of Veterinary Medicine
200 Westboro Road
North Grafton, Massachusetts 01536
(508) 839-5302

Student Population: Approx. 300
Faculty Size: 75
Campus acreage: 634 acres.
Number of Academic Buildings: 23

Names and Numbers:
Dean: Dr. Franklin M. Loew, (508) 839-5302
Assistant Dean for Student Affairs: Barbara Berman, (508) 839-5302
Director of Admissions: Rebecca Russo, (508) 839-5302

Did you know?

The open house held in September at Tufts New England Veterinary Medical Center annually attracts more than 5,000 animal enthusiasts to campus.

Tufts School of Veterinary Medicine is the only veterinary school in New England and one of just 27 schools nationwide.

Over 15,000 animal patients - from million-dollar racehorses to pet mice and everything in between - are treated annually at the school's hospitals.

The school's newsletters, "Catnip" and "Your Dog, " have over 200,000 paid subscribers nationwide.

The school's campus covers one square mile and is one of the loveliest in the region.

University of Massachusetts Medical Center

Worcester, MA

Concern over a national shortage of physicians led the Massachusetts legislature to adopt legislation in 1962 creating the state's only publicly-funded medical school. Three years later, Worcester was chosen - over Amherst and Boston - as the site of the school. In 1970, while the first class of 16 medical students started classes in a nearby building, campus construction began on the hillside between Plantation Street and Lake Avenue North. The first medical school class was graduated in 1974.

Today, the University of Massachusetts Medical Center is a thriving academic health center composed of the Medical School, Graduate School of Biomedical Sciences (established as a doctorate program in 1978), Graduate School of Nursing (opened in 1986), and the UMass Hospital (opened in 1976 and now licensed for 416 beds) and outpatient clinics. The Medical Center's mission is to serve the people of the commonwealth through excellence in health care education, service and research.

Other milestones include: the designation of UMass Hospital as the state's first Level 1 trauma center in 1981; the launching of the Life Flight air ambulance program in 1982; the 1990 establishment of the Program in Molecular Medicine at Two Biotech in the adjacent Massachusetts Biotechnology Research Park; and the opening of the Cancer Center in 1983.

Degree programs at UMass Medical Center include the MD and MD/PhD degrees as well as seven masters and 10 doctoral degree programs. The Medical School continues its founding mission to train students - all of whom are Massachusetts residents - to pursue primary care specialties, such as general medicine, family needs and general pediatrics. The school offers a tuition incentive program to encourage graduates to practice in Massachusetts following residency training. Fifty-one percent of all Medical School graduates currently practice in the commonwealth. Of those graduates, 45 percent practice in primary care medicine.

Students enroll at UMass for a variety of reasons. They describe faculty members as open, accessible and supportive. Class sizes usually are no greater than 10 or 12 students for each faculty member, except in some base-level courses. A high level of student interaction and group studies creates an atmosphere of community among the students. Some graduate students continue research at the Medical Center after completion of their degrees.

Important Information

Address: 55 Lake Ave. North,
Worcester, MA 01655
Telephone: (508) 856-0011
Student Population: In addition to 633 students enrolled in the Medical School, Graduate School of Nursing and Graduate School of Biomedical Sciences, the UMMC learning community includes: 486 resident physicians and fellows; 601 allied health students; and 7,400 registrants in continuing education programs.

Faculty Size: 709 (636 full time, 73 part-time)
College President: Aaron Lazare, MD, Chancellor, also Dean of the Medical School.
Dean Of Students: Mai-Lan Rogoff, MD, Associate Dean for Student Affairs
Admissions Director: Jane Cronin
Student Activities Director: Nancy Salmon, Registrar and Coordinator of Student Services.
Academic Buildings: The schools and hospital are housed in one complex.
Campus Acreage: Approximately 62 acres.

Did You Know:

Founding Dean Lamar Soutter was a respected surgeon at the Massachusetts General Hospital in Boston when he was selected as the dean for the state's first publicly funded medical school. For several years, he had no school buildings and no students as plans for the school worked their way through the Massachusetts legislature.

The location of the Medical Center was once a grassy field where cows grazed.

Eight years after approval of legislation that created the school, the first class of 16 students began classes. Today several of the early group are reaching levels of prominence in the medical field:

James L. McGuire, MD, '74 one of the 16 members of the first medical school class, is currently chief of staff at the Stanford University Medical Center in Palo Alto, California.

Donald L. Abbott, MD, '74 is president of the Maine Medical Center in Portland.

Richard Chaisson, MD, '76, a specialist in infectious disease, is director of AIDS services at Johns Hopkins Medical Center in Baltimore, Md. He is also an advisor to the World Health Organization on AIDS-related issues.

Christine Cassel, MD '76, is chief of general internal medicine at the University of Chicago's Pritzker School of Medicine, and has been featured on national news programs.

Closer to home, Richard Aghababian, MD '74 is chair of emergency medicine at UMass and is a nationally recognized expert on disaster and emergency medical training and disaster planning and has lectured around the world.

UMMC will mark its 25th anniversary beginning in 1995. During that time, the institution has produced 1,736 fully certified physicians, bestowed 82 doctorate degrees in biomedical sciences and 220 graduate nursing degrees.

The Medical Center performs more than 12,000 inpatient and outpatient surgeries a year, and handled more than 300,000 outpatient clinic visits in 1994. The hospital emergency room received 47,960 visits in 1994.

Worcester Polytechnic Institute

Worcester, MA

Worcester Polytechnic Institute, founded in 1865, is the third-oldest private university of engineering and science in the United States. Since its founding, WPI has been a pioneer in technological education. Today, WPI provides its students with a thorough conceptual foundation in science, engineering, the humanities, management and the social sciences.

WPI requires its students to demonstrate their ability to apply what they learn in the classroom to real-world problems, and to gain an appreciation for how the solutions to those problems might impact the world around them. This approach has proven to be uniquely well-suited to preparing young men and women for challenging professional careers and rewarding lives. It has also earned WPI widespread recognition. For example, in recent years WPI has consistently ranked at or near the top of its category in U.S. News & World Report's annual review of colleges and universities. In 1970 WPI adopted a new educational program called the WPI Plan that has all undergraduates complete three independent projects that challenge them to identify, investigate and report on open-ended issues. Project sponsors include leaders in major corporations, senior officers in government, and key representatives of professional societies throughout the world.

Alumni report that the Plan's three projects are excellent preparation for managing team efforts and for communicating - orally and in writing - in a professional manner. In the Sufficiency, students choose a sequence of five courses in an area outside the sphere of their major field of study and complete a project on a theme arising from these courses. In the Interactive Qualifying Project (IQP) students explore in-depth issues at the intersection of science, technology, society and culture. The Major Qualifying Project (MQP) is an intensive, hands-on research or design experience in the student's major field of study. MQP teams often work like colleagues with graduate students and faculty members on leading-edge projects.

WPI has taken the lead in globalizing technological higher education. WPI students currently account for more than 10 percent of all U.S. engineering students studying abroad. WPI's Global Perspective Program has grown from a simple conviction: to be successful in business, engineering and science in our increasingly interdependent world, one must understand and appreciate other cultures and be able to work with - and compete against - people from all nations and backgrounds. WPI's residential project centers and programs offer students the opportunity to complete projects at one of 20 locations around the world. Under the WPI Plan, students may pursue a wide range of majors in the arts and sciences, engineering, and management. Students are not restricted to specific majors, however, and may design interdisciplinary majors in areas in which faculty members are able to help them learn and evaluate their performance on a professional level.

Important Information

Address:
Worcester Polytechnic Institute (WPI)
100 Institute Road
Worcester, MA 01609-2280
(508) 831-5000

Student Population: (fall 1994)

Undergraduate: 2,676 full-time; 57 part-time
Graduate: 387 full-time; 546 part-time

Faculty Size:188 tenure track; 57 part-time & non-tenure track

Campus acreage: 80
Buildings: 31

College President: John Lott Brown (Interim)
Provost: Diran Apelian
Dean of Students: Assistant VP for Student Affairs: Janet Begin Richardson
Admissions Director: Kay Dietrich
Student Activities Director: Chris Jachimowicz

Did You Know:

That WPI is the nation's third oldest private college of engineering and science, founded in 1865. Only MIT (1862) and Rensselaer (1824) are older among the nation's 300 plus engineering institutions.

That W1YK, founded in 1909, was the first college club radio station in the U.S. and is one of the oldest continuously operating amateur radio stations in the world.

That WPI's Alumni Gym, built in 1916, features 36 gargoyles around the top of the building, playing different sports.

That Robert H. Goddard (1882-1945), the father of modern rocketry and space flight, was a 1908 gradaute of WPI. He authored the "Old Tech" song, was editor-in-chief of his yearbook, and voted the "brightest senior" by his classmates.

That one of the oldest football rivalries in the nation exists between WPI and Rensselaer. They first played in 1895 and the record now stands at 41-40-5 in favor of Rensselaer.

That more than 10 percent of all U.S. engineering students studying abroad come from WPI.

That WPI has its share of inventors: Richard T. Whitcomb '46 formulated the area rule, a fundamental principle in the design of high-speed aircraft; Carl C. Clark '45 invented the air-bag system; Robert C. Stempel '55, former chairman of General Motors, developed the catalytic converter; Herman Hollerith '17 invented the IBM punch card; George E. Comstock '43 invented the daisy wheel used in many computer printers; Waldemar E. Carlson '30 was the inventor of detergent oil; and Professor William Wadsworth invented the familiar "Mickey Mouse" ear protectors used at airports.

And that WPI's first astronaut, Professor Albert Sacco Jr., head of the Chemical Engineering Department, a crew member aboard the space shuttle Columbia in the fall of 1995, part of the U.S. Microgravity Laboratory. The 16-day mission was planned to be the longest U.S. space flight to date.

WORCESTER STATE COLLEGE

Worcester, Massachusetts

Founded in 1874 as a normal school, Worcester State College has developed into a comprehensive liberal arts institution with 171 faculty members and more than 5,300 undergraduate students and 1,700 students enrolled in graduate and career-oriented programs.

Since its inception 120 years ago, Worcester State College has remained steadfast in its resolve to provide quality education that is both accessible and affordable to a diverse student population including students matriculating after high school graduation as well as non-traditional students. Worcester State College has remained affordable during difficult transition periods throughout the 1980's and 1990's. The total educational cost at the College has been maintained at the lowest level possible, even though the tuition and fees at other state public colleges have risen substantially. Historically, Worcester State College has been the last institution to approve an increase and remains the most competitive institution among all the state colleges in terms of tuition/fees.

Today, the College offers degrees at the bachelor and master levels and a wide variety of continuing education programs. A diverse curriculum emphasizes a liberal arts core which provides students a solid foundation for career and life choices. Upon this foundation is a dynamic variety of arts and sciences majors in addition to professional programs in business, health and education responsive to student career needs in an ever changing economic environment.

Located in the metropolitan center of Worcester, the College is situated on 58 acres and is about 40 miles west of Boston, 45 miles north of Providence, RI and 60 miles northeast of Hartford, CT.

The College provides cultural, social and recreational programs and offers many convenient services for students. The Athletic Department coordinates a variety of programs for all students to participate in intercollegiate and intramural athletics. Other extracurricular offerings include lectures, films, arts and crafts exhibits, performing artists, dances, and charter travel services. Students have access to the Counseling and Placement Center which provides, free of charge, information on careers and graduate schools. The Learning Resources Center integrates the traditional academic library with audiovisual services. In addition to accommodating a book collection of 125,000 volumes, the building houses the Media Center, which provides student access to television, radio, and film production facilities. The Learning Resources Center also encompasses a complex of modern telecommunications and electronic learning facilities.

THE WSC STUDENT

The College maintains a steady enrollment of a predominately commuting student body from Central Massachusetts. The economic background of students ranges from disadvantaged to upper middle class. Many students are the first generation in their families to attend college. Worcester State College also provides an environment that is accessible and sensitive to the special needs of students with physical disabilities and limitations. Additionally, international students from 27 different countries attend Worcester State College.

More than 22,000 Worcester State College alumni are successful men and women from all walks of life who have earned a reputation for outstanding professional and personal achievement An accomplished Worcester State College graduate can be found in virtually every prominent profession. More than 10,000 alumni live in Worcester County.

Important Information

ADDRESS:
Worcester State College
486 Chandler St.
Worcester, MA 01602-2597
(508) 793-8033

College Personnel:
President:
Dr. Kalyan K. Ghosh, ext. 8020
Vice President of Academic Affairs:
Dr. Bonnie M. Kind, ext. 8039

Vice President of Administration & Finance: K. Robert Malone, ext. 8080
Vice President of Student Affairs: Dr. James Rauker, ext. 8070
Assoicate Vice President: Dr. Stefanie Sullivan, ext. 8031
Exec. Dir. of Grad. & Continuing Ed.: Dr. Michael Massouh, ext. 8125
Exec. Dir. of Development & External Relations: Joseph Webber, ext. 8096
Dir. of Diversity & Affirmative Action: Edna Spencer, ext. 8783
Exec. Assistant to the President: Dr. Vicki DeLorey, ext. 8010

Did You Know:

Worcester State College was the first Massachusetts college accredited by the American Association of Teachers Colleges.

The former Rockwood Park is now the location of the Worcester State College baseball field.

The Child Study Movement, a precursor to Child Psychology, was developed at Worcester State College.

In 1970, the Worcester State College Women's Softball team made its debut.

The Worcester State College softball team won the 1990 ECAC championship.

Worcester State College softball team won the National NCAA Division 3 Batting Title with a .396 average.

Worcester State College is the home of the oldest oak tree in Worcester.

Chapter 12

The Towns of Worcester County: Profiles and Key Statistics

by Ann Lindblad

I grew up in the South, where remnants of Confederate pride and propaganda still pervade grade school history lessons. Civil War history is taught as passionately there as Revolutionary war history is taught in New England - with an "it happened here" sense of importance. We kids only had to count the number of states on each side (Union: 23; Confederacy: 11) to realize the South fought a lost cause.

But it wasn't until writing this book that I fully realized how foolish southern generals were to ever think themselves a match for the North's industrial strength. Overeager Confederate commanders need only have looked at just one county - Worcester County - to measure their folly. Besides the scores of mills along the Blackstone River, "America's hardest working river," there was a mill or factory on nearly every backwater brook in this county. Even tiny towns had their own mill villages, and Holden eventually had 12.

The decisive battle of Gettysburg is said to have started with General Lee's search for shoes. In Worcester County, the town of Milford alone had 11 shoe manufacturers. Throughout the war, the Confederate Army was ill clothed, but here the factories were humming. In Uxbridge, textile mills worked 24-hour shifts filling government orders. In Fitchburg, Ebenezer Butterick's first paper patterns were for Army uniforms. And Stevens Linen in Dudley has manufactured continuously since 1846.

Douglas made axes, wool and carriages. Worcester made telegraph wire, iron for rifle barrels, caissons, blankets for the soldiers and railroad cars for troop transport. Textile machinery was made in Hopedale and Northbridge. Leominster made buttons, buckles and knife handles. Clinton made shoes, boots, clothing and had a cluster of foundries and machine shops. Millbury had a powder mill and manufactured guns. And no doubt, many a Union soldier in the field ate crackers made in Westminster. Perhaps the generals formulated battle plans while sitting on folding "camp chairs" made in Worcester.

Information for Today

Besides a touch of history, this chapter's town profiles also include statistics useful today - timely current information for anyone considering a move to the county, or within the county – tax rates, average house prices, average income, per pupil expenditures, average SAT scores and crime statistics. For accuracy, each section was checked with town representatives in January 1995 so the information is quite up-to-date, but things do change. If you spot a fact that his since changed, or know some fun historical facts, please let us know. Send your notes and comments to: Favorite Places c/o Tatnuck Bookseller, 335 Chandler Street, Worcester, MA 01602 or FAX (508) 7556-9425.

Ashburnham

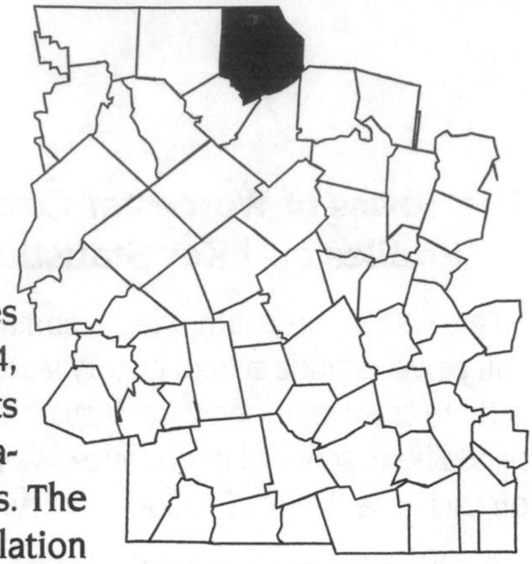

The World's One and Only

The unofficial "snow capital" of Worcester County, where about 140 inches of the white stuff fell in the winter of 1994, Ashburnham is also a town that sees its population double every summer as vacationers flock to its many lakes and ponds. The town saw a dramatic 40 percent population increase during the 1980s, with newcomers attracted by the town's clean air, mountain views and moderate taxes, home prices, and plenty of space; with 41 square miles of land, Ashburnham had room for the influx. From some parts of town, it's a 10 mile drive to the town center. Today, many residents work in Gardner, Fitchburg, Worcester, Boston and Nashua and Manchester, NH.

Ashburnham borders New Hampshire, and Mt. Watatic in the Ashburnham State Forest is included on the Mid-State Trail, which runs through Worcester County from Rhode Island to New Hampshire. The trip to Watatic's summit is a moderate hike, a little over 2 miles long, using the Wapack and Blueberry Ledges Trails. From the top, hikers can see Boston's skyline to the east, the Vermont mountains to the northwest, and Mt. Greylock in the Berkshires to the southwest.

Land grants were a common method of paying for services rendered in Colonial America. The Massachusetts Bay Colony mustered 2,000 men for an expedition to Canada in 1690, but had nothing to pay the survivors, who included some 60 soldiers from Dorchester. Eventually grants of land were provided as compensation and the six square miles that now comprise part of Ashburnham were designated Dorchester Canada.

Early on, the settlers began making potash, using the abundant forests of virgin timber in the town. Potash, an essential ingredient needed to make soap, fertilizer, glass and gun powder, was in much demand, and the village was soon shipping a ton of potash to market in Boston every year. Upon applying for incorporation as a town in 1765, the settlers requested the name, *Ashfield*. Imagine their surprise when the charter came back with *Ashburnham* instead. The governor had substituted the name of a friend, the Second Earl of Ashburnham. The settlers didn't object, and a good thing — *Ashburnham is the only town of that name in the world.*

Like Gardner, Ashburnham was a wood-working town, producing more than 40,000 chairs yearly at the turn of the century. Today, a new business in town is Afina Winery, whose owners are making high quality wines from the 75 different blueberry varieties on their farm. After pressing the first crop of berries by hand, one owner of Afina had hands so blue the locals nicknamed him "Blueberry Bob."

Sources: Town of Ashburnham, Ashburnham Historical Society; Mass. EOCD Community Profile; The Worcester Telegram & Gazette; The Worcester Business Journal; The Boston Globe; Best Hikes with Children in Connecticut, Massachusetts and Rhode Island, Cynthia C. Lewis, Thomas J. Lewis, The Mountaineers, 1991; Massachusetts Bi-Centennial Commemorative.

Year incorporated: 1765
Population: 5,433 (1990 census)
Density: 140 per square mile
Total area: 41.00 sq. miles
Elevation: 1,028'
Mt. Watatic 1,832'
Distance from:
Boston: 55 miles
Worcester: 31 miles
Providence: 75 miles
Hartford: 92 miles
Springfield 66 miles
Transportation:
Highways: Rtes. 12, 101, 119.
Rail: Commuter rail to Boston available in neighboring Fitchburg.
Bus: Ashburnham is a member of the Montachusett Regional Transit Authority. Services for the elderly and disabled available through the Council on Aging.
Airport: Fitchburg Municipal Airport, a General Aviation facility.
Tax Rate:
$13.73 per thousand
(1994, Mass. Div. of Local Services))
Median House Price:
$95,000 (1993, County Data Corporation)
Median Household Income: $42,442 (1990 Census)
% of state average: 114.9%
Per Capita Income: $15,595
% of state average 90.5%
Form of Government:Board of Selectmen, Town Administrator, open town meeting
Municipal Offices: (508) 827-4102
Services: Ashburnham Municipal Electric, no natural gas, no municipal sewer service, surface water.
Nearest Hospital: Burbank Hospital in Fitchburg, 10 miles away.
Registered Voters : (Secretary of State 1992): 2,921
Legislative Districts:
U.S. Congress: 1st District: John W. Olver (D)
State Senate: Worcester, Franklin, Hampden & Hampshire: Robert D. Wetmore (D)
State Representative: 2nd Worcester: Robert D. Hawke (R)
Public Schools
Ashburnham Westminster: Veterans Memorial (K); Westminster Elem (K-06); Briggs Elem (K-06); Oakmont Regional High School (07-12). Montachusett Voc- Tech: (09-12)]

Superintendent: William E. Allen ED.D. (508) 874-1501
School Choice: Yes
Private Schools:
Cushing Academy - world renowned college preparatory school.
Per Pupil Cost:
(State Exec. Office of Education -1992-93) $3,961.
State average $5,023
Average Teacher Salary: (State Exec. Office of Education 1992-93)
statewide $38,774
Ashburnham Westminster $36,323
Montachusett $37,563
Mean SAT scores 1993

	(reported by town)	State Average
Math	511	
Verbal	452	
Combined:	963	903

Student Population (Dept. of Education)

Total students 1991-92:	1,168
at public schools	94.9%
at private schools	`5.1%

Educational Attainment (1990 census)

High School graduate or higher	83.1%
Bachelor's Degree or higher	23.9%

Largest Employers: (supplied by community, 1993)

	# of employees
Cushing Academy	80
Lombards Furniture	40
Spectra Polymer	35
Town of Ashburnham	35

Commuting to Work (1990 Census)
Average time to work (mins.) 26.8
Houses of Worship: Ashburnham Community Church, St. Denis Catholic, St. Anne's Catholic, People's Congregational, Apostolic Lutheran.
Crime Rate:
(1993, Mass. State Police Crime Reporting Unit)

		statewide
Total crimes reported:	112	
rate per 1,000 persons	20.61	37.46
Violent crimes	8	
rate per 1,000 persons	1.47	5.65
Property crimes	104	
rate per 1,000	19.14	31.83

Libraries: Stevens Memorial Library
Museums: Ashburnham Historical Society, Museum of Local History, Main St.

Athol

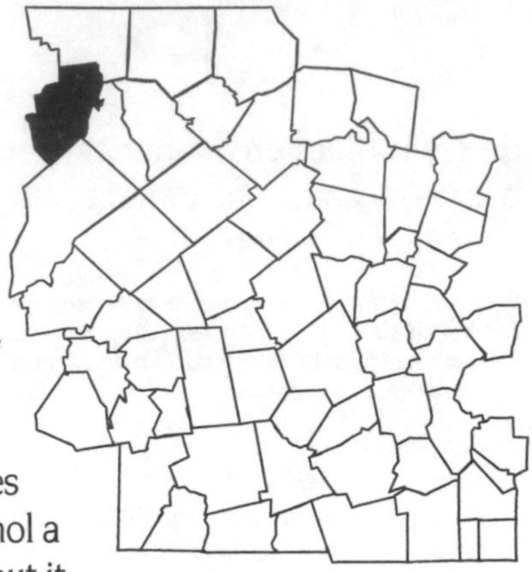

"Tooltown" and the River Rat Race

Athol is an "in-between" place. The largest of the North Quabbin towns, its residents vote in Worcester County, but their services are in Franklin County, and the town has close ties to Orange, just five miles away. Its location north of Rte. 2 makes Athol a bit removed from the state's largest cities, but it is ideally situated not only for Quabbin excursions, but also for trips to the mountains of New Hampshire, Vermont and New York.

First settled in 1735, the area was named "Pequoig," after a local native tribe. When incorporated in 1762, settler John Murray chose the name Athol after his family home in Blair-Atholl, Scotland. For the town's 225th anniversary in 1987, descendant George Iain Murray of Scotland, the 10th Duke of Atholl, paid a visit.

Nicknamed "Tooltown," Athol has a long manufacturing heritage, with various local "shops" over the years making cotton, shoes, iron, tools, blankets, kegs, cribs and cradles. Immigrants coming to work in the factories have given the town a diverse population, which includes French-Canadians, Lithuanians, Italians, Jews, Irish and Asians. Litton Industries closure of its Union Butterfield plant dealt a blow in the '80's, but toolmaker L.S. Starrett remains in Athol, employing over a thousand people.

The zany "River Rat Race" on the Millers River from Athol to Orange is an annual April event drawing hundreds of serious and fun-loving canoeists and thousands of spectators. Legend has it the race started in 1964 in an Athol bar as a bet between regulars "Whip" and "Sput." Now the race has a loyal following, a "Rat Pack Theme Song," and usually ends up with more than a few dunkings during its course.

It was across the Millers River in Athol that native warriors escaped on rafts with captive Mary Rowlandson in 1675, (*see Lancaster*) and a large boulder in the river called "Rowlandson Rock" marks the crossing. The area's proximity to Canada made it a stop on the Underground Railroad, and a native trail from the shores of Connecticut to hunting grounds in Canada passed through the town. Famous sons of Athol include Hollywood choreographer Busby Berkeley, and rocker Dave Bargeron with the '60's group, Blood, Sweat and Tears, the "Durango Kid," movie star of the '30's and '40's (known locally as Charles Starrett) and William J. (Candy) Cummings, who invented the curve ball, which transformed the game of baseball.

Sources: North of the Quabbin, A. Young; Commonwealth of Mass. EOCD profile; The Boston Globe, The Worcester Telegram & Gazette Massachusetts Towns, I. Sandrof.

Year incorporated: 1702
Population: 11,451 (1990 census)
Density: 351 per square mile
Total area: 33.40
Elevation: 535'
Distance from:
Boston: 72 miles
Worcester: 38 miles
Providence: 88 miles
Hartford: 80 miles
Springfield 55 miles
Transportation:
Highways: Rtes. 2, 2-A, 32, 122.
Bus: Athol is a member of the Franklin Regional Transit Authority. No fixed route services, but services for elderly and disabled through Orange Council on Aging.
Airport: Orange Municipal Airport, a General Aviation facility.
Tax Rate: $12.50 per thousand (1994 Mass. Division of Local Services)
Median House Price: $80,000 (1993, County Data Corporation)
Median Household Income: $27,095 (1990 Census)
% of state average: 73.3%
Per Capita Income: $12,444
% of state average 72.3%
Form of Government: Board of Selectmen
Municipal Offices: (508) 249-2368
Services: Mass. Electric, no natural gas, town sewer.
Nearest Hospital: Athol Memorial Hospital
Registered Voters
(Secretary of State 1992) 5,715
Legislative Districts:
U.S. Congress: 1st District: John W. Olver (D)
State Senate: Worcester, Franklin, Hampden and Hampshire: Robert E. Wetmore (D)
State Representative: 1st Franklin District: Stephen Kulik (D)
Public Schools
Athol-Royalston: Ellen Bigelow, (K-4); Pleasant St, (K-6); Riverbend (5-6); Sanders St.(K-4); South Royalston (3-6); Raymond (K-2); Athol Jr. High (7-8); Athol High (9-12).
Montachusett Voc-Tech: (9-12).

Superintendent: Allen KoHogdon (508) 249-2400
School Choice: No
Per Pupil Cost: (State Exec. Office of Education -1992-93) $3,695 State average: $5,023
Average Teacher Salary: (Dept. of Education -1992-93)

Athol-Royalston	$33,727
statewide 1992-93	$38,774
Montachusett	$37,563

Mean SAT scores 1993

	(reported by town)	State Average
Combined:	854	903

Student Population (Dept. of Education)

Total students 1991-92:	2,164
at public schools	94.4%
at private schools	5.6%

Educational Attainment (1990 census)

High School graduate or higher	75.2%
Bachelor's Degree or higher	11.2%

Largest Employers: (supplied by community, 1993)

	# of employees
L.S. Starrett Company	1,100
Town of Athol	377
Athol Royalston School District	300
Athol Memorial Hospital	131
Athol Table, Inc.	30

Commuting to Work (1990 Census)
Average time to work (mins.) 19.3
Houses of Worship: 2 Catholic, 1 Congregational, 2 Methodist, 1 Episcopal, 1 Christian Science, 1 Seventh-day Adventist, 1 Unitarian, 1 Salvation Army, 1 Jewish Temple
Crime Rate: (1993, Mass. State Police Crime Reporting Unit)

	town	statewide
Total crimes reported:	482	
rate per 1,000 persons	42.09	37.46
Violent crimes	127	
rate per 1,000 persons	11.09	5.65
Property crimes	355	
rate per 1,000 persons	31.00	31.83

State Register of Historic Places:
Old Town Hall, 1307 Main St.
Pequoig Hotel, Main St.

ATHOL

Auburn

From Strawberries to the Stratosphere

In Worcester County, it doesn't take a rocket scientist to know that Dr. Robert Goddard launched the world's first liquid-fueled rocket in Auburn on March 16, 1926. Goddard's name is written in stone - literally - at the new Worcester Airport terminal, part of a floor mosaic welcoming passengers to the area. And if you tee off on the 9th hole at Auburn's Pakachoag Golf Course, your ball might land near the spot of the first "lift-off." There's a commemorative marker on the fairway and another one nearby dedicated by the American Rocket Society. At the time of his launch, Goddard was a professor at Worcester's Clark University and his work made modern space flight possible. Models of Goddard's first rocket and a Polaris A2 Rocket are found in Goddard Park near Auburn's business center.

Rocketry aside, Auburn is best known today as the home of the Auburn Mall, built in 1971 on the site of Mirror Lake, which was filled in to accommodate the construction. Auburn approved a $45 million mall expansion plan to add a second floor to the mall and bring in a third anchor store. Key to the mall's success is Auburn's location at the crossroads of several major highways, including the Mass. Pike, I-290, I-395, Rte. 20 and Rte. 12. Access to these highways has made Auburn a gateway to Worcester, and the town's growth makes it hard to tell where its development stops and Worcester's begins.

Many residents work next door in Worcester, but Auburn is quite accessible and nearly equidistant to four other major cities: 44 miles to Boston, 50 miles to Providence and Springfield, and 60 miles to Hartford. It's no coincidence that Federal Express and other firms have distribution centers in Auburn. The choice of Auburn as a distribution center for the U.S. Mail in 1825 resulted in a name change for the town, which was originally called Ward. This was too often confused with Ware, 40 miles west, and the citizens voted the new name of Auburn in 1837, after Oliver Goldsmith's poetic phrase, "Sweet Auburn, loveliest village of the plain." This may have referred to the town's start as a farming village known for its sweet strawberries. Farming declined as Worcester's industry boomed, drawing workers from Auburn. Streetcar service to Worcester from Auburn was available by the turn of the century. After WWII, most remaining farms were subdivided into house lots.

Visitors to Auburn Town Hall can view a unique stained glass window depicting Auburn's history designed by 3rd graders at the Julia Bancroft School. Entitled, "Through the Innocent Eyes of Youth," the window's centerpiece is a rocket, and accompanying scenes are of railroads, peach orchards and parks.

Sources: Commonwealth of Mass. EOCD Community Profile; The Boston Globe; The Worcester Telegram & Gazette; A Guide to the Heritage of Worcester County, Montachusett Girl Scout Council; The Auburn Guide & Community Telephone Directory, published by The Worcester Telegram & Gazette.

Year incorporated: April 10, 1778 as Ward; name changed to Auburn, 1837

Population: 15,005 (1990 census)

Density: 977 per square mile

Total area: 16.40 sq. miles

Elevation: 498'

Distance from:
- Boston: 44
- Worcester: 6
- Providence: 50
- Hartford: 60
- Springfield 50

Transportation:

Highways: Rtes. 90, 290, U.S. Rte. 20, Rte. 395; Rte. 12

Rail: Passenger rail service to Boston, Providence, Hartford, and all other points on Amtrak is available through neighboring Worcester. The Providence and Worcester Railroad provides freight rail service to Auburn.

Bus: Auburn is a member of the Worcester Regional Transit Authority, which provides fixed routes service from the Auburn Mall to Oxford, Webster, and Worcester. The Worcester Regional Transit Authority also offers paratransit services to the elderly and disabled. Commuter service is available from Auburn to Boston via Worcester on the Peter Pan Bus Line.

Airport: Worcester Municipal Airport, a primary commercial facility.

Tax Rate: $10.57 per thousand (1994, Mass. Div. of Local Services)

Median House Price: $111,000 (1993, County Data Corporation)

Median Household Income: $39, 913 (1990 Census)
- % of state average: 108.0%
- Per Capita Income: $17,500
- % of state average 101.6%

Form of Government: Board of Selectmen, Representative Town Meeting

Municipal Offices: (508) 832-7720

Services: Mass. Electric, Commonwealth Gas, town sewer, ground water.

Nearest Hospital: Several in Worcester

Registered Voters 9,733 (Secretary of State 1992)

Legislative Districts:

U.S. Congress: 2nd District: Richard E. Neal (D)
3rd District: Peter Blute (R)

State Senate: 2nd Worcester: Matthew Amorello (R)

State Representative: 7th Worcester: Paul Kollios (D)

Public Schools

Auburn: Julia Bancroft (03-06); Bryn Mawr (K-03); Pakachoag (04-06); Mary D Stone (K-03); Auburn Junior High (07-08); Auburn Senior High (09-12).

Superintendent: Patricia Martin (508) 832-7755

Southern Worcester County: Bay Path Reg Voc Tech High School (09-12)

School Choice: No

Colleges and Universities: none

Per Pupil Cost (State Exec. Office of Education - 1992-93): Auburn:$5,104. State average: $5,023

Average Teacher Salary:
- (State Exec. Office of Education) Auburn: $38,598
- statewide 1992-93: $38,774
- Southern Worcester County: $39,355

Mean SAT scores 1993

	(reported by town)	State Average:
Math	445	
Verbal	411	
Combined	856	903

Student Population (Dept. of Education)

Total students 1991-92: 2,346

at public schools 93.1%

at private schools 6.0%

Educational Attainment (1990 census)
- High School graduate or higher 83.3%
- Bachelor's Degree or higher 22.1%

Largest Employers: (supplied by community, 1993)

	# of employees
R. H. White Construction Company	284
Montrose Company	280
Worcester Envelope	240
Imperial Distributors	183
Automatic Rolls	175

Commuting to Work (1990 Census)

Average time to work (mins.) 18.6

Houses of Worship: 2 Roman Catholic, 6 Protestant

Crime Rate: not available

Libraries Auburn Free Public Library

State Register of Historic Places 1993:
- Goddard Rocket Launching Site
- Joseph Stone House

Barre

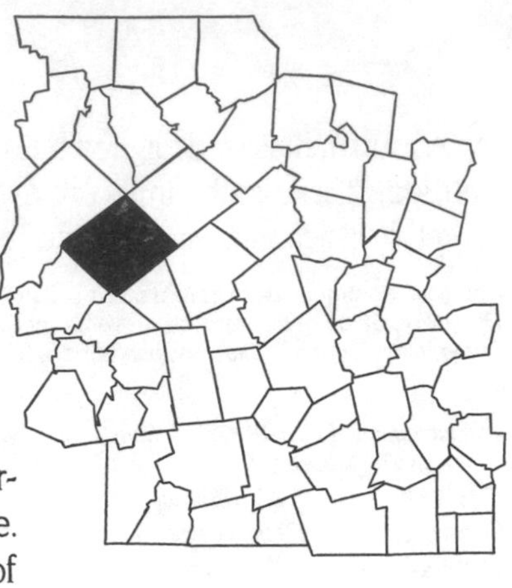

An Uncommon Common and the Barre Slave Case

Once a crossroads, with nine hotels and six stage coach lines, Barre today is a place unto itself. The Quabbin Reservoir cut the town's link to the west, and between watershed and Audubon Society land, Barre is surrounded on three sides by protected acreage. The result is a perfectly preserved example of small town America.

Barre's huge town common, listed on the National Register of Historic Places, was enlarged by the town in 1792 to accommodate militia drills. Band concerts have been performed here regularly since 1859. Perhaps Barre's greatest performance on the Common was an 1840 election year debate between legendary orator Daniel Webster and Worcester historian and diplomat George Bancroft. Speaking to a crowd of thousands, Webster supported fellow Whig William Henry Harrison, and Bancroft endorsed Democrat President Martin Van Buren. Campaign rallies like the one in Barre were new that year, and Harrison's famous slogan, "Old Tippecanoe and Tyler, Too" swept him into office, where he died of pneumonia just one month later.

Settled in 1774 as the Rutland District's northwest quarter, the town was called Hutchinson after a royalist governor. After the battles of Lexington, Concord and Bunker Hill, the rebels of Hutchinson flinched at the Tory name, and asked to be renamed "Wilkes" after the sympathetic mayor of London. The General Court had a better idea, and named the town after Colonel Isaac Barre, a member of Parliament who, in an impassioned speech opposing the Stamp Act, coined the term, "Sons of Liberty."

The "Barre Slave Case" of 1783 provides early evidence of the state's distaste for slavery. Quork Walker, a black slave from Barre who was beaten by his master, Nathaniel Jennison, sued Jennison for assault and battery, asking for 300 pounds in damages. The Supreme Court of Massachusetts threw out Jennison's claim that he was legally free to discipline his "property", agreed that Walker was a free man, and awarded him 50 pounds in damages. Blacks in Massachusetts lived free from then on.

The lack of a railroad line to its center and the advent of steam power caused a decline in Barre's early mills and manufacture of linseed oil, palm leaf hats, and its distribution of cheese. Today Barre attracts newcomers with its affordable house prices, and keeps them with its quality of life and its location, within 90 minutes of Boston, Worcester, Springfield, Hartford and Providence.

Sources: Commonwealth of Mass. EOCD Community Profile; The Boston Globe; An American Town, Barre, Massachusetts 1774-1974, J. Sullivan; A Guide to the Heritage of Worcester County, Montachusett Girl Scout Council; Massachusetts Bicentennial Commemorative; Massachusetts Towns, I. Sandrof; Academic American Encyclopedia.

Year incorporated: 1774
Population: 4,546 (1990 census)
Density: 103 per square mile
Total area: 44.61 sq. miles
Elevation: 886'
Distance from:
Boston: 61
Worcester: 22
Highways: Rtes. 32, 62, 122.
Rail:.The Massachusetts Central Railroad provides freight rail service in Barre.
Airport: The Worcester Municipal Airport, a primary commercial facility.
Tax Rate: $15.10 per thousand (1994, Mass. Div. of Local Services)
Median House Price: $96,000 (1993, County Data Corporation)
Median Household Income: $36,846 (1990 Census)
% of state average: 99.7%
Per Capita Income: $14,012
% of state average 81.4%
Form of Government:Board of Selectmen, Administrative Assistant, open town meeting
Municipal Offices:(508) 355-5003
Services: Mass. Electric, some town sewer and water, ground water, no natural gas.
Nearest Hospital: Athol, Gardner, Worcester, Ware
Registered Voters (Secretary of State 1992) 2,827
Legislative Districts:
U.S. Congress: 1st District: John W. Olver (D)
State Senate: Worcester, Franklin, Hampden and Hampshire: Robert E. Wetmore (D)
State Representative: 5th Worcester: Stephen M. Brewer (D)
Public Schools
Quabbin Regional School District: Barre Ruggles Lane (K-6), Hardwick Elem (01-06); Hubbardston Center (K-06); New Braintree Grade (K-06); Oakham Center (K-06); Quabbin Regional Middle School and High School (7-12)
Montachusett: Montachusett Voc-tech (09-12)
Superintendent: Maureen Marshall
School Choice: Yes

Per Pupil Cost:
(State Exec. Office of Education -1992-93): $4,080.
State average 1992-93: $5,023
Average Teacher Salary:
(State Exec. Office of Education)
statewide 1992-93 $38,774
salary 1992-1993 $31,577
Mean SAT scores 1993

	(reported by town)	state average
Math	459	
Verbal	430	
Combined	889	903

Student Population (Dept. of Education)
Total students 1991-92: 865
at public schools 98.4%
at private schools 1.6%
Educational Attainment (1990 census)
High School graduate or higher 77.4%
Bachelor's Degree or higher 20.6%
Largest Employers: (supplied by community, 1993)

	# of employees
Quabbin Regional School District	280
Stetson School	100
Martone Trucking/Resource Control	40
Charles G. Allen Company	35
I.G.A. (grocery store)	30
Town of Barre	25

Commuting to Work (1990 Census)
Average time to work (mins.): 31.9
Houses of Worship: Barre Congregational; Christ Episcopal; New Life Assembly of God; Barre Center for Buddhist Studies
Crime Rate: not available
Libraries
Woods Memorial Library
Museums
Barre Historical Society,
Woods Memorial Library Museum.
State Register of Historic Places 1993:
Barre Common Historic District
Barre District #4 School house
Barre Town Hall

Berlin

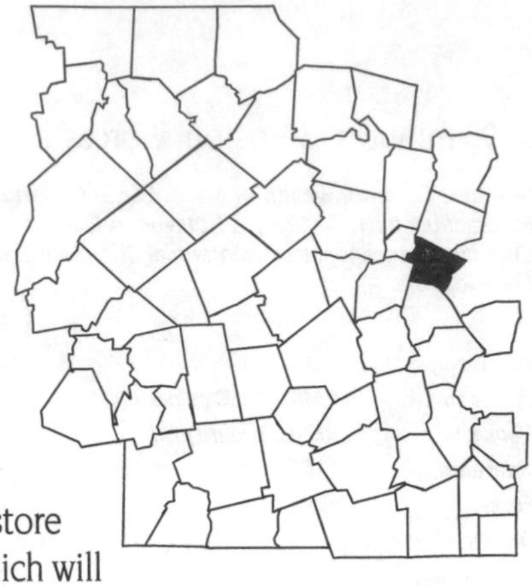

More than Spooky World

Despite its prime location with exits on Rtes. 495 and I-290, the 2,000 or so residents of Berlin lead the quiet small town life, enjoying their easy access to Boston, Worcester and Nashua, NH. But the quiet life is changing, with increased demand for new homes and plans underway for a 100-store mall on the Berlin-Marlborough border, which will have Jordan Marsh, Sears, Filene's and J.C. Penney's stores. "All of a sudden, they found us," said Town Clerk Mary Ellen Matthew.

Before, Berlin's lack of town sewer and water kept out development, but now the town is getting spill-over in new construction from Acton and Concord. Some people are even moving here from Wayland and Boston. The reason? "We still have land available," Matthew said.

The town's Forty Caves rock formation is evidence that it has long been a stop-over for travelers going north. It's believed native tribes sought shelter in the caves on their way to hunting grounds in NH. and Canada. Located off Lancaster Rd., the caves are part of a ravine cut between solid rock, which exposes cliffs and precipices some 50' in height. "It's a miniature Purgatory Chasm," said Matthew. (*See Sutton*).

Berlin might have gone unnoticed a bit longer if it weren't for Spooky World, "America's Horror Theme Park," which opened here in 1990 and draws nearly 200,000 visitors during the Halloween season. Owners Linda and David Bertolino call themselves "hauntrepreneurs," and have built the 24-acre site into a theatrical extravaganza combining horror, comedy, music and the thrill of seeing a famous celebrity. Among the "names" who have appeared here are Elvira, Tiny Tim, the "Exorcist's" Linda Blair, and "Monster Mash" singer Bobby "Boris" Pickett. Spooky World houses the American Horror Museum, with original props from scary Hollywood films, and has a year-round staff of 10 which grows to some 500 during the Halloween season.

Sources: The Worcester Telegram & Gazette; Worcester Magazine; Town Clerk Mary Ellen Matthew; Commonwealth of Mass. EOCD Community Profile.

Year incorporated: 1812
Population: 2,293 (1990 census)
Density: 177 per square mile
Total area: 13.09 sq. miles
Elevation: 300'
Distance from:
Boston: 34
Worcester: 15

Highways: Rtes. 62, and Interstate Rte. 495.

Rail: Conrail services a freight rail line through Berlin.

Airport: The Worcester Municipal Airport, a primary commercial facility.

Tax Rate: $13.90 per thousand (1994, Mass. Div. of Local Services)

Median House Price: $138,000 (1993, County Data Corporation)

Median Household Income: $49,556 (1990 Census)
% of state average: 134.1 %
Per Capita Income: $19,118
% of state average 111.0%

Form of Government: Board of Selectmen, Open town meeting

Municipal Offices: (508) 838-2442

Services: Mass. Electric, Commonwealth Gas, no municipal sewer, ground water.

Nearest Hospital: Marlborough or Clinton

Registered Voters (Secretary of State 1992): 1,437

Legislative Districts:

U.S. Congress: 3rd District:
Peter Blute (R)

State Senator: Middlesex & Worcester:
Robert A. Durand (D)

State Representative: 4th Middlesex:
Daniel J. Valianti (D)

Public Schools
Berlin: Berlin Memorial (K-06)
Berlin Boylston: Tahanto Regional High (07-12)
Assabet Valley: Assabet Valley Voc High School (09-13)

Superintendent: Donald E. J. Dupont

School Choice: Yes

Per Pupil Cost: (State Exec. Office of Education - 1992-93)
$4,749 primary
$7,843 secondary

State average 1992-93: $5,023

Average Teacher Salary: 1992-1993 (State Exec. Office of Education)
Berlin: $36,629/$40,762
statewide: $38,774

Mean SAT scores 1993

	(reported by town)	State Average:
Math	494	
Verbal	440	
Combined	934	903

Student Population (Dept. of Education)
Total students 1991-92: 378
at public schools 87.6%
at private schools 12.4%

Educational Attainment (1990 census)
High School graduate or higher 86.5%
Bachelor's Degree or higher 27.9%

Largest Employers: (supplied by community, 1993)

	# of employees
Berlin Fun Farm (seasonal)	120
Town of Berlin	55
Coldwell's, Inc.	20
A. Risi & Sons Building Supplies, Inc.	10
Village Power Equipment Company, Inc.	6

Commuting to Work (1990 Census)
Average time to work (mins.): 22.8

Houses of Worship: First Parish Church (Protestant - Federated); St. Joseph the Good Provider

Crime Rate: (1993, Mass. State Police Crime Reporting Unit)

	town	statewide
Total crimes reported:	48	
rate per 1,000 persons	20.93	37.46
Violent crimes	3	
rate per 1,000 persons	1.31	5.65
Property crimes	45	
rate per 1,000 persons	19.62	31.83

Libraries
Berlin Public Library

Museums
Berlin Art and Historical Collections

BERLIN

Blackstone

The Blackstone Gorge and the Triad Bridge

In Blackstone, there remains the one untouched spot along the whole of the famous Blackstone River. Beginning in 1793 with Samuel Slater's Pawtucket RI mill, the river was drastically changed, becoming "America's hardest working river" and the birthplace of the Industrial Revolution. With 42 dams, hundreds of mills, and later the Blackstone Canal and towpath cutting through it from Providence to Worcester, the river was forever transformed (*see Webster*).

The only natural part left is the Blackstone Gorge. Because of the rock ledge and drastic 25' drop, the canal builders found it easier to go around the gorge, and left the area unspoiled. According to Blackstone historian Thomas Bik, "All of the other banks along the entire Blackstone River have been altered, either by the towpath and canal, or by dams and mill sites."

Still existing Nipmuc trails lead to the gorge, winding from the river level up to rock precipices towering some 90' above. "Walking through the hemlocks along the forested banks here transports you to a different point in time," Bik observed. To reach the gorge, turn right off Rte. 122-South onto County Street, a dead end. Park here, and you'll see the Rolling Dam and signs to the gorge.

A contrast to the gorge is the "Triad Bridge" on the Blackstone - Millville line. A testament to the bustling railroad age, three bridges intersect here, criss-crossing the river at three different heights. "It was built so three trains could cross the river at the same time on their own bridges," Bik noted. One was owned by Penn Central, the other was part of the unfinished Grand Trunk line, and the third is still in use today by the Providence & Worcester Railroad. The Triad Bridge can be viewed from Rte. 122 South heading into Blackstone from Millville. "If you're lucky, you'll see a train pass," Bik ventured.

Despite its close proximity to Woonsocket and Providence, RI, most people moving to Blackstone today commute to Metro West and Boston, easily accessing I-495 via two exits in nearby Bellingham. Although its mills are gone, Blackstone has historic mercantile buildings in Monument Square, one now housing the Union House Pub, overlooking the Saranac Dam. The Station House Pub is in the former fire station.

Sources: Thomas Bik, Blackstone Historian; The Boston Globe; Commonwealth of Mass. EOCD Community Profile.

Year incorporated: 1845
Population: 8,023 (1990 census)
Density: 736 per square mile
Total area: 11.23 sq. miles
Elevation: 186'
Distance from:
Boston: 37
Worcester: 22
Providence: 15
Highways: Rtes. 122, 126.
Rail: The Providence & Worcester Railroad provides freight rail service to Blackstone.
Airport: The Norfolk Airport, a general aviation facility.
Tax Rate: $13.12 per thousand (1994, Mass. Div. of Local Services)
Median House Price: $115,885 (1993, County Data Corporation)
Median Household Income: $38,687 (1990 Census)
% of state average: 104.7%
Per Capita Income: $15,791
% of state average 91.7%
Form of Government: Board of Selectmen, Town Administrator, open town meeting
Municipal Offices: (508) 883-1500
Services: Mass. Electric, Blackstone Gas Co., no municipal sewer service.
Nearest Hospital: Landmark, Woonsocket, RI
Registered Voters: 4,364
Legislative Districts:
U.S. Congress: 2nd District: Richard E. Neal (D)
State Senate: Worcester & Norfolk District: Louis P. Bertonazzi (D)
State Representative: 8th Worcester Pct. 1: Paul Kujawski (D)
10th Norfolk Pct. 2 and 3: James E. Valle (D)
Public Schools
Blackstone Millville: Longfellow (K-06); John F. Kennedy (K-03); A F Maloney (04-06); Blackstone Millville (07-12)
Blackstone Valley: Blackstone Valley Voc Tech (09-12)

Superintendent: Aldo Cecchi (508) 883-6633
School Choice: No
Per Pupil Cost:
(State Exec. Office of Education -1992-93): $4,466
State average 1992-93: $5,023
Average Teacher Salary:
(State Exec. Office of Education)

	salary 1992-93	statewide 1992-93
Blackstone Millville	$37,597	$38,774
Blackstone Valley	$37,714	

Mean SAT scores 1993

	(reported by town)	State Mean
Math	412	
Verbal	484	
Combined:	896	903

Student Population (Dept. of Education)
Total students 1991-92: 1,564
at public schools 97.5%
at private schools 2.5%
Educational Attainment (1990 census)
High School graduate or higher 75.2%
Bachelor's Degree or higher 13.3%
Largest Employers: (supplied by community, 1993)

	# of employees
Town of Blackstone	250
NET and Company	100
ALMACS	50

Commuting to Work (1990 Census)
Average time to work (mins.): 26.6
Houses of Worship: 1 Federated
Crime Rate:
(1993, Mass. State Police Crime Reporting Unit)

	town	statewide
Total crimes reported:	141	
rate per 1,000 persons	17.57	37.46
Violent crimes	10	
rate per 1,000 persons	1.25	5.65
Property crimes	131	
rate per 1,000 persons	16.33	31.83

Libraries: Blackstone Free Public Library

Bolton

From Cattle to Commuters

Drovers herding cattle to graze the cool pastures of Princeton used to drive their cows down Bolton's Main Street, and one year the "head count" topped 1,200. Today the morning commuter count easily beats that — some 9,000 cars a day drive through Bolton. The town's location, rustic scenery, and the fact that it spends 75% of its property taxes on its schools make it quite desirable for executives and professionals working in Boston or along the 495 corridor.

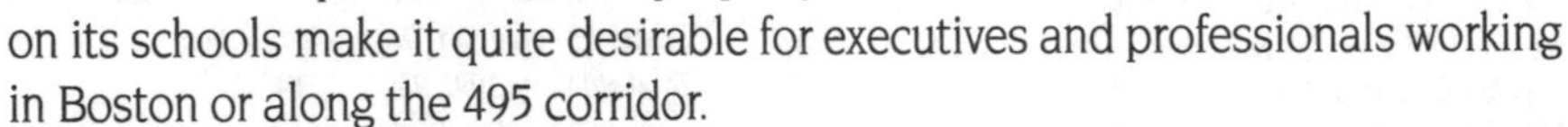

Bolton's Wattaquadoc Hill, at about 650', is the highest point between Mt. Wachusett and the Massachusetts Bay, and from its top Boston's Prudential and John Hancock towers are clearly seen. (Wattaquadock is an Indian name meaning a tract of open land where trees have fallen, a "wood-land.") Author Ivan Sandrof wrote in 1965 that from the the summit, "the dome of the State House is a golden pinhead." Rattlesnake Hill, once the site of a marble and lime quarry, has more than 27 minerals — including the rare Boltonite. The only other place in the world where Boltonite is found is near Italy's Mt. Vesuvius.

The town's history is mostly agricultural — its meadows and apple orchards exist today because the lack of water power limited the build-up of mills early on. Bolton's most famous business and most popular destination is the award-winning Nashoba Valley Winery on Wattaquadoc Hill Road, which makes premium wines from the best native fruit. These high quality wines complement even elegant gourmet meals. Rather than being overly sweet, Nashoba's best blueberry wines are dry and have a smooth and velvety texture equal to a fine Cabernet Sauvignon. A tantalizing hint of blueberry is detected only in the aftertaste.

Eight bridges to Lancaster and the high cost to maintain them caused Bolton's founders to break away from their "mother town" of Lancaster in 1738. A town ordinance In 1817 put an interesting twist on "for whom the bell tolls." Whenever there was a death in town, the village bell would ring five times, and after a pause, would ring three times for a man, twice for a woman, and once for a child. After another pause, the bellringer would then toll the person's age.

Sources: The Boston Globe; Commonwealth of Mass. EOCD Community Profile; A Guide to Nashaway, North Central Massachusetts...a land of uncommon beauty, Marge Darby, Jean C. McCrosky, Mildred A. Chandler, New Guide Group, 1994; More Massachusetts Towns, Ivan Sandrof, Barre Publishers, 1965; Worcester Business Journal.

Year incorporated: 1738
Population: 3,134 (1990 census)
Density: 157 per square mile
Total area: 20.00 sq. miles
Elevation: 387'
Distance from:
Boston: 31
Worcester: 17
Highways: Rtes. 85, 110, 117 and Interstate Rte. 495.
Airport: Minute Man Airport, a Reliever facility located in Stow.
Tax Rate: $13.58 per thousand
(1994, Mass. Div. of Local Services)
Median House Price: $192,500
(1993, County Data Corporation)
Median Household Income: $ 63,757 (1990 Census)
% of state average: 172.5%
Per Capita Income: $24,546
% of state average 142.5%
Form of Government: Board of Selectmen, Administrative Assistant, open town meeting
Municipal Offices: (508) 779-2297
Services: Mass. Electric, Commonwealth Gas, no municipal sewer service, ground water.
Nearest Hospital: Marlborough, Nashoba, Emerson, Worcester
Registered Voters: 2,164
Legislative Districts:
U.S. Congress: 5th District: Martin T. Meehan (D)
State Senate: 2nd Worcester & Middlesex:
Robert A. Antonioni (D)
State Representative: 3rd Middlesex:
Patricia A. Walrath (D)
Public Schools
Bolton: Emerson (K-08)
Nashoba: Nashoba Regional (09-12)
Minuteman: Minute Man Voc Tech High (09-13)
Superintendent: Roland Miller
School Choice: No, primary grades: Yes, high school
Per Pupil Cost:
(State Exec. Office of Education -1992-93)
$4,964 primary $6,767 secondary
State average 1992-93 $5,023

Average Teacher Salary: 1992 - 93
(State Exec. Office of Education)
statewide 1992-92, $38,774
Bolton $38,545/$38,069
Mean SAT scores 1993

	(reported by town)	State Mean:
Math	513	
Verbal	446	
Combined	959	903

Student Population (Dept. of Education)
Total students 1991-92: 625
at public schools: 94.7%
at private schools 5.3%
Educational Attainment (1990 census)
High School graduate or higher 93.3%
Bachelor's Degree or higher 44.2%
Largest employers:
Yankee Atomic 470
Future Electronics 300
Commuting to Work (1990 Census)
Average time to work (mins.): 26.0
Houses of Worship: Catholic, Protestant
Crime Rate:
(1993, Mass. State Police Crime Reporting Unit))

		statewide
Total crimes reported:	2	
rate per 1,000 persons	26.16	37.46
Violent crimes	3	
rate per 1,000 persons	.96	5.65
Property crimes	79	
rate per 1,000 persons	25.21	31.83

Libraries:
Bolton Public Library
Museums:
Bolton Historical Society
State Register of Historic Places 1993:
Roemer House

Boylston

Tower Hill and Wachusett Reservoir

Boylston is home to one of the area's true gems, Tower Hill Botanic Garden, home of the Worcester County Horticultural Society, which maintains 132 acres of meadows, gardens, woodlands, a restored 1742 farmhouse, educational center, and sponsors more than 250 public programs a year. Tower Hill's views of Mt. Wachusett and the Wachusett Reservoir are unsurpassed.

Incorporated in 1786, Boylston is named for Boston's prominent Boylston family, as was Boylston Street in Boston. A branch of this family was instrumental in garnering support for the American Revolution.

In 1894, the state changed Boylston forever by taking over 4,000 acres for the Wachusett Reservoir and displacing a third of its population. Nearly 50 homes were razed, and all of the town's manufacturing was wiped out. More than 25% of the town is part of the reservoir and Metropolitan District Commission (MDC) land, and large housing complexes have been restricted here due to damage the sewerage might cause to the reservoir.

The town common typifies New England with a gazebo, white church, burying ground, town hall and library. The town hall, built in 1830 from Boylston granite, is one of the state's oldest in continuous use, and is now the headquarters of the Boylston Historical Society. Town stocks were once used for public punishment and stood next to the cemetery, just off the main green.

Today, Boylston is a bedroom community to Worcester, but despite its seven mile proximity to the city, the town has protected its quaint, rural charm with large lot zoning and commercial building restrictions. Boylston's population has grown by only 800 residents in the past 20 years. Although the town doesn't have a grocery store, shopping of all kinds can be found just a few minutes away in all directions.

Sources: Commonwealth of Mass EOCD Community Profile, Worcester Magazine, The Boston Globe, The Worcester Telegram & Gazette, the Boylston Historical Society.

Year incorporated: 1786
Total area: 19.67
Elevation: 519'
Population: 3,517 (1990 census)
Density: 219 per square mile
Distance from:
Boston: 38 miles
Worcester: 7 miles
Highways: State Rtes. 70 and 140; I-290 passes just south of Boylston's border.
Rail: Commuter rail to Boston available from Worcester
Bus: The Worcester Regional Transit Authority provides service between Boylston and Worcester.
Airport: Worcester Airport, a primary commercial facility
Tax Rate: $12.82 per thousand (1994, The Central Mass. Fact Book)
Median House Price: $128,500 (1993, County Data Corporation)
Median Household Income: $52,424 (1990 Census)
% of state average: 141.9%
Per Capita Income: $22,571
% of state average 131%
Form of Government: Board of Selectmen; Administrative Assistant, open town meeting
Municipal Offices: (508) 869-2234
Services: Boylston municipal light, Commonwealth Gas, no sewer, partial water, Greater Media Cable
Nearest Hospital: several in Worcester
Registered Voters (Secretary of State 1992): 2,382
Legislative Districts:
U.S. Congress: 3rd District: Peter Blute (R)
State Senate: 1st Worcester District: Robert A. Bernstein (D)
State Representative: 12th Worcester District: Harold P. Naughton (D)
Public Schools
Boylston Elementary: K-6
Berlin-Boylston Tahanto Regional High: 7-12
Superintendent: Donald Dupont (508) 869-2837
School Choice: No for primary; yes for high school.
Per Pupil Cost:
(State Exec. Office of Education -1992-93)

Primary	$4964
Secondary (Regional)	$7,843
State average 1992-93	$5,023

Average Teacher Salary:
(State Exec. Office of Education)

	Boylston 1992-3	statewide 1992-93
Primary	$38,935	$38,774
Secondary	$40,762	

Mean SAT scores 1993

	(reported by town)	State Mean
Math	494	
Verbal	440	
Combined	934	903

Student Population (Dept. of Education)
Total students 1991-92:

Boylston	276
Berlin-Boylston	305

Educational Attainment (1990 census)

High School graduate or higher	90.9%
Bachelor's Degree or higher	34.7%

Largest Employers: (supplied by community, 1993)

	# of employees
Town of Boylston (+seasonal,part-time)	213
Boylston Elementary and Tahanto H.S.	100
Atlas News, Inc.	56
New England Telephone	50

Commuting to Work (1990 Census)
Average time to work (mins.): 19.9
Houses of Worship: 1 Protestant, 1 Catholic
Crime Rate:
(1993, Mass. State Police Crime Reporting Unit)

	town	statewide
Total crimes reported:	24	
rate per 1,000 persons	6.82	37.46
Violent crimes	0	
rate per 1,000 persons	0	5.65
Property Crimes	24	
rate per 1,000 persons	6.82	31.83

Libraries:
Boylston Public Library, 695 Main St., (508) 869-2371
Museums:
Worcester County Horticultural Society/Tower Hill Botanic Garden,
11 French Drive (508) 869-0314.
State Register of Historic Places 1993:
Boylston Historic District, Main, School, Church Sts. and Sear Hill
John B. Gough House, 215 Main St.
Deacon Cyprian Keyes Home, (Barlin Acres), 284 School St.

Brookfield

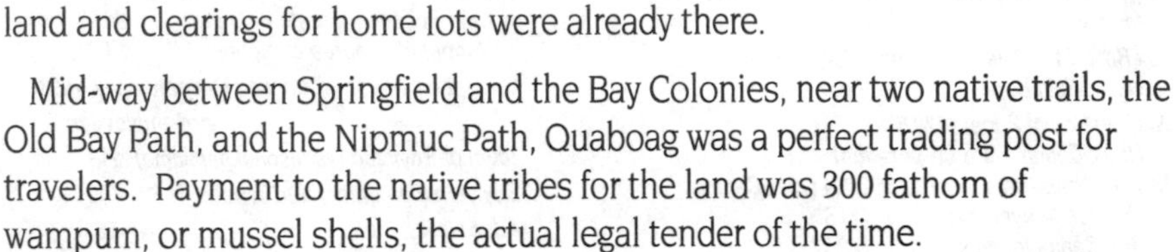

From the Quaboag Plantation

The Ipswich farmers who settled Quaboag Plantation (now Brookfield) in 1660 weren't the area's first planters. Rather than finding virgin forest, these colonists picked the area because it had been continuously cultivated for nearly 13 centuries by the Quaboag tribe, who spoke Algonquin like the Nashaways and Nipmucs. When the farmers arrived, meadow land and clearings for home lots were already there.

Mid-way between Springfield and the Bay Colonies, near two native trails, the Old Bay Path, and the Nipmuc Path, Quaboag was a perfect trading post for travelers. Payment to the native tribes for the land was 300 fathom of wampum, or mussel shells, the actual legal tender of the time.

Quaboag settlers changed the village name to Brookfield in 1673, and built their own Bay Path running northeast to Worcester and west to Warren and Springfield, and the Hadley Path to Ware and Hadley. Portions of both paths can still be traced.

Puritan life had interesting punishments. Babies born on the Sabbath were considered conceived on the Sabbath, and parents were fined for not keeping the day holy. The law was repealed when a minister's wife delivered twins on a Sunday. The Quaboag Magistrate book records the fate of a sharp-tongued Goodwife Hunter, who for "railing, scolding and other exorbitancys of the Toung" was sentenced to be gagged, or set in a stool and dunked under water.

After 10 years of peace, Brookfield was ambushed by native tribes at the start of King Philip's war in 1675. Nearly 100 people crowded into Ayres Tavern for safety and endured a harrowing three-day siege before help arrived. The town was burned and not resettled until 1686. Later it became an important stage stop on the Upper Boston Post Road. The town was subdivided into East Brookfield, West Brookfield, Warren and North Brookfield. Today Brookfield's location is still key, home to many commuters who travel 22 miles to Worcester or 37 miles to Springfield.

Sources: Commonwealth of Mass. EOCD Community Profile; Quaboag Plantation, alias Brookefeild, Roy; The Old Post Road, Holbrook

Year incorporated: 1673
Total area: 16.57
Elevation: 700'
Distance from:
Boston: 57 miles
Worcester: 22 miles
Springfield 37 miles
Transportation:
Highways: State Rte. 9. U.S. Rte. 20 and the Mass. Turnpike are easily accessible.
Bus: The Worcester Regional Transit Authority (WRTA)provides fixed route service between Brookfield Center, Leicester and Worcester.
Airport: Worcester Airport
Tax Rate: $13.84 per thousand (1994, The Central Mass. Fact Book)
Median House Price: $106,000 (1993, County Data Corporation)
Median Household Income: $30,349 (1990 Census)
% of state average: 82.1%
Per Capita Income: $12,368
% of state average 71.8%
Population: 2,968 (1990 census)
Density: 191 per square mile
Form of Government: Board of Selectmen, Administrative Assistant, open town meeting.
Municipal Offices: (508) 867-2930
Services: Massachusetts Electric, Boston Gas, no sewer.
Nearest Hospital: Mary Lane Hospital, Ware; Harrington Memorial Hosp., Southbridge
Registered Voters (Secretary of State 1992): 1,636
Legislative Districts:
U.S. Congress: 2nd District: Richard E. Neal (D)
State Senate: Worcester-Franklin-Hampden & Hampshire District: Robert D. Wetmore (D)
State Representative: 6th Worcester District: Stephen M. Brewer (D)
Public Schools

Brookfield Elementary	K-6
Tantasqua Regional Jr. High	7-9
Tantasqua Regional Sr. High	10-12
Tantasqua Regional Voc.	9-12

Superintendent: David Roach (508) 347-3077
School Choice: No

Per Pupil Cost:
(State Exec. Office of Education -1992-93)

Brookfield	$3,891
Tantasqua	$5,629
State average 1992-93	$5,023

Average Teacher Salary:
(State Exec. Office of Education 1992-93)

Brookfield Primary	$30,119
Secondary	$40,026
Statewide	$38,774

Mean SAT scores 1993

	(reported by town)	State Mean
Math	489	
Verbal	438	
Combined	927	903

Student Population (Dept. of Education)
Total students 1991-92: 2,968
Educational Attainment (1990 census)
High School graduate or higher 71.3%
Bachelor's Degree or higher 11.2%
Largest Employers: (supplied by community, 1993)
Gavitt Wire and Cable
Town of Brookfield
Brookfield Motors
R.L. McCarthy & Son
Custom Pallets
Commuting to Work (1990 Census)
Average time to work (mins.): 27
Houses of Worship: 1 Catholic, 1 Congregational, 1 Unitarian
Crime Rate: not available
Libraries:
Merrick Public Library, Common St., P.O. Box 258; (508) 867-6339
State Register of Historic Places 1993:
Adena Burial Site
Brookfield Common Historic District
Elm Hill Farm Historic District, East Main St. and Brookfield Rd.
Milestone, 1767, Elm Hill Rd., east of North Brookfield Rd.
Milestone, 1767, Elm Hill Rd., west of North Brookfield Town Line
Milestone, 1767, Rte. 9

Charlton

Anesthesia and Grizzly Adams

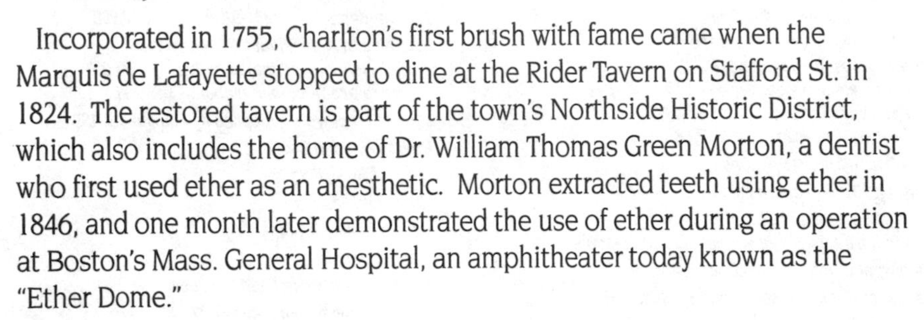

Once home to dairy farms, apple orchards and strawberry fields, Charlton is now the address of a growing number of commuters who enjoy its easy access to the Mass. Pike and its location within 50 miles of five major cities: Boston, Worcester, Springfield, Hartford and Providence. Most commuters work in Worcester, just 17 miles northeast.

Incorporated in 1755, Charlton's first brush with fame came when the Marquis de Lafayette stopped to dine at the Rider Tavern on Stafford St. in 1824. The restored tavern is part of the town's Northside Historic District, which also includes the home of Dr. William Thomas Green Morton, a dentist who first used ether as an anesthetic. Morton extracted teeth using ether in 1846, and one month later demonstrated the use of ether during an operation at Boston's Mass. General Hospital, an amphitheater today known as the "Ether Dome."

Another famous native son was James Capen Adams (1807-1869), better known as mountain man "Grizzly Adams." An unhappy cobbler, Adams headed west in 1852 to spend eight years with the grizzlies in the Rockies. Having survived many close encounters with the bears, Adams toured with famed showman, P.T. Barnum. Adams' grave in Charlton's Bay Path Cemetery is marked by a headstone ordered by Barnum which features a carving of "Grizzly" dressed in buckskin.

The town of Charlton itself had a close encounter with disaster in 1955 when a dam at Glen Echo Lake burst, sending a 30' wall of water rushing towards neighboring Southbridge. Five people died, and many homes, roads and bridges were destroyed. The only thing saving Charlton from obliteration by the surging water was a huge mound of dirt fill piled up by construction crews building the Mass. Pike.

The view towards Southbridge from Charlton's Dresser Hill is among the best in the county, particularly during autumn foliage. Charlton's scenic beauty and central location have caused a population surge over past years. The number of children in town rose by 69% between 1970 and 1990. To handle the increase, the town recently built one new elementary school and built an addition to another.

Sources: Commonwealth of Mass. EOCD Community Profile; The Boston Globe; More Massachusetts Towns, Ivan Sandrof, Barre Publishers, 1965; A Guide to the Heritage of Worcester County, Simone E. Blake, Montachusett Girl Scout Council, 1973.

Year incorporated: 1755
Population: 9,025 (1994 town census)
Density: 224 per square mile
Total area: 43.95
Elevation: 895'
Distance from:
Boston: 40 miles
Worcester: 17 miles
Springfield 36 miles

Highways: Massachusetts Turnpike (I-90); U.S. Route 20; State Rtes. 31 and 169. Interstates 84, 395 and 290 are minutes away.

Airport: Worcester Airport: Southbridge Municipal Airport, a General Aviation (GA) facility in nearby Southbridge has a 3,500' x 75' asphalt runway. Instrument approaches available: Non-precision.

Tax Rate: $11.02 per thousand (1994, The Central Mass. Fact Book)

Median House Price: $117,500 (1993, County Data Corporation)

Median Household Income: $42,461 (1990 Census)
% of state average: 114.9%
Per Capita Income: $15,128
% of state average 87.8%

Form of Government: Board of Selectmen; Executive Secretary, open town meeting.

Municipal Offices: (508) 248-5900

Services: Mass. Electric, city sewer, no natural gas, full time police and fire, Pegasus cable TV.

Nearest Hospital: Harrington Memorial Hospital, Southbridge

Registered Voters: 6,032 (1994 town voters list)

Legislative Districts:

U.S. Congress: 2nd District: Richard E. Neal (D)

State Senate: Worcester & Norfolk District: Louis P. Bertonazzi (D)

State Representative: 6th Worcester: David Peters (R)

Public Schools

Superintendent: Acting Superintendent: Albert L. Thibaudeau (508) 943-6888

Dudley/Charlton:

School	Grades
Dudley Elementary	2-4
Mason Rd. School	K-1
Charlton Elementary	K-2
Heritage School	3-6
Dudley Intermediate	5-6
Shepherd Hill Reg.High	7-12

Southern Worcester County

School	Grades
Bay Path Reg. Voc Tech H.S.	9-12

School Choice: No

Per Pupil Cost:
(State Exec. Office of Education -1992-93)
Charlton: $3,611
State average 1992-93 $5,023

Average Teacher Salary:
(State Exec. Office of Education-1992-93)

Charlton	statewide 1992-93
$36,878	$38,774

Mean SAT scores 1993

	(reported by town)	State Mean:
Math	459	
Verbal	420	
Combined:	879	903

Student Population (Dept. of Education)

Total students	1991-92:
Dudley Charlton	3,397
Southern Worc. County	1,000

Educational Attainment (1990 census)

High School graduate or higher	78.1%
Bachelor's Degree or higher	16.7%

Largest Employers: (supplied by community, 1993)

	# of employees
Masonic Home, Inc.	160
Town of Charlton (non-school personnel)	148
Bay Path Regional Vocational School	141
Dudley-Charlton Regional School District	100
Marriott Travel Plaza	50

Commuting to Work (1990 Census)

Average time to work (mins.): 24.4

Houses of Worship: 1 Catholic, 5 Protestant

Crime Rate: (1993, Mass. State Police Crime Reporting Unit)

		statewide
Total crimes reported:	145	
rate per 1,000 persons	15.14	37.46
Violent crimes	25	
rate per 1,000 persons	2.61	5.65
Property crimes	120	
rate per 1,000 persons	12.53	31.83

Libraries:
Charlton Public Library, Main St. Box 10 (508) 248-2052

State Register of Historic Places 1993:
Northside Village Historic District (Stafford St., Northside, Cemetery, Smith Rds.)
Rider Tavern, Stafford St., opposite Northside Rd.
Spurr House, Main St.
Charlton Center Historic District, Main St.

Clinton

In the Machine Age for 200 Years

Using a 30' drop along the Nashua River's course, a force of 70 horsepower, Clinton's early entrepreneurs redefined the term "mill." Moving beyond sawmills and grist-mills, in operation since 1654, David Poignand's cotton mill here was the first in the country to use power looms. Brothers Charles and Eurastus Bigelow bought Poignand's "Factory Village" operation and patented the carpet loom in 1842, which used the Jacquard system to weave patterns in carpet and upholstery fabric. By 1885, the Bigelow mill was the world's largest carpet manufacturer, with the slogan, "*A title on the door rates a Bigelow on the floor.*"

It was the Bigelows' fondness for New York City's Clinton House hotel that gave the town its name when it separated from Lancaster in 1850. Along the way the Bigelows' Lancaster Mills operation became the world's leader in manufacturing gingham cloth. Their success spawned supporting industries — foundries, machine shops, and factories for clothing, shoes and boots. Another Clinton inventor, William Goodale, patented machinery to make paper bags in 1859. The mills attracted a diverse ethnic population, including Irish, German, Scots and English immigrants, as well as hundreds of Yankee farm girls from New Hampshire and Vermont.

Although the Bigelow mill moved and the Depression ended Clinton's manufacturing reign, the town's mill buildings aren't standing empty. NYPRO, an international precision injecton molding company, has won awards for its rehabilitation of the mill at 101 Union Street. And Dunn & Co. renovated Lancaster Mills Building #13, which had been empty for five years and had 2,000 broken windows. Today, the company operates the world's largest "book hospital" and rebindery business and recycles used book covers into gift items. Owner David Dunn was named 1994 SBA "Business Person of the Year" for Massachusetts.

The Wachusett Reservoir, which doomed the original West Boylston (*see West Boylston*), was created by an impressive dam on the Nashua River at Clinton - the north dike is nearly two miles across and 114 feet high. About 17% of Clinton's land area is either under the reservoir or part of the dam, which was built from 1901-1905. A 12-mile long aqueduct connects Wachusett to the Sudbury Reservoir. Moving caskets from Clinton's soon-to-be-flooded cemeteries took eight months, with workers sometimes averaging 50 coffins per day. One old graveyard, now "Cemetery Island" in the resevoir, is visible from the dam.

Clinton's resilience was one reason President Carter chose it for one of his televised town meetings in 1977. He stayed in a private home for his visit, and the ensuing publicity put Clinton on the map. Town leaders also lobbied to convince President Clinton to visit Clinton.

Sources: Commonwealth of Mass. EOCD Community Profile; The Boston Globe; A Guide to Nashaway, M. Darby, J. McCrosky, M. Chandler; The Lancastrian Towns, Tymeson; A Guide to the Heritage of Worcester County, Blake, Montachusett Girl Scout Council; Run of the Mill, Dunwell.

Year incorporated: 1850

Population: 13,222 (1990 census)

Density: 2,320 per square mile

Total area: 7.29 sq. miles

Elevation: 325'

Distance from:
- Boston: 35
- Worcester: 13

Highways: Rtes. 62, 70 and 110.

Rail: Freight rail service is available from Conrail and from the Springfield Terminal Railway.

Bus: Clinton is a member of the Worcester Regional Transit Authority.

Airport: Worcester Municipal Airport

Tax Rate: $10.92 per thousand (1994, Mass. Div. of Local Services)

Median House Price: $110,000 (1993, County Data Corporation)

Median Household Income: $ 34,091 (1990 Census)
- % of state average: 92.3%
- Per Capita Income: $15,328
- % of state average 89.0%

Form of Government: Board of Selectmen, Administrative Assistant, open town meeting

Municipal Offices: (508) 365-4119

Services: Mass. Electric, Boston Gas Co., town sewer, ground water.

Nearest Hospital: Clinton Hospital, Leominster Hospital, several in Worcester

Registered Voters : 7,659

Legislative Districts:

U.S. Congress: 3rd District: Peter I. Blute (R)

State Senate: 1st Worcester: Robert A. Bernstein (D)

State Representative: 12th Worcester: Harold P. Naughton, Jr. (D)

Public Schools

Clinton: Parkhurst (-K); Clinton Elem (01-03); Clinton Middle (04-08); Clinton Senior High (9-12)

Superintendent: Richard L. Slaven Ph.D. (508) 365-4201

School Choice: Yes

Per Pupil Cost: (State Exec. Office of Education -1992-93):
- Clinton: $3,959
- State average $5,023

Average Teacher Salary: (State Exec. Office of Education 1992-93)

Clinton	statewide 1992-93
$36,592	$38,774

Mean SAT scores 1993

	(reported by town)	State Mean
Math	440	
Verbal	417	
Combined	857	903

Student Population (Dept. of Education)

Total students 1991-92: 1,984
- at public schools 92.1%
- at private schools 7.9%

Private Schools: St. Mary's Elementary

Educational Attainment (1990 census)
- High School graduate or higher 78.0%
- Bachelor's Degree or higher 15.8%

Largest Employers: (supplied by community, 1993)

	# of employees
NYPRO, Inc.	650
Delta Surprenant, Inc.	400
The Clinton Hospital	330
The Weetabix Company	230

Commuting to Work (1990 Census)

Average time to work (mins.): 21.6

Houses of Worship: 1 Jewish Synagogue, 3 Catholic, 1 Greek Orthodox, 2 Congregational, 1 Episcopal, 2 Presbyterian, 1 Assembly of God, 1 Abundant Life Fellowship, 1 Faith Bible Baptist, 1 Christian Science, 1 Lutheran, 1 Methodist.

Crime Rate: (1993, Mass. State Police Crime Reporting Unit)

	town	statewide
Total crimes reported:	342	
rate per 1,000 persons	25.87	37.46
Violent crimes	69	
rate per 1,000 persons	5.22	5.65
Property crimes	273	
rate per 1,000 persons	20.65	31.83

Libraries:
- Bigelow Free Public Library

State Register of Historic Places 1993:
- Bigelow Carpet Company Woolen Mills
- Bigelow Carpet Mill
- Bowers School
- Clinton Central Business District
- First Methodist Church
- Holder Memorial
- Van Brode Mill
- Wachusett Aqueduct Linear District
- Wachusett Dam Historic District
- Water Supply System of Metropolitan Boston

Dana

The Lost Town of Worcester County

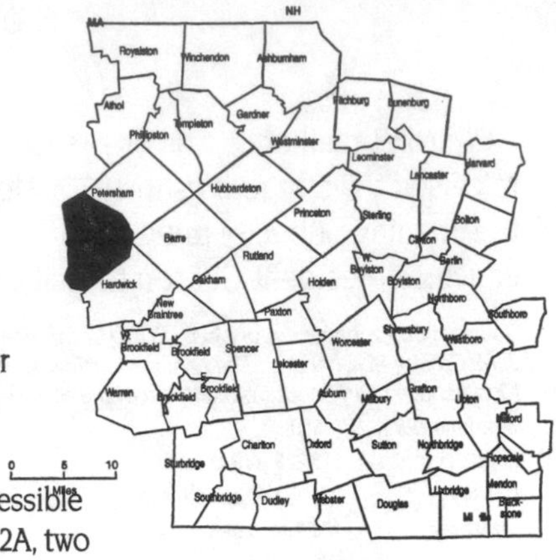

Many assume that Dana, the "ghost town" of Worcester County, drowned beneath the waters of the Quabbin Reservoir, but you can still hike or bike to Dana's town common. Instead of homes and buildings however, only cellar holes remain.

The road to Dana (born 1801; died 1938) is accessible from Quabbin Gate 40, on the west side of Rte. 32A, two miles north of the Petersham-Hardwick boundary sign. There are several parking spaces between Rte. 32A and the gate. J.R. Greene's *Historic Quabbin Hikes* is a detailed guide (*available in libraries or by calling* 1-800-64-*Books*). Visitors to Dana should note that bikes are allowed only on paved roads within the Quabbin, and dogs should be left at home. Quabbin rules are posted at each gate.

Boston began to outdrink its own water supply as early as 1795, and looked west for a solution. Beginning in 1895, the Clinton dam on the Nashua River was built to create the Wachusett Reservoir, which opened in 1907 (*see Clinton, Boylston, West Boylston*).

But Wachusett wasn't enough for thirsty Boston, and Metropolitan District Commission (MDC) engineers set their sights on the Swift River Valley. Their plans for the Quabbin Reservoir spelled the end of the four tiny towns of Prescott, Enfield, Greenwich and Worcester County's own Dana. Just west of Barre and north of Hardwick, Dana Center was near the East Branch of the Swift River. North Dana was on the river's Middle Branch, and the village factories made hats, piano legs and pocketbooks. The majority of Dana's land reverted to Petersham.

The Quabbin's master plan called for diverting the Ware River in Barre, building the Winsor Dam and the Goodnough Dike on the lower portion of the Swift River to create a huge reservoir in the valley, and building a 24.6 mile aqueduct from Quabbin to West Boylston to connect it all to the Wachusett Reservoir. The tunnel, which was blasted through underground rock is at places 750' down, is 13' high and 11' wide and big enough for a truck to drive through. Periodically, the aqueduct is drained, and engineers walk along its length inside to check it.

When reservoir rumors first surfaced in the 1890's, the 3,000 or so valley residents dismissed them as sheer fantasy. But as plans became real, an exodus began in 1927, and people moved and got on with their lives. Others lingered, wanting to stay "home" as long as possible.

Real estate in the valley was evaluated by MDC appraisers, and property owners tried to fight for fair compensation. But during the Great Depression, settlements were not generous, and the four towns were not politically powerful. Some felt those displaced by the Wachusett Reservoir a generation earlier were paid more fairly for their property.

Seven Years to Fill

Some 7,500 graves in the valley's 34 cemeteries were relocated; buildings were bulldozed and burned, and the four towns were disincorporated in 1938. A "Farewell Ball" was held in April; in June the schools held final graduation ceremonies. The flooding began in August, 1939, but it wasn't until 1946 that the reservoir was filled completely.

When it was over, the valley was a lake 18 miles long, 150' deep in some places, covering 39 square miles and filled with 412 billion gallons of water. The reservoir's distinctive "jagged finger" shape is easy to spot from the air, even from jetliners flying at 30,000 feet. Appropriately, Quabbin is the Nipmuc name for "great waters".

Where Eagles Dare

The tops of the valley's hills are now islands in the lake, and the 87.5 square mile Quabbin Reservation, termed an "accidental wilderness" by author Thomas Conuel, is a wildlife haven. "What started off as a land grab by Boston...produced a reservoir, a wildlife refuge, and superb fishing ground."

Today, the Quabbin is home to coyotes, rabbits, turkeys, and a deer herd estimated at 1,500. But by far the most famous Quabbin inhabitants are its bald eagles, carefully reintroduced to Massachusetts in 1982 by Jack Swedberg, former chief photographer for the Mass. Division of Fisheries and Wildlife. The first two eaglets, Betsy and Ross, were shipped from Michigan and placed in artificial nests in the Quabbin. The theory was to imprint upon the eaglets the memory of Quabbin as home so they would return later to mate.

The theory worked with Ross, who stayed and mated in 1989 with an eagle released in 1985. They were the first pair of bald eagles to nest in Massachusetts in nearly 100 years. The eagle program was declared successful after seven years and 42 transplanted eagles.

Some parts of the Quabbin, like the wild Prescott Peninsula, are off-limits, but nearly half a million people visit the Quabbin Park annually. Located at the southern end of the reservoir, just north of Rte. 9 in Belchertown and Ware, the park has picnic spots and a visitor's center just west of Winsor Dam, which is open year-round, including weekends. On a clear day, nearly the whole reservoir can be seen from the glassed-in observation floor of the 85-foot stone tower on top of Quabbin Hill. What used to be Dana lies to the northeast. The summit is accessible by car and directions to the tower are available at the visitor's center (413) 323-7221.

Dana may be gone, but throughout Worcester County's watershed towns controversy still rages about who pays to keep Boston's drinking water clean. The state's "Cohen bill" has increased development restrictions near the region's reservoirs and their tributaries. Boston water users still grumble about rising rates, Central Massachusetts landowners still grumble about unfair land-taking, and the eagles still fly over the Quabbin.

Sources: Quabbin Reservoir, Walter E. Clark, Hobson Book Press, 1946; Reprinted by Athol Press, Inc., 1994; Strange Tales From Old Quabbin, J.R. Greene, Highland Press, Athol, MA, 1993; Historic Quabbin Hikes, J.R. Greene, Highland Press, Athol, MA, 1994; The Creation of Quabbin Reservoir, The Death of the Swift River Valley, J.R. Greene, Highland Press, Athols, MA, 1981; Clif Read, Supervisor of Interpretive Services, MDC.

Douglas

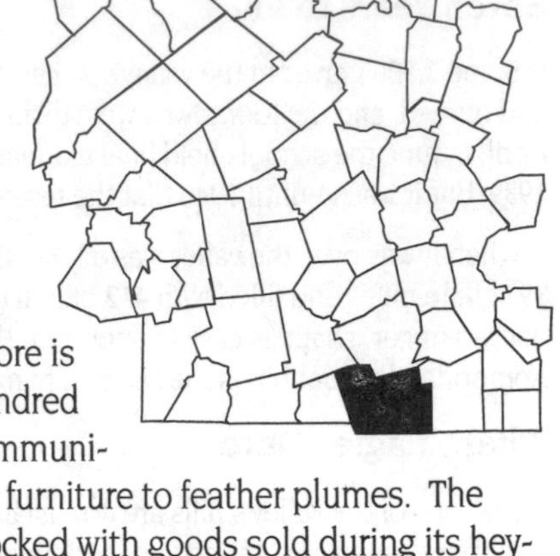

Country Store Snapshot of the Past

History books and war memorials may preserve life's big events, but the E.N. Jenckes Store and Museum preserves the small, everyday ones. Restored by the Douglas Historical Society, the Jenckes Store is a typical small town country store of a hundred years ago that was the lifeblood of the community, selling everything from ladders to lace, furniture to feather plumes. The store's original well-worn counters are stocked with goods sold during its heyday — galoshes and boots, brushes, bed linens, bow ties, shirt collars, straw hats, shaving soap and razors. The dry goods section has original (but empty) tins of codfish, cocoa, cereals, baking powder, mincemeat, mustard, molasses and more.

When Edward Jenckes bought the store in 1883, Douglas was a thriving manufacturing and transportation center. The main industry was the Douglas Axe Mill, with buildings clustered along the banks of the Mumford River, where many town residents worked as forgers, polishers, inspectors or agents of the firm. Other businesses included the Hayward & Company Woolen Mills, a carriage manufacturer and a grain mill. Douglas' Main Street was also the turnpike to Boston and Hartford, and the depot for the New York and New England Railroad was nearby. What wasn't carried at the E.N. Jenckes store could easily be ordered for delivery via railroad. The store's "route men" traveled the countryside in horse-drawn wagons, taking orders one day, and delivering the next.

Mill-sponsored baseball teams from Douglas played in the fiercely competitive Blackstone Valley Industrial league. Home-run hitter Hank Greenberg starred for the East Douglas team before joining the Detroit Tigers. A legendary 1946 exhibition game between the New York Yankees and the Boston Red Sox at Soldiers Field in East Douglas drew 12,000 fans and signalled the decline of the mill leagues (*see Millville*).

Douglas is the Blackstone Valley's largest town in land area, but nearly one third of it is part of the 4,555-acre Douglas State Forest, where Wallum Lake is popular for swimming and boating. The forest is a terminus of the 95-mile Mid-State Trail, which crosses Worcester County connecting New Hampshire and Rhode Island, from Douglas north to Mt. Watatic in Ashburnham. Besides Wallum Lake, the state forest offers a delightful Cedar Swamp boardwalk trail, which begins just past the park's interpretative center.

Sources: Commonwealth of Mass. EOCD Community Profile; The Boston Globe; The Worcester Telegram & Gazette; the Douglas Historical Society "E.N. Jenckes General Store;" A Guide to the Heritage of Worcester County, Simone E. Blake, Montachusett Girl Scout Council, 1973; Natural Wonders of Massachusetts, A Guide to Parks, Preserves & Wild Places, Nancy Prajzner, Country Roads Press, 1994.

Year incorporated: 1746
Population: 5,595 (1994, town)
Density: 150 per square mile
Total area: 37.71 sq. miles
Elevation: 580'
Distance from:
Boston: 40
Worcester: 18
Providence: 35, approx.
Highways: Rtes. 16 and 146.
Airport: The Worcester Municipal Airport
Tax Rate: $14.16 per thousand
(1994, Mass. Div. of Local Services)
Median House Price: $120,900
(1993, County Data Corporation)
Median Household Income: $38,362 (1990 Census)
% of state average: 103.8%
Per Capita Income: $14,660
% of state average 85.1%
Form of Government: Board of Selectmen, open town meeting
Municipal Offices: (508) 476-4000
Services: Mass. Electric, no natural gas, Douglas WWTF sewer.
Nearest Hospital: Milford/Whitinsville Regional Hospital, Milford; Hubbard Hospital, Webster
Registered Voters 3,079 (Secretary of State 1992)
Legislative Districts:
U.S. Congress: 2nd District: Richard E. Neal (D)
State Senate: Worcester & Norfolk District: Louis P. Bertonazzi (D)
State Representative: 8th Worcester: Paul Kujawski (D)
Public Schools
Douglas: East Douglas Elem (K-5); Douglas Memorial High (6-12)
Blackstone Valley: Blackstone Valley VocTech (09-12)
Superintendent: Concetta Verge (508) 476-7901
School Choice: Yes
Per Pupil Cost:
(State Exec. Office of Education -1992-93):
Douglas: $3,724
State average : $5,023

Average Teacher Salary: (State Exec. Office of Education): 1992-3,
Douglas: 1992-93, $43,384
statewide 1992-93, $38,774

Mean SAT scores 1993

	(reported by town)	State Mean
Math	464	
Verbal	430	
Combined	894	903

Student Population (Dept. of Education)
Total students 1991-92: 1,110
at public schools 90.0%
at private schools 10.0%

Educational Attainment (1990 census)
High School graduate or higher 80.3%
Bachelor's Degree or higher 14.9%

Largest Employers: (supplied by community, 1993)

	# of employees
Town of Douglas	155
Guilford Industries	75
Guaranteed Builders, Inc.	20
Axe Mill Tavern	15
Granutec, Inc.	15

Commuting to Work (1990 Census)
Average time to work (mins.): 29.2
Houses of Worship: 2 Congregational, 1 Methodist
Crime Rate: (1993, Mass. State Police Crime Reporting Unit) adjusted to 12 months

	town	statewide
Total crimes reported:	197	
rate per 1,000 persons	36.23	37.46
Violent crimes	24	
rate per 1,000 persons	4.41	5.65
Property Crimes	173	
rate per 1,000 persons	31.81	31.83

Libraries:
Simon Fairfield Public Library

State Register of Historic Places 1993:
Hayward Mill Historic District
E. N. Jenckes Store

Dudley

An Education in Business - and Wine

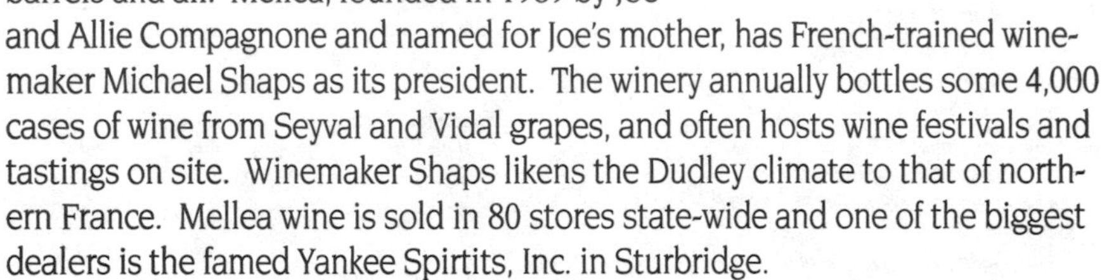

People traveling to Dudley these days are likely going to take a college course or sip some wine. Best known as the home campus of Nichols College, Dudley is also home to the award-winning Mellea Winery, which makes wine in the traditional European way, oak barrels and all. Mellea, founded in 1989 by Joe and Allie Compagnone and named for Joe's mother, has French-trained winemaker Michael Shaps as its president. The winery annually bottles some 4,000 cases of wine from Seyval and Vidal grapes, and often hosts wine festivals and tastings on site. Winemaker Shaps likens the Dudley climate to that of northern France. Mellea wine is sold in 80 stores state-wide and one of the biggest dealers is the famed Yankee Spirtits, Inc. in Sturbridge.

Mellea often taps a local resource to help market its wines — business interns from Nichols College. Nichols, which started In 1931 as a junior college, expanded in 1958 to a four-year business administration curriculum. The school began offering MBA's In 1965, and has built a strong continuing education division, which caters to working professionals by offering evening and Saturday classes. The school now has three other campuses: in Southborough, Leominster, and Auburn, and uses the slogan, "Nichols is everywhere you are."

Other Nichols selling points are easy access and its safe 210-acre-campus. Despite Dudley's proximity to I-395, which helped open up the area, and Rtes. 12, 31, 131, and 197, Dudley remains rural. As late as 1989, it still had more chickens than people. Although it now has its own zip code, it still shares its Main Street and phone prefix with Webster, which is larger and more developed. Dudley residents have lots of commuting options — the town borders Connecticut, and is just 22 miles from Worcester, 59 from Boston and 40 miles from Springfield.

Dudley's mills on the French and Quinebaug Rivers weren't as famous as those further south in Connecticut, but one textile firm, Stevens Linen, has manufactured continuously in Dudley since its founding in 1846. Housed in a 135-year old stone factory building, the firm recently sold its upholstery fabric division, and is best known for its decorative dish towels and linen "calendars."

Sources: Commonwealth of Mass. EOCD Community Profile; Worcester Business Journal, The Boston Globe, The Getaway Guide; Nichols College pamphlet; A Guide to the Heritage of Worcester County, Blake, Montachusett Girl Scout Council; Massachusetts, off the Beaten Path, A Guide to Unique Places, Patricia Mandell.

Year incorporated: 1732

Population: 9,151 (1994, town)
Density: 453 per square mile
Total area: 22.06 sq. miles
Elevation: 650'
Distance from:
Boston: 59
Worcester: 22
Providence: 50
Hartford: 50
Springfield 40
Highways: Rtes. 31, 131, and 197.
Rail: The Providence & Worcester Railroad provides freight rail service to Dudley.
Airport: Southbridge Municipal Airport, a General Aviation facility.
Tax Rate: $9.28 per thousand (1994,town)
Median House Price: $114,500 (1993, County Data Corporation)
Median Household Income: $ 34,139 (1990 Census)
% of state average: 92.1%
Per Capita Income: $13,708
% of state average 79.6%
Form of Government:Board of Selectmen, open town meeting
Municipal Offices: (508) 949-8000
Services: Mass. Electric, Boston Gas Co., no municipal town sewer, ground water.
Nearest Hospital: Hubbard Regional, Webster
Registered Voters: 4,753
Legislative Districts:
U.S. Congress: 2nd District: Richard E. Neal (D)
State Senate: Worcester & Norfolk District: Louis P. Bertonazzi (D)
State Representatives:
6th Worcester:
David M. Peters (R)
7th Worcester: Paul Kollios (D)
8th Worcester: Paul Kujawski (D)
Public Schools
Dudley Charlton: Dudley Elem (02-04); Mason Rd School (K-01); Charlton Elem (K-02); Heritage School (03-06); Dudley Intermediate (05-06); Shepherd Hill Reg High (07-12)
Southern Worcester County:
Bay Path Reg Voc Tech H S (09-12)
School Choice: No
Colleges and Universities: Nichols College, successor to an 1800's era "Nichols Academy"
Per Pupil Cost:
(State Exec. Office of Education -1992-93): $3,611
State average 1992-93 $5,023
Average Teacher Salary:
(State Exec. Office of Education) 1992-3
Dudley:$36,878, statewide, $38,774
Mean SAT scores 1993

(reported by town)		State Mean
Math	459	
Verbal	420	
Combined	879	903

Student Population (Dept. of Education)

Total students 1991-92:	1,613
at public schools	91.2%
at private schools	8.8%

Educational Attainment (1990 census)

High School graduate or higher	76.0%
Bachelor's Degree or higher	16.5%

Largest Employers: (supplied by community, 1993)

	# of employees
Gentex Corporation	223
Ardluck/Stevens	130
Stevens/Guildford of Maine	106
Shield Packaging	80
Park N Shop	80

Commuting to Work (1990 Census)
Average time to work (mins.): 23.5
Houses of Worship: First Congregational Dudley Hill; St. Anthony of Padua, Catholic; St. Andrew Bobola, Catholic; St. Columba's Anglican, Episcopal.
Crime Rate: (1993, Mass. State Police Crime Reporting Unit) - adjusted for 12 months

	town	statewide
Total crimes reported:	292	
rate per 1,000 persons	30.61	37.46
Violent crimes	68	
rate per 1,000 persons	7.13	5.65
Property Crimes	224	
rate per 1,000 persons	23.48	31.83

Libraries:
Crawford Memorial Library
State Register of Historic Places 1993:
Black Tavern- a visible remnant of Dudley Hill, a village center of the original agricultural community preceding the industrial revolution.
Dudley Grange - Building on "the hill," a converted early school-town building.

East Brookfield

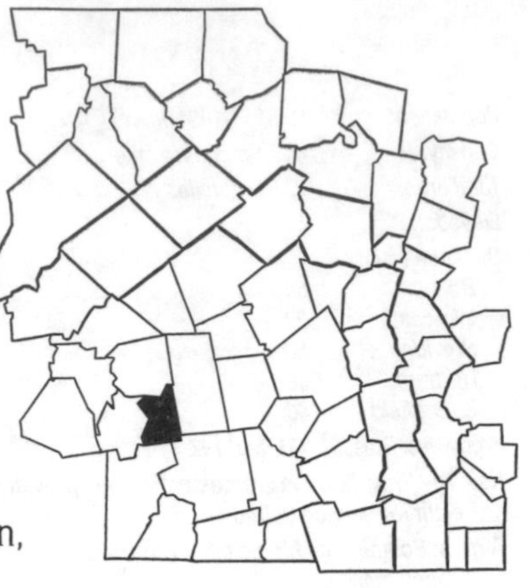

Podunk, U.S.A.

The rest of the country may think "Podunk" is a "place of utter insignificance," but everyone in East Brookfield knows it's right off Rte. 9 on the way to Quaboag Pond, which really is Podunk Pond. In East Brookfield, in fact, there's also an historic Podunk Lower School and a Podunk Mansion, (*appropriately located on* Podunk Road).

According to *Indian Place Names of New England*, "Podunk" means "a boggy place," or "at the place where the foot sinks in." It's hard to trace how the term spread, but you'll find it in the Randam House dictionary, as "any small and insignificant town."

East Brookfield is hardly insignificant in the annals of baseball, since Cornelius Alexander McGillicuddy was born here in 1862. Better known as "Connie Mack," he was a professional baseball manager for 53 years, a major-league record. He was player/manager for the Pittsburgh Pirates for three years (1894-96), and later served 50 years as manager (and later owner) of the Philadelphia Athletics, from 1901-50. His teams won nine pennants, and five Words Series match-ups. Today, there are Connie Mack youth baseball leagues across the country.

Part of the original Quaboag Plantation along with Warren and the other "Brookfields," East Brookfield became its own town in 1920. It is officially the youngest town in the Commonwealth, even though it is located on the historic Old Bay Path and parts of it were settled in the 1600's.

Today, plans are underway for a 60-acre, $11 million auto distribution center on Rte. 49, "The Podunk Pike," near the Spencer/East Brookfield line. The facility is expected to process 200,000 cars per year, and will unload, clean, repair and accessorize American-made cars before shipping them on truck carriers to dealers all over New England.

Sources: Commonwealth of Mass. EOCD Academic Profile; The Worcester Telegram & Gazette; The Smithsonian; Indian Place Names of New England; Academic American Encyclopedia.

Year incorporated: 1920- officially the youngest town in the Commonwealth

Population: 2,033 (1990 census)

Density. 207 per square mile

Total area: 10.37 sq. miles

Elevation: 620'

Distance from:
- Boston: 54
- Worcester: 14
- Springfield 36

Highways: Rtes. 9, 148, and 149.

Rail:Conrail provides freight service through East Brookfield.

Airport: The Worcester Airport

Tax Rate: $ 8.23 per thousand (1994, Mass. Div. of Local Services)

Median House Price: $ 104,900 (1993, County Data Corporation)

Median Household Income: $ 38,226 (1990 Census)
- % of state average: 103.4%
- Per Capita Income: $14,988
- % of state average 87.0%

Form of Government: Board of Selectmen, open town meeting

Municipal Offices: (508) 867-6769

Services: Mass. Electric, Boston Gas Co., no municipal sewer, ground water.

Nearest Hospital: several in Worcester; Mary Lane Hospital, Ware; Harrington Memorial Hosp., Southbridge.

Registered Voters 1,210

Legislative Districts:

U.S. Congress: 2nd District: Richard E. Neal (D)

State Senate: Worcester-Franklin-Hampden & Hampshire District: Robert D. Wetmore (D)

State Representative: 1st Hampden District: Patrick Landers (D)

Public Schools

Spencer East Brookfield: Grove Street (K-03); Lake Street (K-04); Memorial (K-05); Pleasant St. (K-03); Maple St. (05-06); West Main Street (K-03); David Prouty Jr High (07-08); Lashway J H (06-08) David Prouty High (09-12)

Superintendent: John Begley (508) 885-8507

School Choice: No

Per Pupil Cost:
(State Exec. Office of Education -1992-93):
- State average $5,023
- E. Brookfield: $4,217

Average Teacher Salary: (State Exec. Office of Education)

E. Brookfield	statewide 1992-93
$33,224	$38,774

Mean SAT scores 1993

	(reported by town)	State Mean
Math	461	
Verbal	417	
Combined:	878	903

Student Population (Dept. of Education)

Total students 1991-92: 399
- at public schools 99.2%
- at private schools .8%

Educational Attainment (1990 census)
- High School graduate or higher 78.6%
- Bachelor's Degree or higher 12.5%

Largest Employers: (supplied by community, 1993)

	# of employees
Howe Lumber	20
Lamoureux Ford	20
Petruzzi-Forrestor Construction	15
Hyde Shoe	10
New-Tech	10

Commuting to Work (1990 Census)

Average time to work (mins.): 25.4

Houses of Worship: 1 Baptist; 1 Catholic

Crime Rate: not available

Libraries

East Brookfield Public Library

Fitchburg

Paper City Recycles

Fitchburg has come a long way since the days when the Nashua River turned a different color every day based on what dyes the city's paper mills were using. Today, the river is clean and has the Nashua River Watershed Association to protect it. Fitchburg now has two water treatment plants, and no longer pollutes the river. And one of its largest paper mills has turned from a paper producer to a paper recycler - turning office waste into pulp suitable for printing and writing-grade paper.

Fitchburg's role as a paper manufacturer dates back to 1807, and the city was also a leading producer of wool, gingham, yarn, chairs, machine tools, saws, scythes, guns and bicycles. At times over the years, Fitchburg has made all the paper for The New York Herald, The Saturday Evening Post and The Ladies Home Journal. And paper patterns for Ebenezer Butterick's company (*see Sterling*) were also made here.

Plentiful jobs in the mills attracted immigrants from Boston via the Fitchburg Railroad. At the turn of the century, nearly 100 daily passenger trains - one every nine minutes.- brought Finns, French-Canadians, English, Irish, Italians, Swedes, Norwegians, Germans and Greeks to work in Fitchburg's mills.

The latest ethnic group to seek factory jobs in Fitchburg is from the mountains of Laos, Vietnam and Burma. The Hmong were agricultural people who were recruited by the CIA during the Vietnam war and fought for the U.S. Fitchburg is believed to have the largest Hmong population in the state, and has started a Hmong bilingual program in its schools.

Fitchburg has kept its railroad link to Boston, now used by commuters to North Station and points in between. The city, just 10 miles from New Hampshire and 25 minutes to Worcester, is the county's second largest, and offers a host of cultural and educational opportunities at Fitchburg State College, the Fitchburg Art Museum, Fitchburg Historical Society, Stratton Playhouse and the Wallace Civic Center and Planetarium. The golf course at Oak Hill Country Club is said to be among the country's best, and the famed Longsjo Bicycle Race is the country's second oldest, and is named after Olympic speed skater and bicyclist Arthur Longsjo.

The city's legendary rivalry with its "twin city," Leominster is best evidenced at the annual Thanksgiving Day high school football game. "The Game" is over

100 years old, and married couples have been known to sit on opposite sides if one is from Leominster and the other from Fitchburg.

Sources: Commonwealth of Mass. EOCD Community Profile; The Boston Globe; The Worcester Telegram & Gazette; Bike Routes of Northern Worcester County; The Guide to North Central Worcester County; Massachusetts Towns, An 1840 View, Ivan Sandrof, Barre Publishers, 1963; A Guide to the Heritage of Worcester County, Simone E. Blake, Montachusett Girl Scout Council, 1973.

Year incorporated: 1764 (town) ; 1872 (city)
Population: 41,194 (1990 census)
Density: 1,484 per square mile
Total area: 28.06 sq. miles
Elevation: 458'
Distance from:
Boston: 46
Worcester: 25
Highways: Rte. 2, Rte. 12, Rte. 31
Rail: Commuter rail service is available to North Station, Boston. Conrail and the Springfield Terminal Railway offer freight service to Fitchburg.
Bus: The Montachusett Regional Transit Authority provides fixed route service within Fitchburg and to Leominster, Gardner and Fort Devens. The Montachusett Regional Transit Authority also offers paratransit services to the elderly and disabled.
Airport: The Fitchburg Municipal Airport is a General Aviation facility.
Tax Rate: $12.76 per thousand (1994, Mass. Div. of Local Services)
Median House Price: $87,000 (1993, County Data Corporation)
Median Household Income: $27,101 (1990 Census)
% of state average: 73.3%
Per Capita Income: $12,140
% of state average 70.5%
Form of Government: Mayor-Council
Municipal Offices: (508) 345-9550
Services: Fitchburg Gas & Electric Light Co., town sewer, surface water.
Nearest Hospital: Burbank Hospital, Inc.
Registered Voters: 18,102
Legislative Districts:
U.S. Congress: 1st District: John W. Olver (D)
State Senate: 2nd Worcester-Middlesex District: Robert Antonioni (D)
State Representative: 4th Worcester:Mary Jane Simmons (D)
State Representative: 3rd Worcester : Emile J. Goguen (D)
Public Schools
Fitchburg: Crocker Elem (K-05); Goodrich Kdg Ctr (-K); Reingold (K-05); South Fitchburg (K-03); South Street (01-05); B F Brown Junior High (06-08); Memorial Middle (06-08); Mckay Campus-FSC (K-05); Fitchburg High (09-12)
Montachusett:
Montachusett Voc Tech (09-12)
Superintendent: Phillip Fallon (508) 345-3200
School Choice: Yes

Colleges and Universities: Fitchburg State College and Fisher Junior College
Per Pupil Cost:
(State Exec. Office of Education -1992-93):
State average : $5,023
Fitchburg: $4,238
Average Teacher Salary:
(State Exec. Office of Education 1992-93)

Fitchburg:	statewide 1992-93
$34,029	$38,774

Mean SAT scores 1993

	(reported by town)	State Mean:
Math	411	
Verbal	392	
Combined	803	903

Student Population (Dept. of Education)
Total students 1991-92: 6,278
at public schools 84.7%
at private schools 15.3%
Educational Attainment (1990 census)
High School graduate or higher 70.7%
Bachelor's Degree or higher 11.5%
Largest Employers: (supplied by community, 1993)

	# of employees
General Electric Company	850
Burbank hospital	775
Fitchburg State College	502
Simonds Industries	400
ChemDesign Corp.	265
Asher Winer Company	200

Commuting to Work (1990 Census)
Average time to work (mins.) 19.8
Houses of Worship: more than 30, representing 18 denominations; the majority are members of the Montachusett Council of Churches.
Crime Rate:
(1993, Mass. State Police Crime Reporting Unit)

	town	statewide
Total crimes reported:	2570	
rate per 1,000 persons	62.39	37.46
Violent crimes	628	
rate per 1,000 persons	15.24	5.65
Property Crimes	1942	
rate per 1,000 persons	47.14	31.83

Libraries:
Fitchburg Public Library
Museums:
Fitchburg Art Museum
Fitchburg Historical Society
State Register of Historic Places 1993:
Calvanistic Congregational Church
Civil War Monument
Duck Mill
Fay Club
Fitchburg Armory

Gardner

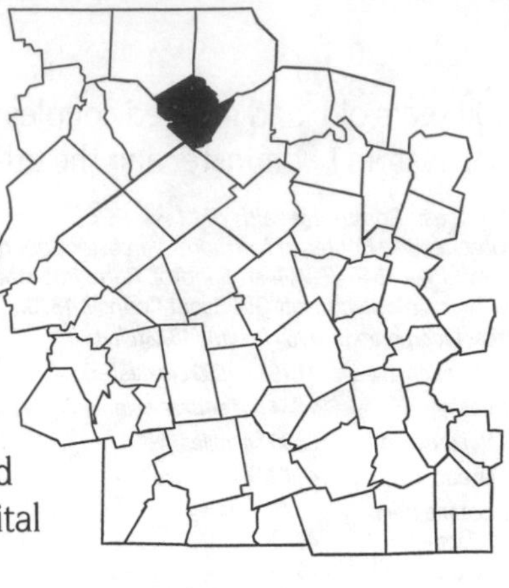

Chair City Heritage

Gardner's furniture industry began in 1805 when James Comee started making chairs out of his home. In 1826, the five Heywood brothers began their empire. The Heywood-Wakefield company closed its household furniture operation in 1979, but the Heywood name is still associated with Gardner's hospital and library.

The furniture factories attracted waves of immigrants. The Levi Heywood factory employed its first Irish workers in the 1830s; more fled the potato famine a decade later. Next came French Canadians from Quebec in the 1850s; Acadians from New Brunswick arrived in the 1890s. Swedes, Finns, Jews and Poles all left various miseries at home and followed the furniture jobs to Gardner.

In its heyday in the 1920s, Gardner was home to some 39 furniture companies, turning out 4 million chairs a year, earning it the nickname "Chair City." The world's largest chair stands on Elm Street in tribute to the city's chair making past, and the front entrance to the Gardner Museum is chair-shaped. Although the furniture industry has largely moved south, and the city has developed a more broad and diversified manufacturing and industrial base, Gardner's remaining factory outlets still draw bargain-hunters from as far away as Boston, 59 miles east via Route 2. Visitors to Gardner's Heritage State Park can see historical furniture exhibits and get a map of the city's furniture outlets.

Furniture manufacturing helped shape the identity of the Greater Gardner area. The city's architectural legacy is diverse and includes Colonial farmhouses, Greek Revival, Victorian and Romanesque styles, a legacy from more than 150 years of thriving furniture manufacturing. The card punch time clock was first used in Gardner's factories. Today, Simplex Time Recorder Co., the city's largest employer, is a world leader in the manufacture of time clock equipment.

Sources: Commonwealth of Mass. EOCD Community Profile; The Boston Globe; A Guide to Nashaway, North Central Mass., Darby, McCrosky, Chandler.

Year incorporated: 1785 as a town; 1923 as a city
Total area: 23 square miles
Population: 20,125 (1990 census)
Density: 907 per square mile
Elevation: 1190'
Distance from:
Boston: 59 miles
Worcester: 28 miles
Highways: Routes 2; 2-A, 68;140,101
Rail: Commuter rail service is available to North Station Boston from neighboring Fitchburg (travel time 85-94 mins., no parking) via connecting Wilson and MART buses. For information call 1-800-392-6100.
Bus: The Montachusett Regional Transit Authority (MART) has two routes from Gardner to the Fitchburg/Leominster area. For information, call (508) 632-7373. Vermont Transit Lines provides service from Gardner to New Hampshire, Vermont, and to Boston via Fitchburg, Ft. Devens, Concord and Newton. Call (508) 537-6669.
Airport: The Gardner Municipal Airport, a General Aviation (GA) facility located 2 miles SW of the city, has a 3,000' x 75' asphalt runway. Instrument approaches available: Non-precision. (508) 632-9794.
Tax Rate: $ 14.59 per thousand (1994, The Central Mass. Fact Book)
Median House Price: $88,000 (1993, County Data Corporation)
Median Household Income: $28,035 (1990 Census)
% of state average: 75.9%
Per Capita Income: $13,207
% of state average 76.7%
Form of Government: Mayor-Council
Municipal Offices: (508) 632-1900
Services: Mass. Electric, municipal water, Fitchburg Gas & Electric Light Co., sewer
Nearest Hospital: Heywood Hospital
Registered Voters (Secretary of State 1992): 9,763
Legislative Districts:
U.S. Congress: 1st District - John W. Olver (D)
State Senate: 2nd Worcester-Middlesex District - Robert A. Antonioni (D)
State Representative: 2nd Worcester: Robert D. Hawke (R)
Superintendent: Michael Pregot, (508) 632-1000
School Choice: Yes (9-12)
Public Schools

Elm St. School	1-6
Prospect	1-3
Helen Mae Sauter	1-3
Waterford St.	1-3
Gardner Jr. High	7-8
Gardner High	K, 9-12
Montachusett:	
Montachusett Voc-tech	9-12

Colleges and Universities:
Mount Wachusett Community College
Per Pupil Cost:
(State Exec. Office of Education -1992-93)
Gardner $3,618
State average $5,023
Average Teacher Salary:
(State Exec. Office of Education 1992-93)

Gardner	statewide
$31,893	$38,774

Mean SAT scores 1993

	(reported by town)	State Mean
Math	481	
Verbal	438	
Combined	919	903

Student Population (Dept. of Education)
Total students 1991-92: 2,576
Educational Attainment (1990 census)
High School graduate or higher 68.6%
Bachelor's Degree or higher 13.6%
Largest Employers: (supplied by community, 1993)

	# of employees
Simplex Time Recorder Co.	1,300
Mt. Wachusett Community College	650
Heywood Memorial Hospital	590
North Central Corrections Institution	400
H and R 1871, Inc.	240

Commuting to Work (1990 Census)
Average time to work (mins.) 19.9
Houses of Worship: all denominations
Crime Rate:
(1993, Mass. State Police Crime Reporting Unit)

	town	statewide
Total crimes reported:	726	
rate per 1,000 persons	36.07	37.46
Violent crimes	167	
rate per 1,000 persons	8.30	5.65
Property crimes	559	
rate per 1,000 persons	27.78	31.83

Libraries:
Levi Heywood Memorial Library, 57 City Hall Ave. (508) 632-5298
Museums
The Gardner Museum, 28 Pearl St., Route 101, (508) 632-3277
Gardner Heritage State Park Visitor's Center, 26 Lake Street. (508) 632-2099
State Register of Historic Places 1993:
Elm St. Fire Station, 58 Elm St.
First Minister's House, 186 Elm St.
Garbose Building, 3 Pleasant St.
Gardner News Building, 309 Central St.
Heywood-Wakefield Company Complex, 206 Central St.
Levi Heywood Memorial Library, 28 Pearl St.
Lake St. Fire Station, 2 Lake St.
Jabez Partridge House, 81 Partridge St.
F.W. Silversmith, 60 Chestnut St.

Grafton

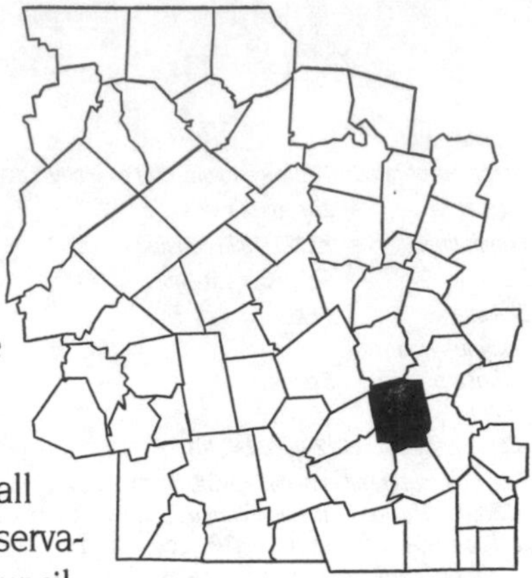

Native Land And Museum-Quality Clocks

Tucked away in Grafton is a 4 1/2 acre patch of land that has never been sold. The Hassanamisco Indian Reservation on Brigham Hill Road has always remained in native hands. Its name means "place of small stones," and it is the oldest and smallest reservation in the state. Owned by the Nipmuc Council of the Hassanamisco band, the area is opened to the public in the summer for tribal meetings.

Among Grafton's first Colonial settlers were the legendary clock-making Willard brothers, Simon, Benjamin, Ephraim and Aaron. Their house and shop at 11 Willard St. was built in 1718, and is not only the oldest House in Grafton, but the country's only 18th century American clock shop still on its original site. Today, it is the Willard House and Clock Museum, featuring 60 clocks - the largest Willard collection in New England. The brothers were known for their "tall case," or grandfather's clocks, and for their clocks with scenes painted on the faces. Simon invented what is often called the "banjo" clock for its distinctive shape. One of the museum's showpieces is a musical case clock by Simon that plays one of seven tunes every hour.

View a copy of the vintage 1935 film *Ah, Wilderness*, and you'll see what Grafton's famous town Common looked like in 1935. The Hollywood movie company built a bandstand on the green, and hired 200 townspeople as extras for the scene. So typically "New England" is the common that it has also been featured in car rental commercials. Surrounded by three churches and numerous historic buildings, it has lots of shade trees, a rarity in Grafton in the 1800's, when the forests were cut for firewood and cleared for pastures.

Part of the Blackstone River Valley, South Grafton had several mill villages along the river - Fisherville, Farnumsville and Saundersville. Today, the major industry is the huge North Grafton facility of Wyman Gordon, a manufacturer of forged metal components for the aerospace industry. Tufts University School of Veterinary Medicine is also in North Grafton, and is working on plans for a biotechnology park and an MBTA commuter rail station on the Worcester-Boston route. The planned Rte. 146 connector to the Mass. Pike in nearby Millbury should also be a boon to Grafton, which is just six miles from Worcester, 30 miles from Boston, and less than an hour from Providence.

Sources: Commonwealth of Mass. EOCD Community Profile; The Boston Globe; Worcester Magazine; A Guide to the Heritage of Worcester County, Simone E. Blake, Montachusett Girl Scout Council, 1973; Massachusetts, off the Beaten Path, A Guide to Unique Places, Patricia Mandell, The Globe Pequot Press, 1992; Historical Markers of the Massachusetts Bay Colony, Samuel Eliot Morison, The Commonwealth of Massachusetts, 1930; Massachusetts Towns, An 1840 View, Ivan Sandrof, Barre Publishers, 1963.

Year incorporated: 1735
Population: 13,035 (1990 census)
Density: 573 per square mile
Total area: 23,27 sq. miles
Elevation: 632'
Distance from:
Boston: 30
Worcester: 6
Providence: 40

Highways: I-90, Rtes. 140, 122, 122-A.

Rail: Amtrak passenger rail service is available from neighboring Worcester. Conrail and the Grafton and Upton Railroad provide freight rail service to North Grafton. The Providence and Worcester Railroad serves Grafton and Upton.

Bus: The Worcester Regional Transit Authority which provides fixed route service between Grafton, Millbury, and Worcester and offers para-transit services for the elderly and disabled.

Airport: The Worcester Municipal Airport, a primary commercial facility.

Tax Rate: $13.46 per thousand (1994, Mass. Div. of Local Services)

Median House Price: $129,500 (1993, County Data Corporation)

Median Household Income: $42,310 (1990 Census)
% of state average: 114.5%
Per Capita Income: $17,313
% of state average 100.5%

Form of Government: Board of Selectmen, Town Administrator, open town meeting

Municipal Offices: (508) 839-4722

Services: Mass. Electric Co., Commonwealth Gas Co. and town sewer, ground water, also Grafton and S. Grafton Water Districts.

Nearest Hospital: several in Worcester

Registered Voters: 8,209

Legislative Districts:

U.S. Congress: 3rd District: Peter I. Blute (R)

State Senate: 2nd Worcester: Matthew J. Amorello (R)

State Representative: 9th Worcester: George N. Peterson, Jr. (R)

Public Schools

Grafton: South Grafton Elem (K-04); North Grafton Elem (K-04); Grafton Middle (05-08); Grafton Memorial Senior (09-12)

Blackstone Valley:
Blackstone Valley Voc Tech (09-12)

Superintendent: Dr. Gail K. Rowe (508) 839-5421

School Choice: No

Per Pupil Cost: (State Exec. Office of Education - 1992-93):
Grafton: $4,058
State average $5,023

Average Teacher Salary: (State Exec. Office of Education 1992-93)

Grafton	statewide
$37,188	$38,774

Mean SAT scores 1993

	(reported by town)	State Mean
Math	504	
Verbal	461	
Combined	965	903

Student Population (Dept. of Education)
Total students 1991-92: 2,088
at public schools 94.8%
at private schools 5.2%

Educational Attainment (1990 census)
High School graduate or higher 81.5%
Bachelor's Degree or higher 22.5%

Largest Employers: (supplied by community, 1993)

	# of employees
Wyman Gordan	880
Tufts U. School of Veterinary Medicine	350
Town of Grafton	295
Tredegar Industries	175
Washington Mills Abrasive	112

Commuting to Work (1990 Census)
Average time to work (mins.): 23.1

Houses of Worship: 4 Catholic, 1 Evangelical Congregational, 1 Unitarian Universalist, 1 Baptist, 1 Methodist, 1 Congregational

Crime Rate:
(1993, Mass. State Police Crime Reporting Unit)

	town	statewide
Total crimes reported:	152	
rate per 1,000 persons	11.66	37.46
Violent crimes	50	
rate per 1,000 persons	3.84	5.65
Property crimes	102	
rate per 1,000 persons	7.83	31.83

Libraries
Grafton Public Library, Nelson Library, South Grafton Public Library

Museums
Willard House and Clock Museum

State Register of Historic Places 1993:
Grafton Common Historic District
Grafton Inn
Willard House and Clock Museum

Hardwick

From Wombemesscook to Lambstown

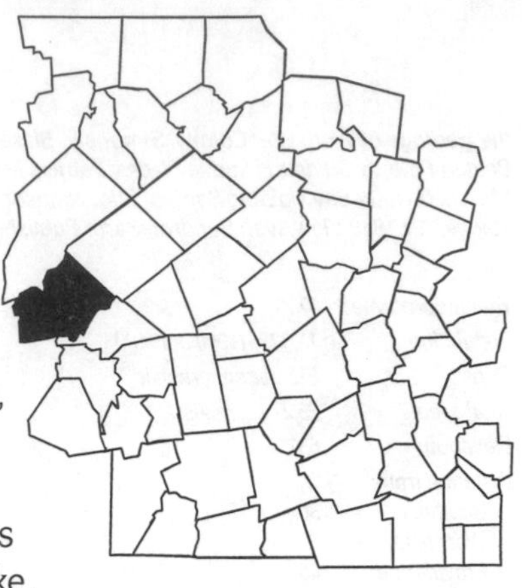

The native Nipmucs called Hardwick, "Wombemesscook," and the early settlers called it "Lambstown," not for grazing herds, but for Joshua Lamb of Roxbury, one of eight men who bought the area for twenty pounds in 1687. Incorporated in 1739, it was named for English nobleman Lord Hardwicke.

Located on the Old Turnpike #6 from Amherst to Worcester, Hardwick, by the time of the Revolution, had become a thriving farming community. At one time, Hardwick's farmers were the richest people in town. One of the largest herds of Guernsey cattle in the world was owned by the Mixters, an early Hardwick family. Four distinct villages grew up: Hardwick Center, Old Furnace, Wheelwright, and Gilbertville. Old Furnace smelted iron and made cannonballs for the Revolutionary War. Wheelwright had a paper mill, and Gilbertville had a large textile mill complex.

The Depression closed the textile mills and the paper mill; Hardwick's population of 2,385 in 1990 is almost the same as it was in 1890. Six working dairy farms remain. Hardwick lost 30,000 acres to the Quabbin Reservoir. It now has about 5 miles of shore frontage on the Reservoir, and many of its most scenic vistas include the Quabbin's waters.

Recent growth in town has filled the elementary school, built in 1990, as commuters to Worcester and Springfield, both approximately 25 miles away, move here for the rural atmosphere and more affordable home prices. Hardwick town common is a classic village green surrounded by a quaint general store, post office, a town hall and two churches. Every August it's the site of the Hardwick Fair, reported to be oldest country fair in the United States. In 1994, Hardwick was pinpointed as the epicenter of an earthquake, felt as far away as southern NH and measuring 3.6 on the Richter scale.

Sources: Commonwealth of Mass. EOCD Community Profile; The Boston Globe; Worcester Magazine; A Guide to the Heritage of Worcester County, Simone E. Blake, Montachusett Girl Scout Council, 1973; Quabbin Reservoir, Walter E. Clark, Hobson Book Press, 1946; Reprinted by Athol Press, Inc., 1994, Myron Goddard, Hardwick Historical Society.

Year incorporated: 1739
Population: 2,385 (1990 census)
Density: 62 per square mile
Total area: 40.84 sq. miles
Elevation: 880'
Mileage from:
Boston: 69
Worcester: 22
Providence: 64
Hartford: 53
Springfield 28
Highways: Rtes. 32 and 32A.
Rail: The Massachusetts Central Railroad provides freight rail service in Hardwick.
Bus: The Montachusett Regional Transit Authority provides paratransit services for the elderly and disabled through the Council on Aging.
Airport: Metropolitan Airport, a general aviation facility located in neighboring Palmer.
Tax Rate: $13.60 per thousand (1994, Mass. Div. of Local Services)
Median House Price: $79,900 (1993, County Data Corporation)
Median Household Income: $30,139 (1990 Census)
% of state average: 81.6%
Per Capita Income: $13,387
% of state average 77.7%
Form of Government: Board of Selectmen, Administrative Assistant, open town meeting
Municipal Offices: (413) 477-6197
Services: Mass. Electric Co., no natural gas service, town sewer in some areas, ground water.
Nearest Hospital: Mary Lane Hospital, Ware, MA.
Registered Voters: 1,254
Legislative Districts:
U.S. Congress: 1st District: John W. Olver (D)
State Senate: Worcester, Franklin, Hampden and Hampshire: Robert E. Wetmore (D)
State Representative: 5th Worcester: Stephen M. Brewer (R)
Private Schools: Eagle Hill School
Public Schools
Quabbin:
Hardwick Elementary (K-06); Quabbin Regional Jr.-Sr. (07-12)
Superintendent: Maureen Marshall
School Choice: Yes

Per Pupil Cost:
(State Exec. Office of Education -1992-93):
Hardwick: $4,080
State average 1992-93: $5,023
Average Teacher Salary:
(State Exec. Office of Education-1992-93)

Hardwick	statewide
$31,577	$38,774

Mean SAT scores 1993

	(reported by town)	State Mean
Combined:	889	903

Student Population (Dept. of Education)
Total students 1991-92: 474
at public schools 98.7%
at private schools 1.3%
Educational Attainment (1990 census)
High School graduate or higher 76.3%
Bachelor's Degree or higher 16.6%
Largest Employers: (supplied by community, 1993)

	# of employees
Hardwick Kilns	75

Commuting to Work (1990 Census)
Average time to work (mins.): 27.6
Houses of Worship: St. Aloysius, Trinitarian Congregational, Calvinistic Congregational, The First Universalist, St. Augustine.
Crime Rate:
(1993, Mass. State Police Crime Reporting Unit)

	town	statewide
Total crimes reported:	25	
rate per 1,000 persons	10.48	37.46
Violent crimes	3	
rate per 1,000 persons	1.26	5.65
Property crimes	22	
rate per 1,000 persons	9.22	31.83

Libraries:
Gilbertville Public Library and Paige Memorial, Hardwick.
Museums: Hardwick Historical Society
State Register of Historic Places 1993:
Gilbertville Historic District
Hardwick Village Historic District
Ware - Hardwick Covered Bridge

Harvard

Shakers, Fruitlands and Superior Schools

"There was such a repose and quiet here...we could not but help contrasting the equanimity of Nature *with the bustle and impatience of man."* - Henry David Thoreau, 1842.

Thoreau's words still describe Harvard, a town determined to protect its rural acreage, rich architectural history, and to limit commercial development, despite its proximity to Route 2 and I-495. Harvard's school system is among the state's best, and is attended through school choice by students commuting from as far away as Worcester, 22 miles south. To the east, Boston's skyscrapers can be seen 32 miles in the distance, but when Bostonians think of Harvard, it's usually as a place to go apple-picking in the fall at one of the town's many orchards.

Incorporated in 1732, Harvard has always been home to free thinkers. The most famous group, the Shakers, came to Harvard in 1780 led by Mother Ann Lee, thought to be the "Daughter of God." They lived by the creed, "Hands to work and hearts to God," and practiced honesty, frugality, charity, temperance — and celibacy. Predictably, the sect's members diminished, and the village closed in 1918, but the historic Shaker Village buildings still exist.

One of these buildings was moved to the Fruitlands Museum in 1922, where it became the first Shaker Museum in the country. Fruitlands is actually four museums in one. The Bronson Alcott farmhouse, called Fruitlands, is where Louisa May Alcott's father and fellow believers briefly experimented with Utopian living, intending to live off the "fruit of the land." Visitors can see artifacts of the transcendental movement belonging to Alcott, Emerson and Thoreau, and "read passages" from 10-year-old Louisa's journal. Also at Fruitlands are the Indian Museum, housing Native American treasures, and the Picture Gallery, containing landscape paintings of the Hudson River school.

Thousands of acres in Harvard are protected conservation land, most notably the Oxbow National Wildlife Refuge, home to great blue herons and the endangered Blandings turtles. With the closing of Ft. Devens, 890 additional acres have been donated to the refuge, more than doubling its size. The view west from Prospect Hill is a fall "must-see," and includes a panorama of the Nashua River Valley, Mt. Wachusett and Mt. Monadnock in New Hampshire.

Sources: Commonwealth of Mass. EOCD Community Profile; The Telegram & Gazette; Worcester Magazine; The Boston Globe; A Guide to Nashaway; North Central Mass., Darby, McCrosky, Chandler.

Year incorporated: 1732
Population: 5,082
(Town census, does not include Ft. Devens);
1990 census: 4,662
Density: 468 per square mile
Total area: 26.36
Elevation: 421'
Distance from:
Boston: 32 miles
Worcester: 22 miles
Highways: Interstate 495; State Routes 2, 110, 111
Rail: Commuter rail service to North Statin, Boston is availabe from the neighboring towns of Ayer (travel time: 66-73 mins., no MBTA parking) Littleton (travel time 55-62 mins., 40 MBTA parking spaces) and in South Acton.
Airport: Minute Man Airport, a Reliever (RL) facility located in Stow, is easily accessible. It has a 1,600' x 50' gravel runway and a 2,743'x 50' asphalt runway. Instrument approaches available: Non-precision.
Tax Rate: $15.15 per thousand (1995, Town)
Median House Price: $240,100
(1995, Town, citing Banker & Tradesman)
Median Household Income: $80,028
(1990 Census adjusted by town, does not include Ft. Devens)
% of state average: 188%
Form of Government: Board of Selectman, Executive Secretary, open town meeting.
Municipal Offices: (508) 456-4100
Services: Mass. Electric, Boston Gas, Suburban Propane, United Cablevision no town sewerage, some town water, full time police, volunteer fire dept.
Nearest Hospital: Nashoba Valley Deaconess Hospital
Registered Voters: 3,290 (supplied by town)
Legislative Districts:
U.S. Congress: 5th District: Martin T. Meehan (D)
State Senate: Middlesex & Worcester District: Robert A. Durand (D)
State Representative: 2nd Middlesex District: Geoffrey Hall (D)
Public Schools

Harvard Elementary	K-6
Bromfield	7-12
Montachusett Voc-Tec	9-12

Superintendent: Lois Haslam (508) 456-4140
School Choice: Yes (K-12)
Per Pupil Cost:
(State Exec. Office of Education -1992-93)
Harvard $5,545
State average 1992-93 $5,023
Average Teacher Salary:
(State Exec. Office of Education 1992-93)

salary 1992-3	statewide 1992-93
$46,310	$38,774

Mean SAT scores 1993

	(reported by town)	StateMean
Math	537	
Verbal	505	903
Combined	1042	

Student Population (Dept. of Education)

Total students (supplied by town)	1994-95
Harvard (includes school choice)	1,047
Montachusett Voc Tec	1,060

Educational Attainment (1990 census)

High School graduate or higher	96.9%
Bachelor's Degree or higher	31.5%

Largest Employers: (supplied by community, 1993)

	# of employees
Carlson Orchards	50
Modtap Systems	25
Manchester Corporation	15

Commuting to Work (1990 Census)
Average time to work (mins.) 27
Houses of Worship: 2 Catholic, 1 Congregational, 1 Unitarian, 1 Episcopal
Crime Rate:
(1993, Mass. State Police Crime Reporting Unit)

	town	statewide
Total crimes reported:	16	
rate per 1,000 persons	3.43	37.46
Violent crimes	1	
rate per 1,000 persons	.21	5.65
Property crimes	15	
rate per 1,000 persons	3.22	31.83

Libraries:
Harvard Public Library, Harvard Common, Box 666
(508) 456-4114
Museums:
Fruitlands Museums, 102 Prospect Hill Road
(508) 456-3924
Harvard Historical Society, Still River Road, Still River, (5080 456-8285
State Register of Historic Places 1993:
Ft. Devens Historic District (Harvard/Ayer)
Fruitlands Farmhouse Museum, Prospect Hill Rd.
Harvard Common Historic District
Harvard Shaker Village Historic District, Shaker Rd.

Holden

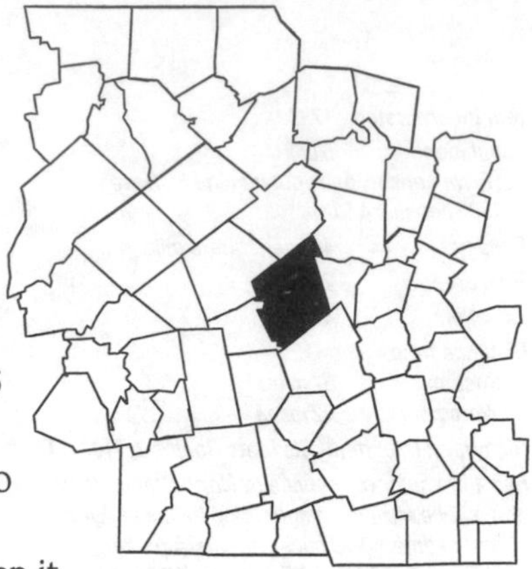

The Day it Rained Frogs

Normally a quiet bedroom community next door to Worcester, Holden was turned upside down, literally, when a tornado barreled through town with wind speeds of 325 miles per hour, the highest ever recorded. The "Tornado of 1953" had already killed two people in Barre and two in Rutland when it slammed into Holden, killing 11 more. When it was over, 94 people were dead, 15,000 people were homeless, and damage topped $53 million along a 42-mile swath from Petersham to Southborough.

Homes in Holden's new Brentwood housing development were completely destroyed. As the funnel headed out of town, it sucked up everything in Chaffins Pond. Later, a boy in Worcester said, "Look Ma, it's raining frogs." Area residents reported cows spinning in mid-air and the paint scoured off automobiles. Chickens plucked from their coops in Rutland were found among the debris in Holden.

For most of its 200 years before the tornado, Holden was known for its many mills, and it had an extraordinary number for a small town. At the peak of its textile manufacturing, Holden had over 20 mills and 12 distinct mill villages, among them Jeffersonville, Dawsonville, and Eagleville on Rte. 122-A, whose mill and millpond still exist. Demand for flannel and twill fabrics made at Dawsonville was so high, the mill ran shifts night and day. Many of the other mill villages were razed to protect watersheds, and land for Worcester's Kendall Reservoir was taken by eminent domain.

Historic buildings in Holden's center include the Congregational Church built in 1789, the Davis House Starbard building, circa 1797, and the Town Hall and First Baptist Church, circa 1835. The 1888 Damon Memorial once housed the high school, and is now the Gale Free Library, which has one of the area's finest children's rooms. When a library addition was built, even the Damon's stone "out house" was saved and is now used as a storage shed.

Sources: A Pictorial History of Holden, Massachusetts, Charles T. Skillings, Clare M. Nelson and Ross W. Beales, Jr., Holden Historical Society, Inc., 1991; History of theTown of Holden Massachusetts, 1667-1941, Florence Newell Prouty, Stobbs Press, 1941; "Experience Holden," The Landmark, June 23, 1994; Commonwealth of Mass. EOCD Community Profile.

Year incorporated: 1741
Population: 14,628 (1990 census)
Density: 418 per square mile
Total area: 36.22 sq. miles
Elevation: 818'
Distance from:
Boston: 46
Worcester: 7
Springfield 55
Transportation:
Highways: Rtes. 31, 122A.
Rail: Passenger rail service to Boston, Springfield, Providence, and all other points on Amtrak is available through neighboring Worcester, the Providence & Worcester Railroad provides freight rail service to Holden.
Bus: The Worcester Regional Transit Authority provides fixed route service between Holden and Worcester and Paratransit services for the elderly.
Airport: The Worcester Municipal Airport
Tax Rate: $15.92 per thousand (1995, Town Assessors))
Median House Price: $130,000 (1993, County Data Corporation)
Median Household Income: $49,143 (1990 Census)
% of state average: 133.0%
Per Capita Income: $20,974
% of state average 121.8%
Form of Government: Board of Selectmen, Town Manager, Open Town Meeting
Municipal Offices: (508) 829-0225
Services: Holden Municipal Light Dept., Commonwealth Gas Co., some town sewer provided, ground surface water.
Nearest Hospital: Several in Worcester
Registered Voters: 9,449
Legislative Districts:
U.S. Congress: 3rd Congressional District: Peter Blute (R)
State Representative: 1st Worcester; Rep. Hal Lane (D)
State Senate: 1st Worcester: Robert A. Bernstein (D)
Public Schools
Wachusett Regional School District (K-12)
Holden:
Chaffins Elem (K-05); Dawson Elem (K-05); Jefferson Elem (K-05); Rice Elem (K-05); Mountview Jr H (06-08)
Wachusett:
Wachusett Regional High

Superintendent: Alfred Tutela (508) 829-6631
School Choice: No
Per Pupil Cost:
(State Exec. Office of Education -1992-93)
Primary $3,983
Secondary $6,374
State average $5,023
Average Teacher Salary:
(State Exec. Office of Education-1992-93)

	Holden	statewide
Primary	$38,362	$38,774
Secondary	$40,951	

Mean SAT scores 1993 : 40,951

	(reported by town)	State Mean:
Math	488	
Verbal	434	
Combined	922	903

Student Population (Dept. of Education)
Total students 1991-92: 2,740
at public schools 93.0%
at private schools 7.0%
Educational Attainment (1990 census)
High School graduate or higher 91.1%
Bachelor's Degree or higher 36.7%
Largest Employers: (supplied by community, 1993)

	# of employees
Reed Rico	300
Astrofoam	165
ECC Corporation	145
Reed Spectrum	110
Inner-Tite Corporation	70

Commuting to Work (1990 Census)
Average time to work (mins.): 21.2
Houses of Worship: 2 Congregational; 2 Baptist; 1 Evangelistic; 1 Lutheran, 1 Episcopal, 1 Catholic, 1 Christ Centered, Nondenominational.
Crime Rate: not available
Libraries
Gale Free Library
State Register of Historic Places 1993:
Boyden Road Historic District
Holden Center Historic District
Rogers House

Hopedale

Why the Mills Left New England

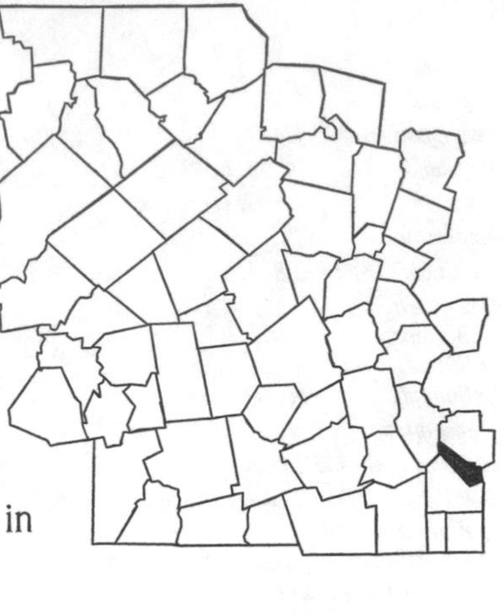

The end of New England's textile supremacy began in Hopedale. In 1842 two mechanically talented brothers, Charles and Ebenezer Draper, were trying to make a go of "practical Christianity" in the Utopian Hopedale Community started by Universalist Adin Ballou (*see Oxford*). The commune failed in 1856, and the Drapers went on to change to course of history.

From their "Little Red Shop," which still exists, the Drapers made not textiles, but textile machinery. They soon held 400 patents and with their Northrop Automated Loom in 1892, the Drapers became the largest textile machinery producers in the world. The Northrop automatic bobbin changer, an engineering marvel, automated a series of very intricate tasks previously performed by hand. By WWI, most of the country's 400,000 mechanized looms were made by Draper, and the company was shipping overseas as well.

Ironically, the Draper loom doomed New England's mills. Using less power and run by untrained workers, they erased a key New England "edge" — its skilled labor force. Steam engines made water power unnecessary, but many New England mill owners were reluctant to automate. The textile industry moved south in search of cheaper, unskilled labor and to escape New England's restrictive child labor laws.

In Hopedale, the Drapers planned a model community. Believing that "good houses make good workers," they erected quality duplex homes and company parks. They built roads, sidewalks, sewers, gas lines, and donated a high school, playground and a bandstand to the town. The Draper baseball team played in the competitive Blackstone Valley Industrial League. Former Boston Red Sox Manager Joe Morgan played shortstop for the Draper team from 1949-51 (*see Millville*).

In 1886, Hopedale officially separated from Milford. Today, Hopedale has one of the best collections of architecturally significant double houses in the country, and many elaborate homes built for Draper executives. The Rockwell Co. liquidated the Draper business in 1967. Now with a lack of industry, Hopedale residents voted to maintain town services even though the result is one of the state's highest tax rates. The town is a bedroom community for Boston and Worcester. Commuter rail to Boston is in nearby Franklin, and Route 495 passes through neighboring Milford.

Sources: The Boston Globe; Commonwealth of Mass. EOCD Community Profile; The Run of the Mill, A Pictorial Narrative of the Expansion, Dominion, Decline and Enduring Impact of the New England Textile Industry, Steve Dunwell, David R. Godine, 1978; The Old Post Road, The Story of the Boston Post Road, Stewart H. Holbrook, McGraw-Hill Book Company, Inc., 1962.

Year incorporated: 1886
Population: 5,666 (1990 census)
Density: 1,100 per square mile
Total area: 5.32 sq. miles
Elevation: 300′
Distance from:
Boston: 31
Worcester: 20
Highways: Rtes. 16 and 140, Interstate 495 accessible in neighboring Milford.
Airport: The Worcester Municipal Airport
Tax Rate: $20.18 per thousand (1994, Mass. Div. of Local Services)
Median House Price: $135,000 (1993, County Data Corporation)
Median Household Income: $44,961 (1990 Census)
% of state average: 121.7%
Per Capita Income: $16,677
% of state average 96.8%
Form of Government: Board of Selectmen, Town Coordinator, open town meeting
Municipal Offices: 508) 634-2203
Services: Mass. Electric Co., Commonwealth Gas Co., town sewer, ground water.
Nearest Hospital: Milford Hospital
Registered Voters 3,247
Legislative Districts:
U.S. Congress: 3rd District: Peter I. Blute (R)
State Senate: 1st Worcester & Middlesex: Matthew J. Amorello (R)
State Representative: 10th Worcester Pct. 1: Marie J. Parente (D)
Public Schools
Hopedale:
Hopedale Kdg (N-K); Hartford Ave (01-04); Memorial (K-06); Park Street (01-02); Hopedale Jr Sr High (07-12)
Blackstone Valley:
Blackstone Valley VocTech (09-12)
Superintendent: Donald Hayes: (508) 478-1471
School Choice: Yes

Per Pupil Cost: (State Exec. Office of Education 1992-93)
Hopedale $4,250
State average $5,023

Average Teacher Salary: (State Exec. Office of Education-1992-93)

Hopedale	statewide
$38,542	$38,774

Mean SAT scores 1993

	(reported by town)	State Mean
Math	494	
Verbal	411	
Combined:	905	903

Student Population (Dept. of Education)
Total students 1991-92: 994
at public schools 95.5%
at private schools 4.5%
Educational Attainment (1990 census)
High School graduate or higher 84.8%
Bachelor's Degree or higher 26.6%
Commuting to Work (1990 Census)
Average time to work (mins.): 25.6
Houses of Worship: 1 Catholic, 1 Unitarian, 1 Union Evangelical
Crime Rate:
(1993, Mass. State Police Crime Reporting Unit)

	town	statewide
Total crimes reported:	46	
rate per 1,000 persons	8.12	37.46
Violent crimes	4	
rate per 1,000 persons	0.71	5.65
Property crimes	42	
rate per 1,000 persons	7.41	31.83

Libraries:
Bancroft Memorial Library

HOPEDALE

Hubbardston

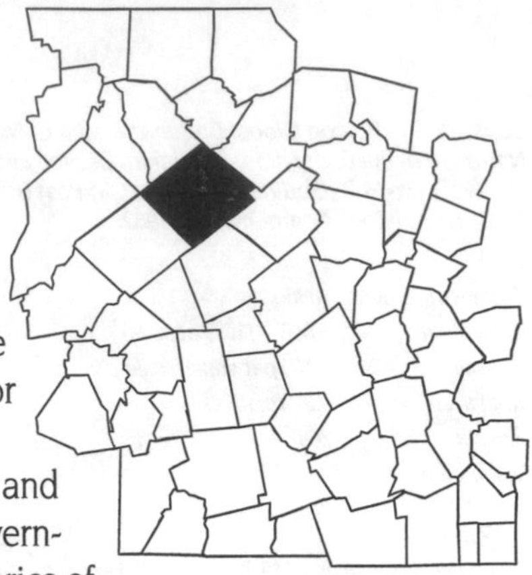

When Hubbardston Marched on Worcester

During the Revolution, three quarters of Hubbardston's men went off to war, and the tiny town nearly went bankrupt providing for the wives and children left behind. The returning soldier/farmers faced heavy taxes and skyrocketing inflation, caused when the government printed too much paper money. The price of corn soared to $150 a bushel, and farmers who couldn't pay their taxes lost their land. Rumors flew about Boston's wealthy merchants grabbing land to turn farmers into peasants.

What happened next is in every American history textbook — Shays Rebellion. Although Daniel Shays got most of the "press," it was Hubbardston farmer Captain Adam Wheeler, hero of Bunker Hill, who led local men marching with Shays on the Worcester Court House to stop farm foreclosures. With leveled bayonets, they canceled court twice — first in September 1786, and at the next session two months later. Massachusetts hit a snag in stopping the rebellion — its own militiamen were sympathetic to the cause, and the federal government was too weak to help.

Eventually, the state militia did catch the rebels (*see Petersham*) and Wheeler escaped to Canada. In the end, all the rebels were pardoned, but some didn't get the good news until they had nooses around their necks. Shays Rebellion caused Governor John Hancock to lower taxes and outlaw imprisonment for debts. Nationally, the rebellion showed the need for a stronger federal government.

A hundred years after Hubbardston marched on Worcester, another local man, Jonas Clark, founded Worcester's Clark University with an endowment of $1 million (considered huge at the time). Clark built his fortune locally in hardware and increased it by supplying California's gold miners and investing in New York City real estate. His gift to Hubbardston, the Jonas Clark Library built in 1874 , is still in use.

Today, a quarter of Hubbardston's acreage is owned by the MDC as part of the Quabbin watershed. Most people know the town, not for Shays Rebellion, but for the Rietta Ranch Flea Market, held every Sunday on Rte. 68. And area gourmet diners can taste a bit of Hubbardston in goat cheese from Westfield Capri Farm, also on Rte. 68.

***Sources:** Commonwealth of Mass. EOCD Community Profile; The Boston Globe; A Guide to the Heritage of*

Worcester County, Simone E. Blake, Montachusett Girl Scout Council, 1973; Quabbin Reservoir, Walter E. Clark, Hobson Book Press, 1946; Reprinted by Athol Press, Inc., 1994; Profiles of the Past, Tom Malloy, Millers River Publishing, Inc., 1984; A Guide to Nashaway, North Central Massachusetts.Marge Darby, Jean C. McCrosky, Mildred A. Chandler, New Guide Group, 1994; Massachusetts Towns, An 1840 View, Ivan Sandrof, Barre Publishers, 1963.

Year incorporated: 1767
Population: 3,495 (1994, town)
Density: 68 per square mile
Total area: 41.95 sq. miles
Elevation: 993'
Distance from:
Boston: 56
Worcester: 19
Highways: Rtes. 62 going E-W and 68 running N-S.
Rail: The Providence & Worcester Railroad provides freight rail service.
Bus: The Montachusett Regional Transit Authority provides paratransit services to the elderly and disabled through the Council on Aging.
Airport: The Worcester Municipal Airport
Tax Rate: $12.48 per thousand (1994, Mass. Div. of Local Services)
Median House Price: $102,900 (1993, County Data Corporation)
Median Household Income: $42,650 (1990 Census)
% of state average: 115.4%
Per Capita Income: $15,575
% of state average 90.4%
Form of Government:: Board of Selectmen, Administrative Assistant, open town meeting
Municipal Offices: (508) 928-5735
Services: Mass. Electric Co., no natural gas or town sewer service, ground water.
Nearest Hospital: Henry Heywood Memorial Hospital, Gardner
Registered Voters : 1,806
Legislative Districts:
U.S. Congress: 1st District: John W. Olver (D)
State Senate: Worcester, Franklin, Hampden and Hampshire: Robert E. Wetmore (D)
State Representative: 1st Worcester; Rep. Hal Lane (D)
Public Schools
Quabbin: Hardwick Elem (01-06); Hubbardston Center (K-06); New Braintree Grade (K-06); Oakham Center (K-06); Ruggles Lane (K-06); Quabbin Regional Jr.- Sr. High, Barre, MA. (07-12)
Superintendent: Maureen Marshall (508) 355-4668
Montachusett: Montachusett Voc Tech (09-12), Fitchburg, MA.
Superintendent: Stratos Dukakis
School Choice: Yes

Per Pupil Cost: (State Exec. Office of Education - 1992-93)
Hubbardston: $4,080
State average: $5,023
Average Teacher Salary: (State Exec. Office of Education)

salary 1992-3	statewide 1992-93
$31,577	$38,774

Mean SAT scores 1993

	(reported by town)	State Mean
Math	459	
Verbal	430	
Combined:	889	903

Student Population (Dept. of Education)
Total students 1991-92: 674
at public schools 95.5%
at private schools 4.5%
Educational Attainment (1990 census)
High School graduate or higher 86.0%
Bachelor's Degree or higher 20.0%
Largest Employers: (supplied by community, 1993)

	# of employees
Wain-Roy, Old Boston Tunpike	44
Wachusett Lumber (Central N.E. Distributing)	19
Sisco Lumber	8
Country Hen	4
Mr. Miko's	3

Commuting to Work (1990 Census)
Average time to work (mins.): 30.9
Houses of Worship: Federated Church and Congregational Church
Crime Rate: not available
Libraries
Hubbardston Public Library

HUBBARDSTON

Lancaster

Capture, Redemption Make a "Bestseller" in 1682

What happened to Lancaster's Mary Rowlandson more than 300 years ago is thrilling enough for a movie plot. Captured by native warriors who sacked and burned the settlement in 1675, she wrote of her ordeal in the 1682 book, *Narrative of the Captivity and Restoration*, becoming New England's first female author. Originally published in both London and Cambridge, Massachusetts, her book has been reprinted over three dozen times, and provides an accurate eyewitness account of Native American life of the time.

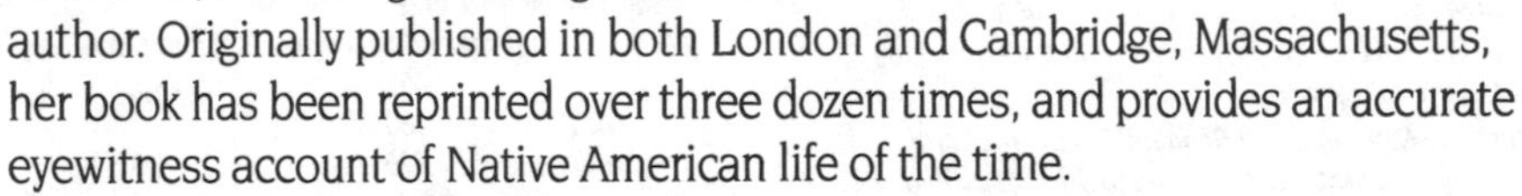

Mary and two children were captured and forced on an arduous journey to Vermont. Daughter Sarah, wounded by a bullet which also pierced Mary's side, died along the trail. After four months, a ransom was paid to release Mary and her son at "Redemption Rock," along Route 140 (also known as Redemption Rock Trail) in Princeton. Mary's carved oak cabinet - a Wethersfield joined chest - can be seen in the town library's rare book room by request.

Lancaster's renowned 1816 Bulfinch Church has a Paul Revere bell, and is considered the finest church by architect Charles Bulfinch, who also designed the U.S. Capitol and the Massachusetts State House. The town is also the birthplace of botanist Luther Burbank, who pioneered plant breeding. Many of the town's architectural treasures are mansions built by the Thayer family. Blue-gray slate quarried in Lancaster was called the world's best, and was used for chalkboards, tombstones, and for roofing slate on Boston's Old State House.

Originally a land grant of over 80 square miles, Lancaster was subdivided to create many of its surrounding towns. Today many residents work in nearby Clinton, Leominster or Worcester, 18 miles south. The town is home to Atlantic Union College, South Lancaster Academy, and the Dr. Franklin Perkins School. When nearby Ft. Devens is closed, some of the South Post acreage could again become part of Lancaster, which has voted to protect much of the land by extending the Oxbow National Wildlife Refuge.

Sources: Commonwealth of Mass. EOCD Community Profile; The Lancastrian Towns, M. Tymeson; The Boston Globe; A Guide to Nashaway, North Central Massachusetts, M. Darby, J. McCrosky, M. Chandler; Massachusetts Towns, I. Sandrof, Barre Publisher, 1963.

Year incorporated: 1653
Population: 6,661 (1990 census)
Density: 241 per square mile
Total area: 28.20 square miles
Elevation: 300'
Distance from:
Boston: 36 miles
Worcester: 18 miles
Highways: Interstate 190; Routes 110 and 117, and Rte. 2 just to the north.
Rail: Commuter rail to Boston's North Station is available in neighboring Leominster (travel time 78-87 mins.) and Shirley (travel time 71-79 mins.) Each stop has 60 MBTA parking spaces.
Bus: The Montachusett Regional Transit Authority (MART) provides service for the elderly and disabled through the Council on Aging.
Airport: Worcester Airport, also Shirley airport, a privately owned public use facility with asphalt runway and copter approach.
Tax Rate: $13.14 per thousand (1995, town))
Median House Price: $115,000 (1993, County Data Corporation)
Median Household Income: $41,552 (1990 Census)
% of state average: 112.4%
Per Capita Income: $14,619
% of state average 84.9%
Form of Government: Board of Selectmen, Executive Secretary, open town meeting
Municipal Offices: (508) 365-3326 or 368-4001
Services: Mass. Electric, Boston Gas Co., partial municipal sewer, partial town water, full-time police, volunteer fire, Continental Cablevision.
Nearest Hospital: Clinton
Registered Voters (Secretary of State 1992): 2,315
Legislative Districts:
U.S. Congress: 3rd District: Peter Blute (R)
5th District: Martin Meehan (D)
State Senate: 2nd Worcester & Middlesex: Robert Antonioni (D)
State Representative: 3rd Middlesex Pct. 1: Patricia Walrath (D)
12th Worcester District: Harold P. Naughton, Jr.
Public Schools
Superintendent: Roland Miller (508) 779-2257
Nashoba Regional School System K-12
Lancaster Middle School 5-8
Memorial School Complex K-4
Nashoba Regional High School 9-12
Minuteman Voc Tech High 9-13
School Choice: Yes
Colleges and Universities: Atlantic Union College
Per Pupil Cost: (State Exec. Office of Education - 1992-93)
Lancaster $3,563
Nashoba $6,767
State average $5,023
Average Teacher Salary:
(State Exec. Office of Education) 1992-93
Lancaster $25,781
Nashoba $38,069
statewide $38,774
Mean SAT scores 1993

	(reported by town)	State Mean
Math	513	
Verbal	446	
Combined	959	903

Student Population (Dept. of Education)
Total students 1991-92: 969
at public schools 81.8%
at private schools 18.2%
Educational Attainment (1990 census)
High School graduate or higher 83.1%
Bachelor's Degree or higher 22.8%
Largest Employers: (supplied by community, 1993)

	# of employees
Dr. Franklin Perkins School	250
Atlantic Union College	150
Town of Lancaster	150
Mass. Correctional Institute, Lancaster	102
Maharishi Ayur Veda/Prod. Int.	90

Commuting to Work (1990 Census)
Average time to work (mins.) 20.3
Houses of Worship: 4 Protestant, 1 Catholic
Crime Rate: (1993, Mass. State Police Crime Reporting Unit)

	town	statewide
Total crimes reported:	126	
rate per 1,000 persons	18.92	37.46
Violent crimes	20	
rate per 1,000 persons	3.0	5.65
Property crimes	106	
rate per 1,000 persons	15.91	31.83

Libraries:
Lancaster Town Library, Main St., (508) 368-8928
Museums:
Fifth Meeting House, Town Common (508) 365-2427
State Register of Historic Places 1993:
Atherton Bridge, Bolton Rd.
Center Village Historic District
First Church of Christ, Fifth Meeting House, Town Green
Founder's Hall, Atlantic Union College
Lancaster Industrial School for Girls, Old Common Rd.
Anthony Lane House, Seven Bridge Rd.
North Village Historic District
Ponakin Bridge, Ponakin Rd.
Shirley Shaker Village (Lancaster/Shirley), Harvard Rd.
South Lancaster Engine House, 282 South Main St.
Nathaniel Thayer Estate, 438 South Main St.

Leicester

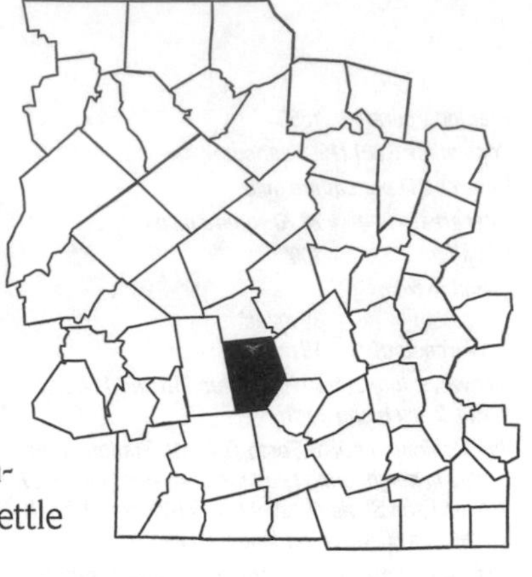

Dead Horse Hill and the Cherry Valley Flood

With brooks feeding the Blackstone River and a long history of textile mills, Leicester has applied to join the Blackstone River Valley National Heritage Corridor. A local Blackstone Pride Committee is already planning hiking trails and working to keep the Kettle Brook tributary clean.

Leicester and its villages of Cherry Valley and Rochdale were known for their mills, and local inventor Pliny Earle improved the design of machine cards used in textile manufacturing. By 1890 the town was producing a fourth of the nation's supply of cards. Earle also experimented with mulberry trees, during a brief silkworm craze.

Disaster struck Cherry Valley and its mills in 1876 when the Lynde Brook Reservoir dam failed, sending 3 million tons of water crashing through town and on into "New Worcester," or Webster Square, washing out bridges there and as far away as Southbridge St. Entire mills in Cherry Valley were washed away as its Main Street turned into a river some 400 yards wide. Word of the spectacular flood spread fast, and gawkers came on trains from Fitchburg, Nashua and Lowell just to view the damage. Streetcars to the flood scene were packed, and The Gazette estimated 40,000 people came to gape at the destruction.

Some 40,000 spectators also turned out for Leicester's famous "Dead Horse Hill" automobile climb in 1909. (*So steep is the incline here it was said that no one horse carrying a heavy load ever reached the top and survived*). The first Dead Horse Hill race, sponsored by the fledgling Worcester Automobile Club in 1905, saw 70 drivers in dusters and goggles attack the one mile course from Stafford St. in Worcester over the Leicester line to the summit, a grade of 843 feet to the mile. The Worcester Telegram described the first racers as dangerous "speedophics in benzine chariots." The 1909 winner broke the course record in 54 seconds driving a Stanley Steamer.

Today, Leicester is home to Becker College, founded in 1784 as Leicester Academy. Becker also has a Worcester campus which includes some 35 historic buildings near Elm Park. Leicester is also the home of Hot Dog Annie's, a haven for hot dog afficionados from all over New England. To the uninitiated non-native, pronouncing Leicester, as well as Petersham and Worcester, is a quick way to prove you're not from Worcester County. (P.S. - *that's* "LES*Ster,*" "*PetersHAM*" *and* "WUH*ster*").

Sources: A Guide to the Heritage of Worcester County, Simone E. Blake, Montachusett Girl Scout Council, 1973; Massachusetts Towns, An 1840 View, Ivan Sandrof, Barre Publishers, 1963; Once-Told Tales of Worcester County, Albert B. Southwick, Databooks, 1994; The Coghlin Story 1885-1985, LaVerne Dickinson, The Coghlin Companies, 1985.

Year incorporated: 1722
Population: 10,191 (1990 census)
Density: 436 per square mile
Total area: 24.68 sq. miles
Elevation: 1,009'
Distance from:
Boston: 46
Worcester: 6
Providence: 48
Hartford: 55
Springfield 50

Highways: Rtes. 9 going E-W, 56 running N-S, and Interstate 90.

Rail: Amtrak passenger rail service is available to all points in neighboring Worcester.

Bus: The Worcester Regional Transit Authority provides fixed route service between Leicester and Worcester and Paratransit services for the elderly and disabled.

Airport: The Worcester Municipal Airport

Tax Rate: $12.96 per thousand (1994, Mass. Div. of Local Services)

Median House Price: $108,000 (1993, County Data Corporation)

Median Household Income: $40,321 (1990 Census)
% of state average: 109.1%
Per Capita Income: $15,806
% of state average 91.8%

Form of Government: Board of Selectmen, Town Administrator, open town meeting

Municipal Offices: (508) 892-7000

Services: Mass. Electric, Boston Gas Co., Commonwealth Gas Co., Deer Island STP sewer, ground water.

Nearest Hospital: several in Worcester

Registered Voters: 5,696

Legislative Districts:

U.S. Congress: 2nd District: Richard E. Neal (D)

State Senate: 1st Worcester & Middlesex: Matthew J. Amorello (R)

State Representative: 17th Worcester: John J. Binienda, Sr. (D)

Public Schools

Leicester: Leicester Center Elem (04-05); Leicester Primary (K-04); Leicester Memorial Middle (06-08); Leicester High (09-12)

Superintendent: Norman Limoges (508) 892-7840

School Choice: No

Colleges and Universities:
Becker Junior College - Leicester Campus

Per Pupil Cost:
(State Exec. Office of Education -1992-93)
Leicester $3,796
State average 1992-93 $5,023

Average Teacher Salary:
(State Exec. Office of Education-1992-93)

Leicester	statewide
$34,944	$38,774

Mean SAT scores 1993

	(reported by town)	State Mean
Math	443	
Verbal	427	
Combined:	870	903

Student Population (Dept. of Education)
Total students 1991-92: 1,790
at public schools 93.4%
at private schools 6.6%

Educational Attainment (1990 census)
High School graduate or higher 80.4%
Bachelor's Degree or higher 16.8%

Largest Employers: (supplied by community, 1993)

	# of employees
Millbrook Distributors	300
Antanavica Construction	25
Minuteman Corrugated	20
Leicester Savings	20
Dryden Machine	20

Commuting to Work (1990 Census)
Average time to work (mins.): 22.5

Houses of Worship: 3 Catholic, 2 Baptist, 1 Church of Christ, 1 Federated (Cong. & Unitarian), 1 Episcopal, 1 Jehovah's Witnesses

Crime Rate: (1993, Mass. State Police Crime Reporting Unit)

	town	statewide
Total crimes reported:	173	
rate per 1,000 persons	16.98	37.46
Violent crimes	33	
rate per 1,000 persons	3.24	5.65
Property crimes	140	
rate per 1,000 persons	13.74	31.83

Libraries
Leicester Public Library

State Register of Historic Places 1993:
Milestone, 1767
Shaw Site

Leominster

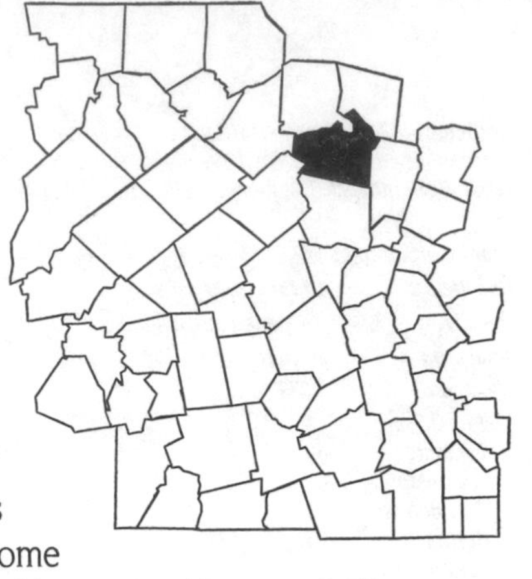

Johnny Appleseed, Plastics and Pink Flamingoes

What do longhorn cattle, Stalin, and Chinese hogs have to do with Leominster? Believe it or not, all contributed to Leominster's dominance in plastics manufacturing. Today, this city 20 miles north of Worcester is the heart of the state's plastics industry, the fourth largest in the nation. Some 150 plastics firms are found here and in neighboring Fitchburg and Clinton, supplying products to the medical, automotive, defense and household products markets. And that enduring symbol of Americana, the ubiquitous pink flamingo lawn ornament, was first manufactured by Leominster's Union Products in 1957.

Leominster craftsmen of the 1800's made a handy living fashioning horn products — combs, hairpins, buckles, buttons, knife handles — all made from the horns of longhorn cattle. When railroad refrigerator cars began shipping beef to the East, the public found longhorn beef tough, preferring the meat of horn-less beef cattle. The demise of the longhorn threatened Leominster's economy until Bernard Doyle switched to pyroxylin plastic to make these products, founding the Viscoloid Company in Leominster in 1898. Du Pont bought the firm in 1925. Enter the hog connection.

The Leominster plant joined Du Pont's research effort to make a synthetic toothbrush bristle. At the time, these were made with hog bristles, specifically the tough long bristles of Chinese and Siberian hogs. By the 1930's Stalin and the Japanese invasion of China were putting the squeeze on hog bristle supplies. Du Pont's breakthrough - nylon - came just in time, and Leominster began exclusive manufacture of Dr. West's Miracle Tuft nylon-bristled toothbrushes. Leominster's plastics heritage is documented at the National Plastics Center and Museum, 210 Lancaster Street.

Of course, Leominster is more famous as the birthplace of Johnny Appleseed, who was born John Chapman in 1774. He was more than a seed-scattering wanderer with a tin pot on his head. Rather, he was a skilled nurseryman who foresaw the pioneers' need for apple seeds and seedlings. He started numerous nurseries in the Midwest, and no doubt apple trees planted from his seeds survive in New England today. A stone marker off Mechanic St. in Leominster marks the site of his home.

Sources: Commonwealth of Mass. EOCD Community Profile; The Guide to North Central Mass., (North Central Mass. Chamber of Commerce); The Worcester Telegram & Gazette; The Boston Globe; The Du Pont Magazine; History of Du Pont's Plastics Dept.; Du Pont, One Hundred and Forty Years, William S. Dutton; Fitchburg Sentinel & Enterprise.

Year incorporated: 1740 as a town; 1915 as a city
Population: 38,145 (1990 census)
Density: 1,321 per square mile
Total area: 29.76
Elevation: 400'
Distance from:
Boston: 41 miles
Worcester: 20 miles
Highways: Interstate 190; State Routes 2, 12,13,31, 117
Rail: Commuter rail service is available from North Leominster to Boston's North Station, via South Acton, Concord, Brandeis, Waltham, Belmont, and Porter Square. Travel time: 78-87 mins.; 60 MBTA parking spaces. For information, call 1-800-392-6100.
Bus: The Montachusett Regional Transit Authority (MART) provides service to Fitchburg, Gardner and Fort Devens, (508) 345-7711. Peter Pan Bus Lines provides limited service to Worcester, with connections to Hartford and New York City. 1-800-237-8747.
Airport: The Fitchburg Municipal Airport, a General Aviation (GA) facility, is easily accessible. It has 2 asphalt runways, 4,511' and 3,502' long. Instrument approaches available. Non-precision.
Tax Rate: $16.31 per thousand
(1994, The Central Mass. Fact Book)
Median House Price: $115,000
(1993, County Data Corporation)
Median Household Income: $35,974 (1990 Census)
% of state average: 97.4%
Per Capita Income: $15,960
% of state average 92.7%
Form of Government: Mayor Council
Municipal Offices: (508) 534-7500
Services: Mass. Electric, Boston Gas, MDC sewer,
Nearest Hospital: Leominster Hospital
Registered Voters (Secretary of State 1992) 20,086
Legislative Districts:
U.S. Congress: 1st District: John W. Olver, Jr. (D)
State Senate: 2nd Worcester-Middlesex District: Robert Antonioni (D)
State Representative: 4th Worcester: Mary Jane Simmons (D)
Public Schools
Superintendent: Carol Kelly (508) 534-7700
School Choice: Yes

School	Grades
Fall Brook	K-6
Johnny Appleseed	K-6
Northwest	1-6
Priest St.	K-6
Southeast Elementary	K-6
Gallagher Jr. High	7-8
Leominster Sr. High	9-12
Leominster High Trade	10-12

Per Pupil Cost: (State Exec. Office of Education -1992-93)
Leominster: $4,141
State average 1992-93 $5,023
Average Teacher Salary:
(State Exec. Office of Education)

salary 1992-3	statewide 1991-92
$39,554	$38,774

Mean SAT scores 1993

	(reported by town)	State Mean
Math	468	
Verbal	423	
Combined:	891	903

Student Population (Dept. of Education)
Total students 1991-92: 5,298
Educational Attainment (1990 census)
High School graduate or higher 75.8%
Bachelor's Degree or higher 18.2%
Largest Employers: (supplied by community, 1993)

	# of employees
Leominster Hospital	810
Eusey Press	320
Tucker Housewares	300
Union Products	275
Victory Button	210

Commuting to Work (1990 Census)
Average time to work (mins.) 20.6
Houses of Worship: 12 Protestant, 5 Catholic, 1 synagogue
Crime Rate: (1993, Mass. State Police Crime Reporting Unit)

	town	statewide
Total crimes reported:	1842	
rate per 1,000 persons	48.29	37.46
Violent crimes	157	
rate per 1,000 persons	4.12	5.65
Property crimes	1685	
rate per 1,000 persons	44.17	31.83

Libraries:
Leominster Public Library, 30 West St. (508) 534-7522
State Register of Historic Places 1993:
Cluett Peabody and Company, 123 First Ave., Leominster
Monument Square Historic District, Main, Park and Church Streets, Leominster
Wachusett Shirt Company, 97-100 Water St.
Wellington Piano Case Company, 22-60 Green St.
F.A. Whitney Carriage Co. Complex District, 142 Water St.

Lunenburg

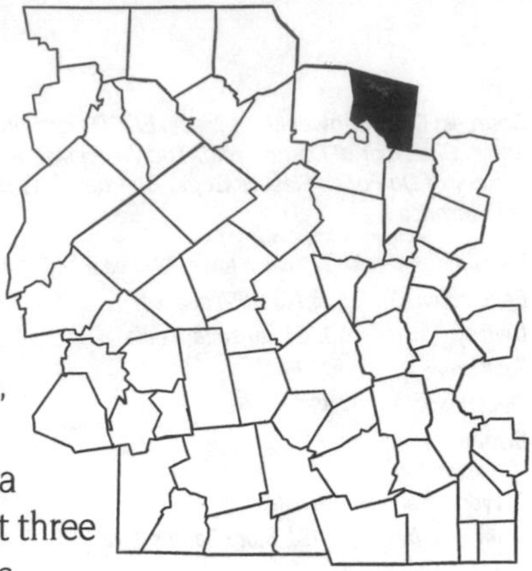

The Lake of the Magician

In native legends, the 95-acre spring-fed pond in Lunenburg was called "Unketchewalom," or "Lake of the Magician." It has proved to be an apt name, because Whalom Park, "New England's Coney Island," has survived two tornadoes, a hurricane, the Great Depression and at least three major fires. Still in operation today, it draws about a quarter of a million vistors annually, who enjoy its 35 rides, including its classic roller coaster, built in 1940, and two water slides.

Whalom was built by the Fitchburg and Leominster Street Railway Company in 1893 to use surplus electricity on nights and Sundays. On opening day in 1903, streetcars hooked six together ran constantly on double tracks bringing thousands from Fitchburg and Leominster. Attractions included an open-air dance hall, theater, a water slide, roller-skating rink, bowling alleys, and the "McKinley Cruiser," a small scale gunboat built in Fitchburg in 1897 and used in President McKinley's campaign.

Lunenburg had a brief industrial history in the 1800's, but the early mills closed due to a lack of water power and railroad service. The town was linked to Boston by a stage line as early as 1807, when a one-way trip cost $1.75 and took 12 hours. Book publishing and binding flourished here briefly, including Bibles and popular titles like *Robinson Crusoe* and *Gulliver's Travels*. In 1837 some 16,000 books were shipped to Boston in horse-drawn wagons. Legend has it that a wagon full of Bibles was exchanged for a wagon full of rum.

Patent medicine queen Lydia Pinkham began in Lunenburg in the 1870's, manufacturing her "compound" for "woman's troubles" here using roots from Mulpus Brook. She later built a factory in Lynn, MA, and printed *Lydia E. Pinkham's Private Text-Book upon Ailments Peculiar to Women*, to stimulate medicine sales.

Today, Lunenburg is attracting more retail development, and residents can work and shop in town, in nearby Fitchburg, and Leominster, or even in Nashua and Manchester, NH. Many commute to Boston via Rte. 2 or to Worcester using Rte. 190 in Leominster.

Sources: A Guide to Nashaway, North Central Massachusetts...a land of uncommon beauty, Marge Darby, Jean C. McCrosky, Mildred A. Chandler, New Guide Group, 1994; Lunenburg; The Heritage of Turkey Hills, Nelde K. Drumm, Margaret P. Harley, Lunenburg Historical Society, 1977; The Boston Globe; Worcester Magazine; A Guide to the Heritage of Worcester County, Simone E. Blake, Montachusett Girl Scout Council, 1973.
Lunenburg

Year incorporated: 1726
Population: 9,117 (1990 census)
Density: 345 per square mile
Total area: 27.69 sq. miles
Elevation: 570'
Distance from:
Boston: 43
Worcester: 29
Highways: Rtes. 2A which runs E-W, and 13 running N-S.
Rail: Commuter rail service to North Station, Boston, is available in the neighboring towns of Fitchburg and Leominster.
Bus: The Montachusett Regional Transit Authority provides limited fixed route service from Fitchburg and Leominster to Whalom Park during the summer and Paratransit service to the elderly and disabled through the Council on Aging.
Airport: The Fitchburg Municipal Airport, a general aviation facility
Tax Rate: $15.19 per thousand (1994, Mass. Div. of Local Services)
Median House Price: $125,000
(1993, County Data Corporation)
Median Household Income: $43,199 (1990 Census)
% of state average: 116.9%
Per Capita Income: $19,166
% of state average 111.3%
Form of Government: Board of Selectmen, Executive Secretary, open town meeting
Municipal Offices: (508) 582-4130
Services: Electric through Fitchburg Gas & Electric Light Co., Boston Gas Co., Fitchburg Gas & Electric Co., no town sewer, ground water.
Nearest Hospital: Burbank Hospital, Inc., Leominster Hospital
Registered Voters: 5,647
Legislative Districts:
U.S. Congress: 5th District: Martin T. Meehan (D)
U.S. Congress: 1st District: John W. Olver (D)
State Senate: Worcester-Middlesex District: Robert Antonioni (D)
State Representative: 1st Middlesex: Robert S. Hargraves (R)
Public Schools
Lunenburg: Thomas C Passios Elem (K-04); Turkey Hill Middle (05-08); Lunenburg High (09-12)
Montachusett: Montachusett Voc Tech (09-12)
Superintendent: Richard Carlson (508) 582-4100
School Choice: Yes
Per Pupil Cost: (State Exec. Office of Education -1992-93)
Lunenburg $4,120
State average $5,023
Average Teacher Salary:
(State Exec. Office of Education-1992-3)

Lunengurg	statewide 1992-93
$34,545	$38,774

Mean SAT scores 1993

	(reported by town)	State Mean
Math	505	
Verbal	474	
Combined:	979	903

Student Population (Dept. of Education)
Total students 1991-92: 1,576
at public schools 95.2%
at private schools 4.8%
Educational Attainment (1990 census)
High School graduate or higher 84.0%
Bachelor's Degree or higher 24.1%
Largest Employers: (supplied by community, 1993)

	# of employees
Whalom Park Amusement Company	375
Town of Lunenburg	302
Ecological Fibers	51
P. J. Keating	50
Maki Home Center	33

Commuting to Work (1990 Census)
Average time to work (mins.): 23.8
Houses of Worship: 4
Crime Rate: not available
Libraries:
Ritter Memorial Library
Museums: none
State Register of Historic Places 1993:
Lunenburg Historic District

Mendon

Lions and Tigers and Bears or Washington Almost Slept Here

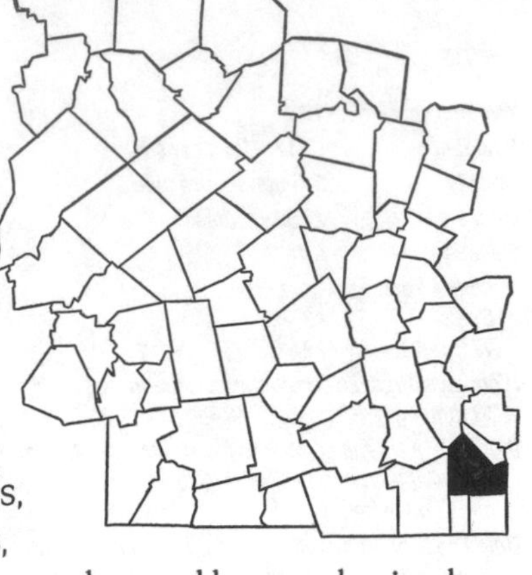

New England's largest zoo? You won't find it in Boston, but rather in tiny Mendon. Once a rural dairy farming town with more cows than people, Mendon is now home to Southwick's Zoo, with more than 500 animals, including rhinos, lions, tigers, bears, chimps, monkeys, camels, zebras, giant tortoises, llamas, deer and barnyard animals. Tres, the proud offspring of Uno and Dos, is the only giraffe born in New England.

Mendon, incorporated in 1667, is the second oldest town in the county behind Lancaster. Like Lancaster, it was the "mother" to many neighboring towns, including Milford, Blackstone, Millville, Upton, Northbridge, Hopedale and Uxbridge. It was the first town destroyed by King Philip's Nipmuc warriors, who burned it in 1675. Resilient settlers rebuilt five years later.

Part of the Blackstone River Valley National Heritage Corridor, Mendon also has one of the best preserved Federal/Greek Revival town centers in the state, and visitors often say it's like stepping back in time. Its annual country fair is legendary and attracts upwards of 14,000 people.

Washington almost slept here in 1789. Returning from Boston, he planned to stay in Mendon with his old friend, Col. Amidon. However, a maid answering the door didn't recognize Washington and refused to let him in. Rebuffed, he traveled on to the Taft Tavern in Uxbridge, where he spent the night (*see Uxbridge*).

Sources: Commonwealth of Mass. EOCD Community Profile; The Boston Globe; A Guide to the Heritage of Worcester County, Simone E. Blake, Montachusett Girl Scout Council, 1973; More Massachusetts Towns, Ivan Sandrof, Barre Publishers, 1965; The Old Post Road, The Story of the Boston Post Road, Stewart H. Holbrook, McGraw-Hill Book Company, Inc., 1962.

Year incorporated: 1667
Population: 4,301 (1994, town census)
Density: 222 per square mile
Total area: 18.26 sq. miles
Elevation: 387'
Distance from:
Boston: 33
Worcester: 20
Providence: 28
Hartford: 60
Springfield 60
Highways: Rtes. 16 and 140
Airport: The Norfolk Airport, a general aviation facility.
Tax Rate: $12.89 per thousand (1994, Mass. Div. of Local Services)
Median House Price: $166,000 (1993, County Data Corporation)
Median Household Income: $55,914 (1990 Census)
% of state average: 151.3%
Per Capita Income: $19,023
% of state average 115.1%
Form of Government: Board of Selectmen, open town meeting
Municipal Offices: (508) 473-2312
Services: Mass. Electric, Bay State Gas Co., Commonwealth Gas Co., no town sewer, ground water.
Nearest Hospital: Milford Hospital
Registered Voters: 2,577
Legislative Districts:
U.S. Congress: 2nd District: Richard E. Neal (D)
State Senate: Worcester & Norfolk District: Louis P. Bertonazzi (D)
State Representative: 10th Worcester Pct. 1: Marie J. Parente (D)
Public Schools
Mendon Upton: Memorial Elem (K-04); Henry P. Clough (K-04); Miscoe Hill Middle School (05-08); Nipmuc Regional High (09-12)
Superintendent: David Crisafulli: (508) 529-7729
School Choice: Yes
Blackstone Valley: Blackstone Valley VocTech (09-12)
Superintendent: Dr. Michael Fitzpatrick (508) 529-7758
Per Pupil Cost: (State Exec. Office of Education -1992-93)
Mendon $4,411
State average $5,023
Average Teacher Salary: (State Exec. Office of Education)

salary 1992-3	statewide 1992-93
$31,230	$38,774

Mean SAT scores 1993 (reported by town)
Math 477
Verbal 459
Combined: 936 State Mean: 903
Student Population (Dept. of Education)
Total students 1991-92: 691
at public schools 98.0%
at private schools 2.0%
Educational Attainment (1990 census)
High School graduate or higher 84.5%
Bachelor's Degree or higher 24.0%
Largest Employers: (supplied by community, 1993)
Mendon-Upton Regional School
Town of Mendon
Commuting to Work (1990 Census)
Average time to work (mins.) 26.9
Houses of Worship: Baptist, Catholic, Friendship Bible Church, Unitarian, Bethany Assembly of God.
Crime Rate:
(1993, Mass. State Police Crime Reporting Unit)

	town	statewide
Total crimes reported:	41	
rate per 1,000 persons	10.22	37.46
Violent crimes	1	
rate per 1,000 persons	0.25	5.65
Property crimes	40	
rate per 1,000 persons	9.98	31.83

Libraries:
Taft Public Library

Milford

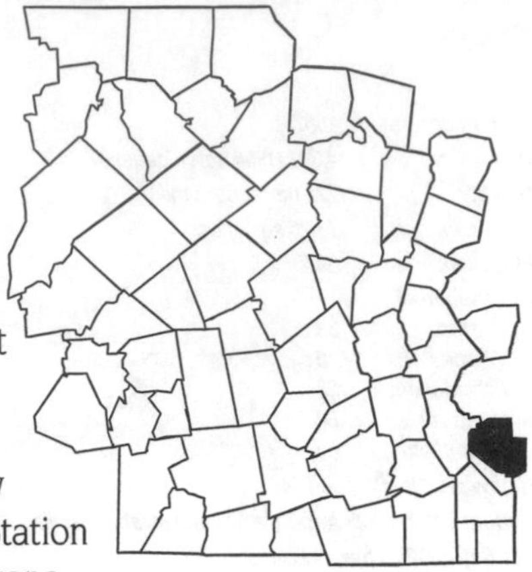

Pink Granite and a Golden Triangle

Touch the base of the Statue of Liberty, and you'll feel Milford's most famous export - fine-grained, handsome pink granite. Prized the world over, Milford pink granite was used to build the Boston Public Library and both Penn Station and Grand Central Station in New York City. Discovered in 1850, the stone was used to build St. Mary's Church and an Irish Round Tower, a replica of one in Ireland where monks hid with precious manuscripts from attacking Danes and Norsemen.

As demand grew for the granite, master Italian stone cutters moved to Milford to quarry the stone, along with workers from Ireland, Sweden, Armenia and Portugal. Many historic buildings in downtown Milford feature the granite, including the Milford Armory, the Milford Cultural Center, the police station and Milford Middle School West and Stacy complex.

Milford's location in a "golden triangle," nearly equidistant to Boston, Worcester and Hartford, has placed it on major transportation routes for over 200 years. President George Washington traveled through Milford on the Boston Post Road, and the railroad came through in 1845. The town's two exits on Rte. 495 make Boston an easy commute. Since the building of I-495, Milford's population has doubled.

Over the years, Milford has hosted one successful industry after another. In the mid-1800's, there were 11 shoe manufacturers in town, and later the straw hat industry here supported 700 milliners. Today, Waters Associates employs 900 in Milford and makes liquid chromatography equipment for medical labs around the world. Benjamin Moore Paints makes interior and exterior house paints in nearly 1,000 colors at its Milford plant.

Milford native Dr. Joseph E. Murray conducted the first successful organ transplant — a kidney from Ronald Herrick to his twin brother, Richard — in 1954. Dr. Murray's work in transplants and the use of immunosuppressive drugs to solve organ rejection earned him the 1990 Nobel Prize in medicine, shared with oncologist Dr. E. Donnall Thomas of Seattle. Dr. Murray, Milford High Class of 1936, went on to Holy Cross College and Harvard Medical School, where he is active today as Professor of Surgery Emeritus.

Sources: Commonwealth of Mass. EOCD Community Profile; The Boston Globe; The Old Post Road, The Story of the Boston Post Road, Stewart H. Holbrook, McGraw-Hill Book Company, Inc., 1962; Massachusetts Towns,

An 1840 View, Ivan Sandrof, Barre Publishers, 1963; A Guide to the Heritage of Worcester County, Simone E. Blake, Montachusett Girl Scout Council, 1973.

Milford

Year incorporated: 1780
Population: 25,355 (1990 census)
Density: 1,737 per square mile
Total area: 14.87 sq. miles
Elevation: 312'
Distance from:
Boston: 30
Worcester: 18
Providence: 32

Highways: Rtes. 495, 16, 140, 90.

Rail: Commuter rail service to Back Bay Station and South Station Boston, is available from neighboring Franklin.

Bus: Brush Hill Transportation provides rush hour service to Boston M-F; bus service to Framingham connects with Boston buses and trains.

Airport: The Norfolk Airport, a general aviation facility.

Tax Rate: $14.58 per thousand (1994, Mass. Div. of Local Services)

Median House Price: $139,900 (1993, County Data Corporation)

Median Household Income: $38,180 (1990 Census)
% of state average: 103.3%
Per Capita Income: $15,980
% of state average 92.8%

Form of Government: Board of Selectmen, Exec. Secretary, Representative Town Meeting

Municipal Offices: (508) 634-2303

Services: Mass. Electric, Commonwealth Gas Co., town sewer, ground water.

Nearest Hospital: Milford Hospital

Registered Voters : 13,318

Legislative Districts:

U.S. Congress: 2nd District: Richard E. Neal (D)

State Senate: Worcester & Norfolk District: Louis P. Bertonazzi (D)

State Representative: 10th Worcester Pct. 1: Marie J. Parente (D)

Public Schools

Milford: Memorial (K-03); Brookside (03-05); Woodland (K-05); Milford Middle West (06-07); Milford Middle East (-08); Milford High (09-12)

Blackstone Valley:
Blackstone Valley Voc Tech (09-12)

Superintendent: Thomas Cullen (508) 478-1100

School Choice: Yes

Per Pupil Cost: (State Exec. Office of Education - 1992-93)
Milford $4,238
State average $5,023

Average Teacher Salary: (State Exec. Office of Education-1992-93)

	Milford	statewide
	$35,789	$38,774

Mean SAT scores 1993 (reported by town)
Math
Verbal
Combined: 947 State Mean: 903

Student Population (Dept. of Education)
Total students 1991-92: 4,207
at public schools 93.9%
at private schools 6.1%

Educational Attainment (1990 census)
High School graduate or higher 77.7%
Bachelor's Degree or higher 21.4%

Largest Employers: (supplied by community, 1993)

	# of employees
Millipore/Waters Chromatography	1,000
Milford Whitinsville Regional Hospital	980
Boston Scientific, Milford	230
Fenwal Electronics, inc.	230
Foster Forbes	220

Commuting to Work (1990 Census)
Average time to work (mins.) 25.2

Houses of Worship: 2 Catholic, 1 Episcopal, 1 Congregational, 1 Methodist, 1 Baptist, several Evangelical Christian denominations, 1 Jewish Temple, 1 Unitarian

Crime Rate: (1993, Mass. State Police Crime Reporting Unit)

	town	statewide
Total crimes reported:	260	
rate per 1,000 persons	10.25	37.46
Violent crimes	4	
rate per 1,000 persons	0.16	5.65
Property crimes	256	
rate per 1,000 persons	10.10	31.83

Libraries:
Milford Town Library

Museums:
Milford Historical Museum

State Register of Historic Places 1993:
Gillon Block
Memorial Hall
Milford Town Hall
Prospect Heights Historic District
Thom Block

Millbury

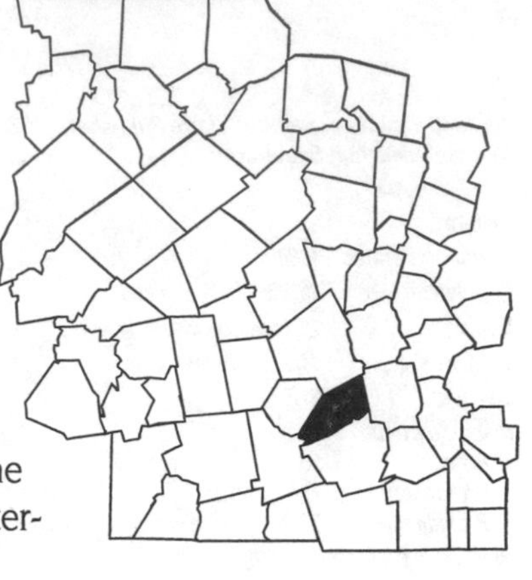

River to the Past; Highway to the Future

The Blackstone River and its old canal bisect Millbury, and Rte. 146 retraces much of this route from Worcester to Providence. The river and canal shaped Millbury's past, but the highway will shape its future, with the 1998 completion of a Rte. 146/Mass. Pike interchange and connector to Worcester.

The project, estimated at $228 million, is second only to Boston's "Big Dig," and many feel it will help correct a 40-year-old mistake made when Mass. Pike planners by-passed Worcester. When the 146 project is completed, Millbury, which also has Rtes. 20, 122, and 122A, will be at the center of traffic flowing between Boston, Worcester and Providence.

Part of the Blackstone River Valley National Heritage Corridor, Millbury has a name that reflects its history. Not surprisingly, it had many textile mills, which reached a peak in 1911. But it also had a powder mill and armory that made guns for the Continental army. Later, Asa Waters got a patent for being the first to turn gun barrels on a lathe.

"Pin Money" wasn't small change in the 1800's, because pins at the time were hand-made in England. This all changed when Millbury's Elijah Waters invented machines both for making pins, and for sticking them into paper. The country's first postage stamp was also manufactured in Millbury.

Today, Millbury's house prices and highways are attracting commuters relocating from Boston's suburbs. The town gets a boost from user fees paid by Wheelabrator, a regional trash-to-energy incinerator in town, which generates 45 megawatts of electricity an hour from the 480,000 tons of garbage it processes annually. Town planners expect more tax revenue to come from development around the Rte. 146 corridor.

Sources: Commonwealth of Mass. EOCD Community Profile; The Boston Globe; A Guide to the Heritage of Worcester County, Simone E. Blake, Montachusett Girl Scout Council, 1973; Massachusetts Towns, An 1840 View, Ivan Sandrof, Barre Publishers, 1963; Visit Worcester County; Worcester County Convention & Visitors Bureau.

Millbury

Year incorporated: 1813

Population: 12,228 (1990 census)

Density: 777 per square mile

Total area: 16.25 sq. miles

Elevation: 415'

Distance from:
- Boston: 43
- Worcester: 7
- Providence: 37

Highways: Interstate 90, U.S. Route 20, State Rtes. 146 running NW-SE.

Rail: Passenger rail service to Boston, Providence, Springfield, and all points on Amtrak is available through neighboring Worcester.

Bus: Paratransit services for the elderly and disabled offered. Peter Pan Bus Lines offers frequent commuter service from the Millbury M.T. #11 commuter lot to Boston and Worcester.

Airport: The Worcester Municipal Airport

Tax Rate: $13.26 per thousand (1994, Mass. Div. of Local Services)

Median House Price: $115,500 (1993, County Data Corporation)

Median Household Income: $37,438 (1990 Census)
- % of state average: 101.3%
- Per Capita Income: $15,474
- % of state average 89.8%

Form of Government: Board of Selectmen, Administrative Assistant, open town meeting

Municipal Offices: (508) 865-4710

Services: Mass. Electric Co., Commonwealth Gas Co., town sewer, ground water.

Nearest Hospital: several in Worcester

Registered Voters: 7,186

Legislative Districts:

U.S. Congress: 2nd District: Richard E. Neal (D)

State Senate: 1st Worcester & Middlesex: Matthew J. Amorello (R)

State Representative: 7th Worcester: Paul Kollios (D)

Public Schools

Millbury: Elmwood Street (K-02); Shaw Memorial Middle School (03-06); Millbury Memorial High (07-12)

Blackstone Valley: Blackstone Valley VocTech (09-12)

Superintendent: (508) 865-9501

School Choice: No

Per Pupil Cost: (State Exec. Office of Education - 1992-93)
- Millbury $4,693
- State average $5,023

Average Teacher Salary: (State Exec. Office of Education-1992-93)

Millbury	statewide
$34,437	$38,774

Mean SAT scores 1993 (reported by town)

Math	489	
Verbal	458	
Combined:	947	State Mean: 903

Student Population (Dept. of Education)
- Total students 1991-92: 1,681
- at public schools 92.2%
- at private schools 7.8%

Educational Attainment (1990 census)
- High School graduate or higher 77.9%
- Bachelor's Degree or higher 14.4%

Largest Employers: (supplied by community, 1993)

	# of employees
Goretti's Supermarket	350
Polyclad Laminates	150
United Counties Industries Corp.	150
Wheelabrator, Millbury	75
New England Newspaper Supply	75

Commuting to Work (1990 Census)
- Average time to work (mins.) 19.1

Houses of Worship: several denominations

Crime Rate: not available

Libraries
- Millbury Public Library

State Register of Historic Places 1993:
- U.S. Post Office - Millbury Main
- Asa Waters Mansion

Millville

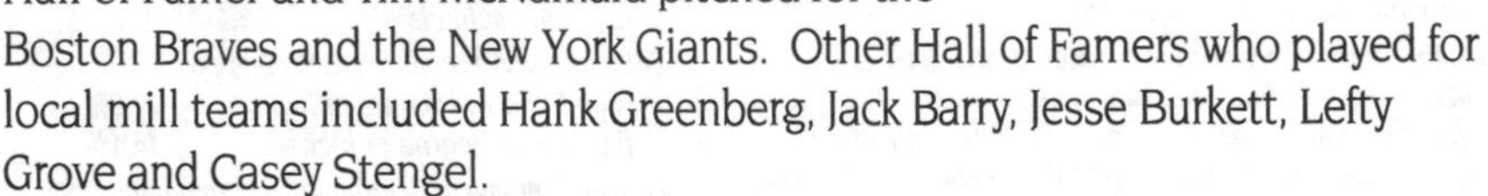

Baseball in the Valley

Blackstone Valley millworkers played hardball and were proud of it. Industrial league baseball played at Millville's "Rubber Shop Oval" approached major league quality. Indeed, two of Millville's own went on to greater fame — Leo "Gabby" Hartnett, a catcher for the Chicago Cubs, was a Hall of Famer and Tim McNamara pitched for the Boston Braves and the New York Giants. Other Hall of Famers who played for local mill teams included Hank Greenberg, Jack Barry, Jesse Burkett, Lefty Grove and Casey Stengel.

Up and down the valley, baseball was a way of life and the competition between mills was fierce. Mill owners started the teams with their own money in 1905 as a way to reduce turn-over, instill company pride and teach the value of teamwork. Baseball teams were another sign of the pervasive paternalism that dominated mill life, with company-owned stores, hospitals, churches and cemeteries. Historians have noted that company hospitals brought workers into the world, and company cemeteries took them out. In between they worked and enjoyed baseball. By the 1920's, mill league games were attracting thousands of spectators.

The "Rubber Shop" that owned the "Oval" in Millville was the U.S. Rubber boot plant. Next to it was the Lawrence Felting Company, which made the boot liners. The mills are gone, but the baseball field is still recognizable. After the Depression, social life began to center around union activities, and the leagues were abandoned by 1955.

The Millville Locks, used to raise and lower the water level on the Blackstone Canal, are still intact, and the town is developing a public trail to the site. Predating the Industrial Revolution is the Chestnut Street Meeting House, a post and beam structure built in 1769. This building has the distinction of being in three different towns without moving an inch. At various times in history, the spot has been part of Mendon, then Blackstone, and finally, Millville. Recently Millville's population has grown enough to necessitate its first new elementary school since 1850. Most new residents commute to jobs in the MetroWest I-495 area.

Sources: Margaret Carroll, unofficial Millville town historian; The Worcester Telegram & Gazette; Commonwealth of Mass. EOCD Community Profile.

Year incorporated: 1916
Population: 2,236 (1990 census)
Density: 454 per square mile
Total area: 5.00 sq. miles
Elevation: 250'
Distance from:
Boston: 42
Worcester: 24
Highways: Rtes. 122, 146.
Rail: The Providence & Worcester Railroad has a mail line through Millville.
Airport: Scheduled passenger flight service is available from airports in Worcester and Providence.
Tax Rate: $17.45 per thousand (1994, Mass. Div. of Local Services)
Median House Price: $114,900 (1993, County Data Corporation)
Median Household Income: $40,154 (1990 Census)
% of state average: 108.7%
Per Capita Income: $15,125
% of state average 87.8%
Form of Government: Board of Selectmen, Executive Secretary, open town meeting
Municipal Offices: (508) 883-8433
Services: Mass. Electric Co., Commonwealth Gas Co., no town sewer, ground water.
Nearest Hospital: Landmark, Woonsocket, R.I.
Registered Voters: 1,344
Legislative Districts:
U.S. Congress: 2nd District: Richard E. Neal (D)
State Senate: Worcester & Norfolk District: Louis P. Bertonazzi (D)
State Representative: 8th Worcester: Paul Kajawski (D)
Public Schools
Blackstone Millville: Longfellow (K-06); John F. Kennedy (K-03); A F Maloney (04-06); Blackstone Millville (07-12)
Blackstone Valley: Blackstone Valley VocTech (09-12)
Superintendent: Aldo Cecchi: (508) 883-6633
School Choice: No

Per Pupil Cost:
(State Exec. Office of Education -1992-93)
Millville $4,466
State average $5,023
Average Teacher Salary:
(State Exec. Office of Education-1992-93)

Millville	statewide
$37,597	$38,774

Mean SAT scores 1993

	(reported by town)	State Mean
Math	412	
Verbal	484	
Combined:	896	903

Student Population (Dept. of Education)
Total students 1991-92: 478
at public schools 97.1%
at private schools 2.9%
Educational Attainment (1990 census)
High School graduate or higher 75.9%
Bachelor's Degree or higher 15.2%
Largest Employers: (supplied by community, 1993)

	# of employees
Millville Elementary School	38
Town of Millville	6
U.S. Post Office	4

Commuting to Work (1990 Census)
Average time to work (mins.) 29.9
Houses of Worship: 1 Catholic, 1 Episcopal, 1 Baptist
Crime Rate: not available
Libraries:
Millville Free Public Library
State Register of Historic Places 1993:
Chestnut Hill Meeting House

New Braintree

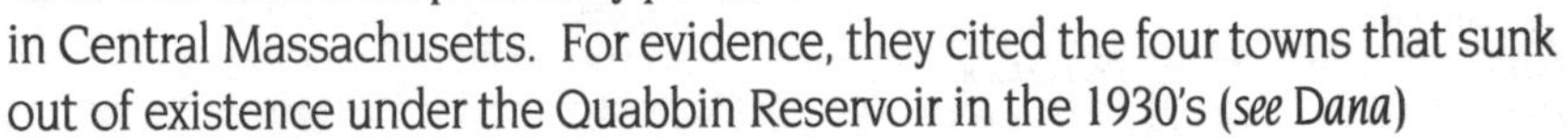

The Little Town That Said "No!"

When New Braintree's Pioneer Valley Academy closed here, it wasn't long before the Boston power brokers cast their eyes toward this tiny town, with only 539 registered voters, and deemed it a perfect place for a prison. Some said this was a familiar pattern for Boston — looking west to solve its problems with land from politically powerless towns in Central Massachusetts. For evidence, they cited the four towns that sunk out of existence under the Quabbin Reservoir in the 1930's (*see Dana*)

The state didn't expect a fight from New Braintree, but they got one. Contending that a huge prison in such a small town would permanently alter its rural character, town residents banded together to form "Conserve Our Small Town," or COST.

They proved to be relentless opponents. Even as the state's machinery inched forward toward a prison opening, COST hung on tenaciously, pleading their case in the press, and making many trips to the State House. At the last minute, the state blinked, and put a police training academy here instead of a prison. Traffic has increased, with "cruisers coming from all over the state and other states for in-service training," said Town Clerk Carolyn Glidden. But some feel it's a more suitable alternative.

New Braintree has been agricultural all its life, shipping dairy products, cheese and beef to Boston beginning in the 1700's. Today, it's losing its dairy farms, but is staying rural through strict zoning. With no town water or sewer, the town requires over 3 acres per house lot. With all the open space, it's no wonder that the "Champion Oak," New England's largest white oak, estimated to be 374 years old, thrives in a field located off Bridge Rd. in the southwest section of New Braintree. It is reported to be more than 97' high, with a 99' spread and a circumference of 21'5".

According to Glidden, there's a population boom underway - by New Braintree standards, anyway — the town has recently grown by 42 people. "Our children are coming back and building, and they're bringing their children. We're quite proud of this." The town must build a new elementary school to handle the growth. "But that's O.K.," said Glidden. "We're putting it right next to our new town hall and our brand new library."

***Sources:** Commonwealth of Mass. EOCD Community Profile; Town Clerk Carolyn Glidden. The Worcester Telegram & Gazette.*

Year incorporated: 1751
Population: 881 (1990 census)
Density: 43 per square mile
Total area: 20.05 sq. miles
Elevation: 945'
Distance from:
- Boston: 53
- Worcester: 14
- Providence: 75
- Hartford: 65
- Springfield 50

Highways: Rte. 67.

Airport: The Tanner-Hiller Airport, a privately owned public access facility.

Tax Rate: $13.02 per thousand (1994, Mass. Div. of Local Services)

Median House Price: $116,000 (1993, County Data Corporation)

Median Household Income: $43,214 (1990 Census)
- % of state average: 116.9%
- Per Capita Income: $15,409
- % of state average 89.5%

Form of Government: Board of Selectmen, Executive Secretary, open town meeting

Municipal Offices: (508) 867-2071

Services: Mass. Electric, no natural gas, no town sewer, ground water.

Nearest Hospital: Mary Lane Hospital, Ware, MA.

Registered Voters 539

Legislative Districts:

U.S. Congress: 1st District: John W. Olver (D)

State Senate: Worcester, Franklin, Hampden and Hampshire. Robert E. Wetmore (D)

State Representative: 5th Worcester: Stephen M. Brewer (D)

Public Schools

Quabbin: Hardwick Elem (01-06); Hubbardston Center (K-06); New Braintree Grade (K-06); Oakham Center (K-06); Ruggles Lane (K-06); Quabbin Regional Jr Sr (07-12)

Pathfinder: Pathfinder Voc Tech (09-13)

Superintendent: Maureen Marshall (508) 355-4668

School Choice: Yes

Colleges and Universities:
Mass. State Police Training Academy

Per Pupil Cost: (State Exec. Office of Education 1992-93)
- New Braintree $4,080
- State average $5,023

Average Teacher Salary:
(State Exec. Office of Education-1992-3)

New Braintree	statewide
$31,577	$38,774

Mean SAT scores 1993 (reported by town)
- Math 459
- Verbal 430
- Combined: 889 State Mean: 903

Student Population (Dept. of Education)
- Total students 1991-92: 179
- at public schools 95.5%
- at private schools 4.5%

Educational Attainment (1990 census)
- High School graduate or higher 76.7%
- Bachelor's Degree or higher 13.0%

Commuting to Work (1990 Census)
- Average time to work (mins.) 28.4

Houses of Worship: Congregational Church (Tri-Parish with Hardwick and Gilbertville)

Crime Rate: not available

Libraries
New Braintree Public Library - Leroy Pollard Memorial Library

North Brookfield

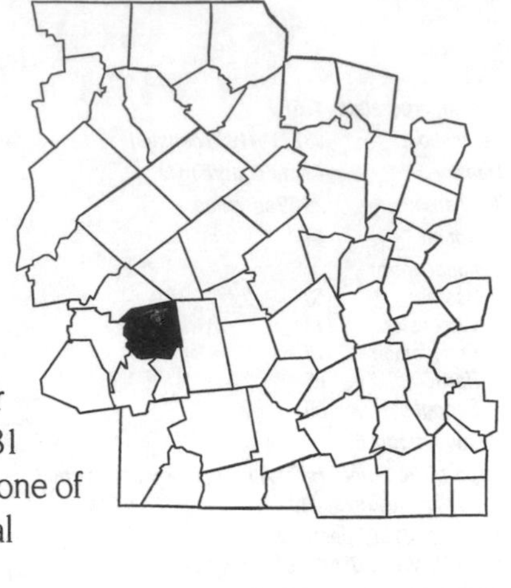

The "Rolling Stones" Gathered Here

Old timers remember that North Brookfield was once home to the world's largest shoe manufacturer, but rock music fans know it as the place where Mick Jagger and The Rolling Stones rehearsed their 1981 tour. The band stayed at Long View Farm, one of the country's few state-of-the-art residential recording studios.

Long View has hosted artists such as Arlo Guthrie, Aerosmith, Stevie Wonder, Dan Fogelberg, Cat Stevens and the Paul Winter Consort. The names of who is recording is never news until after the fact, since Long View strictly protects the privacy of the musicians. The farm has a 24-track recording studio in the house, and another in the 90-year old barn, along with a six foot high stage built especially for the Stones. Known as a recording resort for rock stars, it offers private guest rooms, full kitchen, Jacuzzi, sauna, and workout areas, all on a 100-acre farm. North Brookfield's other claim to fame is the Quabaug Corporation, the only North American maker of the super-durable Vibram soles used by a variety of footwear companies. Recently named "Supplier of the Year" by the industry "Bible," Footwear News, Quabaug is getting raves for its new "Ecostep" sole, which is made from 30% pre-consumer scrap.

"Yankee Doodle Dandy" George M. Cohan used to visit his grandparents in North Brookfield, and he played town hall with his Broadway hit, "Ah! Wilderness." Although baseball Hall of Famer Connie Mack was born next door (*see East Brookfield*), he also lived here. Locals remember that when he brought his Philadelphia Athletics to play an exhibition game against the Quabaug Rubber Company team, the Quabaug team won! (*For more on the excellence of mill league baseball, see* Millville).

During the 1770's smallpox epidemics, Drs. Thomas and Kittredge of North Attleborough used North Brookfield as a base for their experimental vaccine inoculations, and people came from as far away as Worcester for treatment.

Sources: Worcester Magazine; The Worcester Telegram & Gazette; Commonwealth of Mass. EOCD Community Profile; More Massachusetts Towns, Ivan Sandrof, Barre Publishers, 1965.

Year incorporated: 1812
Population: 4,708 (1990 census)
Density: 224 per square mile
Total area: 21.72 sq. miles
Elevation: 915'
Distance from:
Boston: 57
Worcester: 18
Springfield 38
Highways: Rtes. 9 running E-W, and 67 running N-S.
Airport: The Worcester Municipal Airport
Tax Rate: $11.22 per thousand (1994, Mass. Div. of Local Services)
Median House Price: $104,500 (1993, County Data Corporation)
Median Household Income: $31,868 (1990 Census)
% of state average: 86.2%
Per Capita Income: $13,710
% of state average 79.6 %
Form of Government: Board of Selectmen, Administrative Assistant, open town meeting
Municipal Offices: (508) 867-0200
Services: Mass. Electric Co., Boston Gas Co., town sewer, surface water.
Nearest Hospital: Mary Lane Hospital, Ware, MA.
Registered Voters: 2,653
Legislative Districts:
U.S. Congress: 1st District: John W. Olver (D)
State Senate: Worcester, Franklin, Hampden and Hampshire: Robert E. Wetmore (D)
State Representative: 5th Worcester: Stephen M. Brewer (D)
Public Schools
North Brookfield: North Brookfield Elem (K-06); North Brookfield High (07-12)
Superintendent: William S. Leach (508) 867-9821
School Choice: Yes

Per Pupil Cost:
(State Exec. Office of Education -1992-93),
North Brookfield $3,418
State average $5.023
Average Teacher Salary:
(State Exec. Office of Education-1992-93)

North Brookfield	statewide
$28,062	$38,774

Mean SAT scores 1993

	(reported by town)	State Mean
Math	484	
Verbal	449	
Combined:	933	903

Student Population (Dept. of Education)
Total students 1991-92: 880
at public schools 96.3%
at private schools 3.8%
Educational Attainment (1990 census)
High School graduate or higher 82.6%
Bachelor's Degree or higher 12.6%
Largest Employers: (supplied by community, 1993)

	# of employees
Quabaug Corporation	250
Victory Supermarket	50
Chase Precast	50
North Brookfield Savings Bank	20
Optovac	20

Commuting to Work (1990 Census)
Average time to work (mins.) 27.7
Houses of Worship: 4
Crime Rate: not available
Libraries
Haston Free Public Library
State Register of Historic Places 1993:
Camp Atwater
Matthews Fulling Mill Site

NORTH BROOKFIELD

Northborough

Good Roads, Good Schools

For over 200 years, Northborough has been known for its excellence in two things: transportation access and public school support. Situated along the Upper Boston Post Road, Northborough was an early stagecoach stop on the route to Hartford as far back as 1783, when the fare was four pence a mile, or $10 for the trip. The town's first school committee reported in 1825, "...no portion of the public taxes is more cheerfully paid than that which is devoted to the education of youth."

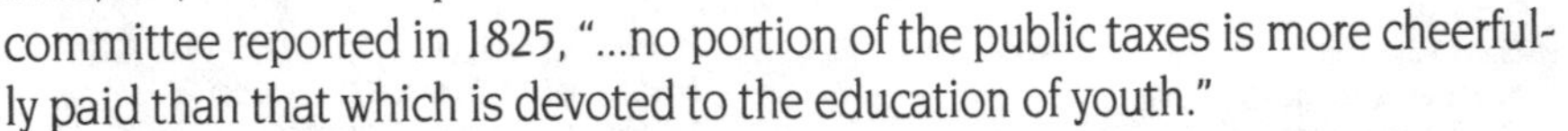

By 1866, the reputation of the schools had traveled east, and the Boston Herald wrote that Northborough "is noted for its interest in public schools." To cope with the post-war population explosion, a "temporary" school housing committee was formed in 1946, but became a permanent fixture for 20 years, planning and building new schools as the town's population tripled.

The early stagecoach routes developed into highways, and today Northborough's commuters can choose between Rtes. 9, 20, I-290 and I-495 to get to Worcester, Boston, Framingham, Providence and points beyond. Many work in the high tech corridor along 495, or in Northborough's own industrial park off 290.

Despite the highways and the town's streetcar link to Worcester and Marlborough beginning at the turn of the century, Northborough retained its small town spirit. For each returning veteran of WWI, the town's fire alarm would blast eight strokes twice, signaling all church bells in town to ring a welcome.

Although Northborough has had its share of successful politicians, teachers and ministers, two local citizens achieved fame elsewhere. The first Texan to yell, "Remember the Alamo!" at the battle of San Jacinto actually grew up in Northborough - Gen. Sidney Sherman. And the founder of what is now George Washington University in Washington, D.C. was Luther Rice, a Baptist missionary born in Northborough in 1783.

Sources: Commonwealth of Mass. EOCD Community Profile; The Boston Globe; The Old Post Road, The Story of the Boston Post Road, Stewart H. Holbrook, McGraw-Hill Book Company, Inc., 1962; Northborough: A Town and Its People, 1638-1975, William H. Mulligan, Jr., Northborough American Revolution Bicentennial Commission, 1982; The Westboro/Northboro Guide, 1994, The Worcester Telegram & Gazette and The Westborough Northborough Area Chamber of Commerce.

Year incorporated: 1775
Population: 12,704 (1994, town census)
Density: 643 per square mile
Total area: 18.76 sq. miles
Elevation: 300'
Distance from:
Boston: 30
Worcester: 10

Highways: U.S. Rte. 20, Interstate 290, 495, 90, and State Rte. 9 and 135.

Rail: Conrail provides freight service to Northborough.

Bus: Northborough is a member of the Worcester Regional Transit Authority.

Airport: The Worcester Municipal Airport, a primary commercial facility.

Tax Rate: $15.97 per thousand (1994, Mass. Div. of Local Services)

Median House Price: $178,000 (1993, County Data Corporation)

Median Household Income: $57,963 (1990 Census)
% of state average: 156.9%
Per Capita Income: $22,795
% of state average 132.3%

Form of Government: Board of Selectmen, Town Administrator, open town meeting
Municipal Offices: (508) 393-5001

Services: Mass. Electric, Commonwealth Gas Co., town sewer, ground water.

Nearest Hospital: several in Worcester

Registered Voters 7,231

Legislative Districts:

U.S. Congress: 3rd District: Peter I. Blute (R)

State Senate: Worcester & Middlesex: Robert A. Durand (D)

State Representative: 12th Worcester Pct. 1 & 2: Harold Naughton (D)

4th Middlesex Pct. 3: Daniel J. Valianti (D)

Public Schools

Northborough: Lincoln Street (K-04); Marguerite E Peaslee (K-04); Fannie E Proctor (K-04); Northborough Middle (05-08)

Northborough/Southborough: Algonquin Reg High (09-12)

Assabet Valley: Assabet Valley Voc H S (09-13)

Superintendent: Dennis M. DiSalvo (508) 351-7000

School Choice: No

Per Pupil Cost: (State Exec. Office of Education - 1992-93)
Northborogh $4,264
State average $5,023

Average Teacher Salary: (State Exec. Office of Education-1992-93)
Primary $43,746
Secondary $44,558
Statewide $38,774

Mean SAT scores 1993 (reported by town)
Math 530
Verbal 463
Combined: 993 State Mean: 903

Student Population (Dept. of Education)
Total students 1991-92: 2,320
at public schools 93.9%
at private schools 6.1%

Educational Attainment (1990 census)
High School graduate or higher 89.7%
Bachelor's Degree or higher 38.9%

Largest Employers: (supplied by community, 1993)
# of employees
Norton Company 250
Nippon Electronics Corporation 205
Digital Equipment Corporation 200
Thornton Nursing Home 100

Commuting to Work (1990 Census)
Average time to work (mins.) 22.7

Houses of Worship: all denominations

Crime Rate: (1993, Mass. State Police Crime Reporting Unit)

	town	statewide
Total crimes reported:	191	
rate per 1,000 persons	16.01	37.46
Violent crimes	26	
rate per 1,000 persons	2.18	5.65
Property crimes	165	
rate per 1,000 persons	13.83	31.83

Libraries Northborough Free Library
Museums Northborough Historical Society

State Register of Historic Places 1993:
Meeting House Common Historic District
Milestone, 1767
Town Hall
Wachusett Aqueduct Linear District
Water Supply System of Metropolitan Boston

NORTHBOROUGH

Northbridge

What? Not Whitinsville?

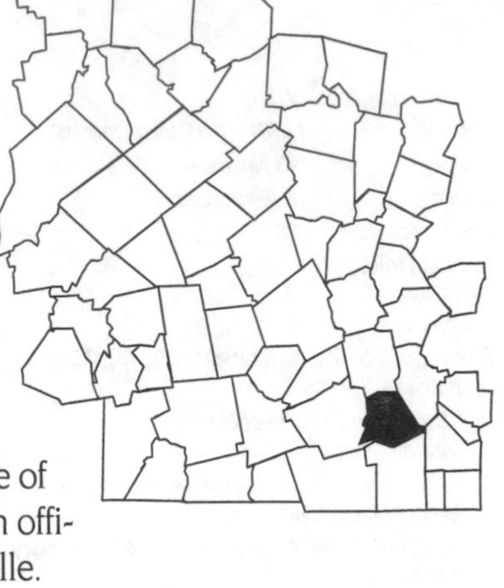

Even the very name of Northbridge was eclipsed by the fame of the Whitin Machine Works, a leading manufacturer of textile machinery based here. At one time the four Whitin brothers each headed a mill in the town's four villages - Rockdale, Riverdale, Linwood and Whitinsville, which was the site of the main mill and the town hall. Today, even official town mail is still addressed to Whitinsville.

The Whitin empire began in 1831 when John Whitin patented a machine to pluck seeds and dirt from raw cotton. By 1940, the firm was a world leader in textile machinery, employing 5,000 people. Closed in 1967, the buildings now offer incubator space for small business development.

Like the Drapers in Hopedale, the Whitins built a self-contained company town, and were, by most accounts, benevolent bosses who didn't even lay off workers during the Depression. The family built the Whitin Community Center in 1923, which today offers swimming, sports, concerts and other family activities. All company housing was meticulously maintained by the Whitins, including the changing of light bulbs. "Climbing the corporate ladder" in Whitinsville meant moving from standard mill worker housing without porches on A Street, up to increasingly more refined company homes on B,C, and D Streets.

Northbridge, like Hopedale, has had to make the tough transition from a company-supported town to one that stands on its own. Its location between Worcester and Providence makes it ideal for commuters, a situation which will improve with the completion of the Rte. 146 highway upgrade to Worcester and connection to the Mass. Pike. The town is part of the Blackstone Valley Heritage Corridor, and architecture preserved from its heyday in the 1800's offers a fascinating look back.

Sources: The Boston Globe; Commonwealth of Mass. EOCD Community Profile; The Worcester Telegram; A Guide to the Heritage of Worcester County, Simone E. Blake, Montachusett Girl Scout Council, 1973.

Year incorporated: 1772
Population: 13,371 (1990 census)
Density: 778 per square mile
Total area: 18.06 sq. miles
Elevation: 300'
Distance from:
Boston: 38
Worcester: 13
Providence: 25
Hartford: 72
Springfield 60
Highways: Rtes. 122 and 146
Rail: The Providence & Worcester Railroad provides freight rail service to Northbridge.
Airport: The Worcester Municipal Airport, and Green Airport, Providence, R.I.
Tax Rate: $12.18 per thousand (1994, Mass. Div. of Local Services)
Median House Price: $119,250 (1993, County Data Corporation)
Median Household Income: $36,634 (1990 Census)
% of state average: 99.1%
Per Capita Income: $14,159
% of state average 82.2%
Form of Government: Board of Selectmen, Town Manager, open town meeting
Municipal Offices: (508) 234-2095
Services: Mass. Electric Co., Commonwealth Gas Co., town sewer, purchased water.
Nearest Hospital: Milford Hospital
Registered Voters: 7,461
Legislative Districts:
U.S. Congress: 3rd District: Peter I. Blute (R)
State Senate: Worcester & Norfolk District: Louis P. Bertonazzi (D)
State Representative: 9th Worcester: George N. Peterson, Jr. (R)
Public Schools
Northbridge: W. Edward Balmer (03-06); Aldrich (-K): Northbridge Primary (K-02); Northbridge Jr-Sr High (07-12)
Superintendent: Henry O'Donnell: (508) 234-8156
Blackstone Valley: Blackstone Valley Voc Tech (09-12)
School Choice: Yes
Per Pupil Cost: (State Exec. Office of Education -1992-93)
Northbridge: $3,632
State average: $5,023
Average Teacher Salary: (State Exec. Office of Education-1992-93)

Northbridge	statewide
$37,885	$38,774

Mean SAT scores 1993 (reported by town)
Math 463
Verbal 421
Combined: 884 State Mean: 903
Student Population (Dept. of Education)
Total students 1991-92: 2,276
at public schools 89.5%
at private schools 10.5%

Educational Attainment (1990 census)
High School graduate or higher 74.3%
Bachelor's Degree or higher 15.4%
Largest Employers: (supplied by community, 1993)

	# of employees
Town of Northbridge	655
Alternatives Unlimited	250
Beaumont Nursing Home	250
Coz Chemical	120
Northbridge Nursing Home	120
Riverdale Industries	115
Duracraft	80

Commuting to Work (1990 Census)
Average time to work (mins.) 24.1
Houses of Worship: 12
Crime Rate: (Office of Public Safety, 1992)

	town	statewide
Total crimes reported:	322	
rate per 1,000 persons	24.08	37.46
Violent crimes	94	
rate per 1,000 persons	7.03	5.65
Property crimes	228	
rate per 1,000 persons	17.05	31.83

Libraries
Whitinsville Social Library
State Register of Historic Places 1993:
Blackstone Canal Historic District
Linwood Mill Historic District
Rockdale Common Housing District
U. S. Post Office - Whitinsville Branch
Whitinsville Mill and Forge
Whitinsville Old Cotton Mill

Oakham

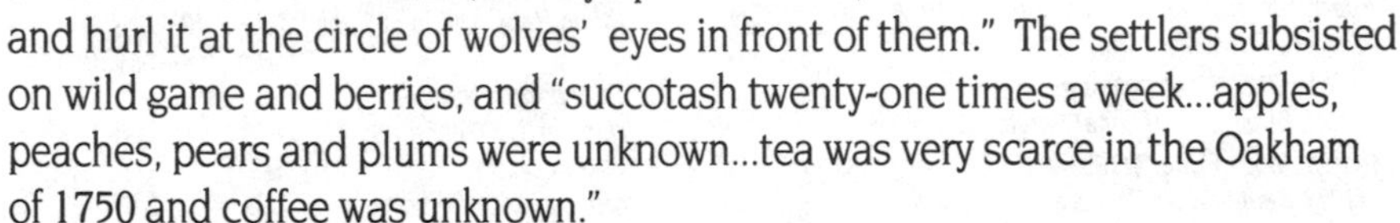

"No Pale Pink Tea Party"

Settling Oakham in 1750 was "no pale pink tea party," according historians H.B. Wright and E.D. Harvey. Faced with felling gigantic trees in a virgin forest, the first Scotch-Irish immigrants also worried about wolves. "...One major sport of boys in the dark winter evenings in Oakham was for them to seize a live coal from the hearth, swiftly open the door, and hurl it at the circle of wolves' eyes in front of them." The settlers subsisted on wild game and berries, and "succotash twenty-one times a week...apples, peaches, pears and plums were unknown...tea was very scarce in the Oakham of 1750 and coffee was unknown."

Oakham was originally "Rutland West Wing," and some hardy settlers were attracted by "good, cheap land in the Wing," but others were given no choice. "Cotton Mather was still a power in the land. He wined and dined the affluent...His influence kept the rich among them permanently in Boston, to the enrichment of its civic life. His equally effective measures sped the poorer artisans on to ...Middleboro, Taunton, Worcester and Rutland."

In early Oakham as elsewhere, inns were the center of town life and inn-keepers were "honored men who stood for the best standards of public manners and morals." In those pre-temperance days, rum, mulled wine or warm "flip" flowed at every social occasion. Indeed, "the bill for 'likker' exceeded the rest of the expenses at the ordination of the first two Oakham ministers."

Today, Oakham protects its rural character with zoning requiring three acres per house lot. The town still has no traffic lights and offers lots of open space - some 30% of its area is watershed protection land. Despite no major roads through town, the population has increased to some 1,600 people. "We were 500 people for a long, long time," observed Town Librarian Maude Stone. "We're really not that far way from Worcester, it only takes half an hour. People come here to get away from all the hubbub."

Sources: The Settlement and Story of Oakham, Massachusettts, H.B. Wright and E.D. Harvey, Ernest L. Hayward, New Haven, CT, 1947; Town Librarian Maude Stone.

Year incorporated: 1762
Population: 1,658 (1994 town census)
Density: 71 per square mile
Total area: 21.53 sq. miles
Elevation: 1,050'
Distance from:
Boston: 56
Worcester: 18
Highways: Rtes. 148 and 122.
Airport: The Worcester Municipal Airport, a primary commercial facility.
Tax Rate: $10.84 per thousand (1994, Mass. Div. of Local Services)
Median House Price: $120,000 (1993, County Data Corporation)
Median Household Income: $41,295 (1990 Census)
% of state average: 111.8%
Per Capita Income: $15,162
% of state average 88.0%
Form of Government: Board of Selectmen, Administrative Assistant, open town meeting
Municipal Offices: (508) 882-5549
Services: Mass. Electric Co., no natural gas, no town sewer, ground or purchased water.
Nearest Hospital: several in Worcester
Registered Voters: 948
Legislative Districts:
U.S. Congress: 1st District: John W. Olver (D)
State Senate: Worcester, Franklin, Hampden and Hampshire: Robert E. Wetmore (D)
State Representative: 5th Worcester: Stephen M. Brewer (D)
Public Schools
Quabbin: Hardwick Elem (01-06); Hubbardston Center (K-06); New Braintree Grade (K-06); Oakham Center (K-06); Ruggles Lane (K-06); Quabbin Regional Jr Sr (07-12)
Superintendent: Maureen Marshall (508) 355-4668
School Choice: Yes

Per Pupil Cost: (State Exec. Office of Education -1992-93)
Oakham $4,080
State average $5,023
Average Teacher Salary:
(State Exec. Office of Education-1992-93)

	Oakham	statewide
	$31,557	$38,774

Mean SAT scores 1993 (reported by town)
Math 459
Verbal 430
Combined: 889 State Mean: 903
Student Population (Dept. of Education)
Total students 1991-92: 346
at public schools 98.0%
at private schools 2.0%
Educational Attainment (1990 census)
High School graduate or higher 84.3%
Bachelor's Degree or higher 23.2%
Commuting to Work (1990 Census)
Average time to work (mins.) 31.0
Houses of Worship: 1
Crime Rate: not available
Libraries: Forbes Memorial Library

Oxford

The Angel of the Battlefield and Religious Freedom

From the French Huguenot settlers in 1687 to the Universalists 100 years later, Oxford has a long history of religious freedom. Even today, this town has 12 churches, quite a lot for a community of only 12,000 people. The Protestant Huguenots chose to immigrate here rather than convert to Catholicism as required under Louis XIV. The foundation of their French fort on Fort Hill Road is visible today.

The liberal Universalists believed that all souls would be saved, and that there was no hell. The church they built in Oxford in 1793 is the oldest standing Universalist building in the world, and the movement's leader, Hosea Ballou, the "apostle of Universalism" was ordained here.

One famous member of this church was Clara Barton, founder of the American Red Cross who was known as "the angel of the battlefield" for tending wounded soldiers on the Civil War's front lines. Clara was born in 1821 in a North Oxford farmhouse that is now the Clara Barton Birthplace Museum. Interestingly, she never trained as a nurse, but got experience tending her brother, who was bedridden after a fall from the barn roof. The museum display includes her field desk, on which she wrote letters for soldiers, and a quilt with 27 blocks signed by Civil War officers.

Oxford was home to another medical legend - Dr. Elliot P. Joslin, a leader in diabetes treatment who founded the famed Joslin Clinic in Boston. He also founded a Diabetic Camp for girls on the site of the Clara Barton birthplace. Both Dr. Joslin and Clara Barton are buried in Oxford's north cemetery on Rte. 12 beyond the center.

Today Oxford's residents enjoy easy access to Worcester, a 15 minute trip along Rte. 395, which runs through town. Travel time to Boston, Springfield and Providence is about 50 minutes each.

Sources: Commonwealth of Mass. EOCD Community Profile; The Boston Globe; A Guide to the Heritage of Worcester County, Simone E. Blake, Montachusett Girl Scout Council, 1973; Massachusetts, Off the Beaten Path, A Guide to Unique Places, Patricia Mandell, The Globe Pequot Press, 1992; Historical Markers of the Massachusetts Bay Colony, Samuel Eliot Morison, The Commonwealth of Massachusetts, 1930; American Academic Encyclopedia.

Year incorporated: 1713
Population: 12,214 (1994 town census)
Density: 473 per square mile
Total area: 27.51 sq. miles
Elevation: 510'
Distance from:
Boston: 51
Worcester: 14
Providence: 37

Highways: Interstate Rte. 90, 395, 95, U.S. Rte. 20, and State Rtes. 12 and 56.

Rail: Freight rail service is available on the Providence & Worcester Railroad.

Bus: The Worcester Regional Transit Authority provides fixed route service between Oxford, Webster, Worcester, and Auburn.

Airport: The Oxford Airport is a privately owned public use facility.

Tax Rate: $14.19 per thousand (1995, town))

Median House Price: $112,900 (1993, County Data Corporation)

Median Household Income: $36,682 (1990 Census)
% of state average: 99.3%
Per Capita Income: $14,337
% of state average 83.2%

Form of Government: Board of Selectmen, Town Manager, Open Town Meeting

Municipal Offices: (508) 987-6032

Services: Mass. Electric Co., no natural gas, no town sewer, ground water.

Nearest Hospital: Harrington Memorial Hospital

Registered Voters: 6,651

Legislative Districts:

U.S. Congress: 2nd District: Richard E. Neal (D)

State Senate: Worcester & Norfolk District: Louis P. Bertonazzi (D)

State Representative: 7th Worcester: Paul Kollios (D)

Public Schools

Oxford: Clara Barton (K-03); Alfred M Chaffee (01-03); Allen Joslin (04-05); Oxford Middle (06-07); Oxford High (08-12)

Southern Worcester County: Bay Path Reg Voc Tech H S (09-12)

Superintendent: Dr. Francis Driscoll (508) 987-6050

School Choice: No

Colleges and Universities: none

Per Pupil Cost: (State Exec. Office of Education-1992-93)
Oxford $3,664
State average $5,023

Average Teacher Salary:
(State Exec. Office of Education-1992-93)

Oxford	statewide
$38,509	$38,774

Mean SAT scores 1993 (reported by town)
Math 442
Verbal 400
Combined: 842 State Mean: 903

Student Population (Dept. of Education)
Total students 1991-92: 2,457
at public schools 90.7%
at private schools 9.3%

Educational Attainment (1990 census)
High School graduate or higher 75.4%
Bachelor's Degree or higher 15.5%

Largest Employers: (supplied by community, 1993)

	# of employees
Town of Oxford	644
Leggett & Platt	300

Commuting to Work (1990 Census)
Average time to work (mins.) 21.7

Houses of Worship: all denominations except synagogue

Crime Rate: (1993, Mass. State Police Crime Reporting Unit)

	town	statewide
Total crimes reported:	307	
rate per 1,000 persons	24.39	37.46
Violent crimes	58	
rate per 1,000 persons	4.61	5.65
Property crimes	249	
rate per 1,000 persons	19.78	31.83

Libraries
Oxford Free Public Library

Museums
Clara Barton Birthplace
Oxford Library Museum

State Register of Historic Places 1993:
Clara Barton Birthplace
15 Charlton Street
Capt. Alijah Davis House
William Hudson House
Huguenot Fort
Allen L. Joslin House
Benjamin Paine House
William H Thurston - Chad B. Carey House

Paxton

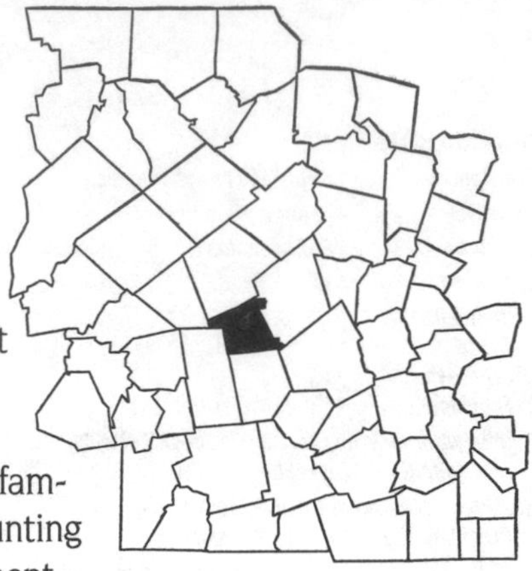

Moore State Park, a Botanical and Archaelogical Treasure

The jewel in Paxton's crown is Moore State Park. With over 600 acres on Rte. 31, it is not one the largest state parks,but it is certainly one of the most beautiful. Once the private country estate of the Spaulding family, the park was used by the Nipmucs as hunting and fishing grounds before colonial settlement. Turkey Hill Brook drops 90' through a steep rocky gorge, so it was a natural choice for Paxton's first mills.

Today, visitors can tour the site of the Eames Sawmill and Mill Village complex with stonework, waterfalls, gardens, stage roads and old foundations. Archaeological experts at Old Sturbridge Village have termed the area, "a potential textbook study of the development of the rural mill village." Locals rave about the peace and quiet and the pristine beauty of the park, especially when the the azaleas and rhododendrons bloom in the spring.

Paxton was a busy stop on the stage coach line from Worcester to Barre and points beyond. An old story tells of a drunken sailor who rode the stage into town, saw bare tree trunks at Bottomley's Pond and thought they were ship-masts. Dubbed the Paxton Navy Yard, the spot later became an amusement area with a miniature train, motorized battleship, restaurant and animal farm. It's now the site of the Paxton Sports Center.

The route into Paxton is lined with many lovely antique homes. The picturesque town common is guarded by the the Congregational Church, the Paxton Inn and the town hall, as it has been for generations. In recent years, the community worked together to build a creative wooden playground at the Center School, designed to the group's specifications by prominent architect Robert Leathers. The Paxton Recreation Commission's summer program provides both organized activities for younger children, and summer jobs as counselors for the town's teen-agers. The town is also home to Anna Maria College, with 775 undergraduates and 1,100 graduate students.

Sources: Commonwealth of Mass. EOCD Community Profile; "Experience Paxton," The Landmark, 1994; Massachusetts Towns, An 1840 View, Ivan Sandrof, Barre Publishers, 1963; The Worcester Telegram & Gazette, Town Historians Edward Duane, Denis Melican.

Year incorporated: 1765
Population: 4,047 (1990 census)
Density: 275 per square mile
Total area: 15.48 sq. miles
Elevation: 1,134'
Distance from:
Boston: 48
Worcester: 9
Highways: Rtes. 31, 56, and 122.
Rail: Passenger rail service to Boston, Providence, Springfield, and all other points on Amtrak available through neighboring Worcester.
Airport: The Worcester Municipal Airport
Tax Rate: $13.85 per thousand (1994, Mass. Div. of Local Services)
Median House Price: $146,000 (1993, County Data Corporation)
Median Household Income: $49, 176 (1990 Census)
% of state average: 133.1%
Per Capita Income: $20,893
% of state average 121.3%
Form of Government: Board of Selectmen, open town meeting,
Municipal Offices: (508) 753-2803
Services: Paxton Municipal Electric, no natural gas, no town sewer, surface water.
Nearest Hospital: several in Worcester
Registered Voters : 2,587
Legislative Districts:
U.S. Congress: 3rd Congressional District: Peter Blute (R)
State Senate: Worcester-Franklin-Hampden & Hampshire District: Robert Wetmore(D)
State Representative: 13th Worcester, Ward 1, Ward 9: Harriette L. Chandler (D)
Public Schools
Paxton: Paxton Center School (K-08)
Wachusett: Wachusett Regional High (09-12)
Wachusett Regional School District- Superintendent Alfred D. Tutela (508) 829-6631
School Choice: No
Colleges and Universities: Anna Maria College
Per Pupil Cost: (State Exec. Office of Education -1992-93)
Paxton Primary $5,023
Secondary $6,374
Average Teacher Salary:
(State Exec. Office of Education-1992-93)
Primary $37,989
Secondary $40,951
Statewide $38,774
Mean SAT scores 1993:

		State Mean
Math	488	
Verbal	434	
Combined:	922	903

Student Population (Dept. of Education)
Total students 1991-92: 677
at public schools 88.8%
at private schools 11.2%

Educational Attainment (1990 census)
High School graduate or higher 91.9%
Bachelor's Degree or higher 35.0%
Largest Employers: (supplied by community, 1993)

	# of employees
Town of Paxton	300
Anna Maria College`	100
Paxton School	36
Forefathers Restaurant	30
Conte Insurance	6

Commuting to Work (1990 Census)
Average time to work (mins.) 25.0
Houses of Worship: 1 Catholic, 1 Congregational
Crime Rate: not available
Libraries:
Richards Memorial Library
Museums:
Moll Art Center, Anna Maria College

Petersham

The "Forest Primeval"

Go to Petersham and you'll see both historic architecture and primeval forest, home to old growth trees, deer, coyotes, bald eagles, and more. The town's regal common is surrounded by elegant Victorian and Greek Revial buildings on the National Register of Historic Places. Petersham is also home to several forest and woodland preserves, and is located next to the Quabbin Reservoir 30 miles north of Worcester.

With its old-growth trees, The Brooks Woodland Preserve is an example of "the forest primeval," and is being developed to show what forests looked like when European settlers first landed. The Fisher Museum of Forestry, owned by Harvard University, houses famous dioramas showing woodland changes brought on by farming, abandonment, erosion and reforestation. As a precaution against bombing in WWII, Harvard hid art treasures by Whistler, Gainsborough and Copley at its Petersham facilities.

Petersham (*pronounced* Peter's HAM), is known as the spot where the famous Shays Rebellion ended. Under Daniel Shays, area farmers rallied to protest taxes and government farm foreclosures. After marching all night during a snowstorm, the state militia captured the Shays band in Petersham on Feb.4, 1787. The rebels had come from Springfield where they attacked the armory for supplies (*see Hubbardston*). The rebellion symbolized the new government's determination to maintain control, and the mistrust of Boston-based government by farmers in central and western Massachusetts.

Petersham was first called by its Nipmuc name, Nichewaug, and later was named Volunteers Town after the volunteer soldiers who won land grants and settled here in 1733. The name Petersham was apparently assigned by officials in Boston. It has the third largest land area in the state, and is one of the highest towns in Worcester County, with views of Mt. Wachusett, Mt. Monadnock, Mt. Grace in Warwick and the Berkshires in the west.

It was on the Quabbin Reservoir in Petersham where a small funnel began in 1953, growing into a deadly tornado as it traveled through Worcester and other towns, killing 94 people, destroying 4,000 homes and causing $53 million in damage. The tornado had the highest winds ever recorded (*see Holden*).

***Sources:** Commonwealth of Mass. Community Profile; North of the Quabbin, A. Young; The Worcester Telegram & Gazette; Worcester Magazine; Mass. Getaway Guide, Massachusetts Towns, I. Sandrof; The Boston Globe.*

Year incorporated: 1754
Total area: 54.24 square miles
Elevation: 1,070
Distance from:
Boston: 69 miles
Worcester: 30 miles
Highways; Rtes. 32, 101. Link to Rte. 2 is in nearby Athol
Bus: The Franklin Regional Transit Authority (FRTA), which provides services for the elderly and disabled through the Council on Aging.
Airport: Worcester Airport and the Orange Municipal Airport, a General Aviation facility.
Tax Rate: $10.26 per thousand (Mass. Dept. of Local Services, 1994)
Median House Price: $134,000 (1993, County Data Corporation)
Median Household Income: $ 39,063 (1990 Census)
% of state average: 105.7%
Per Capita Income: $17,542
% of state average 101.8%
Population: 1,131 (1990 census)
Density: 21 per square mile
Form of Government: Board of Selectmen, open town meeting
Municipal Offices: (508) 724-3353
Services: Mass. Electric, no sewer, no natural gas service.
Nearest Hospital: Athol Memorial
Registered Voters : 851 (Secretary of State 1992)
Legislative Districts:
U.S. Congress: 1st District: John W. Olver (D)
State Senate: Franklin-Hampden & Hampshire District: Robert Wetmore(D)
State Representative:1st Worcester; Rep. Hal Lane (D)
Public Schools

Petersham Center School	K-6
Ralph C. Mahar Regional	7-12
Montachusett Voc-tech	9-12

Superintendent:
Dr. Robert A. O'Meara (508) 724-3363;
Superintendent: Eileen Perkins (508) 544-2920
Mahar Regional H.S., Orange, MA.
School Choice: No

Per Pupil Cost:
(State Exec. Office of Education -1992-93)

primary	$5,758
secondary	$5,250
State average 1992-93	$5,023

Average Teacher Salary:
(State Exec. Office of Education-1992-93)

Petersham	statewide
$33,600	$38,774

Mean SAT scores 1993
Mahar Regional High School does not release SAT scores.
Student Population (Dept. of Education)

Total students 1991-92:	170
at public schools	92.9%
at private schools	7.1%

Educational Attainment (1990 census)

High School graduate or higher	89.9%
Bachelor's Degree or higher	38.9%

Largest Employers: (supplied by community, 1993)

	# of employees
Harvard Forest	50
Center School	23
Sisters of the Assumption,	18
The Country Store	11
Berry Engineering	7

Commuting to Work (1990 Census)
Average time to work (mins.) 25
Houses of Worship: 1 Congregational, 1 Catholic, 1 Unitarian
Crime Rate: not available
Libraries:
Petersham Memorial Library, Common St. (508) 724-3405
Museums:
Fisher Museum of Forestry, Athol Rd. (508) 724-3302
Petersham Historical Society, N. Main St. (508) 724-3380
State Register of Historic Places 1993:
Petersham Historic District - Common St.
Gay Farm, Gay Drive, South St. off Nichewaug Way
Holland-Towne House, Ward Hill Rd, off Rte. 32.

Phillipston

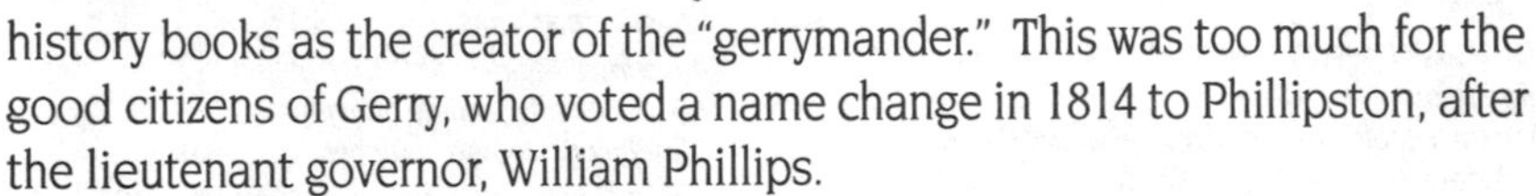

A Name Change and Queen Lake

Once upon a time, this town was called Gerry, Massachusetts, after Elbridge Gerry, a signer of the Declaration of Independence. However, as governor, Gerry supported a sneaky redistricting plan designed to weaken the voting power of his opponents. Drawn on the map, the districts resembled a salamander, and Gerry went into the history books as the creator of the "gerrymander." This was too much for the good citizens of Gerry, who voted a name change in 1814 to Phillipston, after the lieutenant governor, William Phillips.

Phillipston is a small town of steep hills and valleys, and a tiny town green. Although Rtes. 2, 2A and 101 carve through the town, none actually passes through its center. The town began when land grants were given to reward settlers who fought against native tribes in King Philip's War in 1675. Settlement began in 1733, and a road was cut to Athol, then called Pequoig, in 1751.

A fisherman from neighboring Barre was so enamored with Phillipston Pond that he wrote a poem, beginning "Oh, Queen of the Lakes among the hills..." The name stuck when a developer from Athol began using it in ads for summer cottages on the pond. Some years back, divers found on the bottom of the lake a portion of what is thought to be an ancient dugout canoe. The artifact is on display at Phillips Memorial Library.

One enterprising son of Phillipston was Thomas White, whose experiments with sewing machines led to the start of both the New Home Sewing Machine Co. in Orange, and the White Sewing Machine Co. in Cleveland, Ohio. Although Phillipston doesn't have traditional industry today, it is famous for the Baldwin Hill Bakery, which uses a wood-fired brick hearth oven to bake all-natural bread made of stone-ground whole wheat, sea salt and well water. The bakery distributes thousands of loaves per week throughout New England.

Sources: Commonwealth of Mass. EOCD Community Profile; North of the Quabbin, A. Young; Massachusetts Bicentennial Commemorative; The Guide to North Central Massachusetts; Worcester Magazine.

Year incorporated: As Gerry: 1786; as Phillipston: 1814

Population: (1990 census) 1,485

Density: 61 per square mile

Total area: 24.26

Elevation: 1,166'

Distance from:
- Boston: 65 miles
- Worcester: 30

Highways: Rtes. 2, 2-A, 202.

Airport: Orange Municipal Airport, a General Aviation (GA) facility.

Tax Rate: $8.69 per thousand (1994, Mass. Div. of Local Services))

Median House Price: $92,000 (1993, County Data Corporation)

Median Household Income: $35,573 (1990 Census)
- % of state average: 96.3%
- Per Capita Income: $13,216
- % of state average 76.7%

Form of Government: Board of Selectmen, administrative assistant, open town meeting.

Municipal Offices: (508) 249-6828

Services: Mass. Electric Co., no natural gas service, no sewer.

Nearest Hospital: Athol Memorial Hospital

Registered Voters (Secretary of State 1992): 821

Legislative Districts:

U.S. Congress: 1st District: John W. Olver (D)

State Senate: Worcester-Franklin-Hampden & Hampshire District: Robert Wetmore(D)

State Representative: 1st Worcester; Rep. Hal Lane (D)

Public Schools

Narragansett
- Phillipston Memorial K-6
- Baldwinville K-6
- East Templeton 4-6
- Templeton Center K-3
- Narragansett Reg. High 7-12

Montachusett Voc-tech 9-12

Superintendent: William Turner (508) 939-5661

School Choice: Yes for high school

Per Pupil Cost: (State Exec. Office of Education -1991-92)
- Phillipston $4,069
- State average $5,023

Average Teacher Salary: (State Exec. Office of Education-1992-93)

Phillipston	statewide
$33,452	$38,774

Mean SAT scores 1993

	(reported by town)	State Mean
Math	458	
Verbal	437	
Combined:	895	903

Student Population (Dept. of Education)

Total students 1991-92:	292
at public schools	95.5%
at private schools	4.5%

Educational Attainment (1990 census)
- High School graduate or higher 81.8%
- Bachelor's Degree or higher 14.5%

Largest Employers: (supplied by community, 1993)

	# of employees
Phillipston and Narragansett Schools	97
King Phillip Restaurant and Motel	32
Baldwin Hill Bakery	13
Fox Run Restaurant	9
Town of Phillipston	8

Commuting to Work (1990 Census)
- Average time to work (mins.) 24.9

Houses of Worship: Congregatioinal Church

Crime Rate: (1993, Mass. State Police Crime Reporting Unit)

	town	statewide
Total crimes reported:	30	
rate per 1,000 persons	20.20	37.46
Violent crimes	2	
rate per 1,000 persons	1.35	5.65
Property crimes	28	
rate per 1,000 persons	18.86	31.83

Libraries:
- Phillips Free Public Library, The Common, (508) 249-6828

Princeton

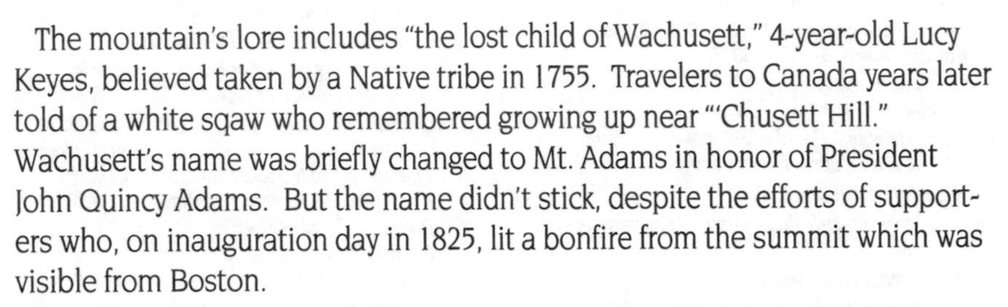

Windmills and Wachusett

Termed "the observatory of the state" by Thoreau, Mt. Wachusett (2,006') was noticed by Gov. Winthrop from a ship in Boston Harbor in 1632. The mountain, whose name means "great hill" in Algonquin, was a gathering place for local tribes. Near the mountain's base at Redemption Rock, captive Mary Rowlandson was returned for ransom in 1676 (*see Lancaster*).

The mountain's lore includes "the lost child of Wachusett," 4-year-old Lucy Keyes, believed taken by a Native tribe in 1755. Travelers to Canada years later told of a white sqaw who remembered growing up near "'Chusett Hill." Wachusett's name was briefly changed to Mt. Adams in honor of President John Quincy Adams. But the name didn't stick, despite the efforts of supporters who, on inauguration day in 1825, lit a bonfire from the summit which was visible from Boston.

In Princeton's glory days as a summer resort in the late 1800's, eight trains a day brought visitors to the town's dozen hotels. Among the guests were Louisa May Alcott, Sarah Bernhardt and Thomas Edison. Working girls from Boston spent their vacations at Fernside on the Mountain Road, now being restored as a Bed & Breakfast. The automobile age changed vacation habits and brought an end to the grand hotels.

Today, Wachusett Mountain Resort draws skiers from all over New England, many coming from Boston, 47 miles away, and Worcester, just 15 miles south. The ski area straddles the Princeton/Westminster line, and has installed a new high-speed quad lift, the first in the state. Many members of WWII's 10th Mountain Division, which saw ski combat in the Alps, learned to ski at Mt. Wachusett, and a monument to their valor is at the summit.

Princeton's Municipal Light Department generates 5% of its power from a windmill farm the town built on the western slope of the mountain. Despite visitors to Wachusett, the town's busiest intersection in town has only a blinking yellow light. The common is graced by a gazebo, the Goodnow library, built of Milford granite in 1884, and the Congregational Church, which has an 1815 Paul Revere bell.

***Sources:** Commonwealth of Mass. EOCD Community Profile; "Princeton, Mass. Illustrated, 1900, Gilbert;"The Princeton Story, 1759-1959; The Boston Globe; The Worcester Telegram & Gazette; Once Told Tales of Worcester County, Southwick; The Guide to Nashaway, Darby, McCrosky, Chandler; Massachusetts Towns, Sandrof.*

Year incorporated: 1771
Population: 3,344 (1993, town census)
Density: 90 per square mile
Total area: 35.85
Elevation: 1,175'
Distance from:
Boston: 47 miles
Worcester: 15 miles
Highways: Rtes. 31, 62 and 140, which connects with Rte. 2 in neighboring Westminster.
Rail: Commuter rail service to Boston's North Station is available in nearby Leominster. Travel time from North Leominster Station: 78-87 minutes; 60 MBTA parking spaces.
Airport: Worcester Airport
Tax Rate: $16.33 per thousand (1994, The Central Mass. Fact Book)
Median House Price: $147,000 (1993, County Data Corporation)
Median Household Income: $52,708 (1990 Census)
% of state average: 142.6%
Per Capita Income: $21,386
% of state average 124.2%
Form of Government: Board of Selectmen, Executive Secretary, open town meeting.
Municipal Offices: (508) 464-2100
Services: Princeton Municipal Light Dept.,no natural gas service, no sewer, no town water.
Nearest Hospital: Fitchburg, Leominster, Worcester
Registered Voters (Secretary of State 1992), 2,007
Legislative Districts:
U.S. Congress: 3rd District: Peter Blute (R)
State Senate: 2nd Worcester-Middlesex District: Robert Antonioni (D)
State Representative: 12th Worcester: Harold Naughton, Jr. (D)
Public Schools
Princeton: Thomas Prince K-8
Wachusett Regional H.S 9-12
Montachusett Voc-Tech 9-12
Superintendent: Alfred D. Tutela (508) 829-6631
School Choice: No

Per Pupil Cost:
(State Exec. Office of Education -1992-93)
Primary $3,935
Wachusett H.S. $6,374
State average 1992-93 $5,023
Average Teacher Salary: (State Exec. Office of Education-1992-93)

	town	statewide
Princeton	$40,021	$38,774

Wachusett High School $40,951
Mean SAT scores 1993 (reported by town)
Math 488
Verbal 434
Combined: 922 State Mean: 903
Student Population (Dept. of Education)
Total students 1991-92: 671
at public schools 87.3%
at private schools 12.7%
Educational Attainment (1990 census)
High School graduate or higher 94.2%
Bachelor's Degree or higher 44.3%
Largest Employers: (supplied by community, 1993)

	# of employees
Mountain Barn	8
E.F.Bufton & Son	6
Photopanels of New England	4

Commuting to Work (1990 Census)
Average time to work (mins.) 26.7
Houses of Worship: 1 Congregational, 1 Catholic
Crime Rate: (1993, Mass. State Police Crime Reporting Unit), adjusted to 12 months

	town	statewide
Total crimes reported:	81	
rate per 1,000 persons	25.40	37.46
Violent crimes	9	
rate per 1,000 persons	2.82	5.65
Property crimes	72	
rate per 1,000 persons	22.58	31.83

Libraries: Princeton
Public Library, 2 Town Hall Drive (508) 464-2115

PRINCETON

Royalston

Land of the Waterfalls

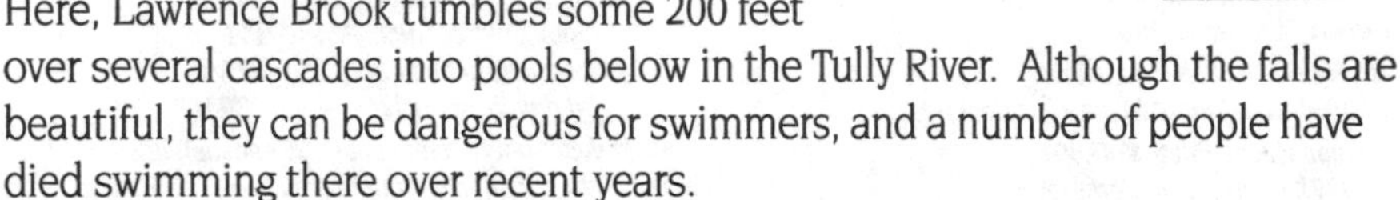

Hard by New Hampshire in the far northwest corner of Worcester County, tiny Royalston is best known for its three lovely and dramatic waterfalls, Royalston Falls, Spirit Falls, and Doane's Falls. Located one mile north of the Athol line, Doane's Falls is the most accessible and best known of the three. Here, Lawrence Brook tumbles some 200 feet over several cascades into pools below in the Tully River. Although the falls are beautiful, they can be dangerous for swimmers, and a number of people have died swimming there over recent years.

Remote Royalston also has one of the most charming town greens in New England, often described as "picture-perfect" and "like a scene from a New England Christmas card." Lined with stately maples and historic Federal and Greek Revival homes, the town center also offers views of Mt. Monadnock and Mt. Wachusett. The Congregational Church steeple is unusually tall, and was rebuilt after blowing over in the hurricane of 1938. Some say Royalston's Common looks the same as it did in the 1940's, and the town is still without a traffic light, subdivision or condominiums. Homes with 100 acres of land are not unusual.

Though small, (its population peaked in 1840 at 1,667), Royalston was a big enough town to spawn two governors in the mid 1800's - Alexander Bullock, who was governor of Massachusetts, and Asabel Peck, who served as governor of Vermont. Today one of Royalston's most interesting artisans is Anthony Cooper, who is thought to be New England's only custom saddle-maker. Cooper, who fled Kennebunkport, Maine when it became over-run with tourists, trained in saddlery in England. Recently he was commissioned by Old Sturbridge Village to re-create a 1830's-era saddle, a project he researched at the Smithsonian Institution in Washington, D.C.

At one time, Royalston was home to mills and factories, which harnessed its abundant water power to make hats, cabinets, furniture and shoe pegs. Farmers found the hilly terrain hard to cultivate, and flocked to the mills, which also attracted a large number of Finnish immigrants. The largest mill was the old Royalston Cotton & Wool Manufacturing Co, which made fine blankets.

Sources: Commonwealth of Mass. EOCD Community Profile; North of the Quabbin, A. Young; Worcester Magazine; The Boston Globe; Mass. Bi-Centennial Commemorative Guide; The Guide to North Central Massachusetts; The Getaway Guide.

Year incorporated: 1765
Population: 1,147 (1990 census)
Density: 27 per square mile
Total area: 42.47
Elevation: 1,000'
Distance from:
Boston: 74 miles
Worcester: 43 miles
Highways: State Rtes. 32 and 68.
Bus:The Montachusett Regional Transit Authority (MART) provides paratransit services between Royalston and Athol.
Airport: The Orange Municipal Airport, a General Aviation (GA) facility
Tax Rate: $8.07 per thousand (1994, Mass. Div. of Local Services))
Median House Price: $105,000 (1993, County Data Corporation)
Median Household Income: $33,333 (1990 Census)
% of state average: 90.2%
Per Capita Income: $12,421
% of state average 72.1%
Form of Government: Board of Selectmen
Municipal Offices: (508) 249-9641
Services: Mass. Electric Co., no natural gas, town sewer
Nearest Hospital: Athol Memorial Hospital
Registered Voters (Secretary of State 1992) 656
Legislative Districts:
U.S. Congress: 1st District: John W. Olver (D)
State Senate:Worcester-Franklin-Hampden & Hampshire District: Robert Wetmore(D)
State Representative: 1st Worcester; Rep. Hal Lane (D)
Public Schools
Athol-Royalston: Ellen Bigelow, (K-4); Pleasant St, (K-6); Riverbend (5-6); Sanders St.(K-4); South Royalston (3-6); Raymond (K-2); Athol Jr. High (7-8); Athol High(9-12).
Montachusett Voc-Tech: (9-12).
Superintendent: Allen Hodgdon, Interim Superintendent, (508) 249-2400
School Choice: No

Per Pupil Cost: (State Exec. Office of Education -1992-93)
Royalston $3,695
State average $5,023
Average Teacher Salary:
(State Exec. Office of Education-1992-93)

Royalston	statewide
$33,727	$38,774

Mean SAT scores 1993 (reported by town)
Math 447
Verbal 407
Combined: 854 State Mean: 903
Student Population (Dept. of Education)
Total students 1991-92: 239
at public schools 96.7%
at private schools 3.3%
Educational Attainment (1990 census)
High School graduate or higher 76.7%
Bachelor's Degree or higher 17.2%
Largest Employers: (supplied by community, 1993)

	# of employees
Athol-Royalston Regional Schools	20
Royalston Highway Department	6
Hubbard Lumber Company	5

Commuting to Work (1990 Census)
Average time to work (mins.) 27.1
Houses of Worship: 1 Catholic, 2 Congregational
Crime Rate: not available
Libraries:
P.S. Newton Public Library, The Common (508) 249-3572
State Register of Historic Places 1993:
Royalston Common Historic District Center

Rutland

Smack Dab in the Center of Massachusetts

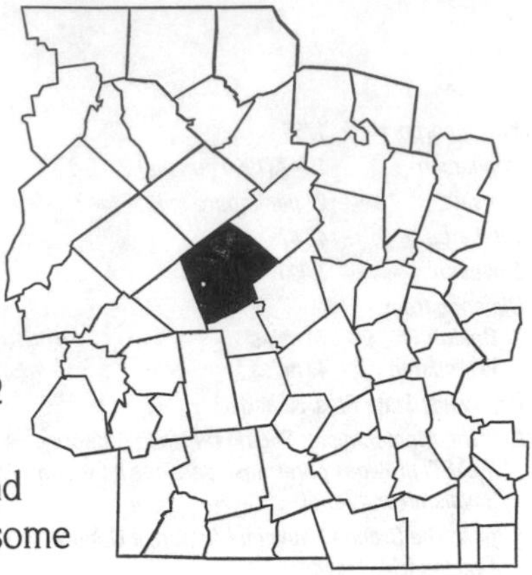

Rutland is located at the exact geographic center of the state and has a tree to mark the spot on Central Tree Road. Just 12 miles northwest of Worcester, Rutland is the highest town between the Berkshires and the Atlantic Ocean. From the town center, some 1200' above sea level, the view includes Mt. Wachusett, Mt. Monadnock and Mt. Watatic in Ashburnham. On clear days, Boston's Prudential Tower can be seen from the Heifer Project International farm. Because of the altitude, Rutland residents know that in winter, when it's raining in Worcester, they can expect snow in Rutland.

Despite a recent population boom, Rutland is still rural, with no traffic lights and six working farms, including Alta Vista Farm, home of Worcester County's only buffalo herd. About 48 percent of the town's acreage is undeveloped and protected watershed land, including Rutland State Park. Town leaders are seeking a use for the 90-acre Maple Ave. campus of the former Rutland Heights Hospital, closed by the state in 1991.

Settled in 1722, Rutland was an isolated frontier outpost frequently attacked by Chief Gray Lock's warriors. Forests stretched northward to Canada, and the settlements at Brookfield and Holden were each a day's walk along narrow trails. The years 1723-24 were particularly bloody, with several settlers attacked and killed in their fields.

During the summer of 1778, the town's Continental Barracks housed British prisoners-of-war and Hessian mercenaries captured from Gen. Burgoyne at the battle of Saratoga. An observer wrote of the Rutland stockade, "You could hardly turn your eyes in any direction without seeing Red Coates." The camp well still exists, and years ago was rumored to contain Continental brass cannon. When pumped out, it yielded a very old Hessian Meerschaum pipe, and a small jewel, but no cannon. Descendants of the Hessians still live in town today.

Rutland resident Gen. Rufus Putnam, "the father of Ohio," led the first expedition to settle Marietta, Ohio, in 1788. His house at 344 Main Street, built in 1765, is now a private home listed on the Register of Historic Places.

Rutland's fresh air and high altitude were thought important in treating tuberculosis, and the state built a sanatorium here in 1898. Private sanitoriums followed, and many homes rented rooms to TB patients. The sanitoriums closed when modern treatment methods made them obsolete. When the Quabbin Reservoir was created, a 12' high tunnel was built under Rutland to carry water from Coldbrook Springs in Oakham to the Wachusett Reservoir in West Boylston.

Sources: The Boston Globe, Once Told Tales of Worcester County, Al Southwick, Commonwealth of Massachusetts EOCD Community Profile; The Landmark Town Guide. History of Rutland in Massachusetts 1713-1968, T.C. Murphy, Northeastern University, 1928; History of Worcester County, Mass. with Biographical Sketches of many of its Pioneers and Prominent Men, D. Hamilton Hurd, J.W. Lewis & Co., Philadelphia, 1889; Quabbin Reservoir, Walter E. Clark, Hobson Book Press, 1946; Reprinted by Athol Press, Inc., 1994.

Year incorporated: 1713
Population: 4,936 (1990 census)
Density: 140 per square mile
Total Area: 36.41 square miles
Elevation: 1205'
Distance from:
Boston: 52 miles
Worcester: 12 miles
Highways: State Routes 56, 68, 122 and 122-A
Tax Rate : $13.82 (1995, Town))
Median House Price: $116,650 (1993 County Data Corporation)
Median Household Income: $44,087 (1990 Census)
% of state average: 119.3%
Per Capita Income: $16,661
% of state average 96.71%
Form of Government: Board of Selectmen, open town meeting
Municipal Offices: 508-886-4103
Services: Town water and sewerage in some parts, Mass. Electric, full-time police and volunteer fire. Cable TV: United Video Cablevision.
Nearest Hospital: Worcester
Registered Voters (Sec. of State, 1992): 2,882
Legislative Districts:
U.S. Congress: 3rd Congressional District: Peter Blute (R)
State Senate:Worcester-Franklin-Hampden & Hampshire District: Robert Wetmore(D)
State Representative: 1st Worcester; Rep. Hal Lane (D)
Public Schools (Dept. of Education)
Wachusett Regional School District- Superintendent Alfred D. Tutela (508) 829-6631
School Choice: No
Naquag Elementary K-8
Wachusett Regional High School (Holden) 9-12
Private Schools: Devereux School for the Emotionally Disturbed
Per Pupil Cost: (Dept. of Education 1992-93)
Rutland $3,916
Wachusett High School $6,374
state average $5,023

Average Teacher Salary: (Dept. of Education-92-93)
Rutland $37,759
Wachusett $40,951
Statewide $38,774
Mean SAT scores 1993:
Math 488
Verbal 434
Combined: 922 State Mean: 903
Student Population (Dept. of Education)
Total students 91/92: 942
at public schools 96.9%
at private schools 3.1%
Educational Attainment (1990 census)
High School graduate or higher 89.6%
Bachelor's Degree or Higher 23.1%
Largest Employers: (supplied by community, 1993):

	# of employees
Devereux School	259
C.B. Blair Builders	80
Sims Cab	40
C&S Builders	20
Mann's Trailer	16
Ladd's Restaurant	16

Commuting to Work (1990 U.S. Census)
Average time to work (mins.) 26.7
Houses of Worship: 1 Congregational, 1 Catholic
Crime Rate: (1993 Mass. State Police Crime Reporting Unit)

	town	statewide
Total crimes reported:	25	
rate per 1,000 persons	5.06	37.46
Violent crimes	0	
rate per 1,000 persons	0	5.65
Property crimes	25	
rate per 1,000 persons	5.06	31.83

Libraries
Rutland Free Public Library, 246 Main Street, 508-886-4108

RUTLAND

Shrewsbury

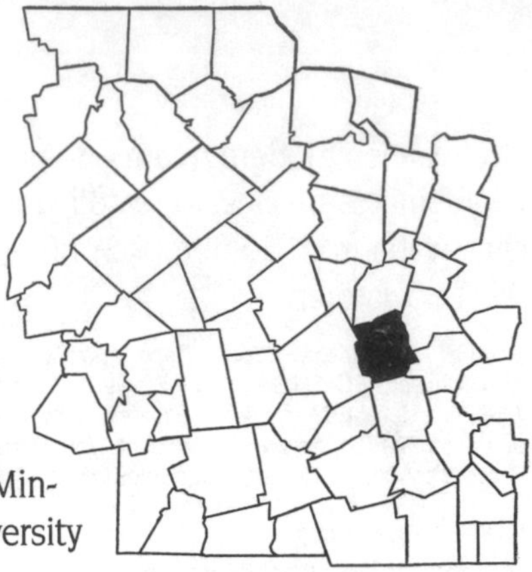

The Pill, Spag's and White Chocolate

The most famous pill in human history was created in Shrewsbury. The birth control pill was developed in the 1950's by Worcester Foundation for Experimental Biology scientists Drs. Gregory Pincus and Min-Chueh Chang. Pincus and fellow Clark University biologist Hudson Hoagland launched the Worcester Foundation in a barn on campus, and later moved it to Shrewsbury, with funding from local businessmen.

In 1951, Pincus was asked to develop an oral contraceptive by birth control activist Margaret Sanger. In just four years, his team began clinical trials and in June, 1960, the world's first birth control pill, Enovoid-10, received FDA approval and was marketed by Searle Pharmaceutical Co. Ironically, the Worcester Foundation got no financial windfall from the discovery because Searle owned the patent. This unfair situation couldn't happen today, because the Foundation now has its own biotechnology company, Hybridon, Inc., with 110 employees working on drugs for gene therapy.

Another Shrewsbury legend is Anthony A. "Spag" Borgatti, Jr., the "granddaddy of all discounters," who started selling auto parts on Rte. 9 in 1934. Today, Spag's Supply is a multi-million dollar retailing complex, carrying 150,000 different items, and drawing 10,000 customers daily to buy everything from tents to toothpaste. According to Spag's daughter, Sandy Travinski, "Dad started with tires and fan belts, but added toys and clothing because they were hard to find during the Depression. His whole premise was to give the working man a break."

It was Shrewsbury's own Hebert's Candies that first introduced white chocolate to the world in the early 1950's. The famous Hebert Candy Mansion headquarters on Rte. 20 was built in 1916 as a summer residence.

Worcester and Shrewsbury are separated by the four-mile long Lake Quinsigamond, which has been spanned at various times by a floating bridge, a causeway, and bridges at the present site on Rte. 9, near the "White City" shopping area, which used to be a popular end-of-the-trolley line amusement park around the turn of the century.

***Sources:** Worcester Magazine; The Boston Globe; Commonwealth of MA EOCD Community Profile; Massachusetts Towns, An 1840 View, Ivan Sandrof, Barre Publishers, 1963. Once-Told Tales of Worcester County, Albert B. Southwick, Databooks, 1994.*

Year incorporated: 1727
Population: 24,146 (1990 census)
Density: 1,165 per square mile
Total area: 21.65 sq. miles
Elevation: 008'
Distance from:
Boston: 34
Worcester: 5

Highways: State Rtes. 140, 9, U.S. Rte. 20 and Interstate Rtes. 290, 495.

Rail: Passenger rail service to Boston, Providence, Springfield, and all other points on Amtrak available through neighboring Worcester.

Bus: The Worcester Regional Transit Authority provides fixed route service to Worcester and paratransit services for the elderly and disabled.

Airport: The Worcester Municipal Airport

Tax Rate: $12.74 per thousand (1994, Mass. Div. of Local Services)

Median House Price: $159,000 (1993, County Data Corporation)

Median Household Income: $44,248 (1990 Census)
% of state average: 119.7%
Per Capita Income: $20,508
% of state average 119.1%

Form of Government: Board of Selectmen, Town Manager, Representative Town Meeting

Municipal Offices: (508) 842-7471

Services: Shrewsbury Municipal Electric, Commonwealth Gas Co., town water and sewer, ground water, cable television is owned and operated by the Shrewsbury Electric Light Dept.

Nearest Hospital: UMASS, several in Worcester

Registered Voters: 15,430

Legislative Districts:

U.S. Congress: 3rd District: Peter I. Blute (R)

State Senate: 1st Worcester, Robert A. Bernstein (D)

1st Worcester & Middlesex:Matthew J. Amorello (R)

State Representative: 11th Worcester: Ronald W. Gauch (R)

Public Schools
Shrewsbury: Beal School (N-01); Calvin Coolidge (01-04); Walter J Paton (01-04); Spring Street (01-04); Shrewsbury Middle (05-07); Shrewsbury Sr High (08-12)

Superintendent: Dr. Anthony Bent (508) 845-5721

School Choice: No

Per Pupil Cost: (State Exec. Office of Education -1992-93)
Shrewsbury $4,702
State average $5,023

Average Teacher Salary: (State Exec. Office of Education 1992 93)

Shrewsbury	statewide
$35,705	$38,774

Mean SAT scores 1993 (reported by town)
Math 479
Verbal 417
Combined: 896 State Mean: 903

Student Population (Dept. of Education)
Total students 1991-92: 3,938
at public schools 85.2%
at private schools 14.8%

Educational Attainment (1990 census)
High School graduate or higher 87.0%
Bachelor's Degree or higher 34.7%

Largest Employers: (supplied by community, 1993)

	# of employees
Digital Equipment Corporation	1,375
Mescaster Company, Inc. UPS	925
U.S. Post Office Processing and Distribution	790
Jamesbury Corporation	479
Spag's Supply	450

Commuting to Work (1990 Census)
Average time to work (mins.) 20.2

Houses of Worship: 2 Catholic, 1 Episcopal, 1 Lutheran, 1 Congregational, 1 Methodist, 2 Baptist.

Crime Rate: 1993 Mass. State Police Crime Reporting Unit

	town	statewide
Total crimes reported:	825	
rate per 1,000 persons	34.17	37.46
Violent crimes	106	
rate per 1,000 persons	4.39	5.65
Property crimes	719	
rate per 1,000 persons	29.78	31.83

Libraries:
Shrewsbury Free Public Library

Museums:
General Artemas Ward Museum

State Register of Historic Places 1993:
Milestone, 1767
Shrewsbury Town Common Historic District
Gen. Artemas Ward Homestead

Southborough

Why Baseball Catchers Still Have Teeth

So well preserved is Southborough's historic center that "someone from the late 19th century standing on a doorstep at the center of town would know exactly where he was today," noted Southborough Historian Nick Noble, author of the town history, *Fences of Stone*. The reason the center is intact is a happy accident — the railroad station was placed to the east, diverting the last century's commercialism. And today, Rte. 9 absorbs the rest.

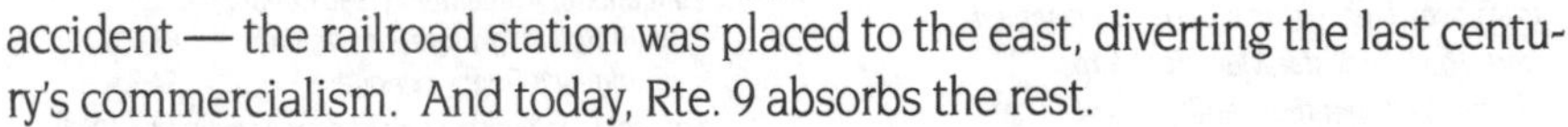

Southborough chemist Joseph Burnett made a fortune manufacturing vanilla extract, and in the 1860's, he and his family founded both of the prestigious private boarding schools in town — St. Mark's (grades 9-12), and the Fay School (grades 1-9), the oldest junior boarding school in the country. The schools attract students from around the world, and both open some of their recreation facilities to town residents.

Although history records that the first baseball catcher's mask was patented by a Harvard University catcher in 1877, Southborough locals know that it really was invented here. Newspaper evidence shows that in April, 1875, a St. Mark's school catcher wore face protection he adapted from a fencing mask to protect his broken nose. The St. Mark's opponents that day were — surprise, surprise — the Harvard freshmen, one of whom obviously saw a future for the mask. His design is very close to what is used today. Later, the St. Mark's catcher was quoted as holding no grudge; his mask idea had merely been an expedient solution for the day.

With 24 percent of its area taken up by the Sudbury Reservoir, Southborough is prized for its open space. Although pricey by some standards, people choose it for its "beautiful open space and water," and because it's "convenient, attractive and comfortable," according to Noble. Most commute to jobs in Boston or along the high tech corridors of Rtes. 128 and I-495, and head to either Framingham or Worcester for shopping. Word has it that most Southborough and Westborough residents prefer the English "borough" spelling to the town's name, but some are "less picky" about that detail.

***Sources:** Southborough Historian Nick Noble; The Boston Globe; Commonwealth of Mass. EOCD Community Profile.*

Year incorporated: July 6, 1727
Population: 6,628 (1990 census)
Density: 468 per square mile
Total area: 15.66 sq. miles
Flevation: 550'
Distance from:
Boston: 25
Worcester: 15
Highways: State Rte. 85, Interstate 495, and the Mass. Turnpike (I-90).
Rail:.Conrail services a freight rail line through Southborough.
Airport: The Worcester Municipal Airport, a primary commercial service.
Tax Rate: $13.30 per thousand (1995, Town Census))
Median House Price: $235,000 (1993, County Data Corporation)
Median Household Income: $61,743 (1990 Census)
% of state average: 167.1%
Per Capita Income: $25,841
% of state average 150.0 %
Form of Government: Board of Selectmen, Administrative Assistant, Open Town Meeting
Municipal Offices: (508) 485-0710
Services: Mass. Electric, Commonwealth Gas, no town sewer, purchased water.
Nearest Hospital: Worcester, Marlboro, Framingham
Registered Voters: 4,577
Legislative Districts:
U.S. Congress: 5th District: Martin T. Meehan (D)
State Senate: Middlesex and Worcester: Robert Durand (D)
State Representative: 8th Middlesex: Barbara Gardner (D)
Public Schools
Southborough: Mary E Finn (K-01); A S Woodward (06-08); Margaret A Neary (02-05)
Northboro Southboro: Algonquin Reg High (09-12)
Assabet Valley: Assabet Valley Voc H S (09-13)
Superintendent: Dennis M. DiSalvo (508) 351-7000
School Choice: No
Per Pupil Cost: (State Exec. Office of Education -1992-93)
Southborough $5,379
State average 1992-93 $5,023
Secondary $6,548

ˀge Teacher Salary:
ᴱxec. Office of Education-1992-93)
ˀry $42,883
Secondary $44,558
Statewide $38,774
Mean SAT scores 1993 (reported by town)
Math 530
Verbal 463
Combined: 993 State Mean: 903
Student Population (Dept. of Education)
Total students 1991-92: 1,197
at public schools 90.8%
at private schools 9.2%
Educational Attainment (1990 census)
High School graduate or higher 91.6%
Bachelor's Degree or higher 43.9%
Largest Employers: (supplied by community, 1993)
NYNEX
Commonwealth Gas
CHIPCOM
New England Frozen Foods
Data General
Commuting to Work (1990 Census)
Average time to work (mins.) 23.3
Houses of Worship: 1 Congregational, 2 Catholic, 1 Episcopal, 1 Baptist, 1 Federated
Crime Rate: (1993 Mass. State Police Crime Reporting Unit)

	town	statewide
Total crimes reported:	74	
rate per 1,000 persons	11.16	37.46
Violent crimes	5	
rate per 1,000 persons	0.75	5.65
Property crimes	69	
rate per 1,000 persons	10.41	31.83

Libraries:
Southborough Library
State Register of Historic Places 1993:
Marlborough Brook Filter Beds
Sudbury Dam Historic District
Sudbury Reservoir Circular Dam
Wachusettt Aqueduct Linear District
Water Supply System of Metropolitan Boston
Weston Aqueduct Linear District

SOUTHBOROUGH

Southbridge

"Eye of the Commonwealth" Sees Fiber Optic Future

A smokestack town in the 1800's, Southbridge had its share of mills and factories on the Quinebaug River making cotton, wool, shoes and shuttles. But it was a gold and silver spectacle-making firm, founded by G.W. Wells in 1835, that grew into America's largest lens maker and manufacturer of ophthalmic products - American Optical - which employed thousands in Southbridge.

So commanding was AO's presence, that the Southbridge town seal bears the motto, "The Eye of the Commonwealth." AO's founding family sold the firm to Warner Lambert in 1967, and many of the company's buildings on Optical Drive fell empty, with only the AO Tech division left behind.

Today, Southbridge is one of the world's major centers for fiber optics technology, and some of the former AO buildings are used for fiber optic research. Now called the Southbridge Business Center, the site will house the newly formed Center for Advanced Fiber Optic Applications (CAFA), which won a $1.3 million grant from NASA to do research. CAFA, which was founded by Mass. Electric Co. and five local fiber optic companies, expects in the future to introduce a new fiber optic product every six months.

Fiber optic cables carry light waves through thin strands of plastic or glass, and are used in voice, picture and data transmission and as sensors in bridges and buildings to detect faults and cracks. Fiber optics are used in pollution detection and in projection TV and cable television systems.

The Southbridge Business Center was also chosen, after a national search and lots of local legislative lobbying, as the site of a Defense Department training center with a full-time staff of 450 and 350 trainees. Southbridge is nearly equidistant from Hartford, Springfield, Providence and Worcester and, due to its industrial past, offers many services, including a modern hospital, cultural center, and YMCA with indoor pool and programs.

Sources: The Worcester Telegram & Gazette; Commonwealth of Mass. EOCD Community Profile; The Boston Globe; More Massachusetts Towns, Ivan Sandrof, Barre Publishers, 1965.

Year incorporated: 1816
Population: 17,816 (1990 census)
Density: 883 per square mile
Total area: 21 sq. miles
Elevation: 600', 1000' variation
Distance from:
Boston: 59
Worcester: 21
Providence: 34
Hartford: 39
Springfield 45

Highways: State Rtes. 131, 169, 198, U.S. Rte. 20 and Interstate Rte. 90.

Rail: The Providence and Worcester Railroad provides freight rail service to Southbridge.

Airport: The Southbridge Municipal Airport, a general aviation facility.

Tax Rate: $17.12 per thousand (1994, Mass. Div. of Local Services)

Median House Price: $92,500 (1993, County Data Corporation)

Median Household Income: $27,834 (1990 Census)
% of state average: 75.3%
Per Capita Income: $12,924
% of state average 75.0%

Form of Government: Town Council, Town Manager,

Municipal Offices: (508) 764-5408

Services: Mass. Electric, Boston Gas Co., town sewer, surface water.

Nearest Hospital:Harrington Memorial Hospital

Registered Voters: 8,288

Legislative Districts:

U.S. Congress: 2nd District: Richard E. Neal (D)

State Senate: Worcester & Norfolk District: Louis P. Bertonazzi (D)

State Representative: 6th Worcester: David Peters (R)

Public Schools
Southbridge: Charlton Street (2-3); Eastford Rd. (K-1); West Street (4-5); Mary E Wells Jr High (06-08); Southbridge High (09-12)

Southern Worcester County: Bay Path Reg Voc Tech H S (09-12)

Superintendent: Jo Ann D. Austin (508) 764-5414

School Choice: No

Per Pupil Cost: (State Exec. Office of Education -1992-93)
Southbridge $4,931
State average $5,023

Average Teacher Salary: (State Exec. Office of Education-1992-93)

Southbridge	statewide
$37,484	$38,774

Mean SAT scores 1993 (reported by town)
Math 434
Verbal 391
Combined: 825 State Mean: 903

Student Population (Town figures)
Total students 1994-95: 2,795
at public schools 89.7%
at private schools 10.3%

Educational Attainment (1990 census)
High School graduate or higher 65.8%
Bachelor's Degree or higher 12.3%

Largest Employers: (supplied by community, 1993)

	# of employees
American Optical Corporation	583
Harrington Memorial Hospital	574
Cabot Safety Corporation	528
Schott Fiber Optics	377
Hyde Group	325

Commuting to Work (1990 Census)
Average time to work (mins.) 18.7

Houses of Worship: 17

Crime Rate: not available

Libraries:
Jacob Edwards Memorial Library

State Register of Historic Places 1993:
Hamilton Woolen Mills Co. Historic District
Dresser House
"The Wells"
Bacon-Morse Historic District
Oak Ridge Cemetery

Spencer

One House, Three Inventors

The "cradle of invention" might literally have existed in Spencer's Howe homestead where three world-famous inventors were born — Elias Howe, who created the first lockstitch sewing machine, and his uncles William Howe, who developed the wooden truss bridge named for him, and Tyler Howe, who patented the spring bed. The foundation of their family home is on the grounds of the Howe Memorial State Park off Rte. 49.

Although his invention changed the world, and possibly the course of the Civil War, Elias Howe didn't have an easy go of it. He spent years in poverty developing his sewing machine, which was the first to use two threads, one from an eye-pointed needle which locked with a bobbin thread below. Unable to market his invention, he sailed for England, hoping for better luck. He returned home destitute to find his wife dying and dozens of imitators selling sewing machines which infringed on his 1846 patent. Only after nine long years of litigation did Howe get paid for his invention. He entered the world's first patent pool, and had earned $2 million from royalties when his patent expired in 1867.

Originally part of Leicester, Spencer separated in 1753 and was named by Lt. Governor Spencer Phipps. Beginning in 1784, Spencer was a stop-over on the Boston Post Road where stages from Boston and Hartford switched passengers. It's still an important transportation center, with Rtes.9, 31 and 49 converging in town. For those living north of Worcester, the back roads of Spencer are the best shortcut to Sturbridge and New York.

Today, Spencer is the international headquarters of FLEXcon, an industrial laminating firm, and the monks at St. Joseph's Abbey have been making jams and jellies since 1954 on Rte. 31. Down the road, you'll find Christmas begins in March at the Oakwood Farm Christmas Barn, which sells ornaments and unique holiday accessories from a 175-year old barn. And family operated Bay Path Furniture, also on Rte. 31, has a complete furniture showroom and gift shop in a very rural setting.

Sources: Commonwealth of Mass. EOCD Community Profile; The Boston Globe; Academic American Encyclopedia; The Old Post Road, The Story of the Boston Post Road, Stewart H. Holbrook, McGraw-Hill Book Company, Inc., 1962; Forty Immortals of Worcester and Its County, Worcester National Bank, 1920.

Year incorporated: 1753
Population: 11,645 (1990 census)
Density: 354 per square mile
Total area: 34.05 sq. miles
Elevation: 925'
Distance from:
Boston: 51
Worcester: 11
Highways: Rtes. 9, 31, 49.
Rail: Conrail provides freight rail service through Spencer.
Airport: The Worcester Municipal Airport
Tax Rate: $9.34 per thousand (1994, Mass. Div. of Local Services)
Median House Price: $100,000 (1993, County Data Corporation)
Median Household Income: $33,201 (1990 Census)
% of state average: 89.9%
Per Capita Income: $14,222
% of state average 82.6%
Form of Government: Board of Selectmen, open town meeting
Municipal Offices: (508) 885-7500
Services: Mass. Electric Co., Boston Gas Co., town sewer, ground water.
Nearest Hospital: several in Worcester
Registered Voters: 6,456
Legislative Districts:
U.S. Congress: 2nd District: Richard E. Neal (D)
State Senate: Worcester-Franklin-Hampden & Hampshire District: Robert D. Wetmore (D)
State Representative: 6th Worcester District: Stephen M. Brewer (D)
Public Schools
Spencer East Brookfield: Grove Street (K-03); Lake Street (K-04); Memorial (K-05); Pleasant St. (K-03); Maple St (05-06); West Main Street (K-03); David Prouty Jr High (07-08); Lashway J H (06-08); David Prouty High (09-12)
Superintendent: John H. Begley (508) 885-8507
School Choice: No
Per Pupil Cost: (State Exec. Office of Education -1992-93)
Spencer $4,217
State average $5,023

Average Teacher Salary:
(State Exec. Office of Education 1992-93)

Spencer	statewide
$33,224	$38,774

Mean SAT scores 1993

	(reported by town)	State Mean
Math	461	
Verbal	417	
Combined:	878	903

Student Population (Dept. of Education)
Total students 1991-92: 2,193
at public schools 96.2%
at private schools 3.8%
Educational Attainment (1990 census)
High School graduate or higher 75.6%
Bachelor's Degree or higher 13.7%
Largest Employers: (supplied by community, 1993)

	# of employees
FLEXcon Company, Inc.	878
Mercury Wire Products	115
Spencer Products	63

Commuting to Work (1990 Census)
Average time to work (mins.) 25.7
Houses of Worship: 2 Catholic, 4 Protestant
Crime Rate: (1993 Mass. State Police Crime Reporting Unit) adjusted to 12 months

	town	statewide
Total crimes reported:	593	
rate per 1,000 persons	50.92	37.46
Violent crimes	108	
rate per 1,000 persons	9.27	5.65
Property crimes	485	
rate per 1,000 persons	41.65	31.83

Libraries:
Richard Sugden Public Library
State Register of Historic Places 1993:
Milestone, 1767
Shaw Site (4,5,6)
Spencer Fire Station
Spencer Town Center Historic District

Sterling

Apples and "Mary Had a Little Lamb"

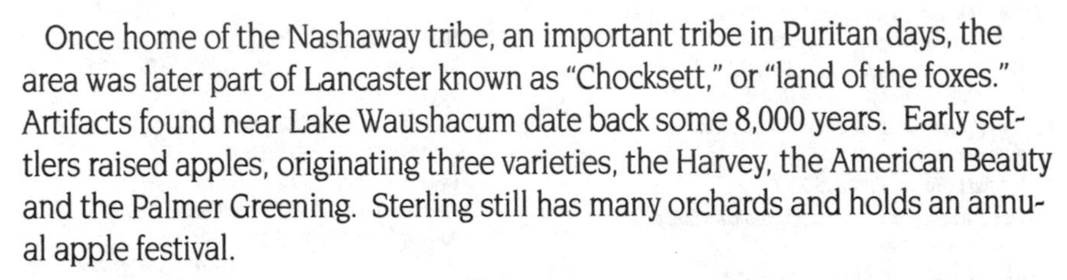

Rural charm and a rich history still define Sterling, despite its location at the crossroads of I-190, Routes 140, 62 and 12. Just 12 miles north of Worcester, the town is minutes from Route 2 and commuter rail service to Boston. Incorporated in 1781, Sterling is named after Scotland's Lord Stirling, who helped the Colonists during the Revolution.

Once home of the Nashaway tribe, an important tribe in Puritan days, the area was later part of Lancaster known as "Chocksett," or "land of the foxes." Artifacts found near Lake Waushacum date back some 8,000 years. Early settlers raised apples, originating three varieties, the Harvey, the American Beauty and the Palmer Greening. Sterling still has many orchards and holds an annual apple festival.

But it is the children's poem, "Mary Had a Little Lamb" for which Sterling is most famous. Written by John Roulstone in 1816, the poem describes a real visit to school by Mary Sawyer's pet lamb. Subsequent verses were added by Sarah Josepha Hale and became a lesson in the *MacGuffey Reader*. A lamb statue on Sterling Common commemorates the poem.

Philosopher Henry David Thoreau made a pilgrimage to Mt. Wachusett in 1842 and stayed at Sterling's Richardson Tavern. Two decades later, Sterling's Silas Stuart invented an apparatus to make sewing machine needles, and Ebenezer Butterick began making and selling dress patterns. Butterick patterns are still sold today (*see chapter* 2). Sterling was an major center of chair manufacturing in the 19th century, making some 70,000 chairs annually, which were shipped country wide and to the West Indies.

According to legend, Sterling had a stop on the Underground Railroad. The Moses Smith house, built in 1788, was connected to a shop by a long tunnel used for storage and as a hiding place for slaves escaping to Canada.

Sources: Commonwealth of Mass. EOCD Community Profile; A Guide to Nashaway, North Central Massachusetts, M. Darby, J. McCrosky, M. Chandler; The Landmark Town Guide; The Boston Globe; The Telegram & Gazette; Mass. State Register of Historic Places, 1993.

Year incorporated: 1781
Population: 6,481 (1990 census)
Density: 212 per square mile
Total area: 31.61 square miles
Elevation: 505'
Distance from:
Boston: 41 miles
Worcester: 12 miles

Highways: Interstate 190 (N-S); State Routes 12, 62 and 140.

Rail: Commuter Rail to North Station from neighboring North Leominster station: 78-87 mins; 60 MBTA parking spaces. For information call 1-800-392-6100.

Bus: The Montachusett Regional Transit Authority (MART) provides services to the elderly and disabled through the Council on Aging.

Airport: Worcester Municipal Airport, Sterling Airport, privately owned.

Tax Rate: $13.87 per thousand (The Fact Book for Central Mass.)

Average House Price: $144,500 (1993 County Data Corp.)

Median Household Income: $49,345
% of state average: 133.5%
Per Capita Income: $17,830
% of state average 103.5%

Form of Government: Board of selectmen, open town meeting

Municipal Offices: (508) 422-8111

Services: Town water in some areas, no sewage; municipal electric; full-time police; volunteer fire; Cable TV: Continental Cablevision.

Nearest Hospital: Clinton Hospital; Leominster Hospital

Registered Voters (Secretary of State 1992), 4,047

Legislative Districts:

U.S. Congress: 3rd Congressional District: Rep. Peter Blute (R)

State Senate: 2nd Worcester-Middlesex District: Robert Antonioni (D)

State Representative: 12th Worcester Harold P. Naughton, Jr. (D)

Public Schools

Chocksett Elementary, 1-3
Houghton Elementary, K, 4-8
Wachusett Regional High, 9-12 (Holden)

Montachusett Voc-tech, 9-12 (Fitchburg)

Wachusett Regional School District - Superintendent Alfred D. Tutela (508) 829-6631

School Choice: No
Per Pupil Cost:
(State Exec. Office of Education -1992-93)

Primary and Middle School	$3,533
Wachusett High School	$6,374
State average 1992-93	$5,023

Average Teacher Salary: (State Exec. Office of Education -1992-93)

	Sterling	statewide
Primary and Middle School	$36,167	$38,774
Wachusett High School	$40,951	

Mean SAT scores 1993
(State Exec. Office of Education

		State Mean
Math	488	
Verbal	434	
Combined	922	903

Student Population (Dept. of Education)
Total students 1991-92 1,316
at public schools 92.6%
at private schools 7.4%

Educational Attainment (1990 census)
High School graduate or higher 88.3%
Bachelor's Degree or higher 29.9%

Largest Employers: (supplied by community, 1993)

	# of employees
Town of Sterling	140
Carbolon Corporation	64
Northeast Poly Bag	55
Morse Manufacturing	45
Lee Plastics	40

Commuting to Work (1990 Census)
Average time to work (mins.) 23.9

Houses of Worship: 1 Unitarian, 1 Catholic, 1 Baptist, 1 Adventist

Crime Rate: (1993 Mass. State Police Crime Reporting Unit) adjusted to 12 months

	town	statewide
Total crimes reported:	138	
rate per 1,000 persons	21.29	37.46
Violent crimes	28	
rate per 1,000 persons	4.32	5.65
Property crimes	110	
rate per 1,000 persons	16.97	31.83

Libraries:
Conant Free Public Library
4 Meetinghouse Hill Rd., Box 428, (508) 422-6409

State Register of Historic Places:
Sterling Center Historic District
Ebenezer Buss House, 382 Redemption Rock Trail
Hasting-Jones-Wheaton House, 14 Campground Road

Sturbridge

A Treasure of Recreated History

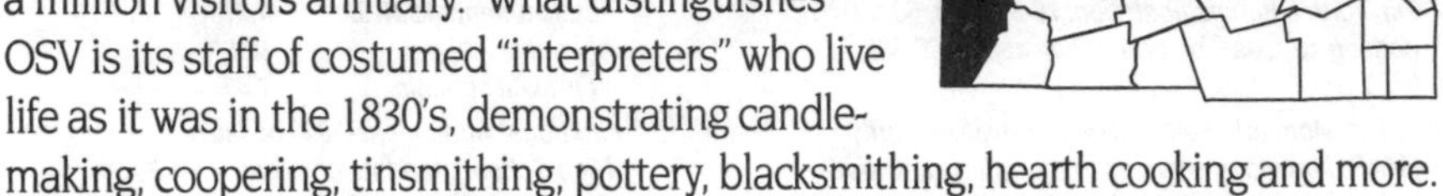

The Worcester County town most associated with the past is Sturbridge, site of the famous Old Sturbridge Village (OSV), a 200-acre "living history museum" with more than 40 restored buildings, which draws nearly half a million visitors annually. What distinguishes OSV is its staff of costumed "interpreters" who live life as it was in the 1830's, demonstrating candle-making, coopering, tinsmithing, pottery, blacksmithing, hearth cooking and more.

Ironically, this village "where time stopped" never really existed. Many of the buildings were moved here from other towns, and Sturbridge's own beginnings were more humble. Albert Southwick's *More Once Told Tales of Worcester County* gives us a description of Sturbridge during the Revolution from Edward Parry, a Tory kept under house arrest, "I found it very lonely - no public road of any consequence thro' it...(the house) was a very miserable one ..." Parry describes the food as "boiled to rags - and brought to table in one dish...the knives and forks - black and dirty - never Scoured - seldom whetted, and sometimes washed."

Today, Sturbridge is home to some of the finest restaurants in New England, and they all wash the silverware! The Publick House, now a world famous historic resort on the Common, was founded in 1771 by Col. Ebenezer Crafts, who lead a Revolutionary cavalry company. Southwick notes that Crafts was so strong "he could lift a barrel of cider and drink from the bung hole." The Publick House logo still sports Crafts on horseback.

Sturbridge's Tantiusques Reservation is the site of the first mine in New England, and possibly the country. Early travelers noticed native tribes wearing shiny black ornaments made of lead, or graphite. In 1641, Gov. Winthrop's son was granted "ye hill at Tantousq...in which the blackleade is..." Even though it was essential to making plumbago, a tarry coating used on the sides of wooden ships, the lead proved too difficult to extract. Over its 250 year history, the mine never made a profit.

Today, however, Sturbridge is a tourist "goldmine" - ideally situated at the junction of I-84 and the Mass. Pike. Visitors spilling over from OSV can choose from hundreds of shops and outlets offering antiques, artwork, crafts, furniture, folk art, candles, curtains and more. Scores of restaurants offer a range of cuisine from fast food to gourmet dining to special occasion Colonial feasts. Weary travelers can choose from motels, resorts and an array of Bed & Breakfasts.

The world famous Brimfield Flea Markets, held every year in adjacent Brimfield, attract hundreds of thousands of bargain hunters every May, July and September. For complete information on Sturbridge offerings and special events, travelers can call the Sturbridge Area Tourist Association at 1-800-628-8379.

Sources: Commonwealth of Mass. EOCD Community Profile; Sturbridge Area Tourist Association; More Once-Told Tales of Worcester County, Albert B. Southwick, Databooks, 1994.

Year incorporated: 1738
Population: 7,775 (1990 census)
Density: 208 per square mile
Total area: 38.95 sq. miles
Elevation: 620'
Distance from:
- Boston: 60
- Worcester: 22
- Providence: 50
- Hartford: 45
- Springfield 32

Highways: I-90 (Mass. Pike), I-84, and U.S. Rte. 20, State Rtes. 131 and 148, 49 and 15.

Bus: Peter Pan Bus Lines offers a daily excursion to Old Sturbridge Village from New York City and Boston, which stops in Sturbridge and Worcester.

Airport: Southbridge Municipal Airport, a general aviation facility.

Tax Rate: $16.45 per thousand (1994, Mass. Div. of Local Services)

Median House Price: $126,100 (1993, County Data Corporation)

Median Household Income: $40,734 (1990 Census)
- % of state average: 110.2%
- Per Capita Income: $16,642
- % of state average 96.6%

Form of Government: Board of Selectmen, Town Administrator, open town meeting

Municipal Offices: (508) 347-2500

Services: Mass. Electric Co., town sewer, ground water, no natural gas.

Nearest Hospital: Harrington Memorial Hospital, Southbridge

Registered Voters: 4,586

Legislative Districts:

U.S. Congress: 2nd District: Richard E. Neal (D)

State Senate: Worcester & Norfolk District: Louis P. Bertonazzi (D)

State Representative: 6th Worcester Pct. 1: David Peters (R)

State Representative: 5th Worcester District: Pct. 2: Stephen M. Brewer (D)

Public Schools
- Sturbridge: Burgess Elem (K-06)
- Tantasqua: Tantasqua Reg Jr High (07-09); Tantasqua Reg Sr High (10-12); Tantasqua Regional Vocational (09-12)

Superintendent: David Roach (508) 347-3077

School Choice: No

Per Pupil Cost:
(State Exec. Office of Education -1992-93)
- Primary $4,734
- Secondary $5,629
- State average $5,023

Average Teacher Salary:
(State Exec. Office of Education-1992-93)
- Primary $3[illegible],510
- Secondary $40,026
- Statewide $38,774

Mean SAT scores 1993 (reported by town)
- Math 489
- Verbal 438
- Combined: 927 State Mean: 903

Student Population (Dept. of Education)
- Total students 1991-92: 1,456
- at public schools 96.6%
- at private schools 3.4%

Educational Attainment (1990 census)
- High School graduate or higher 80.6%
- Bachelor's Degree or higher 24.9%

Largest Employers: (supplied by community, 1993)

	# of employees
Publick House, Inc.	400
Old Sturbridge Village	359
Galileo Electro-Optics Corporation	261
Sturbridge Host Hotel	255
Spectran Corporation	150

Commuting to Work (1990 Census)
- Average time to work (mins.) 23.2

Houses of Worship: 1 Federated, 1 Catholic

Crime Rate: (1993 Mass. State Police Crime Reporting Unit)

	town	statewide
Total crimes reported:	175	
rate per 1,000 persons	22.51	37.46
Violent crimes	27	
rate per 1,000 persons	3.47	5.65
Property crimes	148	
rate per 1,000 persons	19.04	31.83

Libraries: Joshua Hyde Public Library

Museums: Old Sturbridge Village

State Register of Historic Places 1993:
- Sturbridge Common Historic District
- Tantiusques Reservation Site
- Oliver Wight House

Sutton

This Purgatory Is Delightful

Created by an ancient earthquake, Sutton's Purgatory Chasm is a geological wonder, a gorge 70' deep, 60' across and a half-mile long. A maze of caves and crannies with names like "Devil's Coffin" and "Devil's Pulpit," Purgatory is a great spot for a family outing, as kids love to scramble and play hide-and-seek among the rocks. "If ever a geological fault was created with kids in mind, this is it," write Cynthia and Thomas Lewis in *Best Hikes With Children.*

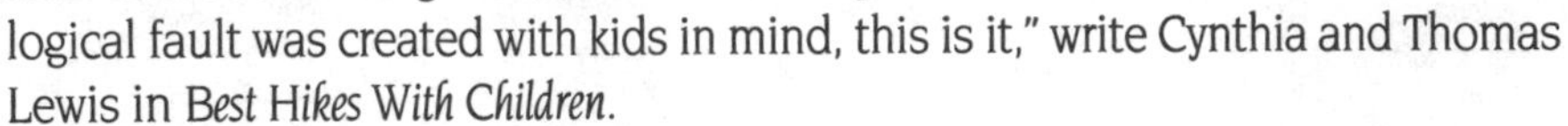

To the reckless, the chasm can also be dangerous. Sutton's rescue teams are equipped with rappelling gear and are called to the gorge an average of five times a year. One 1991 accident was re-enacted on the TV program, "Rescue 911." Purgatory Chasm is part of a 2,660 acre state reservation, and a trail marked with blue blazes leads through the gorge from the parking lot. The park is on Purgatory Rd., one-half mile off Rte. 146 on the left, (508) 278-6486.

Colonists who settled Sutton in 1716 endured a harsh winter the next year, when "Ye Great Snow" fell so heavily it covered one house entirely, including the chimney. The town had some early mills and factories, but these closed when Sutton was by-passed by the railroads. Today, the town is rural and residential, with most commuters traveling to Worcester, Boston or Providence.

Located in an 1820 Sutton farmhouse, Vaillancourt Folk Art is the country's largest and best known producer of Christmas collectibles, with 40 painters creating original folk art products sold around the world. The shop was recently featured in Yankee Magazine.

A local firm, Polyvinyl Films, makes Stretch-Tite plastic wrap, which local consumers believe beats the big national brands hands down. Sutton snags the sports headlines every year when the Pleasant Valley Golf Club hosts a PGA tournament, the Pleasant Valley Classic.

Sources: The Getaway Guide; The Worcester Telegram & Gazette; Commonwealth of Mass. EOCD Community Profile; Best Hikes with Children in Connecticut, Massachusetts and Rhode Island, Cynthia C. Lewis, Thomas J. Lewis, The Mountaineers, 1991; A Guide to the Heritage of Worcester County, Simone E. Blake, Montachusett Girl Scout Council, 1973; More Massachusetts Towns, Ivan Sandrof, Barre Publishers, 1965; Natural Wonders of Massachusetts, A Guide to Parks, Preserves & Wild Places, Nancy Prajzner, Country Roads Press, 1994.

Year founded: 1716
Population: 6,824 (1990 census)
Density: 211 per square mile
Total area: 33.93 sq. miles
Elevation: 706"
Distance from:
Boston: 45
Worcester: 12
Providence: 32
Highways: Rtes. 122A, and 146.
Airport: The Worcester Municipal Airport
Tax Rate: $14.78 per thousand (1994,town)
Median House Price: $142,500 (1993, County Data Corporation)
Median Household Income: $46,491 (1990 Census)
% of state average: 125.8%
Per Capita Income: $16,937
% of state average 98.3%
Form of Government: open town meeting - Board of Selectmen,Town Administrator
Municipal Offices: (508) 865-8725
Services: Mass. Electric Co., Commonwealth Gas Co., town sewer, ground water.
Nearest Hospital: several in Worcester
Registered Voters: 4,333
Legislative Districts:
U.S. Congress: 2nd District: Richard E. Neal (D)
State Senate: 1st Worcester & Middlesex: Matthew J. Amorello (R)
State Representative: 9th Worcester: George Peterson (D)
Public Schools
Sutton: Sutton Elem (K-06); Sutton Pre-School (N); Sutton High School (09-12)
Blackstone Valley: Blackstone Valley Voc Tech (09-12)
Superintendent: William P. Conners (508) 865-9270
School Choice: Yes
Per Pupil Cost: (State Exec. Office of Education -1992-93)
Sutton: $3,628
State average 1992-93 $5,023

Average Teacher Salary: (State Exec. Office of Education-1992-93)

Sutton	statewide
$39,325	$30,774

Mean SAT scores 1993 (reported by town)

Math	409	
Verbal	412	
Combined	881	State Mean: 903

Student Population (Dept. of Education)

Total students 1991-92:	1,378
at public schools	90.3%
at private schools	9.7%

Educational Attainment (1990 census)

High School graduate or higher	84.3%
Bachelor's Degree or higher	21.3%

Largest Employers: (supplied by community, 1993)

	# of employees
Town of Sutton	200
Polyvinyl Films	100
Package Industries	100

Commuting to Work (1990 Census)
Average time to work (mins.) 23.1
Houses of Worship: Catholic, Congregational, Baptist, Episcopalian
Crime Rate: (1993 Mass. State Police Crime Reporting Unit)

	town	statewide
Total crimes reported:	11	
rate per 1,000 persons	1.61	37.46
Violent crimes	5	
rate per 1,000 persons	0.73	5.65
Property crimes	6	
rate per 1,000 persons	0.88	31.83

Libraries:
Sutton Free Public Library
State Register of Historic Places 1993.
Freegrace and Mary Marble Farm Historic District
Waters Farm

Templeton

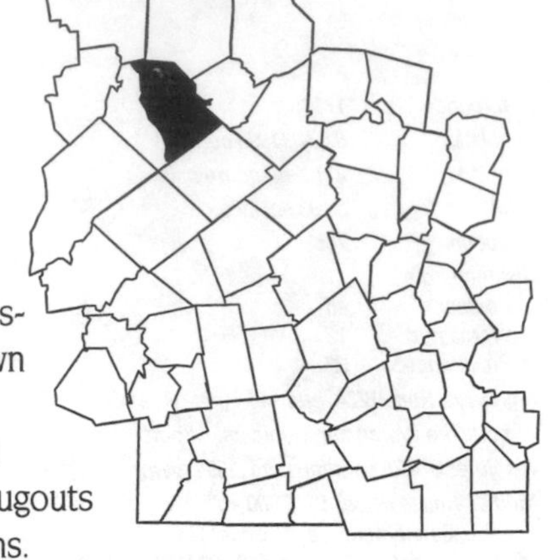

The Tinman's Legacy

As in many towns, land grants in Templeton were given as rewards to the families of veterans who fought against hostile native tribes in King Philips War. Known simply as Narragansett Number Six when settled in 1751, Templeton's colonists had some rough early years, living in hillside dugouts and in caves while building their first cabins.

Templeton was still quite a wilderness in 1760 when a newly assigned minister, Rev. Ebenezer Sparhawk, following only marked trees as a guide, became lost en route from Rutland. Lost in the dark, Sparhawk tied his horse to a tree, and then began walking around the tree — *all night long* — to keep from freezing.

Before Colonial settlement, the Templeton area was frequented by hunters from the nearby Nashaway tribe living in what is now Sterling. A native legend of unrequited love is still told about Princess Rock, a large outcropping along the present Barre Rd. The rock is named for Princess Star Fire, whose father promised her to a chief even though she loved another man. On the eve of the wedding, the lovers met at the rock and were found dead in each others' arms the next morning. Legend has it that their death song could be heard at the rock for many years afterward.

A Templeton "tinman" was the founder of Worcester Polytechnic Institute (WPI). John Boynton, born in Templeton in 1791, was a skilled metalworker who made a fortune in tin, dealing in pots, pans, dippers, cups and plates. Boynton's salesmen loaded their wares onto wagons for week-long forays into neighboring towns, and were the popular news sources upon their return. After retiring to Worcester, Boynton sunk his life savings of $100,000 into founding his dream, a school of technology, which he started in 1851 and called "Worcester County Free Institute of Industrial Science." The school, which changed its name to WPI in 1887, was one the first technical schools in the country, and was the first to stress laboratory and workshop training for mechanical engineering.

Templeton has three other distinct villages within its borders: Templeton, East Templeton, Baldwinville and Otter River, of which Baldwinville is the largest, and Otter River houses the town offices.

***Sources:** Profiles of the Past, T. Malloy; Commonwealth of Mass. EOCD Community Profile; More Massachusetts Towns, I. Sandrof;*

Year incorporated: 1762
Population: 6,438 (1990 census)
Density: 201 per square mile
Total area: 32.42 sq. miles
Elevation: 1,141'
Distance from:
- Boston: 62
- Worcester: 30

Highways: State Rtes. 2, 101, and U.S. Rte. 202.
Bus: MRTA provides paratransit services to the elderly and disabled through the Council on Aging.
Airport: The Gardner Municipal Airport, a general aviation facility.
Tax Rate: $8.03 per thousand (1994, Mass. Div. of Local Services)
Median House Price: $97,000 (1993, County Data Corporation)
Median Household Income: $34,395 (1990 Census)
- % of state average: 93.1%
- Per Capita Income: $13,347
- % of state average 77.5%

Form of Government: Board of Selectmen, Administrative Assistant, open town meeting
Municipal Offices: (508) 939-8801
Services: Templeton Municipal Electric, no natural gas, town sewer, ground water.
Nearest Hospital: Athol Memorial Hospital
Registered Voters: 3,545
Legislative Districts:
U.S. Congress: 1st District: John W. Olver (D)
State Senate: Worcester, Franklin, Hampden and Hampshire: Robert E. Wetmore (D)
State Representative: 1st Worcester; Rep. Hal Lane (D)
State Representative: 2nd Worcester, Pcts. 3 and 4· Robert D. Hawke (R)
Public Schools
- Narragansett: Phillipston Memorial (K-06); Baldwinville (K-06); East Templeton (04-06); Templeton Center (K-03); Narragansett Reg High (07-12)
- Montachusett: Montachusett Voc Tech (09-12)

Superintendent: William Turner (508) 939-5661
School Choice: Yes for high school

Per Pupil Cost:
(State Exec. Office of Education -1992-93)
- Templeton $4,051
- State average $5,023

Average Teacher Salary:
(State Exec. Office of Education-1992-93)

Templeton	statewide
$32,647	$38,774

Mean SAT scores 1993 (reported by town)
- Math 458
- Verbal 437
- Combined: 895 State Mean: 903

Student Population (Dept. of Education)
- Total students 1991-92: 1,312
- at public schools 93.2%
- at private schools 6.8%

Educational Attainment (1990 census)
- High School graduate or higher 72.5%
- Bachelor's Degree or higher 9.8%

Largest Employers: (supplied by community, 1993)
- Seaman Paper Company
- Lily Chemicals
- Glenwood Kitchens
- Fernald School

Commuting to Work (1990 Census)
- Average time to work (mins.) 23.3

Houses of Worship: 1 Protestant, 3 Catholic, 1 Methodist, 1 Baptist, 1 Congregational,
Crime Rate: not available
Libraries:
- Boynton Public Library

Museums:
- Narragansett Historical Society

State Register of Historic Places 1993:
- Baldwinville Village Historic District
- Templeton Common Historic District

TEMPLETON

Upton

Hats Off to a Small Town Survivor

The decision by women to forego hats as a fashion statement could have spelled doom for Upton, but it didn't. Home of the old Knowlton Hat Factory, once the world's leading maker of ladies' hats, Upton has adapted and survived, preserving the best of the Knowlton legacy. Today, the Knowlton factory building has been restored as elderly housing, and a Knowlton dormitory for female stitchers survives as the Upton Inn. Both are on the National Register of Historic Places.

William Knowlton expanded the straw braid industry and founded his company in 1847. At its peak, the mill employed 1,000 workers and was a social center, where the many dances and parties attended by Knowlton factory girls earned the town the nickname of "Capertown." The Knowlton reign lasted until 1914, ended by fast-changing hat styles, federal income tax and higher wages. Subsequent owners survived until 1973, and during WWII, the factory made work caps, mosquito tents, raincoats and sleeping bags.

Upton has a large number of historic buildings because William Knowlton hated to tear things down. Rather, he moved buildings and used them for worker housing. Parts of the huge Warren Tavern, reputed to be the world's longest tavern, were used in least five other buildings. Today, a Knowlton building walking tour brochure by Eagle Scout Thomas Gorman is available from the Upton Historical Society.

Another of Upton's historic structures - a man-made stone cave - may have been built by Europeans pre-dating Columbus. Located off Elm St., the cave is a circular chamber made of granite slabs with a domed roof and long narrow passageway. Various theories suggest the cave was built by Norsemen, by Irish monks fleeing Viking raiders, or by Mediterranean mariners. A 1980 report by the Early Sites Research Society dated the cave at 710 A.D. based on its astronomical alignment with related rock cairns on Pratt's Hill, and pointed to similarities with stone chambers built by Irish monks.

Sources: The Boston Globe; Commonwealth of Mass. EOCD Community Profile; Facts and a Walking tour of the Knowlton Buildings, Thomas Gorman, Troop 132; The Upton Historical Society; More Massachusetts Towns, Ivan Sandrof, Barre Publishers, 1965; Upton's Heritage, the history of a Massachusetts town, Donald Blake Johnson, Town of Upton, 1984.

Year incorporated: 1735
Population: 5,435 (1994 town census)
Density: 217 per square mile
Total area: 21.73 sq. miles
Elevation: 301'
Distance from:
Boston: 36
Worcester: 15
Springfield 51

Highways: State Rte. 140, Interstate Rte. 90 and 495.

Rail: The Grafton and Upton Railroad provides freight rail service in Upton.

Airport: The Worcester Municipal Airport,

Tax Rate: $9.51 per thousand (1994, Mass. Div. of Local Services)

Median House Price: $158,734 (1993, County Data Corporation)

Median Household Income: $45,962 (1990 Census)
% of state average: 124.4%
Per Capita Income: $20,292
% of state average 117.8%

Form of Government: Board of Selectmen, Administrative Assistant, open town meeting

Municipal Offices: (508) 529-6901

Services: Mass. Electric Co., Commonwealth Gas Co., town sewer, ground water.

Nearest Hospital: Milford Hospital, several in Worcester

Registered Voters: 3,235

Legislative Districts:

U.S. Congress: 3rd District: Peter I. Blute (R)

State Senate: 1st Worcester & Middlesex: Matthew J. Amorello (R)

State Representative: 9th Worcester: George N. Peterson, Jr. (R)

Public Schools

Mendon Upton: Superintendent: David Crisafulli: (508) 529-7729
Memorial Elem (K-04); Henry P Clough (K-04); Miscoe Hill Middle School (05-08); Nipmuc Regional High (09-12)

Blackstone Valley: Blackstone Valley Voc Tech (09-12)

Superintendent: Michael Fitzgerald

School Choice: Yes

Per Pupil Cost: (State Exec. Office of Education -1992-93)
Upton $4,411
State average $5,023

Average Teacher Salary: (State Exec. Office of Education-1992-93)

Upton	statewide
$31,230	$38,774

Mean SAT scores 1993 (reported by town)
Math 477
Verbal 459
Combined 936 State Mean: 903

Student Population (Dept. of Education)
Total students 1991-92: 725
at public schools 92.0%
at private schools 8.0%

Educational Attainment (1990 census)
High School graduate or higher 84.9%
Bachelor's Degree or higher 29.7%

Largest Employers: (supplied by community, 1993)

	# of employees
Mendon-Upton Regional School District	28
Town of Upton	26
Knowlton Manor Nursing Home	25
Liquid Solids Control, Inc.	16
Upton Fuel and Construction	8
Nahra Bus Company, Inc.	4

Commuting to Work (1990 Census)
Average time to work (mins.) 26.0

Houses of Worship: United Parish, Holy Angels, Emmanuel Chapel, One Body in Christ, Buddist Chapel.

Crime Rate: not available

Libraries:
Upton Town Library

State Register of Historic Places 1993:
Knowlton Hat Factory

Uxbridge

The Heart of the Blackstone

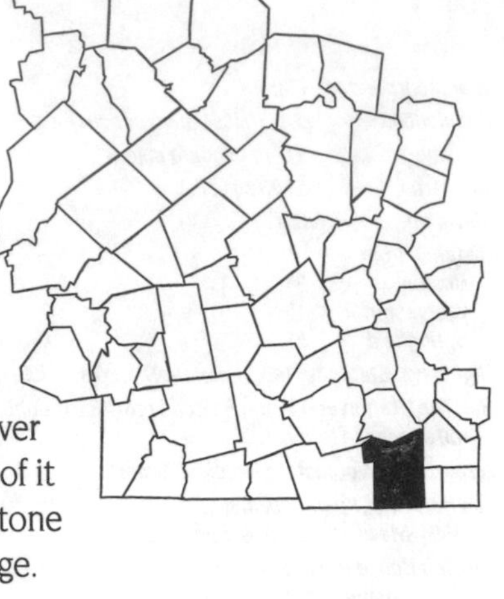

The Blackstone River was America's hardest working river and the birthplace of the Industrial Revolution. With a 438' vertical drop along its course from Worcester to the Narragansett Bay, it once had 42 dams and more mills per square mile than any other river in America. And Uxbridge was at the center of it all. Today, the Visitor's Center for the Blackstone Valley Heritage Corridor is located in Uxbridge.

Equidistant from Providence and Worcester, the town became an overnight stopping point for boats plying the Blackstone Canal which linked the two cities in 1828. When railroads made the canal obsolete, tracks ran through Uxbridge parallel to the canal. The town's first woolen mill, built in 1810, was one of the country's earliest. Its Crown and Eagle Mills, built in 1823, were considered one of the finest examples of New England textile complexes.

Today, the Stanley Woolen Co. still manufactures textiles part-time, and the Calumet Mill here lasted until 1983. At one time, Uxbridge was the "yarn producing capital of the world." During the Civil War, mills here worked 24-hour shifts to fill government orders; in WWI, khaki overcoats for the allies were made here; and in WWII, the town was world famous for its "Uxbridge Blue" army uniforms. Granite from Uxbridge was used to build Ellis Island and to rebuild Boston after its "great fire of 1872."

President George Washington stopped at an Uxbridge inn in 1789. Flattered that innkeeper Taft's daughters were named in his honor, the President sent them chintz and five guineas, cautioning "... the less said about it, the better you will please me."

Today, Uxbridge is a bedroom community for those working in Worcester and Providence. It was the first town to offer school choice, and now more than 100 students from other towns attend its schools, and nearly that many are on a waiting list.

Sources: Commonwealth of Mass. EOCD Community Profile; The Boston Globe; The Worcester Telegram & Gazette; A Guide to the Heritage of Worcester County, Simone E. Blake, Montachusett Girl Scout Council, 1973; More Massachusetts Towns, Ivan Sandrof, Barre Publishers, 1965; Run of the Mill, Pictorial Narrative of the Expansion, Dominion, Decline and Enduring Impact of the New England Textile Industry, Steve Dunwell, David R. Godine, 1978.

Year incorporated: 1727
Population: 10,415 (1990 census)
Density: 352 per square mile
Total area: 30.38 sq. miles
Elevation: 270'
Distance from:
- Boston: 38
- Worcester: 15
- Providence: 25

Highways: Rtes. 122 146, and 16.
Rail: The Providence & Worcester Railroad provides freight rail service to Uxbridge.
Airport: The Worcester Municipal Airport
Tax Rate: $14.49 per thousand (1994, Mass. Div. of Local Services)
Median House Price: $117,500 (1993, County Data Corporation)
Median Household Income: $40,059 (1990 Census)
- % of state average: 108.4%%
- Per Capita Income: $16,531
- % of state average 96.0%

Form of Government: Board of Selectmen, Administrative Assistant, open town meeting
Municipal Offices: (508) 278-8608
Services: Mass. Electric Co., Commonwealth Gas Co., town sewer, ground water.
Nearest Hospital: Milford-Whitinsville Regional Hospital, Milford, MA.
Registered Voters: 5,554
Legislative Districts:
U.S. Congress: 2nd District: Richard E. Neal (D)
State Senate: Worcester & Norfolk District: Louis P. Bertonazzi (D)
State Representative: 8th Worcester: Paul Kujawski (D)
Public Schools
- Uxbridge: Earl D. Taft (01-04); Virgina A Blanchard (N-K); Whitin Intermediate (05-08); Uxbridge High (09-12)
- Blackstone Valley: Blackstone Valley Voc Tech (09-12)

Superintendent: Michael Ronan (508) 278-8648
School Choice: Yes
Per Pupil Cost: (State Exec. Office of Education -1992-93)
- Uxbridge $3,564
- State average $5,023

Average Teacher Salary: (State Exec. Office of Education- 1992-93)

Uxbridge	statewide
$37,909	$38,774

Mean SAT scores 1993

	(reported by town)	State Mean
Math	464	
Verbal	423	
Combined	887	903

Student Population (Dept. of Education)
- Total students 1991-92: 1,718
- at public schools 90.0%
- at private schools 10.0%

Educational Attainment (1990 census)
- High School graduate or higher 77.8%
- Bachelor's Degree or higher 18.8%

Largest Employers: (supplied by community, 1993)
- Town of Uxbridge
- NELMOR
- EMX
- AC Technologies
- Lampin

Commuting to Work (1990 Census)
- Average time to work (mins.) 25.8

Houses of Worship: True Vine Assembly of God, North Uxbridge Baptist, Church of the Nazarene, Unitarian Church, St. Mary's Church, Church of the Good Shepherd, First Congregational, United Methodist,
Crime Rate: (1993 Mass. State Police Crime Reporting Unit)

	town	statewide
Total crimes reported:	179	
rate per 1,000 persons	17.19	37.46
Violent crimes	70	
rate per 1,000 persons	6.72	5.65
Property crimes	109	
rate per 1,000 persons	10.47	31.83

Libraries:
- Uxbridge Free Public Library

State Register of Historic Places 1993:
- Blackstone Canal Historic District
- John Cornet Farnum House
- Friends' Meetinghouse
- Rogerson's Village Historic District
- Uxbridge Common District
- Uxbridge Town Hall
- Waucantuck Mill Complex

Warren

Sewing Supplies and Submarine Pumps

A former mill town of some 4,500 people, Warren hopes to set a new course for the next century and so does one of its largest employers, Warren Pumps, Inc., which makes specialty pumps for industry and government, most notably for the U.S. Navy Seawolf submarines. "Their pumps sail the seven seas," said Library Director Sylvia Buck.

The firm began in town 97 years ago, and employs 250, many of them skilled machinists, down from a high of 340 in 1989. Not surprisingly, Defense Department cuts have caused the firm to diversify. Government contracts still account for 40 percent of the company's sales, and pumps for the petroleum, chemical, pulp and paper industries make up the rest.

Warren's other big employer, sewing notions manufacturer William E. Wright Company, was a family owned firm until 1985. Wright came to Warren in the depths of the Depression, when most other New England textile firms were shutting their doors. According to Buck, "They came here to an empty factory building, horrified at how much empty factory space was available. In effect, they 'huddled in a corner,' operated on a shoestring at first, and built the company bit by bit." Today the company employs 325.

Had famed feminist Lucy Stone been born on the other side of Coy Hill, Warren would be her birthplace, instead of West Brookfield (*see West Brookfield*). "She used to come to the top of Coy Hill and enjoy the view," Buck related, adding that Stone was a member of the first graduating class in 1842 at Warren's Quaboag Seminary.

She went on to Oberlin College, where she was class valedictorian. "In those days, women weren't allowed to speak on stage," recounted Buck. "Told that she was allowed to write her speech, but not deliver it, she declined to abdicate the position of a woman's equal right to speak in public. If she wasn't permitted to deliver her speech, no one would."

Returning home to Worcester County, she promptly started a long and financially lucrative career speaking out for women's rights and abolition. One of her first talks was delivered at her brother's church in Gardner. To enjoy her favorite view, take Rte. 67 West through Warren, and turn right on Coy Hill Road.

Sources: Sylvia Buck, Library Director, Warren Public Library; The Worcester Telegram & Gazette.

Year incorporated: 1834
Population: 4,437 (1990 census)
Density: 161 per square mile
Total area: 27.62 sq. miles
Elevation: 605'
Distance from:
Boston: 64
Worcester: 24
Springfield 27
Highways: State Rtes. 19, 67, 9, and Interstate 90.
Rail: Conrail services a freight rail line through Warren.
Bus: The Worcester Regional Transit Authority provides services to elderly, handicapped and other Warren residents, by appointment.
Airport: Metropolitan Airport, a general aviation facility in neighboring Palmer.
Tax Rate: $14.35 per thousand (1994, Mass. Div. of Local Services)
Median House Price: $90,000 (1993, County Data Corporation)
Median Household Income: $30,423 (1990 Census)
% of state average: 82.3%
Per Capita Income: $12,805
% of state average 74.3%
Form of Government: Board of Selectmen, Administrative Assistant, open town meeting
Municipal Offices: (413) 436-5701 located in Charles E. Shepard Municipal building, High St., Warren.
Services: Mass. Electric Co., Boston Gas Co., town sewer, ground water.
Nearest Hospital: Mary Lane Hospital, Ware; Harrington Memorial Hosp., Southbridge
Registered Voters 2,446
Legislative Districts:
U.S. Congress: 2nd District: Richard E. Neal (D)
State Senate: Worcester-Franklin-Hampden & Hampshire District: Robert D. Wetmore (D)
State Representative: 6th Worcester District: Stephen M. Brewer (D)
Public Schools
Quaboag Regional: Warren Elem (K-06); West Brookfield Elem (K-06); Quaboag Regional High (07-12)
Superintendent: William J. Haggerty (413) 436-5991
School Choice: No
Per Pupil Cost: (State Exec. Office of Education -1992-93)
Warren $4,271
State average $5,023
Average Teacher Salary:
(State Exec. Office of Education-1992-93)

Warren	statewide
$31,316	$38,774

Mean SAT scores 1993 (reported by town)
Math 497
Verbal 428
Combined 925 State Mean: 903

Student Population (Dept. of Education)
Total students 1991-92: 857
at public schools 97.0%
at private schools 3.0%
Private Schools: Seventh-day Adventist, Southbridge Rd. (K-6)
Educational Attainment (1990 census)
High School graduate or higher 69.4%
Bachelor's Degree or higher 7.2%
Largest Employers: (supplied by community, 1993)

	# of employees
William E. Wright Company	325
Warren Pumps, Inc.	250
Handwick Knitted Fabrics	165
Warren Dry Cleaners and Launderers	60
Edward H. Spencer, Inc.	14

Commuting to Work (1990 Census)
Average time to work (mins.) 21.9
Houses of Worship: Federated Church, United Methodist, St. Paul's (Catholic), St. Thomas's (French Catholic), Stanislaus (Polish Catholic), Seventh-day Adventist
Crime Rate: not available
Libraries:
Warren Public Library, Main St., Warren;
West Warren Library Association, Main St., West Warren.

Webster

Samuel Slater and Lake Chargoggagogg-manchaug...etc.

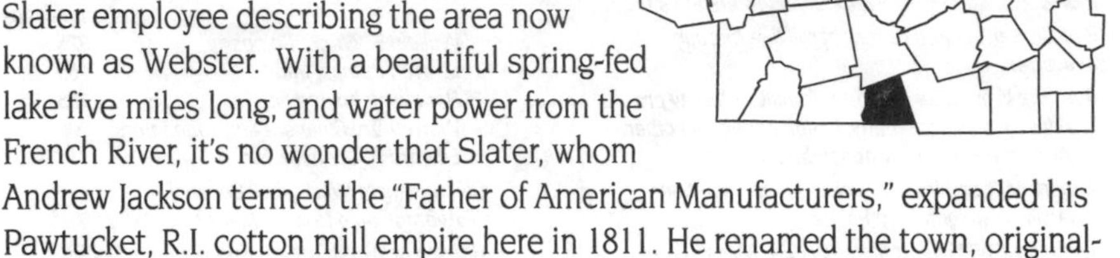

"Wondrous water power...the most God-forsaken place on earth," wrote a Samuel Slater employee describing the area now known as Webster. With a beautiful spring-fed lake five miles long, and water power from the French River, it's no wonder that Slater, whom Andrew Jackson termed the "Father of American Manufacturers," expanded his Pawtucket, R.I. cotton mill empire here in 1811. He renamed the town, originally part of Oxford, in honor of Daniel Webster.

Webster hopes to join the Blackstone River Valley National Heritage Corridor by virtue of the fact that Slater founded the town, owned a house here, and died here in 1835. Mill worker houses built for Slater employees are still occupied in the town's North Village. Rte. 12 is known as Samuel Slater Memorial Highway, and a Slater monument is on Rte. 16 near I-395's exit 2.

As a young indentured servant in England, Slater memorized the superior Arkwright system of cotton manufacturing and emigrated to the U.S. in 1789, passing British customs disguised as a farmer. He modified machinery for Rhode Island's Moses Brown and opened the first water-powered cotton mill in America in 1790. His success started an epidemic of "Cotton Fever" throughout New England, and by 1810, there were 238 textile mills, including 26 in R.I. and 54 in Massachusetts.

Although Slater was the first to start Sunday School in the U.S., his mills also employed children, prized for their finger dexterity and nimble access to cramped spaces. Children as young as seven worked in the mills, earning around 80 cents per week. One reason he picked Webster was its abundance of poor farm families with many children accustomed to hard work. In summer, mill hours were 5 a.m. to 7 p.m.; in winter, workers toiled from dawn until 7:30 p.m., six days a week. Although cramped, company housing was usually far better than what workers could afford on their own.

As for Lake Chargoggagoggmanchauggagoggchaubunagungamaugg, it's easy to see why locals now call it Webster Lake. Encompassing about one sixth of the town's area, it was fished by the Nipmucs, whose name for it means "boundary fishing place — the neutral fishing ground." Modern myth has expanded the meaning to "you fish on your side, I'll fish on my side, and nobody fishes in the middle."

Sources: A Guide to the Heritage of Worcester County, Simone E. Blake, Montachusett Girl Scout Council, 1973; The Run of the Mill, A Pictorial Narrative of the Expansion, Dominion, Decline and Enduring Impact of the New England Textile Industry, Steve Dunwell, David R. Godine, 1978; Forty Immortals of Worcester and Its County, Worcester National Bank, 1920; The Worcester Telegram & Gazette; The Boston Globe; Commonwealth of Mass. EOCD Community Profile.

Year incorporated: 1832

Population: 16,196 (1990 census)

Density: 1,297 per square mile

Total area: 14.53 sq. miles

Elevation: 450'

Distance from:
- Boston: 56
- Worcester: 18
- Providence: 33
- Hartford: 60
- Springfield 60

Transportation:

Highways: State Rtes. 12 and 16, Interstate Rte. 395.

Rail: Freight rail service is provided by the Providence & Worcester Railroad.

Bus: The Worcester Regional Transit Authority provides fixed route service between Auburn, Oxford, Webster, and Worcester.

Airport: Southbridge Municipal Airport, a general aviation facility.

Tax Rate: $10.05 per thousand (1994, Mass. Div. of Local Services)

Median House Price: $105,900 (1993, County Data Corporation)

Median Household Income: $30, 067 (1990 Census)
- % of state average: 81.4%
- Per Capita Income: $14,624
- % of state average 84.9%

Form of Government: Board of Selectmen, Town Administrator, open town meeting Municipal Offices: (508) 943-0033

Services: Mass. Electric Co., Boston Gas Co., town sewer, ground water.

Nearest Hospital: Hubbard Regional Hospital

Registered Voters 8,224

Legislative Districts:

U.S. Congress: 2nd District: Richard E. Neal (D)

State Senate: Worcester & Norfolk District: Louis P. Bertonazzi (D)

State Representative: 8th Worcester: Paul Kujawski (D)

Public Schools

Webster: Park Avenue Elem (K-02); Webster Middle School (03-06); Bartlett Jr Sr High School (07-12)

Southern Worcester County: Bay Path Reg Voc Tech H S (09-12)

Superintendent: Anthony L. D'Acchioli, Ed.D.(508) 943-0104

School Choice: No

Per Pupil Cost: (State Exec. Office of Education -1992-93)
- Webster $4,403
- State average $5,023

Average Teacher Salary: (State Exec. Office of Education-1992-93)

Webster	statewide
$37,406	$38,774

Mean SAT scores 1993

	(reported by town)	State Mean
Math	442	
Verbal	413	
Combined:	855	903

Student Population (Dept. of Education)
- Total students 1991-92: 2,725
- at public schools 73.5%
- at private schools 26.5%

Educational Attainment (1990 census)
- High School graduate or higher 68.8%
- Bachelor's Degree or higher 12.5%

Largest Employers: (supplied by community, 1993)

	# of employees
Commerce Insurance Company	1,200
Cranston Print Works	700
Anglo Fabrics	200

Commuting to Work (1990 Census)
- Average time to work (mins.) 20.8

Houses of Worship: 1 Faith Assembly, 2 Baptist, 1 Episcopal, 1 Lutheran, 1 Methodist,

Crime Rate:
(1993 Mass. State Police Crime Reporting Unit)

	town	statewide
Total crimes reported:	676	
rate per 1,000 persons	41.74	37.65
Violent crimes	59	
rate per 1,000 persons	3.64	5.65
Property crimes	617	
rate per 1,000 persons	38.10	31.83

Libraries:
- Chester C. Corbin Public Library

State Register of Historic Places 1993:
- District Five Schoolhouse
- Eddy Block
- Main Street Historic District
- Rock Castle School
- Shumway Block
- Spaulding Block
- Thompson School

West Boylston

The Town that Moved to Higher Ground

When West Boylston's Baptists built their new stone church in 1892, little did they know the state would own it, and most of their town, just three years later. Today, the church stands alone on a point overlooking Wachusett Reservoir, the only untouched building left from the once-thriving town forever buried under the reservoir waters.

A hundred years ago, after centuries of urban development and pollution, Boston needed more drinking water. The state Legislature responded, and approved damming the south fork of the Nashua River at Clinton, meaning the bustling town of West Boylston would be obliterated. Construction of the Wachusett Reservoir between 1896 and 1907 was the largest project ever undertaken by the state. But it proved to be just a "practice run" for the building of the Quabbin Reservoir 40 years later, which wiped out four towns to provide more clean water for Boston.

In all, the Metropolitan District Commission evicted 1,700 West Boylston residents, razed six mills, eight schoools, four churches, one hotel and 360 homes to make way for the 63-billion gallon reservoir, which is in places 100' deep. The state paid a mere 60 cents on the dollar for the property taken, and agreed to pay $12,000 a year forever to replace the town's lost tax revenue. Many residents left. Others jacked up their homes and buildings, put them on sleds, and dragged them with teams of horses to new locations on higher ground.

During construction, West Boylston was a roustabout town, and residents worried about excessive drinking and carousing among the hundreds of laborers, many of them recent immigrants, living in camps and shanty towns. When the dam was completed in Clinton and the gates closed, the people of West Boylston watched for months as the waters slowly rose, covering their valley forever.

Today, West Boylston is a somewhat affluent bedroom community bordering Worcester, with many of its residents commuting via easy access to I-190. Its commercial strip along Rte. 12 gives it the look of a larger town, and residents recently voted a new high school addition and sewer upgrades. The quality of the school system attracts students from other towns through the state's school choice option.

Sources: Commonwealth of Mass. EOCD Community Profile, Once-Told Tales of Worcester County, A. Southwick; The Boston Globe; The Worcester Telegram, A Guide to the Heritage of Worcester County, S. Blake, Montachusett Girl Scout Council.

Year incorporated: 1808
Population: 6,611 (1990 census)
Density: 512 per square mile
Total area: 13.85 sq. miles
Elevation: 481'
Distance from:
 Boston: 41
 Worcester: 7
Highways: Rtes. 12, 110, 140, I-190.
Rail: Passenger rail service to Boston, Springfield, Providence, and all other points on Amtrak from neighboring Worcester.
Bus: The Worcester Regional Transit Authority provides fixed route service between West Boylston and Worcester and paratransit services to the elderly and disabled.
Airport: The Worcester Municipal Airport.
Tax Rate: $15.00 per thousand (1994, Mass. Div. of Local Services)
Median House Price: $125,000 (1993, County Data Corporation)
Median Household Income: $42,830 (1990 Census)
 % of state average: 115.9%
 Per Capita Income: $17,416
 % of state average 101.1%
Form of Government: Board of Selectmen, open town meeting, Town Administrator Municipal Offices: (508) 835-6091
Services: West Boylston Municipal Electric, Commonwealth Gas Co., no town sewer, ground water.
Nearest Hospital: Several in Worcester
Registered Voters: 3,925
Legislative Districts:
U.S. Congress: 3rd District: Peter Blute (R)
State Senate: 1st Worcester District: Robert A. Bernstein (D)
State Representative: 12th Worcester District: Harold P. Naughton (D)
Public Schools
West Boylston: Major Edwards Elem (K-06); West Boylston Jr-Sr High (07-12)
Superintendent: Leo Sullivan (508) 835-2917
School Choice: Yes

Per Pupil Cost: (State Exec. Office of Education - 1992-93)
 West Boylston $4,534
 State average $5,023
Average Teacher Salary: (State Exec. Office of Education-1992-93)

West Boylston	statewide
$36,848	$38,774

Mean SAT scores 1993 (reported by town)
 Math 488
 Verbal 431
 Combined: 919
 State Mean: 903
Student Population (Dept. of Education)
 Total students 1991-92: 885
 at public schools 95.9%
 at private schools 4.1%
Educational Attainment (1990 census)
 High School graduate or higher 81.6%
 Bachelor's Degree or higher 25.6%
Commuting to Work (1990 Census)
 Average time to work (mins.) 22.0
Houses of Worship: 1 Congregational, 1 Methodist, 1 Catholic
Crime Rate: not available
Libraries:
 Beaman Memorial Public Library
State Register of Historic Places 1993:
 Bigelow Tavern Historic District
 Old Stone Church
 Quinapoxet River Bridge
 Water Supply System of Metropolitan Boston

West Brookfield

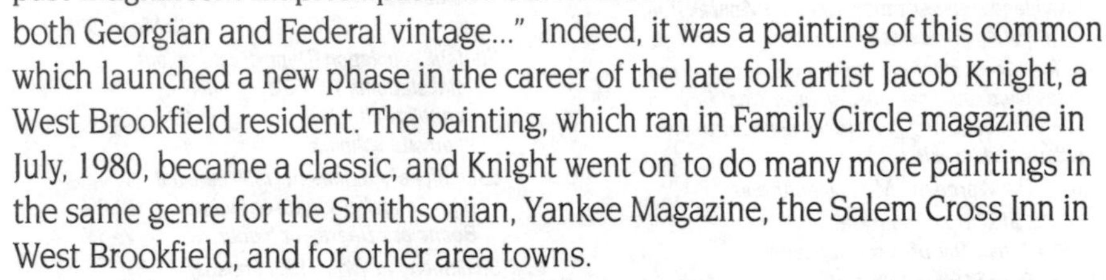

Lucy Stone, Jacob Knight and a Famous Common

West Brookfield's town common is big and beautiful - big enough for a baseball diamond, and beautiful enough to typify New England charm. Author Stewart Holbrook described it "as a great green oval, longer than Lexington Green, curving gracefully past magnificent maples...past fine old houses of both Georgian and Federal vintage..." Indeed, it was a painting of this common which launched a new phase in the career of the late folk artist Jacob Knight, a West Brookfield resident. The painting, which ran in Family Circle magazine in July, 1980, became a classic, and Knight went on to do many more paintings in the same genre for the Smithsonian, Yankee Magazine, the Salem Cross Inn in West Brookfield, and for other area towns.

George Washington stopped to dine at the David Hitchcock Tavern in 1789. The tavern, now called "Ye Olde Tavern," also hosted President John Adams in 1821, and LaFayette in 1825. One of the village's most famous independent thinkers was Lucy Stone, an early leader of the womens rights movement, who was born in West Brookfield in 1818. Looking at her lot as a female in 1834, and overwhelmed with the drudgery of cooking, weaving, spinning, milking and making butter, she asked her mother, "Is there nothing to put an end to me?"

Later, Lucy's marriage to Henry Brown Blackwell in 1855 made news around the world for the "Protest" she and her groom read after the ceremony. They stated that the legal existence of the wife is suspended in marriage. Lucy did not become Mrs. Henry B. Blackwell, but rather Mrs. Lucy Stone, after which the term a "Lucy Stoner" was coined to describe other feminists of the day.

Foster Hill on the east side of town, was the original site of the Quaboag Plantation, later known as Brookfield. West Brookfield became a town in 1848, when it separated from Brookfield. Today, West Brookfield is home to people commuting to Worcester and Springfield. Its adoption of a two-acre residential zoning law in 1972 has helped protect its small-town atmosphere. The town is just a few miles from Sturbridge, and is well-known for Rock House Reservation, 80 acres off Rte. 9 owned by the Trustees of Reservations and named for a massive rock out-cropping legend says was shelter to native tribes. Another landmark is the Salem Cross Inn, which still uses its roasting jack spit, circa 1700, to cook in the Colonial manner for its Hearthside Feasts.

Sources: Commonwealth of Mass. EOCD Community Profile; The Worcester Telegram & Gazette; The Boston Globe; The Old Post Road, Holbrook; Worcester Magazine;

Year incorporated: 1848
Population: 3,621 (1994 town street census)
Density: 172 per square mile
Total area: 20.48
Elevation: 633'
Distance from:
Boston: 60 miles
Worcester: 20 miles
Springfield 30 miles
Highways: Rte. 9, Rte. 67, minutes from Rte. 20 and the Mass. Turnpike
Bus: Member of Worcester Regional Transit Authority, no scheduled services.
Airport: Served by Worcester Airport
Tax Rate: $ 11.25 per thousand (1994, The Central Mass. Fact Book)
Median House Price: $111,000 (1993, County Data Corporation)
Median Household Income:$39,055 (1990 Census)
% of state average: 105.7%
Per Capita Income: $14,238
% of state average 82.7%
Form of Government: Board of Selectmen, Administrative Assistant, open town meeting
Municipal Offices: (508) 867-6874
Services: Mass. Electric, Boston Gas, town water, no sewer
Nearest Hospital: Mary Lane Hospital, Ware; Harrington Memorial Hosp., Southbridge
Registered Voters (Secretary of State 1992): 2,086 (town 1994 voter list)
Legislative Districts:
U.S. Congress: 1st District: John Olver (D)
State Senate: Worcester-Franklin-Hampden & Hampshire District: Robert D. Wetmore (D)
State Representative: 6th Worcester District: Stephen M. Brewer (D)
Public Schools
Quaboag Regional Schools:
Warren Elementary K-6
West Brookfield Elem. K-6
Quaboag Regional High School, Warren 7-12
Superintendent: William Haggerty (413) 436-9256
School Choice: No
Per Pupil Cost: (State Exec. Office of Education -1992-93)
West Brookfield $4,217
State average $5,023
Average Teacher Salary: (State Exec. Office of Education-1992-93)

West Brookfield	statewide
$31,316	$38,774

Mean SAT scores 1993 (reported by town)
Math 497
Verbal 428
Combined: 925 State Mean: 903

Student Population (Dept. of Education)
Total students 1991-92. 637
at public schools 93.7%
at private schools 6.3%
Educational Attainment (1990 census)
High School graduate or higher 78.2%
Bachelor's Degree or higher 16.8%
Largest Employers: (supplied by community, 1993)

	# of employees
Quaboag Nursing Home	160
Brookfield Machine	60
Regency Thermographics	47
Brookfield Wire Company	30
Quirk Wire	24
Precision Wire Shapes	14

Commuting to Work (1990 Census)
Average time to work (mins.) 25
Houses of Worship: 1 Catholic, 1 Methodist, 1 Congregational, 1 Baptist
Crime Rate: not available
Libraries:
Merriam-Gilbert Public Library, and Quaboag Historical Society, Main St. P.O. Box 364 (508) 867-8784
State Register of Historic Places 1993:
Milestones 1797 "Ben Franklin Markers: Foster Hill Rd., East end of town common, and 147 East Main (Rte. 9)
Salem Cross Inn, Ware Rd., Rte. 9
West Brookfield Center Historic District

Westborough

At the Crossroads

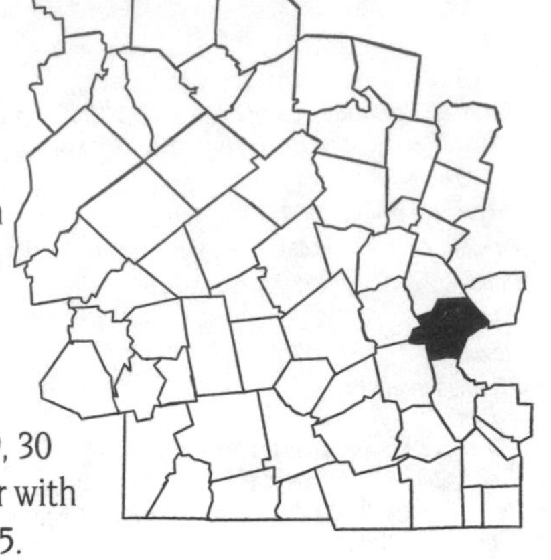

The railroad first came to Westborough in 1834, and by 1889 travelers could pick from seven daily trains to Boston, or eight to Worcester. The town has been a "happy medium" for commuters and corporations ever since. Already criss-crossed by Rtes. 9, 30 and 135, Westborough was changed forever with the opening of the Mass. Pike and Rte. I-495.

Today, these highways put the town within 40 minutes of Boston and Providence, and only 15 minutes from Worcester. Trips "up country" or "down the Cape" are an easy shot from Westborough, and major shopping exists along Westborough's own stretch of Rte. 9, with other large malls nearby in Framingham, Natick and Worcester.

Its prime location and superior highway access have made Westborough a magnet for corporations. The guest cabins, flower farms and small restaurants lining Rte. 9 have given way to sleekly designed corporate centers on Computer and Research Drives. New England Electric's huge facility on 67 acres built in 1964 paved the way, followed by Data General, GTE, Koch Process Systems, Astra Pharmaceuticals and hundreds of other companies which built in a cluster of executive parks, technology parks, business parks and office parks.

But Westborough is more than just highways and high tech. The town's most famous citizen was Eli Whitney, born in 1765 and renowned for inventing the cotton gin, which removed seeds from raw cotton. Whitney was the first to make muskets by machine; before, they had been tediously hand-crafted. His breakthroughs of standard, interchangeable parts and the division of labor laid the foundation for today's mass production methods. Most baby-boomers remember the award-winning children's book, *Johnny Tremain*, written by Westborough's Esther Forbes. She won the 1943 Pulitzer Prize in history for *The Life and Times of Paul Revere*, and was the first female member of Worcester's American Antiquarian Society.

Sources: Commonwealth of MA EOCD Community Profile; The Boston Globe; On the Beaten Path: Westborough, Massachusetts, Kristina Nilson Allen, Westborough Civic Club and Westborough Historical Society, 1984; Forty Immortals of Worcester and Its County, , Worcester National Bank, 1920; Westborough, Northborough Facts and Fancy, Westborough/ Northborough Area Chamber of Commerce.

Year incorporated: 1717
Population: 14,455 (1992 town census)
Density: 689 per square mile
Total area: 21.62 sq. miles
Elevation: 300'
Distance from:
Boston: 29
Worcester: 12

Highways: State Rtes. 9, 30, 135, Interstate 495, and the Massachusetts Turnpike I-190.

Rail: Conrail offers freight service to Westborough and operates an auto transloading facility in the town.

Bus: Westborough is a member of the Worcester Regional Transit Authority, which provides para-transit services for the elderly and disabled. Peter Pan Bus Lines provides local service from Westborough between Worcester and Boston every 2 hours.

Airport: The Worcester Municipal Airport, a primary commercial service facility.

Tax Rate: $10.53 per thousand (1994, Mass. Div. of Local Services)

Median House Price: $195,000 (1993, County Data Corporation)

Median Household Income: $44,044 (1990 Census)
% of state average: 119.2%
Per Capita Income: $20,922
% of state average 121.5%

Form of Government: Board of Selectmen, Town Coordinator, open town meeting

Municipal Offices: (508) 366-3030

Services: Mass. Electric Co., Commonwealth Gas Co., town sewer, ground water.

Nearest Hospital: Several in Worcester

Registered Voters: 8,917

Legislative Districts:

U.S. Congress: 3rd District: Peter I. Blute (R)

State Senate: Worcester & Middlesex: Robert A. Durand (D)

State Senate: Middlesex, Norfolk and Worcester: Pct. 3: David P. Magnani (D)

State Representative: 11th Worcester: Ronald W. Gauch (R)

Public Schools

Westborough: Armstrong (5); Annie E Fales (K-04); Hastings Elem (K-04); Gibbons Middle School (06-08); Westborough High (09-12)

Superintendent: Dr. John P. Doherty Jr. (508) 836-7700

Assabet Valley: Assabet Valley Voc H S (09-13)

School Choice: No

Per Pupil Cost: (State Exec. Office of Education -1992-93)
Westborough $6,271
State average $5,023

Average Teacher Salary: (State Exec. Office of Education-1992-93)

Westborough	statewide
$43,390	$38,774

Mean SAT scores 1993 (reported by town)
Math 506
Verbal 466
Combined: 972 State Mean: 903

Student Population (Dept. of Education)
Total students 1991-92: 2,261
at public schools 95.2%
at private schools 4.8%

Educational Attainment (1990 census)
High School graduate or higher 90.2%
Bachelor's Degree or higher 37.3%

Largest Employers: (supplied by community, 1993)

	# of employees
Data General Corporation	1,500
Massachusetts Electric Company	1,060
Commonwealth Of Massachusetts	850
Federal Deposit Insurance Corp.	678
Astra Pharmaceutical	660

Commuting to Work (1990 Census)
Average time to work (mins.) 22.7

Houses of Worship: 10 - all denominations

Crime Rate: (1993 Mass. State Police Crime Reporting Unit)

	town	statewide
Total crimes reported:	364	
rate per 1,000 persons	25.76	37.46
Violent crimes	46	
rate per 1,000 persons	3.25	5.65
Property crimes	318	
rate per 1,000 persons	22.50	31.83

Libraries
Westborough Public Library

State Register of Historic Places 1993:
Cedar Swamp Archaeological District
Nathan A. Fisher House
Joseph Lothrop House
Maples Cottage
West Main Street Historic District

Westminster

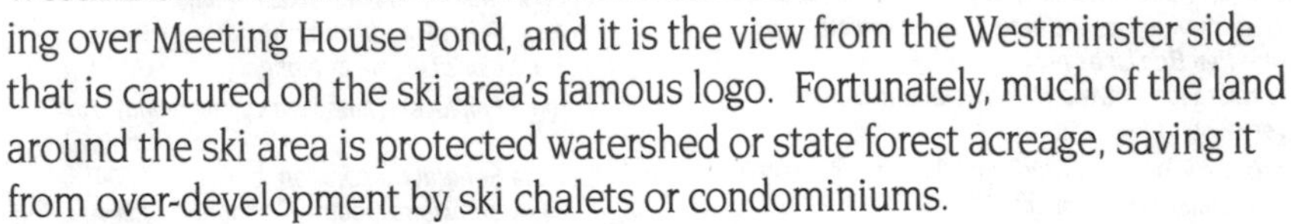

Wachusett's Real Home

Skiers may think they're schussing in Princeton, but with the exception of the summit and one lift, the rest of Wachusett Mountain Ski Area is in Westminster. Residents don't mind the confusion, as long as their town continues to get most of the ski area's tax revenue. Indeed, the scene on Westminster's town seal is of Mt. Wachusett rising over Meeting House Pond, and it is the view from the Westminster side that is captured on the ski area's famous logo. Fortunately, much of the land around the ski area is protected watershed or state forest acreage, saving it from over-development by ski chalets or condominiums.

Chances are the cracker barrel in most New England country stores in the last century contained world-famous Westminster Crackers — either saltines, oysters, the "Westminster XXX Common," or "Boss Lunch" varieties. At one time, the firm, started in 1828, shipped crackers to San Francisco, Chicago, Honolulu and points in between. Westminster Crackers were even taken on an Arctic expedition. Check the oyster crackers restaurants serve with soup, and you may find a picture of the famous red Westminster Cracker building, which still stands in the town center. Pillsbury bought the company in 1982, and today the crackers are baked in Rutland, Vermont.

Another Westminster product making a name for itself today is all natural milk from the micro-dairy Brookside Farm, still delivered to 200 customers and sold in regional stores and bakeries. Brookside's largest customer is the Bread and Circus supermarket chain, which sells the milk in traditional glass quart containers with foil caps featuring the face of a dairy cow. Brookside's veteran dairy cow, "Daisy," produces 50 gallons of milk daily. As the state's only certified organic dairy, the farm doesn't use pesticides on its fields, doesn't give hormones or antibiotics to its cows, and doesn't put additives in its milk.

The popular Old Mill Restaurant on Rte. 2A originated as the Bemis Saw Mill in 1761, producing lumber for early homes in the area, and later wooden organ pipes and shingles. Today the restaurant is known for its early American atmosphere, its traditional menu, and for flocks of ducks and geese making their home in the old mill pond.

Sources: Commonwealth of Mass. EOCD Community Profile, The Boston Globe; Worcester Magazine; A Guide to Nashaway, North Central Massachusetts...a land of uncommon beauty, Marge Darby, Jean C. McCrosky, Mildred A. Chandler, New Guide Group, 1994, Profiles of the Past, An Illustrated History of Ashburnham, Gardner, Hubbardston, Templeton, Westminster and Winchendon, Massachusdtts, Tom Malloy, Millers River Publishing, Inc., 1984.

Year incorporated: 1759
Population: 6,191 (1990 census)
Density: 174 per square mile
Total area: 37.34 sq. miles
Elevation: 1,064'
Distance from:
Boston: 53
Worcester: 24
Highways: State Rtes. 2 and 140.
Rail: Commuter rail service to North Station, Boston, is available in the neighboring towns of Fitchburg, and Leominster.
Bus: The Montachusett Regional Transit Authority, which provides paratransit services to the elderly and disabled through the Council on Aging.
Airport: The Fitchburg Municipal Airport, a general aviation facility.
Tax Rate: $12.13 per thousand (1994, Mass. Div. of Local Services)
Median House Price: $105,700 (1993, County Data Corporation)
Median Household Income: $46, 292 (1990 Census)
% of state average: 125.3%
Per Capita Income: $16,798
% of state average 97.5%
Form of Government: Board of Selectmen, Town Coordinator, Open Town Meeting
Municipal Offices: (508) 874-7400
Services:Mass. Electric Co., Fitchburg Gas & Electric Light Co., town sewer, ground water.
Nearest Hospital: Burbank Hospital, Fitchburg; Henry Heywood Memorial Hospital, Gardner
Registered Voters : 3,839
Legislative Districts:
U.S. Congress: 1st District: John W. Olver, Jr. (D)
State Senate: 2nd Worcester-Middlesex District: Robert Antonioni (D)
State Representative:2nd Worcester: Robert Hawke (R)
Public Schools
Ashburnham Westminster Regional School District: Meetinghouse Elem. (K-2); Westminster Elem (3-6); Oakmont Regional H S (07-12)
Superintendent: William E. Allen, Ed.D. (508) 874-1501
Montachusett: Montachusett Voc-Tech (09-12)
School Choice: Yes

Per Pupil Cost: (State Exec. Office of Education -1992-93)
Westminster $3,961
State average $5,023
Average Teacher Salary: (State Exec. Office of Education-1992-93)

Westminster	statewide
$36,323	$38,774

Mean SAT scores 1993 (reported by town)
Math 511
Verbal 452
Combined: 963 State Mean: 903
Student Population (Dept. of Education)
Total students 1991-92: 1,257
at public schools 97.7%
at private schools 2.3%
Educational Attainment (1990 census)
High School graduate or higher 85.7%
Bachelor's Degree or higher 23.3%
Largest Employers: (supplied by community, 1993)
Simplex Time Recorder
W. E. Aubuchon Hardware
Westminster Village Inn
T.R.W.
Wachusett Mountain Associates
Commuting to Work (1990 Census)
Average time to work (mins.) 24.0
Houses of Worship: 1 Catholic, 5 Protestant
Crime Rate: not available
Libraries Forbush Memorial Library
State Register of Historic Places 1993:
Westminster Village - Academy Hill Historic District
Ahijah Wood House
Ezra Wood- Levi Warner Place
Nathan Wood House

WESTMINSTER

Winchendon

From "Shingletown" to "ToyTown"

In Winchendon, the name Converse means toys, not sneakers. In 1914, the town's Morton E. Converse Company was the largest wooden toy manufacturer in the world, and mail would often arrive marked simply "Toy Town." Converse employed 1,000 people and yearly turned 3 million feet of lumber into children's rocking horses, dollhouses, toy trunks and drums. The factory made over 60 varieties of drums, requiring 600 sheepskins daily for the covers. No major toy firms survive in Winchendon today, but a 12' wooden rocking horse stands at the junction of Rtes. 12 and 202 as a reminder of town's toy-making past.

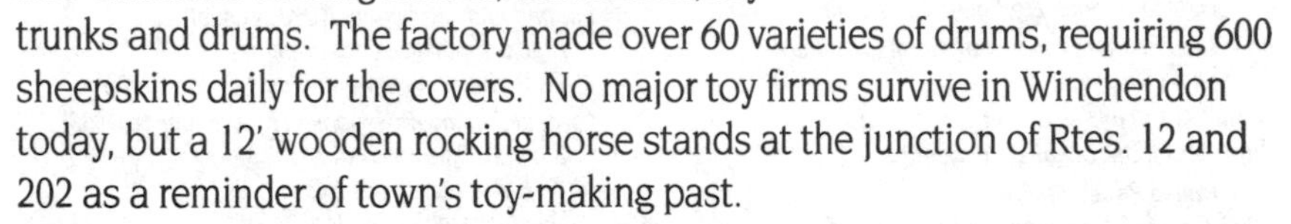

When Morton Converse died in 1917, he left the town an interesting legacy, a $7,000 trust fund which, under the reinvestment stipulations of his will, should exceed $1.5 million when it matures in the year 2117. Part of the interest earned is set aside for an annual "play day" for Winchendon's elementary school children.

Lots of mills harnessed the water power of the Millers River, and in the early 1800's, Winchendon workers made so many shingles, the town earned the nickname "Shingletown." Other mills made chairs, tubs, clothespins and developed innovative woodworking machinery. While most of the wood-working firms are gone, one firm in Winchendon Springs still makes hockey sticks and many furniture outlets remain in the area.

A less well-known legacy is that of Eden London, a black slave from Winchendon who at 23 became one of the 5,000 Black troops to serve in the Continental Army. London, who had been bought and sold nine times by the age of 18, served in the place of his master, Winchendon Selectman Daniel Goodridge. Not only did Goodridge get Eden London's enlistment bonus, he also got part of the soldier's wages. London was freed at the end of his three-year hitch, and when he became destitute some 25 years later, the Worcester County Supreme Court ordered the town of Winchendon to support him. His grave in Winchendon's Old Centre Burying Ground is marked with a Revolutionary War veteran's marker.

The "Old Centre" is a beautiful tree-lined common flanked by white, 18th century buildings. Winchendon has just built a new middle school / high school; house prices are more affordable than some neighboring communities, and many residents enjoy its location. As Joyce Kendall put it, "All of the suggested (favorite place) categories are available from Winchendon within an hour by car. This leaves you living in a standard small town with the option to enjoy all of the things you have in a city."

Sources: Commonwealth of Mass. EOCD Communicty Profile, The Boston Globe; Massachusetts, Off the Beaten Path, A Guide to Unique Places, P. Mandell; Profiles of the Past, T. Malloy; Worcester Magazine.

Year incorporated: 1764
Population: 8,805 (1990 census)
Density: 203 per square mile
Total area: 44.07 sq. miles
Elevation: 1,000'
Distance from:
Boston: 63
Worcester: 44
Springfield 62
Highways: State Rte. 140 and U.S. Rte. 202, Rte. 12.
Airport: The Fitchburg Municipal Airport, a general aviation facility.
Tax Rate: $13.52 per thousand (1994, Mass. Div. of Local Services)
Median House Price: $86,900 (1993, County Data Corporation)
Median Household Income: $32,362 (1990 Census)
% of state average: 87.6%
Per Capita Income: $13,143
% of state average 76.3%
Form of Government: Board of Selectmen, Town Manager, open town meeting
Municipal Offices: (508) 297-2766
Services: Mass. Electric Co., no natural gas, sewer, ground water.
Nearest Hospital: Henry Heywood Memorial Hospital, Gardner
Registered Voters: 4,319
Legislative Districts:
U.S. Congress: 1st District: John W. Olver (D)
State Senate: Worcester-Franklin-Hampden & Hampshire District:, Robert Wetmore(D)
State Representative: 1st Worcester: Harold M. Lane, Jr. (D)
Public Schools
Winchendon: Memorial (K-05); Winchendon Middle (06-08); Murdock High (09-12)
Montachusett: Montachusett Voc Tech (09-12)
Superintendent: David Sandmann (508) 297-0031
School Choice: No
Per Pupil Cost: (State Exec. Office of Education -1992-93)
Winchendon $3,513
State average $5,023

Average Teacher Salary: (State Exec. Office of Education-1992-93)

Winchendon	statewide
$35,951	$38,774

Mean SAT scores 1993 (reported by town)

Math	472	
Verbal	428	
Combined	900	State Mean: 903

Student Population (Dept. of Education)
Total students 1991-92: 1,829
at public schools 92.0%
at private schools 8.0%
Educational Attainment (1990 census)
High School graduate or higher 77.3%
Bachelor's Degree or higher 11.9%
Largest Employers: (supplied by community, 1993)

	# of employees
Town of Winchendon	300
Ray Plastic	113
Rural Housing Improvement	95
Kamenstein, Inc.	75
The Winchendon School	50

Commuting to Work (1990 Census)
Average time to work (mins.) 22.1
Houses of Worship: Protestant, Catholic, Bethany Bible Chaple, Cornerstone Church
Crime Rate: (1993 Mass. State Police Crime Reporting Unit)

	town	statewide
Total crimes reported:	183	
rate per 1,000 persons	20.78	37.46
Violent crimes	41	
rate per 1,000 persons	4.76	5.65
Property crimes	142	
rate per 1,000 persons	16.13	31.83

Libraries:
Beals Memorial Library
Museums:
Winchendon Historical Society
State Register of Historic Places 1993:
Old Center Historic District
Old Center Local Historic District
Old Murdock High School
Winchendon Village Historic District

Worcester

Mechanic to the World

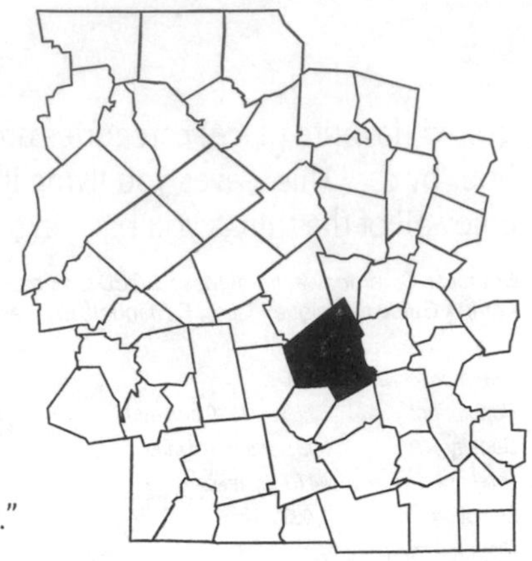

For inspiration as it enters the 21st century, Worcester need only look to itself — 100 years ago. At the turn of the last century, Worcester was vibrant, confident, full of inventors with new ideas, and the mechanics and metalworkers to make them work. Indeed, "the joint was jumpin."

Worcester's "mechanics" were not corner garage grease monkeys. The term "mechanic" had a loftier meaning — they were the pioneers of mass production — skilled workers and factory owners dedicated to converting raw materials into top quality wares. They were enterprising entrepreneurs who built acoustically perfect Mechanics Hall as an expression of their own tastes and skills. When it opened in 1857, all city factories were closed in celebration, and industrialist Henry Washburn called the hall "an offspring of our love."

The Hall — and Worcester — attracted luminaries from around the world — Charles Dickens, Enrico Caruso, Jenny Lind, Ralph Waldo Emerson, Mark Twain, Henry David Thoreau, Oliver Wendell Holmes, John Philip Sousa, and later Theodore Roosevelt, Clarence Darrow, and Woodrow Wilson. Also visiting the city in the last half of the 19th century were Abraham Lincoln, William Lloyd Garrison, and women's rights activists Susan B. Anthony, Lucy Stone and Abby Kelley-Foster, who held the first national women's rights convention here in 1850. In 1994, First Lady Hillary Rodham Clinton spoke here in support of a local legislator.

To these leaders of the day, Worcester was a natural choice for a tour stop, and no wonder, considering what the city was accomplishing. Manufactured goods were pouring from the city, shipped first by stage along the Boston - New York turnpike and the Blackstone Canal, and later by railroad. Worcester's factories turned out machine tools, carriages, corsets, crankshafts, envelopes, boxes, gutters, guns, grinding wheels, parlor stoves, rail cars, rat traps, roller skates, textiles, farm equipment, shredded wheat, sprockets, nuts, axles, washers, and wire — all kinds of wire.

When Worcester Was Wired

Icabod Washburn began "drawing wire" in the 1830's, and quickly improved upon the machinery, increasing production tenfold. He first supplied the wool spinning industry, and later made piano wire for the huge Chickering Piano

Company of Boston. In partnership with his twin brother, Charles, and son-in-law, Philip Moen, Wasburn manufactured the first galvanized telegraph wire, and later diversified to wire for hoop skirts. At its peak, that fashion fad required some 1,500 tons of steel wire annually.

In 1876, Washburn & Moen bought the rights to manufacture twisted barbed wire from its inventor, Illinois farmer Joseph Glidden, and the firm was producing some 300 million pounds of barbed wire by the century's close. Barbed wire from Worcester enclosed much of the western grazing land. In 1899, the firm had 3,000 workers; two years later it became the U.S. Steel Corp., eventually leaving the city. Today, Washburn & Moen's "Northworks" factory survives as a thriving restaurant, retail and office complex on Grove St.

The city's colleges added to the skilled work force. Worcester Polytechnic Institute, (WPI) founded in 1865, trained engineers, and Clark University started as a graduate school in 1889. In 1902 its Physics Dept. Chairman, Albert Michelson, became the very first American to win a Nobel Prize.

Wyman Gordon, founded in 1883 as the Worcester Drop Forge Works, became the world's leading crankshaft manufacturer. (Later,WWII B-17 "Flying Fortress" bombers had 284 W-G parts) Other city firms were thriving: the Royal Worcester Corset Company was the world's largest corset manufacturer, employing hundreds; the Norton Emery Wheel Company began making grinding wheels of clay and emery in 1885. At its peak, Norton's payroll grew to include more than 6,000 local workers. Today, Norton, part of the French Compangnie de St.-Gobain, has facilities in 28 countries, but remains headquartered in Worcester.

Norton's superintendent of the works, the first John Jeppson, encouraged fellow Swedish skilled workers to emigrate, and by 1900, half of the company's work force was Swedish. Attracted by Worcester's prosperity, other waves of immigrants flocked to the city. The Irish first came in the 1820's to build the Blackstone Canal, and were followed by Italians, Greeks, Poles, Lithuanians, Russian Jews, Lebanese and French Canadians.

Diners and Triple Deckers

Plying the lunch trade in the teeming city was Sam Jones, who brought his moveable lunch wagons to town in 1884. Later, the Worcester Lunch Car Company began manufacturing "Worcester Car" diners on Quinsigamond Ave. These classics, with marble counters and oak woodwork, were shipped all over the country, and many are still in operation today (*see Chapter* 7).

By 1890, 28 trolley lines crossed Main and Pleasant Streets. By 1900, the city's population was 100,000, and a train arrived or departed the city every 90 seconds, from the "old" Union Station. The "new" Union Station, the one under renovation in Washington Square, was built in 1911. Worcester's famous "triple deckers," with their fresh air porches, were efficient and practical means to house immigrant workers and their extended families. It's estimated that some 6,000 three-family houses were built in the city, and some of the best surviving examples are on Vernon Hill (*see Chapter* 9).

For entertainment, workers strolled in the nation's first public park — the Olmstead-designed Elm Park. Or they skated at the popular roller skating emporium, Bigelow's Garden. Its developer, Horace Bigelow, offered other entertainment as diverse as opera and indoor polo. A Lake Quinsigamond amusement park was accessible by the narrow-gauge "Dummy Railroad" between Worcester and Shrewsbury. Other attractions included a hotel on one of the islands, and two side-wheeled steamers on the lake.

The bicycle craze hit Worcester in the 1890's, and the "Worcester Whirlwind," black cyclist Marshall "Major" Taylor, won the 1899 world bicycle championship. He moved to Worcester to escape discrimination encountered in Indianapolis.

Anarchy and Ice Cream

Worcester celebrated 50 years as a city in 1898 by building its present City Hall, and the Worcester Art Museum opened the same year, endowed by Stephen Salisbury III. During the 1890's, a wide spectrum of fascinating people called Worcester "home." When Henry Perky was inventing his famous Shredded Wheat cereal in a Jackson Street factory, anarchist Emma Goldman and her lover, radical Alexander Berkman, ran an ice cream parlor on Providence Street!

Certainly, the picture in Worcester in the late 19th Century wasn't all rosy prosperity. The factory smokestacks undoubtedly polluted the air, and the remnants of the Blackstone Canal, put out of business by the railroad became a fetid sewer and had to be capped and covered over. The tenements were overcrowded and the paternalistic factory owners probably weren't always benevolent. Yet, there was progress. Things were happening.

Worcester's Patriot "Spy"

Things were also happening in Worcester at the time of the Revolution. But because no battles were actually fought here, Worcester's importance at the time has been overlooked. The cannon brought from Fort Ticonderoga to drive the British out of Boston were literally dragged through Worcester's streets.

And had Longfellow chosen to write about another of the night riders who warned "The British are coming!" the world would know of Isaiah Thomas, who rode with Paul Revere.

The Massachusetts Spy, Thomas' rebel newspaper, was first printed from Boston, and called the "snake of sedition" by Tories. Fearing they would burn Boston, Thomas sneaked his presses to Worcester and resumed publication in May, 1775, with an eyewitness account of the Battle of Lexington, accusing the British of murder and robbery.

The Spy had the largest circulation in New England. Thomas' Worcester publishing empire also turned out the first dictionary and Bible printed in America. He also printed spelling and music books, almanacs, moral tales, and even the erotic classic, *Fanny Hill*. His legacy to Worcester was his founding of the American Antiquarian Society, which today houses his printing press and the largest collection of early American printed materials in the country.

Worcester's history includes many more famous people (radical Abbie Hoffman and writer Robert Benchley) and fascinating inventions (the monkey wrench, the Valentine and the Steam Calliope). (*For more details, see Chapter* 2).

Sources: Central Mass. Regional Planning Commission; Commonwealth of Mass. EOCD Community Profile; Telegram & Gazette, "Worcester at the Crossroads," Massachusetts Towns, An 1840 View, Ivan Sandrof, Barre Publishers, 1963; More Massachusetts Towns, Ivan Sandrof, Barre Publishers, 1965; Worcester County Convention & Visitors Bureau.

Year incorporated: 1722, 1848 as a city
Population: 169,759 (1990 census)
Density: 4,520 per square mile
Total area: 38.56 sq. miles
Elevation: 400'
Distance from:
- *Boston:* 40
- *Providence:* 43
- *Hartford:* 64
- *Springfield* 51

Highways: State Rte. 9, I-190 and I-290, I-.90 , U.S. Rte. 20.

Rail: Daily commuter Rail to Boston; direct Amtrak passenger rail service to Boston, Springfield, Providence, points beyond. Conrail, the Providence & Worcester Railroad, and the Springfield Terminal Railway all provide freight service and interchange traffic in Worcester.

Bus: Worcester is a member of the Worcester Regional Transit Authority which provides fixed route service within Worcester and to surrounding towns. The WRTA also offers transit services for the elderly and disabled. Peter Pan Bus Lines provides service from Worcester to Boston and points between. Pete Pan connects Worcester directly to Providence, RI, and via Providence, to Cape Cod.

Airport: The Worcester Municipal Airport

Tax Rate: $15.57 per thousand - residential (1994, Mass. Div. of Local Services)

Median House Price: $99,900 (1993, County Data Corporation)

Median Household Income: $28,955 (1990 Census)
- *% of state average:* 78.4%
- *Per Capita Income:* $13,393
- *% of state average* 77.8%

Form of Government: Council-Manager, City Manager

Municipal Offices: (508) 799-1000

City Manager: (508) 799-1175

Services: Mass. Electric Co., Commonwealth Gas Co., Upper Blackstone sewer facility, predominately surface water supply.

WORCESTER

Nearest Hospital: University of Massachusetts Hospital
St. Vincent Hospital
Medical Center of Central Massachusetts
Adcare Hospital of Worcester, Inc.
Fairlawn Rehabilitation Hospital

Registered Voters 75,988

Legislative Districts:

U.S. Congress: 3rd District: Peter I. Blute (R)

State Senate: 1st Worcester & Middlesex: Matthew J. Amorello (R)

State Senate: 1st Worcester District: Wards 1,2,3,4,9,10: Robert A. Bernstein (D)

State Representatives:

17th Worcester: John J. Binienda, Sr. (D)

15th Worcester: Vincent A. Pedone (D)

16th Worcester:William J. Glodis, Jr. (D)

14th Worcester:William J. McManus (D)

13th Worcester:Harriette L. Chandler (D)

Public Schools: 4 high schools, 4 middle schools, 41 elementary schools.

Superintendent: Dr. James L. Garvey (508)799-3115

School Choice: No

Worcester Vocational Schools:

Superintendent: Mr. F. Nelson Burns (508) 799-1940

Worcester Vocational High School (secondary and post-secondary); Worcester Tech. Inst. (post secondary); Career Center (adult ed.)

Colleges and Universities: Assumption College; Becker College - Worcester Campus; Clark University; College of the Holy Cross; Quinsigamond Community College; Worcester State College; Worcester Polytechnic Institute; University of Massachusetts Medical Center

Per Pupil Cost: (State Exec. Office of Education -1992-93)

Worcester	*$4,764*
State average	*$5,023*

Average Teacher Salary:
(State Exec. Office of Education-1992-93)

Worcester	*statewide*
$34,998	*$38,774*

Mean SAT scores 1993 (reported by town)

Math	*431*	
Verbal	*379*	
Combined:	*810*	*State Mean: 903*

Student Population (Dept. of Education)

Total students 1991-92:	*24,745*
at public schools	*86.0%*
at private schools	*14.0%*

Educational Attainment (1990 census)

High School graduate or higher	*74.7%*
Bachelor's Degree or higher	*18.9%*

Largest Employers: (supplied by Worcester Area Chamber of Commerce, 1994)

	# of employees
University of Massachusetts Medial Center	*6,300*
Fallon Health Care System	*5,000*
Medical Center of Central Massachusetts	*3,700*
Allmerica Financial	*3,450*
Worcester Public Schools	*3,000*
Norton Company	*2,500*
City of Worcester	*2,500*
NYNEX	*2,400*
Paul Revere Insurance Group	*1,600*
U.S. Postal Service	*1,302*

Commuting to Work (1990 Census)

Average time to work (mins.)	*18.3*

Houses of Worship: all denominations

Crime Rate:
(1993 Mass. State Police Crime Reporting Unit)

	city	*statewide*
Total crimes reported:	*11,034*	
rate per 1,000 persons	*65.00*	*37.46*
Violent crimes	*717*	
rate per 1,000 persons	*4.22*	*5.65*
Property crimes	*10,317*	
rate per 1,000 persons	*60.77*	*31.83*

Libraries:
Worcester Public Library

Museums:
American Antiquarian Society
Higgins Armory Museum
Iris & B. Gerald Cantor Art Gallery
New England Science Center
Salisbury Mansion
Worcester Art Museum
Worcester Center for Crafts
Worcester Historical Museum

State Register of Historic Places 1993:
Many buildings are listed. For information, call Preservation Worcester: (508) 754-8760.

Chapter 13

Town Rank

Highest Residential Tax Rates:

Rank	Tax rate per thousand 1994
1 Hopedale	$20.18
2 Millville	$17.45
3 Southbridge	$17.12*
4 Westborough	$16.53
5 Sturbridge	$16.45
6 Princeton	$16.33
7 Leominster	$16.31
8 Northborough	$15.97
9 Holden	$15.92*
10 Worcester	$15.57

Lowest Residential Tax Rates:

50 Oakham	$10.84
51 Auburn	$10.57
52 Petersham	$10.26
53 Webster	$10.05
54 Upton	$9.51
55 Spencer	$9.34
56 Dudley	$9.28*
57 Phillipston	$8.69
58 E. Brookfield	$8.23
59 Royalston	$8.07
60 Templeton	$8.03

Source: 1994 Mass. Div. of Local Services:

*figures supplied by town

Highest Median House Prices:

Rank	Median House Price 1993
1 Harvard	$240,100*
2 Southborough	$235,000
3 Westborough	$195,000
4 Bolton	$192,500
5 Northborough	$178,000
6 Mendon	$166,000
7 Shrewsbury	$159,000
8 Upton	$158,734
9 Princeton	$147,000
10 Paxton	$146,000

Lowest Median House Prices:

50 Templeton	$ 97,000
51 Barre	$ 96,000
52 Ashburnham	$ 95,000
53 Southbridge	$ 92,500
54 Phillipston	$ 92,000
55 Warren	$ 90,000
56 Gardner	$ 88,000
57 Fitchburg	$ 87,000
58 Winchendon	$ 86,900
59 Athol	$ 80,000
60 Hardwick	$ 79,900

Sources: 1993, County Data Corporation
*figures supplied by town

Highest Median Household Incomes:

Rank	Median Household Income 1990
1 Harvard	$80,028*
2 Bolton	$63,757
3 Southborough	$61,743
4 Northborough	$57,963
5 Mendon	$55,914
6 Princeton	$52,708
7 Boylston	$52,424
8 Berlin	$49,556
9 Sterling	$49,345
10 Paxton	$49,176

Lowest Median Household Incomes:

50 Winchendon	$32,362
51 N. Brookfield	$31,8652
52 Warren	$30,423
53 Brookfield	$30,349
54 Hardwick	$30,139
55 Webster	$30,067
56 Worcester	$28,955
57 Gardner	$28,035
58 Southbridge	$27,834
59 Fitchburg	$27,101
60 Athol	$27,095

Sources: 1990 Census
*figures supplied by town

Largest Cities and Towns:

Rank	Population, 1990
1 Worcester	169,759
2 Fitchburg	41,194
3 Leominster	38,145
4 Milford	25,355
5 Shrewsbury	24,146
6 Gardner	20,125
7 Southbridge	17,816
8 Webster	16,196
9 Auburn	15,005
10 Holden	14,628

Smallest Towns:

50 Bolton	3,134
51 Brookfield	2,968
52 Hardwick	2,385
53 Berlin	2,293
54 Millville	2,236
55 E. Brookfield	2,033
56 Oakham	1,658*
57 Phillipston	1,485
58 Royalston	1,147
59 Petersham	1,131
60 New Braintree	881

Source: 1990 census
*figures supplied by town

Highest Population Density:

Rank	Population Density people per square mile
1 Worcester	4,520
2 Clinton	2,320
3 Milford	1,737
4 Fitchburg	1,484
5 Leominster	1,321
6 Webster	1,297
7 Shrewsbury	1,165
8 Hopedale	1,100
9 Auburn	977
10 Gardner	907

Lowest Population Density:

50 Ashburnham	140
51 Rutland	140
52 Barre	103
53 Princeton	90
54 Oakham	71
55 Hubbardston	68
56 Hardwick	62
57 Phillipston	61
58 New Braintree	43
59 Royalston	27
60 Petersham	21

Sources: 1990 census
Towns reporting identical figures are ranked alphabetically

Highest Per Pupil Expenditures Primary Grades:

Rank	Per Pupil Cost Primary Grades 1992-93 (state avg. $5,023)
1 Westborough	$6,271
2 Petersham	$5,758
3 Harvard	$5,545
4 Southborough	$5,379
5 Auburn	$5,104
6 Bolton	$4,964
7 Boylston	$4,964
8 Southbridge	$4,931
9 Worcester	$4,764
10 Berlin	$4,749

Lowest Per Pupil Expenditures Primary Grades:

50 Oxford	$3,664
51 Northbridge	$3,632
52 Sutton	$3,628
53 Gardner	$3,618
54 Charlton	$3,611
55 Dudley	$3,611
56 Uxbridge	$3,564
57 Lancaster	$3,563
58 Sterling	$3,533
59 Winchendon	$3,513
60 N. Brookfield	$3,418

Sources: State Executive Office of Education 1992-93
Towns reporting identical figures are ranked alphabetically

Cont. on page 370

(Towns listed in alphabetical order; Rankings listed from highest to lowest)	Residential Tax Rate, 1994	Ranking, Tax Rates	Median House Price, 1993	Ranking, Median House	PriceMedian Household Income, 1990	Ranking, Median Household Income	Population 1990	Ranking Population	Pop. Density (people per sq. mile)	Ranking, Population Density	Per Pupil Expenditure, Primary, 1992-93 (State average: $5,023)	Ranking, Per Pupil Expenditure, Primary Grades	Per Pupil Expenditure, Secondary, 1992-1993 (State avg: $5,023)	Ranking, Per Pupil Expenditures Secondary Grades (58 towns reporting)	Average Teacher Salary Primary Grades 1992-1993 (State avg: $38,774)	Ranking, Avg. Teacher Salary Primary Grades	Combined Mean SAT 1993 (State Mean: 903)	Ranking, SAT Scores (59 towns reporting)	Crime Rate per thousand, 1993, (38 towns reporting)	Ranking: Crime Rate (Highest crime ranking = 1; lowest = 38)
Ashburnham	$13.73	27	$95,000	52	$42,442	24	5,433	38	140	51	$3,961	39	$3,961	45	$36,323	29	963	7	20.61	21
Athol	$12.50	42	$80,000	59	$27,095	60	11,451	19	351	28	$3,695	48	n/a	n/a	$33,727	40	854	54	42.09	5
Auburn	$10.57	51	$111,000	37	$39,913	32	15,005	9	977	9	$5,104	5	$5,104	17	$38,598	10	856	52	n/a	n/a
Barre	$15.10	13	$96,000	51	$36,846	40	4,546	42	103	52	$4,080	30	$4,080	37	$31,577	49	889***	38	n/a	n/a
Berlin	$13.90	22	$138,000	14	$49,556	8	2,293	53	177	44	$4,749	10	$7,843	1	$36,629	27	934	16	20.93	19
Blackstone	$13.12	35	$115,885	30	$38,687	35	8,023	26	736	14	$4,466	15	$4,466	23	$37,597	19	896*	31	17.57	24
Bolton	$13.58	29	$192,500	4	$63,757	2	3,134	50	157	48	$4,964	6	$6,767	3	$38,545	11	959***	9	26.16	11
Boylston	$12.82	39	$128,500	19	$52,424	7	3,517	47	219	35	$4,964	7	$7,843	2	$38,935	9	934	16	6.82	35
Brookfield	$13.84	25	$106,000	41	$30,349	53	2,968	51	191	43	$3,891	44	$5,629	13	$30,119	58	927***	18	n/a	n/a
Charlton	$11.02	48	$117,500	26	$42,461	23	9,025*	24	224	32	$3,611	54	$3,611	54	$36,878	24	879***	46	15.14	28
Clinton	$10.92	49	$110,000	39	$34,091	47	13,222	13	2,320	2	$3,959	41	$3,959	47	$36,592	28	857	51	25.87	12
Douglas	$14.16	21	$120,900	23	$38,362	36	5,595*	36	150	49	$3,724	47	$3,724	49	$43,384	4	894	36	36.23~	7
Dudley	$09.28*	56	$114,500	35	$34,139	46	9,151*	22	453	23	$3,611	55	$3,611	55	$36,878	25	879***	47	30.61~	10
E. Brookfield	$08.23	58	$104,900	45	$38,226	37	2,033	55	207	40	$4,217	25	$4,217	32	$33,224	45	878	48	n/a	n/a
Fitchburg	$12.76	40	$87,000	57	$27,101	59	41,194	2	1,484	4	$4,238	23	$4,238	31	$34,029	39	803	59	62.39	2

Gardner	$14.59	16	$88,000	56	$28,035	57	20,125	6	907	10	$3,618	53	$3,618	53	$31,893	48	919	27	36.07	8
Grafton	$13.46	31	$129,500	18	$42,310	25	13,035	14	573	17	$4,058	36	$4,058	43	$37,188	23	965	6	11.66	29
Hardwick	$13.60	28	$79,900	60	$30,139	54	2,385	52	62	56	$4,080	31	$4,080	38	$31,577	50	889*	39	10.48	31
Harvard	$15.15*	12	$240,100*	1	$80,028*	1	5,082*	39	468	20	$5,545	3	$5,545	15	$46,310	1	1042	1	3.43	37
Holden	$15.92*	9	$130,000	17	$49,143	11	14,628	10	418	25	$3,983	38	$6,374	7	$38,362	14	922***	22	n/a	n/a
Hopedale	$20.18	1	$135,000	15	$44,961	15	5,666	35	1,100	8	$4,250	22	$4,250	29	$38,542	12	905	29	8.12	34
Hubbardston	$12.48	43	$102,900	47	$42,650	22	3,495*	48	68	55	$4,080	32	$4,080	39	$31,577	51	839***	40	n/a	n/a
Lancaster	$13.14*	34	$115,000	32	$41,552	26	6,661	29	241	31	$3,563	57	$6,767	4	$25,781	60	959***	10	18.92	23
Leicester	$12.96	37	$108,000	40	$40,321	29	10,191	21	436	24	$3,796	45	$3,796	48	$34,944	36	870	50	16.98	26
Leominster	$16.31	7	$115,000	33	$35,974	43	38,145	3	1,321	5	$4,141	28	$4,141	35	$39,554	7	891***	37	48.29	4
Lunenburg	$15.19	11	$125,000	21	$43,199	20	9,117	23	345	29	$4,120	29	$4,120	36	$34,545	37	979	4	n/a	n/a
Mendon	$12.89	38	$166,000	6	$55,914	5	4,301*	44	222	34	$4,411	17	$4,411	25	$31,230	56	936	13	10.22	33
Milford	$14.58	17	$139,900	13	$38,180	38	25,355	4	1737	3	$4,238	24	$4,238	30	$35,789	33	947	11	10.25	32
Millbury	$13.26	33	$115,500	31	$37,438	39	12,228	16	777	13	$4,693	13	$4,693	21	$34,437	38	947	12	n/a	n/a
Millville	$17.45	2	$114,900	34	$40,154	30	2,236	54	454	22	$4,466	16	$4,466	24	$37,597	20	896*	32	n/a	n/a

Sources: Tax rates 1994, Mass. Div. of Local Services; Median House Prices, 1993, County Data Corporation; Median HHld Income, Population and Density, 1990 Census; Per Pupil Costs, Avg. Teacher Salary and SAT, State Exec. Office of Education -1992-93; Crime Rates, 1993 Mass. State Police Crime Reporting Unit, from FBI Uniform Report on Crime.

* figures supplied by town

**1995 figure supplied by town

***'94 Public Schools Report Card, Worc. Magazine, 9/7/94

~ crime rate adjusted to 12 monthsNote- where towns have identical figures, as in regional schools, they are ranked alphabetically.

(Towns listed in alphabetical order, Rankings listed from highest to lowest)	Residential Tax Rate, 1994	Ranking, Tax Rates	Median House Price, 1993	Ranking, Median House	PriceMedian Household Income,1990	Ranking, Median Household Income	Population 1990	Ranking Population	Pop. Density (people per sq. mile)	Ranking, Population Density	Per Pupil Expenditure, Primary, 1992-93 (State average: $5,023)	Ranking, Per Pupil Expenditure, Primary Grades	Per Pupil Expenditure, Secondary, 1992-1993 (State avg: $5,023)	Ranking, Per Pupil Expenditures Secondary Grades (58 towns reporting)	Average Teacher Salary Primary Grades 1992-1993 (State avg: $38,774)	Ranking, Avg. Teacher Salary Primary Grades	Combined Mean SAT 1993 (State Mean: 903)	Ranking, SAT Scores (59 towns reporting)	Crime Rate per thousand, 1993, (38 towns reporting)	Ranking: Crime Rate (Highest crime ranking = 1; lowest = 38)
New Braintree	$13.02	36	$116,000	29	$43,214	19	881	60	43	58	$4,080	33	$4,080	40	$31,577	52	889***	41	n/a	n/a
N. Brookfield	$11.22	47	$104,500	46	$31,868	51	4,708	41	224	33	$3,418	60	$3,418	58	$28,062	59	933	17	n/a	n/a
Northborough	$15.97	8	$178,000	5	$57,963	4	12,704*	15	643	16	$4,264	21	$6,548	5	$43,746	2	993	2	16.01	27
Northbridge	$12.18	44	$119,250	25	$36,634	42	13,371	12	778	12	$3,632	51	$3,632	51	$37,885	17	884	44	24.08	16
Oakham	$10.84	50	$120,000	24	$41,295	27	1,658*	56	71	54	$4,080	34	$4,080	41	$31,557	53	889	42	n/a	n/a
Oxford	$14.19	20	$112,900	36	$36,682	41	12,214*	17	473	19	$3,664	50	$3,664	50	$38,509	13	842	56	24.39	15
Paxton	$13.85	24	$146,000	10	$49,176	10	4,047	45	275	30	$3,749	46	$6,374	8	$37,989	15	922***	23	n/a	n/a
Petersham	$10.26	52	$134,000	16	$39,063	33	1,131	59	21	60	$5,758	2	$5,250*	16	$33,600	42	n/a	n/a	n/a	n/a
Phillipston	$08.69	57	$92,000	54	$35,573	44	1,485	57	61	57	$4,069	35	$4,069	42	$33,452	44	895*	34	20.20	22
Princeton	$16.33	6	$147,000	9	$52,708	6	3,344*	49	90	53	$3,935	42	$6,374	9	$40,021	6	922***	24	25.40~	14
Royalston	$08.07	59	$105,000	44	$33,333	48	1,147	58	27	59	$3,695	49	n/a	n/a	$33,727	41	854	55	n/a	n/a
Rutland	$13.82*	26	$116,650	28	$44,087	17	4,936	40	140	50	$3,916	43	$6,374	10	$37,759	18	922***	25	5.06	36
Shrewsbury	$12.74	41	$159,000	7	$44,248	16	24,146	5	1,165	7	$4,702	12	$4,702	20	$35,705	34	896	33	34.17	9
Southborough	$13.30*	32	$235,000	2	$61,743	3	6,628	30	468	21	$5,379	4	$6,548	6	$42,883	5	993	3	11.16	30
Southbridge	$17.12*	3	$92,500	53	$27,834	58	17,816	7	883	11	$4,931	8	$4,931	18	$37,484**	21	825	57	n/a	n/a

Spencer	$9.34	55	$100,000	48	$33,201	49	11,645	18	354	26	$4,217	26	$4,217	33	$33,224	46	878	49	50.92~	3
Sterling	$13.87	23	$144,500	11	$49,345	9	6,481	32	212	37	$3,533	58	$6,374	11	$36,167	31	922***	26	21.29	18
Sturbridge	$16.45	5	$126,100	20	$40,734	28	7,775	27	208	39	$4,734	11	$5,629	14	$33,510	43	927***	19	22.51	17
Sutton	$14.78*	15	$142,500	12	$46,491	12	6,824	28	211	38	$3,628	52	$3,628	52	$39,325	8	881	45	1.61	38
Templeton	$8.03	60	$97,000	50	$34,395	45	6,438	33	201	42	$4,051	37	$4,051	44	$32,647	47	895*	35	n/a	n/a
Upton	$9.51	54	$158,734	8	$45,962	14	5,435*	37	217	36	$4,411	18	$4,411	26	$31,230	57	936***	14	n/a	n/a
Uxbridge	$14.49	18	$117,500	27	$40,059	31	10,415	20	352	27	$3,564	56	$3,564	56	$37,909	16	887	43	17.19	25
Warren	$14.35	19	$90,000	55	$30,423	52	4,437	43	161	47	$4,271	20	$4,271	28	$31,316	55	925	21	n/a	n/a
Webster	$10.05	53	$105,900	42	$30,067	55	16,196	8	1,297	6	$4,403	19	$4,403	27	$37,406	22	855	53	41.74	6
West Boylston	$15.00	14	$125,000	22	$42,830	21	6,611	31	512	18	$4,534	14	$4,534	22	$36,848	26	919	28	n/a	n/a
W. Brookfield	$11.25	46	$111,000	38	$39,055	34	3,621*	46	172	46	$4,217	27	$4,217	34	$31,316	54	925	20	n/a	n/a
Westborough	$16.53	4	$195,000	3	$44,044	18	14,455*	11	689	15	$6,271	1	$6,271	12	$43,390	3	972	5	25.76	13
Westminster	$12.13	45	$105,700	43	$46,292	13	6,191	34	174	45	$3,961	40	$3,961	46	$36,323	30	963	8	n/a	n/a
Winchendon	$13.52	30	$86,900	58	$32,362	50	8,805	25	203	41	$3,513	59	$3,513	57	$35,951	32	900	30	20.78	20
Worcester	$15.57	10	$99,900	49	$28,955	56	169,759	1	4520	1	$4,764	9	$4,764	19	$34,998	35	810	58	65.00	1

Sources: Tax rates 1994, Mass. Div. of Local Services; Median House Prices, 1993, County Data Corporation; Median HHld Income, Population and Density, 1990 Census; Per Pupil Costs, Avg. Teacher Salary and SAT, State Exec. Office of Education -1992-93; Crime Rates, 1993 Mass. State Police Crime Reporting Unit, from FBI Uniform Report on Crime.

* figures supplied by town

**1995 figure supplied by town

***'94 Public Schools Report Card, Worc. Magazine, 9/7/94

~ crime rate adjusted to 12 monthsNote- where towns have identical figures, as in region/al schools, they are ranked alphabetically.

Highest Per Pupil Expenditures Secondary Grades:

Rank	Town	Expenditure
1	Berlin	$7,843
2	Boylston	$7,843
3	Bolton	$6,767
4	Lancaster	$6,767
5	Northborough	$6,548
6	Southborough	$6,548
7	Holden	$6,374
8	Paxton	$6,374
9	Princeton	$6,374
10	Rutland	$6,374
11	Sterling	$6,374

Lowest Per Pupil Expenditures Secondary Grades:

Rank	Town	Expenditure
48	Leicester	$3796
49	Douglas	$3724
50	Oxford	$3664
51	Northbridge	$3632
52	Sutton	$3628
53	Gardner	$3618
54	Charlton	$3611
55	Dudley	$3611
56	Uxbridge	$3564
57	Winchendon	$3513
58	N. Brookfield	$3418

(Based on figures from 58 towns)

Source: State Exec. Office of Education, 1992-93
Towns reporting identical figures are ranked alphabetically

Highest Average Teacher Salary - Primary Grades:

Rank	Town	Avg. Teacher Salary 1992-93 Primary Grades (state avg. $38,774)
1	Harvard	46,310
2	Northborough	43,746
3	Westborough	43,390
4	Douglas	43,384
5	Southborough	42,883
6	Princeton	40,021
7	Leominster	39,554
8	Sutton	39,325
9	Boylston	38,935
10	Auburn	38,598

Lowest Average Teacher Salary Primary Grades:

Rank	Town	Salary
49	Barre	31,577
50	Hardwick	31,577
51	Hubbardston	31,577
52	New Braintree	31,577
53	Oakham	31,557
54	W. Brookfield	31,316
55	Warren	31,316
56	Mendon	31,230
57	Upton	31,230
58	Brookfield	30,119
59	N. Brookfield	28,062
60	Lancaster	25,781

Source: State Exec. Office of Education - 1992-93
Towns reporting identical figures, as in regional schools, are ranked alphabetically

Highest Combined Mean SAT Scores

(59 towns reporting)

Rank	Town	Score
1	Harvard	1042
2	Northborough	993
3	Southborough	993
4	Lunenburg	979
5	Westborough	972
6	Grafton	965
7	Ashburnham	963
8	Westminster	963
9	Bolton	959***
10	Lancaster	959***

Lowest Combined Mean SAT Scores

(59 towns reporting)

Rank	Town	Score
48	E. Brookfield	878
49	Spencer	878
50	Leicester	870
51	Clinton	857
52	Auburn	856
53	Webster	855
54	Athol	854
55	Royalston	854
56	Oxford	842
57	Southbridge	825
58	Worcester	810
59	Fitchburg	803

Source: State Exec. Office of Education 1992-93
****'94 Public Schools Report Card, Worcester Magazine, 9/7/94*
Towns reporting identical figures are ranked alphabetically

Highest Crime Rate:

(38 towns reporting)

Rank	Town	Crime Rate per thousand, 1993
1	Worcester	65.00
2	Fitchburg	62.39
3	Spencer	50.92~
4	Leominster	48.29
5	Athol	42.09
6	Webster	41.74
7	Douglas	36.23~
8	Gardner	36.07
9	Shrewsbury	34.17
10	Dudley	30.61~

Lowest Crime Rates:

(38 towns reporting)

Rank	Town	Rate
28	Charlton	15.14
29	Grafton	11.66
30	Southborough	11.16
31	Hardwick	10.48
32	Milford	10.25
33	Mendon	10.22
34	Hopedale	08.12
35	Boylston	06.82
36	Rutland	05.06
37	Harvard	03.43
38	Sutton	01.61

~ crime rate adjusted to 12 months
Based on 38 town reporting
Source: 1993 Mass. State Police Crime Reporting Unit, from FBI Uniform Report on Crime

About the authors:

Larry Abramoff and his wife, Gloria, both Worcester natives, founded Tatnuck Bookseller in 1975 and live in the city with their two sons, Joe and Mike. Today, Tatnuck Bookseller Marketplace is one of the largest independent bookstores in the country. Housed in a restored factory building at 335 Chandler St., the store also includes a 120-seat restaurant, shops and a book distribution division. Favorite Places of Worcester County is the fourth book published by Tatnuck's Databooks division, following *Tornado! 84 Minutes, 94 Lives* by John O'Toole, the story of the 1953 Worcester tornado; *Once Told Tales of Worcester County* and *More Once Told Tales of Worcester County* by Albert Southwick.

Ann Lindblad, a free-lance writer and head of RFD Communications, lives in Rutland, MA with her husband, Peter, and their three sons, Andy, Matt and Scott. She has lived in the Worcester area since 1979, but grew up in Maryville, Tennessee, near the Great Smokey Mountains. She has held past positions in public relations, advertising, marketing, newspapers and radio, and has a B.A. in Journalism from the University of Georgia.

The People of Worcester County, provided us with over 700 of their "Favorite Places." By sharing what they feel makes Worcester County such a great place to live, they have made Worcester County even better. Our heartfelt thanks to all of you who helped 'write' *Favorite Places*. Keep sending us your hot tips and reviews and the next edition will be even better.

Bibliography

(For information on any of the books listed here, consult your local library or call 1-800-64-BOOKS).

American Town, Barre, Massachusetts, 1774-1974, James E. Sullivan, Barre Historical Society, 1974

Bay State Briefs, Lincoln A. Dexter, Lincoln A. Dexter, 1975

Best Hikes with Children in Connecticut, Massachusetts and Rhode Island, Cynthia C. Lewis, Thomas J. Lewis, The Mountaineers, 1991

City and the River, Vol. I, Doris Kirkpatrick, Fitchburg Historical Society, 1971

Coghlin Story 1885-1985, LaVerne Dickinson, The Coghlin Companies, 1985

Creation of Quabbin Reservoir, The Death of the Swift River Valley, J.R. Greene, Highland Press, Athols, MA, 1981

Forty Immortals of Worcester and Its County, , Worcester National Bank, 1920

Guide to Nashaway, North Central Massachusetts...a land of uncommon beauty, Marge Darby, Jean C. McCrosky, Mildred A. Chandler, New Guide Group, 1994

Guide to the Heritage of Worcester County, Simone E. Blake, Montachusett Girl Scout Council, 1973

Heart of the Commonwealth, Margaret A. Erskine, Windsor Publications, 1981

Historic Quabbin Hikes, J.R. Greene, Highland Press, Athol, MA, 1994

Historical Markers of the Massachusetts Bay Colony, Samuel Eliot Morison, The Commonwealth of Massachusetts, 1930

History of Rutland in Massachusetts 1713-1968, T.C. Murphy, Northeastern University, 1928

History of the Town of Holden Massachusetts, 1667-1941, Florence Newell Prouty, Stobbs Press, 1941

History of Worcester County, Mass. with Biographical Sketches of many of its Pioneers and Prominent Men, D. Hamilton Hurd, J.W. Lewis & Co., Philadelphia, 1889

In and About Worcester, A Guidebook, Beverly H. Osborn, Commonwealth Press, 1983

Jottings from Worcester's History, U. Waldo Cutler, Worcester Historical Society, 1932

Lancastrian Towns, Mildred McClary Tymeson, Barre Publishers, 1967

Lunenberg, The Heritage of Turkey Hills, Nelde K. Drumm, Margaret P. Harley, Lunenberg Historical Society, 1977

Massachusetts, the Beaten Path, A Guide to Unique Places, Patrica Mandell, The Globe Pequot Press, 1992

Massachusetts Beautiful, Wallace Nutting, Bonanza Books, 1923

Massachusetts Bicentennial, The Commemorative Guide, Edited by Georgia E. Orcutt, Yankee, Inc., 1975

Massachusetts Towns, An 1840 View, Ivan Sandrof, Barre Publishers, 1963

More Massachusetts Towns, Ivan Sandrof, Barre Publishers, 1965

More Once-Told Tales of Worcester County, Albert B. Southwick, Databooks, 1994

Natural Wonders of Massachusetts, A Guide to Parks, Preserves & Wild Places, Nancy Prajzner, Country Roads Press, 1994

North of the Quabbin, A Guide to Nine Massachusetts Towns, Allen Young, Allen Young, 1983

Northborough: A Town and Its People, 1638-1975, William H. Mulligan, Jr., Northborough American Revolution Bicentennial Commission, 1982

Old Landmarks in Worcester Massachusetts, William A. and Marion W. Emerson, William A. Emerson, 1913

Old Post Road, The Story of the Boston Post Road, Stewart H. Holbrook, McGraw-Hill Book Company, Inc., 1962

On the Beaten Path: Westborough, Massachusetts, Kristina Nilson Allen, Westborough Civic Club and Westborough Historical Society, 1984

Once-Told Tales of Worcester County, Albert B. Southwick, Databooks, 1994

Pictorial History of Holden, Massachusetts, Charles T. Skillings, Clare M. Nelson and Ross W. Beales, Jr., Holden Historical Society, Inc. , 1991

Profiles of the Past, An Illustrated History of Ashburnham, Gardner, Hubbardston, Templeton, Westminster and Winchendon, Massachusetts, Tom Malloy, Millers River Publishing, Inc., 1984

Quabbin Reservoir, Walter E. Clark, Hobson Book Press, 1946; Reprinted by Athol Press, Inc., 1994

Quabbin The Accidental Wilderness, Thomas Conuel, The Univ. of Mass. Press, 1981

Quaboag Plantation, Alias Brookefeild, Louis E. Roy, M.D., Louis E. Roy, M.D., 1965

Run of the Mill, A Pictorial Narrative of the Expansion, Dominion, Decline and Enduring Impact of the New England Textile Industry, Steve Dunwell, David R. Godine, 1978

Rural Retrospect A Parallel History of Worcester and its Rural Cemetery, Mildred McClary Tymeson, Albert W. Rice, 1956

Settlement and Story of Oakham, Massachusettts, H.B. Wright and E.D. Harvey, Ernest L. Hayward, New Haven, CT, 1947

Some Historic Houses of Worcester, Walton Advertising, Worcester Bank and Trust Company, 1919

Strange Tales From Old Quabbin, J.R. Greene, Highland Press, Athol, MA, 1993

Upton's Heritage, the history of a Massachusetts town, Donald Blake Johnson, Town of Upton, 1984

For information regarding:
Purchasing additional copies of this book;
Custom editions of this book;
Related map, puzzle and card products;
Other Worcester books including:
Once Told Tales of Worcester County,
More Once Told Tales of Worcester County, or
Tornado! 84 minutes, 94 Lives;
Premium giveaways;
Sales for resale;
Retail orders;
To order any book or
Custom publishing

Contact: For retail sales: Tatnuck Bookseller & Sons
335 Chandler Street
Worcester, MA 01602
Phone (508) 756-7644
(800) 642-6657
FAX (508) 756-9425
Internet databooks @delphi.com

For Publishing and Wholesale sales:
Databooks
Sales Department
335 Chandler Street
Worcester, MA 01602
Phone (508) 756-7644
(800) 64206657
FAX (508) 756-9425
Internet D]databooks@delphi.com